The Ancient Greeks

New Perspectives

ABC-CLIO's
Understanding Ancient Civilizations

The Ancient Maya
Ancient Canaan and Israel
The Romans

Forthcoming
The Ancient Celts
The Ancient Egyptians
Ancient Mesopotamia
The Aztecs
The Incas

A B C CLIO
Santa Barbara, California
Denver, Colorado   Oxford, England

The Ancient
Greeks

New
Perspectives

STEPHANIE LYNN BUDIN

Library of Congress Cataloging-in-Publication Data
Budin, Stephanie Lynn.
The ancient Greeks : new perspectives / Stephanie Lynn Budin.
  p. cm. — (Understanding ancient civilizations)
Includes bibliographical references and index.
ISBN 1-57607-814-0 (Hardback : alk. paper) — ISBN 1-57607-815-9 (e-book)
  1. Greece—Civilization—To 146 B.C. I. Title. II. Series.
DF77.B92 2004
938—dc22
2004017620

07 06 05 04 10 9 8 7 6 5 4 3 2 1

This book is also available on the World Wide Web as an e-book.
Visit abc-clio.com for details.

ABC-CLIO, Inc.
130 Cremona Drive, P.O. Box 1911
Santa Barbara, California 93116-1911

This book is printed on acid-free paper.
Manufactured in the United States of America.

Contents

PART 3: CURRENT ASSESSMENTS

Series Editor's Preface

In recent years, there has been a significant and steady increase of academic and popular interest in the study of past civilizations. This is due in part to the dramatic coverage—real or imagined—of the archaeological profession in popular film and television, and to the extensive journalistic reporting of spectacular new finds from all parts of the world. Yet, because archaeologists and other scholars have tended to approach their study of ancient peoples and civilizations exclusively from their own disciplinary perspectives and for their professional colleagues, there has long been a lack of general factual and other research resources available for the nonspecialist. The Understanding Ancient Civilizations series is intended to fill that need.

Volumes in the series are principally designed to introduce the general reader, student, and nonspecialist to the study of specific ancient civilizations. Each volume is devoted to a particular archaeological culture (for example, the ancient Maya of southern Mexico and adjacent Guatemala) or cultural region (for example, Israel and Canaan) and seeks to achieve, with careful selectivity and astute critical assessment of the literature, an expression of a particular civilization and an appreciation of its achievements.

The keynote of the Understanding Ancient Civilizations series is to provide, in a uniform format, an interpretation of each civilization that will express its culture and place in the world as well as the qualities and background that make it unique. Series titles include volumes on the archaeology and prehistory of the ancient civilizations of Egypt, Greece, Rome, and Mesopotamia, as well as the achievements of the Celts, Aztecs, and Inca, among others. Still more books are in the planning stage.

I was particularly fortunate in having Kevin Downing from ABC-CLIO contact me in search of an editor for a series about archaeology. It is a simple statement of the truth that there would be no series without him. I am also lucky to have Simon Mason, Kevin's successor from ABC-CLIO, continue to push the production of the series. Given the scale of the project and the schedule for production, he deserves more than a sincere thank you.

JOHN WEEKS

Preface and Acknowledgments

I suppose the most important question to answer here is: Why another book on the ancient Greeks? After all, people have been studying the ancient Greeks since, well, the days of ancient Greece itself, and the average bookshop and library have no lack of texts on this rich and fascinating society.

What I hoped to accomplish here was to write what I would call a more balanced and complete book on the ancient Greeks, presenting as much of their history and culture as possible as a continuous whole. Thus this book goes from Minoan Crete up through the reign of Cleopatra VII, the last of the Hellenistic monarchs, including information on the so-called Dark Age that separated the Bronze Age from the historic periods. I hope that my presentation of the information in this way will allow the reader to appreciate the long continuity of ancient Greek society and to understand that the glory days of Classical Greece did not spring up out of nowhere, but were the result of several centuries of growth, experimentation, and development.

Likewise, I wanted to correct a somewhat standard practice in the study of ancient Greece, whereby the city of Athens is presented as a microcosm of Classical Greece itself. Granted, we do have more texts from ancient Athens than from all other Greek cities, and the archaeological data for that city are quite extensive. However, one must remember that Athens was also rather weird by ancient Greek standards, the "wild, liberal left" of ancient Greece, and what held true for Athens was not necessarily the case, or even representative of, the other cities. Nevertheless, many books on ancient Greece focus primarily on Athens, with most specialized books focusing exclusively on Athens (Athenian law, Athenian democracy, Athenian religion, etc.). Although there is quite a bit of information on Athens in this book, too, I tried to expand the repertoire to focus on the other important regions of Greece, such as Sparta and Thebes.

Finally, I wanted to present a gender-balanced view of ancient Greek society. Only since the 1970s, with the rise of feminism and feminist theory in academia, has there been much focus on women in ancient societies, Greece included. When women, and then gender, became objects of study, the discipline was somewhat ghettoized, so that a general book on ancient Greece might have a subsection dealing with women, while most studies of ancient Greek women were present in books specifically dedicated to the topic. Here, I tried to present Greek history and society as a combination of men and women (which, let's face it, it was).

A FEW WORDS ON SPELLINGS

The Greek language uses a different alphabet than the one used by most Western languages, which derives from the Latin alphabet. Thus, all Greek words presented in languages other than Greek have to be transliterated (transferred from the Greek alphabet into the Latin one). Furthermore, as discussed in chapter 3 of this book, for a long time the Greek language was "lost" to people in the European West, and most Greek literature, history, and philosophy were only known through Latin translations. As a result, there was a common tendency to present Greek names and words first in their Latin translations (Venus for Aphrodite, for example) and then, when using Greek words themselves, in a Latinized form.

In the past few decades, there has been a growing trend among Hellenists (people who study ancient Greece) to use transliterations closer to the original Greek spellings. Technically speaking, the most common differences between the Latinized versions and the Greek versions are with the letters *k* and *c*, and the endings *-os* and *-us*. The letter *c* did not and does not exist in Greek; they have the letter *kappa* (κ) for the *k*-sound, and *sigma* (σ) for the *s*-sound. When the letter *c* appears in Greek words, it is usually a Latinized replacement for a kappa, thus Socrates (Latinized) versus Sokrates (Greek). The same goes for the Greek letter *khi* (χ), which is transliterated as *ch* in Latinized forms, *kh* in Greek. Likewise, the standard masculine word ending *-us* is actually Latin, being the equivalent of the Greek *-os*, thus the difference between Mt. Olympus and Mt. Olympos.

The problem now with transliterations from Greek is how Greek to keep the words, a decision that is generally up to each individual author. Quite frankly, it is difficult to go 100 percent in either direction. Some Latinized forms now look quite out-of-date, such as Cnossus for the city of Knossos. For other words, though, the Greek form looks completely alien, such as Epikouros for Epicurus.

I originally wanted to keep the transliterations in the book as Greek as possible. However, I polled a group of my students, who overwhelmingly preferred the "normal" (Latinized) spellings. And so, with a few very minor exceptions, such as Olympos for Olympus, the more common, Latinized spellings have been used.

One final note on pronunciation. There is no silent *e* in Greek. *E* is a common word ending in Greek, and in this book I frequently wrote it as *ê* to emphasize its pronunciation. This was mainly so for words that might not be as familiar to the reader, such as Persephonê (per-SEF-o-nee) and the city of Prienê (pre-EN-ee).

ACKNOWLEDGMENTS

I would first like to thank the wonderful folks at ABC-CLIO for all their help and patience in the writing of this book. Cheers to John Weeks for giving me the opportunity to write this book at all, to Kevin Downing and Simon Mason for guiding me in the writing stages (and the rather hopeless task of trying to keep my word count down), and to Gina Zondorak and Michelle Trader for seeing this project through to completion. Many thanks also to Giulia Rossi for the manic task of getting together pictures.

I would also like to thank the various scholars who let me use different aspects of their work in this book. Very many thanks to Simon Ager for letting me use his Linear B syllab chart in the section on "How to Read Linear B." It is definitely the most user-friendly version I have ever seen. My deepest appreciation goes to Paul Cartledge, Robert Garland, Martin Ostwald, Simon Price, and Ronald Stroud for letting me use their translations of philosophical texts, epigraphy, and papyri throughout these pages.

Finally, I send all my love and thanks to my husband, Paul Butler, who provided all the fine drawings throughout this text (except the ground plans, done by me, which are easily distinguishable because they look like they were drawn on an Etch-a-Sketch by a five-year-old with a nervous disorder), is infinitely supportive in all ways, and who had to live with books EVERYWHERE for quite a while.

MACEDONIA

CHALKIDIKE

Corfu

EPIRUS
• Dodona

THESSALY
Petra • • Sesklo
• Iolkos (Volos)

Mt. Othrys

Levkas

ARCARNANIA
AETOLIA

EUBOEA

Krisa • • Delphi • Orchomenos
• Gla • Lefkandi
BOIOTIA
Ithaca • Thebes

Cephalonia

Dymaia • Marathon
ACHEA Ephyra • Eleusis
ATTICA • Perati
• Athens

Iakynthos
(Zante)

ELIS CORINTHIA
Corinth Salamis Laurion
Olympia • Mycenae • Aegina Keos
ARCADIA Argos • Tiryns
Kakovatos • Asine
Malthi Nauplia ARGOLID
MESSENIA Sparta
Routsi • Vapheio
Pylos • Nichoria
Koryphasion LACONIA

Melos Phylak

Kythera

0   50   100 mi

Tylis
CRET

HaghiaTriadha •
Phaistos

THRACE

PHRYGIA

Lemnos

Troy

TROAD

Lesbos

LYDIA

Chios

Smyrna

Ephesus

Samos

Miletus

CARIA

Delos

Iasos

Halicarnassos

Cos

Knidos

Thera

Triandha

Rhodes

Dodecanese

C. Gelidonya

ANATOLIA

Amnisos

Mallia

nossos

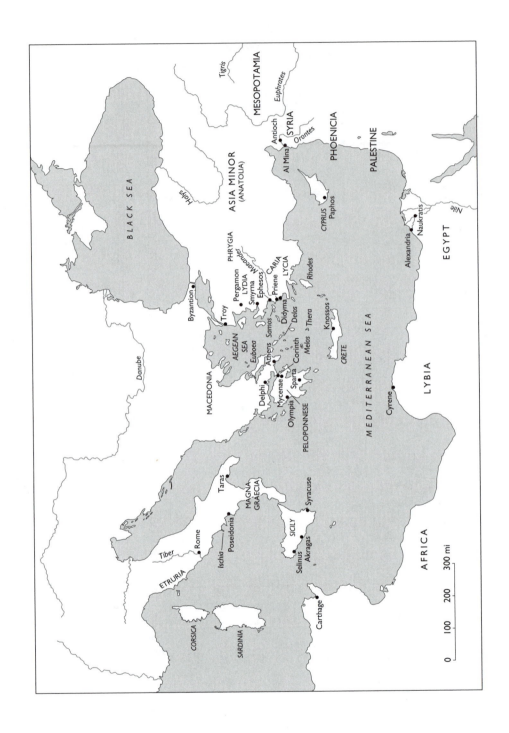

PART I

Introduction

CHAPTER I

Introduction

The ancient Greeks were speakers of the Greek language, who first emerged as a distinct civilization in the region of the Greek peninsula in the eastern Mediterranean during the Bronze Age (before 1000 B.C.E.). They eventually came to occupy Europe and Asia from France in the west to Egypt in the south to India in the east.

The Greek language is an Indo-European language, meaning it is related to languages such as Irish, German, Latin, French, Russian, ancient Hittite, and the dialects of Iran and India. All these languages derive from one postulated original language called *Proto-Indo-European (the * means that the language has never been encountered but is a theoretical reconstruction). The relationships among these languages were discovered by the Grimm brothers, the same men who collected German fairy tales. They noted that several languages used very similar words to express the same concept, leading them to conclude that these languages evolved from a common ancestor. For example, the word for *father* in Latin is *pater,* in Greek *patêr,* in Vedic (India) *pitar,* in Irish *athair* (the *p* has dropped off), in German *Vater,* and in English, of course, *father.* The Greeks were descendants of this large linguistic family, and the Greeks themselves are therefore related to many other inhabitants of ancient and modern Europe, Persia, and India.

The first evidence we have of Greek as a language is its presence in the Linear B tablets from the Greek mainland and the island of Crete (see chapter 3). So we know that the Greeks existed as a Greek-speaking (or, at least, Greek-writing) population from at least 1450 B.C.E. on the Greek mainland, although they almost certainly arrived in the area several hundreds of years before this (see chapter 4).

One very important civilization these early Greeks encountered in their settlement of Greece were the Minoans, a non-Greek, probably non-Indo-European-speaking population that lived on the island of Crete. Even though these Minoans were not Greeks, they greatly influenced the development of early Greek culture, and they must be considered in any early history of Greece.

WHAT DID THE GREEKS CONTRIBUTE TO MODERN SOCIETY?

The modern world, especially the West, is filled with elements of Greek culture, from the languages we speak to the buildings we work in.

Language

About 70 percent of the words in the English language come from either Latin or Greek. The word *acrophobia* derives from the Greek words for *high* (*akros*) and *fear* (*phobos*). *Logos* is the Greek word for *word, study, argument,* or *story,* leading to such combinations as *biology* (*bios* = life), theology (*theos* = god), and anthropology (*anthropos* = human). Other terms in English derive from names of Greek gods, people, and concepts, which continue to be influential in modern thought. For example, we refer to platonic love, which is named after Plato, the philosopher who contrasted sexual attraction with nonerotic love (and wound up being famous for the latter). The term *erotic* itself comes from the name of the Greek god of sexual attraction: Eros. Likewise, a bacchanalia, or wild revelry, was originally named for the Greek god of wine: Dionysos Bacchus.

Literature

Several genres of modern literature have their origins in ancient Greece. Drama is a prime example—the genres of tragedy and comedy were both originally developed in Greece in the sixth and fifth centuries B.C.E. Aristotle, the Athenian philosopher and tutor to Alexander the Great, wrote that all drama should be ordered according to three unities: unity of time, of place, and of action (*Poetics*). Put simply, he said that all plays should deal with one topic in one day in one place. The seventeenth-century French dramatists Corneille and Racine took this notion so seriously that, in their works, a hero can travel from France to Spain (off scene, of course), defeat an Arabic army, return to France, and get married in one day, so as to stick to the Aristotelian unities. The fine art of publicly ridiculing celebrities was also popularized by the Greeks in their comedies, wherein one could watch the philosopher Socrates with his head literally in the clouds, the Athenian and Spartan armies brought low by a sex boycott from their wives, and even the god Dionysos wetting himself on stage.

Beyond merely the form of literature, the Greeks contributed much symbolic language to modern literature. Many allusions in Western literature come from Greek mythology. In his poem "The Raven," Edgar Allan Poe tells us:

> Open here I flung the shutter, when, with many a flirt and flutter,
> In there stepped a stately Raven of the saintly days of yore;
> Not the least obeisance made he; not an instant stopped or stayed he;
> But, with mien of lord or lady, perched above my chamber door—
> Perched upon a bust of Pallas just above my chamber door—
> Perched, and sat, and nothing more.

Pallas is an epithet or nickname for the wisdom goddess Athena, and thus refers to sanity and reason, both of which the narrator is about to lose completely, as evidenced by the Raven overshadowing this image.

More recently, in the song "Wrapped Around Your Finger" by the Police, the narrator claims that he is "caught between the Scylla and Charybdis." Here he refers to two monsters present in Homer's *Odyssey*—Scylla, a six-headed monster who ate sailors for lunch, and Charybdis, who sucked up sea, boat, and, of course, sailors thrice per day for fun. Being caught between these two monsters is a poetic and erudite way of expressing the concept of being stuck between a rock and a hard place.

Architecture and Art

The ancient Greeks not only gave us many elements used in architecture, but they also contributed heavily to modern aesthetics, or a sense of good taste. As discussed in chapter 9, the Greeks developed three orders or styles of public building: the Doric, Ionic, and Corinthian, each of which featured distinctive styles of columns and decoration. The most famous example of Doric architecture is the Parthenon in Athens, a temple dedicated to Athena, the patron goddess of the city. A near replica of this Parthenon can be found in the city of Philadelphia, where the architect William Strickland (1788–1854) designed the Second National Bank in the form of the Greek temple. But elements of Greek architecture are often present even when the building being designed is not intended as a replica. Marble columns with Doric or Ionic volute capitals (curled "caps" on top of the columns) are a common motif in many public buildings, from the United States Capitol Building to the Louvre.

The ancient Greeks, especially during and after the fifth century, achieved a breathtaking skill in the rendering of the human form, most notably in sculpture. Their style of idealized realism contributed to the modern Western taste for realism in art—for having the created object look as much as possible like the item being copied. Such perfection of form influenced the Renaissance artists, inspiring such works as Michelangelo's *David*.

Of course, one might see a certain downside to this desire for realism and perfection in the difficulty that the early Impressionists had in having their less-than-realistic creations accepted as art, much less as good art. This preference for the realistic, especially for an idealized realism (portraying subjects realistically, but with none of the wrinkles, sags, etc., found in real life), has also contributed to a certain snobbery against the so-called Primitive art discovered throughout the past few centuries in regions such as Africa and Polynesia (*poly* = many and *nesos* = island, thus, the land of many islands). Only by considering alternate aesthetics those of the ancient Greeks were modern audiences able to appreciate the meaning, symbolic content, and beauty of non–Classically oriented, non-photo-realistic artistic creations.

Philosophy

Some of the earliest known attempts at organizing the universe into a coherent set of logical precepts were first worked out by the ancient Greeks. This includes not only attempts to classify reality, but the means by which reality itself might be understood and examined. Socrates, through his student Plato, popularized the Socratic Method of inquiry, whereby all assumptions were subjected to a rigorous cross-examination to see if assumptions might stand up in the face of critical reason. Socrates, in the Platonic dialogue *Phaedrus*, also delineated the ideal form for defining a concept or idea. In section 265 D, he argued that all ideas must be defined through a process of grouping and discrimination, whereby one would show the relationships existing between groups of ideas or things and also explain how an idea or thing is distinct from other ideas or things in its grouping.

Aristotle, a student of Plato, took this ideal to logical extremes and attempted to organize the entire universe into an appropriate set of groupings, with ideals and laws established for each category of reality. His classifications extended from grammar to politics to biology, thus paving the way for the Swedish botanist Linnaeus, who established a nomenclature system in the eighteenth century.

Science

The classification and attempt to understand the physical universe did not begin with Aristotle. The Mesopotamians were active in the acquisition of information about mathematics and astronomy centuries before our earliest Greek documents were created. Nevertheless, it was the Greek natural philosophers, whom we would now call scientists, who attempted to understand the laws behind the motions of the universe, thus giving rise to the disciplines of physics and astronomy. Not all of the Greeks' ideas turned out to be correct, however. Aristotle believed that the rate of downward movement of various objects was determined by each object's "natural resting state." A stone clearly wanted to be on the ground and so fell quickly, whereas a feather wanted to be in the air and only fell slowly. He concluded that if you tied a feather to a stone, the stone would fall half as quickly.

But many Greek achievements in these fields did prove to be accurate. Thales of Miletos (625–585 B.C.E.), our first recorded natural philosopher, was the first Westerner to predict a solar eclipse by observing and calculating the paths of the sun and moon. Both he and Anaximander of Miletos (c. 570 B.C.E.) determined that, contrary to popular opinion, the Earth was actually round and suspended in space. Hipparchus of Nicaea (190–126 B.C.E.) studied the problem of parallax (seeing one object from two different perspectives) and determined the size and distance of the sun and moon.

Not only did the Greeks provide us with many of the tools and theories used in modern science; they also gave us many of the names we use in our studies. The name of the element helium, for example, derives from the Greek name for sun—*Helios*. The name of the element hydrogen, which mixes with oxygen to form water, derives from the Greek words for *water creator: hydros* = water, *genos* = family. Likewise, for the human body, the word *thorax* (referring to the chest) comes from the Greek word *thorax*, a piece of armor that protected the chest. The Greek words for *seashore* (*paralios*) and *giant* (*titanos*) give us the name of a very large dinosaur from Egypt, the Paralititan. In fact, most terminology for dinosaurs comes from Greek.

The influence of the ancient Greeks can be felt in many aspects of modern society, from the words we use to the allusions we make, from our means of constructing a building to our means of constructing an argument. Every time we see a play or analyze a statue, every time we sit through astronomy class or study the periodic table of elements, we are in some way indebted to the ancient Greeks.

FURTHER STUDIES

The study of the ancient Greeks (often combined with the study of the ancient Romans) is well entrenched in modern academia. There are very few universities in the world that do not offer some aspect of classical studies (Greeks and Romans), either as its own major or offered under the rubric of (ancient) history. How each institution chooses to present these studies differs. Some schools are very specific in their training, focusing on the languages of Greece and Rome in classics, the physical culture of these societies in archaeology, and the art history as a component of art historical studies. Other institutions combine several aspects of ancient Greek studies into one, so that one might study Plato *and* Mycenaean architecture within one department.

As with university studies, so too with museums. Well before archaeology was a scientific discipline, art connoisseurs acquired and/or stole elements of Greek art to decorate homes and galleries. (Actually, one of the first people to do this was Emperor Constantine, who acquired many pieces of Greek art to decorate his capitol at Constantinople.) From this early period, and certainly since the rise of the archaeological discipline, Greece has been a major focus of archaeological investigations, and many pieces of Greek art and physical culture are displayed in museums throughout the world.

This does cause some controversy. In many instances, Greece wants its artworks back. This is especially so with the Elgin Marbles—sculpture taken from the Parthenon by one Lord Elgin and now on display in the British Museum. In other cases, pieces of art are acquired through illicit sources, such as items stolen from sites and sold on the antiquities market. Since 1977, most of the world's leading museums have agreed not to buy items so retrieved, but this unfortunately has not stopped the spread of illegal "excavations," as private individuals still pay for stolen objects. Nevertheless, many museums throughout the world carry some amount of ancient Greek objects for perusal and study. Notable museums for Greek studies are the National Museum in Athens (which has the side benefit of being in Athens, so the visitor can see the archaeological sites as well) and the Athens Acropolis Museum, the Metropolitan Museum of Art in New York City, the University Museum of Archaeology and Anthropology in Philadelphia, the British Museum in London, and the Louvre in Paris. For a sense of the richness of ancient Greek archaeology and its Greek exhibits, check out http://www.culture.gr.

There are also a number of journals that provide access to the ancient Greek world. Many of these begin with the word "Classical." Thus, one might check out *Classical Quarterly, Classical World, Classical Philology,* or *Classical Antiquity.* Other important periodicals in this discipline are *Transactions of the American Philological Association* (*TAPA*) and the *American Journal of Archaeology* (*AJA*).

For studies ranging from the literary to the artistic, one might consider *Greek, Roman, and Byzantine Studies.* For more cutting-edge literary studies, there is *Arion.* For a full list of all publications in the field of Classics (Greek and Roman studies), one can consult *L'Année philologique.*

Ultimately, ancient Greece is an extremely accessible subject. Literally millennia of interest have guaranteed that peoples, universities, and museums all over the globe offer some aspect of ancient Greek studies to the amateur and enthusiast alike. The bibliography at the end of this book offers some suggestions for books and other Web sites that may prove of particular interest in this regard.

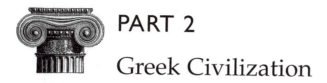

PART 2

Greek Civilization

Location of Greek Civilization
and Environmental Setting

The geography of ancient Greece is a far grander and more complex issue than in modern times. Although the Greek mainland, the island of Crete, and the Cycladic islands started out as the core of ancient Greece, relocation and colonization brought the Greeks all over the ancient world. By 1100 B.C.E., the Greeks had settled on Cyprus and the western coast of Asia Minor (now known as Turkey), including the islands off its coast. By the eighth century, they had settled off the western coast of Italy, and from there they slowly progressed into much of southern Italy and Sicily. Farther west, the Greeks colonized southern France. To the east, they established cities along the Black Sea and in the Ukraine. Under Alexander the Great, they conquered and settled Egypt, Palestine, Syria, Iraq, Iran, and even parts of India. Discussing the geography of ancient Greece, then, can be a tricky topic. This book will discuss the Greek mainland, Greek islands, and Asia Minor—the core area of the Greeks' world.

THE GREEK MAINLAND

The Greek mainland is actually a peninsula. To the west is the Ionian Sea, to the east is the Aegean Sea, and to the south is the Mediterranean Sea. The term *mainland* itself is almost a misnomer, for even this part of the Greek world is composed mostly of smaller peninsulas and islands, such as Euboia and Aigina off the east coast of Attica. (Even the southernmost part of Greece, the Peloponnese, was called Island of Pelops and is only connected to central Greece by a tiny isthmus at Corinth, separating the Corinthian and Saronic Gulfs.) In the extreme south, the landmass of the Peloponnese is cut at its eastern end by the Gulf of Argolis, and the low-lying plain thereabouts is called the Argolid.

The three best words to describe the Greek mainland are *rocky, hilly,* and *mountainous.* The farther south one goes, the more rocky and mountainous the land becomes. Thucydides, in Book 1 of his history of the Peloponnesian War, tells us that the soil of Attica in central Greece was so rocky and poor that when the Dorian invaders came, they passed right by it, looking for "good" land to settle. The mountainous quality of the terrain was significant in the history of Greece and the Greek peoples: It caused many individual city-states to be cut off from their neighbors, and the city-states consequently evolved with a strong sense of regionalism and political independence from one another. This kept the Greeks from uniting into a single power until the rise of Macedon in the fourth century. This also forced the Greeks to travel a great deal by sea, which led very early on to long-distance trade and naval prowess.

In the north, lofty Mt. Olympos dominates the horizon, marking the ancient boundary between Greece and Macedon. The Pindus mountain chain divides northern Greece, running north-south along the western edge of the country all the way down to the Gulf of Corinth. To the east of this range is a series of mountains running east-west, dominated by (north to south) Mt. Olympos, Mt. Ossa, Mt. Pelion, Mt. Othrys, Mt. Parnassos, Mt. Helikon, and Mt. Parnes. The Peloponnese is also dominated by high ground, notably by Mt. Kyllene, Mt. Parnon, and Mt. Taygetos near Sparta. The barriers that these mountains present can be thoroughly appreciated upon a visit to the country. Unlike the rolling slopes of the Rocky Mountains, the mountains of Greece are steep and abrupt. Walking in the suburbs of Sparta, one approaches what appears to be a solid wall stretching straight up into the sky. This is Taygetos. Also of considerable importance in the Peloponnese are the highlands of Arcadia, a high plateau in the center of the landmass. This area is so high as to be freezing most of the year, and it is possible to get frostbite at the Arcadian Temple of Apollo at Bassae in August.

Ancient Macedon abutted the northern border of ancient Greece. To the east was Thrace, which was seen by the Greeks as barbaric and was mainly a source of slaves. Macedon was bordered by Mt. Olympos to the south and cut through by the Haliakmon River, running mostly east to west. To the extreme east of the mainland is the Chalkidikê, an udder-like formation with three peninsulas reaching down into the Aegean Sea.

The ancient Greeks exploited the bounteous natural resources that the land provided. Only the northern regions had flat terrain and rich soil, but some degree of farming and pasturage was possible throughout the land. The region around Sikyon near the Isthmus of Corinth grew rich on timber, which was used to build ships during the Classical period. Otherwise, large trees were restricted to the north, and much of Greece was covered by the smaller, lucrative olive tree, believed to be a gift from Athena. These small, silvery, scrubby trees provided not merely food in the form of olives, but also energy from wood and olive oil. The oil was also useful as a massage oil and skin moisturizer. The other major plant cultivated throughout the land was the grapevine, a gift from Dionysos, and wine was a major export throughout Greek history. (In modern times, the most famous Greek wine is retsina, flavored and preserved with pine. Although this might not sound so appetizing, keep in mind that in the Medieval and early Modern periods, other countries tempered their wine with lead.)

The scrubby, dry, rocky surface of the land is not well suited to raising large cattle but is ideal for sheep and goats, which provided wool, milk, and occasional meat for the ancient Greeks.

Although the land might not have been ideal for large-scale farming, the soil was rich in clay, and the Greeks became famous throughout the Mediterranean region for their exquisite pottery. Almost all major city-states produced their own wares, but the best pottery, used throughout the Mediterranean and now found in millions of museums throughout the world, came from Athens, Corinth, and the Argolid.

Mt. Penteli produced a fine grade of marble; it was one of the very few mainland sources of marble in Greece. Most of this mineral came from the islands, specifically the Cyclades (see below) and the northern island of Thasos, where some of the beaches are actually marble "floors."

Silver came from Macedon (Philip II used it to fund his armies) and from the Laurion mines in Attica (used by the Athenians to fund their navy). Otherwise, there were only sparse deposits of minerals on the Greek mainland, notably iron, and most metals had to be imported.

The climate of mainland Greece is Mediterranean, with hot, dry summers and mild, damp winters. Rainfall varies between heavy storms and drought, so farming was, as previously mentioned, precarious.

CRETE

The island of Crete, located in the eastern Mediterranean, is bathed by the Sea of Crete to the north and the Libyan Sea to the south. It is the largest of the Aegean islands, being 250 kilometers long and between 58 and 12.5 kilometers wide. Like the mainland, the island is very mountainous, with the White Mountains in the west, Mt. Ida in the center, and Mt. Dikte in the eastern-central part of the island dominating the land. The Bay of Mirabello lies at the northeast corner of the island, where smaller islands such as Mochlos and Pseira are located. The south-central portion of the island is a plain called the Mesará, dominated by Mt. Kofina and bounded by the River Ieropotamos to the north. Upland plains are also common on the island, notably the Lassithi Plateau, the Nida Plateau near Mt. Ida, and the Omalos Plateau in the White Mountains. Crete has one freshwater lake, the Kournas, located on the northwest coast of the island.

Like the mainland, Crete has a Mediterranean climate, generally being hot and dry in summer and cold in winter. Changes in temperature can be quite abrupt, however, and the visitor can find herself going from winter coat to T-shirt in the course of one day.

Also like the mainland, Crete is blessed with fine clay for pottery, and Minoan wares were considered a luxury item in the eastern Mediterranean throughout the Bronze Age. The Minoans also sculpted in stone, including serpentine, limestone, and alabaster. Alabaster—also called gypsum—and limestone were also used in architecture in the Minoan palaces, to pave the floors and to construct the stairways. Alabaster was available locally both from Gypsadhes, near Knossos in the north of the island, and from an area near Gortyn in the south.

CYCLADES

As the name indicates, these islands form a cyclical pattern around the sacred island of Delos (see chapter 8) in the Aegean Sea. Twelve to fifteen islands constituted this rather artificial political formation. The climate is, like that of the mainland and Crete, Mediterranean. The most important Cycladic natural resources were obsidian, which was found in abundance on the island of Melos, and marble, especially from the islands of Naxos and Paros.

ASIA MINOR'S WEST COAST

The Anatolian (Turkish) Peninsula was occupied throughout the Bronze Age by a variety of cultures, including the Hittites, Luwians, and Hurrians, many of whom had contact with the Minoans and Mycenaeans. One of the earliest Minoan-Mycenaean settlements in Asia Minor was at the site of Miletos, on the mouth of the Meander River in the region that was later known as Ionia. Hittite documents refer to a great kingdom known as the Ahhijawoi (possibly a version of *Achaean*, one of the Homeric terms for the Greeks), who may have resided at Miletos in the Bronze Age.   ·

When the Greeks arrived to settle the Anatolian Peninsula in the early Iron Age (1100 b.c.e.), there were already a number of peoples inhabiting the land, and the Greeks could only claim the coastal regions and the large islands off the coast. To the northeast were the Phrygians (whose most famous king was the semilegendary King Midas) and the Lydians, to the south were the Carians (whose king, Mausoleus, had a tomb so elaborate that he gave us the term for an elaborate burial structure—the mausoleum), and farther east were the great powers of Babylon and Assyria.

The largest coastal islands near the peninsula are Lesbos (home of the poet Sappho), Chios, Samos, Cos (home of Hippocrates, the father of modern medicine), and Rhodes. Lesbos has an area of 1,632 square kilometers. In shape, it is like a large triangle, cut on the south by the Gulf of Kalloni and to the southeast by the Gulf of Year. The northeast coast faces the Gulf of Edremit, separating it from the mainland. The climate is essentially temperate, allowing for the growing of grapes, and Lesbian wine was famous in antiquity.

Chios, much smaller, is 48 kilometers long and ranges in width from 13 to 24 kilometers. Mountains and hills traverse the island from north to south, with the highest point on the island being Mt. Pelinaion in the north. The island has very fertile soil, and in ancient times it was a major producer of wine, grain, figs, and gum-mastic (nowadays used to make chewing gum). Chios was also a major producer of marble, equaling Naxos and Paros in the Cyclades.

Samos has an area of 492 square kilometers. Like most other areas of the Greek world, it is mountainous, with the main ridge running east-west, with peaks at Karvouni in the center and Kerkis in the west. Although the north of the island is rather rocky, the southern coast has small plains and beaches. Samian wine was not considered to be very good, but the island was renowned for all its other agricultural products.

Cos is 282 square kilometers in area and is a small strip along the edge of Asia Minor, ending in the southwest at the narrow peninsula of Kefalos. The high points of the island are Mt. Dikaios in the northeast and Mt. Latra in the southwest. The lower mountain chain runs along the south from Cape Foka in the east to the region of Pilí in the center. The land is well watered and produces fruit, vegetables, and, of course, wine.

At the southern corner of Asia Minor is the island of Rhodes, one of twelve islands that together were called the Dodecanese (literally "twelve islands"). It is separated from the mainland by the Strait of Marmara. The island's area is 1,398.5 square kilometers, making it one of the largest of the Aegean islands. It is traversed north to south by a range of hills, the highest of which is Mt. Atavi-ros. The climate is generally mild, although the island is rather windy. The island produces a rose-colored rock that may have given it its name (*rhodos* = rose). It also produces a fair number of snakes, most of which are harmless.

The mainland of Asia Minor reaches to the Ionian Sea and the Sea of Marmara in the north, and to the Mediterranean Sea in the south. Although the plateaus of Turkey are quite high, the area around the western coast, especially in the river valleys, is low, lush, and quite fertile. The major rivers are the Skamander, along which lies the site of ancient Troy and the lofty Mt. Ida; the Kaikos to the east of Lesbos; and the Hermos River that runs past the Lydian capital of Sardis and that is joined from the north by the Lykos (or "Wolf") River. The Kayster River runs east-west just south of Mt. Tmolos in the center of Asia Minor, and farther south the mighty Meander cuts deeply into the mainland's interior, emptying into the Mediterranean at Miletos. The southern tip of Asia Minor is dominated by the jutting semipeninsula of ancient Halicar-nassus (modern Bodrum) and the peninsula of Knidos, reaching out almost to touch Cos to the west.

The milder climate and flatter surface of the land in Asia Minor allowed the eastern Greeks a few more agricultural activities than their western cousins. There were more large trees in Asia Minor than in Greece, and the land supported larger cattle. The northern regions were famous, at least since the days of Homer, for horse breeding. Iron was also found in greater abundance in Asia Minor than in Greece.

CYPRUS

Cyprus is the third largest island in the Mediterranean, measuring 222 kilometers from east to west and up to 95 kilometers north to south. The land is dominated by the Kyrenia mountain range, stretching east-west along the northern coast, and the Troodos mountains in the central western portion of the island. The highest point of land is called Mt. Olympos (another Mt. Olympos), located within the Troodos mountains. Between these mountain ranges is the Mesaoria Plain. The southeastern regions of the island are well watered by rivers coming down from the Troodos range, and the coastal plains in the north are likewise well watered and fertile. The climate of Cyprus is semiarid, although the summers are hot and extremely humid.

The single most important resource produced on Cyprus during ancient times was copper. The word *Cyprus* itself comes from the Greek word for copper (*kupros*), and the island was exporting this metal in large quantities at least as early as the early second millennium B.C.E.

REFERENCE

Speake, G., ed. 2001. *Encyclopedia of Greece and the Hellenic Tradition.* London: Fitzroy Dearborn.

CHAPTER 3

Historical and Chronological Setting

THE HISTORY OF GREEK STUDIES

Antiquity

It is difficult to pinpoint a time when the study of ancient Greece began. Our earliest literature from ancient Greece—Homer's *Iliad* and *Odyssey*—deal with the history of the Trojan War and the kings of Mycenaean Greece. As a result, one could argue that the study of ancient Greece dates back as far as the eighth century, before the majority of what we now consider to be "ancient Greek history" actually took place.

The word *history* itself is a Greek term meaning *inquiries,* and it was first used in the modern sense by the Greek historian Herodotus, who wrote the history of the Persian invasions that occurred during the fifth century. This "father of history" was the first non-myth-based historian in Greece. He was followed by his protégé Thucydides who, in the fifth and fourth centuries, wrote the history of the Peloponnesian War. These, in turn, were followed by such fourth-century historians as Xenophon, whose work is one of our main sources for information about Cyrus of Persia, Socrates of Athens, and Sparta in general. Information about Alexander the Great and the Hellenistic kingdoms that sprang up in his wake comes from Diodorus Siculus, who wrote in the late first century B.C.E.; Justinus, who summarized the works of an otherwise lost historian of the first century C.E. named Trogus Pompeius; and Plutarch of Chaeronea, who wrote in the second century C.E. and left us several biographies of the ancient Greeks and Romans.

Other historians important to the study of ancient Greece are Strabo, who lived in the first centuries B.C.E.–C.E. and whose *Geography* sheds much light on the ancient world; and Pausanias, who wrote *The Description of Greece* (the ancient equivalent of a Blue Guide) in the second century C.E. The works of the authors of antiquity, especially those of Herodotus, Thucydides, Xenophon, Pausanias, and Strabo, form the core of our knowledge about the history of ancient Greece.

The Romans conquered Greece and many parts of the Hellenistic kingdoms in the second and first centuries B.C.E. (see chapter 4). Fortunately for Hellenists, several of the later Roman emperors, notably Hadrian the philhellên ("Greek lover"), thought very highly of the achievements of the ancient Greeks and preserved their works, language, and even culture in at least the eastern half of the Roman Empire. It is notable that although Julius Caesar wrote his history of the Gallic Wars in Latin, the second century C.E. philosopher-emperor Marcus Aurelius wrote his Stoic treatise "Meditations" in Greek. The Romans recognized that the Greek language allowed for greater subtleties than did Latin, making the former a better language for philosophy and, later, theology.

This tendency to write in Greek was further enhanced by a trend called Atticism, which began as early as the age of Augustus (first century C.E.) and grew during the second century C.E. By this time, the Greek language had changed considerably from what it had been in the Golden Age of Greece—the fifth and fourth centuries B.C.E.—as is evident in the grammar and vocabulary of the Bible's New Testament. Nevertheless, Roman-period scholars decided that the Attic dialect of Aristotle and Thucydides was the most appropriate form of the language, and, thus, the only form acceptable for the Empire's educated elite. So began a tradition (which still exists to some extent in modern Greece) of writing in a language utterly different from the spoken vernacular. As one can imagine, this fostered several manuals of Attic grammar, syntax, and vocabulary, as well as the repeated publication of the works of the authors of the purest dialects, so that the Roman literati could imitate historians and philosophers who had been dead for at least 400 years.

As in modern times, the great works during the time of the Greeks and Romans were kept in libraries, the most famous of which in the ancient world were those of Athens (Greece), Constantinople/Istanbul (Turkey), Pergamon (Turkey), Antioch (Syria), Beirut (Lebanon), Gaza (Palestine), and Alexandria (Egypt). Each of these libraries had its own areas of specialization: The library at Beirut was a law school, while students of Plato and the later Neoplatonic doctrines held sway in Athens (Wilson 1983, 28 ff.). The library in Alexandria was where Hellenistic scholars began the compilation and criticism of the ancient Greek poets and where the Roman geographer/historian Strabo did much of the research for his *Geography*; at Gaza, the Byzantine historian Procopius wrote a scandalous biography of the Empress Theodora, paraphrased the works of Homer, and possibly invented the ancestor of the modern footnote (Wilson 1983, 30–36). The library at Pergamon was the first of this group to go into decline, specifically when Marc Antony donated many of its contents to the library at Alexandria to make up for losses experienced there in a recent fire (Plutarch, *Antony* 58). Collectively, these libraries were the loci of extensive studies of the ancient Greeks, their culture, and their history.

The Middle Ages: The East

One must remember that the terms *Byzantine* and *Byzantium* are not entirely descriptive of what existed in southeastern Europe and western Asia during the first and second millennia C.E. (Although these terms are misnomers, they are commonly accepted.) This area was actually the continuation of the eastern half of the Roman Empire. It still considered itself to be of the Roman Empire, inhabited by Romans, and controlled by the eastern capital of the Roman Empire, Constantinople (the city was founded on the site of the Greek colony of Byzantion, hence its original name, Byzantium). Even the newly established

Germanic kingdoms of western Europe recognized the authority of the Roman emperor in Constantinople until the coronation of Charlemagne as emperor in 800 C.E. (the Germans apparently were not willing to recognize the suzerainty of the Byzantine empress Irene). So although Greek studies did go into decline in the West after the fall of Rome in 476 C.E., the classical culture persevered in the East, with a particular emphasis on Hellenism. By the sixth century C.E., Greek had replaced Latin as the primary language of this vestigial Roman Empire.

It was only during the Iconoclasm Controversy (eighth to ninth centuries C.E.) that there was a minor dark age in classical studies: During this time, intellectual focus shifted from the literature of the past to theological debates about the use of icons in Christian ritual and devotion (Neoplatonic philosophy did ultimately aid the cause of the iconophiles). Nevertheless, while the Byzantine "Romans" debated their religious beliefs, Asian scholars worked assiduously at translating the Greek and Roman classics into Syriac, Armenian, and Arabic. Many medical and scientific texts were so translated, leading to their eventual circulation in the Muslim empires and reintroduction into western Europe by way of Sicily and Spain (see below).

The Iconoclasm Controversy came to an end in 843 C.E., ushering in a minor renaissance in classical studies in the leftover Rome/Byzantium. At the vanguard of this renaissance was Leo the Mathematician (c. 790–869), who was a high church official of Thessalonica (northern Greece) until the end of the iconoclasm issue and then was head of the philosophy department at the University of Magnaura. Here he taught and edited the works of Plato as well as studying Aristotle, Epicurus, Euclid, Ptolemy, Homer, and Hesiod (Karlin-Hayter 2000b, 944).

The most famous classical scholars of this time were Photius (810–893), a civil servant and, eventually, Byzantine patriarch, and Arethas (860–935), archbishop of Caesarea in Cappadocia (modern Turkey). Photius is most famous for his *Lexicon*, which provides both definitions and commentary on the Greek language, and for his *Bibliotheka* (*Library*), which is one of our earliest and most extensive commentaries on ancient Greek literature, consisting of 280 chapters of commentary about 386 books (Littlewood 2000, 1314). Although Photius was a brilliant scholar, Arethas was most famous as a book collector. Within his personal library were annotated versions of works by Plato, Aristotle, Euclid, Marcus Aurelius, Pausanias, Pindar, Aelius Aristides, and Lucian (the last two were Roman-age authors who wrote in Attic style), among others (Karlin-Hayter 2000a, 150).

Two practical inventions aided this ninth-century renaissance. The first was paper, a new medium for writing that the Byzantines learned from the Arabs (who, in turn, had learned about it from the Chinese). Being much less costly to produce and prepare than animal-skin-based parchment and vellum, paper greatly reduced the cost of publications. The second development was a new style of writing known as miniscule, which used the existing letters written smaller but also included new characters. This miniscule text replaced the much larger uncial scripts of the Roman period, which was used for both

Greek and Latin. The small script not only allowed more text to fit on any given page, it also prompted the Byzantine scribes to "translate" as many of the classical texts as possible into the new hand. Many of our surviving manuscripts of classical Greek texts derive from the great "translating" effort of the ninth century (Wilson 1983, 63–68).

One of the most important aids in the study of ancient Greece was created in the tenth century, probably during the reign of John Tzimisces (969–976 C.E.). This was the *Suda,* an encyclopedia of classical knowledge, texts, and scholia (commentaries on the classical texts). This work provides biographical information, textual criticism, and many sources and fragments whose original texts are now lost from the classical repertoire (Reynolds and Wilson 1991, 66).

The eleventh and twelfth centuries saw important strides in the field of ancient Greek philosophy, particularly under the auspices of Michael Psellus (1018–1078) and Anna Komnena (1083–1153). The former was director of the school of philosophy at the university in Constantinople. Although much of Psellus's scholarship was directed toward Christian themes, he was also particularly interested in the ancient Greek novel, and his work dealt with commentaries on such authors as Heliodorus and Achilles Tatius. Most importantly, his energetic teaching at the university led to a renewed interest in Plato and Aristotle. This interest was taken up by Anna Komnena, daughter of the emperor Alexius I and patron of the scholars Eustratius of Nicaea and Michael of Ephesus. Although Anna wrote the history of her father's reign (Alexius I, 1081–1118), a work that itself is replete with classical references and allusions, Eustratius and Michael wrote commentaries on Aristotle's work. It is significant that they not only focused on Aristotle's works in the humanities, but on his scientific treatises as well (Reynolds and Wilson 1991, 69).

It is commonly assumed that all classical learning was "lost" during the Dark Ages, only to be rediscovered when Crusaders coming home from the "Orient" brought back with them the great works of the classical authors—presumably as wrapping paper for the loot and booty brought back as gifts for their loved ones back home. Very little could be further from the truth. Although it is true that Greek studies were in severe decline in the West during this period (see below), it was actually the arrival of Crusaders from the West that devastated the study of classical texts in the East: In 1204, the soldiers of the Fourth Crusade, apparently deciding that the Holy Land was too far away for their efforts, decided instead simply to attack the Byzantine Empire. The year 1204 marks the greatest single devastation of Greece since the fall of the Bronze Age more than 2,000 years previously (see chapter 4). Great works of art were looted (usually finding their way to Venice), and many classical texts were destroyed and lost forever. From this date until 1261, Constantinople was under the rule of the Latin West, with only a small Byzantine aristocracy holding out in Nicaea. During this period, there were virtually no classical studies in the East.

Once the Byzantines regained power (c. 1261), there was a new, if final, surge in the study of ancient Greece, led by the two great scholars of the day—Maximus Planudes (1255–1305) of Constantinople and Demetrius Triclinius

(1280–1340) of Thessalonica. The former was active in every possible branch of Greek studies, from grammar to the collation of literary texts (he is responsible for the preservation of many plays by Euripides) to the emendation of mathematical and astronomical texts. He is perhaps most unusual in the field of classics for his efforts in translating Latin texts into Greek (usually, as we shall see, translations went the other way around). His collection and comparison of many texts provided materials for the classical scholars of the Renaissance in the West (Fisher 2000, 1330–1331).

Triclinius's greatest achievement was the reconstruction of Greek poetic meter, which accompanied his vast study of ancient Greek lyric poetry, especially that of Pindar. He then studied great works in Greek drama, in terms of both meter and overall literary criticism (Nesselrath 2000, 1672). Both he and Planudes are considered to be the last great Byzantine scholars of any note, and the works of Triclinius are still considered relevant to the study of ancient poetry.

The Middle Ages: The West

Although all these developments occurred in the Greek East, Hellenic studies were all but extinct in the Latin West during the time period discussed above. The one exception was southern Italy and Sicily, which had had a large percentage of Greek-speaking inhabitants since the first arrival of the Greek colonists in the eighth century B.C.E. This eastern orientation was reaffirmed in the sixth century C.E. when Emperor Justinian, with the help of his chief general Belisarius, reconquered this territory for the vestigial eastern Roman Empire. Hellenism then remained common in southern Italy and Sicily throughout the Middle Ages. When Robert Guiscard of Normandy conquered Sicily in 1059, he ushered in a cosmopolitan age featuring greater contacts with the Muslim populations of Spain and northern Africa, where there was already a well-entrenched study of Greek texts.

Very significant in the Medieval study of ancient Greece was the work of Henricus Aristippus, archdeacon of Catania in southern Italy. Toward the end of his life (d. 1164), he oversaw a large-scale attempt to make Greek writings accessible to the West. He himself translated Plato's *Phaedo* and *Meno*, as well as some of Aristotle's medical texts, into Latin. Others working under him translated Euclid's *Geometry*, Hero's *Pneumatica* (a compendium of mechanical gadgets), the works of Proklus, and Ptolemy's *O Magistê*, which ultimately came to be known by the Arabic rendering of its title, *Almagest* (Reynolds and Wilson 1991, 110, 119–120).

In this same century, Arabic commentaries on Aristotle written by Avicenna and Averroes were translated into Latin and passed through Spain for study in Europe. But in spite of this apparent new Western zeal for ancient Greek texts, access to the language still proved difficult, and Greek studies were limited either to a few Hellenic enthusiasts or to the study of Latin translations.

The study of ancient Greece was truly reborn in the West during the Renaissance. The most important individual in this respect was Manuel Chrysoloras, a Greek scholar who came to Florence in 1397 at the invitation of Coluccio

Salutati, humanist scholar and chancellor of Florence, and stayed three years before moving to Pavia, where he remained until about 1403. During the period when he lived in Florence and then in Pavia, he lectured on Greek language and Greek topics; he eventually wrote the *Erotemata*, the first standard Greek language textbook in the West. The book went to press in 1471, and it served as the Greek primer for no less illustrious men than the Dutch scholar Erasmus (Reynolds and Wilson 1991, 147).

Greek studies gained pace in the fifteenth century. At first there were some holdovers from the Middle Ages, notably the interest in translating Greek texts into Latin for study. This especially occurred under the enthusiastic eye of Pope Nicholas V (1447–1455) who commissioned translations of Herodotus, Thucydides, Xenophon, Plato, Aristotle, Theophrastos, Ptolemy, and Strabo (Reynolds and Wilson 1991, 148).

But soon the works of the ancient Greeks were to receive widespread appreciation in their own language. This was primarily due to the fall of Constantinople to the Turks in 1453. Countless Greek refugees arrived in western Europe, especially in Italy, during the latter half of the fifteenth century, many of whom settled in the Latin West as teachers and translators of ancient Greek. For the first time in centuries, Greek teachers were readily available in the West.

Two men who made use of this turn of events were Cardinal Bessarion of Constantinople (1403–1472) and Angelo Politian of Montepulciano (1454–1494). The former was one of the early refugees from the dying remnants of the eastern Roman Empire. The fall of Constantinople in 1453 incited Bessarion to collect many Greek texts from the East before they were destroyed in war. In 1468, he donated his books to the city of Venice, to be of use to the city and its Greek refugees.

The scholar Politian was exceedingly well versed in the Greek language, allowing him to compose in that language as well as to translate and publish documents from the classical world. His scholarship was such that his name still appears in the bibliographies of modern textual editions, and he is most significant for his groundbreaking work in the field of Hellenistic poetry. Politian's use of the work of Callimachus to emend a passage from the author Catullus (who wrote in Latin) was one of the earliest steps in the recognition of the influence of Greek on classical Roman literature (Reynolds and Wilson 1991, 154).

During the fifteenth century, then, the groundwork had been established for the study of ancient Greece. The great Humanists—from Petrarch to Poggio to Erasmus—had collected, copied, and commented upon all of the classical texts from which we work today. Their work was facilitated by the rise and spread of the printing press in the middle of the fifteenth century, and the following 150 years saw the rise of several prestigious printing families who dedicated themselves to the printing of Greek texts. Aldus Manutius, patriarch of the Aldus publishing house, hired Marcus Musurus of Crete to edit and help publish Greek texts in their original language. Between the years 1498 and 1512, the Aldine press in Italy produced editions of Herodotus, Thucydides, Demosthenes, Sophocles, Euripides, and Aristophanes. Meanwhile, to the north, in

Basle, Johan Froben of the Froben publishing house was collaborating with Erasmus to publish Greek texts of the Bible and other church doctrine.

The first Greek book published in France came to light in 1507, and during the sixteenth century the Estienne family became the premier publishers of classical Greek texts. The dynasty's founding father, Robert Estienne, was later obliged to leave France for Switzerland because of his Protestant views. As he continued publishing in Geneva, his son Henri Estienne joined forces with Pier Vittori (the foremost Hellenist of his day) to continue the publication of Greek texts in France. Henri's most important contribution to the spread of Hellenism in western Europe was the publication of his *Thesaurus Linguae Graecae* in 1572. A small series of Greek classics Estienne prepared for the dauphin (the heir to the throne) was the first serial collection of classical texts published in Europe.

The corpus of Greek texts that the modern student now has to work with was mostly complete by the seventeenth century, augmented here and there by the occasional most fortunate discovery. In 1777, for example, the one surviving text of the *Homeric Hymn to Demeter* was discovered in Moscow. Since 1788, various papyri have come to light in Egypt, providing original documents for the study of the ancient world. But in modern times, the most important advances in the study of ancient Greece have been made in the field of archaeology.

Today

Archaeology is a recent science, although interest in antiquarianism has certainly been around since earliest history (the Assyrian king Ashurbanipal had a museum at his capital in Nineveh c. 630 B.C.E.). Stray objects of historical interest have made their way into private and public collections throughout the centuries, but it was really only with the discovery of Pompeii in the 1730s that the discipline of archaeology—digging in specific places for the purpose of unearthing and studying ancient ruins—came into existence. It was not until the twentieth century that this new discipline acquired specific rules, regulations, and the quantitative rigor that brought it fully into the realms of science.

The art and science of archaeology are of inestimable importance in the study of ancient Greece, and this is especially so of the Greek Bronze Age. Until the late 1800s, Greek civilization was understood to date back only into the first millennium B.C.E.; the great tales of Homer—the *Iliad* and *Odyssey*—were seen as pleasant fairy tales that served to amuse, to educate, and occasionally to drive philosophers to distraction with their unflattering portraits of the deities. But in the 1870s, a German businessman with a talent for languages decided to prove that the age of Greek heroes had actually existed. This man was Heinrich Schliemann.

Having heard the tales of Agamemnon and Odysseus from childhood, it was Schliemann's dream one day to prove that these legendary kings actually existed. Having made a fortune in business with which to fund his efforts, in April 1870 Schliemann began to dig at the site of Hissarlik in western Turkey, known as New Ilium and thought to be a likely site for the ancient citadel of

Troy. The work, at first, was tedious and fruitless—although there was no lack of mosquitoes—but by 1871, Schliemann and his workers did not merely discover "Troy," but nine full layers of Troy. This abundance of stratigraphic layers made identification difficult, and at each and every turn Schliemann believed that he had found Homer's Troy yet again.

One must remember that Bronze Age Aegean archaeology was only just being born, and today's wealth of data concerning pottery, stratigraphy, and chronology (see below) was not yet available for consultation. Schliemann never did quite work out all the ambiguities of his first site, a fact that became evident at the end of his dig.

On June 14, 1873, Schliemann, digging with his wife Sophia, came upon a huge hoard of gold. He quickly dismissed the other workers, bid Sophia grab her shawl, and, as secretly as possible, the Schliemanns gathered together their so-called Priam's Treasure and brought it to Germany, possibly smuggled in Sophia's hair! The name *Priam's* came from Schliemann's belief that the walls in which the treasure was discovered belonged to Priam's city (that is, the city described by Homer). In truth, the gold and the city walls were centuries older than Homer's King Priam.

Schliemann's Trojan discoveries proved to the academic community that the world of Homer, to one extent or another, actually did exist. Fired by his success and still funded by his personal wealth, Schliemann moved to the next great city mentioned by Homer—Mycenae, ruled by Agamemnon, King of Men. Work began on August 7, 1876; by the end of the year, the Schliemanns had discovered the first of two giant grave circles located along the walls of the Bronze Age city. In January 1877, Heinrich and Sophia opened the first of the cists within the grave circle (see chapter 9). They found a total of five graves, containing no fewer than fifteen corpses, including a man covered in gold, a woman covered in gold, and two small children. Immediately, Schliemann's mind flew to the story of the murder of Agamemnon, who was supposedly buried with his concubine Cassandra and their twin children, murdered at the same time. So identifying the tomb's occupants, Schliemann sent a telegram to the king of Greece: "It is with extraordinary pleasure that I announce to Your Majesty my discovery of the graves, which, according to tradition, are those of Agamemnon, Cassandra, Eurymedon, and their comrades, all killed during the banquet by Clytemnestra and her lover, Ægisthus" (Ceram 1986, 50). In reality, the cists of what was later designated as Grave Circle A were at least 500 years older than this legendary king of Mycenae. In spite of this slight gaffe in chronological reckoning, this second site confirmed beyond any doubt the presence of a great civilization in Greece long before the first millennium B.C.E. The Bronze Age Greek civilization was named after this city—"Mycenaean."

Schliemann continued to dig at sites of Bronze Age interest throughout the remainder of his life. He returned to Troy, dug at Orchomenus (where he discovered and named the style of pottery now used for dating the arrival in Greece of the Greeks—Minyan Ware), and conducted a full excavation of the city of Tiryns. At this last site, he was rewarded not only with actual standing, Bronze Age walls of Cyclopean size, but it was here where Schliemann began to record similarities in the painting and pottery styles of the various mainland sites. One might say that the first stirrings of the study of a Bronze Age Aegean style of art came into being at Tiryns (Ceram 1986, 64).

By the end of the nineteenth century, there was no longer any doubt in the historicity of at least some of the Homeric epics, at least as far as dates, setting, and culture were concerned. The Mycenaean civilization was discovered, documented, and, for the most part, recognized for what it was. The next great step in the discovery of the Aegean Bronze Age occurred in Crete, when Sir Arthur Evans, digging at the ancient capital of Knossos, discovered a civilization even earlier than the Mycenaean. In 1900, Evans found the remains of a society that he named Minoan after the legendary King Minos of Crete. This society showed many artistic similarities to the Mycenaean civilization. Yet the styles in Crete were even older than those in Greece, and, to Evans's eyes, superior. So Evans came to the conclusion that this Minoan society was older than the Mycenaean; that at one point early in history these Minoans actually controlled the mainland, holding suzerainty over the Mycenaeans; and that it was only a grand-scale volcanic eruption that brought an end to their brilliant society and allowed the northern "barbarians" to take over Crete.

Although quite a bit of this early hypothesis was inaccurate, Evans is to be credited with some of the earliest scientific studies in Bronze Age Aegean archaeology, especially his attempt to establish a chronology for Crete, the mainland, and the Cyclades. His chronology was mostly based on the changing styles of pottery and on a rudimentary use of stratigraphy (see below). Some of his dates are now known to be off by centuries (he believed that the volcanic eruption that supposedly destroyed the Minoans occurred in 1450 B.C.E.; we now know it was closer to 1640, thus shifting his dates by a full 200 years), but his relative chronology is still used in many aspects of Aegean archaeology. Unlike Schliemann, Evans published his excavations in full in his *Palace of Minos at Knossos*, a 1920s–1930s publication that still proves of use in the study of ancient Crete.

The groundwork set up by Schliemann and Evans allowed for more systematic and scientific studies of these newly discovered civilizations. The Greek archaeologist Tsountas continued Schliemann's work in Mycenae, although with a much greater flair for systemization and the scientific method. The Italian archaeologists Federigo Halbherr and Luigi Pernier excavated the palatial site of Phaistos and its nearby villa at Haghia Triadha beginning in 1900. The American archaeologist Harriet Boyd-Hawes excavated the town of Gournia at around the same time. She is to be credited not only for her attention to a "common," rather than palatial, site, but for her attention to artifacts that shed light on the day-to-day culture of the Minoans rather than just on their gold and lavish architecture. In her 1908 publication, she noted: "We must know the standard of living as well as the aesthetic principles of a race, and to save our studies from becoming a mere discussion of styles, must keep in view the significance of the humblest articles of use" (Dickinson 1994, 2).

On the mainland, Carl Blegen and A. J. B. Wace performed for Greece what Evans had for Crete, namely, determining a chronological system based on physical culture. Much of their data derived from Blegen's excavations at Korokou and his later work at Zygouries and Prosymna. A bitter controversy soon emerged between Evans on the one side and Blegen and Wace on the other. Evans firmly believed that the Minoans were the alpha society of the Bronze Age Aegean, dominating both the mainland and the Cyclades until their civilization was destroyed by an act of God in the form of a volcano. Blegen and Wace, on the other hand, recognized the independent spirit of the Mycenaean (and earlier) civilizations on the mainland. Furthermore, they argued that although the Mycenaeans did adapt much of their culture from the Minoans, many elements were not only independent of, but in some instances superior to, Minoan prototypes. One example is the grand tholos tombs (pl. tholoi) of mainland Greece (see chapter 9), appearing in contrast to smaller, less elaborate examples on Crete. Evans argued that the huge, elegantly decorated examples on the mainland were the original Minoan versions, built during the Minoan thalassocracy (sea-based empire) and that the poorer examples were built by Mycenaeans after the fall of the Minoans. By contrast, Wace argued that the small tholoi in Crete were the earliest versions and that those in Greece represented the Mycenaean pinnacle of the architectural style. Ultimately, Wace was shown to be correct, although at the time Evans had him blackballed from the academic community.

The debate intensified with the discovery of a palace archive at the site of Pylos in Messenia (western Peloponnese). Here were discovered hundreds of tablets covered with a writing style identical to the one Evans had discovered at the palace archives at Knossos. For Evans, this meant that the same Minoan dynasty that controlled Knossos also wielded power on the mainland, strengthening the notion of the Minoan thalassocracy. By contrast, Wace argued that the similarity of the Pylos and Knossos scripts (especially in contrast to a script found exclusively on Crete) proved that both the mainland and the later levels of Knossos were under the control of similar Mycenaean dynasties.

This debate finally ended in 1952, when a young British architect named Michael Ventris, standing on the shoulders of many archaeologists and linguists of the earlier twentieth century, proved that this script found at both Knossos and Pylos, known as Linear B (see below), was the earliest known written form of Greek. The Mycenaeans, he said, were Greeks, and they established their hegemony over the Minoans at Knossos. Ventris's translation of Linear B has proved to be one of the most fruitful discoveries in twentieth-century Greek studies.

Although archaeology and Linear B are now our primary means of studying the Aegean area in the Bronze Age, archaeology has been invaluable for the study of Greece in later periods as well. Greece, Crete, and the Cyclades currently host several long-term, ongoing excavations as well as shorter excavations and survey projects (where surface finds are catalogued and no ground is broken). Space in this book does not permit even a partial list of all the sites excavated in the past 100 years, but a few permanent sites are worth noting. The French have established excavations and a museum at Delphi, and the Germans have done the same at Olympia and the Athenian Kerameikos cemetery.

The Americans continue excavations at the Athenian Agora and the old city of Corinth, and the British maintain studies at Knossos and Pylos. The Minoan-Phoenician site of Kommos in southern Crete is currently in the hands of the Canadians. The Greeks themselves run several excavations throughout the region, both independently and in conjunction with scholars from other countries. Two of the more exciting Greek digs currently in progress are those at Akrotiri on the island of Thera and Kato Symi Viannou on Crete.

SOURCES FOR THE STUDY OF GREEK HISTORY

Our primary source of information concerning the ancient Greeks is writing. In the Bronze Age, the Mycenaeans left copious records concerning the administration of their agriculture, real estate, taxes, military, and religion. After a hiatus in writing during the Dark Age (c. 1200–750 B.C.E.), a mass of new texts appeared in the Greek language, recording poetry, history, philosophy, and science.

Forms of Writing

To date, the earliest forms of Bronze Age Aegean writing are not readable. These are two writing systems used by the Minoans. The earlier of the two is a type of pictographic script that the Minoans learned from the Egyptians and their use of hieroglyphics (it has no name). A simpler script evolved from this relatively elaborate beginning, leading to a second system that became known as Linear A (so named by Sir Arthur Evans, who discovered several tablets of Linear A at the palace of Knossos). The word *linear* refers to the fact that the signs are made with relatively simple lines and curves, as opposed to the pictures used in the previous writing system. The letter *A* serves to distinguish this system from the later script used by the Mycenaeans, Linear B.

Unfortunately, the language, and even the language family, of the Minoans are unknown. Some argue that Minoan is an Indo-European language, but others have suggested that it is a Semitic language, related to Hebrew or Arabic. Others offer that Minoan is unrelated to any currently known language and must be learned on its own terms. Although a few words, usually proper names such as those of deities, have been derived from the Linear A tablets, we still have not translated the language itself, and thus we cannot yet read the documents left by the Minoans.

Linear B, on the other hand, is an early form of Greek, and thus is readable. The documents, if we might call them that, are a bit on the awkward side, as Linear B is not a particularly good writing system for the representation of Greek language (see sidebar, pages 27–29). We have no epics, no histories in Linear B (although some current Linear B scholars do amuse themselves by putting poetry *into* Linear B); what we have are lists: lists of who owns what land, what sheep, what slaves; lists of gifts to the gods, shipments to the king, and food rations to factory workers; lists of supply and demand, tax authorizations, and names of horses in the local community. Although it might not seem like the most engaging reading, quite a bit of information can be gleaned from

How to Read Linear B

The Linear B writing system is a syllabery, in which each sign represents either a vowel sound or the combination of a consonant and a vowel, such as *a* or *ba*. No individual consonant, or pair of consonants together, can be directly expressed. Signs that are not syllabs are called ideograms, meaning that one sign stands for an entire word, much as ☺ means "happy." The [syllabic portion of Linear B looks like this:

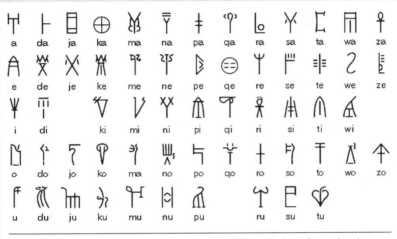

(From http://www.omniglot.com/writing/linearb.htm. Many thanks to Simon Ager.)

Some signs actually express more than one phoneme (sound). What in the picture above is written as *t* actually stands for the sounds/letters τ (*t*) and θ (*th*). The *p* stands for π (*p*), φ (*ph*), and occasionally β (*b*), and the *k* can represent γ (*g*), κ (*k*), and χ (*kh*). The letters *l* and *r* are written with the same signs. The *q* in Linear B usually transforms into a β in Greek, so that "qa-si-re-u" becomes *basileus*. Finally, there was a Minoan phoneme pronounced something like *dl*, which the Mycenaeans, when using vocabulary they got from their southern neighbors, would occasionally write with a *d* and occasionally with an *l*; thus, one gets *labyrinth* as both "ra-pu-ri-to" and "da-pu-ri-to." This also explains why we have the Greek O*dysseus* but the Roman U*lysses*. Some signs have still not been transliterated, meaning we still do not know how they were pronounced. These signs get a number in transliterations, so that you might see a word written 34-ke-ja.

The letter *w*, Greek *digamma*, pretty much fell out of use in post–Bronze Age Greek, but is still prevalent in Linear B. The letter *sigma* (*s*) is not always expressed at the beginning of a Linear B word, and thus the word for "grain," *sperma*, appears in the Linear B as *pe-ma*.

(continues)

How to Read Linear B *(continued)*

Linear B is clearly not well structured to express the Greek language, in which consonant clusters (two consonants together at the beginning or end of a word, or three or more together in the middle of a word) are common. Consider the Greek word for entrails—*splangkhna*. So, a number of techniques were devised to express Greek in Linear B.

Certain consonant clusters appear at the beginning of Greek words, like *sp, mn, kr, tr,* and so forth. When such a consonant cluster appears in Linear B, both consonants are expressed, with a "help vowel" between them. This help vowel is usually an echo of the vowel following the second consonant. So the word *tripod* (*tripode*) would be written "ti-ri-po-de," with the *i* after the *t* "echoing" the *i* after the *r*.

However, if the consonant cluster is one that would not begin a Greek word, the second consonant is dropped. This also occurs with single consonants at the end of a syllable. Therefore, the Greek word for *father, patêr,* in Linear B would be written "pa-te," with the final *r* dropping off. The word for *all, pantes,* would also be written "pa-te," with both the *n* and *s* falling off (*nt* never being a consonant cluster at the beginning of an ancient Greek word). Context, therefore, is quite important for reading Linear B.

Diphthongs (two vowels together) have different means of expression in Linear B. As with final consonants, some vowels seem to "drop off," so that *-a* and *-ai* are both written as *-a*, and *-o* and *-oi* might both be written as *-o*. In some instances, though, it was imperative for the length of the vowel to be recognized. In such instances, two vowels could be written one after the other to lengthen the vowel. One such example is "do-e-ro," the spelling for *doulos,* or *slave.* The *j* phoneme also functioned as a vowel or semi-vowel (like *w* and *y* in English), usually pronounced as a *y*. When together with other vowels, it could create a diphthong, such as the common ending *o-jo = oio*.

Finally, as an aid for a recognizably awkward writing system, the Mycenaeans used ideograms, or signs that were pictures of the object described (there is some overlap between ideograms and syllabs). Thus, after the word *ti-ri-po-de,* this image would be drawn 🝘. Such pictures were of extreme help in the ultimate decipherment of Linear B.

The tablet at the top of the facing page might offer a quick example of how a Linear B document is to be read.

The *PY* indicates that this tablet is from Pylos, as opposed to KN for Knossos, EL for Eleusis, KH for Khania, MY for Mycenae, OR for Orkhomenos, TH

these lists. For example, we learn that the person with the most land in any given district is the wanax, or king, and that he owns three times more land than the next person in the hierarchy, the lawagetas, or "leader of the people."

All these writing systems, Minoan Hieroglyphic, Linear A, and Linear B, were discovered incised into slabs of clay, either rectangular tablets equivalent

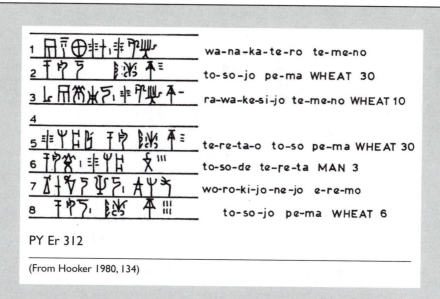

1	wa-na-ka-te-ro te-me-no
2	to-so-jo pe-ma WHEAT 30
3	ra-wa-ke-si-jo te-me-no WHEAT 10
4	
5	te-re-ta-o to-so pe-ma WHEAT 30
6	to-so-de te-re-ta MAN 3
7	wo-ro-ki-jo-ne-jo e-re-mo
8	to-so-jo pe-ma WHEAT 6

PY Er 312

(From Hooker 1980, 134)

for Thebes, or TI for Tiryns. The *Er* tells us that it refers to landholding and grains.

The first word, *wa-na-ka-te-ro* refers to the wanax, the high king. *Te-me-no* is almost identical to the later Greek word for sanctuary land, the temenos, land that is "cut off." *To-so-jo* is a genitive (indicating possession) for "so much," and *pe-ma* refers to the word *sperma,* meaning grain. This is followed by an ideogram for wheat and the unit of measurement 30. Presumably the wanax has a plot of land that can accommodate thirty units of wheat. By contrast, the *ra-wa-ke-si-jo te-me-no* or "temenos of the lawagetas" only accommodates ten units of wheat, letting us know that in Pylian society, the wanax is more wealthy and prestigious than the lawagetas.

In the next section shown, a group of three men called the *te-re-ta-o* (genitive plural) have thirty units of wheat. The number of these men is indicated in the next line, where there are so many (to-so-de) such men (te-re-ta): the ideogram for *man* and the number 3. *E-re-mo* refers to desert or wasteland (*eremos* = *desert* in Greek), which can accommodate six units of wheat grain. *Wo-ro-ki-jo-ne-jo* is still untranslatable.

The Linear B system is difficult to read, but it is also one of the most productive areas of research in Bronze Age Aegean studies. In reading these tablets—grocery lists, sales receipts, and court notes—we derive an understanding of the social, legal, and economic structures of Mycenaean society.

to a very heavy sheet of paper or long "leaves" (see Image 3.1, Linear B Tablet and Leaves)'. When the clay was damp, the scribe would write the signs into the clay with a sharp implement such as a reed or pointed stick. If the Minoans and Mycenaeans also wrote on papyrus (a paper-like plant from Egypt), leather, or some other medium, these writings have not survived. Only pot-

3.1 Linear B Tablet (Roger Wood/Corbis)

tery, with the occasional sign or two, offered an alternate writing surface. These documents on clay tablets were frequently preserved when the storerooms and archives in which they were kept burned down, thus inadvertently firing the clay and making it more durable. However, the Mycenaeans avoided archival clutter by keeping around only current, relevant records: All other tablets and leaves would be remoistened and reused. As a result, the majority of our Linear B documents come from the end of the Bronze Age, around 1250 to 1200 B.C.E., although some date back as far as 1450, such as those from Knossos. No new tablets were produced after the end of the Bronze Age, and the Greeks lost all knowledge of these early writing systems.

Starting around 750 B.C.E., a new form of writing appeared in the Greek world. This new system derived from the writing system used by the Phoenicians, a people living in what is now Lebanon and who spread out to colonize much of the Mediterranean. The Greeks and Phoenicians were active trading partners during and after the Dark Ages, and the Greeks probably relearned the art of writing where these two peoples were in frequent contact. One possible place for this type of contact was the site of Al-Mina in Syria, where Greeks and Phoenicians traded together in a market town. It is somewhat more likely, however, that the Greeks acquired their new alphabet on Cyprus, where both Greeks and Phoenicians had established permanent settlements by the ninth century (Woodard 1997, 48).

Unlike the Bronze Age writing systems, the Phoenician script was relatively well adapted to express the Greek language, at least after some minor adjustments by the Greeks. The Phoenicians did not express vowels in their writing, much as with modern Hebrew, and they had a few phonemes (sounds) that the Greeks did not. So the Greeks took the letters for the unnecessary sounds and turned them into vowels (the Phoenician aleph becoming the Greek alpha, and so forth). Occasionally, the Greeks would develop new letters entirely, such as long and short forms of the letters we would think of as *e* and *o* (eta and epsilon, omicron and omega), or letter combinations—kappa (k) plus sigma (s) yields xi (x). This adjusting did not occur in the same way throughout the Greek world, and different regions of Greece occasionally had different ways of expressing the same sounds or letters. Some Greeks wrote the letter *chi* as χ others wrote it as ψ. Only in 403 B.C.E. did all the Greeks decide to use one common writing system—the Ionic.

This Phoenician system (from which we get the words *phonetic* and *phoneme*) is what the Greeks continue to use up to the present day. All the ancient Greeks' works are recorded in this manner, from dramas on papyrus, to inscriptions on stone, to legends on coins. There are a few major differences, however, between ancient and modern Greek script. The ancient Greeks, especially in the early periods, were not specifically concerned with the direction of their script. Inscriptions could run left to right, run right to left, or even alternate between the two (a system known as boustrophedon, or cow turning, referring to the back-and-forth pattern made by ox-drawn ploughs in the fields). This last system was especially convenient for large inscriptions in high places: Rather than get to the end of a line and have to go all the way back to the far end to start again, the masons doing the carvings could go down one line and then use the next line to work their way back to the far end.

Accents began to be added around 200 B.C.E. (Allen 1991, 125). It appears that ancient Greek was a tonal language, like modern Chinese, and these accents mark the rising and lowering of the voice in pronunciation. One accent mark, the rough or smooth breathing symbol, lets one know if the vowel at the beginning of a word is smooth (as in *ides*) or rough, meaning it was pronounced with an *h* sound (hides). It was a long time before such accents were regularized: Even in the ninth century C.E. they were somewhat optional, and in the fifteenth century, Politian published Callimachus's *Bath of Pallas* without accents, as he thought them anachronistic (Reynolds and Wilson 1991, 154).

The ancient Greeks did not make use of both capital and lowercase letters; all letters were capitals. Furthermore, perhaps in an effort to save space, there were no spaces between words,
ANDTHUSALLOFTHEWRITINGLOOKEDSOMETHINGLIKETHIS.

In the ninth century C.E., lowercase letters were added to the script, and two specific forms of the letter sigma were devised, σ and ς. The first form appeared within a word, and the latter appeared only as the end (sigma being one of the most common final letters in Greek). This helped in seeing where words began and ended.

Other Sources of Study

Another major source of information about ancient Greece is art, artifact, and architecture, which together are aspects of archaeology. This source of information tells us about the physical realities of life for the ancient Greeks, such as what their homes, temples, and cities looked like; how they dressed; and their general levels of health.

One of the most important issues addressed in archaeology is the matter of chronology, or the study of when things happened. The Greeks did not have one specific date that they used to arrange their history, as modern societies do with, for example, the birth of Christ or the Hijra. Sometimes dates might be kept according to which Olympiad they occurred in, that is, in which four-year period since the first Olympics in 776 B.C.E. Or, one might refer to who was priestess at Eleusis when an event took place. Often in Athenian inscriptions, the Archon year is listed, stating who was Archon, or chief executive officer, during that particular year. By consulting a list of priestesses of Eleusis or Archons of Athens, one might deduce the order of events presented, but this only works in limited areas for very limited pieces of knowledge and does not always help in placing these events into modern reckonings of time (e.g., autumn of 403 B.C.E.).

Archaeology provides a number of means to reckon time, both relative (when one event occurred in relation to another) and absolute (exact dates B.C.E. or C.E.). The most basic means of determining relative chronology in archaeology is stratigraphy. Stratigraphy refers to the layers (strata) of discarded and buried materials under the surface of the land. Consider, for example, having a garden. Every year, you add new layers of soil and mulch before planting flowers or tomatoes, and these new layers cover over what had been on the surface the year before. A discarded gum wrapper, a penny, and an old shoelace get covered over by the new layer. The next year, a bottle cap gets covered over, along with a baseball card and a doll's head. In the study of stratigraphy, the archaeologist attempts to discern and study these individual layers, marking the passage of time and the material culture present in each layer (for example, the continued presence of Bazooka bubble gum in year X, as manifest by the discarded gum wrapper).

The basic tenet of stratigraphy is that the deeper the layer and its related objects are, the older it is, with newer layers accruing on top. There are, of course, some exceptions to this rule, including wells, which later might be used for disposing of garbage, and rat holes, which allow one to find a chocolate bar wrapper in fifth-century Athens. But in general this principle of stratigraphy works, and the archaeologist can use it to determine what rooms in a building are older than others, or what style of pottery was popular before another.

Pottery is the single most important tool in the study of the Greek chronology. Pottery has been produced since the Neolithic (New Stone Age) period all the way down to modern times, so it allows for a continuous archaeological record. Once it is fired, pottery is essentially indestructible in small units, although it is still rather fragile in the form of entire vessels. So a pitcher or bowl is used until it breaks and is then tossed into the rubbish heap, where its shards remain forever for later researchers to find. Furthermore, decorative styles of Greek pottery change frequently, at least every quarter century, so there is a massive amount of easily distinguishable material for the archaeologist to study (see chapter 9). For example, one style of pottery from Athens is called Black Figure, as the pictures decorating the vessels are painted in black on a reddish background. This style appears mainly from the late seventh century until about 525 B.C.E. Therefore, objects or building levels found in context with fragments of Black Figure pottery might be dated within this period. But this is only a rough use of pottery for dating, as individual styles and painters can be identified, which narrows the chronological scope even further. In general, pottery may provide a date within twenty-five years at most, and within fewer years if the work of an individual painter is recognized.

Changes in architecture also provide information about chronology, and stratigraphy allows archaeologists to know which layers or portions of a building come before or after others. Just as in modern times, fashions in architecture changed during ancient times, due to both taste and technological innovation. For example, the early Greek temples were long and narrow, because the Greeks did not yet have a good way to roof a broad building. Over the course of the late Archaic and Classical periods, temples become increasingly short and broad, that is, square, as people learned to make wider roofs. This is particularly evident at the Parthenon on the Athenian Acropolis: The remains of the longer, narrower foundations are still visible sticking out from under the still-standing fifth-century structure.

Styles also simply changed over time, most evident in the orders of Greek architecture (see chapter 9). Doric temples with broad, almost pillow-like capitals are older than Doric buildings with rather small, straight capitals, both of which predate the popularity of Ionic buildings on the mainland, which in turn predate the Corinthian style. Fashions in decorative edges and sculptural programs also allow for an understanding of chronological progression in Greek architecture. When a building is considered alongside pottery remains found in the same context as the architectural elements, one might determine that such and such a wall was constructed just when Red Figure pottery was coming into fashion to replace Black Figure, because there is Black Figure pottery under the floor but Red Figure embedded beside the wall. Thus, we might date this wall to c. 520 B.C.E.

Another, although later and less frequent, source of chronology is coinage.

Coins begin to appear in ancient Greece around 600 B.C.E., starting as plain lumps of metal, then with images stamped on one side, and finally with fully decorated obverse (front) and reverse (back) images. The images present on coins, especially images of kings, queens, or other leaders, allow one to know when a coin was minted and, to a certain extent, give information concerning the context in which the coin was found. Coins are less practical for chronology than pottery, as coins might stay in circulation far longer than a broken pot: Think of the penny in the garden scenario given above. It could be a penny from 1947, even though you didn't drop it in the garden until 1999.

Beyond just chronology, archaeology also answers many of our questions about the physical realities of life for the ancient Greeks, in some cases even better than the written sources. For example, classical Athens was a male-dominated society, with many of the arts, sciences, and politics being in the hands of men. As a result, we do not have a "woman's voice" in the records of daily living to tell us about women's thoughts, reactions to life, or even basic education. All we tend to know about women from this period is what the male authors and artists have chosen to tell us. However, certain items produced in classical Athens were made specifically for women, such as White Ground lekythoi pots, in which they brought oils and perfumes to the graves of their family members (a woman's responsibility). Being made for women, these lekythoi are decorated with scenes from women's lives, which provide much information about women's day-to-day realities, including scenes of grave visits, spinning or weaving in the house, and even reading to their siblings and children (one of our few bits of evidence that women were literate at this time). The pictures also let us see what women were wearing, and even give some information as to what the interior of the houses looked like. These lekythoi, beyond just being objects of art worthy of admiration, shed considerable light on the lives of women during a specific period of Greek history. This is just one example of the use of art as a means of understanding the life and mentality of a people.

Modern techniques in archaeological science are uncovering increasingly greater amounts of information about the health, diet, and even class of the ancient Greeks. Careful sifting of soils allows for the recovery of seeds, shells, bones, and even pollen in the ancient layers, showing what the ancient Greeks grew and ate on a daily basis. Likewise, palaeozoology, the study of animal remains, lets us see what animals the Greeks hunted or domesticated and used on a daily basis. Physical anthropology, the study of human remains, lets us see the general health of the Greeks during life, the causes of death and people's ages at death, and even changes in bone structure due to daily activities. Excessive bending of the foot arch, for example, indicates a lower-class female, as this change was produced either crouching by the fire to work or climbing up the hilly terrain in search of sheep or water. A spear wound to the skull, by contrast, seems to indicate a more martial lifestyle.

Finally, the relatively new sciences of neutron activation analysis, applied to pottery, and lead isotope analysis, applied to metals, reveal for the first time where ceramic and metallic items were made (although this does not apply to gold). It is therefore possible to know if a Greek-style pot found in Cyprus, for example, was an import and thus a sign of trade or was actually made on the island and is thus a sign of a relocated Greek population.

CHRONOLOGY

There are different techniques used to understand and express chronology in the study of Greek history. In the study of the Bronze Age, from which absolute dates are more difficult to assess, a specific relative chronology is often used. This relative chronology was established by Sir Arthur Evans based on changes in pottery styles throughout the mainland, Crete, and the Cyclades. In this system, the Bronze Age is divided into three phases: the Early Bronze Age, Middle Bronze Age, and Late Bronze Age. The Bronze Age period on the mainland is called Helladic, and thus the term *Early Helladic* refers to the Early Bronze Age on the mainland. The Bronze Age in Crete is called Minoan, and in the Cyclades, Cycladic. Each of the three chronological divisions—early, middle, and late—is further divided into three subdivisions of I, II, and III, which are themselves subdivided, yielding a relative chronology for the Aegean Bronze Age that looks something like this:

Early Helladic IA, B, C	Early Minoan IA, B	Early Cycladic IA, B, C
Early Helladic IIA, B, C	Early Minoan IIA, B, C	Early Cycladic IIA, B, C
Early Helladic IIIA, B, C	Early Minoan IIIA, B, C	Early Cycladic IIIA, B, C
Middle Helladic IA, B, C	Middle Minoan IA, B	Middle Cycladic IA, B, C, etc.
Late Helladic IA, B, C	Late Minoan IA, B	Late Cycladic IA, B, C, etc.

Each phase is ideally connected with a specific style of pottery, so that Middle Helladic IA is when Yellow Minyan Ware first appeared in Greece, and Late Minoan IB is when the Marine style replaced the Floral style on Crete. Other events and art styles might then be linked with this basic relative chronology to place everything in the Bronze Age Aegean into a correlated sequence. For example, the changeover from Early Minoan IB to II is when the Mycenaeans seized control of Crete and set up their own capital at Knossos. In many texts, the relative dates are abbreviated as EH, MH, and LH for Early, Middle, and Late Helladic; EM, MM, and LM for Early, Middle, and Late Minoan; and EC, MC, and LC for the Early, Middle, and Late Cycladic.

There was enough discontent with Evans's system that a new system was developed for Crete. Rather than using pottery, this system is based on the construction and subsequent reconstructions of the palaces. Thus, there are the Prepalatial, Protopalatial, First Palace, Second Palace, and Third Palace periods. The First Palace period marks the construction of the first large palaces in Crete and is comparable in Evans's chronology to the Middle Minoan period. The Third Palace period marks the Mycenaean takeover, thus it is equivalent to the Late Minoan II phase and after.

Rather than relying too much on either of these systems, some archaeologists prefer to work with the relative dates offered by individual sites. Thus, when referring to a building in Bronze Age Greece, the excavator may refer to it as being from the Lerna IV period, seeing the structure as contemporaneous with the fourth level of construction at the site of Lerna in the Argolid. These more site-specific dates will be avoided in this text, but those who engage in further readings should be able to recognize them.

Following is a chart showing approximate time frames for the different periods in Aegean civilization, as delineated by changes in pottery styles. Dates relating to metal technology and other developments in society may be slightly different from those shown here for pottery; this is not meant to be a comprehensive timeline of Greek civilization.

Several attempts have been made to link these relative dates with absolute dates. One common way to do this is through correlations with Egypt, where a reasonably standard chronology has, more or less, been worked out. Thus, if a scarab import bearing the name of Thutmosis III is found in a stratigraphic layer on Crete, that layer can, with some certainty, be dated to the fifteenth century, around the reign of this Egyptian king.

Another means of discerning absolute dates is through radiocarbon dating: An isotope of Carbon 14 degrades at a predictable rate into Carbon 12 and nitrogen. Scientists analyzing organic compounds from a site (such as a piece of burnt timber) can determine how much of the carbon has changed, thus providing a date for the object and its surrounding matrix. One current area of intense interest in this respect is the attempt to use radiocarbon dating to date accurately the volcanic eruption on the island of Thera, which thoroughly shook Crete and the Cyclades and gave rise to the Second Palace period. The eruption is generally dated to around 1640 B.C.E., although there is continued debate.

Dendrochronology and archaeomagnetic dating are two other techniques in use in the study of Aegean chronology. The former involves the examination of tree rings from wood used in furniture, boats, architecture, etc. Similar tree rings provide a relative chronology among different objects, but, more importantly, the information inherent in the rings themselves might be correlated with known climactic events. One such example is, once again, the eruption at Thera. Dendrochronological data have been of use in dating sunken ships off the coast of southern Turkey (see chapter 5).

Archaeomagnetic dating is the study of changes in the Earth's magnetic field and their effect on fired pottery. Data from pots, furnaces, and other clay samples can be correlated with known fluctuations in the Earth's magnetic field, yielding valuable chronological information. By this means relative dates from pottery shards can be associated with specific years (Fagan 1991, 160).

As one comes forward in time, chronology becomes more precise. A better sense of chronology in Egypt allows for cleaner correlations in the Aegean. Records of leaders' reigns and periods in office (see above) allow archaeologists and historians to count forward and backward once one date is authenticated through scientific or other means. Even astronomical events, such as an eclipse of the sun on May 28, 585 B.C.E. predicted by Thales, come into play, giving us data with which to calculate other historical events throughout the Mediterranean.

Bronze Age Chronology

Date B.C.E.	Crete		Cyclades	Mainland
3300	Early Minoan I	Prepalatial Period	Early Cycladic (3000–2000, with additional subdivisions given below) Pelos	Early Helladic I
3200				
3100				
3000				
2900	Early Minoan IIA		Kampos	Early Helladic II
2800				
2700			Syros	
2600				
2500	Early Minoan IIB			
2400			Kastri	
2300				
2200	Early Minoan III ?------------? Middle Minoan IA		(gap?)	
2100			Phylakopi I	
2000			Middle Cycladic (early)	Early Helladic III
1900	Middle Minoan IB ?---------------? Middle Minoan IIA Middle Minoan IIB ?---------------? Middle Minoan IIIA Middle Minoan IIIB	First Palace		
1800			?---------------? Middle Cycladic (late)	Middle Helladic
1700				
1600		Second Palace		
1500	Late Minoan IA ?---------------? Late Minoan IB		Late Cycladic I ?---------------? Late Cycladic II	Late Helladic I Late Helladic II ?---------------? Late Helladic IIIA
1400	Late Minoan II ?---------------? Late Minoan IIIA1 Late Minoan IIIA2 ?---------------? Late Minoan IIIB	Third Palace	Late Cycladic III early ?---------------? Late Cycladic III middle ?---------------?	Late Helladic IIIB
1300				
1200				
1100	Late Minoan IIIC	Postpalatial	Late Cycladic III late ?---------------? Late Cycladic III final	Late Helladic IIIC
1000	Subminoan			Submycenaean

Chronology is always a matter of debate in ancient history, especially for the Bronze Age. The dates used in this text are those most commonly accepted in the academic community. The reader is reminded that alternate dates (such as Evans's belief that the Thera eruption dates to 1450 B.C.E.) can be encountered both in earlier works and in publications where other chronological criteria or theories are used.

REFERENCES

Allen, W. S. 1991. *Vox Graeca: The Pronunciation of Classical Greek*. 3d ed. Cambridge, UK: Cambridge University Press.

Ceram, C. W. 1986. *Gods, Graves, & Scholars: The Story of Archaeology*. 2d ed. New York: Vintage.

Coleman, J. E. and C. A. Walz. 1997. *Greeks and Barbarians*. Bethesda, MD: CDL.

Dickinson, O. 1994. *The Aegean Bronze Age*. Cambridge, UK: Cambridge University Press.

Fagan, B. M. 1991. *In the Beginning: An Introduction to Archaeology*. 7th ed. New York: HarperCollins.

Fisher, E. A. 2000. "Planudes." In Speake, G., ed. 2000. *Encyclopedia of Greece and the Hellenic Tradition*. London: Fitzroy Dearborn, 1330–1332.

Hooker, J. T. 1980. *Linear B: An Introduction*. Bristol, UK: Bristol Classical.

Karlin-Hayter, P. 2000a. "Arethas of Caesarea." In Speake, G., ed. 2000. *Encyclopedia of Greece and the Hellenic Tradition*. London: Fitzroy Dearborn, 150–151.

———. 2000b. "Leo the Mathematician." In Speake, G., ed. 2000. *Encyclopedia of Greece and the Hellenic Tradition*. London: Fitzroy Dearborn, 943–944.

Littlewood, A. R. 2000. "Photios." In Speake, G., ed. 2000. *Encyclopedia of Greece and the Hellenic Tradition*. London: Fitzroy Dearborn, 1314–1315.

Nesselrath, H.-G. 2000. "Triklinios." In Speake, G., ed. 2000. *Encyclopedia of Greece and the Hellenic Tradition*. London: Fitzroy Dearborn, 1672–1673.

Reynolds, L. D. and N. G. Wilson. 1991. *Scribes and Scholars: A Guide to the Transmission of Greek and Latin Literature*. 3d ed. Oxford: Clarendon.

Walz, C. A. 1997. "*Black Athena* and the Role of Cyprus in Near Eastern/Mycenaean Contact." In Coleman, J. E. and C. A. Walz. *Greeks and Barbarians*. Bethesda, MD: CDL, 1–28.

Wilson, N. G. 1983. *Scholars of Byzantium*. Baltimore, MD: Johns Hopkins University Press.

Woodard, R. D. 1997. "Linguistic Connections between Greeks and Non-Greeks." In Coleman, J. E. and C. A. Walz. 1997. *Greeks and Barbarians*. Bethesda, MD: CDL, 29–60.

CHAPTER 4

Origins, Growth, and Decline of Greek Civilization

CRETE

Prepalatial Period

Crete has been inhabited since at least the seventh millennium B.C.E., with the earliest settlements, probably of farmers, appearing at Knossos. Already at this early date, sea trade is evident from the presence of obsidian on Crete, indicating contacts with either Melos in the Cyclades or western Anatolia (Turkey), the two Aegean sources for this material. The household evidence from this Neolithic period (seventh–fourth millennia B.C.E.) suggests small, nuclear families living together in clan-like villages (Dickinson 1994, 31–34).

The Bronze Age in Crete began around 2800 B.C.E. (Metal technology does not necessarily follow the same dates as pottery, hence the seeming discrepancy with the preceding chart.) As in all areas, the designation "Bronze Age" means that the Minoans began working with metals, specifically copper. Copper is an easily malleable metal with a low melting point. As time went on, the Minoans realized that adding certain other elements, especially tin, to copper made it stronger when cooled and easier to pour when molten. A combination of 90 percent copper plus 10 percent tin yields bronze, a strong metal with a low enough melting point to allow the ancients to make mould-cast objects with it.

The Early Minoan period is subdivided into three periods—Early Minoan I, Early Minoan II, and Early Minoan III—as originally designated by Sir Arthur Evans (see chapter 3). The first two periods are called Prepalatial, as there is no evidence of large-scale communal buildings in Crete at this time. Instead, in the Early Minoan I and Early Minoan II periods, we see the rise of villages, notably at Haghia Triadha (Holy Trinity), Gournia, Knossos, Mallia, Mochlos, Myrtos, Palaikastro (Old Castle), Phaistos, and Vasiliki. The evidence from these sites suggests an undifferentiated society where most people were probably farmers who also took part in other crafts, such as pottery and weaving, during rests from fieldwork. Society seems to have been based on individual family units, with larger family units living together in village-like communities.

Myrtos is an excellent example of such a community. The excavation of this site has revealed an extensive structure built up over several years, beginning with a "core" unit and extending outward. The entire complex was burnt to the ground and never reoccupied, so the objects found in the various rooms were still where such items were generally used. There are at least four or five separate areas of the Myrtos complex where food preparation took place, as well as agricultural storage, vessel storage, specialized work areas (weaving, for example), and what appear to be general living areas (Whitelaw 1990, 328–331). If the entire complex were unified into one large domestic unit, one would not expect to find five separate kitchens. It seems more likely that Myrtos was an early type of townhouse residence, with five, maybe six, families inhabiting a structure with contiguous walls. Considering that the entire structure grew over a period of time, radiating out from an original core "house," archaeologists suggest that the inhabitants were one large, extended family. The core would have been the original home of "great-grandmother and great-grandfather," with rooms being added as the family grew throughout the generations. Roughly similar communal structures have also appeared at Haghia Triadha, Knossos, Mallia, and Phaistos, suggesting that this communal society was island-wide (Branigan 1995, 34).

The burials from this period show a similar picture, although with some interesting differences. There are no known single burials from Early Minoan Crete (although, admittedly, these would be difficult to find). Communal burials were the rule of the day. To the south, in the region known as the Mesará (see chapter 2), people were buried in tholos tombs—round structures built of stone, somewhat beehive-shaped, with perishable ceilings (see chapter 9). Each tholos was used over several generations, the older bones being swept aside to make room for the more recently dead. Furthermore, several tholos tombs were in use at once, even in very close proximity to one another, suggesting that individual families made use of specific tholoi (plural of tholos) over the course of several generations.

A different picture emerges to the north at sites such as Mochlos, Gournia, and Palaikastro (Cherry 1990, 41; Branigan 1995, 37). Here, especially at Mochlos, we find house-like tombs, with great differences in both structure and grave goods. Some tombs were very elaborate, indicating a considerable expenditure of wealth, but others were far more humble. The funerary data from these Early Minoan II–III cemeteries show that social differentiation was already on the rise in Early Bronze Age Crete, with the first blossoming of an elite class.

Further changes occurred in the Early Minoan period that changed the simple, somewhat egalitarian farmer community into a political and social hierarchy. A hierarchy of settlements developed as some Early Bronze Age communities grew much larger than others. Knossos was always the largest, achieving a size of five hectares already in the Early Bronze Age (Dickinson 1994, 52). Phaistos, Mallia, and Mochlos, however, grew enough to absorb their neighbors. The growth of populations at these centers not only indicates a possible migration into "urban" areas, but, combined with data from the tombs, indicates an overall population growth during the Early Bronze Age (Branigan 1995, 34).

At these large sites, orchard horticulture emerged, in which the Minoans cultivated such luxury items as grapes, figs, and the ever-famous olive (Dickinson 1994, 45). These plants, in contrast to, say, wheat, require several years to yield their fruits, indicating that long-term planning went into their cultivation. The spread of specialized drinking vessels suggests that the grapes were being used for wine, an industry requiring both long-term management and agricultural surplus. (It is worth noting that wine, beyond its "cheering" effects, also has hygienic applications. As with beer and other alcoholic beverages, toxins cannot grow in wine as they can in water, thus making wine safer to drink during periods of questionable water cleanliness.)

Finally, as early as the Early Minoan II at Palaikastro and Early Minoan III at Knossos, monumental architecture appeared in Crete (Branigan 1995, 34). These new buildings were much larger than the simple homes of the Early Bronze Age Minoans, and it would appear that one of their original purposes was the storage of agricultural surplus. Another early use of these grand structures was craft production, indicating that the homogenous, agricultural society of Early Minoan I and II was now giving way to a more specialized society (Dabney 1995, 44). Both early functions indicate a communal use for these early protopalaces, suggesting that they were erected not for some political elite, but as a collective project (Dabney 1995, 45). Nevertheless, the ability to organize the workers and supplies necessary in such undertakings shows that, as with the horticulture, at least some manner of "managerial" class was coming into being.

The First Palace Period

Perhaps the most significant development in the (pre-)history of Minoan Crete is the rise of the palaces, which first occurred at the end of the twentieth century B.C.E.—the Middle Minoan period—at Knossos, Phaistos, and Mallia. A palace is a large architectural structure organized around a central court (see Image 9.2, Palace of Knossos). It may contain other courts, as well as substantial storage facilities, production areas, administration and archive rooms, areas for religious ritual, state rooms, and reception halls (Warren 1987, 47). In the midst of all of these were also probably food preparation areas, lavatories, and living quarters. The creation of the palaces indicates a new societal organization in Minoan Crete, with a supposed elite class (those who inhabited the palaces), occupational differentiation and craft specialization, and state control over aspects of life such as long-term planning and trade, both domestic and foreign. The fact that the three earliest palaces are very similar to each other in plan also suggests that there was island-wide trade and communication by the Early Minoan III–Middle Minoan I period, indicating the beginnings of a homogenous Minoan culture (Preziosi and Hitchcock 1999, 35 ff.).

There are countless debates concerning the origins of the palaces and palatial society in Crete. Many scholars, such as Peter Warren, take a gradualist approach, seeing the rise of the palaces as a gradual step in the overall consistent evolution of Minoan society (Warren 1987, passim). Other scholars, such as John Cherry, take a "punctuated equilibrium" approach, seeing the palaces as a very quick development in Crete, sparked by internal developments and external influence (Cherry 1990, passim).

Some of the gradual developments have already been considered above. As early as the Early Minoan II and III periods, sites such as Mallia, Knossos, and Palaikastro begin to show elements of palatial architecture, such as monumental architecture and copious storage facilities. Orchard horticulture at the sites of the future palaces indicated long-term planning and a managerial class. The tombs of Mochlos revealed that social differentiation was already beginning in the Early Minoan period.

By contrast, one significant distinction between Early Minoan Crete and Middle Minoan Crete was the rise of craft specialization. The high quality of such artifacts as metal objects, pottery, stone, and seals, as well as the elaborate palaces themselves, shows that professional stonemasons, metallurgists, etc., were now prevalent in Middle Minoan Crete, where agricultural surplus allowed for a more diverse society (Warren 1987, 50).

But there were other, more significant changes in Middle Minoan society, specifically in foreign relations. There is, at best, minimal evidence for foreign trade in Crete during the Early Minoan period. Early Minoan III levels revealed a few Egyptian goods, mainly ivory and stone vessels, but it is unlikely that Crete had any direct or long-standing links with Egypt at this early date (Dickinson 1994, 240; Cherry 1990, 41). To the north, some Minoan vessels came to light on the island of Kythera, just to the south of mainland Greece, and a few Greek wares appeared in Knossos specifically and western Crete in general. Nevertheless, other than contacts with obsidian-producing regions, Crete was mostly self-sustaining in the Early Bronze Age.

This picture changed dramatically in the First Palace period, when direct contacts emerged between Crete and Egypt (Cherry 1990, 41 ff.). To the north, Minoan wares become more common in the Aegean. But the main contacts occurred between Crete and the Near East. Crete's main trading partners were the western coast of Anatolia, especially the site of Miletos, and the islands off of Turkey's southern coast, especially Rhodes. As early as the Middle Minoan I period, Minoan wares appeared on the island of Cyprus. By the eighteenth century B.C.E., the people of a place called "Kaptara" were mentioned in texts from the ancient Syrian city of Mari. These Kaptarians traded in the Syrian port city of Ugarit, and comparisons between this name and the ancient Egyptian name for Crete—Keftiu—strongly suggest that the Kaptarians were Minoan traders (Dickinson 1994, 241–244).

Palaces, and the highly specialized societies that create them, had existed for centuries in the Near East by the Middle Bronze Age. Several scholars have suggested that it was exposure to the palaces of such sites as Ugarit, Alalakh, and Mari that spurred the Minoans into creating centralized bureaucracies on Crete. It is also possible that a new elite class emerged on Crete who maintained exclusive control of foreign prestige items. By monopolizing the agricultural surplus and organizing the specialized craft industries, this elite became the equivalent of royalty in Minoan society.

The trend toward larger settlements during the Early Bronze Age culminated with the rise of towns in the Middle Minoan period. Large towns such as Gournia and Palaikastro are distinguished by clearly delineated, somewhat regular streets creating blocks of houses (much as in a modern American city). These houses are typically multiroomed and are at least two stories high (Dickinson 1994, 60). By the Second Palace period, such towns grew even larger and maintained community-oriented facilities such as public shrines.

Some villages clearly defined their regional territory in the Middle Minoan period, notably Aghia Photia (Holy Light), which was entirely surrounded by a stone circuit wall punctuated by stone towers. The purpose of these towers is not yet known, but they may have been watchtowers (Preziosi and Hitchcock 1999, 39; Dickinson 1994, 65). Similar structures were also found at the site of Pyrgos, suggesting that interisland hostilities may have been a factor in the transformation to a palace society.

The growing contacts and trade with regions outside of Crete, and especially with the Near East, prompted the growth of port cities. Pseira and Mochlos to the north and Kato Zakro to the south show evidence of foreign trade beginning in the Middle Bronze Age and continuing well into the Late Bronze Age, with Kato Zakro bringing to light such objects as elephant tusks from Egypt and copper ox-hide ingots from Cyprus and the Levant (Preziosi and Hitchcock 1999, 84 ff.; Dickinson 1994, 65).

Finally, it was during this period that the Minoans made their first attempts at colonization outside of Crete. The earliest known colony is at Kastri on the small island of Kythera. Archaeological evidence from Kastri, including pottery and architecture, suggests that the site may have been settled by the Minoans as early as the Early Minoan II period. Another major early colony was at the site of Trianda/Ialysos on the island of Rhodes in the Dodecanese, founded at the end of the First Palace period between Middle Minoan I and Middle Minoan II. On mainland Turkey, the Minoans settled the area of Iasos from the Middle Minoan II period onward (Niemeier 1984, 205; Coldstream and Huxley 1984, passim).

On the whole, the First Palace period was a productive time for the Minoans. Surplus, specialization, and organization mark this era, as do extensions outward into the broader world of the eastern Mediterranean. But, there was one inherent flaw in this almost ideal Minoan society—Crete is located very close to Thera, and Thera is volcanic. A volcano on Thera experienced a massive eruption in approximately 1640 B.C.E., taking much of Thera with it and causing considerable real estate damage on Crete. But the Minoans emerged from the literal ashes of their Middle Bronze Age society to create an even more glorious Late Bronze Age society. The 200 years following the eruption of Thera mark the apex of Minoan civilization.

The Second Palace Period

This apex of Minoan civilization took place between Middle Minoan III and Late Minoan I, roughly between 1640 and 1450 B.C.E. The Minoans took the opportunity after the havoc wrought by Thera to rebuild their palaces on an even grander scale, creating monumental structures at Knossos, Phaistos, Mallia, and Zakro. These palaces share a number of similar features and styles. Although part of this is certainly because they served similar functions (storage, for example), this architectural similarity can also be attributed to close connections throughout Crete during this period. Island-wide communications are also evident in the pottery dating from that period. Coarse wares (simple pots used mainly for food preparation and transportation) from eastern and central Crete show up throughout the island, indicating island-wide trade in specialized commodities (Preziosi and Hitchcock 1999, 84). Furthermore, such vessels were secured by lumps of clay marked by an impressed design known as a seal (as in seal of approval). Each center of production, and probably each individual manager, would own a personalized seal. When the same seal can be identified on impressions throughout the island, as occurs in the Second Palace period, it is yet further evidence of island-wide contacts and trade (Warren 1989, 100).

Perhaps as a result of improved communications and contact, or perhaps resulting in them, the organization of society that was visible in the First Palace period became even more elaborate during this period. At the pinnacle of this society, as previously mentioned, are the palaces, although who actually ran the palaces is still a matter of debate. Greeks who lived 1,000 years later told stories of three brothers—Minos, Rhadamanthys, and Sarpedon—who were the kings of Knossos, Phaistos, and Mallia, respectively. It was King Minos specifically who gave his name to the Minoan culture, not to mention to the dread Minotaur ("Bull of Minos"). By contrast, the Bronze Age evidence seldom depicts kings; rather, females predominate in the artwork from that period, leading some to suggest that Crete was ruled by women, either in the function of queens or priestesses (see chapter 7).

Regardless of who pulled the strings and kept the tablets in the palaces, by the Second Palace period a new level of bureaucracy emerged in Crete, visible in a new architectural structure—the villa. There were three distinct types of villas: country villas, which were fairly independent entities; manorial villas, which were associated with towns and villages; and urban villas, which were located in the cities, including one located right beside the palace of Knossos itself. Such villas sprang up throughout Crete, in Knossos, Zominthos, Vathypetro, Pyrgos, Gournia, Nirou Chani, Tylissos, and Makrygialos. Depending on what type of villa it was, each such structure was prepared to perform different functions. The country villas were equipped for industrial production (such as pottery and wine), storage, and religious/ritual use as well as domestic activities. The manorial villas were usually more oriented toward storage, and the urban villas could provide little more than a household unit with possible religious functions. In spite of these differences, all villas seem to have performed one common function—to serve as a liaison between the centralized and centralizing power of the palaces and the rest of the community. Thus, as opposed to the roughly two-tiered bureaucracy of the First Palace period, the Second Palace period appears to have been a three- or even four-tiered system, with palaces at the top, villas and cities in the middle, and villages and farmlands at the bottom (Betancourt 1997, 91–92). Such a hierarchical evolution is also visible in the artwork from this period, such as the Harvester Vase (see Image 4.1), on which what appears to be a group leader is distinguishable by a different mode of dress (Dabney 1995, 45).

4.1 Harvester Vase (The Art Archive/Herakleion Museum/Dagli Orti)

Nevertheless, although a social hierarchy is apparent in the archaeological record, this hierarchy does not seem to have been as closed or as exclusive as those in many contemporary societies. The boundaries between palace and village, or villa and village, were not so clear (at least in modern excavations), suggesting a certain amount of free access on the part of all members of society to the areas of power (Warren 1989, 92). This freedom of access probably not only contributed to the general lack of warfare on Crete in the Second Palace period, but also served to homogenize the society, whereby all members of the society engaged in similar religious rituals and bureaucratic practices.

The general peace and stability of Crete at this time are particularly significant in light of the general growth in population discernible in the seventeenth
and sixteenth centuries B.C.E. Both surface surveys and full-scale excavations
of all regions of Crete show an intensified use of land, for both farming and
settlement, during the Second Palace period (Warren 1989, passim). At Pseira
in the northeast, for example, the hilly land was cut and terraced so as to maximize the available farming terrain (Dickinson 1994, 69). Eventually, however,
the Minoans decided to stretch out into the eastern Mediterranean, continuing
the process of colonization that they had begun at Kythera and Rhodes during
the preceding era.

Many of the Cretan colonies were new foundations, whereby the Minoans
settled previously uninhabited land (although this currently held picture could
change with future excavations). Such sites were on the Cycladic islands of Cos,
Kaliminos, and Karpathos and along the Ionian coast (western Turkey) at
Samos, Iasos, Knidos, and Miletos (Cadogan 1984, 14). At other sites, the Minoans settled down among the native inhabitants, bringing aspects of Minoan
culture such as pottery and architecture into the native culture. Often these
colonies served not only to relieve overpopulation in Crete, but also to establish
trade networks throughout the Aegean. Settlements at Kea, Melos, and Thera
(or what was left of it) served as ports of call for trade with the Cyclades and
even mainland Greece, and Kasos, Telos, Cos, and Ialysos connected Crete with
the civilizations of ancient Turkey (Schofield 1984, 46; Niemeier 1984, 206).

Evidence of the Minoans living, or at least trading, throughout the Aegean
was studied alongside the ancient Greek myths—such as the tale of Theseus,
the Minotaur, and the Labyrinth—and the writings of Greek historians such as
Thucydides. Combined, they gave rise to the notion of a Minoan thalassocracy
(*thalassa* = sea; *kratos* = power), or Minoan naval empire, ruled, at least according to the myths, by King Minos of Knossos. According to one story, King Minos raised a navy and ruled all of the islands of the Aegean, as well as wielding control over mainland Greece and perhaps even Turkey. There is still little
consensus concerning the extent of Minoan influence throughout the Aegean,
and the thalassocracy is now generally regarded as a combination of colonization and extensive trade in Minoan wares that spread Minoan culture far
throughout the Aegean islands. In the United States, one might think of the
prevalence of Chinese immigrants, "Chinatowns," Chinese restaurants, and
objects labeled "made in China" as a close parallel.

Beyond the Aegean, Minoan Crete had increasingly frequent contact with
the great powers of the Near East during the Second Palace period. In Egypt,
records from the reigns of Queen Hatshepsut and King Tuthmosis III mention
gifts brought by the "Keftiu," who appear in Egyptian wall paintings dressed
in Minoan-style garb. These "gifts" were more likely items for trade, with
Egyptian "gifts" being sent back to Crete in return. Pottery from the island of
Cyprus and the eastern coastal areas of the Mediterranean appeared in increasing quantities in Crete during the seventeenth through fifteenth centuries
B.C.E. Likewise, Minoan pottery began to appear in quantity on Cyprus in the
Late Minoan IA period, and from Cyprus to Canaan to Egypt by Late Minoan
IB (Dickinson 1994, 248).

Such was the power and influence of Minoan Crete at its peak. The island had a stable hierarchy and bureaucracy, with little to no evidence having been found for intraisland warfare. The population had expanded, making full use of resources on Crete while also spreading out into the islands and mainland of the Aegean. Trade in Minoan wares was on the rise, both in the Aegean and in the more exotic lands of the ancient Near East, and the Minoans carried on diplomacy with the Egyptians at least, if not the other great eastern powers.

What brought an end to this great power in the middle of the fifteenth century, at the break between Late Minoan IB and Late Minoan II, was not another natural disaster such as a volcano or earthquake, as the Minoans had already shown that they could deal brilliantly with such problems. To the contrary, what brought about the end of the Minoan civilization and the beginning of "barbarian" settlement in the Third Palace period were invaders from the north—the Mycenaeans.

THE MAINLAND

The Early Greeks

When did the Greeks arrive in Greece? This is a difficult question, as the one defining characteristic of the Greeks—their language—is not preserved in the early material records. It is clear that the Greeks must have arrived in Greece no later than 1450 B.C.E., as the Linear B texts from Pylos and Knossos are written in Greek, showing that the dominant populations of mainland Greece and Crete were Greek by this time.

There have been various dates offered for the coming of the Greeks, some of which have now been rejected. In 1918, excavators Wace and Blegen (1916–1918) noted the arrival of a new style of pottery in Greece—Yellow Minyan Ware—that dated to approximately 1900 B.C.E. This new pottery was considered evidence of a new population arriving in Greece at that time, until it became apparent that there was an older form of Minyan Ware (Gray) dating back into the previous two centuries. Another position lies in the theories of Hood (1973), who rejects the identification of Linear B as Greek and argues that the Greeks did not arrive in Greece until 1100 B.C.E. In another extreme position, Renfrew (1974) argues that the Greeks were indigenous to Greece.

Two dates are now suggested by scholars for the arrival of the Greeks in Greece: 2100 B.C.E., or the beginning of the Early Helladic III period, and 1650 B.C.E., or the beginning of Late Helladic I. Although the earlier date is the one most commonly accepted, evidence for both hypotheses is presented here.

A relatively advanced culture, or cultures, were evolving in Greece in the Early Helladic I and II periods (3000–2100 B.C.E.). Fine artwork and architecture from this period have been excavated at such sites as Eutresis and Orchomenus in central Greece, and in Tiryns and Lerna in the Argolid. At this last site, excavators discovered not only a distinctive style of art, but also fortification walls; houses with sturdy, spacious, square rooms; and even a "palace" (large building)—the so-called House of the Tiles. The refinements in the art and architecture, and the central planning evidenced by the House of the Tiles, point to a sophisticated civilization with a sense of hierarchy, social community, or both.

At some point around 2100 B.C.E., at the boundary between the Early Helladic II and Early Helladic III periods, a new population entered Greece, probably from the north, and wiped out this early society. Lerna, to provide one example, was burnt to the ground. The House of the Tiles was knocked down, buried over, and utterly abandoned. The houses that replaced the old homes at Lerna were small and irregular, and the new population showed no tendencies toward the distinctive art styles that had characterized the Early Helladic II population (Vermeule 1972). By contrast, these newcomers brought with them a new style of pottery known as Gray Minyan Ware, which replaced the previous pottery styles on the mainland. This introduction of a new pottery style, along with the new style of architecture, is significant to modern archaeologists—it suggests that there was a new cultural group moving into Greece, and that these hostilities and warfare were not occurring between the previously established communities. Most scholars accept that this new, rather belligerent, population was the early Greeks moving into Greece for the first time.

An alternate theory is that the Greeks arrived in Greece at the dawn of the Late Bronze Age, around 1650 B.C.E. At this time, there was a surge in the Greek economy and a corresponding change in culture. Gold, silver, ostrich eggs, and even amber from the Baltic region began to appear in Mycenaean graves, which became far more lavish than in previous centuries. A new interest in warfare also became evident in the art from this period, with scenes of charioteers carved onto stelai (commemorative stone pillars) and painted onto walls, and knives and swords decorated with gold and niello (a black inlay made of copper, lead, sulfur, and borax) laid out beside their owners in the new-fashioned burials (see below).

These developments occurred at the same time as a wide-scale interest in horse and chariot warfare spread throughout the Near East, from Egypt to Iran. Drews (1988) has used this as evidence that there was a mass migration of Indo-Europeans (people with languages related to Greek) at the turn of the Late Bronze Age. These people dominated the native populations through their superior weapons technology, especially the chariot. This would account for the simultaneous arrival of the Greeks in Greece, the Vedic populations in India, and the general appearance of chariot warfare in the art of Egypt and Mesopotamia. Thus, the arrival of the Greeks might be correlated with a more general population movement from the Caspian Sea, west to Greece, and east as far as India. Not only would this account for the sudden interest in warfare and chariots in Greece, it also explains how so much wealth entered Mycenaean society so quickly—it was war booty.

Those in favor of the earlier date for the Greeks' arrival in Greece offer alternate theories regarding these changes in Late Helladic society. One idea is that the Mycenaeans served as mercenaries, especially in Egypt. Some Egyptian wall paintings from the seventeenth century show Aegean elements, indicating that Aegean populations made their way to Egypt to be influenced by Egyptian wealth and styles of warfare. If mercenary activity did become popular in Greece starting around 1650—in Egypt or otherwise—it would explain how the new wealth and obsession with militarism came into the area without the introduction of a new population.

There is a strong cultural continuity between 1650 and 1450 on the mainland, so no new population could have arrived before the Late Helladic I population started writing Greek. We can conclude that the Greeks were in Greece from at least as late as 1650 B.C.E., probably as early as 2100 B.C.E., with continual occupation of that land until the present day.

The Shaft Grave Period: Middle Helladic III to Late Helladic I

The Era of the Shaft Graves, as it is sometimes called, marks the transition from the Middle Helladic period to the Late Helladic period. This was an incredibly important time of development in Greece, heralding the apex of Bronze Age Greek culture on the mainland, known as the Mycenaean era. The preceding period, from Early Helladic III through the end of Middle Helladic II, was a "downtime" in Greece. Although the arts and civilizations of Crete and the Cyclades were flourishing, there was very little by way of fine art or fine architecture on the mainland during this period (although this view may change with future excavations). All this was to change, however, at the dawn of the Late Helladic period.

The designation "Era of the Shaft Graves" derives from two extraordinary finds at the site of Mycenae in southern Greece. The first of these is called Grave Circle A, originally discovered by Schliemann in 1876. The second is Grave Circle B, which is actually older than Grave Circle A, but which was discovered later, in the early 1950s.

Grave Circle B was located just outside the later thirteenth-century walls of Mycenae. The circle consists of twenty-four graves: Fourteen were true shaft graves (more than 1 meter deep, rectangular in shape, with beams supporting a wooden roof overlaid with earth); the rest were simple inhumations on bare earth or in cist graves (a much smaller version of the shaft grave, with no supports) (Vermeule 1972, 84). Above several, but not all, of the graves were simple engraved stelai. The pottery and other finds within the burials show that Grave Circle B was in use from 1650 to 1550 B.C.E. (Warren 1990, 120).

Grave Circle A contained only six elaborate shaft graves and a small group of simple inhumations. These burials contained nineteen people, including men, women, and children. In contrast to Grave Circle B, Circle A was already a significant landmark in the Mycenaean period, so that when the citadel of Mycenae was refurbished in the thirteenth century, care was taken to keep Grave Circle A within the city walls. This involved bracing the mound with a stone circuit wall and raising the level of earth above the graves several feet. As with Circle B, many of the burials on Circle A were marked with engraved stelai, which had to be moved and restored during the renovations. The pottery and accompanying artifacts in the burials of Grave Circle A show that it was in use from 1600 to 1500, with a final burial as late as 1450 B.C.E. (Warren 1990, 120).

The items found within these two grave circles attest to a stratified society extremely interested in warfare and hunting and in close contact with the rest of the eastern Mediterranean. Stratification is evident in the energy and resources poured into the burials of only a few members of the society. Unlike the tholoi of southern Crete, where clans worked together to provide burials for all the clan members, it is clear from the sophisticated shaft structures and artifacts in these grave circles that in Mycenae, considerable amounts of specialized labor went into the burials of only a tiny percentage of the entire population—one might say the ruling dynasty.

The fondness for warfare and hunting is abundantly clear when surveying the goods with which these rulers of Mycenae were sent off to the afterlife. Weapons, notably swords and daggers, accompanied many burials. Several weapons were decorated with hunting scenes, allowing simultaneous associations with violence against both humans and animals. Even items not necessarily associated with warfare were decorated with scenes of combat. One example is a silver cup known as the Siege Rhyton (*rhyton* = funnel). This treasure, found badly damaged, was decorated with impressed images of a city wall being attacked by a small invading army, one of our earliest depictions of large-scale warfare in the Aegean. Jewelry, of which there was quite a bit, was often decorated with scenes of human and animal combat. Even the stelai that served as grave markers in Circle A showed scenes of combat (see Image 4.2 Mycenaean Stele). Some of these show lion hunts, and others clearly depict fallen enemies trampled beneath the wheels of the triumphant charioteer. The overall impression of a society, or at least a class, obsessed with conflict and violence led Emily Vermeule to write, "Mycenae's early wealth came more by violence than merchant profiteering" (Vermeule 1972, 104).

And the Mycenae of the Shaft Grave period certainly did possess great wealth. The bodies in the richest of the shaft graves of Circle A were literally covered head to toe with gold, not to mention the elaborate grave goods mentioned above. The wealth evident in the shaft graves also attests to the broad connections that these early Mycenaeans had with the rest of Europe, the Aegean, and the Near East. Buried with the rulers of Mycenae were amber from the Baltic, weapons from the Balkans, obsidian from Melos, pottery from the Cyclades and Crete, faience (a type of proto-glass) from Crete, ostrich eggs from Nubia (south of Egypt) or the Levant, gold from Egypt, lapis lazuli (a blue stone) from Afghanistan, as well as other artifacts from Turkey and Syria (Vermeule 1972, 89).

So, what of the people who were not dead and buried during the Shaft Grave era? This is a more difficult issue, as there is virtually no architecture remaining from this period. Evidence from pottery distribution shows that many sites inhabited during the previous Middle Helladic I–II periods were abandoned at this stage, with former villages being converted into cemeteries. However, no accompanying destruction layer is apparent, suggesting that the village residents may instead have simply relocated to more practical or cosmopolitan living quarters. Some of these new Middle Helladic III sites, such as Kiapha in Attica, Panakton in Boiotia, and possibly Petra in Thessaly, were located in easily defensible areas, such as on hilltops, with the site of Kiapha ac-

4.2 Stele from Shaft Grave V of Mycenae (Courtesy of Paul Butler)

tually having a full-scale fortification system. This may have been due to a new spirit of warfare in Middle Helladic III–Late Helladic I society, as suggested by the shaft grave art, but it may also have been related to a new trend toward far-flung trade. The hilltop sites are generally in a good position to control the various trade routes through Greece (Maran 1995, 67–72).

A spirit of internationalism is the hallmark of the Late Helladic I period. Emily Vermeule noted that the pottery and other arts of this period are marked by a strong influx of Minoan styles and imports—a "Minoanization" of the mainland. To the east, though, Miletos, formerly associated with Crete, appears to have become a Mycenaean colony at this time, and the islands of Lemnos and Knidos and the Turkish site of Halicarnassus served as Mycenaean trading ports. To the west, as early as Late Helladic I, Mycenaean pottery began to appear in the Lipari Islands and on the island of Ischia west of Italy (Taylour 1990, 132–141). The Mycenaeans may have been looking for new sources of metals, especially tin, at this time. To the south, Late Helladic I wares appeared in abundance in Egypt.

A new power had clearly emerged on the Aegean horizon, rich in gold and wielding considerable military might. Over the course of the next 400 years, this new Greek power would come to dominate the Aegean, following in the footsteps of the Minoans before finally conquering them and seizing control of Knossos. The vacuum left by the fall of the Minoans would be replaced by Mycenae, leading Greece into its first great age of international contacts and conquests.

Late Helladic II to IIIA

Although the art of Late Helladic I showed an interest and even reliance on Minoan prototypes, Late Helladic II was marked by an amalgamation of Minoan and Mycenaean influences into a new Aegean style. In architecture, this was the age of the great Mycenaean tholos tombs, which still stand as some of the greatest achievements of ancient Greek architecture. This period ends with the Mycenaean conquest of Knossos, heralding the Third Palace period on Crete.

Much evidence about the society derives from burial practices. Most significant was the construction of colossal tholos tombs (round, elaborate tombs for royalty), which in Late Helladic II appeared in Mycenae, Prosymna, Berbati, Dendra, Kazorma, Koukla, and Pylos, among others (Voutsaki 1995, 58), These tholoi replaced the shaft graves that had marked the earlier period, and they give us some evidence that affluence was spreading throughout the mainland during the Late Helladic II period. After all, these monuments were extremely costly to build, and even more costly to fill. The fact that several families throughout the mainland could afford to flaunt their wealth in this manner strongly suggests that Late Helladic II Greece was composed of several small political units, each with its own upper classes.

By Late Helladic IIIA, however, this scenario begins to change. The tholos tombs that previously had been spread throughout Greece became concentrated only in a few affluent regions, such as Mycenae, Tiryns, Dendra, and Asine. It is possible that the conspicuous consumption of the upper classes was curtailed by a ruling class who wanted to reserve certain forms of display exclusively for themselves. By Late Helladic IIIB, only the royal city of Mycenae was still creating tholos tombs (Thomas 1995, 352).

Beyond the mainland, the Mycenaeans were extending their foreign contacts during the Late Helladic II–Late Helladic IIIA period. Following in the footsteps of the Minoans, the Greeks established a colony on the island of Rhodes in the Late Helladic II period, as researchers have determined from the pottery. Farther east, Late Helladic II pottery appeared in quantity at several sites along the eastern Mediterranean, notably Ugarit (Ras Shamra), Alalakh (Tell Atchana), and Byblos in Syria/Lebanon, and Gezer and Lachish (Tel-ed-Duwair) in Palestine. In the west, the Mycenaeans settled the Italian city of Taranto during the Late Helladic IIB period, possibly as they sought out new sources of important metals such as copper and tin (Taylour 1990, 148–151).

Internationally, though, the most important event during this period was the conquest of Knossos, which occurred c. 1450 B.C.E. How this happened is still in debate. Vermeule (1972) has argued that the Mycenaeans established an initially peaceful and ultimately dominant position within the Minoan infrastructure of Knossos, so that the city gradually turned from Minoan to Mycenaean in terms of language, culture, and so forth. The more common view, however, is that the Mycenaeans, still obsessed with war and violence, brought down Knossos in a military conquest in which horses and chariots featured prominently. In this latter scenario, the Mycenaeans are assumed to have sought to remove their main economic competitor in the eastern Mediterranean, and thus to improve trading and colonizing prospects for the Greeks from Italy to Egypt to Turkey.

Late Helladic IIIB and the Third Palace Period

The years from 1450 to 1200 B.C.E. mark the apex of Mycenaean civilization. For close to 100 years, the mainland Greeks held control over the city of Knossos. To the east, they established further trading posts and colonies, bringing the Greeks into direct contact with the "Great Civilizations" of the ancient Near East (the Hittites, Mesopotamia). At home, palatial centers sprang up throughout Greece as Mycenae consolidated its hold over the land, leading eventually to the myth of mighty Agamemnon, "King of Men."

The Late Helladic IIIB period formally begins with the Mycenaean conquest of Knossos. This was important for three reasons. First, it gave the Greeks a foothold on Crete, allowing for a greater amalgamation of Minoan and Mycenaean artistic styles, as well as closer relations between the mainlanders to the north and the islanders to the south. One must remember that while Knossos was conquered, the other palatial centers of Crete, such as Phaistos, remained strongly under Minoan control. This was the Minoans' Third Palace period.

Second, this closer contact with the Minoans resulted in the first Greek script—Linear B. From this point forward, we can read about Mycenaean culture and society in the tablets where they kept their economic and social records. These tablets have proved invaluable for the reconstruction of such things as Mycenaean social structure (see chapter 6) and religion (chapter 8). Furthermore, it was probably influence from Knossos that gave rise and shape to the palaces that emerged on the mainland during this period.

Finally, with the dominant Minoan city out of the way, the Greek mainland found no intermediary powers between itself and the great powers of the Near East, especially Egypt. Late Helladic IIIB was the greatest period of Mycenaean international relations. To the west, Mycenaean wares appeared in quantity in Sicily and Sardinia. One of the most extraordinary examples of the extent of Mycenaean influence was the Pelynt Dagger, a fragment of a Late Helladic III sword, which has come to light in the tomb of a Wessex chieftain in southern England! This shows how far the Mycenaeans traveled and traded (Taylour 1990, 145, 150). Copious amounts of Mycenaean pottery have been discovered along the Nile dating back to the fourteenth century, including at the temporary capitol of Amarna, constructed under the heretic king Akhnaten. Trade continued with Cyprus and the Levant during this period, and, at least briefly, Greece seems to have entered into relations with the great Near Eastern kingdoms—the Hittites, Assyrians, Babylonians, and Egyptians.

Evidence for such relations is shown not merely by pottery, but in the documents produced by the Near Eastern kingdoms. These documents were written in Akkadian, which served as the lingua franca of the day, much like Latin in the European Middle Ages. (This language, related to Arabic and Hebrew, was written in a script called cuneiform, a name that referred to its wedge-shaped appearance [Latin *cuneus* = wedge]). These cuneiform documents, especially those of the Hittites, Mycenae's closest neighbors, mention a powerful people called the Ahhijawoi, who were related to a place called Millewanda. The term *Ahhijawoi* looks very similar to the Homeric term for the Greeks (*Achaeans*), just as *Millewanda* resembles the place-name *Miletos*. Although there is still debate over this issue, most scholars accept the identification of the Ahhijawoi as Mycenaean Greeks, and so consider the Greeks to have been at least marginally active in the political affairs of the Near East.

Both Crete and the Near East had long been dominated by grand palaces that coordinated the societies and economies of their immediate districts. The Mycenaeans came across such palaces at Knossos; Amarna in Egypt; and Alalakh, Ugarit, and Mari in Syria. Perhaps it was this exposure that led to the establishment of the great palaces in Greece at this time. Or, possibly, the trend toward palatial systems was already present in Greece from an earlier age, only manifesting itself fully with the rise of the Late Helladic IIIB period.

The theory of internal development for palatial systems is supported by two sites in southern Greece. Peristeria (in Messenia) and the Menelaion (a site roughly 3 kilometers from Sparta) both show evidence of monumental architecture as early as Late Helladic I. These could be the earliest palatial structures in Greece (Taylour 1990, 86–92). Even if they were, however, the trend does not seem to catch on until Late Helladic IIIB. During this period, palaces become the main form of grand architecture in Greece, replacing the tholos tombs that had thrived in the previous age. Palaces were constructed throughout Greece, from Iolkos and Thebes in the north, through Athens and Gla in central Greece, to Mycenae, Tiryns, Sparta, and Pylos in the south (Warren 1990, 122). The best examined of these is Pylos in the western Peloponnese.

The palace of Pylos consisted of a series of storage rooms located around a central hall called a megaron (see chapter 9). The storage rooms contained mainly agricultural products, such as wine and olive oil, as well as some luxury goods. Most significantly, several thousand wine goblets were found in this palace, suggesting either a corner on the wine goblet market or a phenomenal rate of alcoholism. Beyond the storage rooms were several manufacturing facilities and workshops, attesting to production as well as storage taking place at the palace. One of the most important discoveries at Pylos was the archive, where several hundred Linear B tablets were stored. Among other details, these tablets revealed that the palace of Pylos was in administrative control of roughly 2,000 square kilometers of the surrounding region, divided into the "Hither" province between the coast and Mt. Aigaleon, and the "Farther" province extending from Aigaleon to Mt. Taygetos (Bennet 1999, 9–10). In short, this palace, like the other palaces of Late Helladic IIIB Greece, was an administrative and commercial center where goods were created, stored, and traded under the auspices of a ruler and bureaucracy (see chapter 5).

As stated above, the rise of the palaces more or less coincides with the decline of the tholos tombs. Some see this as evidence of the rise of a Mycenaean middle class, with the prestigious tholoi—marks of conspicuous consumption—declining as the more generalized, economically prosperous palaces come to the fore (Vermeule 1972, 156–157). Others see the decline of the tholoi in the opposite light, indicating a consolidation of power in Greece. That is to say, fewer people expressed their prestige through opulent burials than in the previous period (Voutsaki 1995, 58–59). As this is clearly not due to inadequate wealth (the palaces show considerable affluence), it appears that the right to be buried in tholoi was restricted by a newly emerging elite. By the end of Late Helladic IIIB in the thirteenth century, only Mycenae was still constructing tholoi, specifically the Treasury of Atreus and the Tomb of Clytemnestra. The lavishness of these tombs, combined with the wealth of the palatial city and the later Homeric legends, gives the impression of a royal city ruled by a high king. Altogether, the Late Helladic IIIB palaces reveal a thriving economy and bureaucracy throughout Greece, and the few grand burials show the consolidation of high royal status in Mycenae alone (Thomas 1995, 352).

And so a picture of a prosperous and civilized land emerges. The Greeks learned the art of writing from the conquered population of Knossos, while incorporating much Minoan art and industry into their mainland culture. The Mycenaeans were trading with lands as far off as England to the west and Babylon to the east, even playing a role in Near Eastern diplomacy. Palaces and a palatial economy were on the rise as a high king kept a loose surveillance over the Mycenaeans. The only indication that something sinister was looming over the horizon was a new interest in fortifications, which swept through Greece in the thirteenth century.

The Mycenaeans had always been interested in war, ever since the time of the first art found in the Middle Helladic III burials in Mycenae. And yet, for all their interest in warfare, the Mycenaeans do not appear to have felt personally threatened by aggression at home. Fortifications were minimal throughout the mainland, with only the occasional circuit wall or watchtower at Pylos or in the slightly more vulnerable Cyclades. In the late fourteenth century, Mycenae and Tiryns began to fortify themselves. The outline of Tiryns shows that there was a clear interest in supporting a large body of either troops or the local population within fortification walls (see Image 4.3, Tiryns). In the thirteenth century, Dendra, Gla, Argos, Asine, Midea, Athens, Thebes, Eutresis, Krisa, Teikhos Dymaion ("Powerful Wall") near Patras, and the isthmus of Corinth all followed suit (Warren 1990, 123). What led to this sudden interest in "national defense" is still unknown. However, it is worth noting that the palatial center of Thebes was destroyed twice during the Late Helladic IIIB period, once in approximately 1375 B.C.E. and again in 1240 B.C.E (Taylour 1990, 157). Either the Mycenaeans were waging more frequent war on each other, as

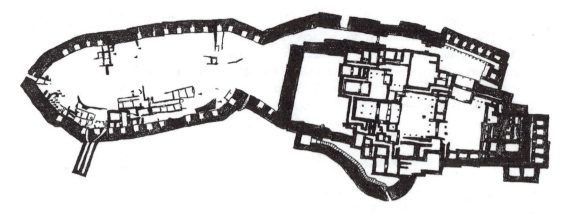

4.3 Plan of Tiryns (Courtesy Stephanie Budin)

is indicated in later myths such as the Seven Against Thebes, or some foreign element was moving in.

In either event (possibly both), by the end of the thirteenth century much of Greece was preparing for siege. At Mycenae, as at other sites, a "secret" cistern was constructed to guarantee reasonably fresh water for the inhabitants, and the fortification wall was renewed, including the famous Lion Gate (Taylour 1990, 103; Vermeule 1972, 215). Only Pylos seems to have remained unaffected by this trend toward siege preparations, probably because it was far from the other Mycenaean centers and shielded from potential enemies from the Near East.

In spite of all this planning, Late Helladic IIIB, and the Mycenaean era in general, ended not just in disaster but in a full-scale series of disasters. Beginning around 1200 B.C.E., all the great palatial centers of Mycenaean Greece were destroyed.

Late Helladic IIIC

Around the year 1200 B.C.E., the transition from Late Helladic IIIB to Late Helladic IIIC, the entire infrastructure of the eastern Mediterranean came crashing down. The Hittite Empire collapsed in Turkey, Egypt was repeatedly attacked by so-called Peoples of the Sea, and the majority of palatial centers in Greece met with fiery ends. Mycenae was burnt down, as were Tiryns and Pylos. In Crete, the palatial centers and harbor towns were slowly abandoned, being replaced by new villages high in the hills.

The causes of this downfall of civilizations in the twelfth century are still a matter of research. Earlier in the twentieth century C.E., theories were put forward suggesting massive earthquakes, drought (and resulting famine), or some manner of epidemic similar to the Black Plague of the fourteenth century C.E. Now, the common consensus is that an overconnected system collapsed domino-style when one of the pieces fell out of place. There is evidence that the Hittite Empire began to lose cohesion as early as the late thirteenth century B.C.E. Desperate (former) Hittites took to the seas as pirate refugees, attacking towns along the Levantine coast, which in turn sent out its own groups of pirate refugees. Soon the entire eastern Mediterranean was in chaos, with trade and travel dangerous at best and halted at worst. Some of the populations of Turkey, the Levant, and Greece took to the seas searching for new farms to till and new governments to serve.

Of extreme importance was the relocation of great portions of the population. As stated above, in Crete the trend was to head to closely knit communities very high up in the mountains. Leaving behind Phaistos and Mallia, the Minoans moved into the regions of Karphi, Vrokastro, and Kavousi (Drews 1993, 29). Today, getting to that last site requires an hour-long trip uphill by bus, another hour-long ride uphill by truck, and a final hour-long hike straight uphill on foot.

In Greece, Mycenae was abandoned forever, as was Pylos. Some people of the Peloponnese fled to Asine, which lasted longer than many other sites. To the north, Attica became a safe haven, possibly because the soil was so bad that nobody would fight for that city. Thucydides (1, 2, 5–6) wrote, "At any rate, Attica from that time was for the most part without internal strife due to its poor soil, the inhabitants being the same continuously. And not the least proof of this fact is that the other regions of Greece did not grow at the same rate as Attica due to emigrations. For when the most powerful people were driven out of the rest of Greece by war and sedition, they relocated to Athens, as it was secure, and becoming citizens straightaway from earliest times they made the city even larger through the multitudes of the population, so that later, Attica not being sufficiently large, they sent off colonies to Ionia."

But linguistic evidence suggests that many Bronze Age inhabitants of Greece also sought refuge in Arcadia in the Peloponnese highlands. The dialect spoken here was quite similar to that preserved in the Linear B tablets, suggesting holdouts from older traditions in a society preserved in the hills (see chapter 6).

This Arcadian dialect is called Cypro-Arcadian, as it shares a number of similarities with the Greek dialect spoken in Cyprus. This brings us to the next group of relocations: those that brought the Greeks out of Greece entirely. Many Greeks of the twelfth century moved east and settled the islands off the coast of Turkey, such as Samos, Lesbos, and Rhodes. Some of these, such as Rhodes, had already been settled by the Mycenaeans, so in many ways the Greeks were heading out to familiar territories. Likewise for a longtime trading partner of the Minoans and Mycenaeans—Cyprus. The Mycenaeans settled on the western edge of Cyprus at Maa-Palaikastro as early as 1190 B.C.E. Within a few decades, they moved into the Cypriot city of Paphos (also called Palaipaphos, to distinguish it from the later Roman town of Nea Paphos) and shared the city with the Cypriot inhabitants. The Minoans also moved to Cyprus, settling the north and east of the island in the early eleventh century. By the tenth century, much of Cyprus was Hellenized.

Farther east, a group of "barbarians" settled in the southern Levant, a group called Philistines in the Bible and Peleset in the Egyptian records. These Philistines appear in the Bible wearing Mycenaean-style armor, including the distinctively Greek greaves on the shins. The biblical book I Samuel 17:4–6 says, "And there came out from the camp of the Philistines a champion named

Goliath, of Gath, whose height was six cubits and a span. He had a helmet of bronze on his head, and he was armed with a coat of mail, and the weight of the coat was five thousand shekels of bronze. And he had greaves of bronze upon his legs, and a javelin of bronze slung between his shoulders" (Revised Standard Version).

Archaeology has shown that the pottery of these Peleset was in most respects similar to that used by the Late Helladic IIIB and Late Helladic IIIC populations of Greece and Cyprus. It appears that some of the disenfranchised Mycenaeans, having attempted some mercenary attacks against Egypt, relocated north and settled in the land that eventually came to take their name—Palestine (from *Peleset*). They set up cities in the Philistine Pentopolis (*Pentopolis* = "five cities") at Ekron, Gath, Ashdod, Ashkelon, and Gaza (Mazar 1985, 308). Unlike Cyprus, where the Greeks became the dominant culture, the Peleset quickly adopted the culture of their Levantine neighbors, such that it was only in the past century that the original Greek origins of the Philistines were discovered.

THE DARK AGE

The period from 1200 to 750 B.C.E. in Greece is called the Dark Age, a period of cultural decline following the previous period of high civilization (much like the later Dark Ages following the fall of the Roman Empire). The monumental architecture that distinguished Mycenae and Tiryns ceased to be produced; literacy was lost entirely; and the pottery—in a style called Submycenaean and Subminoan—was dowdy, unimaginative, and often even lopsided.

Nevertheless, the Dark Age was not a period of utter barbarism in Greece. It was during this period that iron technologies were developed, leading to the dawn of the Iron Age. Foreign contacts were still maintained, especially among Attica, Euboia, Crete, Cyprus, and the Near East. Some Greek regions even prospered at this time, notably Lefkandi on the island of Euboia. And it was probably during this period that the Homeric epics—*Iliad* and *Odyssey*—were composed, reflecting as they did elements of both Mycenaean and Iron Age culture.

Before 1050, worked iron was rare in the eastern Mediterranean. The metal of choice for everything from tools to armor was bronze, an alloy composed of (ideally) 90 percent copper and 10 percent tin. The entire Mediterranean had a ready source of copper in Cyprus, whose name actually means "copper." Tin was more difficult to acquire. Some researchers have suggested that there was a far eastern source for tin, traded through Mesopotamia to Turkey and finally to the Aegean. Others, noting possible trade connections between the Aegean and Britain, have looked to Cornwall for the ancient source of tin. In either event, bronze was the preferred metal for all practical commodities. Iron was seen as a luxury material, used in very small quantities for jewelry. In general, iron was not used for more functional goods for three reasons: First, it rusts, which bronze does not, meaning that iron requires more daily upkeep. Second, raw iron is not as strong as bronze. Third, iron has a higher melting point than bronze, making it far more difficult to shape.

By 1050, however, the breakdown of wide-scale trade in the Mediterranean provoked interest in newer, more local metal technologies. Rather than constantly recycling bronze, the Greeks exploited local iron mines, giving Greece a ready supply of raw materials for arms and gadgets. Additional technological innovations compensated for iron's apparent "weaknesses." The standard means of working iron was to heat it in a furnace and hammer it into shape. These furnaces were often heated by burning peat moss, a readily available source of carbon. Repeatedly exposing iron to the burning moss allowed the metal to acquire up to 3 percent carbon, turning it, functionally, into steel. Furthermore, in an effort not to burn down the foundry, the blacksmiths dunked each newly wrought iron object into cold water. This practice, called quenching, also strengthened the iron. Finally, to render it less brittle, the iron was slightly reheated after quenching (this process was called tempering), which allowed the carbon to respread evenly through the iron.

These techniques of carbonizing, hammering, quenching, and tempering created a material that was significantly stronger than bronze. The only remaining manufacturing problem was that of melting the iron. Not until the fourteenth century C.E. was a furnace created that could get hot enough to melt iron, and so the ancient Greeks were forced to hammer their iron into shape. This eventually resulted in a division of uses between iron and bronze. Iron was used primarily for weapons—swords, daggers, etc.—which could be relatively straight instruments, and bronze was used mainly for armor—helmets, shields, etc.—which required more specialized fittings. Put simply, iron was used for offense, bronze for defense.

The earliest known practical objects made from iron were a pair of daggers discovered in the Perati Cemetery in Attica and dated through the associated pottery to around 1050 B.C.E. From this date forward, iron continuously outstripped bronze for general production. The Iron Age had begun.

Some researchers, such as R. Osborne, have argued that the Greeks learned iron technology from the Cypriots, who first worked the metal as a possible alternative to copper (1996, 25 ff.). This would accord well with the general evidence for contacts among Greece, Cyprus, and the Near East during the Dark Age. The closest contacts were with Crete, Attica, and Euboia. Evidence of close contacts between Crete and Cyprus is also apparent, especially in grave goods from cemeteries at both Knossos and Kavousi as well as general goods from the Idean Cave sanctuary of Zeus in central Crete and the site of Arkhades in southern Crete. Such items include Cypriot- and Phoenician-style jewelry, weapons, metal bowls, faience, and even pottery. More generally, a number of Cypriot artistic motifs begin to appear in Crete at this time, and it may be during this period that the Cretans adopted the goddess Aphrodite from Cyprus. Contacts between Crete and Phoenicia are most evident in a Phoenician shrine established at Kommos in southern Crete, possibly to honor the Phoenician deities Baal, Astarte, and Asherah. Pottery shows this site to have been occupied during the middle of the ninth century, when the Phoenicians were heading westward in their colonizing efforts (Shaw 1989, 165–183).

Concerning the mainland, the best evidence for contacts between Greece and the East is pottery. After a dry spell in contacts between Greece and the Near East from 1050 to about 975–950 B.C.E., Greek trade appears to have resumed with both Cyprus and Phoenicia. At first, the Euboians dominated the trade routes. Euboian pottery appears in quantity at the Cypriot site of Amathus, often regarded as a port of call on the way from Greece to the Levant. Only starting in the ninth century are Attic wares found on Cyprus.

In the reverse direction, Cypriot and Levantine materials begin to appear in Attica in several of the wealthier people's graves in the Kerameikos cemetery as early as the tenth and ninth centuries B.C.E. (Kourou 1997, 221). Imitations of Cypriot pottery were buried with the dead, as were artifacts from Levantine goldsmiths (Coldstream 1977, 55–68). Likewise, Cypriot-style weapons begin to appear in Attica in the ninth century (Demetriou 1989, 75).

The main Greek site at which Dark Age Cypriot and Levantine imports have been found, though, is Lefkandi on the island of Euboia. This site is covered with five cemeteries and a massive burial tomb, each of which brought to light foreign imports. Excavation of tenth-century graves from the Toumba, Palia Perivolia, and Skoubris cemeteries has brought to light Phoenician bowls decorated with sphinxes, Cypriot bronze wheels, Near Eastern faience and pottery, and even a small Cypriot centaur figurine (Popham et al. 1980, 217–264).

Lefkandi, however, is important for more than just the luxury goods in its cemeteries: The one known example of Dark Age monumental architecture was discovered here—the Heroön of Lefkandi. A heroön is a building used to worship a previously mortal hero who is later worshipped like a deity (e.g., Heracles or Achilles; see chapter 8). The Heroön of Lefkandi was not actually a place of worship but a monumental burial structure.

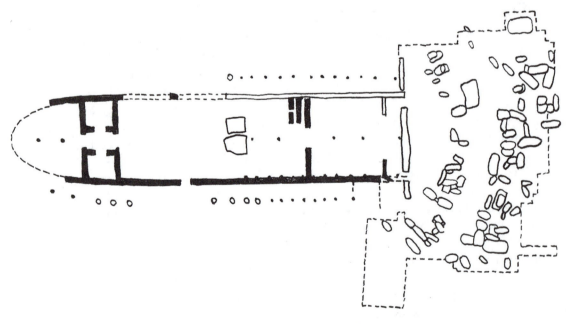

4.4 Plan of Heroön of Lefkandi (Courtesy of Stephanie Budin)

This structure, located in the Toumba cemetery, is an apsidal building, about 45 meters long and 10 meters wide (see Image 4.4, Heroön of Lefkandi)). An apsidal building has a rounded end on one of the long sides. Parts of the wall of this particular building still stand up to 1.5 meters high. Both ends of the structure are destroyed, but it presumably had a porch at the east end and, to judge from the postholes, an ovoid apse on the west end. Internally, it is divided into three connected sections, of which the central one is the largest. This central, largest room is separated from the western, apsidal end by two square rooms on either side of the central passage, and the eastern end is partitioned off by two walls that project into the room. The floor is mostly clay. The roof, which was composed of reeds, to judge from reed remains found on the floor, was supported centrally and at the sides by timbers set against the inner and outer faces of the main walls.

The pottery found within the structure dates to 1050–950 B.C.E. Within the central chamber was a shaft 2.75 meters deep, containing two compartments. The northernmost contained the skeletons of four horses, apparently thrown in headfirst. The southern compartment contained two human burials.

Stretched along the northern wall was the skeleton of a woman, her feet crossed and her hands crossed over her stomach. There were gilt hair coils on either side of her head, a gold pendant decorated with granulated circles on her throat along with a necklace of gold and faience beads, and gold discs embossed with spiral designs on her breasts. At her left thigh was a cluster of bronze and iron pins, the latter covered with gold foil; an iron knife with an ivory handle was beside her head.

In the smaller area at the south of the chamber was a bronze vessel covered over with a bronze bowl. The style of the vessel is clearly Cypriot, and of a make common about 100 years before the burial, suggesting that this piece was an heirloom. Within it were remnants of cloth and, possibly, bone. This burial may be connected with the cremated remains of a man at the far end of the structure. Near the vessel were an iron sword, a spearhead, a razor, and a whetstone, leading the excavators to suggest the presence of a male "hero" with the burial, probably a warrior. At some point soon after its construction, the structure was completely covered over with a burial mound.

The wealth at this site, the imports, the sacrifice of horses, and the fact that one family or set of nobles could coordinate such a massive expenditure of labor for an individual grave all suggest that the economy of Lefkandi was thriving at that time and that the social distinctions that marked the earlier Bronze Age were still in place in some areas of Greece. Clearly, the Dark Age was not equally "dark" everywhere.

It was probably, in part, such a culture that Homer recalled when he (or she, or they—see chapter 10) composed the *Iliad* and the *Odyssey*. Although many aspects of the Bronze Age are recorded within these verses, such as the use of boars' tusks on helmets and the glory of Mycenae, several aspects of Iron Age society are also prevalent. The most significant of these, of course, is the use of iron weapons by Greek warriors, not to mention frequent contact with Iron Age Phoenician traders. Other myths, not as popular now but of considerable importance to the ancient Greeks, are also associated with this period. One was the story of the return of the children of Heracles, also known as the coming of the Dorians. As Thucydides tells it (1, 12):

> Even after the Trojan War Greece continued to emigrate and to colonize, and so did not settle down and expand. For the return of the Greeks from Ilion, taking a long time, brought about changes, and civil strife sprang up for a long time in the cities; those cast out founded new cities. For example, in the 60th year after the capture of Ilion the Boiotians were driven out of Arne by the Thessalians, and they settled in what is now Boiotia, formerly called Cadmeia (there was a portion of them in that land previously, some of whom took the field at Ilion). And the Dorians, 80 years after the war, took the Peloponnese with the descendants of Heracles. And when, after quite a long time, Greece settled permanently and no longer were the peoples compelled to relocate, they sent out colonies. The Athenians colonized Ionia and most of the islands; the Peloponnesians much of Italy and Sicily and some places in Greece itself. All these things occurred after the fall of Troy.

This story helps to explain the different Greek dialects spoken throughout ancient Greece, referring specifically to the Doric dialects of the Peloponnese and Crete, as opposed to the Ionic dialects of Attica and Ionia (see chapter 6). It was previously thought that a large horde of Doric-speakers arrived en masse in Greece during the Dark Age, but this is now considered rather unlikely, and other causes have been sought for the distribution of dialects (Osborne 1996, 33–37).

THE EIGHTH-CENTURY RENAISSANCE AND THE ARCHAIC AGE

The Dark Age came to an end in 750 B.C.E., and the following period, from 750 to 500 B.C.E., was the Archaic Age. The year 750 B.C.E. is the traditional date assigned to the full introduction of an alphabet into Greece (see chapter 3), heralding a new, literate age. During this period, there were new trends in the display of elitism, the initial conglomeration of the Greek city-states, as well as the birth of the idea of "Greece." Finally, it is during this period that the Greeks began their colonization of the Mediterranean.

The word *renaissance* means "rebirth," and the eighth-century renaissance began, as the name implies, with a lot of new births. Judging from the number of settlements discovered in various eras, there was a radical increase in the number of settlements throughout Greece starting just before 800 B.C.E. In Attica, for example, the roughly seventeen sites known from the ninth century increase to more than fifty in the eighth century. There was a proportional increase in the number of graves in Athens, with the numbers rising from about 19 in the year 825 B.C.E., to 27 in the year 775, to 114 by the year 725. Similar statistics exist at other sites for which we have adequate data, such as the Argive Plain and Corinthia (Osborne 1996, 75–79), suggesting a general population increase. The cause of this increase is still in debate. The most likely reason is that as the Greek population settled down and returned to farming (after having engaged in piracy and mercenary fighting), a steady food supply led to better health and a more fertile population.

As the graves became more numerous, however, they also displayed less affluence. The high-quality grave goods that marked the status of previous grave occupants, as at Lefkandi, dwindled during this period to merely a few personal items, a piece of jewelry or an iron knife, maybe a bit of pottery. This was because, during the eighth century, there was a change of focus in conspicuous consumption—the resources originally spent on the grave were now spent on the sanctuary.

There was certainly a logic to this change. Expressing one's wealth through grave goods only works for a very short period of time: The remains of the dead are laid to rest with copious worldly goods, which are visible only during the funerary rituals. Although this might impress those at the funeral, once the dead are buried, the lavish display is over. By contrast, a sanctuary, especially one visited by people from all over Greece, serves as a continuous and more public display of affluence. Thus, the family wishing to flaunt its wealth for the longest period of time to the greatest number of people would have done well to redirect their "investment" from the graves of humans to the houses of gods.

Such large-scale "houses" became especially prominent starting in the eighth century B.C.E., when monumental architecture reemerged in Greece after the Dark Age. There is some evidence that certain cult places remained in use from the Bronze Age into the Iron Age, notably at Kato Symi in Crete and Amyclae in Laconia. But it was only with the eighth-century renaissance that the Greeks elaborately furnished their cult centers and used them as areas of public display.

This is especially evident at one of the earliest great sanctuaries, that of Olympia in the Peloponnese, the original site of the Olympic Games. This sanctuary, dedicated to Zeus and Hera starting in the tenth century B.C.E., served as a place of worship for the peoples of both Messenia and Arcadia during the eighth century. The votive offerings from the site say much about the people who convened there and serve as excellent evidence for class stratification already in this early phase of Greek history. The two most common types of offerings at Olympia were bronze tripods and bronze figurines of sheep, oxen, horses, and chariots.

The tripods were intended as prestige items, saying something about the resources and values of the Greek upper class. (A tripod was a cauldron on a three-legged stand, used for cooking.) Tripods were highly valued as heroic items in the Homeric and Hesiodic epics, as evidenced in this passage from the *Iliad* 23.700–705:

> The son of Peleus straightaway set up the other prizes for the third contest,
> showing them to the Danaans. For strenuous wrestling:
> for the victor a great tripod to stand over the fire,
> the Achaeans valued it among themselves at twelve oxen.
> For the man defeated he set a woman in their midst,
> well-skilled in handwork, they valued her at four oxen.

Tripods were also expensive to manufacture and to transport. At this early date, tripods must have been made in individual villages and brought by wagon to Olympia. The tripods were large, requiring several pounds of bronze to make, several pounds of wood and charcoal to work, and copious amounts of hay for the horses or oxen bringing the dedication to the sanctuary. As a result, the commissioning of a tripod was quite expensive, and everyone from the home village, everyone who saw the tripod at Olympia, and everyone who saw the transport between the village and sanctuary developed a deep appreciation for the resources of the dedicator (Morgan 1995, 24). Olympian tripods were the ancient Greek equivalent of driving a custom Rolls-Royce in public today.

The second type of votive, the bronze figurines, were used by the lower class of worshippers at the sanctuary. Evidence of small-scale bronze casting, and even botched votives, have come to light at the sanctuary from this early date, indicating that these votives were made, purchased, and dedicated right at the site. Thus, there was no similar investment of resources as involved in dedicating a tripod, nor an equivalent return of prestige. Nevertheless, the focus of these dedications—herd animals and horses—shows the dedicators' concerns with farming and with such "noble" pursuits as horse raising and chariot racing. In both cases, the votives not only served as physical tokens of a prayer to the deity, but also acted as testimonials to the dedicator's presence at the sanctuary, for which the travel alone deserved some recognition (Morgan 1995, 23).

Beyond the mere flaunting of wealth by a self-conscious elite, the rise of the great sanctuaries also said something about changes in the social organization of Greece. The display of wealth in a grave or tomb was predominantly a familial affair, with the individual family investing in the grave and the goods therein. There was no higher organizational power than the family. By contrast, the sanctuaries functioned on a suprafamilial level. With the large-scale structures evident at eighth-century sanctuaries like that of Apollo Daphnephoros at Eretria and that of Hera at Samos—and the even larger sanctuaries and temples that rose in the later centuries of the Archaic Age—it becomes clear that the resources and consensus of larger political units were at work: in short, the early stirrings of the Greek city-states (Morgan 1995, 19). The sanctuaries served as some of the earliest unifying factors in ancient Greece, around which the various neighboring families could unify and rally.

There is debate concerning whether the rise of the sanctuaries gave birth to the cities or whether the cities used the sanctuaries as a means of self-unification. In either event, one of the most important developments of the Archaic Age was the rise of the polis (pl. poleis)—the city-state—which became the standard political unit of Greece until the rise of the Hellenistic kingdoms. A polis was a small, independent, self-governing community composed of a city and its surrounding countryside (Murray 1980, 63–64). The criteria for citizenship varied from polis to polis, but citizenship was usually given to all adult male landowners, who expressed their citizenship by meeting in some manner of assembly and by being both subjected to and protected by a common set of laws. Citizenship for women did not hold the same political prerogatives, although citizen women, like citizen men, were protected under the laws of the city. Both male and female citizens participated in the various city cults.

The generally accepted theory among scholars is that up until the population "explosion" of the eighth century, most Greeks lived in small villages, probably composed of only a few families (with some exceptions, of course, as at Lefkandi). With the low population, land was relatively abundant, communications and regulation within the village easy, and those living outside the village not yet entirely important. In short, minimal infrastructure or regulation was required to get by from day to day (Snodgrass 1980, ch. 1).

The Rise of the City-States

Once the population grew, however, new forms of infrastructure were needed to allow the Greeks to live together with minimal conflict. The familial basis of problem resolution and the simple cottage industries that marked most human interaction in the Dark Age villages—the oikos, or household system—gave way to a more complex system that accommodated larger groups of people who not only were not related, but did not necessarily know each other—the polis system. Laws were established to organize the community, to determine and allocate responsibilities, and to protect economic interests (see chapter 7). Armies were organized to protect the cities (see chapter 6). Group labor projects, such as the building and maintenance of city walls, were assigned. Eventually, coinage was struck polis by polis (see chapter 5).

A common cult, a common territory, a common set of laws, and a common defense were the glue that held together the early poleis. This last element—that of the military—was of particular importance during this period, as the new system of hoplite (foot soldier) warfare contributed to the communal, citizen-based society of the poleis (see chapter 6). Another means of creating a sense of unity and citizenship within the newly forming poleis was a common dedication to a common city deity. The Athenians, for example, venerated Athena Polias—Athena of the city. At Corinth, by contrast, Aphrodite was the city goddess and protector, and at Argos, the citizens revered Hera. These manifestations of the deities were closely allied to their respective cities, so that worship of, say, Argive Hera would not translate into worship of Samian Hera; the fact that both Athens and Sparta adopted Athena as a city goddess certainly did not lead to close alliances between these two cities.

However, the common Greek pantheon did lead to an even higher form of unification in Greece as early as the eighth century B.C.E., with the rise of the Panhellenic sanctuaries. The earliest of these was Olympia, later followed by Delphi, Isthmia, and Nemea. Unlike the local sanctuaries, where peoples from the immediate surrounding areas would convene, the Panhellenic sanctuaries received regular visits from all over the Greek world, usually during specific religious festivals. Starting at least as late as the eighth century B.C.E., for example, a great festival of Zeus took place at Olympia. One element of these festivals was the assortment of athletic contests, which legend originally ascribed to Heracles and which were resurrected in 776 B.C.E. at the First Olympiad. According to the later-era Christian author Eusebios, "First Olympiad: from the capture of Troy up the first Olympiad 405 years. The first Olympiad took place in the second year of Aeschylus as judge of the Athenians, and Koroibos of Elis was victorious . . . Iphitos son of Praxonides or of Haimon set up the first Olympiad. From this time Greek history is believed to be accurate in the matter of chronology" (Osborne 1996, 100).

Originally these Olympic Games (and the festival in general) were probably local affairs, composed mainly of Messenians and some Arcadians, with other contestants from the rest of the Peloponnese. In time, however, athletes and worshippers started to come from all over the Greek world, from the islands as well as the northern regions. Because the athletes were taking part in a religious ritual, their safe conduct had to be guaranteed both to and from the games, and so all the Greeks had to acknowledge a period of several months of peace to allow for this safe passage. The notion of all Greeks taking part in the same ritual, and organizing the various aspects of that ritual on a communal basis, marks the beginnings of Panhellenism, whereby the Greeks came to see themselves as an ethnically unified society.

This tendency toward Greek unification was never strong. The topography of Greece (see chapter 2) did more to separate the Greeks than to unite them, and the various dialects and differences in local traditions did not help matters. But there were a few aspects of Greek society that did cause the Greeks to see themselves as one people. The first was language. In spite of the differences among Doric, Ionic, Aeolic, etc., the Greek dialects were mutually understandable, allowing the Greeks to understand and appreciate the same literature and rituals. Religion was also of crucial importance, permitting all Greeks to take part in the same Panhellenic rituals. The alphabet, which came to Greece from Phoenicia (see chapter 3), was also a unifying factor, allowing inscriptions and dedications from any part of Greece to send their message to any reader of Greek. Even the wars became Panhellenic. According to Thucydides, the greatest Greek conflict since the Trojan War was the Lelantine War, fought between the cities of Eretria and Chalkis on the island of Euboia and eventually involving all the other Greek cities. In Book 1, 15, 3, he states, "At best [concerning Panhellenic wars], in the olden times, was the war between the Chalkidians and the Eretrians; the rest of the Greek world divided into camps as allies of one or the other."

The combination of religion, language, and alphabet culminated in what was probably the greatest unifying factor among the Greeks—the epics of Homer and Hesiod (see chapter 10). These works—the *Iliad, Odyssey, Theogony,* and *Works and Days*—in a way created a common religion, history, and ethos for all the Greeks. The lineage of the deities as expressed in Hesiod's *Theogony* became, with variations, the standard Greek pantheon. All Greeks traced their heritage back to the Trojan War (a semi-mythological event), occasionally citing relations between Homeric heroes as bases for "modern" laws and traditions. For example, in the sixth century B.C.E., the cities of Athens and Megara disputed who owned the island of Salamis. Before Spartan arbitrators, both parties presented the relevant myths that associated their own city with the hero Ajax, who in epic tradition had owned the island. The Megarians quoted portions of Homer, which showed that Ajax himself was Megarian; the Athenians used quotes that noted that Ajax "willed" the island to an Athenian, thus establishing their proper inheritance. The Athenians won (Wickersham 1991, passim) Even the Panhellenic games mentioned above were understood in terms of Homeric ideology. The games at Olympia, Isthmia, and Nemea were funeral games for dead heroes, just like the funerary games hosted by Achilles at the end of the *Iliad* for his dead companion Patrocles.

There is debate concerning when these epics were composed, especially those longer ones created by the shadowy figure of Homer. Actual written texts are late, and even ancient Greek testimonia only mention written copies from as early as the sixth century B.C.E. (Osborne 1996, 158). However, as mentioned above, there are cultural and linguistic elements in the epics that show knowledge of the Bronze, Dark, and Iron Ages. The general understanding for Homer is that both the *Iliad* and *Odyssey* were passed down and embellished generation after generation during centuries of oral recitations (see chapter 10). Although some authors, such as Osborne, have argued that the Homeric epics achieved their "permanent" form in the seventh century B.C.E., others, such as Graham, have argued rather convincingly that these epics portray most clearly the world of the eighth century B.C.E. (Osborne 1996, 156–160; Graham 1995, passim). In short, it seems likely that the Homeric epics evolved during the Dark Age and were "standardized" during the eighth century B.C.E.

In contrast to Homer, Hesiod seems to have been a historically verifiable person, living in Boiotia in the eighth century B.C.E., and it is probable that he recited his poetry in the context of the Panhellenic games mentioned above. The fact that Hesiod himself claimed to have sung at a funeral game for a fellow named Amphidamas of Chalkis, who probably lived in the mid- to late eighth century B.C.E., also supports the claim that Hesiod composed during this century.

And so the Archaic Age was a good time for Greece. Temples were under construction, cities were born, games were afoot, and wonderful tales of famous heroes filled the long hours. Nevertheless, all good things bring their difficulties, and the Archaic Age was no exception. While the population was growing, the land failed to expand to accommodate all the new mouths to feed. The finite amount of land also proved problematic in a social sense: Although land was the basis of wealth and prestige, it became increasingly difficult during the Archaic Age to get either. New sources of land and alternate types of wealth had to be found. Thus began the great age of colonization.

Archaic Colonization

It is worthwhile to differentiate here among the Dark Age relocations, the Archaic colonization, and the expansion of Greece under the Hellenistic empires. The colonization in the Archaic Age was an outcome of the polis-based society, whereby a specific polis sent off a colony to a specific region. Afterward, theoretically, the colony maintained at least religious, if not political and legal, links with the founding polis. This differs from the Dark Age migrations, when the homeland was usually abandoned entirely, and from the Hellenistic expansion, when political units greater than the individual poleis were at work (Graham 1983, 1).

The first Greek colonies were to the west of Greece, in Italy and Sicily. The first was Pithekoussai, on the island of Ischia just off the western coast of central Italy, which was settled around 750 B.C.E. Ancient literary sources claim that it was settled by a combined party from Eretria and Chalkis, apparently before these cities fought each other in the Lelantine War. However, both the population as presented in the cemeteries (5,000–10,000 persons, too many deaths to have come from just two cities) and the various scripts and art styles prevalent on the island reveal that colonists came from various parts of the Greek world. The main attraction of Pithekoussai was the prospect of wealth from trade, as the island was too small to offer much agricultural potential. But the site was defensible and was ideally situated to conduct trade with the Etruscans of central Italy. The Greeks probably received metals from the Etruscans in exchange for copious amounts of Greek goods, especially pottery. The Etruscans loved Greek pottery, and the eighth century B.C.E. marked a turning point in Etruscan culture as well as Greek, for from this point, elements of Greek (and Phoenician) art and culture flooded the Italian peninsula.

Henceforth, there was a continual relocation of Greeks to Italy and Sicily, followed by further (and farther) colonization efforts in the later Archaic Age, settling Greeks as far afield as southern France, Libya, Egypt, and the Ukraine. Information about the creation of individual colonies is difficult to ascertain, as many foundation legends were created as late as centuries after the actual foundings of the colonies, and these legends were often influenced by political interests or literary romanticism. Nevertheless, certain aspects of colonization do seem to be fairly well established and consistent. Ideally, it was thought, the move to colonize should be approved by the deities, preferably the oracular god Apollo. So a mother city, or metropolis (from the Greek words *meter* = mother and *polis* = city), would send to, say, the sanctuary at Delphi to find out if they should send a colony to a particular site. If the answer was unfavorable, the city could keep sending consultation parties to the deity until they got a better answer. Next, a person, the oikistes, would be placed in charge of the colony's founding. The colonists would then set out, either establishing themselves in an uninhabited land, conquering the indigenous population, or simply cohabitating with the previous inhabitants. There was no guilt associated with overcoming a native population, as the enterprise was religiously sanctioned by Apollo. To confirm the "Greekness" and sanctity of the new city, a fire sacred to Hestia, the hearth goddess, would be brought from the mother city to the colony. From this point, ideally, the oikistes would set up a system of government in the colony. As early as Homer's time, these responsibilities were spelled out:

> Then leaving, godlike Nausithoos led them,
> And he went to Skheria, far from bread-eating men,
> And he established a wall for the city, and built houses
> and made temples of the deities, and he allotted the shares.
>   (*Odyssey* 2, 7–10)

And so a new Greek city was created. This drive to inhabit new regions was very strong in the later eighth century, and the Greeks established new colonies in Italy and Sicily about every other year from 730 to 700 B.C.E. Eventually, southern Italy and Sicily came to be known as Magna Graecia, or Big Greece. Some cities were extremely active in colonization, such as Chalkis on Euboia and Miletos on the Ionian coast. Others, like Athens, only started colonizing in the later Archaic Age, occasionally stealing land from other cities' colonies. Sparta was unique in that, rather than establishing colonies to solve its land shortage problem, it simply took over and enslaved its next-door neighbor, Messenia. The only Spartan colony was at Taras (later Tarentum) in southern Italy. According to legend, one year when all the Spartan men were at war, their wives at home all got pregnant by the domestic servants. At a loss as to what to do with these partial citizens who were, nevertheless, half-slaves, the Spartans sent them off in 706 B.C.E. to colonize Italy. The inhabitants of Taras were known as Partheniai, those "Born of Maidens."

By the end of the Archaic Age, Greece had developed the political and social systems that typified it for the next several centuries. It was a culturally, religiously, and linguistically cohesive region covering much of the eastern Mediterranean and divided up into poleis, all autonomous and mostly independent of each other. It would take the intrusions of a foreigner in the fifth century B.C.E., however, to get this massive Greek system to come together to act as a unified force.

THE CLASSICAL PERIOD—FROM THE PERSIAN INVASIONS TO THE DEATH OF ALEXANDER

The "Golden Age": Greece in the Fifth Century B.C.E.

The fifth century B.C.E. is the first period of Greek history known fully from written texts. Herodotus of Halicarnassus recorded the events of the early fifth century in his "Inquiries" ("Historia" in Greek), which mainly focused on the rise of Persia and the events leading up to, and through, the Persian Invasions. These "Inquiries" are considered to be the earliest purely historical narratives in the European tradition (as opposed to the more fanciful "histories" preserved in Homer), and thus Herodotus has been dubbed the Father of History. The period following, from the retreat of the Persians and the rise of the Athenian Empire until the middle of the Peloponnesian War, was recorded by Herodotus's protégé Thucydides, an Athenian general who wound up in exile in Sparta. The end of the Peloponnesian War and the events following it in the fourth century were preserved by Xenophon, who also wrote about the Persian royal family. These data are augmented by other written sources, such as epigraphy, plays, and philosophical works referring to the events of this period.

This bounty of written material is a great aid to historians, who no longer find themselves trying to extrapolate civic ideology from, say, the study of the tripods. However, the written histories are never as simple and clear-cut as they appear, and they must be used in conjunction with other sources of data, as well as with a lot of reading between the lines.

For one thing, the majority of written records from the fifth century come from Athens. This gives a rather biased slant to the accounts, especially those concerning Athenian relations with Persia and Sparta. We get no sense of the Spartan, Theban, and Corinthian points of view, except for what the Athenians may have chosen to invent or propagandize for their own purposes. Likewise, by the middle of the fifth century, it was considered impolite to write about women, especially those still alive. As almost no women, and certainly no Athenian women, wrote during this period, this can make it rather difficult to get accurate written information about one-half of the people under study. Finally, Greek historians generally only wrote about "important and interesting" events, tending to exclude the day-to-day activities that form the matrix in which the "important and interesting" events took place. To study the Greeks of the fifth century B.C.E., then, and not just their wars or their ambassadorial embassies, other sources of data are needed.

For this reason, historians augment their study of Greek texts with art, archaeology, and epigraphy. Sometimes these alternate sources confirm the written records, such as the inscriptions that honor those Athenians killed at the Battle of Marathon. Sometimes the artifactual sources contradict those on the written page, as with an inscription from Corinth, which records those citizens who died at Salamis in 480 B.C.E. (Meiggs and Lewis 1992, #24). This inscription contradicts the Athenian version of the battle recorded in the writings of Herodotus, who claimed that the Corinthian fleet fled as soon as the actual fighting started and only returned once the battle was won.

Greece did not evolve in a vacuum. Although Greece's political and national consciousness was growing during the Archaic Age, the great Near Eastern powers were rising, falling, and rising again. The Assyrian Empire, which had dominated western Asia from Iran to Egypt, fell to a combined force of Babylonians, Medes, and Persians in 612 B.C.E. The Babylonian Empire, which replaced it, fell to the Persians under Cyrus the Great (559–530) in 539 B.C.E., after the Persians had already conquered and absorbed the Medes. Farther west, the Lydian Empire of western Turkey expanded under King Croesus (as in the expression "Rich as Croesus"), dominating the Ionian Greek poleis by the middle of the sixth century B.C.E. In 547, Cyrus the Great was victorious over Croesus of Lydia, and in one fell swoop eastern Greece came under the control of the Persian Empire.

At first, this was not really a problem. The eastern Greeks were already used to being under the supervision of an eastern monarch, such as the aforementioned Croesus, and the Persian means of rule consisted of keeping local rulers in their places, making sure only that they were loyal to the Persian king. So the Greek political, legislative, and religious structures were not affected, and life continued as usual. The problem lay in the fact that Cyrus and his heirs wished to maintain political stability in Ionia, and thus they supported tyrants (see chapter 7) who were unpopular with the citizens. Unable to oust these tyrants due to Persian interference, in 499 B.C.E. the Ionian poleis revolted against the Persian Empire, summoning aid from Athens and Eretria. This Ionian Revolt lasted until 494, when it was definitively crushed by King Darius I (522–486 B.C.E.) of Persia and his general Mardonios, whom Darius subsequently placed in charge of Ionia. For the record, Darius and Mardonios were sympathetic to the grievances of the Ionians, and they removed the tyrants.

Darius was not, however, especially sympathetic to Athens and Eretria for assisting the Ionians in their revolt. This derived particularly from the fact that, only a few years previously, Athens had somewhat willingly subjected itself to Persian authority. In 507 B.C.E., the Athenians had sent to Darius to form a common alliance against Athens's greatest rival in Greece—Sparta. The Persian response was "Who in the world are you and where do you come from?" (Herodotus 5, 73). The Persians had never even heard of Athens. Nevertheless, as they did with any political entity seeking audience, the Persians demanded that the Athenian ambassadors offer earth and water to the Persian king, which, it turned out, carried the symbolic meaning of subjugation to Persia. The Athenian ambassadors enacted the ritual as a matter of protocol, but they in no way felt themselves actually owing allegiance to Persia. Thus the considerable slap in the face to Darius when he, in 499, found himself being attacked by his own subjects with the support of what he believed to be his other avowed subjects. This was not to be tolerated.

In 490 B.C.E., Darius led the Persian army into Greece. First, he burned Eretria for helping the Ionians. Then he headed for Athens via the field of Marathon, just north of the city.

This was the most massive army the Athenians, or any Greeks, ever faced. The combined forces of an empire stretching from India to Egypt were converging on one polis in the middle of Greece. The Athenians prepared their hoplites under General Miltiades (c. 550–489 B.C.E.). They sent a runner to summon assistance from Sparta; he covered the roughly 224 kilometers between Athens and Sparta in less than two days with only mild hallucinations along the way (Herodotus 6, 105). Unfortunately for the Athenians, however, the Spartans were in the middle of a religious festival and could not leave the city to aid in the battle. In the end, only the Boiotian city of Plataia sent a contingent to help fight the Persians.

The Greeks faced the Persians on the field of Marathon. In spite of their far fewer numbers, the Greeks defeated the Persian army by dint of superior training and not having just marched several hundred miles before fighting. Once the battlefield was clear, the Athenians and Plataians ran the more than 30 kilometers back to the city to defend it from the Persian navy, which was also attacking Athens. This arduous trek is today commemorated by the athletic competition called the marathon. In the end, the Greeks were completely victorious. The Persians were driven from the Greek mainland, and the Athenian navy, still under Miltiades, ousted the Persian fleet from Greek waters as far as Ionia.

Darius was irked. He planned a larger retaliation against the Greeks, but he did not live long enough to see the preparations brought to completion. His son Xerxes I took up the cause and, in 480 B.C.E., led a much larger army and navy to Greece. This was to be another two-pronged attack, hitting the Greek mainland by both land and sea. The navy sailed directly over from western

Asia, but the army spent seven days crossing the Hellespont (also called the Dardanelles, a strait dividing Asian Turkey from European Turkey) on a series of boats lashed together to form a makeshift bridge.

The Greeks, never having seen such a large contingent before, panicked. Some, especially those to the north such as Thebes, willingly offered earth and water to the Persian king in exchange for being left alone. But to the south, thirty-one poleis formed a coalition headed by Sparta to hold off and fight the Persians. The Spartans were chosen as leaders because they had the best-trained hoplite army in Greece.

An important concern was where to hold off the Persians. Clearly, the Greeks would have to choose some narrow pass to minimize the difference in numbers between the Greek and Persian armies. The Spartans voted for the isthmus at Corinth, it being the narrowest point in Greece and still well north of their own city (the Spartans were never famous for their selflessness). This was hardly pleasing to the Athenians, who happened to live north of Corinth, not to mention the Corinthians themselves, who were not eager to have the battle occur on their own front steps. So the Greeks opted for the narrow mountain pass at Thermopylai ("Warm Gates") just north of Lokris. A troop of 300 Spartans plus their allies under General Leonidas defended the pass. Xerxes was amazed that so few soldiers were sent to confront him, not to mention the fact that much of their battle preparation consisted of hair maintenance.

But the Spartans, who had spent their entire lives preparing for war, held off the Persian army for several days, only falling when a Spartan exile named Ephialtes showed the Persians a secret passage by which they could sneak behind, outflank, and surround the Spartans. The Spartan army was killed to a man. According to Herodotus (7, 277), an inscription set up in their honor told future travelers:

O, passer-by, tell them in Lakedaimon [Sparta]
That here we lie, obedient to their word.

While the Spartans fought the Persians on land, the Athenians and their allies fought them at sea. Ever since 483 B.C.E., when they had discovered a new vein of silver in their mines at Laurion, the Athenians had been building a fleet. Sailing up to the straits of Salamis, east of Attica, the Greek navy used the narrowness of the place to counteract the larger numbers of the Persian fleet. At first, the Persians planned to hold off from battle, waiting for better light and a broader space. But Themistocles (who was also responsible for both the new ships and the coalition under the Spartans) sent one of his slaves to Xerxes, ordering the slave to pretend that he was a runaway with no love for his former Greek masters and to "inform" Xerxes that the Greek naval forces were completely bogged down with internal bickering. If Xerxes struck now, the slave told him, Xerxes would catch the Greeks completely unawares and was sure to win the day.

Xerxes bought the lie and ordered his fleets to attack in spite of the clear disadvantages of the site. First, the Persians lost several ships off the southern coast of Aigina in a freak storm. What was left of the fleet attempted to pin in the Greek ships in the narrows that separate Aigina from Attica. But the Greek ships were far more maneuverable than the clunkier Persian vessels, and the Greeks were highly successful in ramming and sinking the more numerous Persians, who, due to their ships' size, could not maneuver out of each other's way. One captain in the Persian service, Queen Artemisia of Caria (southwestern Turkey), got so frustrated with this state of affairs that she rammed and sank another Persian ship so she could get away from an advancing Greek vessel. This action proved highly successful, as the Greeks, seeing her action, believed that she had changed sides and was fighting for the Greeks, and they left her alone. Xerxes believed she had succeeded in sinking a Greek ship, and subsequently he held her in very high regard.

By this point the Persian army, victorious on land after having defeated the Spartans at the pass of Thermopylai, marched southward to burn, devastate, and destroy Athens. The Greek navy was victorious at sea and succeeded in seeing Xerxes return to Persia. Nevertheless, the Persian king left behind a portion of his army and fleet to continue harassing Greece. By 479 B.C.E., Athens was devastated. Then, after the city burned, the Athenians under the direction of Themistocles and Aristides succeeded in defeating the Persians on land at the Battle of Plataia and by sea at Mykale in Ionia. After that, the Persians finally left Greece for good.

Physically, Greece was in minor shambles, with Athens the hardest hit. Psychologically, though, Greece had never been better. A handful of Greek soldiers and sailors had held off the largest military force any of them had ever seen. Greece was to be a major player in world events henceforth.

The next fifty years (480–430 B.C.E.) marked the rise of the Athenian Empire, starting with Athens and Sparta leading the anti-Persian alliance of Greek poleis, and ending with the outbreak of the Peloponnesian War. In Book 1, 18, 2–3 of his *History,* Thucydides relates:

> By a common effort the Barbarian was repelled. But not long afterwards both those Greeks who fought against the King and those in the alliance parted ways, either siding with the Athenians or the Lakedaimonians [Spartans]. For it became apparent that these were the most powerful states, the one strong on land, the other in ships. And for a short time the defensive league endured; then the Lakedaimonians and Athenians splitting apart waged war with each other along with their respective allies. Concerning the other Greeks, if any should stand aloof, the war was brought to them anyway. So from the time of the Persian Invasion to the present war, they were continually making treaties and fighting either with each other or with allies who revolted, so they became well-prepared and trained for war by constantly dealing with the real thing.

Right after the Persian invasions, Athens, having been trounced, was in utter shambles. Rebuilding began immediately, but there was a problem concerning the erection of a city wall. Sparta encouraged Athens and the other Greek poleis not to wall their cities, as this would give the Persians a lodging place if they ever returned and took a city. The Athenians had no mind to leave their city undefended, but they also did not wish openly to disregard, and possibly insult, the Spartans. Once again, Themistocles saved the day (the same fellow who had encouraged the construction of the Athenians' fleet and caused Xerxes to attack at Salamis). He told the Athenian assembly to send him to Sparta as part of a diplomatic group to discuss the wall issue, but not to send the rest of the group until much later. Meanwhile, the Athenians were to throw together a city wall as fast as possible, using all the rubble left over from the Persian destructions. Themistocles would stall the Spartans, who would therefore not learn about the wall until it was already complete (i.e., until it was too late). Archaeology has verified this story—the remnants of the fifth-century city wall are composed of ruble, broken sculpture marble, and other debris, just as Thucydides described. These walls were built not only surrounding the city, but also extending down to the harbors at Phaleron and Pireus, guarding the Athenians' access to the sea.

In the meantime, an alliance of Greeks under General Pausanias of Sparta were still routing the Persians from the eastern Mediterranean, attacking them at such places as Cyprus. Unfortunately, Pausanias quickly won the hatred of the united Greeks and even the disapproval of the Spartans. Soon he was recalled home to stand trial, and the Greeks gleefully handed control of the alliance over to the Athenians, who had the better navy anyway. (Thucydides 1, 96–97), "The Athenians, having gotten leadership in this way with willingness on the part of the allies through their hatred of Pausanias, established which cities would supply money to fight the Barbarian, and which ships. The pretext was to avenge themselves for what they had suffered by ravishing the King's land. And at that time the office of the Treasurers was first set up by the Athenians. They received the tribute, as they called the monies received. After these events they waged war on the Naxians who had revolted and took them by siege. This was the first allied city to be enslaved contrary to the established rule, and then each of the other cities followed in turn."

Thus began the Delian League, an alliance headed by Athens and centered on the small island of Delos in the Cyclades. Being Panhellenic, Delos was seen as neutral territory, much as Switzerland is today, so it was chosen as the center of the new alliance.

Under the command of Kimon, son of Miltiades, the Delian League did exact some retribution against the Persians. But soon, Athens found itself more interested in maintaining control of the poleis within the League, and the alliance soon became an empire under the Athenians' control. This first became apparent when, as stated above, the island of Naxos attempted to leave the League. Athens attacked Naxos and besieged the inhabitants, forcing them to rejoin and to continue paying their share of tribute.

While this was happening in the north, Sparta experienced an earthquake followed immediately by a revolt of the helots, their Messenian slaves. The revolt centered in Ithomê, where the helots walled themselves in and withstood a long siege. The Spartans were never very good at siege warfare, preferring direct fighting, and they called in the Athenians to help them. The Athenians sent out a large force under Kimon, who was very pro-Spartan and good at maintaining diplomatic relations between Athens and Sparta. Once the Athenians arrived, however, their force's large size made the Spartans nervous, and the Spartans decided to send the Athenians home again, assuring the Athenians they had the situation under control. The Athenians felt justifiably insulted, and so began a long-growing distrust that eventually ended in hostilities between Athens and Sparta. (The Spartans did get the helots under control again without the help of Athens.)

In 451 B.C.E., the Greeks signed a mutual nonhostility treaty with Persia, called the Peace of Kallias. Technically, this removed the original purpose of the Delian League, which then should have dissolved. But the Athenians would not accept the loss of resources and prestige this would entail. The poleis were forcibly held in the League, and the treasury was moved from Delos to the Athenian acropolis (supposedly so the Athenians could guard it better, although they never did specify from whom). Adding insult to injury, the Athenians, under their head statesman Pericles (495–429 B.C.E.), began using Delian treasury funds to rebuild their own city instead of using the money to fund the navy, which protected all of Greece.

From this point on, most power struggles in Greece came one way or another to involve Athens and Sparta. A city would beseech aid from the one; that city's enemies would seek aid from the other. In most cases, though, the Spartans and the Athenians did not confront each other directly, but merely backed different squabbling groups.

All this changed in 431 B.C.E. with the outbreak of the Peloponnesian War. This conflict started when the citizens of the small island of Epidauros tried to expel their aristocracy. Epidauros was a colony of Corcyra, and Corcyra itself was a colony of Corinth. Once expelled, the aristocrats tried to get Corcyra to restore them to power, but Corcyra could not be bothered. So the aristocrats went to Corinth, their grandmother city of sorts, to seek aid. Corinth was happy to re-ally itself with the younger colony, and it stepped in to restore the aristocrats. Corcyra took offense, went right into Epidauros, and expelled the aristocrats *and* the Corinthians. The Corinthians prepared a larger fleet, and the Corcyrans, as was typical for that period, asked Athens for help. The Athenians were really not interested, especially as to offer aid would have violated the Thirty Years' Peace of 446–445 (a recent treaty they had made with Sparta that relegated both poleis to battle only within their own systems of alliances). Epidauros belonged to neither camp, so technically the Athenians did not have the right to get involved there. But the Athenians agreed to send a small fleet just to sit in the harbor and look menacing, so as to frighten away the Corinthian fleet—a bluff of sorts.

The Corinthians, who never liked the Athenians (being rivals of theirs in the ceramics production trade, among other things), immediately went to Sparta, accused the Athenians of breaking the treaty, and demanded that the Spartans put a stop to Athens's political and military power in Greece. The Spartans were persuaded, and so began the Peloponnesian War.

The Peloponnesian War (431–404 B.C.E.) was divided into three phases. The first decade was the Archidamian War, named after King Archidamus of Sparta, who led much of the fighting. This phase ended with the Peace of Nikias, signed between Athens and Sparta in 421 B.C.E. For the next eight years, there were occasional clashes (comprising the second phase of the war) between the two powers, despite the treaty they had just signed. In 415–413 B.C.E., Athens attempted to invade Sicily, which ended in the almost-entire annihilation of the Athenian navy, after which the war reheated. The last phase was the Ionian War, which ended with the defeat of Athens at the Battle of Aigospotamoi in 404 B.C.E.

From the beginning, the war did not go well for Athens. Pericles persuaded the Athenians that the best strategy against the Spartans was to abandon their farms in the countryside and to hide within the walls of Athens. The long walls connecting the city to the harbors provided some living space for the population. The Spartans, never good at siege warfare and never pleased to stay away from Sparta too long (the helots might revolt again), would eventually become frustrated and leave Attica. Meanwhile, the Athenians could use the city's fleet to import food from the city's colonies and to strike at the Spartans and their allies. So, for a while, Sparta was fighting a land war, and Athens a sea war.

All the crowding in Athens led to less than sanitary conditions, and a plague broke out in 429 B.C.E. Thucydides reports that a large percentage of Athenians died, including Pericles. This was especially disastrous to Athens, as Pericles had been the most popular and level-headed statesman they had; after his death, Athenian policy began to crumble.

The lack of competent leadership became acute in the second phase of the war, when the Athenians decided to attack Sicily, having no idea how large that island actually was. The original aim was to harass the Spartan allies on the island and possibly to acquire additional funds in the form of loot and booty. The leader of this Sicilian Expedition was Nikias (the same man responsible for the Peace of Nikias), who stood out among the Athenians as the most vocal objector to the entire plan. Yes, the Athenians placed in charge of the expedition the one man who specifically did not want to go. Another leader was Alcibiades, nephew of Pericles. Right before the expedition set out, a crime occurred in Athens: The city's herms (statues of the god Hermes placed at intersections and property entrances) were mutilated, and Alcibiades was implicated in the crime. Rather than trying Alcibiades before he left for Sicily, when all his friends were present and might rescue him, the Athenians decided to wait until the expedition had left Athens and then recall Alcibiades to stand trial, while all his friends were heading to Sicily. Of course, Alcibiades refused to return to Athens and instead defected to Sparta.

This was not a bad decision, considering how the Sicilian Expedition ended. It turned out that Sicily was very big and quite wealthy, and the Athenians were not prepared to deal with that much space and wealth. At first, they intended merely to sail around the island looking menacing. But when they saw that the Sicilians might send out a navy to confront them, the Athenians decided just to go home. However, at this time there was an eclipse, and Nikias, a religious man, believed that they should wait nine days before sailing. While so waiting, the Athenian ships became waterlogged, and the fleet was surrounded and captured. This, after the plague, was the second great blow to Athens during the war.

Things got worse for Athens by the start of the Ionian War. Alcibiades had informed the Spartans that Athens was completely dependent on its Black Sea colonies for food. So, rather than attacking Athens directly, the Spartans could simply attack or blockade these colonies and starve Athens into submission. In Athens, meanwhile, the democracy was crossing that fine line into mob rule, especially when a gruff commoner named Kleon was suddenly made head of the Athenian army (usually, such posts were held by the more aristocratic families). At first, Kleon did not seem to be so bad a choice; under him the Athenians achieved their greatest success against the Spartans, by capturing an entire retinue of Spartan soldiers on the island of Sphakteria off the western coast of the Peloponnese. If Athens had simply made a peace treaty with Sparta then, it would have emerged from the war victorious. But such level-headedness and practicality were not the strong suits of Kleon or any of the other Athenians at this point, and they decided to continue the war, convinced of their invulnerability.

In the end, Athens lost. Thucydides does not record this part of the war, so we must rely on Xenophon and later Athenian authors such as Plato for our knowledge of what occurred during this period. The Spartans were by now under the command of Lysander, who had—amusingly enough, considering how all these events were set in motion—the backing of the Persian king. In 405 B.C.E., Lysander lured the Athenian fleet into a region of the Dardanelles called Aigospotamoi ("Goat Rivers"). Lysander attacked while the Athenians were still beached for the night, and he took 170 of their 180 ships almost without a fight. Having lost their navy twice within a decade, the Athenians no longer had the resources to fight the Spartans and were forced to admit defeat. The Peloponnesian War thus ended.

The Spartans graciously chose not to slaughter the Athenians wholesale, due to the latter's efforts to protect Greece during the Persian Invasions. They merely undid the final vestiges of the Delian League and replaced, temporarily, the Athenian democracy with a pro-Spartan oligarchy. Athens never fully restored its political power, although it continued to be the Greek center of learning and the arts for centuries. Meanwhile, as the following section of this chapter will show, the Spartans became so obnoxious that many Greeks started rooting for Athens again.

The Fourth Century and the Rise of Macedon

Immediately after the war, the Spartans dismantled the Athenian Empire and placed ten commanders-in-chief in each of the newly "liberated" poleis (Hamilton 1997, 46). According to the peace settlement arranged by an Athenian named Theremenes and the Spartan general Lysander in 404 B.C.E., the Athenian democracy was dismantled and replaced by the Thirty Tyrants, an oligarchy loyal to Sparta. For a year, a "reign of terror" endured, prompting a civil war in 403 led by the Athenian Thrasyboulos, who established himself and his army at Phylê, a border fort between Attica and Boiotia. The Thirty Tyrants summoned Sparta for assistance, but their combined forces could not defeat the "men of Phylê." Finally, King Pausanias of Sparta resolved the situation. The Thirty Tyrants were deposed, a general amnesty was declared, and in September 403, nomothetes ("law-givers") began the process of re-creating the Athenian democracy (Schwenk 1997, 11).

Other than their relative kindness to Athens, however, the Spartans quickly showed themselves to be even less pleasant rulers than the Athenians. For one thing, there was the problem of Persia. Sparta had advertised itself at the beginning of the Peloponnesian War as the "Liberator of Hellas," meaning they were liberating Greece from Athens, which had previously liberated Greece from Persia. In the struggle to defeat Athens, however, Sparta had turned to Greece's old nemesis in 411 and received Persian support and money in exchange for control of the eastern Greek poleis, mainly those of the Ionian coast and the islands. This struck the Greeks as particularly treacherous and began an early distrust of the Spartans even before the Peloponnesian War was over (Hamilton 1997, 45). This pro-Persian position of the Spartans changed somewhat at the very end of the fifth century due to political turmoil within the Persian Empire. As the pro-Spartan Athenian historian Xenophon tells it, after the death of Artaxerxes, the crown passed to Xerxes II. Xerxes II's younger brother Cyrus attempted to seize control of the Persian Empire using several thousand Greek mercenaries, whom he marched all the way to Mesopotamia (modern Iraq). There, at Kunaxa in 401 B.C.E., Cyrus was killed and his forces defeated, and the Greek mercenaries began their long march home—called the Anabasis ("March Up"). Meanwhile, the Greek poleis who had supported Cyrus were in considerable trouble with the local Persian authorities loyal to Xerxes, and it appeared there might be serious repercussions for the Greeks' support of Cyrus. Sparta came to the defense of the eastern Greeks, attempting to undo their pro-Persian reputation and reestablish themselves as liberators of the Greeks. King Agesilaus of Sparta set out to Ionia to do battle with the Persians (Hamilton 1997, 49).

He did not get very far. The Spartans were never a great navy, whereas the Persians had a large fleet under the admiralship of Konon, an exiled Athenian general. In 394 B.C.E. at Knidos, the Persian fleet under Konon defeated the Spartan navy. The Spartans abandoned the eastern Greeks to their fate and returned home.

Meanwhile, the mainland Greeks (the Greeks in Greece as we know it today), Persian attacks notwithstanding, grew increasingly impatient with Sparta for all its inept rulings, so much so that Athens and Corinth, which were traditional enemies, formed an alliance with Thebes and Argos to wage war on Sparta. This Corinthian War began with the Battle of Nemea in 395 B.C.E. and endured until 387/386 (the ancient Greeks reckoned years from summer to summer; thus, one of their years can overlap two "modern" years), when the Spartan navy seized control of the Hellespont and starved Athens into submission by cutting off its main supply route. This brought about the King's Peace, a treaty that was arranged by the Persian king Xerxes II at the instigation of Sparta. According to its stipulations, all empire building in Greece was to cease, and Greece was to function as a collection of independent, autonomous poleis, all under the loose leadership of Sparta. Athens retained control of the islands of Lemnos, Imbros, and Syros, and Sparta maintained its traditional hold on Messenia (Schwenk 1997, 13–17). For a while, the fighting stopped, at least among the Greek "superpowers."

By this point, Athens had recovered from its losses in the Peloponnesian War and was interested in again establishing a network of alliances with the other Greek poleis. In 384 B.C.E., it allied with the island of Chios. In the following years, Byzantion, Methymna, Mitylenê on Lesbos, and the kingdom of Odrysia followed suit. All this culminated in 377 B.C.E. with the formal creation of the Second Athenian League (the first having been the Delian League of the previous century). This political entity was defined on the so-called Aristoteles Decree (IG II2, 43), wherein Athens promised not to infringe upon the sovereignty of its allies, not to seize control of their territories, not to demand tribute, and generally not to act the way it did during the Delian League (see chapter 7) (Schwenk 1997, 21–24).

Simultaneously, Sparta showed that it could be obnoxious even without association with Persia. In general disregard of the King's Peace, Sparta responded to an invitation from a pro-Spartan faction in Thebes to take over the city. Technically, as per the "autonomous poleis" provision in the King's Peace, Thebes should have been left alone, but in 382 B.C.E., a Spartan contingent marched into Thebes and seized control of the Cadmeia, the city's acropolis. They set up a puppet, pro-Spartan government in Thebes until the anti-Spartan Theban coalition managed to expel the opposing forces in 379. The Athenians and their allies pointed out that the Spartans had hopelessly violated the stipulations of the King's Peace, rendering it null and void (Hamilton 1997, 41).

In an effort to avoid another Peloponnesian War, in 375 B.C.E. a renewed King's Peace was established, but this time Sparta and Athens shared hegemony over Greece. However, it was not until 371 that a formal peace treaty—negotiated by a fellow named Kallias—was signed. This peace brought about new problems, again with Thebes. The problem was, just as Sparta represented its allies in the Peloponnesian League (see chapter 7), and Athens represented its allies in the Athenian League, Thebes demanded that it represent its allies in the Boiotian League, of which it was the dominant member. The Spartans refused to recognize Thebes's power, arguing that Thebes was actually infringing upon the Boiotian cities' autonomy. A Spartan army led by King Kleombrotos marched up to Boiotia to end the Theban dominion. At the Battle of Leuctra, the Theban army, lead by Generals Epameinondas and Pelopidas, utterly destroyed the Spartan army. King Kleombrotos was killed, along with almost half the Spartans (an estimated 700 out of the 1,500 they had sent) (Schwenk 1997, 24–25; Hamilton 1997, 42). An inscription set up by the victors and currently housed in the Theban Museum reads (Tod 1985, #130):

Xenokrates | Theopompos | Mnasilaos |
When the spear of Sparta was mighty, then did
Xenokrates receive the right by will of Zeus to erect a trophy,
Not fearing the shield armament from Erotas nor from Lakainas
"Thebans conquered in war!"
The victory-bearing trophy announces by spear,
Nor did we race second to Epamenondas.

From 371 to 362 B.C.E., it was Thebes's turn to be hegemon of Greece (see chapter 7). In reality, Theban power had been growing continually during the fourth century, minus the brief interlude of Spartan power in 382–379 B.C.E. Thebes was especially making headway in allying with its northern neighbors, such as the Macedonians, during the generalship of Epameinondas, who also improved Theban fighting techniques. This training of the soldiers was especially so with the Sacred Band, an elite corps of soldiers of the Theban army trained to the pinnacle of hoplite fighting technique (see chapter 6). With a good army and the support of the other Greek poleis, Thebes had brought down the Spartans—who had been, for the previous 400 years, the premier army of Hellas. No one, not even the Thebans themselves at first, believed it.

The Spartans raced home; the Thebans followed. Under Epameinondas and Pelopidas, the Thebans liberated the Peloponnese from Sparta, freeing the helots and establishing the cities of Messenê and Megalopolis. More so than the defeat at Leuctra, this was Sparta's ultimate undoing, for the creation of an autonomous Messenia deprived Sparta of the majority of its fertile land and almost all of its labor (see earlier section of this chapter, on colonization). Many Spartiates, the citizen-soldiers of Sparta, lost their property, and with it their citizenship. This further depleted Sparta of its army, as only citizens were supposed to fight. New ranks of society were therefore permitted to join the Spartan army in order to keep its ranks from becoming too depleted, such as the neodamodies, or "newly created citizens," and the hypomeiones, or "lower classes" (see chapter 6). Even so, King Agesilaus and his son Agis were henceforth forced to fight as mercenaries from Egypt to Italy to raise money to pay for soldiers to fight for Sparta (see above—they had lost their property). Sparta's glory days were over (Hamilton 1997, 56).

In spite of attempts by other poleis to halt the growing power of Thebes, that city remained dominant in Greece until the Battle of Mantinea in 362 B.C.E., when the Thebans were confronted with a combined army of Spartans, Athenians, and Mantineans. Technically, the superior Theban army won the day, but Epameinondas was killed. Without his inspired leadership, the Thebans could not manage the gains they had won, and, in spite of its victory, Thebes fell from power (Munn 1997, 93–94).

And so a general Greek squabbling began again. By this time, Athens was emerging as the dominant power in southern Greece, while new political rivals were forming in the north, especially in Macedon and Thessaly. The real turning point for Greece in the fourth century came in 360 B.C.E., when Philip II of Macedon ascended the throne.

The Greeks had always thought of the Macedonians as northern barbarians (as opposed to the Persians, who were eastern barbarians). Actually, to the Athenians, the Macedonians were worse than barbarians if we are to believe Demosthenes, who claimed that Philip was "Not only not a Greek nor related to the Greeks, but not even a barbarian from a land worth mentioning. No! He is a pestilence from Macedonia, a region where you cannot even buy a slave worth his salt!" (*Orations* 9.31).

The Macedonians were organized into tribes with minimal international trade and a monarchy that allowed for minimal political development or sophistication. The Macedonians spoke some Greek, and an earlier king—Alexander I—had convinced the deputies of the Olympic Games that his family was descended from Heracles and that he was thus Greek and eligible to compete in the Games (Heskel 1997, 169). Nevertheless, in the eyes of the Greeks, the Macedonians were definitely outsiders at the dawn of the fourth century B.C.E., relevant only when fighting turned northward. Thebes specifically kept an eye on Macedon, as well as on other northern kingdoms such as Illyria and Thessaly. During the reign of Epameinondas, hostages from the Macedonian royal family were sent to Thebes to ensure Macedon's goodwill and alliance, and also to raise a generation of Macedonians with pro-Theban sentiments. These hostages were well treated and were raised with Thebans—being educated and playing sports together helped the two groups develop a sense of camaraderie.

One of those Macedonian hostages was Philip II (see Image 5.4), who learned everything he knew about the Greeks, their diplomacy, and their fighting techniques from Epameinondas. Philip remained in Thebes for three years. In 359/360 B.C.E., the previous king of Macedon, Perdiccas II, died, and Philip returned home to be regent for Perdiccas's son Amyntas. Soon Philip declared himself king (rather in spite of the too-young Amyntas), a position he formalized after the birth of his son Alexander in 356 B.C.E. (Heskel 1997, 178–179).

While these events were unfolding up north, Athens, ever the imperialist, became embroiled in the Social War of 357–355, wherein the majority of its allies attempted to withdraw from the Second Athenian League due to the obnoxious behavior of Athens's general, Khares. Perhaps the most significant event of this war was Athens's loss (to Macedon) of Amphipolis on the Black Sea, an excellent hub of trade and an important source of food for Athens. Much of Athens's foreign policy from this point revolved around getting back Amphipolis, just as the Spartans were fixated on the reacquisition of Messenia. A second important event during the Social War was the seizure of the Delphic sanctuary by the city of Phokis. This led to the Third Sacred War, which began in 356 and involved most of mainland Greece up to and including Macedon. The Third Sacred War continued until the Peace of Philokrates was signed in 346.

The Peace of Philokrates, named for the Athenian ambassador who served as liaison between Macedon and Athens, was essentially, although unofficially, dictated by Philip II. According to its provisions, both Athens and Macedon were to cease fighting, and each was to remain in possession of its current territories—a formalization of the status quo. The Athenians were not content with the treaty, but they signed it for the sake of peace and for their newly emergent empire. However, Amphipolis remained in the possession of Macedon, a state of affairs that the Athenians could not tolerate. The Athenian ambassadors who had signed the treaty were accused of treason, and the Peace was rejected by Athens. Up north, Philip II was not overly scrupulous about keeping his hands out of others' local affairs, either.

After a brief attempt to renew the Peace in 342, war broke out yet again between Macedon and Greece. This time, however, Philip II clearly had the upper hand. Both armies met in Boiotia at the Battle of Chaeronea in 338 B.C.E. Philip led the infantry, and his young and talented son Alexander led the cavalry. Macedon won the day, and they then swept their army through Greece and seized control of the entire mainland. For the first time in history, all of mainland Greece was under the authority of a single king, and that king was a Macedonian "barbarian."

Nevertheless, the Macedonians did not advertise their control of Greece, but instead pulled together the various poleis into a voluntary league convened in Corinth—hence, the League of Corinth. Most of the poleis joined in, but Sparta did not, because the Macedonians had accepted the autonomy of Messenia, which the Spartans would not tolerate under any conditions. The Macedonians accepted the noncompliance of Sparta, as it made the League look that much more voluntary.

Philip II did not get to enjoy his conquest of Greece very long. In 336 B.C.E., he was assassinated at his daughter's wedding, right when he believed himself to be at the pinnacle of security. According to Diodorus Siculus (16.93.1–2), "The theater being packed, Philip himself appeared wearing a white mantle, and by his orders the spear-bearers followed standing a long way off from him. For so he showed to everyone that he was protected by the common good-will of the Greeks, and that he did not need the protection of spear-bearers. So great was his preeminence; and while everyone praised and blessed the man, the unforeseen and completely unexpected plot against the king was revealed along with his death." Philip was assassinated by one of his own guards.

And so Greece fell into the hands of Philip's son Alexander, now known as Alexander the Great. Alexander was only twenty years old when he received the crown of Macedon and Greece, but by this age he had already served as the head of his father's cavalry and knew something about military leadership.

Much of what we know about Alexander and his escapades comes from his biographer Arrian, whose *Anabasis* tells of Alexander's conquests in Europe and Asia. As with most new monarchs, Alexander spent the initial years of his reign consolidating his power. The years 336–334 B.C.E. were spent securing his northern frontiers in Thrace and Illyria and suppressing revolts in Greece. When this was done, Alexander decided to fulfill his father's final wish of conquering the Persian Empire. Before his death, Philip had sent some 10,000 men into Asia to prepare for such a conquest, so, in reality, Alexander was stepping into a war in media res. In the spring of 334 B.C.E., Alexander went to Asia himself, bringing with him about 37,000 men from Greece, Thrace, Thessalia, the northern reaches of Greece, and Macedon itself. Greece (and Macedon) he left in the care of his general Antipater with 13,500 footmen and cavalry (Diodorus Siculus 18, 17, 3–5).

After a brief trip to Troy and a sacrifice to Achilles for appearances' sake, Alexander proceeded to the River Granikos, where he won his first victory and, according to Arrian (*Anabasis* 1, 16, 7), "He sent off to Athens 300 panoplies of Persian armor to be a dedication to Athena in the city, and he commanded this inscription be written: 'Alexander, son of Philip, and the Greeks—minus the Lakedaimonians—from the Barbarians who live in Asia.'"

In the autumn of 333 B.C.E., Alexander and his army came into direct confrontation with King Darius III at the Battle of the Issos River. The army did not capture the king, although Alexander did achieve a stunning victory, which cleared for him the route to Syria and won him several members of the Persian royal family as hostages. While treating with Darius about a ransom for his family, Alexander conquered all of Syria, Palestine, and Egypt. In Egypt, the Pharaoh adopted Alexander as his official heir, not only allowing Alexander and his own heirs legitimately to inherit Egypt, but also raising Alexander to the status of a god. The nature of Macedonian kingship was now beginning to change. In northern Egypt, Alexander established the city of Alexandria, one of the intellectual capitals of the Hellenistic and Roman periods.

In the summer of 331 B.C.E., Alexander and Darius once again met on the field of battle, this time at Gaugamela by the Tigris River in northern Mesopotamia. Once again, Alexander was victorious and pushed the Persian army past Babylon, which he then occupied. From here he proceeded to the capital of the Persian Empire itself: Persepolis. Here, according to Arrian (3, 18, 11), "He burnt the Persian palace, although Parmenio [a general] advised him to save it, in that, among other things, it was not good to destroy what was now his own property, and that similarly the men throughout Asia would not join him, as they would not believe him to be taking rule of Asia for himself, merely invading to conquer it. But Alexander said that he wanted to take revenge on the Persians for what they did invading Greece—trashing Athens and burning the sanctuaries, and for as many other evil deeds done to Greece he took vengeance." (Although Alexander himself was not Greek, and his father had conquered Greece by force, Macedonians liked to think of themselves as Greek—hence Alexander's concern with how Greece had been treated by others.)

Darius himself was assassinated by a usurper named Bessos. In 330/329, Alexander continued his eastward conquest, chasing down Bessos as he went. He finally caught up with the assassin in Afghanistan (then called Sogdiana), where he had Bessos captured, flogged, mutilated, and executed in honor of Darius. In Afghanistan, Alexander made a diplomatic marriage to a princess named Roxana, daughter of the Sogdian leader Oxyartes. This marriage helped to stabilize Alexander's control over, and legitimacy in, Sogdiana. In the summer of 327 B.C.E., Alexander brought his army past the Hindu Kush mountains and into India, the northern portion of which he conquered.

By this point, Alexander's empire stretched from Macedon and Greece in the west, to Egypt in the southwest, to India in the east. Impressive as this was, however, his army was getting tired. When Alexander wanted to move farther east, his soldiers rebelled and refused to follow. Alexander set India as his eastern boundary and returned to Babylon, where he attempted to unite the Macedonian/Greek and Persian elements of his empire into one cultural/political whole (Arrian 7, 11, 9). This he tried to achieve through forced marriages between Greek soldiers and Persian women, as well as through the Persian technique of leaving local authorities in control of their own territories—at least once they had shown their loyalty to Alexander. The Greeks were not thrilled by either notion, and most of the marriages dissolved upon Alexander's death.

Alexander died at age thirty-three on June 13, 323 B.C.E., after a long bout of drinking. His body was transported to Egypt, where he received the most elaborate mummification ritual known in Egypt. As soon as news of his death reached Greece, the Greeks launched into the Lamain War, whereby the various poleis tried to throw off Macedonian hegemony. By 322, the successors of Alexander (see below) crushed the revolt, and Greece remained firmly under Macedonian control until the Roman conquests.

One must remember, though, that the entire notion of "Greece" had changed by Alexander's death. During the reign of Philip II, Greece was the land south of Mt. Olympos to Crete, Ionia, Magna Graecia, and the colonies on the Mediterranean and Black Sea coasts. Macedon was *not* Greece, and Persia certainly was not. After Alexander's conquests, though, what might be considered the Greek world spread. Areas that had been linguistically and culturally distinct, even foreign, to the Greeks now became areas for relocation, where Greek rulers administered different ethnic groups, which were increasingly intermarrying and intermixing. Greek culture spread, which is why modern archaeologists study Greek temples in Afghanistan and statues of Athena from Chandragupta's India. This is why Egyptologists study Egyptian cities with Greek names, such as Heliopolis ("City of the Sun"), and why numismatists study Indian coins bearing pictures of the Buddha identified by Greek writing. For the next 300 years, the "Greek world" stretched from France to Egypt to India.

THE RISE AND FALL OF THE HELLENISTIC KINGDOMS: 323–30 B.C.E.

Maintaining such a vast empire was not particularly wieldy, as Alexander's successors discovered in the decades after his death. The biggest problem was that Alexander had not designated an heir. As of summer 323 B.C.E., there were two claimants to the throne. One was Alexander's half brother Arrhidaios, also known as Philip III. The other was Roxana's unborn child. This turned out to be a son, who was named Alexander IV (Alexander III had already died). Together, Philip III and Alexander IV held power as Alexander the Great's heirs for thirteen years, with Antipater (the aged general who had been left in Macedon to guard the home front during Alexander the Great's foreign conquests), serving as their regent.

Both Philip III and Alexander IV, however, were incapable of ruling the empire at the time of Alexander's death—especially Alexander IV, who was not even born yet, while Philip III was considered to be too "feeble-minded." With the two heirs' hold on the throne being so weak, those who had been in power under Alexander the Great started vying for greater control of Alexander's conquests. The first to do so was Perdiccas, the senior cavalry officer under Alexander the Great (Perdiccas held the same role under Alexander that Alexander had held under Philip II). At first, Perdiccas functioned as an able regulator, assigning administrators to the various lands and institutions of the empire. Antipater was named general of Europe, Antigonos "One-Eyed" was placed as satrap (governor) of northern Turkey, Ptolemy was placed in charge of Egypt, Lysimachus was placed in charge of Thrace, and Seleucus and Cassander (Antipater's son) were established as army generals.

The problem with all this, though, was that Perdiccas set himself up against the semi-established authority in the realm—Alexander's heirs and their official regent, Antipater. Defying their claims, Perdiccas tried to bring the various satraps, armies, and populations under his own authority, ultimately leading to the Civil War of 322–321 B.C.E., during which Perdiccas faced a double front against Alexander's heirs and their regent to the north and the Ptolemies in Egypt to the south. Perdiccas met Ptolemy's army in Egypt in 322–321, suffered a humiliating defeat at their hands, and was murdered by his own soldiers, who no longer cared for Perdiccas's leadership style.

Technically, this should have ended any rivalries for the crown, at least until Alexander IV grew up and the two heirs tried to kill each other for possession of it. But Antipater was quite old by this point (in his eighties). He died in 319 B.C.E., leaving in his place as regent Polyperchon, an old, loyal soldier of Alexander the Great's. Although in many respects this was a prudent choice, Antipater did pass over his own son Cassander, who was as ambitious as any of the other successors of Alexander. And so began the next phase of squabbling, now between Cassander and Polyperchon—and, through Polyperchon, Alexander's heirs. This conflict was mainly set in Greece, where Cassander, under the banner of "autonomous Greek poleis," garnered support from the Greeks. Cassander was victorious, and he maintained his position of authority in Greece and Macedon until his death in 297 B.C.E. His marriage to Thessalonikê, daughter of Philip II, strengthened his claims to the throne.

But not enough. Although Cassander maintained control of the empire's European territories, the other successors kept a literal death grip on their own possessions. To the north, the main threat was Queen Olympias, Alexander's mother (but *not* the mother of Philip III). Seeing Cassander, Philip III, and Philip III's wife Euridikê as threats to the inheritance of her own grandchild Alexander IV, in 317 B.C.E. she led an army from Greece into Macedon, where she killed Philip III and forced Euridikê to commit suicide. In revenge, Cassander brought an army against Olympias's forces; Olympias took refuge in the city of Pydna in the north. After a year under siege, she surrendered, was put on trial, and was executed.

To the east, the main threat was Antigonos, who had seized control of all of

Alexander the Great's eastern possessions, even evicting Seleucus from Babylon, where he had been made satrap in 321 B.C.E. This was a point of concern for Ptolemy, Lysimachus, and Cassander, who, in the winter of 316/315, delivered an ultimatum to Antigonos. Basically, they demanded that he relinquish a small portion of his lands to the three other territories (Egypt, Thrace, and Greece) and reinstate Seleucus, or else the three united would wage war upon him. Antigonos opted for war, and he made his first foray against Cassander with the assistance of Polyperchon. The war proceeded down through the Peloponnese, throughout the eastern Mediterranean, and into northern Egypt. It is a tribute to Antigonos that he held out so long against the combined forces of the other successors with only his son Demetrios as ally (Polyperchon was too old to be of much help).

Nevertheless, by 312 B.C.E., all the successors were in need of rest, and so peace was declared. This peace acknowledged Cassander as general of the European territories, Lysimachus as head of Thrace, Ptolemy as head of Egypt, and Antigonos as head of Asia, all until Alexander IV reached maturity around age sixteen. However, in 310, Alexander IV was killed in secret, probably through the machinations of Cassander (rather justifying his father's decision not to make him regent). As Diodorus relates the results of this (19, 105, 3–4), "Cassander, Lysimachus, Ptolemy, and even Antigonos were freed from the anticipated danger from the king. For, there no longer being anyone to inherit the realm, each of those remaining in power over nations or cities entertained hopes of kingship, and each one held his territory as if it were some spear-won kingdom."

Any notion of reuniting the empire died with Alexander IV. Various successors had themselves crowned kings of their territories shortly thereafter—Antigonos in 306, Ptolemy in 305, and Seleucus in Babylon in 304.

But the fighting continued. The problem now, as it had been twenty years previously, was Antigonos, who continually tried to expand the borders of his territories. This situation was not resolved until 301 B.C.E., when Antigonos and his son Demetrios faced the combined forces of the other successors at the Battle of Ipsos. Antigonos was killed in the battle, and Demetrios was driven from Asia by Seleucus. Armed with only a small fleet, Demetrios took to the seas, where he spent several years trying to restore his fortunes in Greece.

His luck changed slightly for the better after Cassander's death in Macedon in 297 B.C.E. Nevertheless, he was only one of a number of claimants to the Macedonian throne, and the period from 297 to 277 in Macedon and Greece was one of extreme instability. This culminated in 279 with the Gaulish Invasions, when a host of Celts occupied Delphi and eventually established the territory of Galatia in Turkey. Stability was only restored under Antigonos Gonatos, son of Demetrios, who entered Greece in force, drove out the Gauls (see Image 9.25), and established himself as the savior of Greece and the King of Macedon in 276. From this point until 168, the European portions of Alexander's empire were ruled by the Antigonids, the dynasty named for Antigonos Gonatos. In a similar fashion, Asia was ruled by the Seleucids, the descendants of Seleucus, and Egypt was ruled by the Ptolemies.

Thus did the former possessions of Alexander the Great continue down into the second and first centuries B.C.E. The main powers were the Antigonids, Seleucids, and Ptolemies, but there were also other, smaller powers at play, such as the semi-independent commercial republic of Rhodes, the Aetolian and Achaean Leagues in central Greece (see chapter 7), and the small kingdom of Pergamon in Turkey. All of these Hellenistic kingdoms, with the exception of Pergamon, would be overcome and undone by the Romans.

Problems between Greece and Rome began as early as 280 B.C.E., with the commencement of the Pyrrhic War. In 282, Rome had accepted an invitation to help the Greek cities in Italy fight off local hillsmen. Rome was successful, but the Greek city of Tarentum, resenting Roman interference, attacked the Roman forces. Pyrrhos, king of Epeiros in Greece, was the general for the Greeks. In 275, at the Battle of Beneventum, the Romans defeated Pyrrhos, and after this, they annexed the poleis of Magna Graecia. In general, though, relations between the Romans and the western Greeks were good, especially under the Greek king Hiero II of Syracuse (Sicily), who remained loyal to the Romans until his death in 215.

The next round of confrontations between Greece and Rome focused on Illyria, which technically was outside the Greek orbit but which nevertheless brought the Romans increasingly closer to Greece. These confrontations began over problems of Illyrian piracy in the eastern Mediterranean. Although the Romans had persuaded the Illyrian queen Teuta to restrain this piracy, Demetrios of Pharos, a local Greek dynast, blatantly defied her attempts. With Queen Teuta unable to control him, the Romans stepped in, deposed Demetrios, and established themselves in Illyria.

At the end of the third century B.C.E., Rome fought the First and Second Macedonian Wars with King Philip V of Macedon. The first of these (215–205) broke out when Philip, attempting to acquire territory in Roman-occupied Illyria, signed a treaty in 215 with King Hannibal of Carthage, who was then at war with Rome. This put the Romans at war on two fronts, to the south with Sicily and to the northeast with Greece. The First Macedonian War with Philip lasted until the Peace of Phoenice in 205 B.C.E., but hostilities resumed in 200 with a Roman attack on the borders of Macedon. Now, during the Second Macedonian War (200–197 B.C.E.), the Romans, armed with propaganda, portrayed themselves as the liberators of Greece. After Philip's defeat, Polybius, a Roman historian, relates that the Romans made the following proclamation at the Isthmian Games (18, 46, 5): "The Roman Senate and T. Quinctius, proconsul, having defeated King Philip and the Macedonians, leave free—without garrison, free of tribute, governed by their countries' laws—the Corinthians, Phokians, Lokrians, Euboians, Phthiotic Achaeans, Magnesians, Thessalians, and Perrhaebians."

Of course, the majority of these privileges were revoked as soon as the Romans perceived that the Greeks were actually trying to be autonomous, something that had not occurred since the Peloponnesian War. Thus came about, among other things, the Third Macedonian War, which was fought between Rome and Philip V's heir Perseus (r. 172–168). Rome was successful once again, and the Antigonid family was removed from the Macedonian throne. The first of the Hellenistic kingdoms had come to an end. In 148 B.C.E., Macedon became a Roman province.

To the east, the Seleucids were having their own problems with Rome. Already in 192–188 B.C.E., the Romans had come into conflict with Seleucid king Antiochus III when he, attempting to liberate the Greeks (have you noticed this recurring theme?), fought on the side of the Aetolian League in alliance with Rome against Macedon. Between Rome, Pergamon (supported by Rome), and Egypt chipping away at them, the Seleucids continued to lose territory until, by 129 after the death of Antiochus VII, they were left with only a sliver of northern Syria, which was eventually conquered by Rome.

The last Hellenistic dynasty to fall was the Ptolemies of Egypt, whose power lasted until the Battle of Actium in 31 B.C.E. At this time, Queen Cleopatra VII ruled Egypt. She had attempted to bolster her authority in Egypt through a close alliance with Rome, first becoming the ally and lover of Julius Caesar (and bearing him a son), and then, after Caesar's assassination, becoming the wife of Marc Antony, Caesar's comrade. Unlike Rome's problems with the previous two Hellenistic kingdoms, the conflicts between Egypt and Rome had more to do with the political situation in Rome than with any power struggles between Egypt and its neighbors. After the death of Julius Caesar, Rome had split into two factions—those favoring Marc Antony and those favoring Octavian Caesar, Julius Caesar's formal heir. Cleopatra backed Marc Antony, fighting for him at the sea battle of Actium. In the end, however, Octavian's forces won. Marc Antony and Cleopatra committed suicide, Cleopatra's son by Julius Caesar was assassinated, the Ptolemaic line was extinguished, and the Roman Empire eventually annexed Egypt. The Hellenistic kingdoms, the final phase of ancient Greece, thus came to an end.

REFERENCES

Bennet, J. 1999. "Pylos: The Expansion of a Mycenaean Palatial Center." In Galaty, M. L. and W. A. Parkinson, eds. *Rethinking Mycenaean Palaces: New Interpretations of an Old Idea*. Los Angeles: UCLA Cotsen Institute of Archaeology Monograph 41, 9–18.

Berolini, G. 1913– . *Inscriptiones Graecae*. Vol. 1. Berlin: De Gruyter.

Betancourt, P. P. 1997. "The Minoan Villa: The Definition of the Minoan Villa." In Hägg, R., ed. 1997. *The Function of the "Minoan Villa."* Stockholm: Paul Åströms Förlag, 91–92.

Branigan, K. 1995. "Social Transformations and the Rise of the State in Crete." In Laffineur, R. and W.-D. Niemeier, eds. *Politeia: Society and State in the Aegean Bronze Age*. AEGAEUM 12. Liège, Belgium: Université de Liège, 33–42.

Cadogan, G. 1984. "A Minoan Thalassocracy?" In Hägg, R. and N. Marinatos, eds. *The Minoan Thalassocracy: Myth and Reality*. Stockholm: Paul Åströms Förlag, 13–15.

Cherry, J. 1990. "Evolution, Revolution, and the Origins of Complex Society in Minoan Crete." In Krzyszkowska, O. and L. Nixon, eds. *Minoan Society*. Bristol, UK: Bristol Classical, 33–46.

Coldstream, J. N. 1977. *Geometric Greece*. London: Methuen.

Coldstream, J. N. and G. L. Huxley. 1984. "The Minoans of Kythera." In Hägg, R. and N.

Marinatos, eds. *The Minoan Thalassocracy: Myth and Reality.* Stockholm: Paul Åströms Förlag, 107–110.

Dabney, M. K. 1995. "The Later Stages of State Formation in Palatial Crete." In Laffineur, R. and W.-D. Niemeier, eds. *Politeia: Society and State in the Aegean Bronze Age.* AEGAEUM 12. Liège, Belgium: Université de Liège, 43–54.

Demetriou, A. 1989. *Cypro-Aegean Relations in the Early Iron Age.* Studies in Mediterranean Archaeology 83. Göteborg: Paul Åströms Förlag.

Dickinson, O. 1994. *The Aegean Bronze Age.* Cambridge, UK: Cambridge University Press.

Drews, R. 1988. *The Coming of the Greeks: Indo-European Conquests in the Aegean and the Near East.* Princeton, NJ: Princeton University Press.

———. 1993. *The End of the Bronze Age: Changes in Warfare and the Catastrophe ca. 1200 B.C.* Princeton, NJ: Princeton University Press.

Graham, A. J. 1983. *Colony and Mother City in Ancient Greece.* 2d. ed. Chicago: Ares.

———. 1995. "The *Odyssey,* History, and Women." In Cohen, B., ed. 1995. *The Distaff Side: Representing the Female in Homer's Odyssey.* Oxford, UK: Oxford University Press, 3–16.

Hamilton, C. D. 1997. "Sparta." In Tritle, L. A., ed. 1997. *The Greek World in the Fourth Century: From the Fall of the Athenian Empire to the Successors of Alexander.* New York: Routledge, 41–65.

Heskel, J. 1997. "Macedonia and the North, 400–336." In Tritle, L. A., ed. 1997. *The Greek World in the Fourth Century: From the Fall of the Athenian Empire to the Successors of Alexander.* New York: Routledge, 167–188.

Hood, S. 1973. "Mycenaean Settlement in Cyprus and the Coming of the Greeks." In *Acts of the International Archaeological Symposium: The Mycenaeans in the Eastern Mediterranean.* Nicosia, Cyprus: Department of Antiquities, 40–50.

Kourou, N. 1997. "Αιγαιο και Κυπρος κατα την Προιμη Εποχη του Σιδηρου: Νεωτερες εξελιζεις." In *Cyprus and the Aegean in Antiquity: From the Prehistoric Period to the Seventh Century A.D.: Nicosia 8–10 December 1995.* Nicosia, Cyprus: Department of Antiquities, 217–230.

Maran, J. 1995. "Structural Changes in the Pattern of Settlement during the Shaft Grave Period on the Greek Mainland." In Laffineur, R. and W.-D. Niemeier, eds. *Politeia: Society and State in the Aegean Bronze Age.* AEGAEUM 12. Liège, Belgium: Université de Liège, 67–72.

Mazar, A. 1985. *Archaeology in the Land of the Bible: 10,000–586 B.C.E.* New York: Doubleday.

Meiggs, R. and D. Lewis. 1992. *A Selection of Greek Historical Inscription to the End of the Fifth Century B.C.* Oxford, UK: Clarendon.

Morgan, C. 1995. "The Origins of Panhellenism." In Marinatos, N. and R. Hägg, eds. *Greek Sanctuaries: New Approaches.* London: Routledge, 18–44.

Munn, M. 1997. "Thebes and Central Greece." In Tritle, L. A., ed. 1997. *The Greek World in the Fourth Century: From the Fall of the Athenian Empire to the Successors of Alexander.* New York: Routledge, 66–106.

Murray, O. 1980. *Early Greece.* Palo Alto, CA: Stanford University Press.

Niemeier, W.-D. 1984. "The End of the Minoan Thalassocracy." In Hägg, R. and N. Marinatos, eds. *The Minoan Thalassocracy: Myth and Reality.* Stockholm: Paul Åströms Förlag, 205–214.

Osborne, R. 1996. *Greece in the Making: 1200–479 B.C.* London: Routledge.

Popham, M. R., L. H. Sackett, and P. G. Themelis, eds. 1980. *Lefkandi I: The Iron Age.* London: Thames & Hudson.

Preziosi, D. and L. A. Hitchcock. 1999. *Aegean Art and Architecture.* Oxford, UK: Oxford University Press.

Renfrew, C. 1974. "Problems in the General Correlation of Archaeological and Linguistic Strata in Prehistoric Greece: the Model of Autochthonous Origin." In Crossland, R. A. and A. Birchall, eds. *Bronze Age Migrations in the Aegean: Archaeological and Linguistic Problems.* Park Ridge, NJ: Noyes, 263–275.

Schofield, E. 1984. "Coming to Terms with Minoan Colonists." In Hägg, R. and N. Marinatos, eds. *The Minoan Thalassocracy: Myth and Reality.* Stockholm: Paul Åströms Förlag, 45–47.

Schwenk, C. 1997. "Athens." In Tritle, L. A., ed. 1997. *The Greek World in the Fourth Century: From the Fall of the Athenian Empire to the Successors of Alexander.* New York: Routledge, 8–40.

Shaw, J. 1989. "Phoenicians in Southern Crete." *American Journal of Archaeology* 93: 165–183.

Snodgrass, A. 1980. *Archaic Greece: The Age of Experiment.* Berkeley: University of California Press.

Taylour, W. 1990. *The Mycenaeans.* Rev. ed. New York: Thames & Hudson.

Thomas, C. G. 1995. "The Components of Political Identity in Mycenaean Greece." In Laffineur, R. and W.-D. Niemeier, eds. *Politeia: Society and State in the Aegean Bronze Age.* AEGAEUM 12. Liège, Belgium: Université de Liège, 349–354.

Tod, M. N. 1985. *Greek Historical Inscriptions.* Chicago: Ares.

Vermeule, E. 1972. *Greece in the Bronze Age.* Chicago: University of Chicago Press.

Voutsaki, S. 1995. "Social and Political Processes in the Mycenaean Argolid: The Evidence from the Mortuary Practices." In Laffineur, R. and W.-D. Niemeier, eds. *Politeia: Society and State in the Aegean Bronze Age.* AEGAEUM 12. Liège, Belgium: Université de Liège, 55–66.

Wace, A. and C. Blegen. 1916–1918. "The Pre-Mycenaean Pottery of the Mainland." *British School Annual* 22, 175–189.

Warren, P. 1987. "The Genesis of the Minoan Palace." In Hägg, R. and N. Marinatos, eds. *The Function of the Minoan Palaces.* Stockholm: Paul Åströms Förlag, 47–56.

———. 1989. *The Aegean Civilizations.* New York: Peter Bedrick.

West, M. L. 1997. *The East Face of Helicon: West Asiatic Elements in Greek Poetry and Myth.* Oxford, UK: Clarendon.

Whitelaw, T. M. 1990. "The Settlement at Fournou Korifi, Myrtos and Aspects of Early Minoan Social Organization." In Krzyszkowska, O. and L. Nixon, eds. *Minoan Society.* Bristol, UK: Bristol Classical, 323–346.

Wickersham, J. M. 1991. "Myth and Identity in the Archaic Polis." In Pozzi, D. C. and J. M. Wickersham, eds. *Myth and the Polis.* Ithaca, NY: Cornell University Press, 16–31.

CHAPTER 5
Economics

The word *economics* comes from the Greek *oikonomikos,* referring to the orderly running of a household. Xenophon's essay *Oikonomikos* concerned the smooth functioning of an Athenian nobleman's idealized household. More in line with the modern understanding of economics, the same author penned a treatise entitled *Poroi* (Resources), in which he discussed means of increasing revenue in the city. This ideology was pursued by Pseudo-Aristotle (thought to be a student of Aristotle), whose own essay *Oikonomikos* presents various anecdotes concerning fundraising and the use of money in society (Oliver 2000, 526). Ultimately, ancient Greek economics is one aspect of the larger issues of Greek society and politics. Nevertheless, there are elements that one may justly consider as independent aspects of Greek economics—production, trade, and access to goods.

PALACE ECONOMIES OF THE AEGEAN BRONZE AGE

One can expect that, at any given time, at least 95 percent of the Aegean economy was dominated by agriculture. Independent or semi-independent farmers raised grains, fruits, and vegetables; pastoralists grazed sheep and goats, and possibly larger cattle, for milk, meat, wool, and even labor; hunters and fishers supplemented the daily fare. In the home, women and probably children spun wool, wove cloth, sewed clothes, prepared meals, and made the majority of the pottery for household consumption. Trade had existed since the Neolithic period, when obsidian from Melos made its way to all corners of the Aegean. By the Early Bronze Age, copper and then tin appeared throughout the Aegean, copper most likely from Cyprus and tin from much, much farther afield. Also there is evidence that, already during the Early Bronze Age, a more organized, extrahousehold economy was beginning to develop throughout the Aegean. In Crete, monumental architecture began to appear in Early Minoan II Palaikastro and in Early Minoan III Knossos, revealing the early stirrings of an organized labor force. In Greece, the Early Helladic II town of Lerna had what appears to have been a large, central storehouse, where excavators found a collection of clay sealings probably used for identification of producers and for redistribution. Henceforth, one might speak of them having a palace economy—an economic system in which a strong, centralized power controlled the production and distribution of nondomestic goods and, presumably, services.

5.1 Aegean Storage Jars in situ (Courtesy of Tobia Worth)

Minoan Crete

In Palatial Crete, this centralized power consisted of the palaces and, later, the villas. According to Branigan, the five primary economic functions of Minoan palaces from Middle Minoan III to Late Minoan I were (1) production of manufactured goods, (2) consumption of food and manufactured goods, (3) regulation of local and internal exchange, (4) regulation of international and external exchange, and (5) use as depositories (Branigan 1987, 245) (see Image 5.1).

The production and storage of manufactured goods are evident from the digs at Phaistos and Mallia. Excavations of the earliest phases at Phaistos (Middle Minoan I–Middle Minoan II) revealed two areas dedicated to economic activity. Unit A contained several large storage vessels originally filled with foodstuffs, including liquids such as wine and oil. Nearby Unit B was the palace workshop. Here, excavators found tools used for stoneworking (a lapidary workshop), several loom weights (a weaving workshop), and two potter's wheels (a ceramics workshop). Clay sealings from a smaller room in Unit B may indicate where finished products were processed for storage or export. By the second phase of the palace, there were even more food storage vessels present, and an actual archive room was created (Branigan 1987, 247).

Similar finds appeared at Mallia. In the northwest quarter of the palace, excavators discovered obsidian, soapstone, and a reddish stone called rosso antico, all evidently part of the lapidary workshop. A potter's workshop was also present within the palace walls. During the Middle Minoan II period, a bronze smithy was located just outside the palace walls. It is actually surprising that such an industry would be so close to any residential quarters, considering the unpleasant fumes given off by the work and the rather high potential for fires. Nevertheless, by the Middle Minoan III period, the palace walls were actually extended so that the smithy was located within the palace itself. Clearly, this was an industry over which the palace wanted to keep very close control (Pelon 1987, 269–271).

The role of Minoan palaces as depositories and regulators of local distribution and trade may be seen in the koulouras—large stone-lined pits located at Knossos, Phaistos, and in a slightly altered guise at Mallia. There is continued debate as to the purpose of these huge storage bins. Evans suggests that they were rubbish pits. Some modern scholars believe that they were giant tree planters. But the usual interpretation is that they were for grain storage, with the koulouras at Knossos being able to hold enough grain to feed 1,000 people and the koulouras at Phaistos being able to hold enough for 300 people (Preziosi and Hitchcock 1999, 80–81). In such a case, the palace would have received a substantial portion of the agricultural produce of the surrounding farms, stored it, and then distributed it to the more specialized, nonagricultural populace of the palace region.

Palatial control over foreign trade is more difficult to prove archaeologically, as there is often no way to determine where on Crete any specific item found abroad was made. One argument often brought to the fore is that only the palaces would have the capital (to use a modern term) to finance the goods and shipping for long trade journeys, not to mention to handle the risks of possible sea wrecks. Another argument, however, lies in the nature of the Minoan goods found abroad. For example, Kamares Ware pottery (see chapter 9) has come to light on the coasts of Cyprus, Egypt, Palestine, Canaan, and Syria (Wiener 1987, 261). This Kamares Ware is clearly a product of palatial manufacture. The ceramics from before and after the "classical" Kamares wares are clearly local creations—Knossian Ware being distinct from Mallian Ware. By contrast, the Kamares Ware made in the palaces is similar from palace to palace but is utterly distinct from the provincial wares (Walberg 1987, 284). Therefore, we might argue that the Kamares wares found in the Near East are definitely from palatial production centers. The number of foreign goods stored in the palaces, especially Zakro, also gives evidence for the palatial control of international exchange (Wiener 1987, 265).

Mycenaean Greece and Crete

The Mycenaean palatial economy did not differ in many respects from the Minoan. In fact, the Mycenaeans seem to have taken over the trading posts once used by the Minoans, as well as the palace of Knossos, after 1450 B.C.E. (see chapter 4). The fact that the Mycenaean palaces fulfilled the same roles as the Minoan is evident from the archaeology, which reveals palaces on the Greek mainland functioning as producers and storers of manufactured goods. This is particularly evident at the palace of Pylos in southwestern Greece. Surrounding the megaron, or main throne room, was a series of rooms used for the storage of oil and ceramics. One room contained 850 pots of varying shapes, and another a total of 2,853 drinking cups (Vermeule 1972, 167). To the east and northwest of the palace proper were industrial buildings containing storage jars, pieces of bronze, clay sealings from "packaged goods," and even bits of ivory. Farther on were remains of a potter's kiln with discarded bits of pottery lying about it (Vermeule 1972, 166).

The Linear B archives discovered at the Mycenaean palaces (see chapter 3) give further insight into the functionings of the Mycenaean palace economies. The palaces maintained extensive control of the nondomestic areas of production through careful control of the acquisition and distribution of raw materials, the maintenance of several key personnel in the palace industries, and the tallying of produced goods. The similarities and contrasts among three separate industries will serve to show the various machinations of the Mycenaean bureaucracies.

Textiles were an important Mycenaean commodity: Beyond just the household production of cloth and clothing, the palaces produced textiles for their own use as well as export. Numerous Linear B tablets record the various components of this textile industry. For example, the Da–g and Dn series of tablets from the archives at Knossos show that some 80,000 to 100,000 sheep were grazed in central Crete. Some tablets show how much wool was expected from these sheep; others show how much wool and offspring were expected (it seems that one group recorded males; the other, females). Later, the Dk and Kl tablets revealed that these flocks produced about 30–50 tons of wool, which was collected and brought to palatial workshops, where the Lc tablets show how this wool was allocated (Burke 1997, 414). Here, the Linear B A-series of tablets reveals that the workers in these workshops were predominately women, usually identified only through what they did or where they were from (see chapter 6). Many women were listed with girls and/or boys associated with them. Perhaps they were mothers working with their children, or older women training girls and boys too young yet for other employment (Killen 1984, 49–50). Thus, from Pylos, we have one tablet (Ab 573) that says, "Pylos. 16 Miletos women, 3 girls, 7 boys. 5+1 units of wheat, 5+1 units of figs" (Hooker 1980, 102).

It is clear from this document that food rations were provided for the textile workers. This, plus their namelessness and the fact of their foreign origins (in this case Miletos) may suggest that the workers were slaves, although the word do-e-ro = doulos = slave does not appear.

The L series of tablets covers the target production set for these worker groups, including the allocations of raw materials they were given to process. These "allocations" refer to the still rather ambiguous word ta-ra-si-ja in the tablets. Currently, researchers think that the ta-ra-si-ja were individual units of a raw material, be it wool, bronze, or possibly some other material, which the palace gave to workers to turn into finished products—in this case fabric of some sort. When the finished products were collected by palace officials, the amount of fabric (or whatever the commodity) was reckoned against the amount of the original ta-ra-si-ja, to be sure that all necessary materials were used appropriately. In this way, the palaces could administer and control workshops and factories that were not necessarily located within the palaces themselves.

In contrast to the textile industry, bronzesmithing seems to have been under less direct palatial control, and the smiths themselves had a higher status than the textile workers. Unlike the textile industry, not all bronzesmiths received raw materials from the palaces (although many did), suggesting that there was also some noncentralized, free trade taking place. The smiths likewise received no rations from the palaces, and in many instances, they actually owned their own slaves. Thus, tablet Jn 605 from Pylos tells us:

> From the region of Amphinouios the bronze smiths with allocations:
> Stolios: M1 N2 units of bronze; Eidomoneus: M1 N2 units of bronze;
> Mikelion: M1 N2 units of bronze; Phyltas: M1 N2 units of bronze;
> Ywantas: M1 N2 units of bronze; Katharwa: M1 N2 units of bronze.
> Bronze smiths without allocations:
> Witimios, Manouros, Awexeus.
> Number of slaves:
> Of Perigonios: 2; of Aigiewes: 2; of Mikelion: 1;
> Of Phyltas: 1.
>   (Hooker 1980, 116–117; normalizations of names from Landau 1958)

It is interesting to note that the palace bureaucracies kept track of the smiths to whom they did *not* send allocations, showing that the centralized powers kept at least some degree of watch and/or control over what may have been the "free sector." It is of note that no smithies have yet come to light in Mycenaean territories, save one at Nichoria dating back into Middle Helladic times (Gillis 1997, 505). This suggests that the smithies were located away from the more populated areas, no doubt due to the fumes produced by the industry.

Finally, let us consider a third, highly specialized industry—perfumed oil. The tablets referring to this industry, the Un series, mention what appears to be a "master" perfumer who worked at the palace itself and who used several different commodities in the production process, including oil, flowers and spices, wool, and even wine (Killen 2001, 169). However, the term ta-ra-si-ja, "allocations," never appears in these perfume production tablets, in spite of the fact that it seems to be very much a palace-centered industry. This is probably because of the highly supervised nature of the industry itself. One might imagine the master perfumer working (and possibly living) at the palace, organizing his materials and disposing of his perfume all within the very hub of the bureaucratic system and therefore without the need for an official to keep track of goods sent outside the palace to him. Such a system would also be applicable to other industries that made use of specialty items (flowers, spices, precious stones) that were processed at the palaces themselves by master craftsmen and -women. This stands in contrast to the more spread-out and single-material industries, such as the bronzesmiths who required bronze and the weavers who required wool or linen. Only these latter fall into the economic category of the ta-ra-si-ja.

These three examples show a spectrum of industries in the Mycenaean economy. At one extreme were industries such as textiles, for which many steps were required between the most basic raw materials (sheep) and the finished product (fabric); in which many, if not all, of the workers in the industry were maintained directly by the palaces through rations; and in which there did not appear to be a "private" industry operating alongside the palatial one (except, of course, for basic domestic textile production). We might call this a state-owned monopoly based on factories. Contrast this with the bronze industry, for which the palace maintained control over many of the raw materials necessary—but not all of them, to judge from the smiths who worked without ta-ra-si-ja. The smiths were independent, insofar as they were not allocated rations but presumably earned their own living, and some of them even owned slaves. We might see this as a more freelance industry, with independent or semi-independent smithies doing contract work for the palaces. Finally, there were the luxury item industries, such as perfumed oils, in which the workers worked directly in the palaces in positions that must have attained considerable prestige.

TRADE IN THE LATE BRONZE AGE

The wide-scale, international trade prevalent in the Late Bronze Age is imminently evident in a pair of shipwrecks, one found off the southern coast of Turkey, the other off the southern coast of Greece. The first, the Ulu Burun shipwreck, sank with all its cargo (and probably its crew) at the very end of the fourteenth century. The goods aboard the ship included elephant and hippopotamus ivory; Levantine amphorae; gold, silver, faience, and amber jewelry; Mycenaean, Cypriot, Canaanite, and Ugaritic pottery; glass ingots and beads; copper and tin ingots; bronze weapons; Mycenaean seals; an Ugaritic-style gold chalice; and a (possibly) Syrian finger cymbal (Bass 1986, 274). Concerning the Levantine amphorae, the excavator—George Bass—noted that fifty-two were of a style that not only was prevalent in the trading city of Ugarit, but also had attested parallels on the Greek mainland. The glass discovered was of Syro-Palestinian origin, but it was chemically identical to Mycenaean glass amulets (Bass 1986, 282). The Mycenaean seal may attest to the presence of an Aegean merchant on the vessel, as does the presence of a few Mycenaean kylikes (drinking cups). The amber beads attest to trade as far afield as the Baltic, and the ivory points to trade with either Egypt to the south or, more probably, Palestine (Bass 1986, 284 ff.). The presence of the tin ingots may attest to trade from the extreme east, with Iran or even Afghanistan. Ultimately, Bass argues that the abundance of Near Eastern materials, the paucity of Aegean pottery, and the east-to-west orientation of the vessel suggest that the ship was proceeding east to west in a circular route from the Levant to Cyprus to Greece running along the southern coast of Turkey, then proceeding to Egypt, back to Cyprus, ending up again in the Levant (Bass 1986, 296). Thus, Greece was involved in trade from as far afield as Afghanistan to the east and possibly even Nubia to the south.

More information concerning international trade in the Late Bronze Age comes from the shipwreck off the coast of Point Iria in the Argolic Gulf of southern Greece, where we can see strong proof of the close connections among Cyprus, Crete, and Greece (Lolos 1995, 72–76). The pottery salvaged from the sunken vessel is predominantly Cypriot and Mycenaean, including Cretan-Mycenaean stirrup-jars of the Late Minoan IIIB2 style. All of these offer a date c. 1200 B.C.E. for the wreck (Vichos and Lolos 1995, 324; Lolos 1995, 73). Based on the pottery found on board, the excavators—Vichos and Lolos—have derived a hypothetical trade route for the ship's final passage, beginning at a harbor on the southern coast of Cyprus and heading first to the north coast of Crete, then to the west of the island. From here, in decent weather, the ship would probably have passed by the small island of Kythera on its way to the Peloponnese. There it probably stopped at harbors such as at Tiryns and Asine, continued its trading, and then headed out toward the Argosaronic islands, such as Aigina. In all cases, the primary units of trade were probably food-stuffs, such as fruit and oil (Vichos and Lolos 1995, 328–329).

THE DARK AGE

As discussed in chapter 4, the cosmopolitan society of the Late Bronze Age in the eastern Mediterranean came to a violent end between 1200 and 1000 B.C.E. This certainly slowed down trade among the Mediterranean superpowers such as Greece and Egypt, not to mention the production of luxury items. Nevertheless, neither trade nor production for export came to a total halt, and certain parts of Greece flourished during the early Dark Age, especially Athens and the islands of Euboia, the Dodecanese, and Crete.

The primary evidence for contacts between the Greek mainland and Cyprus from the tenth through eighth centuries B.C.E. is imports of Euboian and Attic pottery to Cyprus (Coldstream and Bikai 1988, 42). The earliest find site for post–Bronze Age Greek pottery—exclusively Euboian pottery—on Cyprus is Amathus, a site that probably served as a port of call for east-west trade between Euboia and the Levant (Coldstream and Bikai 1988, 35). This Euboian monopoly on the markets of Cyprus (and the Levant) was maintained throughout the early Dark Age, and it was only in the ninth century that Attic imports began to appear throughout Cyprus (Coldstream and Bikai 1988, 42).

From the opposite direction, both Cypriot and Phoenician artifacts appeared in Greece possibly as early as the late tenth century B.C.E. (Kourou 1997, 220 ff.). This was evident in Euboia, where there is evidence for trade with the Levant via Cyprus at Lefkandi (see chapter 4). The Athenian Kerameikos (the pottery center that gave rise to the word *ceramic*) began to show evidence of eastern contacts in many of its wealthier graves during the tenth and ninth centuries, such as examples of Cypriot pottery and—even more elaborate—Levantine-style gold jewelry (Kourou 1997, 221; Tzedakis 1979; Coldstream

1977, 55–68). Likewise, Cypriot-style weapons began to appear in Attica in the ninth century, notably an early ninth-century spearhead and shield bosses dating to c. 850 B.C.E. (Demetriou 1989, 75).

To the east, in the Dodecanese, renewed contact with the Near East was evident as early as 925 B.C.E. with the appearance of Cypriot materials in Cos (Coldstream 1998, 255). These materials include pottery—such as Bird-vases, pilgrim flasks, and barrel-jugs—as well as at least one sword (Demetriou 1989, 85). There is, however, no evidence of Dodecanese artifacts in Cyprus in the years 1050–700 B.C.E., although it seems that the Dodecanese probably served as one of the main ports of call on the trade routes between Cyprus and the western Mediterranean (Coldstream 1998, 260). Perhaps the new connections between Cyprus and Greece occurred originally between Cyprus and Euboia-Attica, with ships passing through the Dodecanese.

There is even more evidence for Cypriot and Levantine contacts with the island of Crete during the Dark Age. Starting in the mid-tenth century B.C.E., countless Cypriot ceramics made their way to Crete, where they ended up buried with the more affluent members of Cretan society. Of particular interest is a hemispherical bronze bowl of Cypriot style found in the Fortetsa cemetery near Knossos. This item, dated to c. 900 B.C.E., was inscribed with a Phoenician graffito, not only showing evidence of contacts with Phoenicia, but also serving as one of the earliest examples of an alphabetic script in Greece (Coldstream 1977, 257). Further evidence of Cretan-Phoenician trade comes from southern Crete, especially at the site of Kommos, where not only have shards of Phoenician ceramics come to light, but where the Phoenicians themselves set up a small sanctuary, possibly for use during long trading missions (Shaw 1989, 165 ff.).

It is evident, then, that long-range trade continued through the Dark Age, frequently trade in the luxury items we tend to associate with an elite class. In the absence of direct evidence, we might use this information to suggest that grinding poverty was not the norm during this phase of Greek history and that there was an adequate surplus to support the import of gold jewelry and elegant tablewares.

THE EARLY EMPORIA

The overseas trade of the Dark Age led to the rise of large-scale trading centers (emporion, pl. emporia) and eventually colonies (apoikia) throughout the Greek world. An emporion was a settlement of mixed or uncertain founding communities that continued to be inhabited by ethnically mixed communities who survived through industrial production and trade. Apoikia, by contrast, were usually founded by people from one (maybe two) poleis, with a mind toward eventual self-sufficiency, especially in terms of agriculture (Ridgway 1992, 108).

Al Mina

The earliest attested Greek emporion was Al Mina, located at the mouth of the Orontes River in southernmost Turkey and excavated by Sir Leonard Woolley in the 1930s. Once again it seems that the Euboians took the initiative for the Greeks, for Euboian pottery dating to the mid-ninth century B.C.E. has come to light at the earliest levels of the site. This Euboian pottery predominated among the Greek wares, accompanied only by traces of Rhodian Ware and even some early Protocorinthian Ware. Then, around 700, Corinthian pottery suddenly came to dominate the Al Mina market. A number of factors may have caused this shift, most likely the downfall of Euboian power in the early to mid-eighth century (the Lelantine War) and the increased demand for Corinthian pottery in Mediterranean markets in general over the course of the Archaic Age. One must remember, though, that these Greek wares, and Greek inhabitants, existed side by side with an extensive local and Phoenician population, all using Al Mina as a port of call for an east-west trade that brought Greek pottery as far afield as inner Syria and Israel in the Levant, and Phoenician wares all the way to western Spain.

What the Greeks took away from Al Mina in exchange for the pottery is still uncertain, although some have suggested raw metals such as tin (Boardman 1980, 42–48). The switchover from bronze to iron technologies was not total in the Iron Age, and bronze was still heavily in demand for armor. Thus, the Greeks were still in need of tin, especially at the Euboian city of Chalkis, literally "the Brazen City."

Pithekoussai

This interest in metals was even more pronounced at what is considered the first true Greek colony, located at Pithekoussai on the island of Ischia off the western coast of Italy. Yet again we look to Euboia for origins, as the later literature claims that the cities of Chalkis and Eretria together colonized the island (an unusual event, as most colonies have only one metropolis, or mother city). According to Strabo (*Geography,* 5.4.9), "Pithekoussai was settled by Eretrians and Chalkidians. Although prospering through the fruitful soil and goldmines, some abandoned the island on account of internal strife, and later they left because of earthquakes and eruption of fire, sea and hot waters."

Likewise Livy, when discussing the second Greek colony across the shore from Pithekoussai at Cumae, relates (*Early History of Rome,* 8.22.5–6): "Palaepolis was not far from where Neapolis is now; one populus inhabited the two cities. They were Cumaen by origin; the Cumaens trace their origin to Euboian Chalkis. By means of a fleet, with which they had come leaving their homes, they had considerable power along the coast where they dwelled, first on the islands of Aenaria and Pithekoussai, then daring to transfer their seat onto the continent."

Archaeological data also indicate an important Euboian role in the foundation of Pithekoussai: A distinctive style of Euboian drinking vessel called a pendant semicircle skyphos appeared prominently and early at the site. It is possible that the Euboians first became interested in Pithekoussai by hearing references to the western islands from Phoenician traders at Al Mina, and thus we might consider a trail of Euboian traders going from Euboia itself to the Levantine coast to Ischia and finally settling in Italy (Ridgway 1992, 25 ff.).

What most archaeologists and historians studying Pithekoussai notice right away is that, unlike a traditional colony, the island does not offer many possibilities for agricultural self-sufficiency. The island is somewhat hilly and the soil is predominantly volcanic, thus good mainly for growing vines but not for grains. Clearly, then, farming was not a major concern for the settlers. By contrast, Pithekoussai was easily defensible and had two excellent harbors, one to either side of the town, as well as easy access to the metal reserves of Etruria to the west and the island of Elba to the north (where the French later imprisoned Napoleon).

The fact that the Pithekoussans were engaging in metallurgy is evident from the main "factory" area discovered at the ancient site of Mazzola, described as a "suburb" of the residential area. Here, excavator Georgio Buchner discovered an entire industrial complex dating (by the pottery) from the mid-eighth century through the first quarter of the seventh century B.C.E. (Ridgway 1992, 92). One of the rooms (Structure III) contained many pieces of iron bloom (pre- and partially worked metal), slag (metal leftovers), and fragments embedded in the floor. There was a burnt area immediately outside of the room, suggesting a blacksmith's shop with a forge. Right next door, Structure IV had an arrangement of heavily burnt bricks that appear to have been yet another forge, with heavily polished hard stones nearby that may have served as anvils. Just outside this structure were remains of bronze sheet and wire, discarded pieces of half-made bronze jewelry, as well as bits of copper and lead (Ridgway 1992, 93). Clearly, this was the metalworking zone of the ancient community.

Additional evidence for metalworking comes from the literary evidence, wherein Strabo tells us that the settlement prospered—at least in part— through the works of its goldsmiths. Ischia itself had neither gold nor silver, although the latter metal was found in abundance in the local graves, but both metals are attested to on the nearby island of Elba. One can imagine trade and importation of the raw materials to the Greek settlement, which then exported the finished luxury items.

In contrast to the metalworking aspects of the Pithekoussan economy, we have less archaeological evidence for other industries in the colony, such as pottery. Although ceramics were imported from Greece and the Near East, these ceramics served a primary purpose of carrying goods to Ischia, notably wine and oil. Local-made amphorae indicate that the Pithekoussans also had local "brands" of these items, although it is not yet possible to tell if they exported these (Ridgway 1992, 64). Where the amphorae and other ceramics were fabricated remains a mystery, as a potters' quarter to match the metalsmithing complex at Mazzola has yet to reveal itself (Ridgway 1992, 101).

Naukratis

The quintessential Greek emporion was the city of Naukratis in Egypt, founded late in the seventh century B.C.E. According to Herodotus (2, 178), "Pharaoh Amasis, coming to like the Greeks, granted them various privileges, and especially to those who had come to Egypt he gave the city of Naukratis for habitation. But for those of the sea-traders who did not wish to inhabit the place he gave land for the establishment of altars and sanctuaries to the gods."

Rather than as a gift, it is better to understand Naukratis as a restricted area in which the Greeks were allowed to trade with the Egyptians. Up to the seventh century B.C.E., Egypt had been somewhat xenophobic in its foreign relations and trading preferences. However, the conquests of the Neo-Assyrian Empire in the eighth and seventh centuries B.C.E. cut Egypt off from its traditional middlemen—the Phoenicians. As a result, new avenues of commerce were created, including the Greek emporion at Naukratis. Greeks could live here (as residents if not actual citizens), trade here, and worship according to their own traditions within the confines of the city. The participating Greek poleis—listed by Herodotus as Chios, Teos, Phokaia, Klazdomenai, Rhodes, Knidos, Halicarnassus, Phaselis, and Mytilenê—ran a small, local government at Naukratis and traded Greek wine, oil, and silver for Egyptian grain, possibly gold, and luxury items such as faience (Graham 1970, 134). One must also remember that Egypt was a nexus of African trade, and that exotic items from the south, such as ebony and ivory, passed through Egypt to Aegean markets. The service sector also played a considerable role in Naukratian economics; the emporion was famous, among other things, for the number and beauty of its prostitutes (Herodotus 2, 134): "They love how the courtesans in Naukratis are quite lovely, for at that time, as the story goes, one there became so famous that all the Greeks learned the name of Rhodopis. Later it was the name Archidikê, which became well-sung throughout Greece, although she was less spoken of in common talk than the other."

Unfortunately, the oldest parts of Naukratis are now under water due to a rise in the delta's water table and the presence of several canals in the immediate area, so excavation of the earliest remains of the emporion are no longer possible (Coulson and Leonard 1982, 363).

ARCHAIC AND CLASSICAL GREECE

Agriculture, Natural Resources, Theft

It is ironic that although trade, emporia, and industrial production such as at Pithekoussai serve as much of our primary evidence about the ancient Greek economy, the Greeks themselves looked down upon these trades. For the ancient Greeks, the ideal economic standard was agricultural autarkeia, or self-sufficiency. For the Greeks, subsistence should, and usually did, come directly from the land, with factory production and long-distance trade being only a tiny fraction of the daily economy of most Greeks. As far as the pseudo-Aristotelian author of the *Oikonomikos* was concerned, this was only "natural" (1343a25–b2): "First according to nature is agriculture, and second are such trades as come from the earth, such as mining and the like. Agriculture is best because it is just; for it does not take from men, either from those willing as with trade or wage-labor, or those unwilling as with war. And it is according to nature in all respects, for sustenance for everyone comes from the mother, just as for men this comes from the earth."

Based on such an understanding of "natural" economics, the majority of production in ancient Greece did revolve around agriculture, much as it has in the rest of the world up to the present day. The average family's first concern was to provide for itself, growing—where possible—grain, grapes for wine, olives for food and oil (see Image 5.2), various fruits and vegetables, flax for linen, and supplementing this fare from the earth with pasturage of animals such as sheep (wool and meat), goats (wool, meat, milk), and cattle (meat and labor). When these basic concerns were provided for, the family might make something of their surplus, with wine and olive oil being the two most basic commodities.

On the polis level, the city economy began as a direct extension of the family economy, with the accumulated wealth of the citizenry forming the primary basis of the city's economy. This was so instilled in Late Archaic Athens that the four sociopolitical classes were divided upon the basis of their annual agricultural yields (see chapters 6 and 7). At the city level, however, other factors also came into play. The most important was the natural resource factor. At the agricultural level, this might include especially fine wines, such as those from Chios, or high-quality oils, as from Athens. Beyond food were products such as timber for shipbuilding, from which Sikyon made its fortune; fine potters' clay, which boosted the economy of Athens and Corinth; mineral resources such as the silver mines of Laurion in Attica or the gold deposits in Macedon; accommodating harbors and control over critical points of transportation, such as at the Corinthian isthmus; and even unique plants and/or animals, such as the silphium plant of Cyrenê in northern Africa, which was one of the preferred forms of birth control in ancient Greece.

So, natural resources provided a second source of revenue for the poleis. A third source was conquest, in which poleis took loot and booty from one another after military conquest and then placed conquered territories under tribute, leading to a continuous income long after the war, battle, or skirmish. An excellent example is the Spartan conquest of Messenia. Needing land and not wishing to colonize, the Spartans literally mugged their neighbors to the west, seized control of the land, and reduced the native Messenian population to slaves and serfs, a group called helots in Greek. The Spartan economy, and the individual Spartans, thrived on the produce of Messenia. An example of economic gain through tribute is manifest in the Athenian Empire of the fifth century B.C.E., when Athens was able to rebuild the city and develop a full social-democratic system of government based on monies received as tribute (in other words, extortion) from the subject poleis of the Delian League (see chapter 4).

A fourth source of revenues available to the Greek poleis was religion (and anyone who knows anything about the medieval sale of indulgences by the church can appreciate just how profitable religion can be). Religion brought wealth into the poleis in a number of ways. The most direct was the establishment and filling (through donations) of sanctuaries and treasuries (see chapter 8). Such acts of piety and conspicuous consumption on the part of the various poleis brought extreme quantities of wealth to the sanctuaries—such as Delphi, Olympia, and Ephesus—in the form of precious metals, marble sculpture, bronze and iron arms and armor, and coinage. A secondary type of revenue derived from certain religious rituals, such as the Eleusinian Mysteries (see chapter 8), which could cost more than a week's earnings for a lower-class arti-

5.2 Black Figure Vase: Men Harvesting Olives (Bildarchiv Preussischer Kulturbesitz)

san. Finally, religion was a popular impetus for tourism and travel. The Panhellenic games at Olympia, Delphi, Nemea, and the Isthmus brought athletes and spectators from all over the Greek world to the sanctuaries of Zeus, Apollo, and Poseidon. These athletes and spectators spent money on lodging, food, drinks, dedicatory votives, and, of course, souvenirs. Think of the Super Bowl, or World Cup soccer, or today's Olympics, for modern parallels.

Production

Only after all these sources of revenue should we consider nonagricultural production and its role in ancient Greek economics. Perhaps the most traditional, long-standing industry in ancient Greece was textiles, the transformation of wool and linen into cloth and clothing (silk was almost exclusively imported). From as far back as we can reconstruct, this industry was in the hands of women, although men probably did the original shearing of sheep and threshing of flax and, possibly, the dyeing of the cloth. From here, women were

5.3 Black Figure Weaving Vase (The Metropolitan Museum of Art)

responsible for the carding, spinning, weaving, and sewing, and such activities were considered to be the ideal feminine occupations (see Image 5.3). Homer, when describing the perfect society of the Phaiakians in the *Odyssey* (7, 108–111), praises the women in this manner:

> As much as Phaiakian men are most skillful among all men
> at rowing a swift ship on the sea, just so the women
> are skillful at the looms, for Athena gave them
> great understanding of very beautiful works and good minds.

Even royalty were engaged in textile production; the semidivine queen Helen routinely occupied herself with the fiber arts (*Iliad* 3, 125–128; *Odyssey* 4, 131–135):

> [Iris] found [Helen] in the megaron; she was weaving at a large loom
> a double-folded tapestry in purple, in which she wove the many battles
> of the horse-taming Trojans and the bronze-clad Achaeans,
> which they suffered on her account at the hands of the war god.

> She bestowed on [Helen] a golden distaff and a basket with silver
> wheels beneath, gilded with gold along the edges.
> Carrying this the servant Phylo set it by her
> full of fine-spun yarn. And upon it
> the distaff lay holding the violet-colored wool.

For much of early Greek history, textiles were a cottage industry: Clothing was made by the female members of the family for the household. The only exception was the creation of clothing for the deities, specifically the goddesses. The most famous example of this was the Peplophoria, which took place in Athens as part of the Panathenaic Festival (see chapter 8). For a year, two young girls (usually around eleven years old) lived on the Athenian acropolis and wove a peplos, or dress (see chapter 9) for the cult statue of Athena. The Athenians then offered the peplos to the goddess during the city-wide festival.

A change in the strictly domestic nature of textile production may have been visible in Athens after the Peloponnesian War, when mass production and public banking became more prominent in that city. In his *Memorabilia* (2.8.2–14), Xenophon records a conversation between the philosopher Socrates and a man named Aristarchus. Aristarchus was upset because, in the wake of the war, several of his female relations had come to live with him, and he was at a loss as to how to provide for them all. At least part of the problem, he claimed, was that they were "gentle folk," thus, apparently, incapable of working. Socrates inquired as to whether the gentlewomen in question knew how to make garments, to which Aristarchus replied in the affirmative. The obvious solution, then, Socrates, pointed out, was to put them to work making clothing for sale, so as to earn their keep. "But now they understand this to be the work best and most suitable for women, as I believe. And all things so understood are accomplished easily, quickly, beautifully, and with pleasure. Don't delay . . . to mention these things to them, things that will bring both you and them profit, and, I think, they will hear it gladly . . . From these things capital was provided, wool was purchased, and the women worked while lunching, stopping work only at dinner."

Another extremely important and long-standing industry in Greece was the ceramics industry, giving rise to the huge number of pieces of pottery archaeologists and historians pore over. In reality, pottery production can almost be seen as a combination of a natural resources–based economy and a production-based economy, as the primary material—good clay—was a result of the natural geology. However, not all poleis made equal use of their clay resources, and only two—Corinth and Athens—were really active in pottery export in the Archaic Age and following.

As with weaving, pottery no doubt began as, and in many places remained, a household industry, probably practiced exclusively in the summer when the clay and kindling wood were dryer and easier to transport and burn. But evidence of a more concentrated effort at production for export appeared already in the Bronze Age (see above) and continued in the Dark Age, as with the copious export of Euboian skyphoi (drinking cups) to Cyprus, the Levant, and even Italy. These were followed by the Corinthian Thapsos cups and skyphoi, and finally the Athenian kylix (a shallow type of wine goblet). The demand for Greek vessels to drink out of appears to have stemmed from a desire for Greek things to drink, and amphorae and pithoi (storage vessels), especially from Attica, also proliferated in the Mediterranean (Johnston 1991, 208–211).

This need for commercial production led to the rise of workshops and factories. Such workshops were usually family-owned businesses run by the head of the household, his sons (and possibly daughters), and, depending on the size of the industry, additional servants and/or slaves. The general assumption concerning many professional potters is that they were not citizens of the cities in which they worked. In Athens, these were the metics, or resident aliens, as well as slaves. The identity of the workers in the primary ceramic working area in Corinth—the Potters' Quarter—is uncertain. But an inscribed pottery shard naming the Phoenician goddess Astarte suggests that there were Phoenician immigrants working there, or at least a heavy Phoenician influence.

Happily for modern researchers, many artisans signed their works. This gives an idea not only of who these ancient ceramicists were, but also of how labor was divided. Modern scholars have the names of a few potter-families from sixth-century Athens: Nearkhos, who worked with his sons Tleson and Ergoteles; Ergotimos, who was succeeded by his son Eukheiros (literally "Good Hand"); and Amasis and his son Kleophrades, who produced pottery from the mid-sixth century B.C.E. to the dawn of the fifth (Hemelrijk 1991, 255). The signatures indicate, however, that although these men fashioned and fired the ceramics, others were employed to paint the more elaborate figural vases. Such artists traveled around to different workshops, like the sixth-century Epictetus, whose name as painter accompanied about six different names of potters (Hemelrijk 1991, 255–256).

Starting around 550 B.C.E., numbers were scratched onto the bottoms of some vases, often appearing after the name of the vase in full or abbreviated form. These may have been batch numbers, indicating groups of pots fired together and intended for specific merchants or markets. The merchants were also indicated by markings on some vases, whereby a signature sign or abbreviation indicated to which exporter or importer in the receiving city the pottery was destined. In the sixth century B.C.E., such merchants were frequently Ionians, who were responsible for much of the import-export business at Naukratis in the south and Gravisca in the west (Johnston 1991, 221–224).

But the most important markings vis-à-vis economics are the actual "price tags" etched into some pots. One example is a fifth-century Red Figure kylix-krater (wine bowl) from Italy. On the bottom are the letters *ON* (of uncertain reference), "90 le-" (lekythoi—a type of vessel), "17 sky-" (skyphoi—another type of vessel), and "TI 12 3/4." The *TI* refers to timê, or price. Apparently the skyphoi sold for approximately three-fourths of an obol (a Greek unit of currency) each. Such data from the various ceramics indicate a less-than-one-obol price for smaller vessels such as drinking cups, but larger vessels such as kraters could go for 4 to 6 obols at the beginning of the fifth century B.C.E., going up in price to 12 to 18 obols by mid-century. An important difference in price occurred between painted and undecorated vases, with a markup of anywhere from 25 to 50 percent for the figural vases. Clearly, this was because the pottery manufacturer had to pay for the additional labor (see above) (Johnston 1991, 224–228).

Workshops and factories existed in ancient Greece for commodities other than just the ubiquitous pottery. Many were extremely small affairs, such as the household workshop of Simon the shoemaker in the Athenian Agora. Others, such as the shield factory of Lysias, employed up to 120 slaves (Lysias 12.8, 10).

Beyond just factory-style production, however, individual Greeks could also be self-employed, producing goods and offering services at the individual level. Citizen males were actually somewhat excluded from this aspect of the economy. To work for another person for a salary was seen as slavish, the antithesis of the ideal of autarkeia (self-sufficiency). Thus, while a male artisan might take different commissions from a host of patrons, he would generally avoid working too much for any one patron (Cohen 2002, passim).

Metics, semi-independent slaves, and women, however, had no such ego issues, and they were free to employ themselves as they saw most expedient and profitable. In contrast to the standard view of women being sheltered indoors in so-called Oriental seclusion—a leisure available only to the uppermost classes at best—many women did work outside of the home, supporting themselves and their children. At the upper echelons of the working world, women could be priestesses (see chapter 8), midwives, or doctors. More commonly, they worked as wet nurses, nannies (Spartans and Thracians were considered especially good at this), or nurses. As manufacturers, they could produce and sell ribbons and garlands (important for religious rituals), textiles (as mentioned above), and even perfume (a hobby even of Empress Theodora of Byzantium). Some women, probably not citizens, even worked as innkeepers and bath attendants (Brock 1994, 337–341). Many women took pride in their self-sufficiency, recording their prowess and good fortune on stone. Around 350 B.C.E, an Athenian named Melinna had inscribed (S.E.G. [trans. Supplement of Greek Epigraphy] 774), "By her handiwork and skill, and with righteous courage, Melinna raised her children and set up this memorial to you, Athena, goddess of handiwork, a share of the possessions she has won, in honor of your kindness" (translation in Lefkowitz and Fant 1992, 218–219).

Coinage and Currency

In spite of the desire for autarkeia, the Greeks did need to trade, either to acquire additional grain for a burgeoning population; to acquire materials such as silver and gold, which existed only in restricted regions; or to buy and sell fabricated goods such as perfume and armor. From the earliest periods, barter was the main form of trade, whereby the Greeks at, say, Naukratis traded Athenian silver for Egyptian grain, or Rhodian perfume for faience. Homer tells us that a common system of valuation existed among the ancient Greeks, whereby the price or value of an object could be agreed upon by both buyer and seller. Such was the case with prizes at the funeral games of Patrocles (*Iliad* 23.702–705):

> For the victor a great tripod to stand over the fire,
> the Achaeans valued it among themselves at 12 oxen.
> For the man defeated he set a woman in their midst,
> well-skilled in handwork, they valued her at four oxen.

However, it was amazingly difficult to bring oxen on long-distance business trips, not to mention making change with them, so other forms of currency came to be required. The general consensus is that the earliest form of Greek non-barter-based currency was a system of iron spits (long spikes). The evidence for this is etymological, epigraphic, and historical.

Concerning etymology, or word origins, the ancient Greek word for *spit* is *obol,* the name of the most basic division of coinage in the Classical period—comparable to the American or British penny. Furthermore, iron spits were of such a size that the human hand could hold a maximum of six, thus a drachma, or handful. By the Classical period, the term *drachma* referred to six obols, just as ten U.S. pennies today equal one dime. Once coins came into use, the human hand could obviously hold more than six obol-coins, but the terminology remained from the earlier definition, when six iron spits were an actual handful. (Inflation being what it is, they no longer have obols in Greece, and the drachma is today the standard unit of currency.)

Epigraphic and historical evidence derives from sanctuaries, where spits, or groups of spits, were dedicated to the deities. One example is an inscription from the sanctuary of Hera at Perachora, near Corinth, datable to c. 700 B.C.E., which reads, "I am a drachma, O White-(Armed) Hera!" (Jeffery 1961, #17). The excavator—H. Payne—believed that this inscription, found on a piece of stone that had been reused as flooring after a temple redecoration, accompanied six iron spits, possibly attached thermometer-style to the marble inscription base. Similar dedications have come to light at Fortetsa in Crete, the Temple of Apollo at Dreros, a tomb at Argos, and in southern Italy (Kraay 1976, 314). One particularly famous dedication was found at the Temple of Apollo at Delphi, which read, "Rhodopis dedicated." This may be the same dedication Herodotus mentions as being a tithe of the earnings of Rhodopis, the above-mentioned prostitute from Naukratis (Herodotus 2, 135).

But by far the most famous dedication is the offering of 100 to 180 iron spits found in a bundle at the Temple of Hera at Argos. Many scholars like to view these as the dedication of 30 drachmai to Hera by King Pheidon of Argos, as recorded in the *Etymologicum Magnum: Obeliskoi.* This is significant because the historian Ephoros claimed that Pheidon was the first to mint silver coinage in Greece, making use of the silver and silversmiths of the nearby island of Aigina. Perhaps, then, as some have argued, Pheidon replaced the iron spit currency with silver coinage, gathering together the now outdated obols and dedicating them at the local sanctuary of Hera. There are numerous unanswered questions relating to this issue, beginning with when, exactly, Pheidon himself supposedly lived. But the anecdote does hint at the ancient Greeks' understandings of the history of their monetary systems.

A final bit of possible historical evidence for the use of obols comes from Plutarch in his *Life of Lycurgus.* Here the historian Lycurgus tells how, in his attempts to ennoble the Spartans, "He commanded that all gold and silver coin should be called in, and that only a sort of money made of iron should be current, a great weight and quantity of which was very little worth; so that to lay up 20 or 30 pounds required a pretty large closet, and, to remove it, nothing less than a yoke of oxen" (Dryden translation 1952, 36).

This fragment suggests that gold and silver coinage was already the norm in Sparta. But some have argued that this use of iron currency actually refers back to a period of precoinage exchange, to wit, iron spits.

Nevertheless, this does bring up the next question, which is, How and when did coinage first appear in Greece? According to the literature, King Alyattes of Lydia was the first person anywhere to strike coinage from the electrum (gold and silver alloy) that his kingdom derived from the Halys River. This seems to be verified by the discoveries at the Temple of Artemis at Ephesus (see below). A generation later, if we are to trust Herodotus, Alyattes's heir, King Croesus, developed a means of separating out the silver from the gold, and thus was the first to mint coinage in pure metals (Herodotus 1, 94). In Greece, Pheidon of Argos is credited with minting the first coinage (see above}. Such coinage is dated to the first quarter of the sixth century B.C.E., which is a rather late date for the reign of Pheidon, so his name must be used with caution.

Archaeologically, the best evidence about Greek coinage comes from the sanctuary of Artemis of Ephesus in southwestern Turkey (one of the seven wonders of the ancient world). Here, excavations of the temple's foundations have revealed a full chronology and evolution of coins, from the unromantically named dumps to fully legitimate coinage. A dump was simply a small glob of metal, usually silver or, less often, gold or electrum. The problem with

5.4 Coin with Athena and Philip of Macedon (Library of Congress)

dumps, of course, was that it was very difficult to determine whether they were pure metal or not (this was centuries before Archimedes discovered specific gravity). How could one be sure that a dump was solid silver instead of lead covered with a thin coating of silver?

So in the next phase of development, the dumps were struck with a sharp implement such as an awl, which dug into the metal. Thus, one could see the interior of the dump and verify that the metal was solid. Once this idea of striking predetermined weights of metal came into being, the evolution of coinage proceeded rapidly. Rather than striking the dump with a random sharp object, a royal house or polis might choose to strike it with an image relevant to the area of production, such as an initial or city mascot (like the Athenian owl). So long as one side—the obverse—was being struck, it was little effort to decorate the other side—the reverse—as well. And so by 500 B.C.E., standardized coins with identifying images on the front and back were prevalent throughout the Greek world (see Image 5.4). In reality, most coinage remained close to its polis of origin, much as modern monies are supposed to remain within their country of issue. Some poleis, however, had wide-ranging political or economic sway, notably Athens. As the various poleis under Athenian authority in the fifth century both traded with Athens and paid tribute to that city, Athenian "owls" were legal tender far beyond the boundaries of Attica.

However, as noted by several numismatists (people who study coins) such as C. Kraay, the amount of money represented by one coin was very large, much like a modern $100 bill. Most people had little use for such large denominations, especially as, without smaller denominations, it was impossible to make change (see the above example of oxen). So it would appear that coinage was used, at least originally, mainly for large-scale trade. A secondary use for coins was hoarding, whereby a family's wealth was stored up in the form of gold and silver coins kept in a box or jar under the house (many coins have been discovered in such contexts). For day-to-day purchases, barter was still the norm, and not until smaller denominations of coinage—usually in the form of bronze—came into being did the average person make use of coins in daily transactions. Literary evidence from Athens shows that such an economy was in place by the end of the fifth century B.C.E., when the comic poet Aristophanes wrote in his *Assemblywomen* about men receiving their pay in obols for attending the assembly and courts (*Assemblywomen*, ll. 300–316):

> Let's make sure to jostle
> The assemblymen from town,
> Who never used to attend:
> When the pay was only one obol,
> They sat around gossiping
> In the garland-shops,
> But now they fight for seats.
> Never in the good old days,
> With noble Myronides in command,
> Would anyone have dared
> To husband the polis' affairs
> For a handful of money.
> No, everyone would come to assembly
> With a little bag of lunch:
> Something to drink, dry bread,
> A couple of onions and three olives.
> Now all they want is their three obols . . .
>   (Translation by J. Henderson 1996, 160–161)

The obol was the smallest unit of coinage, with 6 obols equaling 1 drachma, as discussed above. A sum of 100 drachmai equaled a mina (mna in Greek), and 6,000 drachmai equaled a talent. In general, by the late Classical period, a skilled artisan was paid 1–1.5 drachmai per day of work (I.G. I^2 373–374—Erechtheion accounts from the years 409–406). A brief period of inflation may be visible in a later set of accounts from Eleusis, where unskilled laborers were paid 1.5 drachmai per day and skilled artisans up to 2.5 per day (I.G. II^2–III^2 1672–1673, for the years 329–326; Cohen 1992, xiv, 22).

Taxation

Taxation might be viewed as a redistributive economic procedure, whereby governmental institutions take resources from their constituencies to pay, ideally, for public benefits. Such systems pretty much date back to the dawn of time—the oldest extant written document in the Western world is a tax record from Egypt dating to before 3100 B.C.E. As such, taxes are premonetary. In the days before coinage, taxes were paid "in kind," meaning predetermined amounts of agricultural goods were handed over to the ruling authority, often with an additional component of required labor.

A simple system of taxation was present in ancient Sparta. At the bottom of the social ladder were the helots, who provided agricultural slave labor for their Spartan overlords. The Spartan citizens turned over a percentage of their own produce to their sysitia, or eating clubs (see chapter 6). Spartan citizenship actually depended on a citizen's ability to pay his full share of the sysitia tax. Beyond this obligatory donation system, additional "taxes" existed in the form of gifts to the kings. Very little bureaucracy or record keeping was required.

More complex systems of taxation appeared in the Archaic Age during the reigns of the tyrants, such as Peisistratos of Athens and Cypselus of Corinth (see chapter 7). At this time, residents were subject to direct taxation on the basis of personal wealth, as well as an annual income tax, a sales tax, and customs duties (although this last was generally levied on foreign traders coming into the cities) (Christesen 2000, 1603).

The situation in Athens became even more complex during the fifth century B.C.E., when Athens received tribute from the Delian League and went from a democracy to a social democracy (see chapter 7) under Pericles. At this time, the city received revenues from five sources: tribute; rents on state properties; direct taxes of resident aliens (metics); indirect taxes on the entire population, including a 10 percent tax on agriculture; and liturgies. A liturgy is the assumption of a work or duty, whereby a wealthy citizen must fund, say, the production of a play or the construction/restoration of a certain number of warships. Such liturgies might be seen as the combination of a direct tax and corvé labor, as it obliged the individual to pay for and oversee goods and services for the state. Such demands could be quite outstanding, as Xenophon expresses in his *Oikonomikos* (2, 6): "I observe that the city has assigned you to provide many things—horse-rearing and funding choruses and gymnastic competitions and presidencies. And should war arise, I know that they would assign to you ship maintenance and taxes of such a sort that you would not easily bear it. And if ever you should appear to do any of these tasks under budget, I know that the Athenians would take vengeance on you no less than if you took something from them by theft."

Eisphora, or emergency taxes, were collected in addition to these other sources of revenue during times of economic crisis, such as during a protracted war. Of all these taxes in Athens, about 35 percent went to maintaining the military, 20 percent to building projects, 20 percent to state services such as attendance of the assembly or jury, 10 percent for religious ceremonies and festivals, and about 6 percent for social welfare (Christesen 2000, 617).

Banking

The ancient and modern Greek word for bank is *trapeza*, literally "table," based on the original conception of a money changer conducting business on a tabletop. By strict definition, as provided by the fourth-century Athenian orator Demosthenes (36.11), a trapeza is "a business operation producing risk-laden revenues from other people's money." In short, the "bank" went from being a money changer to being an entity that guarded and invested other people's money while under constraint to return said money upon demand. Usually, the money entrusted to the bank was invested in interest-bearing loans to a variety of merchants and venturists. (It was a system much like today's, but without the free toasters for opening new accounts.)

The earliest "banks" were, in fact, the temples. As mentioned above, religion was a common form of wealth acquisition in ancient Greece, especially in the form of dedications stored in temples or treasuries. The temples could then invest the money from their treasures as needed. For example, the Temple of Athena in Athens loaned money to the state between the years 433–427 B.C.E. at 6 percent interest. This was a generous arrangement, as interest rates of up to 30 percent were levied on loans made to merchants and shipmasters, obviously to cover the probability of business failure or sinkage (Gkamas 2000, 214).

The earliest known non-temple-oriented banker was Philostephanos of Corinth, who is recorded as having received an investment of 70 talents from one Themistocles. In fourth-century Athens, the most famous banker was Pasio, remarkable not only for his wealth but also because he was a former slave, having inherited the bank from his former masters (see chapter 6). There was nothing especially unusual about this—slave manumission was quite common, especially for highly skilled, highly trained slaves. Furthermore, Athenian citizens seldom held the office of banker. As a profession that ultimately depended on the work and money of others, banking was not seen as a particularly respectable occupation; usually only metics and slaves who were prevented from owning land engaged in it (Gkamas 2000, 214).

By the late Classical and early Hellenistic periods, the poleis were coming to appreciate the benefits of banking, and state banks began to appear, beginning in Miletos and quickly extending to such regions as Cos, Ephesus, and Sardis. Perhaps the largest such establishment was the state bank of Alexandria, established by the Ptolemies and continuing into the Roman era. The primary responsibilities of the Bank of Alexandria were the guardianship of state revenues and the collection of taxes, although private individuals could also invest their money in this bank. Complementing the official state bank was a system of corn banks and private banks. Corn banks functioned in many respects the same way "coin" banks did, especially as corn virtually served as currency in Egypt. Government granaries existed throughout Egypt, all centralized through a main corn bank in Alexandria. The private banks, like the state bank, received monies and made investments. Unlike the state bank, however, the regulations and requirements for obtaining a business loan from the private banks were not so severe, and thus these smaller institutions were more influential in making the loans necessary for the functioning of the non-agricultural aspects of society (Gkamas 2000, 214)

REFERENCES

Bass, G. 1986. "A Bronze Age Shipwreck at Ulu Burun (Kas): 1984 Campaign." *American Journal of Archaeology* 90, 269–296.

Berolini, G. 1913– . *Inscriptiones Graecae*. Vol. 1. De Gruyter: Berlin.

Boardman, J. 1980. *The Greeks Overseas: Their Early Colonies and Trade*. New York: Thames & Hudson.

Branigan, K. 1987. "The Economic Role of the First Palaces." In Hägg, R. and N. Marinatos, eds. *The Function of the Minoan Palaces*. Stockholm: Skrifter Utgivna ac Svenska Institutet, 245–248.

Brock, R. 1994. "The Labour of Women in Classical Athens." *Classical Quarterly* 44 (2), 336–346.

Burke, B. 1997. "The Organization of Textile Production on Bronze Age Crete." In Laffineur, L. and P. P. Betancourt, eds. *TEXNH: Craftsmen, Craftswomen and Craftsmanship in the Aegean Bronze Age*. Liège, Belgium: Université de Liège, 413–424.

Christesen, P. 2000a. "Finance." In Speake, G., ed. 2001. *Encyclopedia of Greece and the Hellenic Tradition*. London: Fitzroy Dearborn, 616–617.

———. 2000b. "Taxation." In Speake, G., ed. 2001. *Encyclopedia of Greece and the Hellenic Tradition*. London: Fitzroy Dearborn, 1603–1604.

Cohen, E. E. 1992. *Athenian Economy and Society: A Banking Perspective*. Princeton, NJ: Princeton University Press.

———. 2002. "An Unprofitable Masculinity." In Cartledge, P., E. E. Cohen, and L. Foxhall, eds. 2002. *Money, Labour and Land: Approaches to the Economies of Ancient Greece*. London: Routledge, 100–112.

Coldstream, J. N. 1977. *Geometric Greece*. London: Methuen.

———. 1998. "Crete and the Dodecanese: Alternative Eastern Approaches to the Greek World during the Geometric Period." In Karageorghis, V. and M. Stampolidis, eds. *Eastern Mediterranean: Cyprus-Dodecanese-Crete Sixteenth–Sixth Centuries B.C.: Proceedings of the International Symposium Held at Rethymon, Crete in May 1997*. Athens: A. G. Leventis Foundation, 255–262.

Coldstream, J. N. and P. M. Bikai. 1988. "Early Greek Pottery in Tyre and Cyprus: Some Preliminary Comparisons." *Report of the Department of Antiquities, Cyprus*, 35–44.

Coulson, W. D. E. and A. Leonard Jr. 1982. "Investigations at Naukratis and Environs, 1980 and 1981." *American Journal of Archaeology* 86, 361–380.

Demetriou, A. 1989. *Cypro-Aegean Relations in the Early Iron Age*. Studies in Mediterranean Archaeology 83. Göteborg: Paul Åströms Förlag.

Gillis, C. 1997. "The Smith in the Late Bronze Age—State Employee, Independent Artisan, or Both?" In Laffineur, L. and P. P. Betancourt, eds. *TEXNH: Craftsmen, Craftswomen and Craftsmanship in the Aegean Bronze Age*. Liège, Belgium: Université de Liège, 505–514.

Gkamas, D. 2000. "Banking." In Speake, G., ed. 2001. *Encyclopedia of Greece and the Hellenic Tradition*. London: Fitzroy Dearborn, 214–216.

Graham, A. J. 1970. "The Colonial Expansion of Greece." In *Cambridge Ancient History*. London: Cambridge University Press, 83–195.

Hemelrijk, J. M. 1991. "A Closer Look at the Potter." In Rasmussen, T. and N. Spivey, eds. *Looking at Greek Vases*. Cambridge, UK: Cambridge University Press, 233–256.

Henderson, J. 1996. *Three Plays by Aristophanes: Staging Women*. New York: Routledge.

Hooker, J. T. 1980. *Linear B: An Introduction*. Bristol, UK: Bristol Classics.

Jeffery, L. 1961. *The Local Scripts of Archaic Greece: A Study of the Origins of the Greek Alphabet and Its Development from the Eighth to the Fifth Centuries B.C.* Oxford, UK: Clarendon.

Johnston, A. 1991. "Greek Vases in the Marketplace." In Rasmussen, T. and N. Spivey, eds. *Looking at Greek Vases*. Cambridge, UK: Cambridge University Press, 203–232.

Killen, J. 1984. "The Textile Industries at Pylos and Knossos." In *Pylos Comes Alive: In-*

dustry and Administration in a Mycenaean Palace. New York: Fordham University, 49–64.

———. 2001. "Some Thoughts on *TA-RA-SI-JA*." In Voutsaki, S. and J. Killen, eds. *Economy and Politics in the Mycenaean Palace States*. Cambridge: Cambridge Philological Society, 161–180.

Kourou, N. 1997. "Αιγαιο και Κυπρος κατα την Πρoιμη Εποχη του Σιδηρου: Νεωτερες εξελιξεις." In *Cyprus and the Aegean in Antiquity: From the Prehistoric Period to the Seventh Century A.D.: Nicosia 8–10 December 1995*. Nicosia, Cyprus: Department of Antiquities, 217–230.

Kraay, C. 1976. *Archaic and Classical Greek Coins*. Berkeley: University of California Press.

Landau, O. 1958. *Mykenisch-Griechische Personennamen*. Göteborg: Uppsala University.

Lefkowitz, M. R. and M. B. Fant. 1992. *Women's Lives in Greece and Rome: A Sourcebook in Translation*. Baltimore: Johns Hopkins University Press.

Lolos, Y. G. 1995. "Late Cypro-Mycenaean Seafaring: New Evidence from Sites in the Saronic and the Argolic Gulfs." In Karageorghis, V. and D. Michaelides, eds. 1995. *Cyprus and the Sea*. Nicosia: University of Cyprus, 68–88.

Oliver, G. 2000. "Economy." In Speake, G., ed. 2001. *Encyclopedia of Greece and the Hellenic Tradition*. London: Fitzroy Dearborn, 526–529.

Pelon, O. 1987. "Minoan Palaces and Workshops: New Data from Malia." In Hägg, R. and N. Marinatos, eds. *The Function of the Minoan Palaces*. Stockholm: Skrifter Utgivna ac Svenska Institutet, 269–271.

Plutarch. 1952. *The Lives of the Noble Grecians and Romans*. The Dryden Translation. Chicago: Encyclopedia Britannica.

Preziosi, D. and L. A. Hitchcock. 1999. *Aegean Art and Architecture*. Oxford, UK: Oxford University Press.

Ridgway, D. 1992. *The First Western Greeks*. Cambridge, UK: Cambridge University Press.

Shaw, J. 1989. "Phoenicians in Southern Crete." *American Journal of Archaeology* 93 (1989), 165–183.

Snodgrass, A. 1980. *Archaic Greece: The Age of Experiment*. Berkeley: University of California Press.

Tzedakis, Y. 1979. "Cypriot 'Influences' on the Geometric Pottery of Western Crete." In *Acts of the International Archaeological Symposium: "The Relations Between Cyprus and Crete, ca 2000–500 B.C."* Nicosia, April 16–22, 1978. Nicosia: Department of Antiquities, Cyprus.

Vermeule, E. 1972. *Greece in the Bronze Age*. Chicago: University of Chicago Press.

Vichos, Y. and Y. Lolos. 1995. " The Cypro-Mycenaean Wreck at Point Iria in the Argolic Gulf: First Thoughts on the Origin and the Nature of the Vessel." In Andreae, B. et al., eds. *In Poseidons Reich: Archäologie unter Wasser*. Zaberns Bildbände zur Archäologie, 23. Mainz am Rhein, Germany: 321–335.

Walberg, G. 1987. "Palatial and Provincial Workshops in the Middle Minoan Period." In Hägg, R. and N. Marinatos, eds. *The Function of the Minoan Palaces*. Stockholm: Skrifter Utgivna ac Svenska Institutet, 281–284.

Wiener, M. 1987. "Trade and Rule in Palatial Crete." In Hägg, R. and N. Marinatos, eds. *The Function of the Minoan Palaces*. Stockholm: Skrifter Utgivna ac Svenska Institutet, 261–266.

CHAPTER 6

Social Organization
and Social Structure

The long-enduring, highly regionalist Greeks did not have a single society, but several, each unique for its own time and place. The Minoans were different from their Mycenaean neighbors, just as the Spartans were viewed as the antithesis of the Athenians (who were seen as the "radical left" of the Classical Greek poleis). Therefore, this chapter is not about "Greek society" per se, but rather about the cultural constructs and institutions that the Greeks shared, each with its own distinctive variations and regional flavors. The chapter is divided thematically into issues of division and unification. The divisions are the categories the Greeks used to organize their society, such as age, gender, and class. Unifications concern how the Greeks joined together as friends, families, and institutions.

DIVISIONS

Language, Dialects, and Ethnê

One of the most important differences between the Minoans and Mycenaeans is that they spoke completely different languages. As discussed in chapter 3, the Mycenaeans who wrote in Linear B used an early form of Greek. If ethnicity is determined by language, the Mycenaeans were Greeks. The Minoans, by contrast, spoke an as-of-yet-unknown language, written in Linear A. The close connections among these peoples, especially after 1450 B.C.E., make it inevitable that at least some people were bilingual.

Although there were probably regional variations in the Greek spoken during the Bronze Age, the dialectical and ethnic variations became significant only during and after the Dark Age. When Greek once again came to be written in the eighth century B.C.E., there were clear regional dialects appearing throughout the Greek world, each with its own history and, to a certain extent, culture. The main dialects of Greek were Cypro-Arcadian, Attic-Ionic, Aeolic, and West Greek, of which the primary dialect was Doric. The first three dialects have more in common with each other than with the last, which is generally seen as some manner of late intruder in the history of Greek linguistics.

For many years, Cypro-Arcadian was seen as the final remnant of Mycenaean Greek. It appeared that at the fall of the Bronze Age, several Mycenaeans either headed for the hills of Arcadia in the central Peloponnese or fled to Cyprus. The common dialect shared between these two distant regions was credited to their common source in Mycenaean Greek. Since then, however, differences in Linear B dialects have been distinguished, suggesting that the Cypro-Arcadian dialect is just the grandchild of one of several versions of Mycenaean, with a close relative being the Aeolic dialect spoken on Lesbos, parts of the coast of Turkey, and areas in central Greece such as Boiotia. The dialectical similarities between Cypro-Arcadian and Aeolic are close enough that they may be grouped together as the Achaean dialect.

Another descendant of Mycenaean is Attic-Ionic. *Attic* refers to the region surrounding Athens. According to the Greeks' history, at the fall of the Bronze Age, invaders came and took over the fertile regions of central and southern Greece, but they ignored the harsh, rocky soil of Attica. Thus, the Attic residents remained mostly in place throughout the Dark Age, sending off some colonies to the islands off the coast of Anatolia. The western coast of Anatolia, along with its islands, is called Ionia, where an Ionic dialect similar to its parent Attic was spoken.

Finally, there is the Doric dialect, spoken in the Peloponnese, Crete, and some of the smaller islands. Tradition had it that the Dorians were latecomers to Greece. Although the Achaeans and Attic residents had been in place since before the Trojan War, the Dorians invaded the Greek peninsula at the end of the Bronze Age, displacing many former residents. For their own part, the Dorians claimed they were the descendants of Heracles—the Heracledai—and that, although "newcomers," they were entitled to the land once owned by their divine ancestor. Until recently, the theory of this Doric invasion was accepted by most classicists and ancient historians, being used to explain both the fall of Mycenaean civilization and the geographic spread of the Greek dialects. Recently, however, it has been suggested that Doric was more likely another Bronze Age dialect, not as clearly expressed in the Linear B tablets. As nothing distinctive of a new ethnic group could be found in the archaeological remains of the Dark Age (see chapter 4), the theory of Dorians as latecomers has been replaced by one of Dorians as an alternate, long-standing linguistic/ethnic group in Greek (pre)history (Osborne 1996, 33–37).

Each of these dialectical groups understood itself to be distantly related to one another, either with a common ancestor, like the Dorians, or through early colonization, like the Ionians. They called these broad divisions ethnê, literally "ethnic groups," and each ethnos (sing.) was understood to share a number of cultural elements. For example, Attic-Ionic speakers shared several religious celebrations; Doric speakers had strong similarities in marriage and educational practices.

Tribes and Brotherhoods

The ethnê were the primary divisions between the ancient Greeks. Further subdivisions occurred within these ethnê, all understood at some level to result from old familial relations. The next division under the ethnos was the phylê, or tribe. The best-known tribes were those of the Dorians (the Hylleis, Pamphyloi, and Dymanes) and the Ionians (the Geleontes, Hopletes, Argadeis, and Aigikoreis). These groupings occurred in all Doric and Ionic regions, no matter how separated in space. The Aetolians and Arcadians also had their tribes, although less is known about them. In the Early Archaic Age, political and military groupings tended to be divided along phylê lines. By the late Archaic, though, many poleis came to object to these traditional tribal groupings, especially as they preserved the hereditary prerogatives of the aristocracy. To counter this, many poleis "restructured" their tribes. In Sparta, the three Dorian tribes were replaced with five tribes based on the five obai, or towns, that united to form the city of Sparta. In 508 B.C.E. in Athens, Kleisthenes replaced the traditional tribes as primary political divisions with demes and trittyes, as discussed in chapter 7.

A further subdivision of the traditional phylê was the phratry. The word comes from the Indo-European (see chapter 3) word for *brother,* and thus it is related to words such as *fraternity* and *fraternize.* This phratry, or brotherhood, was a recognized political/religious body, usually with its own constitution; possessions (including property); religious rites; and annual meetings where decrees were passed, new members were inducted, and officials, including priests, were elected (in Ionian regions, these meetings were called the Apatouria). In Archaic Greece, citizenship was based on membership in a phratry: To be enlisted in the ranks of a phratry was considered proof of citizenship. This changed during the Classical period, especially in the more democratic poleis. In Rhodes, phratriai were replaced with synnomai (partners) in Chios with khiliastyes. In 508 B.C.E., Kleisthenes based Athenian citizenship on deme (see chapter 7) rather than phratry membership. Nevertheless, as Aristotle stated in his *Constitution of Athens* (21.6), Kleisthenes did leave the phratriai intact, and it seems likely that, at least unofficially, phratry membership was still necessary for full civic participation. Most phratriai disappeared during Hellenistic times, although some endured through the Roman period.

As the name suggests, the phratriai, like the phylê, were understood to be kin-based, with phratry members sharing a common ancestor. In theory, then, membership in a phratry would be hereditary, passing from father to son. Apollodoros (Pseudo-Demosthenes 59.122) claimed that marriage was "when a man engenders children and presents his sons to the phrateres [members of the phratry] and demesmen and gives his daughters as being his own in marriage to husbands" (Pomeroy 1997, 79). However, acceptance into a phratry was not automatic and could be influenced by considerations other than genetic ones. This was especially clear in a court case against one Neaira, which took place in fourth-century Athens. At this point, the laws required that for a person to be an Athenian citizen, both of his/her parents had to be Athenian citizens (replacing the earlier rule, pre-451, that only the father had to be a citizen). In the case against Neaira, the prosecutor Apollodoros argued that Neaira was not an Athenian citizen, thus neither was her daughter, who was nevertheless married to an Athenian man as if she were a citizen. This couple, Phano and Phrastor, had a son. Phrastor, discovering his wife's noncitizen status, divorced her and disowned the son. Later, though, when he became seriously ill, Phano nursed him to health, and in return Phrastor agreed to acknowledge his son and introduce him to his phratry, making him an Athenian citizen. The phratry members, however, knew the story of his relationship with Phano and of the scandals surrounding Neaira, and they refused to accept the child, even though he was the son of an Athenian citizen, into their ranks.

Age

Bronze Age. Our main evidence about Minoan age groupings comes from Theran frescoes. Here, according to Davis (1986, passim), up to six age divisions are evident in the iconography. Three of these portrayed childhood, one adolescence and early maturity, one maturity, and one the beginnings of old age. The divisions were clearest for females, less so for males. The main age indicators in paintings are hairstyle, clothing, and eyes.

All three ages of children had shaved heads, a practice that the Minoans may have picked up from the Egyptians. Such shaving is portrayed by blue scalps in Minoan art (see Image 6.1). The youngest children had heads that were almost entirely shaven, with a few locks curling off from the forehead and back of the scalp. Girls at this age are sometimes shown wearing wraparound dresses, as in the above example. Older children still had shaved heads but had longer locks, usually including one on the right side of the head as well as the ones in front and back. By the third stage of childhood, probably prepubescence, the hair began to grow back in, so that a girl had three long locks as well as shorter hair on her scalp. By this age, the girls dressed in styles typical of older Minoan women: flounced skirts and fitted bodices. These younger girls are not shown with breasts, merely dots indicating nipples. Children of all three stages are shown with faint blue lines in their eyes, possibly indicating the "sheen of youth." These blue eye lines also appear in frescoes at Knossos, suggesting that this iconography was typical of the Minoans beyond Thera (Davis 1986, 401, 406).

Full-grown women no longer had these blue eye lines, and their coiffures were both long and even. Often, their hair was bound up in a scarf or snood. They dressed in the traditional garb, and their bodices frame quite ample bosoms. At the oldest age, the blue lines from youth are replaced with red lines, indicating either old age (Davis 1986, 404) or considerable saffron consumption (Rehak 2002, 49). Such reddening of the eyes in art was also used on the mainland at both Tiryns and Mycenae (Davis 1986, 405). The oldest class of women at Thera are shown with pendulous breasts, possibly indicating post-lactation, and they often wore makeup such as rouge (see Image 6.2).

The distinctions between the male age groupings in the iconography can be more ambiguous. Little boys had the same shaved heads as their female counterparts, although unlike the girls, they are often portrayed nude. Adult men had full heads of hair and were clothed in full robes, kilts, or penile sheaths. The adolescent age stages, however, are not so clearly demarcated. Some males are shown with shaven heads but large stature and full musculature, but some are shown with several locks but less muscle definition.

The Linear B tablets reveal variations in how the Mycenaeans categorized childhood. It is important to note that the tablets deal with subjects relevant to

6.1 Fresco of Young Girl from Thera (The Art Archive/National Archaeological Museum Athens/Dagli Orti)

the palaces: We are getting a bureaucratic, not familial, image of children. The texts from Pylos, particularly those in the Aa and Ab series, record what appear to be worker women associated with groups of children. Thus, tablet Aa01 records female grain grinders, along with ten girls and six boys (Ventris and Chadwick 1959, 158). In some instances, boys are referred to exclusively as sons of working women, such as "sons of the weavers" or "sons of the carders." The word *ko-wo* is Linear B for either *son* or *boy*, and *ko-wa* is *daughter* or *girl*. Separate signs were used as shorthand for *man* and *woman,* indicating that adults were viewed as a separate category from the children.

6.2 Theran Older Woman Fresco (The Art Archive/Dagli Orti)

Further subdivisions are apparent at Knossos, possibly through Minoan influence. Here, working women are still listed with groups of children, but the
children are categorized as either older (me-zo-e) or younger (me-wi-jo). Likewise, the women themselves were subdivided by age. Thus, tablet Ak 627
records nine (females) of a-no-zo, two older women under instruction, seven
older girls, ten younger girls, two older boys, and ten younger boys (Ventris
and Chadwick 1959, 163). It is possible that the age distinctions were relevant
for food allotments, older children needing more food than younger ones. The
evidence from Pylos does show that both men and women, and both boys and
girls (of the same age?), received equal rations (Billigmeier and Turner 1981, 6).

The fact that children were under the care of women exclusively suggests that boys' ages were more relevant than girls', as once a boy became old enough, he would be reassigned to the men's labor forces. Girls morphed into women with less occupational disruption.

Historic Periods.   The life of the human body is a continuous process of change, starting with birth and proceeding through growth, puberty, the finding of our first gray hairs, and death. In Greece, as now, there was a need to subdivide and categorize this continual process. At its simplest, the ancient Greeks recognized three ages of life: youth, adulthood, and old age, divisions seen as early as the time of Hesiod and continuously through the Classical period. Plutarch relates that in Sparta, choruses of men were so grouped, with the gerontes (old men) singing first, then the akmazontes (men at their peak, literally acme), and finally the paides, or boys (Garland 1990, 4–5). By contrast, the Pythagoreans (see chapter 10) identified four ages, parallel to the four seasons: There was childhood, like spring; youth, like summer; adulthood, like autumn; and old age, like winter (Garland 1990, 6). Such divisions, with or without the seasonal speculations, clearly influenced the common way of thinking: At the Nemean, Isthmian, and Panathenaic Games, males competed in groups of children, youths, or full-grown men. Likewise, there were three divisions of female competitors at the Heraia festival: girls, maidens, and young women (Calame 2001, 28). These, plus the elderly, comprised the four stages of life. The most elaborate system held that life had seven to ten stages, each composed of seven years. The Athenian statesman and poet Solon claimed (fr. 27):

> A young child still growing first loses baby teeth at seven years.
> When indeed god might complete seven additional years the signs
> of full youth become manifest.
> In the third, limbs still growing, the chin becomes downy, changing
> the bloom of his skin.
> In the fourth seven, all are best in strength, and men have signs of excellence.
> The fifth is the season for a man to think of marriage and producing children
> to follow after him.
> In the sixth the mind of man is educated in all things,
> he wishes as well not to work at impractical tasks.
> At seven sevens he is best in mind and speech;
> as well as at eight–fourteen years for both.
> In the ninth he is still capable, but his speech and wisdom are softer
> in matters of great virtue.
> In the tenth, if one should arrive at this completed measure,
> he'll have his portion of death not out of season.

The Greek neonate was hardly considered to be human. Upon birth, there was a decision whether to keep the child or not. In some areas, such as Athens, the father made this decision, and in others, specifically Sparta, a council of old men chose whether the child was a "keeper." It is unknown whether girls were subject to this scrutiny in Sparta: Our information from Plutarch's *Life of Lycurgus* tells us that the gerousia (council of old men) examined boys to see if they would make fit soldiers; if not, they were abandoned. There is no comparable evidence for girls (Pomeroy 2002, 34 ff.). By contrast, girls were more likely to be abandoned in other parts of the Greek world—up to 20 percent of the girls in Classical Athens (Golden 1981, passim). Even in Hellenistic Egypt, where infanticide appears to have been less common than elsewhere, a letter dated to the first century B.C.E., written by a man named Hilarion to his wife Alis, states: "If—good luck to you—you bear offspring, if it is male, let it live; if it is a female, expose it" (Pomeroy 1997, 224 ff.; Lefkowitz and Fant 1992, 187).

Except for Astyanax, son of Hector, who was thrown from the walls of Troy, exposure was the main form of infanticide, as no one had to take responsibility for actually killing the child. A baby could be left in a public place with hopes of its being adopted. Or, the gods could take pity on it and rescue it themselves, as did Apollo for his own exposed son Ion in Euripides's play of that name. By the Hellenistic period, some poleis tried to curb infant exposure. In Thebes, it became illegal: Should a father claim dire poverty, he could give up a child to the local magistrates, who then sold/adopted away the child. In Ephesus, infant exposure was permissible only in cases of severe famine, when there was little hope of the child surviving anyway (Garland 1990, 93).

If the child was a keeper, it was inducted into the family through the amphidromia ritual (see chapter 8), in which the father ran around the household hearth carrying the child, thus "humanizing" the baby and making it a family member (this was done about three days after birth). At some point between the seventh and tenth days after birth, the child was named. This involved hosting a small party, to which relatives were invited and brought gifts for the baby, something akin to a modern, postnatal baby shower.

How the child was presented to the rest of the community depended on the polis and the child's gender. As one may imagine given the Greeks' patriarchal society, there was more effort to publicize a new son than a daughter. In Athens and the Ionic regions, new sons were presented to their phratriai (see above) on the third day of the Apatouria festival, called the Koureôtis. The Apatouria was an annual religious festival, which, among other things, solidified the phratry's group identity. The Koureôtis was the first occasion when fathers could introduce their sons to the phratry, and fathers had to swear that the child was their own, born in legitimate wedlock. In Athens after the Periclean Citizenship Law of 451/450—whereby citizens had to be born of both a citizen father *and* a citizen mother—the oath included a clause that the mother was also an Athenian citizen. There was no comparable ritual for girls (Garland 1990, 121). A second opportunity to present one's children (definitely sons, possibly daughters) to the Athenian community took place at the Choes festival during the Anthesteria (see chapter 8). All boys (and perhaps girls) aged around three to four received a mini wine jug and got their first taste of wine among the citizenry. Archaeologists have uncovered many such miniature vessels, usually with pictures of small children on them. Toddlers in Attica who died before their Choes ritual were often buried with such items.

Formal education (provided the child was going to get any) began around age seven, and henceforth it was typical for both sexes to associate primarily with members of their own sex and age group. Our clearest evidence for this comes from Sparta, where boys entered the agogê—long-term military boarding school—at this age. The boys were assigned to agela, literally "herds," where they were raised with other boys of their own age (bouai) led by a bouagos. The focus of their education was being good soldiers: Literacy was of minimal importance, but endurance was highly valued. Around age eleven or twelve, things got worse for Spartan boys. According to Plutarch (*Life of Lycurgus*, 16.6), "When 12 years old they continued on without a robe; they received one cloak a year. They were wretched in body and ignorant of baths or ointments, save for very few days a year when they partook in such amenities. They lay down to sleep in the same place by troops and companies upon beds of rushes, which they gathered themselves, breaking off the tips of the grown stalks by the Eurotas with their hands, not iron. In winter they got so-called Lykophon (a plant) and mixed it with the rushes, this stuff believed to provide warmth."

Likewise, around this age, the boys' food rations were severely curtailed, forcing them to steal food whenever possible. According to the fourth-century historian Ephoros, a similar system was in place on Doric Crete as well. Here, boys were taken to the men's cafeterias, where they sat on the ground and ate together, wearing the same shabby clothes winter and summer, waiting on the men. Later they were required "to learn their letters and also the songs prescribed by the laws and certain types of music" (Strabo 10.4.19, quoted in Garland 1990, 139).

Things were better for Spartan girls, although the evidence for when they began their public education is ambiguous. Because girls had to grow up to be good mothers rather than good soldiers, they could spend more time at home with their female family members. Their group/public education seems mainly to have consisted of participation in choruses, where the girls learned to dance (the equivalent of today's gym class) and to sing songs that educated them in the ways of history, philosophy, and ethics (like an ancient, sing-along version of *Schoolhouse Rock*). Boys also took part in choruses, but this was only a small part of their overall education. Both genders seem to have begun choral training as children (paides). (The word is gender-neutral in Greek, so there is no way to determine from the written records whether boys, girls, or both are being discussed.) A second age group of girls who participated in choruses were the parthenoi, or maidens, in this instance probably referring to young teenagers (although see below). Finally, there were the women, or gynaikes, aged from the late teens upward (Calame 2001, 26). As we shall see in upcoming sections of this chapter, age grade divisions were always less pronounced for girls than boys, in Sparta and Athens as well as elsewhere.

Just like today, the teenage years pretty much marked the transition from child to adult in ancient Greece. These years were especially meaningful for females. The two most important life changes for Greek girls were menarche and marriage. Menarche, probably occurring around ages twelve to fourteen, marked a girl as ready for marriage. In many poleis this was all the indication needed that it was time to marry off a daughter. Medical writers even claimed that it was imperative to marry off a girl as soon as her menses began, as the vagina had to be opened by sexual intercourse for the blood to escape. If the girl were left "constricted" for too long, she could suffer a number of physical consequences, including the dire "illness of maidens," which led to insanity and suicide attempts. The best way to "open" a virgin was through penile intercourse, with a husband of course (Hanson 1990, 324), and so in many poleis, girls were married in their early teens.

The terminology for female age grade divisions could be complicated. As children, girls were paides. Next, they graduated to parthenoi, traditionally translated as "maiden" or "virgin." For a brief period they were nymphai, or brides (we get the modern word *nymphomaniac* from this Greek word), and they finally became gynaikes, or women, once they had their first child. An awkward term in this system for modern scholars is *parthenos* (sing. of *parthenoi*). Unlike the modern notion of physical virginity (someone who has never had sex), a parthenos was a girl who had not clearly been shown to have had sex. A new bride might be referred to as a parthenos, as could a woman who had had sex but had hidden the evidence. Kreusa, in Euripides's *Ion,* is the mother by Apollo of Ion (whom she exposes as an infant). Although the play's chorus knows this about Kreusa, they nevertheless call her a parthenos, not because she is physically a virgin, and not even because she is not yet a mother, but because her social standing is that of a woman who is not known to be a mother. Thus, the ancient Greek term *parthenos* had more to do with how one was perceived by society than with the physical state of one's body (Sissa 1990, passim).

As this social identification was so intertwined with motherhood, there was an understandable overlap between the parthenos and the nymphê, or new bride. In any event, the ultimate aim of any Greek female was to be a mother (at least according to the popular ideology; we have no testimonia from ancient Greek women regarding their own feelings on this topic). Thus, once a girl was married and produced an heir, she was officially grown up. No further changes in her status occurred until she reached menopause.

Maturation was more complicated for males, because it involved a series of introductions into the political and military milieux in which the boy would spend the rest of his life. For Athenian boys, at around age sixteen they were once again introduced to their phratriai during the Koureôtis day of the Apatouria, entrenching their identities as Athenian citizens. On this occasion, boys performed a sacrifice and cut off and dedicated a lock of their hair to Apollo, indicating that their childhood was now over. Two years later, Athenian males achieved legal majority and were officially enrolled in their demes (see chapter 7). According to the Athenian Constitution (42.1), "Those who partake of citizenship are from citizen parents on both sides, and they are registered into the demes at eighteen years of age. When they are registered the demesmen on oath vote on them—first if they appear to be of legal age . . . and second if one is free and born according to the laws."

At this age, Athenian males could inherit property and could represent themselves in the law courts, and orphans were declared independent of state care. Perhaps more importantly, males of this age began their two-year period of military duty as ephebes (something like the mandatory military service performed today by Israeli citizens). This function began with a tour of the principal sanctuaries of Athens and proceeded with instruction in the various arts of war, including hoplite fighting, light-armed fighting, and archery. Ephebes also worked on their acting and dancing abilities, as they were called upon to play the part of choruses in dramas (see chapter 10). For the first year of their training ephebes lived together in barracks on the Akte peninsula and on Mounychia Hill in the Piraeus. When their period of ephebe-ship was complete, they received their arms and took an oath before the shrine of Aglauros to protect Attica (see chapter 8 and below) (Garland 1990, 183–184). From this point until they reached age fifty-nine, they were eligible for military service (Garland 1990, 185).

The Athenian model seems to have been standard for most of Greece, where education was very much in the hands of individual families until the period of military training. An exception to this was Sparta, as mentioned previously, where state-sponsored education was the norm for both sexes starting at age seven. Even so, Spartan males had their own final rite of passage to undergo before they could enter into adulthood, and this was the krypteia. The krypteia was like a secret, state-sponsored terrorist organization, composed of boys ages seventeen to nineteen. It was their duty to live on the frontiers between Spartan society and the helots' territory (see below), where they terrorized and slaughtered the serf population. This kept the helots in a state of constant panic and reduced their numbers, while training Spartans to live off the land and to function in "enemy territory." Once the krypteia was complete, Spartan males were ready for normal active military service, although, unlike their Athenian counterparts, they were not yet regarded as full citizens (Garland 1990, 179).

The transition to adulthood for males took place around age twenty and was marked by an increase in emotional maturity; a traveling out from the familial context to form or re-form bonds with other males, preferably warriors; and finally adopting the identity of warrior and protector for oneself. This process could take up to ten years, and men aged twenty to thirty were still thought of as quite young, being called neoi in Athens (literally, "new ones") and hebontes in Sparta (literally "young ones") (Garland 1990, 200–201). Spartan males married at this point, but they were not free to live with their families until well after age thirty (they lived in barracks until they moved in with their wives). Most other Greek males married between the ages of thirty and thirty-six, usually to girls only half their age (see below in the section about marriage). As most men only *began* having children around age thirty, by the time a man turned thirty himself his father was probably dead, meaning that one could acquire a wife and one's inheritance at roughly the same time. And so, in the eyes of the law and state, one was officially a man at age thirty.

"Normal" adulthood lasted until around age fifty-nine for a man and until menopause for a woman (women's lives in Greece were determined by their biology, and men's were determined by their functions in society). For women this meant, socially, an end to their "usefulness" and the beginning of a new age of freedom. Once women could no longer bear children and no one was overly paranoid about issues of illegitimacy of those children, older women had the freedom, even in highly restrictive Athens, to go about their affairs outdoors and with no chaperone. For men, age fifty-nine meant an end to their period of active military duty. This is not to say that men were in constant military service for several decades, but they were now not to be drafted away from their normal affairs during periods of warfare (see the section entitled "The Military," below). Men of this age also became eligible for certain political positions, such as the council of the gerousia in Sparta. The fact that men had to be at least sixty (Plutarch, *Life of Lycurgus*) to join this council shows that such life expectancies were not abnormal.

It appears that men also went through their midlife crises at this age. Plutarch, in his philosophical work "Should Old Men Take Part in Public Life?", talks of men who, "having lived blamelessly for many years under the same roof as his wife, kicks her out when he gets old and either lives alone or takes a mistress instead of his wedded wife" (Garland 1990, 207).

After sixty, a man became a gerôn (old man) and a woman a graia. The same stereotypes about the elderly were present in ancient Greece as now. On the one hand, those over sixty were generally understood to have acquired a lifetime's worth of knowledge, and they could be seen as the most philosophical and temperate of citizens. They were especially accorded respect in Sparta, where the highest political rank short of king was reserved for those above sixty. In Hellenistic Cyrenê in Libya, a Doric community like Sparta, a charter granted by King Ptolemy I in 310 B.C.E. stated that all 500 members of the council, the 100 members of the gerousia, as well as the generals and ephors (see chapter 7), had to be at least forty-nine years old (Garland 1990, 283). In Doric communities, at least, age was granted a considerable amount of respect.

On the other hand, it was commonly thought that old age was a time of physical decay, loss of libido, and possible dementia. This last idea made its way into the law courts, as when Isaios, in his "On the Estate of Nikostratos," argued, "For the law allows no one to dispose of his own property if his reason is impaired by old age or disease or the other causes with which you are familiar" (4.16). This state of being out of one's mind was called paranoia, and it marked the stage at which an old person entered a second childhood, once again needing physical care and being seen as a minor in the eyes of the law.

Gender

Gender is a cultural construct, representing the way a society believes men and women are supposed to act, think, and behave. Nevertheless, notions of gender in ancient Greece had their ideological roots in biological differences, real or imagined, between the sexes. This is presented most clearly by the fourth-century physician Hippocrates, who wrote in his *Diseases of Women,* "A woman's flesh is more sponge-like and softer than a man's: since this is so, the women's body draws moisture both with more speed and in greater quantity from the belly than does the flesh of a man. . . . And when the body of a woman—whose flesh is soft—happens to be full of blood and that blood does not go off from her body, a pain occurs, whenever her flesh is full and becomes heated. A woman has warmer blood and therefore she is warmer than a man. Because a man has more solid flesh than a woman, he is never so totally over-filled with blood that pain results if some of his blood does not exit each month. He draws whatever quantity of blood is necessary for his body's nour-ishment . . ." (translation by Hanson 1975, 572).

Women were seen as bound to bleed, most notably at liminal points of life—menstruation, defloration, and parturition—it was seen as an essential aspect of the prime female role as giver of life. By contrast, it was man's duty to bleed in warfare, which the Greeks saw as the male counterpart to female parturi-tion. Euripides's Medea proclaims that she would prefer to face battle three times rather than give birth once (*Medea*, ll. 250 ff.), and according to Plutarch, Lycurgus (a Spartan reformer and law giver) allowed marked burials only for men who died in battle and women who died in childbirth.

This dichotomy of the "soft, weak" female and the "strong" male pervaded all Greek understandings of gender distinctions. As the female was weak in will and body, excess and temptation received feminine attributes. It was femi-nine deities who personified both strife (Eris) and madness (Lyssa). Neverthe-less, this weakness also counteracted a high potential for destruction and dis-ruption—women were understood as essentially passive, unable to exert active control over the self and often considered to be childlike.

By contrast, the male was seen to be strong in body and mind and essen-tially active in character. As the strong body made men fit for warfare, mental strength gave them more potential for self-restraint, in Greek called sophrosynê. Thus, the male was expected to control his appetites for food, drink, and sex, as well as overweening pride and anything else considered ex-cessive. Therefore, as Aristotle argued in his *Politics* (1254b2), "The male is by nature superior, and the female inferior, and the one rules, and the other is ruled; this principle, of necessity, extends to all mankind." He later goes on to add, "this inequality is permanent."

Beyond these "standard" gender concepts, though, were several exceptions throughout Greek history. Most blatant is the prominence of women in Mi-noan society, where they were portrayed as active, often dominating religious and possibly political scenes. Such iconography led early scholars to suggest that Minoan Crete was a matriarchy. This is now considered unlikely, but de-pictions of prominent and, apparently, responsible women in the Minoan records do suggest that the later Greek ideologies did not apply to their early southern neighbors. Furthermore, nothing in the Minoan iconography depicts women as mothers (Olsen 1998, passim). The Minoans clearly did not limit fe-males to being reproductive entities and caregivers.

It seems more likely that the seeds of Greek sexism were sown in the Myce-naean period, from which the Linear B texts reveal few women in positions of power (depending, of course, on the meaning of the ambiguous word *potnia* in the Linear B corpus; see chapter 8) and no women except priestesses owning land. By contrast, the Linear B texts do reveal that women, but not men, were responsible for childcare in addition to industrial duties in the palaces. This close association between women and maternity was also played out in the iconography, especially in the small figurines known as tau, phi, and psi figurines (see chapter 8). These small, feminine images, almost certainly religious in character, were often portrayed holding or even nursing babies. Thus the concept of woman as mother became extremely common in the Mycenaean repertoire.

The engendering of Spartan women is an interesting variation on the classical theme. When Sparta became a military state, probably in the seventh century B.C.E., all priorities were focused on military perfection. Men were trained to be soldiers and very little else; Plutarch notes in his *Life of Lycurgus* that Spartan citizens were not even expected to engage in trade or production. Women were seen as producers of soldiers (sons) and of soldier producers (daughters). In order that Spartan women give birth to the best possible soldiers, Lycurgus demanded that they train along with the men, eat well, and marry and reproduce at the end of adolescence (rather than around age fourteen, as was common elsewhere in Greece; see "Marriage," below). So Spartan women were rather masculine by Greek standards, being strong, athletic, and not bashful in the presence of males. This masculinization of the women was seen to reinforce their ultimately feminine role as mothers.

Another instance in which the image of strong, temperate male vs. weak, extravagant female was overturned was in Pythagorean philosophy. According to the Pythagoreans (see chapter 10), the ultimate aim of life was balance and harmony, and many believed that women had a greater potential for such balance than men. Furthermore, the Pythagoreans accepted that women had equal intellectual potential to that of men. Not only did they advocate women's education, but several Pythagorean philosophers were women, notably Pythagoras's own wife Theano and his daughter Myia. Nevertheless, these philosophers did not disagree with the general belief in the greater physical strength of males, and they argued that men and women had different, but balanced, roles in life.

From the early Archaic Age through the fourth century B.C.E., Greek society was very much divided along gender lines. Homer himself (or herself) depicts a world where women are expected to remain indoors, like Penelope, while men go off to fight in wars, like her husband Odysseus, or to win glory for themselves by other means, such as Telemachus going in search of Odysseus. In Book 6 of the *Iliad*, Hector is concerned when his wife is not in her chambers but has gone off like a raving woman to the city walls to watch the battle. Even the goddesses in the *Odyssey* are remarkably interior creatures: The nymph Calypso remains in her cave, and we see Circê leaving her mansion only once to join Odysseus down on the beach of her private island.

In Sparta—the most sexually "egalitarian" Greek polis—from age seven, boys and girls were raised and educated separately, the boys in the agogê, the girls in female-only choruses (see above). In Athens, especially in the fourth century B.C.E., the desire to keep females indoors and out of the reach of nonfamilial men was so strong that some orators claimed that truly modest females were ashamed to be seen even by men of their own families (Lysias, *Against Si-*

mon, §6). Males, on the other hand, had more opportunities to mingle with females, mainly through contact with prostitutes.

Some of this changed during the Hellenistic period, when the kingdom replaced the polis as the main form of political organization. As city defense was removed from the shoulders of the citizenry, there was less emphasis on the idealized male soldier. Women acquired greater economic rights, with which came greater opportunities to get involved in regional political affairs. For example, in the second century B.C.E., a woman named Archippe was publicly honored in Kyme (Turkey) with an inscription for financial contributions made to the polis, and an inscription from Histria records the existence of a female archon (Pleket 1969, #2–3). In the first century B.C.E., a woman named Philê of Priene held the office of stephanephoros (crown-bearer) for building, at personal expense, the city aqueduct and reservoir (Budin 2001, 1728). Clearly, these women were interacting with male officials and the citizen body at large. At the apex of Hellenistic society, of course, were the queens, who often ruled side by side with, or instead of, kings. The most famous example is Cleopatra VII Ptolemy, who ruled as consort to her brother before becoming sole (and the last Hellenistic) monarch of Egypt. This is not to say that Greece became a sexually egalitarian society in the Hellenistic period, merely that the social divisions between men and women became less significant than, say, class or ethnicity.

Class and Slavery

As far as modern scholars can tell, the Greeks, and even the Minoans before them, always had a class-divided society. As discussed in chapter 4, for instance, by the Late Bronze Age, Minoan society seems to have been divided into four levels, with the palaces at the top, underneath which were the villas, the cities, and finally the villages. Likewise, the different characteristics of the tombs located in northern Crete at Mochlos (as opposed to the more communal tholos tombs of the south) show that different individuals/families/clans could afford more or less elaborate burials. Whether such differences were due to economic or inherited class differences is uncertain, but it does call into question whether class may have been determined by economic prosperity.

The Mycenaeans were at least as class-conscious as the Minoans, if not more so. As early as the late Middle Helladic/early Late Helladic periods (around 1650–1550 B.C.E.), the elaborate creation and contents of the shaft graves at Mycenae give evidence of the recognition of elite status in the community, a status probably associated with warfare, to judge from the prominent display of weapons and chariot imagery at the graves. As discussed in chapter 7, the evidence from the Linear B tablets also shows a strongly class-oriented society, with the king or wanax at the top of the social ladder, accompanied by his followers (the hequetas), the war leader or lawagetas, and possibly a queen. Below these were the bureaucrats, such as the regional governors (ko-re-te), and the po-ro-ko-re-te, who are thought to have been their assistants.

The Mycenaean economy seems at least partially to have been divided into guilds, at the top level of which were the basileis (a word that later came to mean "king" in Greek). There were men who owned extensive tracts of land and who rented out portions to lesser farmers and the like (see chapter 5). At the bottom of the social ladder were, of course, the slaves. All these titles show that the Mycenaeans had a bureaucratic society. But further data reveal that many, if not all, of these positions may have been determined by inherited class. For example, our evidence about the hequetas Alektruon Etewoklewehios, or Alektruon son of Eteocles ("he who truly has fame"), suggests that he was the son of a nobleman, indicating that this was an inherited status (Deger-Jalkotzy 1999, 128). Likewise, many religious offices seem to have stayed within families, being held by people whose parents were also listed as religious functionaries (see below, under "The Family"). When social functions are (pre)determined by birth, we may comfortably speak of a class-based society, although, as with other aspects of the Aegean Bronze Age, this requires further research.

Even during the Dark Age, when Greek society and civilization reached its nadir, there is still evidence for elaborate class distinctions in the archaeological record. This is clearest at Lefkandi on Euboia. In contrast to the standard view of poverty-stricken times, the graves at Lefkandi show an abundance of foreign luxury goods, such as Phoenician jewelry and Egyptian faience. These slightly poorer, single inhumation burials (nothing like the fancy tholoi or shaft graves of earlier eras) are certainly balanced out by the goods the dead took with them to the afterlife.

This is especially so in the Heroön of Lefkandi (see Image 4.4), a monumental burial structure constructed and used around 1000 B.C.E., located in the midst of the Lefkandi cemeteries. As discussed in chapter 4, this monument, a proto-mausoleum of sorts, contained the buried remains of a woman, horses, and the cremated remains of what scholars think to be a man. The buried woman was covered with gold, and she brought objects of ivory and iron—as well as her horses—with her to the great beyond. Such burial treasure accompanying a structure that clearly required the coordinated efforts of an entire community to build argues that this "hero" and "heroine" of Lefkandi were high-status individuals, possibly a king and queen. Thus, even in the heart of the Dark Age, class distinctions, especially in the upper classes, were visible in Greek society.

Nobility, then, from Mycenaean through Archaic times, was apparently based on birth; one was noble because one was born into a noble family, and there was no other way to achieve this status, just as one could not really overcome a base heritage. One's class influenced how others treated one, and class also created preconceived notions of one's character. Nobles were understood to be superior, morally and intellectually, to commoners, thus the word *aristocracy*, or "power" (*kratos*) "of the best" (*aristos*).

These noble families (genê, sing. genos; see more below under "The Family") held a monopoly on political power before the era of the tyrants (see chapter 7). The clearest example of this comes from Corinth, which was ruled during the early Archaic Age by the Bacchiadae. According to Herodotus, "The government of Corinth was once an oligarchy: one clan—the Bacchiadae, who intermarried only among themselves—were in power there" (5.91). Their power was broken only by one of their own members—the outcast Cypselus (see chapter 7).

Typically in Greek society, the reign of tyrants ushered in economic reforms and thus an economic improvement for the rest of society. With this economic prosperity came greater responsibilities but also prerogatives in the political sphere (such as buying and using hoplite armor in defense of the state—see below), so that a greater percentage of the populace had access to the political machinery once dominated by the noble genê. Only priesthoods remained in the hands of such families by the Classical period.

Although the noble-born and, eventually, the wealthy topped the social register, there were several categories of class beneath these, each recognized as having a specific place in the political and legal system. The largest category of upper-middle-class people were the free men, citizens of the poleis. Their wives held a slightly more ambiguous position, as they could technically be identified as citizens, but this did not put them, politically or legally, anywhere near an equal standing with their citizen husbands. Next after citizens were resident aliens, called metoikoi in Attica, perioikoi in Sparta, and apetairoi in Crete. These resident aliens were extremely important to their local economies, engaging in trade, paying taxes, and serving in war if necessary. At the bottom of the social register were various categories of nonfree peoples, such as serfs and slaves. How each of these categories was distinguished comes across clearly in the Law Code of Gortyn (see chapter 7). In a section on sexual offenses, the law states (§ii.3): "If a man rapes a free person, male or female, he shall pay 100 staters [an amount of money higher than a drachma], and if the [victim] is from the house of an apetairos, 10 staters; and if a slave rapes a free person, male or female, he shall pay double. If a free man rapes a serf, male or female, he shall pay 5 drachmai. If a male serf rapes a serf, male or female, he shall pay 5 staters" (translation from Lefkowitz and Fant 1992).

From this passage, we see that greater compensation was required for crimes committed against citizens than against aliens, and even less compensation was required for crimes against serfs. Likewise, slaves paid greater punishments for their crimes than did the free classes. However, we also see that even nonfree persons (the serfs) were protected by law, and even full citizens were punished for crimes against them.

Although positions of nobility had to be inherited, all other class rankings could be achieved through economic activity or, in the case of slavery, military defeat. That is to say, class was flexible in ancient Greece, both for good and bad. The changeover from hereditary to economic upper-class status is most visible in Athens with the reforms of the statesman Solon in the early sixth century B.C.E. Up to this time, political office had been reserved exclusively for hereditary members of the noble genê. Solon changed the basis of eligibility to one of economic ranking, as recorded by Pseudo-Aristotle in his *Constitution of Athens* (see chapter 7). Although such a structure—one in which only the affluent might hold political office—may seem like the height of classist injustice to a modern reader, one must remember that such a structure actually opened up the political machinery to the entire male population. One could not change the family into which one was born, but anyone, technically, had the opportunity to better his financial status. Thus, in Athens, upward social mobility became a practical reality.

Even in rigid Sparta, social mobility was feasible, although it was much easier to go down the social scale than up it. The Spartan social hierarchy was headed by two kings and their royal families, all of whom inherited their status. Below the kings were the Spartiates, full Spartan citizens who maintained membership in a sysition, or dining club, through annual contributions of foodstuffs used in communal meals. Below the Spartiates were various categories of lower classes, many described by the historian Xenophon in his *Hellenika*. In section 5.3.9 of this work, he describes as follows those noncitizen Spartan residents who fought on behalf of the Spartan army: the perioikoi, noncitizen resident aliens (the word literally means "around the house"); mothakes, mixed-blood members of the lower classes who were educated with Spartan children and raised in the lower to middle class; nothoi, literally "bastards," children of Spartiate fathers and helot mothers, who were not quite slaves and were used to fill the army ranks. Also falling into the lower classes were the hypomeiones, Spartiates who fell on hard times and could no longer maintain their sysition dues (Pomeroy 2002, 97). At the absolute bottom of the Spartan social register were the helots, composed of the conquered population of Messenia and having a status somewhere between slave and serf (slaves were completely unfree and had no rights; serfs had some rights).

Technically, to be a full citizen, a man needed enough economic surplus to maintain his sysition membership. Ideally, such a surplus was almost guaranteed upon the citizen's birth, when, according to Plutarch's *Life of Lycurgus*, he would receive an allotment of land with which to sustain himself and his family. This would be in addition to any private, familial lands he might own. However, by the fifth century B.C.E., it seems that either the system of public land allotments had ceased to function or, more probably, they never existed at all. More and more Spartiates fell into economic duress during this time, forcing them to sell land, lose their surpluses, lose their sysition memberships, and thus lose full citizenship—hence the existence of hypomeiones. As the land continued to be concentrated into ever fewer hands, it became increasingly impossible for the vast majority of Spartans to recover citizen status.

Slavery. With the possible exception of Minoan Crete, all Greeks made use of slave labor, such that many economic historians (notably M. I. Finley) have asked whether we might consider ancient Greece to have been founded on slavery. The presence of slaves in Mycenaean society seems confirmed by references to do-e-ro, or the Greek douloi ("slaves"), in Linear B texts. What status this word indicated, however, is debatable. For example, some individuals in the texts are specifically do-e-ro te-o, literally "slaves of the God/dess." Were these slaves as we understand the term today, or cult functionaries, possibly of quite high status? In either case, it appears likely that a do-e-ro, not accompanied by the te-o, may in fact have been a slave, one person owned by another and used for profit.

Although being a slave did place one in the lowest ranks of society, such a status did not necessarily come from an inherited class. Quite to the contrary, slavery was often inflicted on formerly free individuals who were unfortunate enough to be conquered in war or kidnapped. Such was the fate of Eumaios,

Odysseus's swineherd in the *Odyssey*, who, as related in Book 15, was actually the son of the king of Syria (a small island, not the modern country of Syria). He was kidnapped by a household slave woman and handed over to Phoenician traders, who sold him as a slave in Ithaca. Thus, the man went in one fell swoop from prince to slave. Enslavement was the usual fate of women in conquered cities. Although the warriors were killed in or after battle, the women, and sometimes children, would be taken back to the conquerors' lands in servitude. Such was (almost) the fate of Princess Cassandra of Troy, the daughter of King Priam, who was enslaved and brought back to Mycenae to be Agamemnon's bedfellow.

One might assume that slaying an entire population of males and enslaving all the women and children were purely endemic to the barbaric Dark Age and not at all appropriate for the high civilization of Classical Greece. However, during the Peloponnesian War, during the "Golden Age" of Greece—one of the "Golden Ages" of humankind in general—the Athenians did the same thing to the Melians. As Thucydides recounts it (5, 116), after a long siege, "[T]he Melians surrendered at the discretion of the Athenians, who put to death all the grown men whom they took, and sold the women and children for slaves, and subsequently sent out 500 colonists and inhabited the place themselves." So, slavery as a "punishment" for losing a war was still common even at the height of Greek civility.

Generally, though, the Greeks preferred non-Greek slaves. Most were imported from the regions of Thrace (north of Greece), Turkey, and Scythia (modern-day Ukraine). Scythians were especially good archers, and many poleis used them as a police force. Such "policemen" often appeared in Athenian comedies as humorous characters, being portrayed either as cowardly, as in Aristothanes's *Lysistrata,* or lecherous, as in his *Thesmophoriazousai.* On the other hand, Thracian women were thought to be especially good nurses, and many families put such slaves in charge of rearing their children. Likewise, slaves were sometimes employed to educate children, as many slaves were well educated, such as a conquered philosopher enslaved after a battle.

Having foreign slaves, especially a variety of them, lessened the probability of escape and revolt. A foreigner with an easily distinguished accent would have trouble blending into normal Greek society. Having slaves of different ethnicities and languages inhibited communication, and thus plotting, among them. The reverse of such a scenario—having a multitude of Greek (-speaking) slaves, and the problems and fears so engendered—is evident in the relations between the Spartans and their slaves, the Messenian helots. The helots were the conquered population of Messenia, enslaved by the Spartans and forced to work their own land for Spartan profit. Unlike other slaves in Greece, they lived in their own communities in a familial structure, and so the potential for plots and uprisings was high. It is largely agreed that the primary impetus toward Spartan militarism was fear of a helot revolt, an event that occurred more than once in Spartan history.

And so the Spartans had an awkward relationship with the helots. On the one hand they were completely dependent on the helots for labor and food. On the other, this dependency bred anxiety, an anxiety that was in no way alleviated when, in the later fifth century B.C.E., the population-diminished Spartans realized that they needed helot soldiers to fill their army's ranks (much as they had sired children with helots previously). Although in other poleis, service in war was grounds for manumission, the Spartans had a far more ambiguous approach to helot soldiers, especially as recounted by Thucydides. Having fought side by side with their Spartan masters in battle during the Peloponnesian War (4, 80, 3–4), "The Spartans proclaimed that the Helots pick out as many of them they believed to have been the bravest among them in the wars, so that they might be freed. It was a test—the Spartans believed that the very ones judged the first to be freed might attack them through their daring spirits. So, having picked out 2,000, those Helots crowned themselves and went about the sanctuaries as being liberated. But not much later the Spartans did away with them, and no one knew by what means they were offed." Apparently it was okay to arm helots and to send them off to war, so long as they didn't actually come back again.

The relationship between the Spartans and the helots was an extreme case in Greece (as was just about anything involving the Spartans). Elsewhere, slaves had legal status and rights, and their lots could vary considerably, ranging from member of the family to abject laborer to multimillionaire. The most wretched slaves were the heavy laborers, like those in Attica who worked in the Laurion silver mines. There is some debate as to whether these slaves belonged directly to the city or whether the government rented them out from individual owners. The latter seems more likely, indicating that wealthy Athenians could own very large numbers of slaves indeed.

More commonly, however, Greek families owned only a few slaves. After a period of successful war, one might imagine that the cost of slaves went down, so that even poorer families could afford at least one. More affluent households probably had a few male and female slaves: the men to help with outdoor farming duties, the women to help the mistress of the house with her chores. Xenophon, in his *Oikonomikos,* related that one of the most important duties of a young wife was to train the slaves in domestic duties like spinning and weaving. The master of the house, or one of his trusted servants, was likewise responsible for training and supervising the male slaves.

Greek slaves generally had more rights and opportunities than slaves in recent history. They had at least minimal protection under the laws, and they received payment for their work. An adequately skilled slave could eventually earn enough money to buy his/her freedom. Or, just as likely, he/she would be manumitted (freed) upon the death of the master, a common occurrence in ancient Greece. Such manumissions were inscribed on stone in public places such as the sanctuary at Delphi, thus publicizing the new status of the freed man or woman. Some lucky former slaves were so dear to their masters that they not only got their freedom but inherited their masters' property as well. The best-known example of this, and the best possible example of social and class mobility in ancient Greece, is the story of Pasio, Phormio, and Archippe of Athens, whose tale comes to light in the writings of the orator Demosthenes.

Pasio was born a slave around the year 430 B.C.E., although whether he was foreign or Greek is unknown. He was owned by Arkhestratos, a banker, who used Pasio as his banking manager. Pasio proved to be such an expert manager that Arkhestratos came to value him more than he did his own son; by 394 he manumitted Pasio and left the entire bank, with all its assets, to him. Upon his manumission, Pasio married Archippe, who was possibly a (former) slave, although she may also have been free-born, possibly even a lower-class citizen. Pasio grew quite wealthy, being extremely successful in his profession, and it is evident that he made many generous donations to the city of Athens. In exchange for this, at some point between his manumission and 376 B.C.E., the city granted him full citizenship. Thus, Pasio went from slave (perhaps even foreign slave) to upper-class citizen.

Continuing the story, Pasio himself acquired a slave to help in his banking business—Phormio. Phormio was a foreign slave who did not originally even speak Greek. However, like Pasio, he was industrious and trustworthy, so much so that Pasio came to think of Phormio as family. Upon his death in 370 B.C.E., Pasio manumitted Phormio and left him in his will not only the bank and all its assets, but also his wife Archippe, along with a hefty dowry and custody of their two sons (Demosthenes 45.29G).

Like Pasio before him, it seems that Phormio was also quite generous with the people of Athens, such that he was granted citizenship in 361 B.C.E. With Archippe as his wife, Phormio had two stepsons, Apollodoros and Pasikles (Pasio's sons). Phormio and Archippe also had two sons of their own, Archippus and Phormio "Jr." Pasikles eventually inherited the banking business, and Apollodoros married into a prestigious and wealthy family. Years later, the younger Phormio was recorded as one of the citizens eligible for liturgies (see chapter 5), the high-cost "donations" to the state, such as building ships or financing plays. Only the wealthiest and most prestigious citizens were so enlisted. In roughly one generation, Archippe saw her family go from slavery to borderline nobility (Pomeroy 1997, 183–191).

UNIONS

Xenia

Xenia, often translated as "hospitality" or "guest-friendship," was one of the most important aspects of Greek culture. It referred simultaneously to basic hospitality to strangers and to the formation of long-lasting, reciprocating friendships formed through the exchange of gifts and goodwill. Xenia made it possible for a lone person traveling through Greece to proceed safely, while also creating a means by which the highly competitive and belligerent Greeks might form alliances and build camaraderie. Xenia could occur between individuals, between individuals and communities, and between communities (Thorburn 2001, 775).

Although there is no direct evidence for it from the Bronze Age, the importance of xenia in Homer's poetry is so strong that we might suggest that the concept was important from the Mycenaean period at least. The Trojan War was blamed on a breach of xenia, whereby Paris, after enjoying the guest-friendship of Menelaus, responded by stealing his host's wife and her possessions. This infuriated Zeus Xenios, god of guest-friendships, and Menelaus came under a religious obligation to punish the xenia-violator.

All classes of Greeks could, and were required to, show hospitality to strangers. This is revealed in the ultimate tale of xenia—the *Odyssey*. At the highest level of the practice, royal families and communities showed xenia to destitute strangers, as did the Phaiakians to the unknown Odysseus (7, 155–166). Entering the palace of Alkinöös and Aretê, Odysseus found the Phaiakian nobility dining in the megaron. Odysseus went to the queen, clasped her knees, and implored her to receive him and help him on his journey home. Then he went to sit in the hearth ashes, a suppliant's position. At first there was shocked silence in the halls (the Phaiakians did not get many visitors). Then:

> At length the elder hero Ekhenos replied,
> who indeed was oldest of the Phaiakian men
> and excelled in words, very old in countenance.
> He thinking well addressed them and replied:
> "Alkinöös, this is neither fair nor seemly,
> that a guest [xenos] sit on the ground among the ashes.
> These others hold back waiting for you.
> But come, have the guest get up and sit on a
> silver-studded throne, and you bid the heralds
> to mix wine, so that we might pour libations to Zeus
> Delighting-in-Thunder, who accompanies reverend suppliants.
> Let the housekeeper give dinner to the guest from her stores."

The Phaiakians gave the stranger a royal welcome, not only feeding and clothing him, but promising to return him home, celebrating a festival for him, and giving him countless treasures. All before they even asked his name!

At the other end of the social register, even the humblest slave recognized his duties as host. When Odysseus returned to Ithaca in disguise, he was taken in by his own slave, the swineherd Eumaios. The poor man welcomed the stranger into his squalid hut and there prepared a small feast of pork, bread, and wine for the visitor. When it came time to sleep, Eumaios found whatever bed coverings were available and set them on Odysseus to protect him from the cold. He apologized for the scant resources he could offer the stranger, but assured him that Telemachus the prince would give him fine clothing and send him wherever he needed to go.

Those who failed to show xenia were punished. Paris's breach of xenia caused his community to be destroyed in the Trojan War; Polyphemos, a Cyclops who chose to eat rather than feed his guests, was blinded; and the highly uncivil suitors of Penelope were slaughtered one and all.

The end results of xenia relationships were considerable, played out both in literature and in life. A good example of the former occurs in Book 6 of the *Iliad* (6, 215 ff.), when the enemies Diomedes (Greek) and Glaukos (a Trojan ally) meet in battle. They stop briefly to identify themselves to each other, each giving his lineage up through the times of his grandfathers. It turns out that

Glaukos's grandfather Bellerophontes was once a xenos-guest to Diomedes's grandfather Oineus. A xenia relationship had been established that lasted generations, bonding the two heroes in a friendship that outweighed their allegiances to their own armies. The following description expresses not only the endurance of such unions, but also the gift-giving and continued hospitality that were seen as an essential aspect of the formation of the xenia relationship:

> See now, you are my xenos from the days of our fathers.
> For godly Oineus once received noble Bellerophontes
> in our halls, keeping him for 20 days.
> They offered each other fine friendship gifts:
> Oineus gave a shining purple belt,
> and Bellerophontes a two-handled golden cup
> which I left in my house, coming here.
> . . . .
> So now I am your dear friend in the midst of Argos,
> and you in Lykia, when I should come to that land.
> Let us avoid each other's spears even in the throng.
> . . . .
> Let us exchange armor with each other, so that others
> might know that we swear to be friends from the days of our fathers.

A real-life example of the power and endurance of xenia appears in Book 2 of Thucydides. At the inception of the Peloponnesian War, Pericles (see chapter 4) convinced the Attic populace to abandon their farms and seek refuge within the city walls of Athens. The Spartans were excellent in land battles, but seldom had the patience for long sieges, so Pericles's idea was that the Spartans would come in and devastate the farms and countryside, but the people would survive intact. His major concern was that, while the people's farms would all be destroyed, his own would be spared due to his guest-friendship with Archidamas, the Spartan general. So as not to provoke the ill will of the Attic people, Pericles promised that if his lands were spared through his friendship with Archidamas, he would donate those lands to the state when the war was over.

A historic example of xenia between a person and an entire city is recounted by Herodotus, when the Lydian (western Turkey) king Croesus established a xenia relationship with Sparta. In Book 1, §69 of his *Histories*, Herodotus relates that Croesus sent messengers with gifts to Sparta, asking for xenia with the Greeks as per the dictates of an oracle, probably of Apollo. The king specifically went to Sparta, having heard that the Spartans were the most eminent of their people. The Spartans, having heard tell of the same oracle, and having once received a favor at Croesus's hands (he gave them a golden statue of Apollo), agreed to the union.

Feasts and Symposia

Like most peoples, the ancient Greeks came together to eat and drink. Although normal meals generally took place within individual families (much like today), the banquet/feast (deipnon) and the drinking party (symposion) brought together different subsets of the community.

The feast was closely linked to religion, as the animal(s) consumed was usually first offered as a sacrifice to the deities. As discussed in chapter 8, sacrifice was the core religious ritual for the Greeks, probably dating back into Minoan times. An animal was slaughtered at the altar of a deity, and then certain parts of that animal, such as the thigh bones, were burnt as a sacrifice to the heavens. The rest of the animal, though, was butchered and eaten by those participating in the sacrifice. Thus, a feast was a ritual communal meal. The Minoans probably had a similar practice, to judge from the evidence found at Kato Symi Viannou in Crete (see chapter 8). This site, dating back to the Middle Minoan period, was a sacred enclosure, something like an early form of sanctuary. Many early remains—bones and dishware—indicate that large, communal picnics took place there. Thus, from the mid-second millennium B.C.E., we have evidence of ritual meals eaten by large segments of the community. Mycenaean portrayals of bulls trussed up on altars suggest that the Mycenaeans had similar rituals.

The "Heroic" feast was an important aspect of early Greek society, to judge from its prevalence in Homer's work, and it seems to have been a core aspect of ancient Greek xenia. In Book 9 of the *Iliad* (ll. 199–221), Achilles welcomes his friends Odysseus, Ajax, and Phoinix with a modest feast:

> So speaking godly Achilles led them forth,
> he sat them on couches and rugs of purple.
> Immediately he spoke to Patrocles, who was nearby:
> "Set forth a larger krater, son of Menoitios,
> and mix in more wine, prepare a cup for each.
> For the men dearest to me are under my roof."
> So he spoke, and Patrocles obeyed his dear companion.
> He tossed down a great meat-tray in the fire's gleam,
> and on it he set the back of a sheep and a fat goat,
> and the lower portions of a fat pig, rich in lard.
> Automedon held them for him; godly Achilles carved.
> And he carved them well and pierced them with spits.
> The son of Menoitios, peer of the gods, lit a great fire;
> and when the fire burned down and the light dimmed,
> scattering the embers he set the spits upon the fire,
> and sprinkling them with salt he set them on the fire-dogs.
> But when they were cooked and set upon platters,
> Patrocles, taking bread portioned it out on the table
> in fair baskets, but Achilles portioned out the meat.
> He sat down opposite godly Odysseus
> by the other wall; he bade Patrocles, his companion, sacrifice to the deities.
> And he cast the offerings onto the fire.
> And they put their hands to the good things laying before them.

With the rise of the city-states, the deipnon came to take on more political meanings, especially as regarded the distinction between citizen and foreigner.

Such is the case in the fourth-century Athenian epigraphy. The Athenians, as a political entity, bestowed various honors on individuals and communities alike. One was honorary Athenian citizenship, including full protection under Athenian laws. Another was ritual friendship—the xenia discussed above. Both groups of honorees received certain benefits when visiting Athens, including a free meal in the Prytaneion, or city hall. For citizens, this was called a deipnon; for noncitizens, xenia. In 342 B.C.E., when Arybbas the Molossian was made an Athenian citizen, the commemorative stele mentions that he was invited to the Prytaneion for deipnon, his noncitizen friends for xenia. Two years later, when the entire population of Elaeus was granted Athenian citizenship, they were also invited for a deipnon (Tod 1985, 214–219). The feast therefore served as a bonding element not only between individuals, but also between citizens and allied communities.

The ritual banquet, as an important aspect of Greek religious and civic life, continued in use throughout Greek history. More exclusive in nature, however, and ultimately more important in the development of Greek culture and society, was the symposion. The symposion (from *syn* = with, *posis* = drinking) was a drinking party, attended by men and by less reputable females, such as prostitutes. In its standard enactment, the men lay on couches (klinai), one or two per couch. Wine was mixed with water in a krater (a special bowl for this purpose)—the Greeks believed that it was barbaric to drink wine straight, an idea thought to be proven by the fact that the Macedonians did not mix their wine.

Serving boys ladled out the mixed wine into the guests' wine cups, or kylikes. Prayers were offered to Dionysos, god of wine, and the other deities. Entertainment consisted of music, possibly provided by a flute-girl (a type of prostitute); poetry composed and recited by the guests themselves; sex, provided by slave girls and boys, not to mention the other guests; and, quite possibly, intellectual conversations. Even the intellectual conversations tended to revolve around the themes of the symposion, such as drinking and sex, with the most famous example being Plato's *Symposion,* the great philosophical treatise on the nature of love. It was this last category of "entertainment" that led to the modern notion of the symposium as an intellectual/academic gathering.

When and how the symposion emerged in Greek society is still a matter of debate, considering the paucity of early evidence. Communal drinking is an age-old aspect of Greek society attested to even in Mycenaean data. Perhaps the earliest portrayal of a symposion forerunner is the Knossos Camp Stool Fresco, painted during the period of Mycenaean hegemony (see chapter 4). On this fresco groups of seated men drink from chalices in the presence of two larger females, sometimes interpreted as either goddesses or priestesses. The fact that these women have "sacred knots" in their hair—a motif associated with religion in the Minoan iconography—may indicate that some manner of sacred or ritualized function was intended (Preziosi and Hitchcock 1999, 166–167). Religious or not, this is our earliest depiction of groups of men sharing wine in a communal setting. Rehak has suggested that a primary function of the Mycenaean megaron was for communal wine-drinking, where men, presided over by (perhaps royal) women, drank wine as a cohesive element in Mycenaean society (Rehak 1995, passim).

Although Homer frequently referred to males drinking wine together, there are significant differences between the Bronze Age and Dark Age portrayals of communal drinking and the institution of the symposion practiced in later Greek history. As the Knossos fresco shows, the drinking was originally done seated, not reclining as with the later fashion. For Homer, drinking was merely one part of a feast, and entertainment was not necessarily provided. When, then, did the traditional form of the symposion come into being, and under what stimulus?

Our earliest evidence for the traditional symposion is actually our earliest piece of Greek writing: the Nestor Cup. This drinking vessel (a kotylê) was buried with an adolescent boy around 725 B.C.E. at Pithekoussai. Inscribed on the vessel are the following lines:

> Of Nestor, in this wine cup a pleasant drink;
> who would drink this beverage, immediately
> will desire for fair-crowned Aphrodite seize him.

The lines are dactylic hexameter, the meter of epic poetry (see chapter 10). "Nestor" almost certainly refers to Pylian Nestor, Homer's garrulous advice-giver. In some ways, then, the cup seems to refer to the epic-style drinking discussed above. However, the reference to Aphrodite, goddess of sex, is far more in line with the later conception of the symposion, and it may indicate that by the end of the eighth century the symposion-as-center-of-revelry idea was taking hold (Murray 1994, passim). This would synchronize the changes in the symposion with the influx of Near Eastern practices and motifs that characterizes this phase of Greek history, known as the Orientalizing Revolution. The practice of reclining on couches certainly comes from Near Eastern influence, where depictions of men so poised were common in Assyrian wall reliefs. The change from warrior banquet to symposion, then, probably began in the eighth century B.C.E.

The full evolution, however, probably occurred in the seventh to sixth centuries, to judge from our artistic and literary evidence. The earliest portrayal of a symposion in vase painting is on a Corinthian krater dating to c. 610, depicting Heracles drinking with a youth named Eurytios. The seventh-century lyric poet Alcman (fr. 116) refers to the layout of a typical symposion in one of his verses, mentioning the "seven couches and as many tables crowned with poppy cakes . . ." (Murray 1994, 48). In the mid-sixth century B.C.E., the lyric poet Anacreon, considered by some to be *the* sympotic (relating to the symposium) poet, wrote:

> I do not like him who, drinking wine by the full krater,
> speaks of strife and tearful war,
> but whoever calls to mind lovely cheer, mingling
> the Muses and the shining gifts of Aphrodite . . .

These lines suggest that Anacreon experienced the transition from heroic-style drinking party to the purely frivolous and sexual.

Every house that could afford it had a room for the celebration of the symposion; the room was called the andrôn, literally "men's room," and was a place where respectable women were not supposed to go. As this was a room for entertaining and, in typical Greek fashion, showing off, it was often the most elaborate room in the house, decorated with fancy mosaics. For archaeologists, the andrôn is the easiest room in a Greek house to make out: Unlike other rooms, the door to the andrôn is offset to accommodate the long couches set against the walls. One full couch plus the end of another could fit against the door wall. A modest house's andrôn may have been able to accommodate about seven klinai at a time; Alexander's palace at Pella had several andrôns, each able to accommodate more than twenty.

Marriage

Marriage served two main functions in ancient Greece: the creation of family alliances and the production of legitimate children. Although romances from as early as the Hellenistic period do narrate tales of young lovers who overcome any number of obstacles to marry and be together, love was not the usual basis for marriage.

To date, scholars have no information regarding marriage or weddings in Bronze Age Greece. Some have interpreted the festive flotilla fresco from Thera as a wedding procession, but there is no clear evidence for this. We know that women were the primary caregivers for children as mentioned in the Linear B texts, but these texts deal mainly with palatial affairs, not the daily lives of "housewives," so we know little about the workings of Mycenaean marriages.

We learn more about marriage during the Dark Age and Archaic Age through Homer and Hesiod. Much can be gleaned from a short passage in Book 9 of the *Iliad* (ll. 144–148). Agamemnon, attempting to assuage Achilles's wrath, makes the following offer:

> There are three daughters of mine in the well-built hall,
> Khrysothemis and Laodikê and Iphianassa,
> Of them let him lead her whom he wishes without bride-price
> to the house of Peleus. And I will give as dowry
> many things, as many as never before anyone gave with his daughter.

What is first evident is that the father has the right to marry off the daughter, without either her or her mother's consent. As in later Greek history, marriage arrangements were conducted between either the groom or his family and the bride's kyrios, or legal guardian. Usually this was her father, although in his absence it could be a brother, or even a son.

Two financial transactions were involved in marriages: the bride price and the dowry. In contrast to later understandings of these, both transactions ultimately benefited the wife. The bride price consisted of goods offered by the groom or his family to the bride and her family. Such a tradition recognized the value of daughters to their families, especially their economic contributions vis-à-vis textiles and labor; the groom's family had to "buy" her from her parents. The bride price might also include presents to the intended bride herself, especially if she were in high demand. In Book 18, 291–300, of the *Odyssey*, Penelope, one of Greek tradition's most sought-after wives, reminded her suitors of their obligations and got some lovely jewelry.

Somewhat the opposite of the bride price, the dowry was property given by the bride's family into the keeping of the groom. In reality, the dowry was the bride's inheritance from her natal family, usually around one-half or one-third of each of her brothers' portions, although she received it upon marriage rather than the death of her father. Laws varied throughout the poleis concerning what property could be included in a dowry. For example, land was acceptable in Sparta, but categorically not so in Athens. In the story quoted above, Agamemnon includes copious tracts of land as dowry for whatever daughter Achilles would choose to marry, indicating that land was transferable as dowry in Homer's world.

Although technically the husband had use of the dowry while married to his wife, the dowry actually belonged to her and her natal family. If the marriage were ended for any reason other than the wife's infidelity (and sometimes not even then), her entire dowry had to be restored to her or her family. This helped to prevent "frivolous" divorces. Furthermore, the wife continued to have use of her dowry after the death of her husband, providing her with a type of life insurance. Upon her death, she left her dowry to her children. In this way, some inheritance went through the female line as well as the male's. Typically, the bride who offered the largest dowry had a greater share of suitors, and poorer families could find the dowry a heinous burden on family resources, especially as the father had to produce it while still alive (in contrast to his sons' inheritance). The dowry has continued in use even into the present day in Greece (although since the 1980s it has technically been illegal). The bride price was more restricted in use.

Hesiod, more "working-class" in his concerns than Homer, strongly advises the listener against getting a bad wife while offering advice on how to get a good one in his *Works & Days* (ll. 695–705):

> Lead a wife to your home when you are of age,
> neither much less than 30 years
> nor much more, this being the appropriate age to wed.
> And let the woman be four years from youth; marry her in the fifth.
> Marry a virgin, so you might teach her good ways.
> Best of all to marry someone who lives near you,
> having looked all about, so your marriage is not a joke to the neighbors.
> For a man acquires nothing better than a wife of
> the good sort, but nothing's worse than the bad kind,
> a parasite!

As discussed below, many Greeks took Hesiod's advice. Greek men generally married at around age thirty, when their own fathers might be near death, thus releasing the family land for inheritance. Women—girls, really—married for the first time while in their teens. In Sparta, this was seldom younger than age eighteen, when women were considered to be better able to bear children. In Athens, the more common age was fifteen, although in the fourth century B.C.E., girls could be married as young as thirteen. Men generally preferred virgins as their first wives, so as to ensure the paternity of their children. However, both divorced and widowed women could and did remarry, so female virginity was hardly a prerequisite for marriage.

Athens. As is typical for ancient Greece, the two regions we know the most about concerning weddings and marriage are Athens and Sparta. Athens was certainly the more traditional of the two, and it might be accepted as the template for weddings in other Greek poleis. The full affair was composed of three basic parts: the betrothal (engyê), the giving away of the bride (ekdosis), and the union (gamos). As was customary, the betrothal was made between the bride's kyrios and either the bridegroom himself or his family, "for the ploughing of legitimate children" (Menander). The dowry, dependent on the bride's family's assets, would be established at this time (Rehm 1994, 2–18).

The actual wedding ceremony commenced before the ekdosis. Both families would preside over preliminary sacrifices in honor of the event and to reaffirm the familial unit. The bride herself would make offerings to different deities such as Hera, goddess of marriage, and Aphrodite, goddess of sex. But most importantly, she made offerings to Artemis, including childhood toys and a lock of her own hair specially grown for this occasion. Artemis protected the girl as a child, and it was she who would preside over the bride during defloration and childbirth (see chapter 8).

On the day of the wedding, both bride and groom would take a ritual bath. In Athens, the water was brought from the Kallirrhoê ("fair flowing") Spring in special vases called loutrophoroi—"bath water carriers." Both bride and groom would then be decked out in their finest clothing and crowned with garlands. The bride also wore a veil. The groom and his family arrived at the house of the bride for a banquet, probably also involving a number of smallish sacrifices and libations. From here, the groom took the bride by the wrist and led her out of her paternal home to bring her to his own. If circumstances allowed, they would ride there on a cart; if not, it was customary to ride a mule. (If a man married the girl next door, he could probably just walk his bride to their new home.) This leading out by the wrist formally constituted the ekdosis.

At the groom's house, the couple was greeted at the door by the groom's mother, who led them to the hearth, where they were showered with seeds, dried fruits, and candies (much like the modern throwing of rice). This act performed two functions. First, the hearth, domain of the goddess Hestia, was where new people were ritually inducted into the family; newborn babies were also brought to the hearth to make them family members. Second, the shower of fruits and seeds had fertility connotations. It may have been at this point that the bride removed her veil, the anakalypteria, thus formally giving herself to her new husband.

Finally, the couple went to bed to consummate the marriage—the gamos itself. The next day, friends and family came by to visit, to sing wedding songs, and to give wedding gifts. From this point forth, the bride lived with her husband's household and produced his heirs (Rehm 1994, 12–18).

Sparta.   The Spartans believed that the purpose of marriage was the production of children, although they were somewhat less concerned than the Athenians about the "legitimate" aspect: What was important was the creation of good soldiers. Because they believed that good soldiers could be only produced by healthy and strong mothers, Spartan girls did not marry until they were around eighteen years old, in contrast to the Athenian brides. It also appears that the bridegrooms in Sparta were not much older than the brides, probably in their mid-twenties, meaning that there was far less of an age gap between Spartan couples.

Much of what we know about the Spartan marriage ritual(s) comes from Xenophon and Plutarch, two authors quite removed from the time and/or place about which they were writing. As such, the accuracy of either of their descriptions is debatable. Nevertheless, from what researchers can tell, the Spartans seem to have practiced what to modern Westerners would seem a rather bizarre wedding rite. According to Plutarch (*Lycurgus* 15.3–4), "They married through seizure, not when the bride was small or underage for marriage, but being at the peak of youth and ready. After she was seized the so-called bride's-maid took charge of her, cropping her hair to the skin, dressing her in a man's cloak and shoes, and then laying her on a mat alone in the dark. The bridegroom, neither drunk nor enfeebled, but sober like always, having dined in the mess hall, slips in and loosens her belt, lifts her and carries her to the bed. Having spent a short time together he leaves in an orderly fashion, returning to his usual place and sleeping among the other young men."

So long as the man was stationed with his troop (see above, the section about age), the marriage was carried on in secret, the man sneaking away whenever possible to tryst with his wife, then returning to the barracks. The marriage was officially proclaimed once the woman became pregnant. In this way, a couple could be certain they were fertile before establishing a formal marriage. Only when the man was discharged from constant active duty around age thirty did he and his wife share a house (until this point, the bride remained in her parents' house), and Plutarch remarks that some couples had several children before getting to see each other face-to-face in daylight! However, the fact that Spartan girls practiced athletics, in the nude even, outdoors alongside the boys makes it unlikely that any Spartan couple had not seen each other before the wedding, indicating some possible misconceptions on the part of Plutarch.

In contrast to the other Greeks, the Spartans exhibited a remarkable lack of concern with either virginity or marital fidelity. The fact that a marriage was only made official once a couple produced a child (or a pregnancy, at least) suggests that some couples who did not conceive moved on to try other partners. Furthermore, Xenophon tells us that wife-sharing was common among Spartans, whereby a husband might lend his wife to another man for the production of healthy children. More likely than not (Pomeroy 2002, 37–39), the wives had a considerable say in these "spouse-swapping" arrangements. Both of these differences from the other Greeks might be attributed to the Spartan obsession with having a large, powerful army, but another factor was the Spartan system of landownership and inheritance.

It is generally understood that before the end of the fifth century B.C.E., the Spartans had two types of landholdings, one type that belonged to an individual family (private property), and one type that belonged to the state and was apportioned out to citizen males in exchange for military service. As all citizen males were guaranteed a chunk of land, the concern with the inheritance of private property was less rigorous, thus less concern with the parentage of children. This notion has recently been severely challenged by historians such as Hodkinson, who argues that there were actually two types of *private* property, one of which was called the ancient portion. There were some laws regulating what the owner could do with his land—for example, he could not sell any of the ancient portion—but he could bequeath any of his land as he saw fit (Hodkinson 2002, 88). Thus, the landowner could distribute his land as he chose; he was not obliged to pass on his property to his sons. Furthermore, women had, for Greece, extraordinary property rights themselves, so that passing land and possessions through the female line was common. Without the strict need for father-son inheritance, marriage, sexuality, and reproduction were more casual in Sparta than in many of the other Greek poleis. The only exception to this rule was the Spartan royal family, wherein adultery of women could be quite scandalous. Once again, this was not because of inheritance issues, but rather for the royal bloodline: Spartan kings had to be legitimate members of the royal families (Pomeroy 2002, 73–74).

Hellenistic Egypt.   In the Hellenistic period, women attained far more power, especially economic rights, than they had held in the Classical period. This is especially evident in the marriage contracts that accompanied Hellenistic marriages. Many of these documents were preserved in Egypt because of the dry climate. A contract that sheds considerable light on Hellenistic marriages is the one between Heraklides and Demetria of Cos, who wed in 311 B.C.E. According to this document:

> Heraklides takes as his lawful wife Demetria of Cos from her father Leptines of Cos and her mother Philotis. He is free; she is free. She brings with her to the marriage clothing and ornaments valued at 1000 drachmai. Heraklides shall supply to Demetria all that is suitable for a freeborn wife. We shall live together in whatever place seems best to Leptines and Heraklides, deciding together.
>
> If Demetria is caught in fraudulent machinations to the disgrace of her husband, she shall forfeit all that she has brought with her. But Heraklides shall prove whatever he charges against Demetria before three men whom they both approve. It shall not be lawful for Heraklides to bring home another woman for himself in such a way as to inflict contumely on Demetria, nor to have children by another woman, nor to indulge in fraudulent machinations against Demetria on any pretext. If Heraklides is caught doing any of these things, and Demetria proves it before three men whom they both approve, Heraklides shall return to Demetria the dowry of 1000 drachmai

which she brought, and also forfeit 1000 drachmai of silver coinage. . . . (Translation, Pomeroy 1975, 127–128)

It is evident that some previous ideas about marriage were still maintained in the Hellenistic period. The bride was given away by her father as before, although now we note that Demetria's mother is also mentioned. A dowry (but no bride price) is documented, and it was Heraklides and Leptines who decided where the new couple would live. Furthermore, as per tradition, the dowry belonged to Demetria; if there were a divorce for any reason other than her adultery, she would take her dowry with her. Somewhat new is the contract itself. Even more so are the stipulations placed upon Heraklides. In a classical Greek marriage, there was little evidence that a wife, especially one of the middle or lower classes, had any redress against a husband's philanderings. Here, not only is Heraklides expressly forbidden to engage in any relationship with a woman not approved by his wife, but, failing that, upon their divorce he must pay a 100 percent surcharge to her dowry. Similar contracts existed throughout the Hellenistic period, especially in Egypt.

Heiresses. Normally in ancient Greece, inheritance went from father to son, especially as far as land and buildings were concerned. A secondary line of inheritance went through women by means of their dowries (see above). What happened, then, if a family had no sons to inherit their property? In the absence of any children at all—a rare occurrence in Greece—a man's estate was divided up among his closest relatives on his father's side, keeping the patrimony within the paternal unit. It was far more common, however, that a couple had at least one daughter, and the patrimony would "travel" through her. There were different names for such a girl throughout Greece. In Athens she was an epikleros, meaning "attached to the family property." In Sparta she was called a patroukhos; in Gortyn, a Doric community like Sparta, she was the patroiokos—"of the father's house." In all cases, the idea was to have the heiress marry her closest male relative on her father's side. Her children, then, would inherit the paternal estate from the grandfather.

The legal procedures regarding heiresses varied from city to city, with some of the harshest laws existing in Athens, as we know through the court cases of Isaios and Demosthenes. According to Athenian law, an epikleros was obliged to marry her closest male relative on her father's side. The order of preferable spouses was firmly set: first paternal uncles, then first cousins who were sons of paternal uncles, then first cousins who were sons of paternal aunts. There was some room for maneuvering on the part of the potential grooms; if they did not wish to marry the epikleros, they could pass her on to the next relative, possibly being obliged to provide her with a dowry if the girl were poor.

The epikleros herself, however, had no say in the matter whatsoever, *even if she was already married.* That is to say, if a family lost its sons and was left with only a daughter who was already married, she was forcibly divorced from her husband and married to the appropriate paternal relative. Isaios (3.64) claimed in the fourth century: "many men who have already been living with their wives have been deprived of them thus." As for the (new) husband, his role in the continuation of the paternal line was highly valued. Husbands of epikleroi were legally obliged to have sex with their wives at least three times a month, and they were released from military duties to fulfill their obligations. (In other words, a man could explain to the authorities that he could not be sent to war because he legally had to stay home to have sex with his first cousin.)

The laws concerning heiresses in other parts of Greece were less severe, as we can determine from the Gortyn law code (see chapter 7). Section vii.15 of this code relates:

> The heiress is to marry the oldest of her father's living brothers. If her father has no living brothers but there are sons of the brothers, she is to marry the oldest brother's son. . . . If the heiress is too young to marry, she is to have the house, if there is one, and the groom-elect is to have half of the revenue from everything. If he does not wish to marry her as prescribed by law, the heiress is to take all the property and marry the next one in succession, if there is one. If there is no one, she may marry whomever she wishes of those who ask her from the same phratry (see above). If the heiress is of age and does not wish to marry the intended bridegroom, or the intended is too young and the heiress is unwilling to wait, she is to have the house, if there is one in the city, and whatever is in the house, and taking half of the remaining property she is to marry another of those from the phratry who ask her, but she is to give a share of the property to the [rejected] groom. If there are no kinsmen as defined for the heiress, she is to take all the property and marry from the phratry whomever she wishes. (Translation from Lefkowitz and Fant 1992, adapted)

Although there was obviously some attempt here to have the heiress marry within the paternal family, this was not strictly enforced. The girl could "buy" out of her obligations by renouncing a percentage of her inheritance to a possible claimant rather than marrying him. And in other respects, she could marry "whomever she wishes," indicating a fair amount of autonomy for girls from Gortyn. Something similar seems to have been practiced in Sparta. According to Herodotus, Spartan kings had the right to pick husbands for heiresses; or a father, knowing he was going to die, could "bequeath" his daughter(s) to a preferred groom. But by the Late Classical period, Spartan women were more or less able to decide for themselves whom they would marry. As women could own land and resources in Sparta, inheritance of the paternal estate through the female line was legitimate and uncomplicated (Pomeroy 2002, 84–86).

Sex

Like gender, sex is a cultural construct, with different societies understanding aspects of sex and sexuality in different ways. This becomes especially evident when studying the ancient Greeks. The usual assumption is that the Greeks had a lot of homosexuality in their society. The word *lesbian*, in fact, derives from the supposed homosexual inclinations of Sappho and her "girls," who lived on the island of Lesbos.

In reality, the ancient Greeks did not have our concepts of homo- and heterosexuality; they saw all people as being essentially bisexual. Their delineation of human sexuality distinguished between the dominator/penetrator and the submissive/penetratee. In all heterosexual unions, the male was (as they chose to understand it) the penetrator, the woman the penetratee. For homosexual unions, there were different sets of rules governing the relationship between two males, and the specifics of Greek female-female unions are still a matter of debate among researchers.

Heterosexual Unions. For "proper" women, heterosexual sex took place exclusively with one's husband, although adultery was a reality in ancient times just as now. Men had a bit more freedom; neither virginity before nor fidelity during marriage was demanded of them (at least until the Hellenistic period). This, of course, leads to an obvious paradox: If girls are not supposed to have sex but boys can, with whom are the boys having sex? "With other boys" was part of the answer, especially in certain communities. But another part was the traffic in female sex workers in ancient Greece. Men of affluence could afford hetairai (sing. hetaira). The word technically means "female companion," although a closer definition in English might be "courtesan" or "call girl." These were the upper-class sex workers, who set their own hours and booked their own clients. At the opposite end of the spectrum were the pornai (sing. pornê), literally "whores," usually slaves who worked in brothels for a madam. Somewhere in between were flute-girls, semitrained musicians who entertained at parties such as the symposia and who often had sex with their clients.

Same-Sex Unions. Sex got complicated between males. It was thought by the Greeks that men were dominant sexually, meaning they were the penetrators. This was not too much of a problem with heterosexual intercourse, but was definitely problematic with homosexual ones, as, inevitably, one of the males had to play the feminizing role of the penetratee. As this could be a source of extreme shame in ancient Greece, there were rules governing what kind of males men could be attracted to, and how these relationships might unfold. As with everything else in Greece, these rules differed from polis to polis.

In Athens, the "norm" was that older men might fall in love with youths, *youths* usually being defined as before the first whiskers appeared on the chin. Depending on when body hair started to appear, this probably indicated boys sixteen to nineteen years old. Boys at this age were not yet entirely masculinized, so assuming a passive role in a love affair was not as shameful for them. Older men, then, felt/expressed attraction for younger men; even Socrates, the supposed bastion of self-restraint, claimed that he got "hot" looking down the robes of the handsome youth Kharmenides. In these relationships, the dominant, older male was called the erastes, literally "lover." The object of his affections was the eromenos, literally "beloved."

Such crushes, as we might call them, were expressed quite openly. In art, a lover might have the name of his beloved painted on a vessel, accompanied by the word *kalos* ("beautiful"). More demonstrative were scenes of actual courtship, in which the erastes would offer the young eromenos tokens of his affection, such as a hare, sometimes pointing to the young man's genitalia (the Greeks were not big on subtlety). One of the most famous literary examples of the erastes-eromenos relationship (although not an especially successful one) appears in Plato's *Symposion*. Here, the playboy of Athens—Alcibiades—sees Socrates reclining on his klinê (couch). In a twist of the usual older man–predator/younger man–prey scenario, it becomes clear that Alcibiades has turned the tables on his erastes (213 c–e): "Socrates: Agathon [the host], see if you might protect me, as the love of this man for me is no trivial matter! For since that time when I fell in love with him, it hasn't been possible for me to look at or chat with any handsome fellow, as he being jealous has fits of envy and abuse, and he hardly keeps his hands off me! . . . His mania and violent sexuality have me scared off my ass!"

Usually, though, younger fellows were not supposed to be quite so openly amorous. It was seen as an honor to receive the attentions of a distinguished man (like Socrates), but not necessarily to be dominated/penetrated by one. The crush on the young boy either was intended to remain sexually unfulfilled or a less penetrating form of sex was preferred. Vase paintings suggest that intercrural sex (between the thighs) was common. What was typical from the Socrates-Alcibiades scene was the location: Symposia were venues for flirtation and erotic contact between not only men and the flute-girls, but also between men and boys. An even more common trysting space was the palaistra, what we might call a health club or sports club. Here, males exercised in the nude (the Greek word *gymnô* = to strip naked, thus the gymnasium was where people stripped naked to exercise), giving them a wonderful opportunity to see each other, perform for each other, and express varying degrees of admiration.

In Doric areas like Sparta and Crete, male homosexuality was less stress-inducing and may actually have been part of a boy's education. The fourth-century B.C.E. author Ephoros relates that in Crete, it was customary for an older erastes to take a fancy to a younger eromenos. The erastes would inform the eromenos's family of his intentions; if they approved, he would "kidnap" the object of his affections. The erastes then took the boy out to the country for two months, where they camped and slept together while the older man educated the younger. At the end of the two months, the lover returned the beloved home with many fine gifts, including clothing (Dover 1989, 189–190). This type of relationship may be what is represented artistically in the lead figurines from the Cretan sanctuary of Kato Symi Viannou, where pairs of hunters of different ages are shown (see Image 6.3).

There is no clear evidence for similar customs in Sparta, but much classical Athenian literature ascribes strong homoerotic inclinations to the Spartans, with expressions such as "doing it Spartan-style" referring to anal intercourse. Amusingly, this expression applies to both homosexual and heterosexual unions (Dover 1989, 187–188). Other pieces of evidence have also been put forward to explain Spartans' connection with homosexuality. Xenophon and Plutarch, when describing Spartan marriage customs (see above), mention that Spartan brides were dressed as men for their wedding night, even shaving their heads. This ritual transvestitism may have been intended to comfort the

6.3 Kato Symi Hunters Figurine (Courtesy of Paul Butler)

bridegroom in his transition from homoerotic to heteroerotic sexuality. Furthermore, the fact that Spartan males spent the first thirty years of their lives living mainly in the company of other men in their barracks has led some to suggest that in such an all-male, military situation, homosexual liaisons between boys and men should be expected.

Two other places where male-male homoeroticism was considered common were Elis and Boiotia, in central Greece. Xenophon, in his *Constitution of the Lakedaimonians,* says, "In other Greek states, for instance among the Boiotians, man and boy live together, like married people; elsewhere, among the Eleans, for example, consent is won by means of favors" (2.13). Both Xenophon and Plutarch stated that in Elis and Thebes (the capital of Boiotia) the strongest military units were composed of pairs of homosexual lovers, all of whom would want to impress each other on the battlefield and who would be willing to die for each other. The epitome of this sentiment was the Theban Sacred Band, established around 380 B.C.E. and composed exclusively of pairs of homosexual lovers (see below) (Dover 1989, 192).

Researchers know far less about female homosexual relations than they would like, as is true for most aspects of women's lives in ancient Greece. Fewer than twenty pages of Sir Kenneth Dover's book *Greek Homosexuality* (Dover 1989) are dedicated to lesbianism, with the majority of that focusing on Sappho's poetry (see chapter 10).

One cannot deny, though, that Sappho is one of our best early sources for female homoeroticism. In reality, not all of her poetry (all but one poem existing exclusively as fragments) can be understood as referring to the first person. That is, when Sappho talks about how "I" love "her," the "I" is not necessarily Sappho. Sappho wrote wedding songs, and in some instances we may understand the "I" as the bridegroom. In other poems, however, Sappho is more clearly speaking as herself, especially in the one complete poem that has been recovered, in which she addresses herself by name in the text (see chapter 10 for a full translation). In this same poem, she prays to Aphrodite to help her turn the affections of an unresponsive beloved, referred to as a female. This would appear to be clear evidence of homoerotic affections in Sappho's poetry, while other fragments relate the close affections her students had for each other (see below).

Other than Sappho's voice, our slim evidence for female homoeroticism comes from men, both in literature and in vase paintings. The problem with both sources is the matter of intention and audience: Were men simply expressing their own conceptions to other men, or were they portraying lesbianism as it actually occurred, with women in the artistic audience? Some of the more obvious portrayals of lesbian sexual encounters appear on wine cups, a form of pottery usually used only by men. Were these scenes of reality, or merely images meant to titillate a male audience? If men were using these cups in symposia, were the scenes intended to stimulate the sexual revelries associated with that forum?

In some instances, though, homoerotic images appeared on items associated with women, such as dishes or trinket boxes or oil jars. In such cases, we might understand the images as being intended for a female audience, and thus more true to their own lives. In one example from Thera on Crete, two women holding garlands stand face-to-face, one stroking the chin of the other. The proximity of their bodies and the affection portrayed in the scene strongly suggest a romantic encounter. Likewise, a Black Figure lekythos (small oil jug) from Athens shows two women sharing a shawl or mantle. Such imagery, for both females and males, is generally symbolic of erotic contact in Greek iconography (Rabinowitz 2002, passim).

From both Ionic (Athens) and Doric (Thera) regions, then, we have imagery that presents female homoerotic encounters. The literary evidence of such encounters is more sparse. From Athens, Aristophanes shows a group of Athenian women fondling the Spartan woman Lampito in his play *Lysistrata*. In Sparta, Plutarch, in his *Life of Lycurgus*, reports that women often maintained erotic relations with girls (perhaps following the model of the older erastes/younger eromenos among the men). The choral hymns composed by Alcman (see chapter 10) for Spartan girls make references to their love for exemplary older girls, possibly a reference to the homoerotic affections hinted at in Sappho's poetry.

Bisexuality. It appears the ancient Greeks went through phases of sexual orientation, being more homoerotic in adolescence and more heteroerotic in adulthood. When boys and girls were separated during childhood and adolescence, it was customary for them to form romantic and sexual relationships with members of their own sex. Societies, however, cannot perpetuate themselves without heterosexual unions, so all societies have to inculcate to some degree heterosexual inclinations in their members. In Greece, marriage was a heterosexual union existing for the creation of children (see above). Children would therefore go from their adolescent homosexual relationships to marital (and otherwise) heterosexual relationships. Such a transition may have been somewhat traumatic. As stated above, Spartan brides dressed as boys on their wedding nights, possibly to make their grooms feel more at ease, the grooms perhaps being used to sexual encounters with other males. Much literature (Boedeker 1974, 85–91) refers to girls being raped or seized out of the all-female chorus by males (all over Greece), thus being brutally ripped out of the "safe" female environment to be incorporated into the harsher world of heterosexual intercourse. Sappho's poetry reveals some of this anxiety on the part of young brides. In a poem about a departed friend, who probably left Sappho's "school" upon her marriage, Sappho wrote (fr. 83):

[. . .]
I truly wish to die.
She left me crying
very much, and she said to me,
"We know what awful things we suffer,
Sappho, as unwillingly I leave you behind."
And I replied to her,
"Go in joy and remember me,
for you know how we are fettered
who cannot go with you.
But I want you to remember, if you forget,
how many sweet and lovely things we shared,
how many garlands of violets

and roses you wove sitting by me;
how many necklaces
twined about your soft neck
were made of lovely flowers,
and you anointed your fair-tressed head
with copious, regal myrrh oil;
and lying on soft beds girls
with all they most wished for beside them."

"All they most wished for" was probably the other girls, whose company and affections they lost upon their (unwilling) marriages to men. Other poems of Sappho recount the fear of defloration, and men's sexual ineptitude in general.

So it seems that there were different phases of homosexuality and heterosexuality in Greek society. These divisions were certainly not concrete, and both continuously influenced the lives of most Greeks. Sappho's daughter complains that she cannot weave, so overwhelmed is she for love of a boy. In Athens, the wealthy man Timarchus was brought to trial for prostituting himself to other men, mainly so he could afford female prostitutes for himself (see chapter 7).

GROUPS

The Family

Bronze and Dark Ages.   Any assertions about the family in the Minoan period are, of necessity, speculative. We have no readable documents dating from that period, and the frescoes that have been found do not portray any clearly familial relationships. Nevertheless, the archaeology, especially the architecture, does reveal some data concerning the construction of the family in Early and Middle Minoan times. As early as the 1920s, G. Glotz (1921) argued that the communal nature of the Messarà tholos tombs (see chapter 9), along with the "extended family" layout of Early Minoan dwellings, suggested that the Minoans organized themselves according to clan lines, or in extended families. The organization and growth of Myrtos especially (an area excavated after Glotz's work) suggested that the community began as a nuclear family in the original dwelling, with the later generations adding on to the original structure over the course of generations. Thus, the Early Minoan family was actually the clan.

In the Middle Minoan period, however, the dwellings became smaller, and the burials were more likely to be of smaller groups of people, often only one or two people buried together. This trend continued into the Late Minoan period, indicating that the larger clan structure was replaced by smaller family units, possibly even conforming to the modern nuclear family of two, possibly three, generations of blood kin living together (grandparents, parents, and children) (Billigmeier 1985, 13).

The archaeological evidence from pre-Mycenaean Greece, as with Middle Minoan Crete, shows a society of smaller family units. What domestic architecture remains, especially at sites such as Dorion-Malthi in Greece, shows small houses with work and storage rooms sufficient for small families. Early Helladic burials were mainly of two types: simple inhumations of individuals, and groups of people cast down into chasms. These latter group burials hardly seem like good evidence for the use of family burial plots. Even the more elaborate cemeteries at Chalkis on the island of Euboia had individual burials (Vermeule 1972, 43). During the Middle Helladic period, although single inhumations remained the norm, sometimes as many as three people could share a single grave—a possible indication of familial units. Even more indicative of a family structure was a new type of burial, in which both children and adults could be buried inside actual houses, either under the floors, between or behind walls, or in passages (Vermeule 1972, 79). Such intramural infant burial was not uncommon in the ancient Near East, but persons of all ages buried within houses do give evidence for family units being attached to specific domestic dwellings.

The idea that some notion of an extended family, at least in the sense of a dynasty, was in place in the Late Helladic/Mycenaean period is attested to by the shaft graves at Mycenae (see chapter 4). It is probable that the smaller groups of individuals in the individual cists were nuclear family members, such as a husband and wife. When Schliemann first discovered a gold-covered man, woman, and two children in one of the cists, he was convinced that he had discovered the tomb of Agamemnon, Cassandra, and their children (see chapter 3). Although the names were a bit fantastic, the notion of familial connection among the individuals found is certainly logical. Those buried in the two grave circles at the site, then, may have been one large, extended family, buried over the course of several generations. The rise of tholos tombs throughout Greece in the following Late Helladic II (see chapter 4) also suggests that Mycenaean Greece was dominated by fairly affluent families who could afford the time and wealth necessary to construct such huge funerary structures for their members.

By the late Mycenaean period (fifteenth through thirteenth centuries), the palaces give some evidence that at least royal dynasties/extended families existed, although whether this principle affected the lower classes is difficult to tell. Further information about familial units is offered in the Linear B tablets, where the earliest Greek kinship terms are found. Pylos tablet An 42, discussing women who belong to the ki-ri-te-wi-ja group (see chapter 8), records the professions of both the mothers and fathers of the group members. The ki-ri-te-wi-ja seem to have been cult functionaries of some sort, and it is significant that all of their parents are either slaves of deities (= cult functionaries) or smiths. This would indicate that certain professions, such as priestess, were inherited along family lines, much as in later Greek society (see below) (Ventris and Chadwick 1959, 166–167; Billigmeier and Turner 1981, 8).

Of particular interest in the Linear B tablets are the uses of patronymics and metronymics. A patronymic is a name composed of one's father's name. Thus, Paul Anderson is Paul, son of Anders. Patronymics were one of the most common means of indicating family relationships throughout Western civilization, and they are still used in Iceland. Metronymics are far less common; in fact, the word *metronymic* is not even listed in many dictionaries. Both types of names appear in the Linear B tablets. At the uppermost levels of society, patronymics were in place, as in the case of the "Follower" (see chapter 7), Alektruon Ete-woklewehios, Alektruon son of Eteocles (Billigmeier and Turner 1981, 6). Some patronymics were used for the lower classes as well, but metronymics were far more common in these classes. Children of workers were identified with their mothers' names, or, more likely, their mothers' trades or even ethnicities, thus "George, son of the Weaver-Woman." Some have argued that these women were either slaves or refugees, working in the Mycenaean kingdoms separated from their men. Thus, the metronymics may derive from the absence of fathers after whom to name the children. Such a hypothesis is strengthened by evidence from Pylos tablet Vn 1191, which lists women identified by male names in the genitive (meaning essentially "possession of"), such as Helen (wife of) Menelaus. Such means of identification (identifying women merely by the genitive form of a father's or husband's name) were extremely common in Greece in the historic period; one might think of Margaret Atwood's *The Hand-maiden's Tale*, recounted by Offred, Fred's handmaid. The fact that this practice appears in the tablets suggests that already by this time, wives were understood to "belong" to their husbands, and a patriarchal form of marriage and family was in place. Only in unusual circumstances would a child in a patriarchal system be identified in reference to a mother.

Unfortunately, we do not possess very much information about "normal" families from the Linear B tablets. The tablets were concerned with palatial affairs, and matters of the average family were essentially kept private. Therefore, we do not know much about the composition and workings of the average family, although the tablets do attest to husband-wife, mother-son, mother-daughter, mother-son, and father-son relationships (Billigmeier 1985, 15). Although it might be too much to ask to find further familial terms in the tablets, such as cousin, grandmother, and uncle, the terms that are mentioned refer to nuclear-style families at most, single-parent families at least.

The evidence from archaeology and literature suggests that the compact, nuclear family remained the norm in Greek society during the Dark Age, even during the massive upheavals that marked the end of the Bronze Age. For a long time, it was believed that Homeric-style warriors left Greece to invade and colonize territories around the Mediterranean, such as Cyprus, and that apparently, women just disappeared from the equation. However, excavations in Cyprus and artistic representations of the Dark Age relocations show that families relocated together. In Egypt, the Medinet Habu reliefs decorating the funerary temple of Ramses III show Egyptian battles against the Sea Peoples (see chapter 4) who invaded Egypt around 1186 B.C.E. (see Image 6.4). In the midst of all the fighting and drowning are depictions of families—men, women, and children—in carts, not war chariots, apparently in the process of household relocation.

The fact that such families populated the later Mediterranean settlements is evident at the Cypriot site of Maa-Palaikastro, settled by the Greeks in 1190 B.C.E. Here, excavators have discovered not only Mycenaean pottery typical of

6.4 Medinet Habu Relief detail (Erich Lessing/Art Resource)

the period, but also Greek cookware and loom weights, implements traditionally used by women. As cooking vessels are customized to accommodate the
food to be prepared in them, cooking vessels are highly indicative of the ethnicity of the user. The presence of Greek cooking pots indicates the presence of
Greek women (Bunimovitz and Yasur-Landau 2002, 216). So, Mycenaean families literally packed up their households and moved across the sea. The small
size and individual kitchen and storage spaces of the houses at Maa also attest
to the presence of nuclear families.

The Homeric-era family, as a possible example of Late Bronze Age, Dark
Age, or even Archaic society, could be quite extensive, including not only parents, siblings, and in-laws, but also distant ancestors. This is brought into
sharp relief in Book 6 of the *Iliad,* both in the confrontation between Diomedes
and Glaukos (see above, in the section about xenia) and in the meeting of Hector and Andromachê.

As stated above, both Diomedes and Glaukos identified themselves to each
other by means of long genealogies stretching back several generations.
Clearly, a warrior's (or perhaps any man's) sense of identity derived from his
place within a lineage, and he conceived of his functional family as comprising
as many generations as could be recalled. Furthermore, the actions of earlier

generations (grandfathers in this instance) continued to affect the warrior's interactions with others. One might say that a strong vertical bond existed in the Homeric family.

Strong horizontal bonds also existed, especially between husband and wife and between in-laws. When Hector returns to Troy to see his family, he is confronted, in escalating degrees of affection (Arthur 1981, 27 ff.), by his mother, brother, sister-in-law, and wife. The last instance is especially compelling for the evidence it gives concerning the Homeric family. Andromachê, imploring Hector not to go back to the battle, laments that Achilles has already killed every other member of her family: father, seven brothers, and mother (of a broken heart). In the end, she has no family but Hector. Although pathos is the emotion of the moment, Andromachê (and through her, the author, Homer) does reveal here that she has no other clan to turn to, and that with Hector dead, she will be utterly alone. Aunts, uncles, and cousins do not seem to figure into Homeric families, and Andromachê seems to suggest that even her connections to her family-in-law would be severed upon her husband's death. Later, when Hector is dead, the women come out to mourn him, Helen last of all confessing (*Iliad*, 24.767–772):

> But never have I heard from you a word mean or degrading,
> but if someone else in the halls should rebuke me
> of my sisters- or brothers-in-law, or their well-dressed wives,
> or mother-in-law—but my father-in-law was always gentle, as a father ought—
> then you rebuking them held off those words
> by your own kindness and gentle words.

This speech also gives a good indication of the people who constituted a woman's family in the Homeric world. These were her lord/husband, her brothers- and sisters-in-law, the wives of her brothers-in-law, and her mother- and father-in-law. In short, the family was constructed around her husband: his parents, his siblings, and their spouses. In this quote, Helen's own family is entirely absent. Although this could easily be blamed on circumstances (Helen having run off to Troy), it does agree with later conceptions of the family in ancient Greece, where women were somewhat cut off from their natal families upon marriage (see below). What is surprising in Priam's family as here described is that even Hector's married sisters still live in the palace, although, once again, this may be due to extreme circumstances. In all respects, the family presented in Homer conforms to the image we receive from the Late Archaic Age and Classical period as well.

Archaic Age and Classical Period. The ancient Greek construction of the family existed on both macrocosmic and microcosmic levels. On the macro level, the Greeks recognized the previously mentioned institutions of phylê, phratry (see above), and genos (or clan)—groups of (aristocratic) males who supposedly shared a common ancestor and on whom each city's political system was based. Of these groupings, only the genos (and maybe the phratry) may actually have been kin-based, in the sense of a large, extended family. The different genê (pl. of genos) worshipped their ancestors as well as Zeus Herkeios and Apollo Patroos (gods of clans), thus binding them together into a somewhat artificial family unit. The genê then monopolized certain political and priestly positions. For example, before the days of Solon, only the noblest genê, called Eupatridai ("well-fathered"), could hold the office of archon in Athens (see chapter 7). Between Solon and Kleisthenes most of the political prerogatives of the Eupatridai were removed. Some noble clans did, however, manage to retain their exclusive priestly duties, with the Eumolpidai and Kerykes, the high priests and priestesses of the Eleusinian Mysteries, being an excellent example (see chapter 8).

On the micro level were the syggeneia, the anchisteia, and the oikos, those familial units composed of blood relatives and augmented through marriage and adoption. The syggeneia consisted of all relatives on both sides of the family as far as anyone could actually remember or trace the bloodline. Thus, your fifth cousin twice removed on your mother's side would be a member of your syggeneia, although you may not know this person.

The anchisteia was the group of people who actually related to each other as family. The word means "closest," and the anchisteia usually included family up to either first cousins once removed or possibly even second cousins. A funerary law from late fifth-century Keos defined the immediate female members of a dead man's family, and thus those who were legally prescribed to formal mourning, as "the mother and wife and sisters and daughters, and in addition to these not more than five women, the daughters' children and cousins, and no one else" (Lefkowitz and Fant 1992, 59). These family members had certain responsibilities to each other as established by both custom and law, including burying the family's dead and providing dowries for females (Pomeroy 1997, 19).

The oikos was literally the household, and consisted of all the family members who lived together in one house. As the Greeks were patriarchal and patrilocal, this household would belong to the oldest male family member and would consist of him, his wife, their sons and the sons' wives and children, and unmarried daughters. Except in cases of adoption, males remained in their oikos for life, but females switched oikoi upon marriage. Children were understood to belong to their father's oikos, providing for an interesting twist on modern practices: If a couple divorced, the children stayed with the father and his family; they did not go with the mother. In the case of widowhood, if the wife had given birth to at least one son, she was permitted to remain in her husband's oikos instead of going back to her own family. If she remarried, however (which was generally expected of young widows), she would leave her children to her first husband's family, unless they were specifically adopted (through the will of their father) by the next husband, who may have belonged to the first husband's anchisteia anyway.

Beyond just blood relations, there were other practical considerations relating to the oikos and anchisteia. At the most concrete level, this concerned land: Land belonged not to individuals but to families, and it was transmitted by inheritance down the oikos generations. In much of Greece, this went exclusively through the paternal line: Women could not inherit or transmit land (save for epikleroi and their kind). In Sparta, though, women could and did own land, and transmission of familial estates went through both lines.

But land was not the only resource "managed" at the familial level, for occupations were also often transmitted down family lines. This must not be confused with the situation at the end of Late Antiquity, when sons were legally obliged to take up their fathers' trades. Rather, in ancient Greece, it was seen as the responsibility of the parents to train their sons (and frequently daughters) in a trade—generally the one the parents knew best, which was, of course, their own. Such practices were established by law: In Athens, Solon regulated that a father who had not taught his son a trade could not expect in old age to be cared for by that son (Plutarch's *Life of Solon*).

Children were not required to take up the familial trade, especially in Hellenistic times, but it was common and certainly expedient for them to do so. This was especially the case when families were internationally renowned for their trade, such as politicians, athletes, artists, physicians, and philosophers, or when trades were tied to individual families, as with priesthoods. Such trades went through both paternal and maternal lines. For example, one of the most famous athletes of the fifth century B.C.E. was Diagoras of Rhodes, a boxer. Three of his sons were also athletic victors: Damagetos in the pankration (a no-holds-barred combination boxing/wrestling sport), Akusilaos in boxing, and Dorieus in both. Two grandsons of his were also Olympic victors: Peisirodos and Eukles, both in boxing. Peisirodos was the son of Diagoras's daughter Pherenicê, and Eukles was the son of his daughter Kallipateira. Thus, the second generation of athletes was seen to have derived their prowess from their father, but the third generation through their mothers (Pomeroy 1997, 88).

In addition to the practical aspects of the oikos—people living together in a household and sharing familial bonds—there were theoretical aspects: the manifestation of a paternal line, the descendants of revered ancestors, and the owners of certain properties. In this way, the oikos actually existed beyond just the immediate members of the household, and there was a need, almost at a religio-civic level, to perpetuate the oikos. To have one's oikos die out was seen as the ultimate tragedy in ancient Greek life. As early as the seventh century B.C.E., Hesiod (*Theogony*, ll. 603–607) noted:

> He, fleeing marriage and the baneful works of women,
> who wishes not to wed, destructive old-age comes upon him
> with no one to care for him; not lacking a livelihood
> while he lives, once dead his property is divided by his kinsmen.

Many Greek tragedies, especially the tales of Oedipus, have as their final end the utter destruction of the hero's household, and in the Late Classical law courts, men such as Timarchus could be brought to trial for squandering their paternal estate, thus impoverishing and endangering their oikoi. The oikos was the core of the polis; to endanger it not only threatened individual families, but also threatened the stability of the state. Furthermore, one important responsibility of the oikos was the maintenance of the reverence of ancestors. Should the oikos cease to exist, the ancestors would fall out of memory.

Also extremely important in ancient Greece was the notion that honors and disgraces ran through a family. On one level, this was both practical and readily explainable. The fact that, say, athletic honors ran in a family probably had a lot to do with the idea that athleticism ran in families (as in the case with Diagoras above). Along with what we would recognize as a genetic tendency toward speed or strength was the fact that excellent coaches, in the form of other talented family members, were readily available. As a modern parallel, consider how many movie stars are the children of actors, like Michael Douglas and Gwyneth Paltrow. A similar situation was in place for family priesthoods, which in some cases were the highest honors available in a polis.

Far more influential, though, were familial dishonors. On its most immediate level, the disgrace of one family member could harm the entire family. In Sparta, for example, not only were male cowards ostracized, but neither they nor their sisters were allowed to marry and reproduce, thus bringing an end to their oikoi: "In Lakedaimon everyone would be ashamed to take a coward with him to the mess hall, as would they all to be matched with him in wrestling . . . he must support the maidens of his household and explain to them why they are manless. He must suffer a hearth devoid of a wife, and he must pay a penalty for it. He must not wander about cheerfully nor imitate the innocent, or he must suffer blows from his superiors" (Xenophon, *Constitution of the Lakedaimonians*, 9.5).

On a practical level, political benefits could be stripped from the family of a criminal or debtor. In Athens, one who attempted to impose a tyranny or upset the laws was punished with kathapax atimia, "immediate loss of civil rights," for both himself and all his descendants, legitimate and illegitimate. Similar atimia devolved on state debtors. Those who died in debt passed that debt and the accompanying atimia along to their descendants, who could only have their rights reinstated by paying the debt or being adopted into another family (Pomeroy 1997, 85). Although that latter move could be economical, it led to the extinction of the oikos and was thus highly undesirable.

But by far the worst disgrace to come down the family ranks was that of ritual impiety, which left the family cursed. On one level, this could be seen as a simple pollution, such as the one that affected the female relatives of a recently dead person. The pollution was temporary, and had only short-term effects of the inability to socialize. By contrast, a family could acquire a very serious pollution to itself that would be remembered for generations. The best example is that of the Alcmaeonidai in Athens. In 632 B.C.E., several members of this family slaughtered Kylon, a would-be tyrant, while he was under the protection of a sanctuary (see chapter 8). Generations afterward, the family was seen as polluted, possibly contributing to the ostracism of its descendant Xanthippos "the Accursed" in 490 (Pomeroy 1997, 84).

In general, families of the Classical period were fairly close-knit, on both paternal and maternal sides. Up to three generations shared a house (and farm and/or occupation); brothers inherited land equally and sometimes chose to work it collectively. In spite of a woman's transfer to another oikos upon marriage, women kept in touch with their natal families. This is evident not only after widowhood or divorce, when a woman usually returned to her natal family, but also during marriage, when a woman would participate in funerary rituals for someone in the natal family or assist sisters or their children financially. As families were often associated with plots of land, they tended not to move around too much, and individual families were linked to specific regions for generations.

Hellenistic Era. Much of this changed in the Hellenistic era, when all forms of association were changed in the wake of new political structures. As mentioned above, the institution of the phratry was extinguished in the Hellenistic era. Families were certainly not dismantled, but the greater potential for travel and relocation that typified the Hellenistic era shook up the settled oikoi of the Classical period. It became far more common for a son, say, to leave the family farm to find work as a mercenary in Egypt or Afghanistan, to earn money and buy land there, and thus to establish a new oikos for himself on foreign soil, possibly with a foreign bride and a different conception of family. This began with Alexander himself, who dismissed the Greek ideal of monogamy and strengthened his political control over many of his new territories by marrying local princesses, such as the Sogdian princess Roxana.

Further blendings of local and Greek conceptions of the family are evident in Hellenistic Egypt, where Egyptian practices such as bigamy, polygyny, and sibling marriage came to influence the structure of the Greek family. The most famous example of this is the case of Cleopatra VII: Contrary to standard Greek tradition, but very much in line with the Egyptian tradition, Cleopatra was the official wife and consort of her younger brother, Pharaoh Ptolemy XII. This does not mean that they had sex and produced children together: The Egyptian pharaoh had a harem (although Ptolemy XII was probably too young to do much with his) for "normal" wives; his consort served as queen and joint ruler/administrator. Nevertheless, in western eyes, the brother and sister were seen as married, and upon the death of Ptolemy XII, Cleopatra was his exclusive heir.

The Military

Bronze Age. *Crete.* The study of militarism in Minoan Crete has always been plagued by paradoxes. The ancient Greeks believed that Crete under King Minos had ruled a thalassocracy—a naval empire—as attested to as late as in the works of Thucydides. However, Evans, who did support this notion, also believed the Minoans were an inherently peaceful society, not marked by the warlike aspect of their northern neighbors, an opinion emphasized by the lack of fortifications throughout the island. However, as early as the Early Bronze Age, Crete had several times more weapons than mainland Greece and the Cyclades combined (Branigan 1999, 88). However, the majority of these weapons were daggers and rather flimsy swords, none of which were especially fit for combat. What does it all mean?

With very rare exceptions, such as the Middle Minoan I villa at Aghia Pho-tia, there really were no fortified settlements in Minoan Crete. This strongly suggests that defense was not a major concern, probably indicating that (1) there was general stability among the urban and palatial centers of Crete, and (2) the sea helped to keep any other potential aggressors at bay (literally!). One must remember, though, that the extremely martial Mycenaeans (see below) also had few major defensive structures until the fourteenth century B.C.E.

In contrast to the martial Mycenaeans, though, the Minoans made no use of war imagery in their art. The scenes of hunting and battle endemic to Myce-naean art are strikingly absent in the Minoan repertoire. But, as Gates has ar-gued (1999), societies do not depict actual life in their art; they depict items re-lating to their own values and aesthetics. The popularity of paintings of shepherdesses in eighteenth-century France does not mean that the nobility all went out and tended sheep (with the exception of Marie Antoinette), but that they liked the *idea* of the pastoral life. Therefore, the absence of martial scenes in Minoan art may reflect Minoan tastes rather than life, and it cannot be used as evidence of noncombative tendencies in their society.

In the end, based on an assessment of the fighting capabilities of Minoan swords and daggers and the funerary contexts in which they are found, along with the overall lack of interest in military art and trappings, Peatfield (1999) has suggested that "militarism" in Minoan society was mainly an elite affair. Daggers have come to light in several tombs, and they routinely appear on male figurines, suggesting that the dagger was both a status symbol and marker of social identity, whether or not it was actually used in knife fights. The idea that daggers could have been used as actual weapons is apparent from their double-edged blades, more effort than necessary for paring knives (Peatfield 1999, 68). The various types of swords developed and supposedly used by the Minoans were slender rapier styles (the type used for thrusting rather than hacking). Much as in modern fencing, they could be effective in single combat, but they were hardly practical in full-scale combat, especially against cutlass-style weaponry.

Furthermore, in the Late Minoan funerary remains, swords appear in graves accompanied by jewelry, indicating the elite, or at least wealthy, status of the interred. Based on the class of the owner and the potential of the swords, Peat-field has suggested that "combat" in Minoan (or at least Knossian) society was a ritualized affair between members of an elite class, possibly even for reli-gious purposes. No one appears to have been using weapons to defend his or her life (Peatfield 1999, 71). This accounts for the prevalence of weapons in Mi-noan Crete along with the general absence of fortifications.

Cyclades. The situation was quite different in the Cyclades, where fortifica-tions appeared by the Early Bronze Age at Kastri on Syros, at Panermos and Spedos on Naxos, and at Phylakopi on Melos, and by the late Middle Bronze Age–early Late Bronze Age at Haghia Irini on Keos (Ducrey 1986, 21; Branigan 1999, 90; Barber 1999, 134). In truth, the early fortification walls were compara-tively flimsy in contrast to the "Cyclopean" walls of Mycenaean Greece, but they at least had visual impact, possibly enough to ward off potential aggres-sors. Those potential aggressors were probably other Cycladists; evidence of ships and trade (see chapter 5) indicate that Aegean residents traveled quite a bit among the various Cycladic islands. Large-scale combats were hardly the norm in the early Cyclades, though. Analyses of the ships suggest that they could transport only about twenty-five to thirty men, traveling at a speed of 6–12 mph (Branigan 1999, 91). Also, as no one would have wanted too many warriors to be out of town for too long (this would leave the town defenseless), this would have resulted in short, small-scale piratical raids, in which the different towns just attacked each other and went home. So, violence was common, but it was limited and local, probably enacted by part-time pirates who were really full-time farmers.

Evidence for larger combat scenarios is present in the frescoes at Thera, a Minoan colony but physically part of the Cyclades. The image in question is the Miniature Fresco in the West House, specifically the one entitled *Shipwreck and Landing Party*. In the lower part of the image, one sees naked (= dead) bodies in water next to ships still afloat. Above the scene is a rural village with small-scale architecture and residents in simple clothing. To the right is a line of soldiers carrying spears, animal-hide shields, and boar's tusk helmets (see chapter 9). The fact that none of the village folk seem overly concerned with the soldiers, and the fact that the soldiers are walking away from the town, suggest that whatever violence did/will occur is happening outside the village. The corpses in the sea may indicate that the soldiers are coming home after a successful battle. However, the soldiers' arms and armor are typical of the Mycenaeans, especially the boar's' tusk helmets. Minoan shields as they appear in the iconography were generally shaped like a figure-eight (see chapter 9). Therefore, it is possible that what we see here is some manner of early Greek infantry, making their way throughout the Aegean before the real conquest of Minoan territories in the fifteenth century B.C.E. One theory explaining the amazing wealth suddenly apparent in Mycenaean Greece at the time of the shaft graves (c. 1650) is that the early Greeks served as mercenaries in northern Africa; we may be seeing a depiction here of early Greek mercenary soldiers.

In the Late Helladic III period, the Cyclades came under the direct influence, if not control, of the Mycenaeans. This is evident in the copious imports of Mycenaean wares into the islands, as well as Mycenaean elements in Cycladic architecture, such as the megaron. Likewise, in the mid-thirteenth century, there was an intensification of fortifications in the Cyclades, occurring in tandem with similar developments on the mainland. Although the Theran frescoes do give evidence for Mycenaean soldiers possibly fighting in the Cyclades (although northern Africa is also likely) in the eighteenth century B.C.E., it appears that this military escalation did not occur in the Cyclades in the face of Mycenaean aggression, but as an extension of Mycenaean defensiveness at the end of the Bronze Age (Barber 1999, 134–138).

Greece.   As with the Cyclades, it is evident that the mainland had belligerence problems from very early on. The generally accepted theory concerning the first arrival of the Greeks in Greece (see chapter 4) is based upon a series of destructions—accompanied by a new style of pottery—evident at the dawn of the Early Helladic III period. Although these Indo-European newcomers came in with a literal crash, they seem to have calmed down a bit between the end of the Early Bronze Age and the middle of the Middle Bronze Age. Starting in the late Middle Bronze Age, though, the earliest stirrings of what would become Mycenaean civilization were accompanied by a renewed interest in violence. This is evident in the artwork of the shaft graves at Mycenae (see chapter 4), where aboveground commemorative stelai and goods buried with the deceased show a marked interest in aggression. Not only were the interred buried with weapons, but items such as knives were decorated with battle and hunting scenes. Clearly, violence, real or imagined, played an important role in the early Mycenaeans' sense of self and social identity.

Nevertheless, the apparent aggressiveness of the Mycenaean period was not consistent, and there was an evolution in militaristic ideology over the course of the Middle and Late Helladic periods. In the Middle Helladic, Grave Circle B at Mycenae (the older of the two grave circles) and a similar burial at Pylos were filled primarily with men. Furthermore, study of the physical remains has shown that these fellows were rather young when they died, in spite of the fact that they were in good health. These data, plus the interest in war-oriented art, suggest that the grave occupants were warriors who died in battle and were "rewarded" with an ostentatious and glorious burial (Acheson 1999, 99)

The purpose of this relatively prevalent warfare appears to have been for territorial acquisition (and the rewards that came with it) and for prestige. In fact, prestige was probably how the warriors were able to maintain their newly conquered territories, and so the intense interest in military paraphernalia probably had a lot to do with advertising one's martial status—there was a combined need to *be* a good warrior and be *known* as a good warrior. As Sigrid Deger-Jalkotzy put it, "The claim of social and political leadership, as well as the chance of accumulating wealth by monopolizing the access to the economic resources seems to have rested upon the performance of military excellence. Moreover the ostentation of military prowess was certainly prominent among those factors which shaped the lifestyle, the self-awareness and the corporate identity of those individuals who formed the upper social group(s) and who claimed to political leadership" (Deger-Jalkotzy 1999, 122).

Once one had acquired territory, though, it behooved one to find nonviolent means of keeping it. This was certainly easier on the knees. In the earlier years of the Late Helladic, the Mycenaeans did just that—they replaced military domination with domination through religious justification and a well-entrenched bureaucracy. This is evident in changes in elite burials. Although the late Middle Helladic burials focused on young male warriors, the early Late Helladic graves featured more women and children. Noble families, rather than individual warriors, were now being honored (Acheson 1999, 99). Such nobility and bureaucracy were embodied in the palaces themselves, which were under the dominion of the wanakes (pl. of wanax). As stated in chapter 7, the wanax had only a minimal military component to his duties, which were more geared toward religious function. In such a way, the land was ruled not through military force, but through the auspices of a divinely sanctioned king, whose religious role no doubt encouraged obedience from his constituency. Furthermore, this wanax maintained close social bonds with his bureaucracy, the nobility, probably through communal feasting and drinking in the megaron (see above, in the section on symposia). The combination of divine right and a closely bonded administration lessened the need for ostentatious display of militarism.

At this point, then, Mycenaean Greece went from having a military based on individual warriors to having one based on a regular army. The Linear B tablets show that the palaces kept track of weapon and armor production, chariot maintenance, and muster rolls. But the army as such (as well as the navy) was just another piece of the bureaucracy, under the auspices of the lawagetas, who, while socially significant, was still below the wanax in status. Although some art did depict militaristic themes, such as in the subsidiary Southwestern Building at Pylos (Davis and Bennet 1999, 108 ff.), the "official" art program sponsored by the palaces was far more pacific in nature, featuring lovely ladies, fantastic creatures, and banquet scenes.

Such a system works well during periods of peace and stability, two words that do not mark the end of the Mycenaean period. The fact that the threat of violence increased toward the end of the Late Helladic period was evident in a new concern to fortify the palace centers such as those at Mycenae. These were real fortifications, much sturdier than those of the Cyclades, containing access to water and room for the general population. By the end of the Mycenaean period (Late Helladic IIIC), the palaces were burnt down and the hierarchy apparently dismantled, with the last of the Linear B tablets referring to increased calls for rowers and "watchers of the coasts." At this time, there was a reversal in the militaristic downplay of the preceding centuries, as once again the welfare of the state came into the hands of the warriors, now relying more on personal valor than on the efficient operations of the palatial machinery. Military scenes again took precedence in art, such as on the Late Helladic IIIC Warrior Vase (see Image 9.31). Such a world fraught with violence and dependent on the personal fighting prowess of its heroes is very much in line with Homeric society, which was primarily based on the realities of life at the end of the Bronze Age.

Dark and Early Archaic Ages. The evidence from Egypt and Palestine, such as the Medinet Habu reliefs mentioned above, shows that at the end of the Bronze Age many Greeks went off into the world to seek their fortunes as mercenaries—often bringing their families with them. Thus Greek cohorts like the Peleset (see chapter 4), one of the tribes composing the Sea Peoples, originally attacked Egypt on behalf of the king of Libya. Later, they went to work for the Pharaoh, settling in southern Palestine to maintain the region for Egypt. Such soldiers brought many aspects of Greek military life with them, such as greaves, but they also borrowed elements from their new neighbors, such as scop (scale) armor. Eventually, these mercenary-settlers so thoroughly merged with the indigenous populations that all traces of their Greek origins were lost.

Nevertheless, many Greeks also stayed in Greece after the fall of the Bronze Age. For this period, some of our best evidence for military culture is the Homeric epics, which show the armies to be composed primarily of aristocrats: nobles fighting under the auspices of individual princes, themselves under the authority of a "high king"—the wanax. In the *Iliad*, Agamemnon, "King of Men," was the high king and general-in-chief of the Greeks. He received the greater share of booty, even though he was not necessarily the best fighter (who was, of course, Achilles). So, in Book 1 (ll. 163–168), Achilles complains:

> Never do I have a prize equal to yours, whenever the Achaeans
> sack the well-peopled city of the Trojans,
> although my hands took on a greater part
> of furious warfare. But when the apportioning comes,
> to you goes the greater prize; but with some small, dear thing
> I return to the ships, when I'm weary of fighting.

Thus, status in this society depended not on good fighting, but on birth and possessions. Under Agamemnon were the kings of Greece, such as Achilles, Odysseus, and even Agamemnon's brother Menelaus. These in turn brought fighting men from their territories: Achilles, for example, brought his subjects the Myrmidions, who fought under Achilles and obeyed his orders, not those of Agamemnon. So it would seem that the chain of command went only one link at a time. Agamemnon more or less (often less) controlled the princes, while they controlled their subjects rather independently of the high king.

The various princes had different reasons for going to Troy. Menelaus had to win back his wife and punish the Trojans for taking her. Agamemnon, as wanax, had to care for the concerns of his brother and subject Menelaus. Other warriors went for the glory and booty to be won. As Sarpedon and Glaukos discuss in Book 12 of the *Iliad*, they receive the status of kings in Lykia in exchange for their feats of daring on the front lines. In short, individual soldiers were seeking prestige for themselves, and so they had to accomplish impressive feats independently on the battlefield. Fighting, then, was predominantly one-on-one during this period, hero against hero, with the winner receiving honor for killing his opponent (and probably ultimately enslaving that opponent's wife).

Contemporary with the Homeric epics, though, a revolution was occurring in Greek military organization. Starting in the eighth century B.C.E., to judge from archaeological remains (see chapter 9) and the poetry of the time, the every-man-for-himself style of warfare was giving way to hoplite warfare. A hoplite was a heavily armed soldier, usually clad in helmet, chest plate, possibly greaves, and, most importantly, a new style of shield. He was armed with two spears and, as a last defense, a short sword. It was the shield specifically that brought about the revolution. Before this, the usual shield had been large and extremely unwieldy, hanging from a strap around a person's neck and which he maneuvered with an arm that had to support much of the shield's weight. By contrast, the new, round shield had two straps on the interior, at-

6.5 Chigi Vase (Hirmer Fotoarchiv)

taching to the elbow and the hand, making the shield much easier to hold and maneuver.

There was, however, one slight problem: The shield covered the left side of the body and went just past it, but it left the right side of the body exposed. To compensate, the soldier had to stay as close as possible to the soldier on his right, to protect his right side with the left overhang of his comrade's shield. This created a need for order in battle, as lines and ranks had to be maintained for the protection and safety of the troops. So the Greeks came to fight in phalanx formation, with lines of men (usually around eight) standing close enough together that the shield of one covered the man next to him, several ranks deep. Such is the style of fighting portrayed on the seventh-century Chigi Vase (see Image 6.5), and such is the description we get from Tyrtaios, a poet of the same century. In fragment 11, he writes:

> For those who endure, standing by each other,
> going into hand-to-hand combat and the front lines,
> very few die, preserving the host behind them.
> The virtue of fleeing men is totally destroyed;
> no one would ever finish telling of these things:
> how many shames he suffers, the evils existing for this man.

For it is appealing to pierce the mid-back
of a fleeing man in dreadful war,
but disgraced is the corpse lying in the dust
with the point of a spear running through his back.
But let one stand fast, holding with both feet
firmly planted on the ground, biting his lips.
Thighs and knees below, and chests and shoulders
covered over by the belly of the broad shield.
In the right hand let him extend the mighty spear,
let him shake the dread crest upon his head.
Accomplishing mighty deeds let him learn to fight,
nor may he stand far from the missiles, holding his shield.
But one going close in combat, let him seize a man
with his long spear, or attacking with a sword.
And going foot-to-foot and shield-to-shield,
crest-to-crest and helm-to-helm
and heart-to-heart let him fight drawing near his man,
seizing him with sharp sword or long spear.
And you, O light-armed ones! Crouching beneath another's shield
cast your large boulders,
hurling smooth javelins against them,
standing by the hoplites.

For all its interdependence, though, hoplite warfare was still quite aristocratic. Each warrior had to provide his own armor and weapons, which were extremely expensive; only the wealthy could afford to fight. Slightly lower classes of fighters filled the ranks of the light-armed soldiers mentioned by Tyrtaios. They wore less armor, if any at all, and their arms consisted of slingshots and other simple weapons. Armies, nevertheless, were generally composed of the upper class, and for many years, fighting as a hoplite was a requirement for full citizenship, producing effective oligarchies (see chapter 7).

Classical Period. This new style of fighting radically changed the approach to warfare. Individual displays of heroism, which had been the core of Homeric battle, were the bane of the phalanx—no one was likely to appreciate having the fellow to his right racing off after the enemy and leaving his spear arm exposed. So the heroic ethos changed from one of individual prowess to one of group identity. It also created a need for training, as people are seldom able just to fall into and maintain the ranks of phalanx warfare. A certain amount of group training became necessary.

As discussed above in the section on age, different poleis took different approaches to this need for training. The Spartans, the most militaristic of the Greeks, made military training a lifelong process for males, starting at age seven in the agogê, graduating from the krypteia at age nineteen or twenty, being on active military duty through the thirties, and being on military call up until age sixty. For most other poleis, the process was far less rigorous (which, of course, is why the Spartans could usually beat them). For the Athenians, for example, group military training took place in the ephebeia, between ages seventeen and nineteen, when boys learned military drills and formations as well as literature and history. Upon "graduation" from the ephebeia, the Athenian boys went to the shrine of Aglauros on the Acropolis and took a vow to protect their homeland. The wording of this vow has been preserved in a fourth-century inscription:

> I shall not disgrace my sacred weapons nor shall I desert my comrade at my side, wherever I stand in the ranks. I shall fight in defense of both sacred and secular things and I shall not hand down a fatherland that is reduced in size, but one that is larger and stronger as far as in me lies and with the assistance of all. I shall be obedient to those who on any occasion are governing prudently and to the laws that are established and to any that in the future may be wisely established. If anyone tries to destroy them, I shall resist both as far as in me lies and with the assistance of all, and I shall honor the sacred rites that are ancestral. These gods are witnesses: Agraulos [sic], Hestia, Enyo, Enyalios, Ares and Athena Areia, Zeus, Thallo, Auxo, Hegemone, Heracles, and the boundary-markers of the fatherland, the wheat, barley, vines, olive trees and fig trees. (Translation by Garland 1990, adapted)

The comparatively little training non-Spartans received in ancient Greece casts into sharp relief the different understanding they had of the idea of an army. Before the late Classical and Hellenistic periods, there was no such thing as a professional army outside of Sparta (where there was no other official industry). Elsewhere, soldiers were literally amateurs. Men had their various employments, usually farming for someone of hoplite status, and they took up military duties only during times of war. Granted, for the Greeks this was almost perpetual, but the idea was that any individual Greek male was first and foremost a farmer, merchant, potter, etc., and a soldier only on special occasions. There was no such thing as a professional army, in terms of either long-term commitment or payment (which is another reason hoplites had to be well-off financially). Any "payment" received by soldiers was in the form of booty—not too different from Homeric days, really. One effect of this amateur nature of the soldiers was that wars generally were not held during busy farming seasons. Wars were scheduled around other industries and generally took place during agricultural downtimes.

Until the fifth century B.C.E., then, warfare was remarkably classist. Only those who could afford a full hoplite complement could fight in the ranks, although it was less so for the light-armed fighters. Slaves were prohibited from fighting at all except under really bad circumstances. This elitist regime started breaking down, primarily in Athens, at the dawn of the fifth century in response to a new influx of money and two full-scale Persian invasions (see chapter 4). The new influx of money came from the Laurion silver mines, when a new vein of metal was discovered. After debating what to do with the new funds, Themistocles convinced the polis's assembly to invest in a naval fleet. This fleet could not only ameliorate trade, he contended, but it could help to defend the city in times of war. At the Battle of Salamis in 479 B.C.E., this navy thoroughly routed the Persians, saving the day and effectively instigating Athens's sea-based empire. Henceforth, Athens was a naval power.

So, what did this mean on a social level? As stated above, it took money to be a soldier, to invest in armor and weapons. It took no money whatsoever to use an oar. As the need for oar-based warships increased, the lower classes had an opportunity not only to get jobs, but to get jobs defending Athens. Suddenly, *all* members of society (males, at any rate) were involved in the defense of the homeland. As military service was accepted as an important component of civic status, the rise of the navy increased the military contributions of the lower classes, thus increasing their participation and rights in government. A revolution in warfare led to a revolution in class ideology.

Professionalism.   By the fifth century B.C.E., notions of full-time or professional soldiers started to play a role in the Greek military. This started with light-armed mercenaries from the "fringes" of the Greek world. Crete was famous for its archers, as was Scythia, and Thrace provided peltasts—soldiers with short swords and small shields. These mercenaries, probably landless, lower-class residents in their own poleis, sold their services throughout Greece. According to Thucydides, a contingent of Thracian peltasts was originally supposed to go along with the Athenians on the Sicilian Expedition. They arrived late, and they cost a drachma each per day (quite expensive at the time), so the Athenian Assembly just decided to send them home (Sage 1996, 152).

By the fourth century, professionally trained troops were definitely coming into fashion. The vanguard of this development was Thebes, which defeated Sparta at the Battle of Leuctra in 371, thus ending the Spartan military glory days. The most famous "professional" soldiers of the Late Classical period were the Theban Sacred Band. There is some debate as to when this institution first came into being, although evidence for them mainly exists for the fourth century, fighting against both the Spartans and the Macedonians. According to Plutarch in his *Life of Pelopidas* (18–19):

> They say that Gorgidas first formed the Sacred Band from 300 picked men, for whom the city provided training and maintenance while they inhabited the Cadmeia, and because of this the band was called "of the city." For at that time acropoleis were, reasonably, called cities. And some say that this corps was composed of lovers and beloveds . . . [for] a corps bound together by amorous affection is indissoluble and unbreakable, since the lovers regard the beloved with affection and the beloveds are ashamed to disgrace their lovers; they stand fast together in danger . . . It was natural, then, that the Band was called "Sacred," as even Plato called the lover a god-inspired friend. It is said the band remained undefeated until the Battle of Chaeronea.

Chaeronea, the great battle between Philip II of Macedon and the Greeks headed by Athens and Thebes, was a watershed in Greek history. It ended Greek independence, as the poleis came under the rather direct hegemony of

Macedon. The institution of the polis itself started to unravel as Greece came to be subsumed into a larger political, and cultural, entity. The Sacred Band was killed off forever, as was the entire institution of hoplite warfare. In place of the amateur, heavily clad, heavily armed soldiers, Philip, and Alexander after him, made increased use of well-trained, light-armed troops, still fighting in phalanx formations. The heavy hoplite shield was replaced with a lighter one; the spears and sword were replaced with the sarissa, a pike ranging from 16 to 24 feet in length, made of wood and balanced by an iron spear tip at one end and an iron butt at the other. As one might imagine, considerable choreography and trained maneuvering were required for the use of this weapon.

Furthermore, especially under Alexander, the fighting was carried much farther afield than in earlier periods. During the Classical period, most battles were relatively close to home. The Spartans could travel up to Attica, burn the fields, fight the battle, and be home again easily within a month. This ceased to be the case when Alexander's troops were fighting along the Kashmir. To be a soldier during this period inherently implied professional/full-time/paid status, insofar as it was functionally impossible to travel with the armies and hold any other type of job. Thus, between the necessary training and the time/travel commitment, professional armies completely replaced the amateur armies of earlier periods. The flip side of this, of course, was that the average man on the street ceased being a soldier. Put simply, there was a functional demilitarization of day-to-day society. The former farmer-soldier was replaced by the farmer on the farm and the soldier out abroad.

The extensive travel died down some during the Hellenistic period, when armies were linked to empires that had established boundaries. In the Late Classical tradition, these armies were professional, paid, and trained by the government. Such armies could be huge, containing up to 80,000 men (Sage 1996, xxvi). This, of course, put great pressure on the governments to pay so many bodies. Coinage was well in use by this time, which helped. Another common payment was the granting of land allotments based on military service. These allotments were called klerukhies, based on the Greek kleros, or royal lot. The idea was that, in return for fighting for the king, the king would grant a soldier the use of a plot of land technically owned by the crown. So long as the soldier remained in service, he kept the land. This allowed the soldier and his family to live off of their farm produce and to earn money, and it kept them bound to the area and to the king.

At first, this land returned to the crown upon the death of the soldier. A letter from mid-third-century Egypt from Asclepiades to Artemidoros in the Egyptian district of Arsinoë recorded the names of various soldiers who died and, thus, whose klerukhies had to be restored to the royal treasuries (Sage 1996, 222). The trade of being a soldier, however, was often inherited, and a son could pick up the klerukhy of his father upon the latter's death. After a while, the plots came to be seen as being inherited. At first this was only from father to son, but by the first century B.C.E., women were also eligible to inherit klerukhies, pretty much signaling the death knoll of the land-for-military-service system, as women did not serve in the military (Sage 1996, 222).

REFERENCES

Acheson, P. E. 1999. "The Role of Force on the Development of Early Mycenaean Polities." In Laffineur, R., ed. 1999. *Polemos: Le Contexte guerrier en Égée à l'Âge du Bronze.* Liège, Belgium: Université de Liège, 97–103.

Arthur, M. B. 1981. "The Divided World of *Iliad* VI." In Foley, H., ed. 1981. *Reflections of Women in Antiquity.* New York: Gordon and Breach Science Publishers, 19–44.

Barber, R. L. N. 1999. "Hostile Mycenaeans in the Cyclades?" In Laffineur, R., ed. 1999. *Polemos: Le Contexte guerrier en Égée à l'Âge du Bronze.* Liège, Belgium: Université de Liège, 133–138.

Billigmeier, J.-C. 1985. "Studies on the Family in the Aegean Bronze Age and in Homer." *Journal of Family History* 3 (3/4), 9–18.

Billigmeier, J.-C. and J. A. Turner. 1981. "The Socio-Economic Roles of Women in Mycenaean Greece: A Brief Survey from Evidence of the Linear B Tablets." In H. Foley, ed. 1981. *Reflections of Women in Antiquity.* New York: Gordon and Breach Science Publishers, 1–18.

Boedeker, D. D. 1974. *Aphrodite's Entry into Greek Epic.* Leiden, Netherlands: E. J. Brill.

Branigan, K. 1999. "The Nature of Warfare in the Southern Aegean during the Third Millennium B.C." In Laffineur, R., ed. 1999. *Polemos: Le Contexte guerrier en Égée à l'Âge du Bronze.* Liège, Belgium: Université de Liège, 87–95.

Budin, S. L. 2001. "Women." In Speake, G., ed. 2000. *Encyclopedia of Greece and the Hellenic Tradition.* London: Fitzroy Dearborn, 1727–1729.

Bunimovitz, S. and A. Yasur-Landau. 2002. "Women and Aegean Immigration to Cyprus in the Twelfth Century B.C.E." In Bolger, D. and N. Serwint, eds. 2002. *Engendering Aphrodite: Women and Society in Ancient Cyprus.* Atlanta: ASOR Publications.

Calame, C. 2001. *Choruses of Young Women in Ancient Greece: Their Morphology, Religious Role, and Social Functions.* Lanham, MD: Rowman & Littlefield.

Davis, E. N. 1986. "Youth and Age in the Thera Frescoes." *American Journal of Archaeology* 90, 399–406.

Davis, J. L. and J. Bennet. 1999. "Making Mycenaeans: Warfare, Territorial Expansion, and Representations of the Other in the Pylian Kingdom." In Laffineur, R., ed. 1999. *Polemos: Le Contexte guerrier en Égée à l'Âge du Bronze.* Liège, Belgium: Université de Liège, 105–120.

Deger-Jalkotzy, S. 1999. "Military Prowess and Social Status in Mycenaean Greece." In Laffineur, R., ed. 1999. *Polemos: Le Contexte guerrier en Égée à l'Âge du Bronze.* Liège, Belgium: Université de Liège, 121–131.

Dover, K. J. 1989. *Greek Homosexuality.* Cambridge, MA: Harvard University Press.

Ducrey, P. 1986. *Warfare in Ancient Greece.* New York: Schocken.

Garland, R. 1990. *The Greek Way of Life: From Conception to Old Age.* Ithaca, NY: Cornell University Press.

Gates, C. 1999. "Why Are There No Scenes of Warfare in Minoan Art?" In Laffineur, R., ed. 1999. *Polemos: Le Contexte guerrier en Égée à l'Âge du Bronze.* Liège, Belgium: Université de Liège, 277–283.

Glotz, G. 1921. *La Civilization minoenne.* Paris: N.p.

Golden, M. 1981. "The Exposure of Girls at Athens." *Phoenix* 35, 316–331.

———. 1990. *Children and Childhood in Classical Athens.* Baltimore: Johns Hopkins University Press.

Hanson, A. E. 1990. "The Medical Writers' Woman." In Halperin, D. M., J. J. Winkler, and F. I. Zeitlin, eds. 1990. *Before Sexuality: The Construction of Erotic Experience in the Ancient Greek World.* Princeton, NJ: Princeton University Press, 309–338.

Hodkinson, S. 2002. "Spartiate Landownership and Inheritance." In Whitby, M., ed. 2002. *Sparta*. New York: Routledge, 86–89.

Lefkowitz, M. R. and M. B. Fant. 1992. *Women's Lives in Greece and Rome: A Sourcebook in Translation*. Baltimore, MD: Johns Hopkins University Press.

Morpurgo Davies, A. 2002. "The Greek Notion of Dialect." In Harrison, T., ed. 2002. *Greeks and Barbarians*. New York: Routledge, 153–171.

Murray, O. 1994. "Nestor's Cup and the Origins of the Symposion." *Annali di Archeologia e Storia Antica*, vol. 1, 47–54.

———. 1999. *Sympotica: A Symposium on the Symposion*. Oxford, UK: Clarendon.

Olsen, B. 1998. "Women, Children, and the Family in the Late Aegean Bronze Age: Differences in Minoan and Mycenaean Constructions of Gender." *World Archaeology* 29 (3), 380–392.

Peatfield, A. 1999. "The Paradox of Violence: Weaponry and Martial Art in Minoan Crete." In Laffineur, R., ed. 1999. *Polemos: Le Contexte guerrier en Égée à l'Âge du Bronze*. Liège, Belgium: Université de Liège, 67–75.

Pleket, H. W., ed. 1969. *Epigraphica II: Texts on the Social History of the Greek World*. Leiden, Netherlands: E. J. Brill.

Pomeroy, S. B. 1975. *Goddesses, Whores, Wives, and Slaves: Women in Classical Antiquity*. New York: Schocken.

———. 1997. *Families in Classical and Hellenistic Greece: Representations and Realities*. Oxford, UK: Clarendon Press.

———. 2002. *Spartan Women*. Oxford, UK: Oxford University Press.

Preziosi, D. and L. Hitchcock. 1999. *Aegean Art and Architecture*. Oxford, UK: Oxford University Press.

Rabinowitz, N. S. 2002. "Excavating Women's Homoeroticism in Ancient Greece: The Evidence from Attic Vase Painting." In Rabinowitz, N. S. and L. Auanger. 2002. *Among Women: From the Homosocial to the Homoerotic in the Ancient World*. Austin: University of Texas Press, 106–166.

Rehak, P. 1995. "Enthroned Figures in Aegean Art and the Function of the Mycenaean Megaron." In Rehak, P., ed. 1995. *The Role of the Ruler in the Prehistoric Aegean*. AEGAEUM 11. Liège, Belgium: Université de Liège.

———. 2002. "Imag(in)ing a Woman's World in Bronze Age Greece: The Frescoes from Xeste 3 at Akrotiri, Thera." In Rabinowitz, N. S. and L. Auanger. 2002. *Among Women: From the Homosocial to the Homoerotic in the Ancient World*. Austin: University of Texas Press, 34–59.

Rehm, R. 1994. *Marriage to Death: The Conflation of Wedding and Funeral Rituals in Greek Tragedy*. Princeton, NJ: Princeton University Press.

Sage, M. M. 1996. *Warfare in Ancient Greece: A Sourcebook*. New York. Routledge.

Sissa, G. 1990. "Maidenhood without Maidenhead: The Female Body in Ancient Greece." In Halperin, D. M., J. J. Winkler, and F. I. Zeitlin, eds. 1990. *Before Sexuality: The Construction of Erotic Experience in the Ancient Greek World*. Princeton, NJ: Princeton University Press, 339–364.

Thorburn, J. E. 2001. "Hospitality." In Speake, G., ed. 2000. *Encyclopedia of Greece and the Hellenic Tradition*. London: Fitzroy Dearborn, 775–777.

Tod, M. N. 1985. *Greek Historical Inscriptions from the Sixth Century B.C. to the Death of Alexander the Great in 323 B.C.* Chicago: Ares.

Ventris, M. and J. Chadwick. 1959. *Documents in Mycenaean Greek: 300 Selected Tablets from Knossos, Pylos, & Mycenae*. Cambridge, UK: Cambridge University Press.

Vermeule, E. 1972. *Greece in the Bronze Age*. Chicago: University of Chicago Press.

CHAPTER 7

Politics

A ristotle, in his *Ethics* (VIII), claimed that there are three types of political rule, each with good and bad manifestations. Rule by one individual is, at best, a monarchy (*mono* = one, *arkhos* = rule) and at worst a tyranny. Rule by a few is an aristocracy (*aristos* = best, *kratos* = power); if gone bad, an oligarchy (*oligos* = few). Rule by many is a democracy, or mob rule. Variations of the rule of one individual existed throughout Greek history, from the kings and queens of the Bronze Age through the Archaic tyrants to the Hellenistic monarchies. In between, most Greek poleis had some manner of constitutional government, usually incorporating aspects of at least two of these aforementioned forms of government.

MINOAN CRETE: KINGS? QUEENS? PRIESTESSES? PRIESTS?

The presence of palaces on Crete since the Middle Bronze Age has led to the belief that some manner of ruler must have been present at least since the First Palace period. Sir Arthur Evans, inspired by the semidivine kings of the Near East, suggested that a "priest-king" ruled Crete, who reigned over the island from his palace at Knossos. However, Minoan iconography contains no pictures of recognizable kings. Evans originally identified such a monarch in a reconstructed fresco from Knossos known as the Lily Prince Fresco, which shows a striding male with an elaborate floral headdress (perhaps a crown) and jewelry. Since the original publication, though, it has been shown that the Lily Prince Fresco is actually an amalgam of three different frescos. The head with its fancy cap is actually the head of a sphinx. The two halves of the body—torso and legs—belong to females, which is evident from the white-painted skin (males were usually shown red; see chapter 9). The torso belongs to either a boxer or an acrobat; the legs are actually walking in the opposite direction from the torso. The entire fresco would have been dismantled and reconstructed long ago if not for the fact that Crete's largest travel agency had already adopted it as a logo. Nevertheless, with the removal of the "prince," the Minoan repertoire suddenly became king-free.

In its place, a new iconography of male authority figures was recognized. One example of this is a staff-bearing male recognizable on such Minoan items as the Chieftain Cup (see Image 7.1) and the Harvester Vase (see Image 4.1), both from Haghia Triadha. The other is an axe-bearing "priest-king" prominent on Minoan seal stones.

7.1 Chieftain Cup (Courtesy of Paul Butler)

The Harvester Vase shows a group of males carrying what appear to be win-nowing tools. One male has what looks like a rattle and has his head back and mouth open as if singing; perhaps he is the group musician. Another man with longer hair than the rest wears an elaborate shawl and carries a long staff over his shoulder. The length of his hair, and his costume, make him stand out as the older member of the group, most likely the authority figure in charge of the scene. The scene on the Chieftain Cup is a much simpler affair. A taller (per-haps older) youth with elaborate jewelry stands before a smaller (perhaps younger) youth wearing a helmet and carrying a sword over his shoulder. The older youth holds a long staff in his hand, which he appears to be handing over to the younger fellow, whose hand is outstretched to receive it.

This pose of holding out a staff appears frequently in the Minoan glyptic art (art engraved on seals), where deities hold such implements or hand them to humans. The use of this staff as a divine symbol suggests it has an authoritative meaning. In similar art from the Near East, deities often extend staffs to men to show their investiture with kingship. As such, it appears that in the Minoan art the staff is an emblem of either kingship or queenship, or the authority of the person holding it. For the Harvester Vase, the interpretation is fairly straightforward—the staff-bearing male is the leader of the troop. However, we have no idea if this translates into "king," "priest," or something else. Concerning the Chieftain Cup, Koehl has argued that the scene is the final act of an initiation ritual, in which the young boy "graduates" to adult status in the community (Koehl 1995, 99–110). Thus, the helmet and sword show the boy-turned-man's adult status in the community, and the staff indicates either the authority of the male completing the initiation or the symbolic bestowing of power and authority onto the initiate. Once again, though, although the staff seems to imply authority, the type of authority (king, priest, etc.) remains open to debate.

An equally ambiguous figure is the axe-bearing male in the Minoan glyptic. This character, clearly an older fellow as indicated by his frequently appearing with a beard, routinely appears dressed in a distinctive wrap-around outfit that goes from shoulders to feet—a much more elaborate affair than the usual Minoan male garb of a simple kilt. Sometimes this figure seems to be a deity, as he stands next to fantastic creatures such as griffins. Often, the seals depicting these men have a bull's head on the reverse. As bulls were sacred in Minoan Crete, the males are interpreted as priests, and the bulls—or other animals they are shown holding, such as birds—as sacrificial victims.

Some have suggested that the axe the man holds is similar to the later European scepter, serving, like the staffs, as an emblem of authority. If so, then we might have here a portrayal of Evans's priest-king, a religious functionary who also wields some manner of secular power. However, as this figure never appears with other people, and as he is sometimes shown with fantastic creatures, it is difficult to tell if he is intended as a human at all or if he is a deity, possibly "imported" from the east where both his style of clothing and axe were common. In the end, it is perhaps safest to suggest that the staff-bearing individual represents an authority figure in the Minoan repertoire, be it a deity or human, and the axe-bearing priest-king is a (perhaps divine) character in need of further study.

Of course, there is a certain irony to this search for the Minoan male authority figure, as most Minoan portrayals of authority figures were female. In fact, the notion of a Minoan matriarchy is still prevalent in some literature, although notions of *any* ancient matriarchies have now come under serious debate. Nevertheless, females, be they women or goddesses, do appear prominently in Minoan art, far outstripping males in most categories.

Amusingly, the most important datum in the search for Minoan royalty has

7.2 Throne Room at Knossos (Roger Wood/Corbis)

no human portrayals in it at all. This is the throne in the so-called throne room of the palace at Knossos (see Image 7.2). This elaborately frescoed room has a fancy, carved-stone throne attached to one of the walls. Griffins rest on either side of the throne. Evans originally believed that this was the priest-king's seat and that the griffins' presence confirmed that this king was somehow beyond mortal realms. However, parallels in Minoan art show that the character usually standing or seated between a pair of griffins was a female (Rehak 1995, 109–110). So it seems more likely that the person intended to sit on the Knossos throne was not a "king" but a "queen."

Of course, there are no easy answers in Minoan studies. The females portrayed between griffins, by the very fantastic nature of the griffins themselves, may have been goddesses. Who then, or what, actually sat on the Knossos throne? Perhaps the throne served as a seat for a deity, and no actual human sat there. Or, as is usually suggested, perhaps a priestess serving as a manifestation of a goddess sat on the throne during religious rituals. In such a

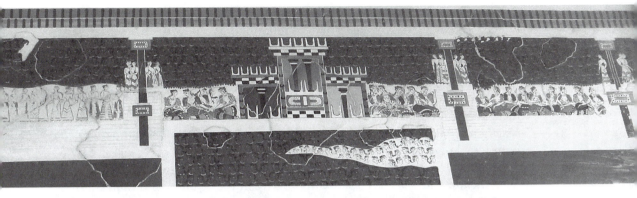

7.3 Above: Grandstand Fresco, Knossos (Kathleen Cohen/Herakleion Archaeological Museum)
7.4 Below: Sacred Grove Fresco, Knossos (Kathleen Cohen/Herakleion Archaeological Museum)

case, did the Minoans have a priestess-queen instead of the priest-king? Or did they have a secular queen who used divine imagery to enhance her perceived power and closeness to the gods, as Medieval patrons had their portraits placed in paintings of the Holy Family? Such questions are not yet resolved.

Nevertheless, other art confirms the power of women in Minoan society, although whether these artworks are to be understood as secular or religious is debatable. In the Knossos Grandstand Fresco (see Image 7.3) and Sacred Grove Fresco (see Image 7.4), as well as much glyptic art and the (later) Haghia Triadha Sarcophagus (see chapter 8), females have the positions of prominence and control (Davis 1995, 14). In the First Palace period's Sacred Grove Fresco, women and men congregate in what is identified as one of the Knossos palace courtyards. In the center of the scene are trees, possibly sacred in nature. Below the trees on the courtyard floor are fully depicted women (head to foot) with their arms raised in a gesture of praise and/or prayer. Past the trees, in the courtyard seating, are partially portrayed women; outside of this group are men, often only shown as faces in the fresco. At least part of this division of the sexes must be for ease of painting. Huge swaths of white paint are detailed with female faces, swaths of red with male. Nevertheless, one must note the detailed portrayals of women actually enacting the ceremony and the division of first-class and second-class seating between the females and males in the seating area. Clearly the women, and not just the "priestesses," have the higher status in this image.

In the Second Palace period's Grandstand Fresco, two groups of women are seated on either side of a tripartite shrine. Around these women, in what appear to be the "second-class" seats, are the faces of men, who are portrayed much smaller than the far more prominent females. The palatial setting argues against the notion that the females are goddesses, leaving us with the idea that their larger size compared to the men is due to their greater importance (a common artistic motif in both Egypt and ancient Turkey). As with the Sacred Grove Fresco, this Knossian image portrays a higher status for women than men.

In the end, we have little idea concerning who "ruled" the Minoans, or even if any one person did, king or queen. Tradition claims an especially important role for Knossos and its supposed king Minos, but throughout Minoan history the other palaces were often just as wealthy as Knossos. Some have argued that all the palaces belonged to the king of Knossos, who used them as bases of operation throughout the island. Others have argued that there must have been several rulers on the island, each controlling his/her own territory through their personal palaces. The fact that neither the conquest of Knossos circa 1450 B.C.E. nor its destruction around 1375 brought about the total downfall of Minoan civilization suggests that there was some independence among the different palatial regions, and even independence among the cities and villas. It is entirely possible that the notion of monarchy did not even exist in Minoan society.

BRONZE AGE GREECE

Mainland Greece went through a slow process of political evolution. This was partially due to the mountainous nature of the land, which made overland travel and communication difficult, and partially because of the destruction of the Early Helladic II civilization by the makers of Minyan Ware, giving Greece a somewhat later start than the palatial civilizations farther south. The independent nature of most early Greek settlements is summarized nicely by C. G. Thomas:

Permanent agrarian villages existing from 6000 B.C. continued as the foundation for the Bronze Age culture. The number of small villages grew steadily from Early Helladic to Late Helladic and, over time, some nucleation drew neighboring settlements together into cooperative activities. Until late in the Bronze Age, however, independent villages constituted community for the largest share of the population. Only in Late Helladic did centralization within larger regions begin; citadel centers emerged and enlarged their control over increasing numbers of villages, but even then towns and villages retained a pronounced identity. (Thomas 1995, 350)

As remarked in chapter 4, the Middle Helladic period was a "downtime" in Greece, especially in contrast to the contemporaneous brilliance of the island societies. Although we have no writing and little architecture to work with from this period, the political structure of the Middle Helladic in Greece is generally understood as a series of chiefdoms. A chiefdom was a loose political structure in which a chief held power through charisma and personal force. This chief served as political leader, high priest, and economic sovereign simultaneously, with all his/her assistants being loyal to the person of the chief directly. There were no departments, no official bureaucracy, no elected positions. The large Middle Helladic structures on the acropoleis (pl. of acropolis) of Tiryns and Mycenae were probably the homes of such chiefs (Wright 1995, 69; Laffineur 1995, 85).

It was only in the Mycenaean period, beginning in Middle Helladic III and continuing through the end of the Bronze Age, that kingdoms came into being on the mainland. Although this was most evident with the prestigious shaft graves at Mycenae, such kingdoms evolved at several sites throughout Greece, where local chiefs consolidated their power and established systems beyond the purely personal (Wright 1995, 64). Much of this consolidation probably came about through contacts with the Minoans and, later, the Near Eastern civilizations. These contacts provided the Greek chiefs with prestige items ranging from Minoan gold trinkets to imported Egyptian ivories and Levantine ostrich eggs. Such items already appeared in quantity in the shaft graves (Palaima 1995, 126). Possession of such objects created a visual distinction between the political elite (the "haves") and the rest of the population (the "have-nots") that made the elite seem distinct, superior, and thus worthy of political power.

The development of these various kingdoms throughout Greece probably continued rather peacefully, with the rise and spread of the tholos tombs serving as evidence for the growing power of several royal families (see chapter 4). This began to change in Late Helladic II, when expanding kingdoms started bumping into each other. From this point, the tholos tombs come to be associated with only the most powerful palaces, particularly in the south, and warrior tombs indicated a new (or renewed) interest in belligerence in the society (see chapter 6). Possibly to reaffirm their power, both to their own populations and to their neighbors, the Mycenaean monarchs began building palaces at Pylos, Mycenae, Tiryns, Thebes, Orchomenus, Athens, and the Menelaion at Sparta. By Late Helladic III, fortifications appeared at Mycenae, Midea, Tiryns, Argos, Geraki, Teikhos ("Wall") Dymaion, Kris, Thebes, and Athens. In addition to serving as strongholds in the face of potential danger, such monumental architecture was directed toward public display. Large ramparts directed the eyes toward the royal residences, which were intimately connected with the cult centers that helped to legitimize the king's authority (see below), to the open courts for public gatherings, and to the royal megara (pl. of megaron; see chapter 9) used for public feasts and drinking. Such displays assured the population of the economic and religious power of the king, as well as his potential for sharing his wealth and prestige (Wright 1995, 73–74).

Conveniently, from this point forward we have textual evidence from the Mycenaean palaces in the form of the Linear B tablets (see chapter 3). Although none of these documents spell out the political structure of the Mycenaean kingdoms in the style of the U.S. Constitution, the various functions and properties listed do give a helpful glimpse into their systems.

Two separate systems, a central and a local, operated in the Mycenaean kingdoms. At the top of the central hierarchy was the wanax (wa-na-ke), what we might call the king. In later Greek, this word is preserved as *anax* and was applied to King Agamemnon of Mycenae (*anax andron* = king of men) and to gods such as Zeus and Hermes. The fact that this individual owned at least three times as much land as any other person in the Linear B tablets, and that various industries, such as the purple dye industry, were described with the adjective wa-na-si-jo ("belonging to the king"), shows that this was a wealthy and important member of the Mycenaean hierarchy. To quote T. Palaima:

> No other title appears in quite so many diverse and important contexts. The *wanax* is the only person who undergoes or presides over an initiation (Un 2). The *wanax* is the only person who appoints (or buries?) another official . . . (Ta series). With the exception of the *lawagetas*, the *wanax* alone possesses a *temenos* [sanctuary], and his is three times bigger than the military leader's. The *wanax* alone at Knossos has a purple-dye workshop or workers or purple dye itself under his control. (Palaima 1995, 133)

What exactly the king's responsibilities were, though, remains in question. The fact that his role was at least partially religious comes across in tablet Un 2 from Pylos, which refers to the "initiation" or induction of the wanax, thus perhaps indicating that he was some manner of priest-king (Davis and Bennet 1999, 116). By contrast, there is minimal evidence for the king's role in military affairs, especially in contrast to the *lawagetas* (see below). Such evidence from the Linear B, combined with archaeological evidence such as the palaces and megara mentioned above, give us a picture of a wanax whose primary duty is to serve as intermediary between the people and the gods, while more mundanely organizing the local economies—a combination priest-king/CEO of sorts.

The presence of a queen is a more difficult matter. The adjective *wa-na-se-wi-jo/ja* appears at Pylos describing oil, and this appears to be the Linear B word for *queenly* or *queen's*. However, there is no independent attestation of a feminine form of *wanax* in the singular (a dual form, referring to two, does appear, but it probably refers to a pair of goddesses). The Linear B tablets recovered to date offer no evidence for a queen. By contrast, the iconography is replete with images of powerful women, especially those seated on thrones. However, these may have been an import from Minoan iconography, with far less meaning for the Mycenaeans. The fact that the well-attested wanax never appears in the art strongly hints that there was quite a divide between political realities and royal iconography.

The wanax was assisted in his bureaucratic functions by the e-qe-ta—the hequetai or followers. These fellows took care of the king's business throughout the kingdom, in return for which they received land and slaves (Pylos tablets Ed 317 and 847) (Chadwick 1988, 72). The wanax, aided by the hequetai, served as the centralized political body of Mycenaean Greece and Crete.

Different functionaries existed at the more local levels, people who were probably at least partially under the control or influence of the wanax. One of the most important local functionaries was the qa-si-re-u, or basileus, a word that would eventually come to mean "king" in Greek (from which we get such words as *basilica, basilisk,* and the herb *basil*). Unlike the wanax, several basileis (pl. of basileus) existed simultaneously, much like the later Homeric epics in which several basileis ruled, all loosely under the authority of Anax Agamemnon. As is typical with Linear B studies, we are not completely certain of the responsibilities of the basileis. Some tablets list them as associated with bronze workers and what appear to be worker collectives or workshops. In some respects, then, they functioned as foremen. But their roles went beyond just the economic, and the general understanding is that the basileus was the head of the local aristocracy, the local chieftain whose authority was minimized with the rise of the wanax (Palaima 1995, 124–125). After the fall of the Aegean Bronze Age palatial centers, the wanax fell from power and the basileis remained as the pinnacles of the now more localized societies, with the word thus coming to mean "king" in the Iron Age.

The various Mycenaean kingdoms were subdivided into administrative units. Pylos, for example, comprised sixteen such administrative units, each controlled by a ko-re-te and a po-ro-ko-re-te (tablet Jn 829) (Chadwick 1988, 73; Palaima 1995, 124). A ko-re-te was a sort of mayor, and the po-ro-ko-re-te was an assistant mayor or vice mayor. These individuals were bureaucrats in the purest sense, insofar as they kept close records of all happenings within their districts, for which they were presumably responsible before the wanax. Also important in the local hierarchies were the te-re-ta, or telestai, whom the tablets record as being large-scale landowners. At least forty-five of them owned territory in the region of Knossos (tablet Am 826), and they had some relationship with the local citizenry, called the damos (tablet Un 718) (Thomas 1995, 351–352).

This damos was the lowest level of "political" category mentioned in the Linear B tablets (as opposed to the lowest level of society, which were slaves; see chapter 6). This word continues in later Greek as the demos, or the "people," as in "We the People" and the word *democracy*. This was the local population, presumably landowning, probably residing in the spread-out villages of Greece and Crete. One functionary—the da-mo-ko-ro—may have been the local organizer or spokesperson for each of these individual villages.

The final person to consider in the Mycenaean hierarchy was the ra-wa-ke-ta, or lawagetas. The word seems to mean "leader of the laos," where the laos is a military contingent, what we might call a host, or local aristocracy. Like the wanax, there was only one lawagetas; he owned, or was responsible for, crafts-men and boat-rowers, and like the wanax he owned a temenos or reserved parcel of land, although his was only one-third that of the wanax (see sidebar, "How to Read Linear B," in chapter 3) (Palaima 1995, 129). Based on his land-holdings and the etymology of the name, this lawagetas is understood as the Mycenaean military commander-in-chief, whose responsibilities extended from the centralized palace bureaucracy to the localized administrative units and villages. He was probably the second most important person in the Myce-naean hierarchy after the wanax.

THE DARK AGE AND "EPIC" KINGSHIP

The word *politics* comes from the Greek word for city: *polis*. When Aristotle claimed, "Man is a political animal," he meant that humans were naturally in-tended to live in cities. With the fall of the Bronze Age, the Aegean urban and palatial centers disappeared, and, as a result, one could argue that there were no politics during this phase of Greek history.

This is not to say that there was utter anarchy (*an* = non-, *arkhos* = leader). It appears, rather, that for a while the Greeks reverted back to the system of chiefdoms postulated for the Middle Helladic period (see above). Once again, there was no formal bureaucracy, but leadership was based on charisma and personal power. In this unstable period, a good part of that personal power was probably military in nature, and authority went to that individual best ca-pable of protecting a village, clan, or region. Of course, not all areas of Greece were equally damaged by the end of the Bronze Age, the island of Euboia be-ing an excellent example (see chapter 4). Here, the continued wealth present in the graves, and especially in the large-scale Heroön of Lefkandi, suggests that a king and queen in control of economic goods and prestige items still ruled the local population.

Such holdovers were rare, though. As mentioned above, the person of the wanax almost entirely disappeared during the Dark Age, as, it would appear, did the lawagetas, leaving the local basileis at the top of the political ladder. Except for the unique Anax Agamemnon, the basileis are the military/political leaders we encounter in the works of Homer and Hesiod, which are as close as we might come to a written account of the Dark Age. These epics—the *Iliad* and *Odyssey* by Homer, and the *Works and Days* and *Theogony* by Hesiod—are an amalgam of several different periods of Greek history, extending back into the Bronze Age but recording aspects of even Archaic society as well. Thus, Homer recalled the boar's tusk helmet in use in the Mycenaean period (see chapter 9) but also referred to the synoecism of Rhodes (see below). Therefore, one cannot rely too heavily on his works for information on any specific pe-riod of Greek history. By contrast, Hesiod seems to have written about his own here-and-now, providing a somewhat clearer picture of Greek society in the eighth century B.C.E.

Both poets show a society dominated by basileis, each in command of a small territory. From what we can gather from the epics, kingship ran in the family, kings were military leaders, and kings were responsible for justice and proper religious observances in their kingdoms. The idea that kingship was hereditary is evident in the Homeric epics, where son succeeds father into kingship, such as Odysseus and Telemachus, and Agamemnon and Orestes. Of course, these being epics, such transitions are seldom entirely smooth. Furthermore, the role of the queen appears to have been significant in this period, and transmission of power seems to involve her at least as much as the king. For example, in the *Iliad*, we discover that Menelaus, Helen of Sparta's husband, is king of Sparta through his marriage to Helen, even though she has at least two living brothers. It appears that although patrilineal descent was the ideal form of passing along kingship, other forces were at play.

The fact that kings were military leaders is most evident in Homer, where warfare is a dominant theme, especially in the *Iliad*. This ideology comes across most strongly in a conversation (Book 12, 310–321) between the two warriors Glaukos and Sarpedon:

> Glaukos, why indeed are we two most honored,
> with a seat of honor and meats and full cups
> in Lykia, all beholding us as gods?
> And we dwell on great land holdings on the banks of the Xanthos,
> fair in orchards and wheat-bearing fields.
> Now it is necessary for us two to stand among the foremost of the Lykians
> And face the raging battle,
> so that someone of the thorax-clad Lykians might say:
> "Not inglorious are our kings, ruling
> over Lykia, they eat fat sheep
> and excellent honeyed wine. But their strength
> is good, when they fight among the first of the Lykians."

The idea that kings were, ideally, responsible for justice and proper religious observations comes across in both Homer and Hesiod. In Books 6–8 of the *Odyssey*, Homer portrays a "perfect" society, the Greek ideal, in the Phaiakians who live on the island of Skheria. These people are ruled by no fewer than thirteen kings, the heads of whom are Alkinóòs and his wife Aretê. When Odysseus is washed ashore on this island, it is Alkinóòs's responsibility to see that the hero is treated according to the dictates of the gods, an example of Greek xenia or hospitality (see chapter 6). Alkinóòs's concern for divine piety and xenia, as well as the diffuse nature of royal authority on Skheria, is evident in the king's reception of the yet-unnamed Odysseus in Book 7, 186–196:

> Listen, leaders and rulers of the Phaiakians,
> to what I say and the heart in my breast bids me.
> Now having dined go home and rest;
> come dawn, having summoned more elders,
> we shall entertain our guest-friend and to the gods
> we shall offer fine sacrifices; and then towards his homecoming

we shall turn our minds, so that our friend, without labor and sorrow
might return to his fatherland by our conveyance,
rejoicing greatly, even if it is quite far away.
Nor, in the meanwhile, should he suffer hardship
before he sets foot on his own land.

Hesiod takes a more blatant approach to kings, for both good and evil.
When sweet-talking the kings who are judging his performance of the
Theogony (ll. 79–90), Hesiod waxes on kingship with a honeyed tongue:

And Kalliope; she is superior to them all.
for she accompanies reverend kings.
Whomever of the god-reared kings the daughters of Zeus
will honor and see at birth,
on his tongue they pour sweet dew,
words flow from his mouth like honey
and all the people look to him to settle cases
with straight justice. And he steadfastly
speaking with wisdom resolves great strife.
For in this respect kings are wise, because
when the people are in a quarrel in the meeting-place,
easily he ends vengeful deeds
with mild, encouraging words.

When having legal difficulties with his brother, however, Hesiod takes a
harsher view of the kings, lashing out at them in his *Works and Days* (ll. 35–40):

But here now let us resolve the quarrel
through straight judgments, which are best,
coming from Zeus.
For already we have divided up the inheritance,
but seizing it you carried off more,
greatly honoring [bribing] the gift-swallowing kings,
who are eager to judge a case such as this.
Fools!

The kings Hesiod discusses in his epics were probably the heads of various local, dynastic families, the aristocracies that ruled in the newly emerging city-
states until the age of the tyrants.

THE ARCHAIC AGE:
SYNOECISM, ARISTOCRACY, AND TYRANNY

Whatever the exact nature of political authority in the Dark Age, come the Archaic period, Greece transformed from a land of small village-kingdoms to a
land of city-states, called poleis (pl. of *polis*). There were two ways that a polis

could come into being. The simpler, and generally later, way was through colonization, as described in chapter 4. Here, a designated leader, the oikistes, led a group of people to a new land to establish a new city of residence. The oikistes was the first ruler of the people, and the colonists each received equal portions of land on which to begin their homesteads. A sense of community was created by the common colonizing experience of the original settlers, which was passed down to their children along with the land.

However, colonization, except in the Dark Age, presupposes an original city from which the settlers set out, such as the Eretrians and Chalkidians who went to Pithekoussai (see chapter 5) or the Spartans who settled Italian Taras. How, then, did these original poleis come into being, after the tribulations that ended the Bronze Age? In general, the original Greek poleis came into being through synoecism, which means literally "houses together," and refers to the process by which individual homes, families, and clans united into the political unit of the polis. Such processes are recorded literarily and archaeologically.

For literary evidence, we might consider Athens, whose synoecism was recorded by the fifth-century historian Thucydides. In Book 2, §15, 1–2, of his *Peloponnesian War*, the historian tells us:

> For in the time of Kekrops and the first kings up to the time of Theseus Attica always existed in individual cities, each having their own city halls and magistrates, and if not compelled by some common fear, they did not come together to join in council with the king, but each separately conducted civil affairs and city planning. And some of them even waged war on the kings, like the Eleusinians in the time of Eumolpos with Erechtheus. But when Theseus was king, having power in addition to intelligence, he marshaled together the land in many respects, and having disbanded the other cities' councils and magistracies, he made them now into one city, creating one city council and city hall. He bound them together, all those who still lived separately as before, and made them use the one city [Athens]. And the city became great, what with all those tax-payers, handed down by Theseus to his successors, and from that time even to now the Athenians celebrate the Synoikia festival at public expense in honor of the goddess.

For archaeology, two sites provide excellent evidence for the synoecism of Corinth. The earlier evidence comes from the acropolis of Corinth—Acrocorinth—where Protogeometric cups were discovered; these may have served as cult items or votives, indicating an active cult from as early as the tenth century B.C.E. (Williams 1994, 33–36). The temple on Acrocorinth—dedicated to the city's goddess Aphrodite—was originally constructed at the end of the seventh century, to be replaced by a more elaborate version in the fifth. This shows that at least by the late seventh century, there was sufficient political unity in the area to provide for the mass effort, and mass expense, of a city sanctuary to an official city goddess. Perhaps more indicative of political unity is the evidence from the cemeteries. In the mid-eighth century, the small "family plot" burials around the city were consolidated into a new, common burial ground in the lower plain below the city, and the North Cemetery came into common usage (Williams 1994, 33–36). Thus, from a small series of family plots, a larger, more communal ideology developed.

This synoecism of Corinth probably occurred under the auspices of their dominant aristocratic family—the Bacchiadae. Almost every ancient Greek polis was originally dominated by at least one such family. Sparta, as we shall see below, had two. We might imagine that these families were the original defenders, judges, and even priests of their respective poleis, thus functioning much as the basileis of Homer and Hesiod. Also in keeping with Dark Age tradition was the practice of keeping royal authority within the family. Although such political "hoarding" may have been practical during the unsettled times of the Dark Age, it became increasingly intolerable to the Greeks beginning with the eighth-century renaissance. This was because the colonizing efforts of the Greeks created new patterns of settlement and distribution of power in the newly settled poleis. Every (male) settler received an equal allotment of land and a say in local affairs. Such diffusion of political power was probably responsible for the earliest inklings of democracy in Greek political thought (Robinson 1997, passim). Furthermore, the economic prosperity that began to rise in the eighth century instigated the rise of a middle class—that population with copious economic resources but no "royal blood." In short, people outside of the royal families were coming into power, either through amassing wealth or through relocation. Inevitably, there would be a confrontation between the traditional power holders and those demanding a bigger piece of the political pie.

The resolution to this conflict in most Greek poleis, except Sparta and Aigina, was tyranny. For the record, an ancient Greek tyrant was not, at least originally, the same thing as a despot, as we now tend to think of the concept. A despot was, and is, an "evil ruler"; an ancient tyrant was a man who held power in a nontraditional and/or nonconstitutional way. In some cases, these men actually were kings, but kings who acted in unorthodox ways. Or, more often, they were related to the ruling family but used their "reign" or "tyranny" to change the political and even social composition of the city they ruled. In this way, tyrants actually tended to be good for the Greek poleis, allowing for a transition between the hereditary monarchies of the Early Archaic Age and the constitutional governments of the Classical period. Although in later times the tyrants were demonized and portrayed as violent, if not actually perverted, in their own period they were tolerated and praised. They were the alternative to violent revolution.

The word *tyrant* is non-Indo-European (see chapter 1). Although the etymology is still under debate, the ancient Greeks seemed to think that the word, if not the concept entirely, came from the east, specifically from Lydia in what is now western Turkey. The word first appears in a poem of the seventh-century poet Archilochus, who said:

> The things of Gyges rich in gold do not concern me,
> neither has jealousy yet taken me, nor do I reproach
> the works of the gods; I do not desire a great tyranny,
> for that is far off from my vision.

Tyranny first appeared in Greece in the seventh century B.C.E. The first figure who could be considered a tyrant was Pheidon of Argos, who established the weights and measures of the Greeks and once seized control of the Olympic Games. Unfortunately, Pheidon is an amorphous creature to modern researchers. The dates of his supposed exploits span 150 years, from the early seventh century down through the mid-sixth, and this makes it difficult to say anything concrete about Pheidon's life or reign. The more historic first tyrant was Cypselus of Corinth, for whom we have excellent (if biased) evidence from both Herodotus and Nicolaus of Damascus. This Cypselus ruled from about 657–625 B.C.E., and his son Periandros after him ruled circa 625–585. The fullest account of the Cypselid rise to power is preserved in Book 5 of Herodotus's *Histories* (Book 5, 91), in which a Corinthian named Sosikles is trying to prevent the Spartans from returning the Athenian tyrant Hippias to power in Athens. As a result, Sosikles puts a very negative spin on tyranny in general, and the earliest tyrants come across in a very harsh, if amusing, light:

For the government of the Corinthians was thus: it was an oligarchy, and those called Bacchiadae governed the city, and they gave and took [wives] only among each other. Among these men, one belonging to Amphion, was a lame daughter, whose name was Labda. Since no one of the Bacchiadae wanted to marry her, Eetion, son of Ekhekratos, of the deme of Petras but by descent of Lapithes and Kaineides, married her. But no children came to him, either from this wife or any other woman, so he set forth to Delphi concerning his family. At his arrival straightaway the Pythia greeted him with these words:

"Eetion, no one honors you, being most honorable.
Labda is pregnant, she'll bear a boulder, which will
Fall upon the monarchs, bringing justice to Corinth."

These things she prophesized to Eetion were likewise announced to the Bacchiadae, to whom there had been a previously unintelligible prophecy in Corinth concerning them and Eetion, which went thus:

"An eagle gives birth among the rocks, will bring forth a lion
strong and ravening, it will loose the knees of many.
Well pay heed to these things, Corinthians, who
Live around lovely Pirene and rocky Corinth."

Previously this was incomprehensible to the Bacchiadae, but then with the speech to Eetion they understood, as immediately they saw the similarity between the two, their prophecy and that of Eetion. Getting together in secret, they decided to destroy the child of Eetion as soon as it was born. Just as soon as his wife gave birth, they sent 10 of their own to the deme in which Eetion lived to kill the child. Arriving in Petras and approaching Eetion's courtyard, they asked for the child. Labda, knowing nothing of why they came and thinking that they were there for love of his father, handed the child over to one of them. Their plan had been that the first of them to get hold of the child would dash it onto the street. But when Labda carrying the child handed him over, by good chance the child smiled at the one of the men who took him, and seeing this pity, kept him from killing anyone, and having compassion he handed him over to the second guy, who gave him to the third, and so on until, having been passed about, the child went around to all 10 of them, none of them wanting to do the deed. Having handed the child back to its mother and heading outside, they stood around by the gates upbraiding each other, especially accusing the first guy who took the child, in that he didn't act according to the plan. Then, after a time, they decided to go back and all take part in the murder.

But it was fated that an evil for Corinth would sprout from the family of Eetion. For Labda heard everything they said standing by the gates. Fearing lest they change their minds and, getting a hold of the kid a second time, kill him, she carried him and hid him in the most unlikely place she could think of—a storage bin (cypselus)—believing that if they returned they would conduct a thorough search, looking everywhere they could think of. And this in fact did happen. They returned, and when they looked everywhere and could not find the child, it seemed best to them to leave and to tell those who sent them that they did everything that they were supposed to. And this is what they did. And after this the son of Eetion grew up, and because he escaped danger in a storage bin, they named him Cypselus.

When Cypselus grew up he consulted an oracle in Delphi and got a double-edged prophecy. Relying on it he prepared to take Corinth. The prophecy went thus:

> "Best is the man who walks into my house,
> Cypselus, son of Eetion, King of glorious Corinth,
> And your children, but not your children's children"

Such was the prophecy, and Cypselus, becoming a tyrant, was such a man as this: he banished many Corinthians and stole their property, while from many others he stole their lives. Having ruled 30 years and come to the end of his life in style, his son Periandros was heir to his tyranny. Now this Periandros was at the beginning milder than his father, but then he associated by messenger with Thrasyboulos, tyrant of Miletos. Then he became far more bloodthirsty than his father. For he sent a messenger to Thrasyboulos to find out by what means he should most securely set up his affairs and best manage his city. Thrasyboulos went along with Periandros's man. Leading him out of town, and going to a cultivated field he went along through the grain stalks questioning and cross-examining the messenger about why he had come from Corinth, and whenever he saw some one of the ears of grain projecting up above the others he cut it down and threw it away, and so he destroyed the finest and tallest of the grain. Having gone through the fields and not offered a word of advice, he sent the messenger away. When the messenger returned home to Corinth, Periandros was eager to inquire as to the advice. The messenger said that Thrasyboulos hadn't advised a thing, and that he [the messenger] was amazed that Periandros should have sent him to such a man, being so loony and destructive (for he described to Periandros the things he saw Thrasyboulos do). But Periandros understood what he did and believed that Thrasyboulos advised him to kill the prominent citizens. So then he unleashed the most unpleasant acts on the Corinthians. For whatever Cypselus left [undone] in terms of killing and banishing, Periandros accomplished, and furthermore in one day he stripped naked all the women of Corinth on account of his wife Melissa. For he sent a messenger to the Thesprotons by the Akheron River for a necromancer so as to inquire about the property of a friend, and Melissa said that she would neither point out nor relate where the goods lay in the land, for she was cold and naked because they buried her with clothes that were unburnt, ergo useless to her. And to prove that what she said was true, she mentioned that Periandros tossed loaves of bread into a cold oven. This was then related to Periandros, and the latter comment was meaningful to him, since he had had sex with Melissa's corpse. As soon as the messenger gave him this message, Periandros sent all the Corinthian women to the temple of Hera, and they went to the "festival" decked out in their finest apparels. But Periandros, having placed spearmen in ambush, stripped them all at once, both free woman and servant, and bore the clothing to a hole and burnt them, calling upon Melissa. Having done these things and having sent a second time to the necromancer, the ghost of Melissa told him where in the land he had put his friend's property.

The version of Cypselus's tyranny as preserved in the works of Nicolaus of Damascus appears less judgmental, showing Cypselus to be a mild and effectual ruler, as was his son after him. Seeing how their reign lasted for some sixty years, one has to imagine that there was more to their work than bloodshed and necrophilia. According to Nicolaus, Cypselus began his political career as a polemarch, the officer who judged criminal cases, exacted fines, and imprisoned the guilty. The previous Bacchiadae who had held this position were "overwhelming and violent," whereas Cypselus was "prudent and public-minded." Becoming popular with the common folk, Cypselus garnered support and, in a sudden coup d'état, killed the Bacchiad king. From here, Cypselus attempted to correct the injustices committed by the Bacchiadae against the Corinthians, such as recalling exiles and restoring their citizenship. Ultimately, Nicolaus claimed that Cypselus ruled in a mild manner, did not need a bodyguard, and was not hateful to the Corinthians (Fragments of the Greek Historians 90 F 57.4–57.8). As for Periandros, even Herodotus admitted that the man was world-famous for his wisdom and just judgments (McGlew 1993, ch. 2).

Furthermore, the Cypselids greatly improved the Corinthian economy, which had already been flourishing since the seventh century. They sent out several new colonies to Italy and Sicily, many founded by the illegitimate sons of Cypselus. With the exception of Corkyra, all these colonies remained friendly with Corinth throughout their histories. The Cypselids initiated trade relations with Egypt, which had been a very standoffish country up to that point. Periandros established the diolkos, a "strip" that allowed ships to be dragged between the Corinthian and Saronic Gulfs—an ancient Greek Panama Canal—greatly increasing Corinth's role in overseas trade. In general, it was in any tyrant's best interest to improve the lives of his constituents, especially those of the middle class, as it was through their goodwill that the tyrannies endured.

Tyranny need not have been the result of a bloody coup, as is evident in the rise of another famous tyrant—Gelon of Syracuse, founder of the Deinomenid dynasty. This man used his status as a war victor to rally public support. In 479 B.C.E., Gelon successfully led the city's defense against an attack from Carthage (a Phoenician colony located on the north shore of Africa). Diodorus Siculus tells us that upon returning home, Gelon, as general, called an assembly of the Syracusan demos, at which he appeared completely unarmed to deliver an account of his actions and victory. At the end of his address, he offered to relinquish his role as defender of the city; the demos shouted down the offer and proclaimed him benefactor, savior, and king (basileus) (McGlew 1993, 137).

Although many tyrants supported each other, as the episode between Periandros and Thrasyboulos makes clear, in other cases they were perfectly willing to take advantage of each other, overthrowing rival tyrannies and proclaiming themselves "liberators" of the people. Such were the actions of Gelon's brother and successor Hieron. According to Diodorus Siculus (11.53.4–5), Thrasydaios, tyrant of nearby Acragas and Himera, attacked Syracuse in the 470s B.C.E. After some confusion, Hieron defeated the attacker, who was packed off to exile in Megara on the Greek mainland. Immediately upon his removal, the demoi of both cities, Acragas and Himera, established themselves as democracies and sent ambassadors to Hieron with terms for peace. Technically, Hieron had just conquered both cities, and it could have been in his interest to extend his tyranny over both. Instead, he accepted their offerings of peace and let them remain independent democracies, allied to, but not controlled by, Syracuse. In later years, these cities would show their gratitude to the Deinomenids by taking in Thrasyboulos, son of Hieron, when he was ousted from Syracuse.

The Deinomenids were, for their brief period of power at the beginning of the fifth century B.C.E., mild and apparently well liked, a sharp contrast to what later political commentators would consider to be "tyrannical." Their reign was particularly fruitful in the realms of literature, and their dynasty was the subject of, or referred to by, several odes from the Greek poet Pindar (see chapter 10). Concerning Hieron, Pindar wrote in his sixth *Olympian* for the victor Hagesias (ll. 92–98):

> And I said to remember Syracuse and Ortygia,
> which Hieron manages with a pure scepter,
> contriving perfection, he honors purple-footed
> Demeter and the festival of the white horse and her daughter
> and the might of Aitnian Zeus. Sweet songs
> and chanting lyres know him. Let not encroaching time
> ruin his joy,
> but with loving, friendly greetings may he receive
> Hagesias' band of revelers
> from one home to another, approaching from the
> walls of Stymphalos,
> leaving behind mother Arcadia rich in sheep.

Many tyrannies shared certain characteristics. The tyrant was usually somehow related to the ruling family, as was the case with Cypselus, or was at least related to another tyrant through blood or marriage. Thus, he was *of* the aristocracy, but not *for* the aristocracy. He had legitimacy to rule, but could garner public support from the masses by being in a position to defend them against the atrocities of the ruling regime, or, as with Gelon, against an external enemy. Thus, tyrants came to power by offering freedom to the people. The inherent flaw in this, of course, was that eventually the people actually wanted their freedom, meaning freedom from tyranny. This was why few tyrannies lasted longer than two generations—refer back to the prophecy quoted about Cypselus above: "And your children, but not your children's children." By the time a tyranny was over, the polis usually had a new social and political composition in which a greater percentage of the male population had access to the wheels of power and in which economic prosperity extended to a larger portion of the people.

FORMS OF RULE IN THE CLASSICAL PERIOD: OLIGARCHY AND DEMOCRACY

Between the tyrannies that marked the Late Archaic Age and the kingdoms of the Macedonian and Hellenistic regimes, monarchy was not a common form of rule in Greece. Instead, the governments, or politeia, of the various poleis were poised somewhere on the continuum between aristocracy/oligarchy—the rule of the few/best/richest—and democracy—the rule of the people/masses. In truth, these terms are somewhat anachronistic—the words *oligarchy* and *democracy* appeared for the first time only in the fifth-century writings of Herodotus, and they became topics of political/philosophical discussion only in the later fifth- and fourth-century works of Thucydides, Plato, and Aristotle (Ostwald 2000, 386). Oligarchy in Greece was not the narrow junta we might think it in modern times. Rather than specific "governments of the rich," the more mild oligarchies in Greece limited the franchise to those citizens who possessed property, with the amount of property required varying from city to city. In this respect, they were no different from the early United States, where the right to vote was dependent on landownership. This had a practical basis: Only those citizens with adequate means could afford to take part in day-to-day political affairs. It was not until the reforms of Pericles in fifth-century Athens that pay was implemented for governmental services in that city, such as jury duty, so that even the poorest citizens could afford to take part in the political machinery. Aristotle, in his *Politics* (1293a12–34), noted four different types of oligarchy, ranging from the mild to the blatantly dynastic closed system:

> When a great number of people own estates of smaller and not excessive size, we have the first type of oligarchy. They permit a property-owner to participate, and, with a large number of men having a share in governing, authority will necessarily be vested not in men but in the law. For the further removed they are from monarchy, the less likely it will be that their estate will either be so large that they can enjoy leisure without concern for their property, or so small that they have to be maintained from public funds. It follows that they think it right that the law should rule over them and not they.

When the number of estate owners is smaller but their estates larger, we get the second type of oligarchy. Their greater influence, they believe, entitles them to greater prerogatives. Accordingly, they take it upon themselves to choose from the rest those who will be admitted to the governing body; but since they are not quite influential enough to rule without law, they enact a law to that effect.

If they narrow it by having fewer people own larger estates, the third stage of oligarchy is reached. They keep the offices in their own hands but adopt a law stipulating that sons succeed their fathers.

When they confine membership to an extreme extent, requiring large estates limited to a network of relationships, we have a narrow power-group, a dynasty, which is close to monarchy, in which authority rests with the men and not the law. This is the fourth type of oligarchy. . . . (Translation by Ostwald 2000, 392–393)

Thebes

The only oligarchy for which we have adequate documentation is Thebes of the fifth and very early fourth centuries B.C.E. This documentation comes from the so-called Oxyrhynchos Historian, who wrote at some time in the middle fourth century and whose work is preserved in papyri from Oxyrhynchos, Egypt (see chapter 3). This author wrote a history of Greece, continuing the work of the more illustrious fifth-century historian Thucydides. Some have suggested that the Oxyrhynchos Historian was Thucydides's daughter, charged with carrying on his work. According to this text (*Hell. Oxy.* 11.2), "At that time the political situation in Boiotia [the region of Greece containing Thebes] was as follows. There were four councils established at that time in each of the poleis. Not every one of the citizens was allowed to share in these, but only those who met a certain property qualification. Each of these councils in turn would sit and pre-deliberate about policy, and refer matters for decision to the other three. What was deemed acceptable to all four became authoritative policy" (translation by Cartledge 2000, 399, used with kind permission).

Here we have a system of at least two classes. The "upper" class consisted of those possessing a certain minimum amount of property, probably enough to supply themselves with military equipment and sufficient slaves that they did not need to be "at work" every day. Only members of this upper class could sit on the councils. The "lower" classes did not own sufficient property to be on the councils, although where this left them in the political machinery is uncertain. Clearly they could not be members of the councils, but what their political and legal rights were is unknown, assuming they had any (Cartledge 2000, 399–404).

Where the dividing line between mild oligarchy and moderate democracy lay is a matter of debate, especially considering that even in the most radical Greek democracy—Athens—the right to vote in the assembly and take any part in any governmental machinery was denied to women (who *were* considered to be citizens) and to resident aliens and slaves (who were both expected to pay taxes and to fight in wars). It is perhaps better to think of the Classical and later constitutions as lying, and even moving, along a continuum, with oligarchic and democratic—and even monarchic—elements existing side by side in the same system.

Sparta

This side-by-side existence of oligarchic, democratic, and monarchic elements was especially the case in Sparta, which pulled together all three ancient Greek political manifestations into one constitution—having kings, an aristocracy, representatives, and a semidemocratic state assembly all at once. This system provided stability for so many centuries that it attracted the admiration of several philosophers, notably Xenophon and Aristotle, both of whom wrote treatises entitled *Constitution of the Lakedaimonians [Spartans]*. In modern times, unfortunately, much of what remains is what the later Roman author Plutarch extracted from these works. His *Life of Lycurgus* provides the most direct information we have about the origins of the Spartan government, although much of it is suspect in terms of historical accuracy.

From Plutarch's *Life of Lycurgus:*

Of the many innovations enacted by Lycurgus, the first and the greatest was the establishment of the *gerousia* [council of elders], which, Plato said, being added to the feverish rule of the kings and having equal vote with them in the most important matters of safety, brought rationality to the polity. For the civil government was wavering, and on the one hand was about to have the kings become tyrants, while on the other hand the majority was moving toward democracy. Like a steady keel, Lycurgus established the rule of the gerousia between these extremes and set the state in balance, and so he had the most dependable arrangement and institution. For there were always 28 elders standing by the kings so as to resist the trend toward democracy, while they also strengthened the people in their resistance of tyranny. Such things Aristotle said concerning the number of the gerousia, that at first there were 30 elders set in place by Lycurgus, but two of them abandoned the project through cowardice. But Spairos says that from the beginning 28 was the number of those sharing Lycurgus's confidence. In my opinion it seems best to accept the 28 elders, so that all together they would be 30—the 28 elders plus the two kings.

Lycurgus was so zealous about his new regime that he got an oracle from Delphi about it, called the *Rhetra* [Decrees]. It went thus: "Having established a sanctuary for Zeus Sullanious and Athena Sullania, set the tribes into tribes and the subdivisions into subdivisions. Establish 30 elders with the leaders, and from time to time call assemblies between the Babuka and Knakion Rivers, so as to introduce and rescind (decrees). Let the rule and power be with the people." In these clauses, "set the tribes into tribes and the subdivisions into subdivisions" meant to divide up the multitudes into clans, called phratries by some and obes by others. The "leaders" were the kings, and "calling assemblies" meant to convene the people for civic purposes. So Lycurgus linked the rule and the course of the civil government to Pythian Apollo . . .

When the people were assembled, it was not permitted for anyone to put forth a motion, but the assembly was to decide on matters brought before them by the gerousia and the kings. Later, however, when the people distorted and constrained the motions by deleting parts or adding on riders, Polydoros and Theopompos the kings added another clause to the Rhetra, saying: "If the people should adopt a crooked measure, let the elders and leaders put an end to it." That is, they should not enact such a motion, but dismiss it altogether and dissolve the assembly, as it was twisting and altering a motion against the best interests. And the kings persuaded the city that these additions were added on by the god. So the poet Tyrtaios memorialized in these words:

Hearing and performing the words of the god and oracle
Brought home from the Pythian
To rule over the council belongs to god-honored kings.
The delightful city of the Spartans is their concern,
Second are the elders, then the men of the people
Obeying in turn proper decrees.

In this way, the constitution of Lycurgus came together, but even still the oligarchic element was unfazed and too strong, "swelling and foaming" as Plutarch put it, "so they threw the power of the ephors about the city like a leash." Some 130 years after Lycurgus, the first of the ephors (see below) were established—Elatos and those with him, during the reign of Theopompos. And when the king's own wife berated him, saying that he would hand over to his sons a worse kingship than he had received, he answered her, "Actually a better one, for it will last longer."

The most ambiguous element of Plutarch's narrative is the existence of Lycurgus himself. In reality, he was probably a mythical character, created by the Spartans to give a divine element to their laws, making them inviolate. So, we really have no idea when or under what auspices the Spartan "constitution" was created, although a date in the seventh century B.C.E. is generally accepted (Whitby 2002, 46).

Other aspects of Plutarch's account are more easily addressed. As he mentioned, Sparta had not one but two kings, one each from the city's two royal families (so the two kings were not brothers or otherwise related). This is probably a result of Sparta's own synoecism between four or five separate villages, two of which already had royal families when the union occurred. Each king had his own agenda, and rather than oppressing the people, the two kings appear to have balanced each other out. This was especially true during times of war (the Spartans' favorite pastime): One king would be the general-in-chief, leading the armies, and the other would remain home tending to the affairs of the city. Besides their civil duties, the kings were also priests, conducting important rituals for all the Spartans.

Gerousia literally means "group of old men," much as the word *senate* is based on the same root as *senior* and *senile*. The gerousia officers were a minimum of sixty years old and were voted in for life by the Spartan demos. These twenty-eight men, together with the two kings, formed the council or boulê, which prepared issues, decrees, and laws for consideration by the assembly. They were also the highest law court in Sparta, the only ones who could exile or condemn someone to death (Andrewes 2002, 67). The two kings plus the gerousia formed the monarchic and aristocratic aspects of the Spartan state.

Between the gerousia and the people were five ephors elected on an annual basis to serve as the "executive branch" of the Spartan government. For basic duties, the ephors convened both the Spartan boulê of kings and elders and the assemblies. In times of war, the ephors were responsible for mustering troops, determining what age groups of soldiers would be sent out to battle, and determining how many would be sent. They also sent messages to those in the field regarding strategy and tactics, although one must imagine that the king who served as commander-in-chief was the ultimate strategist. During periods of crisis, the ephors could act without consulting the assembly. Thus in 405/404, during a siege at the end of the Peloponnesian War, it was the ephors, not the Spartan assembly, who treated with the Athenians, as Xenophon tells us in his *Hellenica,* Book 2, 2, 13. Finally, the ephors had the right to arrest the kings and put them on trial, as Thucydides records in Book 1, 131, 2: "And first Pausanias was tossed into prison by the ephors—it is possible for the ephors to do this even to the kings." Although this was not a common occurrence, such power did give them considerable leverage with the kings, allowing them to make very strong suggestions about state affairs. In some cases, the ephors could merely fine the kings, as in a story attributed to Theophrastos, when the ephors fined King Archidamus for marrying too short a wife, on the grounds that she would give birth not to kings, but kinglets (Andrewes 2002, 60). Ultimately, the ephors were the voice of the people in the face of the oligarchic powers of the gerousia and the kings. They guaranteed that the laws, and not any individual person, were sovereign in Sparta.

Finally, there was the assembly, the ekklesia. This consisted of the damos—Spartiates, males who were members of a sysition or eating club (see chapter 6) and who were either of or past the age of military service. The Rhetra mentioned in Plutarch is ambiguous about the Spartiates' status in Spartan politics. Apollo himself declared that "rule and power" should be with the people, suggesting that the Spartans were a democratic lot and Apollo a political liberal. But, Spartiates could not propose motions in the assembly meetings, only saying "yea" or "nay" to motions introduced by the boulê. Nevertheless, it seems logical that such restrictions were in place during the meeting itself, meaning that no one could simply stand up in the crowd and put forth proposals while in session. Rather, the Spartiates may have been able to bring up matters with the ephors, gerousia, and even kings at times outside of the assemblies, which suggestions would be digested by the boulê and then presented to the ekklesia. Furthermore, except for times of crisis, matters of both internal and external policy were determined by vote in the assembly. The kings literally could not act in opposition to, or without, the consent of the demos. To do so would result in fine or imprisonment at the hands of the ephors.

Athens

The path from aristocracy/oligarchy to democracy by way of tyranny is best viewed in Athens, where an unnamed follower of Aristotle recorded this process in a work called *Constitution of Athens* (classicists refer to it as the *Ath.Pol.—Athenaiôn Politeia*). The following extract is a paraphrase of that political development as preserved in this work. The numbers in this extract refer to sections of the *Ath.Pol.* Dates are, of course, modern (as opposed to the ancient system of dating).

[2] In the later seventh century, there were considerable tensions between the upper and lower classes. Not only was the constitution at this time entirely oligarchic, but the poorer classes—men, women, and children—were the slaves of the rich. [3] At this time, the government consisted of the following offices. First was the king, a position that had existed since ancient times. Second was the polemarch ("war leader"), or head of the military; the office was instituted because some kings proved feeble in times of war. Finally, there were the Archons ("leaders"). At first there were three Archons; later, six thesmothetai, or junior Archons, were added, with the position becoming an annual office. It was their responsibility to record all legal decisions and act as guardians of the law. After the year of service, the ex-Archons were inducted into the Areopagos council, in which they remained for life. The original purpose of this body was to protect the laws and to serve as the highest law court in the state, especially trying cases involving murder or treason. In reality, though, at this time, the Areopagos council administered many of the important aspects of government. In all cases, all offices were reserved exclusively for the nobility, based on birth and wealth.

[4] In 621 B.C.E., Drakon revised the Athenian constitution, enacting extremely harsh laws that gave rise to the term *Draconian*. For example, he prescribed the death penalty for every infraction of the law. Citizenship, along with the right to vote, was given to all males who could provide themselves with military equipment. They elected the Archons and city treasurers from among those citizens who owned at least 10 minas of property (the equivalent of a few million dollars today); generals and cavalry officers from those who possessed 100 minas and had children at least 10 years old; and lesser officials from among themselves. Drakon also instituted a council of 401 members, chosen by lot from all the male citizens over thirty years old. No one could serve on the council twice until every citizen had had his turn once.

[5] Such revisions still did not resolve the class crisis in Athens, and in 594, when civil war was about to break out, the citizens elected Solon as an Archon and asked him to fix the government. The Athenians considered Solon the ideal choice, as his moderate views convinced both rich and poor that he was on their side. [6] Solon's first action was the Seisakhtheia, or "Shaking-Off of Burdens," by which he cancelled all debts in Athens, ending much of the hold the rich had on the poor. Furthermore, he liberated all citizens who had become slaves through their inability to pay off debts, and he made borrowing off one's person (i.e., using one's liberty as collateral, so that if one cannot pay off a debt, one must become the loaner's slave) illegal, so that this would not happen again.

[7] Next, Solon changed the Athenian class structure, creating four new classes. At the top were the pentakosiomedimnoi, whose property furnished 500 units of grain, wine, oil, etc. annually. Next were the knights (literally "horsemen"), whose property furnished 300 units and who could afford to buy and maintain a warhorse with full accoutrements. Third were the zeugetai, with 200 units and at least one pair of oxen; and fourth the thetes, or basic laborers. All government positions were available only to the top three classes, although the thetes did have the right to vote. [8] Solon also

created (or possibly re-created from the time of Drakon) a council of 400, called the boulê, with one hundred representatives coming from each of the four tribes [see chapter 6]. The Areopagos continued its function as guardian of the laws and protector of the constitution. These reforms benefited all levels of society, although ultimately they did not satisfy anyone. The poor were lifted out of the lowest levels of poverty and had their debts removed. The middle classes now had access to the political machinery, as candidacy was based not on noble birth but on wealth. The wealthy did not have their land taken or their prerogatives touched, in contrast to the general call from the poor for land redistribution. Still, the poor were poor, the wealthy were ambitious, and problems resumed.

[13] Within 15 years of the Solonic reforms, political strife reemerged in Athens. The factions were divided based on residence and political ideology. First was the Coast faction, led by Megakles the Alcmaeonid, which wanted a moderate form of government. Second were the Plainsmen, led by Lycurgus, who wanted an oligarchy. Third were the Highlandsmen, led by Peisistratos, who wanted a radical democracy. [15] It took three attempts over ten years for him to become tyrant, but from 546 to 527, Peisistratos was tyrant of Athens.

[16] Peisistratos was a mild and beneficent tyrant. He was merciful in justice, and he advanced money to the lower classes to improve their farms, so they might make a comfortable living through agriculture. One reason for this was so the people, being busy at their farms, would not come into the city to cause problems. But Peisistratos also began the agriculture tax, claiming one-tenth of all produce [see chapter 5] for the city. He established regional justices, even going to the countryside himself to hear cases. This made the legal system infinitely easier for the common folk to access, and, once again, kept them out of the city. Peisistratos greatly improved the city's culture—he commissioned great works of architecture, such as the new temple of Athena on the Acropolis, and instituted new religious festivals, such as the Greater Dionysia. It was during his reign that Athenian pottery experienced a renaissance, and from this time forth Athens was Corinth's major rival in the pottery trade.

[17] Peisistratos died in 527 and left the city to his Athenian sons Hipparchus and Hippias (he also had two sons from his Argive wife Timonassa—Iophon and Hegesistratos, also known as Thessalos). [18] Hippias administered the city, being more politically minded, and Hipparchus functioned more in the realms of literature and art. For a while, the beneficial and mild tyranny of Peisistratos persevered under these brothers. Unfortunately, their half brother Thessalos was a liability, being highly visible and very temperamental. He fell in love with a youth named Harmodios, who did not return the affections. Thessalos took revenge by refusing to allow Harmodios's sister to take part in the Panathenaic procession, claiming she came from a disreputable family. This was quite an insult in status-conscious Athens, and Harmodios, along with his friend Aristogeiton and others, took revenge by plotting the tyrants' assassination at the very religious festival from which his sister was barred. The assassination did not go as planned, and the two wound up killing Hipparchus, but not Hippias. As a result, Harmodios was killed instantly, Aristogeiton was tortured to death, and Hippias went from tyrant to despot.

[19] This tyranny came to an end in 510, when Hippias was expelled from Athens by the Spartan king Kleomenes. It seems that Delphi needed a new temple, and the

noble Athenian family Alcmaeonidai agreed to finance the building, using the best marble money could buy. In exchange, they persuaded (bribed) the Delphic priests that, whenever any Spartan came for an oracle, they were to tack onto the answer that it was the will of Apollo that the Spartans free Athens from tyranny. Eventually the Spartans got the hint and freed Athens by expelling Hippias.

[20] From this point, two rival factions sought political control of Athens, one led by Isagoras, who favored tyranny, and one by Kleisthenes, an Alcmaeonid, who favored democracy. [21] Kleisthenes won out, and he instituted the next round of democratic reforms. Starting in 508 B.C.E., he broke down the traditional four tribes of Athens [see chapter 6] and created ten. Each tribe was composed of three thirds, or trittyes: a third of coastal dwellers, a third of country dwellers, and a third of city dwellers. Having one third of each tribe in each location meant there could be no strong opposition between, say, the interests of the coastal sailors against those of the country farmers. Furthermore, because the political machinery was within the city itself, each tribe had equal access to the city. The trittyes were each composed of several demes. A deme was like a neighborhood, headed by a demarch who controlled local affairs. Membership in a deme was the most basic level of citizenship, and henceforth people in the literature and inscriptions were identified by name, father's name, and deme name.

Kleisthenes enlarged the boulê from 400 to 500, with each tribe contributing 50 members, all picked by lot. For each tenth of the year, the 50 members of each tribe took turns being on 24-hour call, living in the Tholos in the Athenian Agora. Thus, if there were a crisis at, say, 4 A.M., there would be a governmental body already convened to deal with it. Boulê positions were open to all male citizens. The more important positions, like Archon and general, were voted on rather than picked by lot and were open to only the top two economic classes. [22] Finally, Kleisthenes instituted ostracism, a procedure by which the people of Athens could vote to have someone banished from the city for ten years. This was intended to keep anyone with too much power from becoming tyrant.

[25] After the Persian Invasions [see chapter 4], the two most significant politicians in Athens were Ephialtes and Pericles, Kleisthenes's nephew. Ephialtes, in 462 B.C.E., stripped the Areopagos of most of its functions, returning it to the status of treason- and homicide-jury. All other functions were turned over to the boulê. The following year, Ephialtes was assassinated, and one must savor the irony that the people in charge of prosecuting his assassin were, of course, the Areopagos. [26] From this point, Pericles, as a continually reelected general, was functional master of Athens, and he turned the city from a democracy (as established under Kleisthenes) to a social democracy. He allowed the Zeugetai, the third economic class, to hold governmental offices such as Archon. [27] He instituted pay for attending governmental functions, such as the assembly or juries. This allowed those too poor to miss even a day of work to take part in the political machinery. The wealth pouring into Athens from the Delian League financed these reforms. Furthermore, Pericles started a huge building campaign in the city, replacing all the public monuments that were destroyed by the Persians half a century before. Between pay for political service, wages for the building program, and the pay for the continued maintenance of the navy with its rowers (usually from the poorest classes), Pericles raised the standard

of living for all the lower classes without infringing on the assets or prerogatives of the wealthier classes.

[26] To limit the number of people who would benefit from these benefits, however, Pericles restructured the citizenship requirements. Previously, one only had to have an Athenian father, enrolled in a deme, to be a citizen. As of 451 B.C.E., Pericles mandated that, for a person to be a citizen, his/her father *and* mother both had to be Athenian citizens. This limited the number of those drawing money from the state while strengthening the notion of Athenian community, especially in the upper classes. Up to this point, it was customary for the Athenian elite to intermarry with the elite of other poleis, forming aristocratic, familial unions that could be stronger than civic ties. With this new law, Athenians were forced to marry other Athenians or risk loss of citizen status for their children and rights to property in Attica. (Amusingly, Pericles was one of the first people to contravene this law. His sons from his Athenian wife, whom he had divorced, died, leaving him only with his son Nothos by his Milesian concubine Aspasia. He begged the assembly to grant this son citizenship, which they did.)

Other Democracies: Argos and Rhodes

Athens was not the only, or even the first, democracy in Greece—although this is a popular misconception. As mentioned above, many colonies began on a basis of at least partial egalitarianism, leading to democratic structures and ideologies. Likewise, it is probable that the hoplite warfare that evolved in the Archaic Age led to a belief that all members of a city who fight in its defense should share in its administration. Later, the Athenians "inflicted" democratic reforms on many of the poleis in their empire, popularizing the trend. Finally, many poleis simply opted for democracies.

One was Argos in the Peloponnese. Argos appears to have adopted a democratic system around 470–460 B.C.E. The base of the government was the damos (an alternate form of the word *demos*), which was equated early on with the Aliaia, or Assembly. This Aliaia convened about once per month (more in periods of crisis) to discuss sacred matters and legislation, as well as foreign affairs when necessary. The laws and decrees of the Aliaia were authenticated by an assembly president and a council secretary. This secretary probably served an annual term, but the president himself served for four months at a time. The Aliaia, the president, and the secretary served as the "legislative branch" of government (Piérart 2000, 303–310).

Part of the "executive branch" was the Eighty. They, along with the city treasurer, ensured that decrees were made public, and they served as judicial functionaries and arbitrators. Like the assembly, they had a president and, unlike the assembly, two secretaries. Also functioning in an executive capacity were the Artynai, known only through a reference in Thucydides. These men probably were the equivalent of the Athenian archons, the magistrates in charge of implementing the will of the assembly. Finally, at least until 420 B.C.E., there was a government official called the king, or basileus. This was probably a hereditary title for an official with traditional religious responsibilities to the city (Piérart 2000, 303–310).

Another democracy was established on Rhodes. This Rhodian democracy existed among the three poleis on the island—Ialysos, Kameiros, and Lindos—which had synoecized over a gradual process, culminating mainly between 411–407 B.C.E. During this period, they founded the city of Rhodos to serve as a political and military center (much like Washington, D.C., in the United States), and started minting a common coinage for the entire island (Gabrielsen 2000, 195–196).

The political base of the community was the damos, usually called the *pas damos* or "entire people." This damos enjoyed freedom of speech (parresia) and especially the right to submit proposals (isegoria) to the ekklesia/assembly. This ekklesia was the highest political authority in the state. It met in the theater of Rhodos monthly to debate national and foreign issues and to pass laws and decrees. Thus, it might be seen as the legislative branch of the Rhodian government. The ekklesia worked in conjunction with a boulê, whose members were chosen by lot from the damos to serve six-month terms. As with other democratic systems, this boulê prepared materials for presentation in the ekklesia. Along with these two bodies were five prytanies, officials who presided over sessions of the ekklesia and probably the boulê as well. As with Periclean Athens, there was pay for governmental service, such as attending the assembly, serving on juries, or even for serving various military and civic functions. In all, the system on Rhodes was what we might term a radical (social) democracy, where pay for service allowed even the poorest members of society to take part in government (Gabrielsen 2000, 190–191).

(Please note: This book uses terms like *legislative branch* and *executive branch* to make these functions more familiar to the modern reader. The ancient Greeks themselves did not share our concepts of checks and balances, and there was no strict segregation of governmental functions.)

POLITICS BEYOND THE POLIS

Although independence and self-sufficiency were the ideals of ancient Greece, both for individuals and poleis, reality forced the Greek poleis to deal with each other from time to time. Often, as discussed in chapter 4, this interaction was in the form of war. But the Greeks also had peaceful forms of political alliance, notably the amphictiony, the hegemonic league, and the ethnic league. As with the various forms of government (monarchic, oligarchic, democratic), these political arrangements could overlap or evolve from one into another.

Amphictionies

The oldest type of political alliance between poleis was the religiously based amphictiony (*amphi* = around; *khthonos* = earth, land; *amphictiony* = those living around the same area). In such organizations, several independent poleis organized themselves around the cult and sanctuary of a deity, and these poleis came together mainly for religious festivals. As time went on, perhaps to maintain goodwill between the participants, codes of conduct were set down for the amphictiony members. Known amphictionies included the Boiotian Amphictiony of Onkhestos and that of Kaluria on the Saronic Gulf, both dedicated to

Poseidon; the Panionian of Ionia, and the Amphictionies of Delos and Delphi dedicated to Apollo (Ehrenberg 1969, 108–109)

The most famous amphictiony was that at Delphi, site of the famous oracle and Panhellenic games. From what can be deduced from the epigraphic evidence, this amphictiony had twelve members, each of whom had two votes in the meetings held biannually at the site of Pylaia. These meetings were composed of two parts—a synedrion, or council, and an ekklesia, or assembly. The council was composed of formal representatives from the member poleis, specifically the hieromnemones, the pylagori, and the agoratri (all three names of the representatives' offices). The council was the amphictiony's leading authority and high court. The assembly consisted of any citizens who happened to be around for the meetings (Ehrenberg 1969, 110–111). In most cases, the meetings concerned purely religious matters, dealing with aspects of cults or festivals, with the organization of the games, or with religious infractions committed within the poleis. The members of the amphictionies could not interfere politically or legally with other members, making for rather loose alliances.

Hegemonic Leagues

Although amphictionies were regionally and religiously based, with no specific polis having a political edge over the others, hegemonic (*hegemon* = leader) leagues were politically based and organized, with one polis being the dominant member. The earliest such league was the Lakedaimonian League, begun in the sixth century B.C.E., led by Sparta as the most militarily prestigious of the group, and including both Tegea and Corinth.

The three most famous and, in the fourth century, influential hegemonic leagues were the Second Athenian League, the Boiotian League (although some might argue that this belonged to the next category—ethnic leagues), and the Corinthian League. The last was established by Philip II of Macedon in 337 B.C.E. and included all the Greek poleis except Sparta. Macedon, specifically Philip, was the clear hegemon, and in reality the league existed as little more than a means of organizing the newly conquered Greek poleis for Macedonian domination (see chapter 4). Still, one must give Philip II some credit—this was probably the first thing the Greeks had ever done as a unified nation.

More typical was the Second Athenian League—"Second" because it came after the "First" Athenian League, also known as the Delian League and/or the Athenian Empire. The Athenians were clearly trying to be more equitable at the inauguration of this later alliance, established in 377 B.C.E. in the face of Spartan aggression and annoyance. Much of what we know about its inception comes from the Aristoteles Decree, a marble inscription discovered in the Athenian Agora (see chapter 9) (Tod 1985, 123):

In the Archonship of Nausinikos
Paionieus secretary

In the 7th prytany [of Nausinikos] in the month Hippothontis [February or March]. This seemed good to the *boulê* and to the demos, with Kharinos Athmoneus presiding and Aristoteles speaking:

Good Fortune to the city of the Athenians and to the allies of the Athenians.

So that the Lakedaimonians leave the Greeks free and autonomous in peace, each one having their own territories in security and so that a common peace be maintained forever, the Greeks and the King [of Persia] swore to this agreement, voted on by the demos.

If any Greek or barbarian, on the mainland of any island, who is not subject to the King wished to become an ally of Athens and her allies, he may do so enjoying his freedom and independence and any constitution he pleases, without the imposition of a garrison or governor or the payment of tribute, on the same terms as the Khians, Thebans, and other allies.

The people guarantees to surrender all Athenian landed property, either privately or publicly owned, in the territory of members of the League, and if there are at Athens inscribed records unfavorable to any of the league states, the boulê receives full authority to destroy them. From the current year onward no Athenian may, privately or publicly, acquire house or land in the territory of allies by purchase or mortgage or in any other way whatsoever. If he does do so, any ally may lodge information with the allied assembly (synedrion), which shall sell the property and give half the proceeds to the informant, retaining half in the common fund of the allies.

The Athenians and her allies shall give the utmost assistance to any member of the League who is attacked.

If any magistrate or citizen proposes or puts to the vote any measure contrary to this decree, he shall lose his citizenship, his property shall be confiscated and a 10th shall be given to Athena. Further, he shall be tried before the Athenians and the allies and punished with death or with banishment from the league territory. If sentenced to death, he may not be buried in Attica or in league soil.

The secretary of the council shall erect a marble stele bearing this decree beside the statue of Zeus Eleutherios, and the treasurers of the goddess shall defray the cost— 60 drachmas, from the "ten talents." On this stele shall be inscribed the names of the existing allies and all future accessions. Three envoys shall forthwith be elected to visit Thebes and secure what benefits they can.

[Names of envoys]

[Names of allies]

(Translation adapted from Tod 1985)

The synedrion met regularly in Athens and was summoned by an Athenian official. It elected its own president and voted on affairs concerning the entire league. The league's hegemonic aspect was evident in the synedrion's voting policy—all states except Athens had only one vote; Athens had more. Furthermore, the decrees passed by the synedrion then went before the Athenian boulê or assembly, and it is unknown who actually had final say in league decisions (Ehrenberg 1969, 114–115).

The Boiotian League actually began as an amphictiony—the Onkhestos Amphictiony—in the sixth century B.C.E., centered on the Panboiotia Festival at the sanctuary of Athena Itonia (Ehrenberg 1969, 122). The League became politicized in two distinct phases. The first lasted from 447 until 386, when it was dissolved by the Spartan king Agesilaus; the second emerged in 379/378 and lasted into the Hellenistic period.

Much of what we know about the earlier manifestation of the League comes from the Oxyrhynchos Historian (see above). In the *Hell. Oxy.* 11, 2–4, she tells us:

> Boiotia-wide matters were arranged in the following way. All who lived in that area were distributed into 11 divisions, and each provided a Boiotarch, as follows. The polis of Thebes contributed four (two on its own behalf, two for Plataia, Skolos, Erythrai, Skaphai and the other regions previously sharing a common citizenship with them but at the time subject to Thebes); Orchomenus and Hysiai provided two Boiotarchs between them; Thespiai with Eutresis and Thisbai provided two; Tanagra one; and Haliartos, Lebadeia and Koroneia between them provided a further one, whom each of the poleis would send in turn; and in the same manner one would come from Akraiphnion, Kopai and Chaeronea (jointly). In this way the divisions returned their officials. They provided also 60 councilors per Boiotarch, whose daily expenses they paid . . . In accordance with the number of their officials, they drew on the common funds, paid taxes, appointed jurymen, and in general shared alike in all the public burdens and benefits. This, then, was how the set-up of the whole ethnos was arranged, and the meetings of the council and other common assemblies of the Boiotians would sit on the Cadmeia. (Translation by Cartledge 2000, 399, used with kind permission)

The League was divided into eleven administrative units, called merê in Greek. Each meros (sing.) contributed equal numbers of soldiers and taxes to the League, suggesting that the merê were roughly equal in size/population/resources. The League's main administrative unit was a federal boulê/council, to which each of the merê sent sixty annual representatives, for a total of 660 councilors. This boulê was divided into four parts, with each quarter in permanent session for three months of the year (much as the local Theban government was at this time). Furthermore, each meros contributed one boiotarch (Boiotian leader), elected by the enfranchised populace of each division, to serve as the League's executors. They levied troops, commanded the field, served as diplomats, and may have helped to organize the affairs of the boulê itself (Cartledge 2000, 405).

In theory, there was an equitable division of power throughout the League. However, one must note that different poleis controlled different numbers of merê—Thebes had four, Orchomenus had two, and Akraiphia, Kopai, and Chaeronea had one among the three of them. Thus, Thebes alone had 240 councilors in the boulê, while Akraiphia, Kopai, and Chaeronea together had only 60. By natural extension, Thebes provided four of the Boiotarchs, and the others provided Boiotarchs in like proportion. This, plus the fact that the council met in Thebes itself, gave Thebes a considerable majority over the other members of the League, thus classifying it as hegemonic (Cartledge 2000, 405).

After the interlude of Spartan rule from 386 to 379 B.C.E., a new Boiotian League formed, mostly on the same lines as the previous one. Now, however,

Thebes was in even greater control of the League, being recognized as formal hegemon and providing four of the now seven boiotarchs. Furthermore, Thebes now adopted a more democratic constitution, with lower property requirements for enfranchisement. Thus, a larger number of Thebans were taking part in League affairs than previously, along with the city's proportionately higher representation.

Ethnic Leagues

The ethnic leagues, so named as they usually began with a confederation of neighboring, ethnically related poleis, were different from the hegemonic leagues in that no one polis clearly dominated the rest. Rather, these leagues attempted to create a "nation" out of the member poleis, where league citizenship overshadowed the more narrow polis citizenships. Such leagues included the Cretan League, the Aetolian League, the League of Islands, and the Achaean League.

The most influential of these was the Achaean League, founded in 280 B.C.E. by the union of four Peloponnesian cities. Over time, not only did all the other Achaean poleis join this league, but so did cities from other ethnic regions, such as the Arcadians. Eventually the League incorporated some sixty cities and around 13,000 square kilometers of territory. All poleis were admitted on a basis of equality, but their self-sovereignty was eliminated as they came under League authority. Rather than a system based on individual poleis, the League was divided into administrative districts, called synteleiai, thus helping to diminish traditional loyalties (Ehrenberg 1969, 126–127).

According to the historian Polybius, "For the first 25 years these cities shared in a league, appointed a common secretary according to a rhota (formal, written terms), and two generals. Later they made a new decision to elect a single general and to entrust him with substantial authority. Margos of Kerynia was the first." From 280 to 255 B.C.E. two elected generals stood at the head of the League. After 255, only one general was in control. No general could serve two consecutive terms, so power was, to a certain extent, rotated among the more powerful League members. Below the generals were the demiourgoi, the main administrators who presided over the League assemblies. As with many poleis, the main legislative bodies were a boulê and an ekklesia, open to all males over age thirty. Originally, before about 220, the boulê and ekklesia met about four times per year in meetings called synodoi ("roads together," from which we get the modern word *synod*). In cases of emergency, an extraordinary council might be summoned, called a synkletos. At the end of the third century B.C.E., however, a law was passed forbidding the ekklesia from attending the synodoi, which became reserved exclusively for the boulê. The ekklesia could only attend the synkletoi, arranged and announced in advance by the boulê. Thus the more democratic arrangement of the League became increasingly oligarchic/centralized over the course of the third to second centuries (Ehrenberg 1969, 125–130). As will soon become evident, this was probably done to compete with the infinitely more centralized political systems of the Hellenistic monarchies.

ALEXANDER AND THE HELLENISTIC MONARCHIES

With the rise of the Hellenistic monarchies, beginning under Alexander the Great and continuing with his successors, Greek politics came full circle. During this period, leagues and a defiantly independent Sparta notwithstanding, Greece came under the authority of semidivine kings assisted by companions, much like the Mycenaean wanakes with their e-qe-ta. The change derives primarily from eastern influence in which Hellenistic kings and queens ruled populations long accustomed to divine monarchs.

Divine Right

Up through the reign of Philip II, the Macedonian king was technically just the first among equals, a high-functioning bureaucrat rather than an omnipotent emperor. The prerogatives of the Macedonian nobility had to be honored, and Greece was governed through legally constructed leagues (like the Corinthian League) and alliances. In many ways, Philip II was little more than a new hegemon for the Greeks, following in the footsteps of Athens, Sparta, and Thebes (see chapter 4).

It was Alexander who divinized the Macedonian royalty. According to Arrian, after Alexander's conquest of Persia with all its domains, he traveled to the oracular sanctuary of Amun in Libya, where he was told that he was, in fact, the son of Amun, the Egyptian equivalent of Zeus. Furthermore, the final non-Greek pharaoh of Egypt adopted Alexander as a son, making Alexander a legitimate pharaoh. Since, according to Egyptian beliefs, the pharaoh is the human manifestation of the god Horus, this made Alexander the son of the king of the gods for the Greeks *and* the god Horus for the Egyptians. As the rule of Egypt continued through the Ptolemaic dynasty, the Ptolemaic pharaohs continued to be so regarded. Cleopatra was, technically, the god Horus.

The situation was different in the Near East. Although some early Mesopotamian kings did claim to be gods (such as Naram-Sîn of Akkad), this was the exception rather than the rule. More common, both in earlier Mesopotamia and in Persia, was the idea that the king was responsible for his people before the gods. Divinity, therefore, was not at issue. However, the Persians did have their own concept of monarchy, which placed the king well above the common man. The Persian king ruled absolutely, and the population revered him, if not as a god, then as something between divinity and humanity. Ritual self-abasement before the king was an absolute necessity in his court, and it was absolutely anathema to the Greeks.

As one might imagine, this caused problems after Alexander's conquest of Persia, when both Greek and Persian functionaries were functioning next to each other in Alexander's court. The Persians treated Alexander with all due Persian respect, most notably an action called the proskynesis, which seems to have involved either physical prostration or blowing a kiss to the king from a bowed or prostrate position (Walbank 1992, 38). Whatever it was, the Greeks found it to be completely demeaning, and one courtier—Kallisthenes—utterly refused to perform it. Alexander had him tortured and killed but later absolved his Greek followers from having to do it. Nevertheless, between the Egyptian and Persian influences, Alexander and his successors completely changed Greek notions of monarchy. In contrast to the irritating tyrannies or constitutional kings, the Hellenistic monarch emerged as an absolute ruler whose word and will were law, and who could claim legitimacy not through ancestral custom or elected laws, but through divine right.

The Rhetoric of Freedom

Of course, all Hellenistic rulers did die at some point, starting with Alexander, so claims of godhood could only go so far. In truth, the Hellenistic monarchs did have to manage their power carefully, keeping as much as possible on the good side of the Greeks (who were more likely to chafe under the new regimes than, say, the Egyptians, for whom there was little change in government). A large part of this management was maintaining the traditional Greek rhetoric about liberty, claiming that the kings stood for the independence of the poleis. Diodoros records that in 319 B.C.E., when Polyperchon tried to rally support against the faction of Cassander, Antigonos, and Ptolemy (see chapter 4), he claimed that he intended ". . . to free the cities throughout Greece and to overthrow the oligarchies established in them by Antipater: for in this way they would best decrease the influence of Cassander and also win for themselves great glory and many considerable allies" (Diodoros 18.55). Years later, Antigonos made a similar cry for the freedom of the Greek poleis, once again recorded in Diodorus (19.61–62):

> And it stated that all the Greeks were free, without foreign garrisons and autonomous. When the soldiers voted on the matters stated, Antigonos sent off men in all directions to announce the decree. For he undertook on the one hand to have the Greeks as eager allies in the war through their hope for freedom, while on the other hand to have the generals and satraps of the upper satrapies, who suspected that Antigonos would overthrow the kings succeeding Alexander, change their minds and be willing to follow his orders if they saw him blatantly taking up the war on their behalf. . . . At the same time that these things were happening, Ptolemy, hearing the intentions of the Macedonians along with Antigonos to free the Greeks, issued a similar proclamation himself, wanting the Greeks to see that he was concerned about their autonomy no less than Antigonos. For each seeing it to be no small matter to acquire the good will of the Greeks, they strove with each other in bestowing benefits on them.

The Greeks never did regain their autonomy. They did, however, have a reasonably beneficial rapport with the various monarchs. Although much of the land was destroyed by the wars between Alexander's successors, the kings and queens were generous in their attempts to ward off financial and cultural destitution among the poleis. In a pinch, a king could take on the role of public magistrate or priest, funding the city's affairs until the economy improved. Thus, Alexander served as magistrate in Miletos in 334, as did Demetrios in 295 and Antiochus in 280. At other times, the monarchs could simply send either money or goods to sustain the poleis in times of crisis, as in 195 when the Seleucid queen Laodikê sent grain to the population of Iasos in southwestern Turkey, from which the poorer citizens could derive dowries for their daughters. Likewise, in 159, King Attalos II of Pergamon sent 18,000 drachmai to Delphi to pour into their school system, to pay teacher salaries and to educate the children (Shipley 2000, 85–86).

Bureaucracy

Lysimachus once identified the government as "Ourself [the king], our friends, our army, and our administration" (Ehrenberg 1969, 159). We have already considered much of what constituted the monarch himself or herself. The Friends (philoi) started out as Alexander's companions (hetairoi), all Macedonian. As time passed and the empires grew, the official Friends of the king(s) were a combination of Macedonians and local natives, the latter usually the elite of loyal cities. Informally, these Friends served as liaisons between the king and his subjects, and they were instrumental in securing benefits for their cities. At other times, these Friends might meet more formally in a type of synedrion or council to advise the king (Shipley 2000, 76)

The army was unique in Greek history, insofar as it consisted primarily of professional mercenaries rather than the common populace (see chapter 6). This had the distinct benefit of keeping those with arms more closely loyal to the crown than to any individual polis, at least as long as they were paid. This loyalty was not only important in the face of possible mutinies by the poleis, but also when matters of succession were in debate. A long-standing Macedonian tradition maintained throughout the Hellenistic period was that the king was formally pronounced and accepted by the army. Having the army on one's side made it infinitely easier to have one's preferred candidate set upon the throne in cases of contested inheritance.

Finally, there were the administrations (pragmata in Greek, literally "things"), which in the Hellenistic governments were combinations of traditional bureaucracies and Macedonian innovations. At the head of each bureaucracy were the king and queen, who were responsible for the proper functioning of their administrations. Complaints about inefficiency or corruption eventually wound up on their desks: "King Ptolemy (II) to Antiochus, greetings. Concerning the billeting of soldiers we hear that there has been increased violence as they are not receiving lodgings from the oikonomoi (governmental officials) but break into the houses themselves, expel the inhabitants and settle there by force. Give instructions therefore that in the future this is not repeated, but that preferably they provide themselves with accommodation [= barracks]" (translation by Austin 1981, 249, adapted).

Assisting the king and queen throughout the different empires were strategoi—generals—each of whom controlled a limited territory and a certain percentage of the army. Likewise, all administrations possessed a bevy of scribes, who were almost exclusively Greek among the Macedonian Antigonids, but probably mainly Hellenized natives in the other kingdoms where, at minimum, bilingualism was required. These scribes recorded and publicized the letters and edicts of the monarchs, the foundation of all Hellenistic law, policy, and action. The most famous example is the Rosetta Stone, an edict written in 196 B.C.E. on the anniversary of the coronation of Ptolemy V Epiphanes. The text is a list of benefits conferred upon Egypt by the king. More significant (at least for later Egyptologists) is that the edict appears in three scripts—Greek, demotic, and hieroglyphic, leading to the translation of hieroglyphics by Champollion in the 1820s.

The Ptolemaic and Seleucid dynasties made use of the bureaucratic systems already in place when Alexander conquered Egypt and Persia, respectively. Egypt was divided into cantons/nomoi (in place since the Old Kingdom, 2650–2180 B.C.E.), districts/topoi, and villages/komai. Strategoi and nomarchs controlled the various regions of the country, and the pharaoh was assisted by the Egyptian vizier, an age-old position. The Seleucids maintained the divisions of their land established by the Persians. These were called satrapies, each governed by a satrap and/or a strategos (Ehrenberg 1969, 180).

In spite of the huge territories and the mixture of ethnicities involved, the Hellenistic bureaucracies were nevertheless "personal." All functionaries functioned directly for and by the will of the monarch and were responsible to him/her personally. The rule of law that characterized Classical Greece was replaced by an absolutism the Archaic tyrants could not have imagined.

ANCIENT GREEK LAW

The Early Years

The Greeks believed that their first lawgivers were King Minos of Knossos and his brother Rhadamanthys. These men were so successful in their art that they went on to be judges of the dead in Hades. Beyond the "laws of Minos," however, we know very little about law and legal practices in the Bronze Age Aegean. Some Linear B tablets record disputes over landholdings, such as between the damos and the priestess Erita, and we may assume that one purpose of the Linear B documents was to keep legal records.

The earliest evidence we have for legal procedure comes from Homer and Hesiod. The references in Hesiod have already been discussed above in the section on Dark Age kingship, wherein kings, for better or worse, decided legal judgments for their people. The evidence in Homer comes from Book 18 of the *Iliad* (ll. 497–508), where Homer describes the scenes of civilized life that Hephaistos—the smithy god—wrought on the shield of Achilles:

> But the people were assembled in the agora where a contention
> emerged, and two men fought over the blood-money
> of a murdered man, the one swore to have paid it all
> declaring this to the demos, but the other man refused to accept anything.
> Both put the issue before a judge, hoping to win.
> The people chattered about them both, favorable to both sides.
> The herald held back the people; the old men
> sat on polished stones in a sacred circle

holding in their hands the scepter of the loud-voiced heralds.

Then they sprang up, giving judgments in turn.

In their midst lay two talents of gold,

to be given to him who among them spoke the straightest judgment.

The picture derived from portrayals like this is that early Greek law was a matter of voluntary arbitration, wherein aggrieved parties came together, picked a judge or judges (possibly the basileus/eis, as per Hesiod), and had that judge decide a resolution to the problem. If we are to trust Homer, it is possible that several judges offered advice and that a prize (court fees, perhaps) went to the judge who suggested the best course of action (Gagarin 1989, 42–43). Such a course must have proved the most pleasing to both parties, soothing feathers for all involved. This was certainly preferable to a Hatfield-and-McCoy-style long-term family vendetta, which, if we are to trust Homer, was the other major form of justice in the Dark Age and Early Archaic Age.

The Late Archaic Age

Starting in the seventh century B.C.E., the Greeks put their laws into writing. The evidence for this is both literary and epigraphic. Our earliest epigraphic evidence comes from the city of Dreros on Crete, dating to 650–625 B.C.E. The laws are only partially preserved, but the most intact shows concern for legal procedure and city administration: "May God be kind. The city has thus decided: When a man has been kosmos, the same man shall not be kosmos again for ten years. If he does act as kosmos, whatever judgments he gives, he shall owe double, and he shall lose his rights to office, as long as he lives, and whatever he does as kosmos shall be nothing. The swearers shall be the kosmos and the damioi and the twenty of the city" (translation by Meiggs and Lewis 1992, 2).

The kosmos appears to have been some manner of judge who decided cases, clearly a rotating function to be held by any citizen for only one year, once per decade. The presence of anxiety that someone would try to hold the office more frequently may indicate that financial gain was to be had from this duty, and the citizens of Dreros were concerned with avoiding abuses of power in their legal proceedings.

Another early law is the homicide law of Drakon, the early Athenian lawgiver (see above). The original version of this law, composed around 620 B.C.E., no longer survives, but it was copied verbatim in 409/408, and thus the text remains:

Even if someone kills someone without premeditation, he shall be exiled. The Basileis are to adjudge responsible for the homicide either . . . or the one who instigated the killing. The Ephetai are to give verdict. Pardon is to be granted, if there is a father or brother or sons, by all, or the one who opposes it shall prevail. And if these do not exist, pardon is to be granted by those as far as the degree of cousin's son and cousin, if all are willing to grant it; the one who opposes it shall prevail. And if there is not even one of these alive, and the killer did it unintentionally, and the Fifty-One, the Ephetai, decide that he did it unintentionally, then let ten members of the phratry admit him to the country, if they are willing. Let the Fifty-One choose these men according to their rank. And let also those who killed previously be bound by this ordinance. A proclamation is to be made against the killer in the agora by relatives as far as the degree of cousin's son and cousin. The prosecution is to be shared by cousins, sons of cousins, sons-in-law, fathers-in-law, and members of the phratry . . . responsible for homicide . . . the Fifty-One. . . . If someone kills the slayer or is responsible for his being killed while he is avoiding a frontier market, games, and Amphictionic rites, he shall be treated on the same basis as one who kills an Athenian. The Ephetai shall bring in the verdict . . . one who is the aggressor . . . slays the aggressor . . . the Ephetai bring in the verdict . . . he is a free man. . . . And if a man immediately defends himself against someone who is unjustly and forcibly carrying away his property and kills him, the dead man shall receive no recompense. . . . (Translation by Stroud 1968, 6–7. Used with kind permission)

Essentially, this law states the legal procedure for dealing with homicides. The accused murderer had to leave Athens and was banned from the markets at the edges of Attica and the peripheral religious ceremonies. While he was gone, judges worked with the victims' families to determine if the slaying was accidental, in self-defense, or actual murder. If self-defense, the killer was acquitted. In the other cases, the family to the degrees specified had the option of accepting money as recompense for their loss. Until the case was settled, no one was allowed to harm the accused (provided he kept out of the forbidden areas); if someone did, then *he* was accused of murder. Thus, the law provided for the safety of the accused, gave a step-by-step procedure for dealing with the problem, and made allowances for issues of self-defense.

Other early law codes come from Chios, Eretria, and possibly Gortyn in Crete (a code that may be older than its fifth-century writing). With the possible exception of Dreros (so little remains that it is difficult to say anything definite about it), the early written codes seem to represent entirely new sets of laws created in the seventh and sixth centuries B.C.E., rather than the eventual recording in writing of old laws. The majority of these new laws were procedural: They dealt with the carrying out of legal functions rather than establishing what people could or could not do. One must assume that the Greeks already had a number of traditional notions of right and wrong to which they adhered. It would appear that starting in the seventh century, though, the poleis came to need new means of arbitrating disputes among citizens, probably resulting from the growth of the cities in the eighth century and the rising power of the middle classes. This was especially the case with the colonies, where a new sense of egalitarianism met with a break from the traditions of the mother city/cities: The colonists had to come up with new means of resolving conflicts.

Perhaps this is why the earliest literary evidence for the early lawmakers concerns the colonies. According to tradition, the earliest man to draw up a full set of new, written laws was Zaleukos, for the colony at Epizephyrian Lokris in Italy in 662 B.C.E. (Gagarin 1989, 52). According to Aristotle (fr. 548

Rose), "When the Lokrians asked the oracle how they might find relief from the turmoil they were experiencing, the oracle responded that they should have laws enacted for themselves, whereupon a certain shepherd named Zaleukos ventured to propose to the citizens many excellent laws. When they learned of these and asked him where he had found them, he replied that Athena had come to him in a dream. As a result of this he was freed and appointed law-giver" (translation by Gagarin 1989, 58).

There are some interesting aspects to this story. First, the lawmaker was a slave. Second, the laws were not only officially ordained by an oracle, but were, technically, dictated by a goddess—Athena. These aspects are significant because they fall in line with several other stories about the origins of the early law codes. Typically, the laws arose during periods of turmoil within the individual poleis. The lawmaker was either an outsider, from a liminal class within the city, or a god. Additionally, several traditional lawmakers either killed themselves or left the city after the implementation of their laws, so that they would not have to hear any complaints and could not be forced to amend their decisions.

Many of these motifs come together in the (semi-)mythical persona of Diokles, who supposedly wrote the laws of Syracuse. Pinning down this individual is quite a challenge. According to Diodorus (and supported by the author of the *Homeric Hymn to Demeter*), Diokles was originally from Eleusis in Attica, from where he migrated to Megara. Here, he invented the law code adopted by the Corinthians, and then he moved to Syracuse, where the Syracusans established a cult in honor of Diokles the Lawgiver. According to Aristotle, Diokles's tomb lay in Thebes, where he traveled with his lover Philolaos ("Lover of the People"). According to Diodorus, Diokles killed himself after accidentally breaking one of his own laws. It seems he forbade anyone to bring weapons into the agora on pain of death. During a period of military strife, Diokles rushed out with his weapons when a disturbance in the agora caught his attention. Entering, he was reprimanded for contravening his own law. Claiming in all honesty that he was actually fulfilling the laws, he killed himself with his sword (Sealey 1994, 24).

The presence of the Diokles cult in Syracuse and the possible Hero cult (see chapter 8) in Thebes suggests that Diokles may have been a local hero, if not a minor deity, to whom the Syracusans later attributed their laws (thus the divine connection). Likewise, the legend of his suicide in fulfillment of his own laws echoes the motif mentioned above of the lawgiver who disappears after the instigation of the new code. Kharandas, who was responsible for many of the law codes in Magna Graecia, died a similar death, adding to the mythic quality of such stories (Sealey 1994, 24).

By the dawn of the fifth century B.C.E., there were considerable changes in Greek legal practice from what Homer recorded in Book 18 of the *Iliad*. Many laws were written down into codes, rather than being at the discretion of arbitrator-judges. Furthermore, mutual agreement was no longer an aspect of the law, either for seeking arbitration or for rendering judgments. In Athens, starting with the laws of Solon, new legal categories came into being that allowed citizens to prosecute each other without mutual consent. The simplest was the dikê (literally "justice"), or private suit, which occurred between two individuals. Above this was the graphê (literally "writing"), which was a public suit whereby any person could demand justice for an offense against anyone else. Thus, if a man were murdered, leaving only female relatives (who were ineligible to enact court actions), any male citizen could bring suit against the alleged murderer. The ultimate embodiment of this sentiment was the eisangelia, whereby any male citizen could bring someone up on charges of antistate activities. This would be the only way, for example, to arrest someone on charges of establishing a tyranny, which was forbidden by the laws of Solon (Gagarin 1989, 79).

Solon gave the Athenians several other legal tools in the pursuit of justice. The ephesis allowed a party to appeal a ruling of the jurors, much like the modern appeals process. Also aware of problems of perjury, Solon instituted the episkepsis, whereby a party at a trial could formally announce his intention to sue a witness for perjury after the trial was over. Two other types of lawsuit were the dikê exoules and the apagogê. The first was a standard suit brought against a party who had been previously found guilty but who refused to pay the penalty established by the courts. The latter, in a similar vein, called the city officials to enforce a verdict if the guilty party refused to comply. Thus, in all ways, justice was removed from the hands of individuals and placed in the hands of the city. Arbitration turned into written laws prescribing certain penalties for specific crimes, with definitive procedures for handling the unhappy lawsuit loser who refused to comply with the courts' will (Gagarin 1989, 79). Similar laws existed in other poleis, including fines set not only for those who refused to comply with court mandates, but for the governmental officials who refused to enforce court decisions. So a law from the great code at Gortyn reads, "He is to pay fifty cauldrons in each case. If the kosmos in charge [of the case] does not exact full payment, he shall owe the penalty himself, and the titas, if he does not exact full payment, [shall himself pay?]" (translation by Gagarin 1989, 93).

The Classical Period

The Greeks were traditionalists, and their laws, however they came into being, were generally maintained, with "reforms" often being the reestablishment of earlier laws. Thus, in the fifth century B.C.E., the inscription of Drakon's homicide law (see above) was reestablished in Athens, and in Syracuse, the legislators Kephalos (c. 340) and Polydoros (c. 250) claimed not to have revised the laws of divine Diokles but simply to have reinterpreted them (Sealey 1994, 28).

Nevertheless, it is from this period that we have the main texts concerning the laws of the ancient Greeks. These might be divided into two categories—actual inscribed laws, of which the enormous law code of Gortyn is the most complete, and the speeches of litigants who fought cases in fifth- and fourth-century Athens. Although the laws themselves might be much older, these two categories show how the laws finally manifested themselves and how they were used and interpreted in actual courts of law.

The Great Code of Gortyn.   The law code of Gortyn in southern Crete was inscribed on twelve columns of a 9-meter-long circular wall that may have once been part of a courthouse. The writing is boustrophedon, and the letters suggest a fifth-century B.C.E. inscription, although the laws themselves might have been much older. Unlike earlier codes, the majority of laws from Gortyn are not procedural in nature but substantive, indicating what actions are and are not legal. After an introduction beginning with an invocation to the gods, the code deals with sexual offenses, dissolution of marriage by divorce or death, rules of inheritance and personal property, mixed marriages between free people and slaves, the purchase of slaves, the rights of female orphans, rules regulating debt, and adoption. The code ends with miscellaneous decrees (Sealey 1994, 38). Issues relating to families and households predominate, and it is notable that the laws protect women's property as assiduously as men's, quite a change from the traditions farther north.

Concerning procedural law, the Gortyn code stated that judges (who served one at a time) had two types of functions. In simpler cases, the judge determined whether adequate evidence was brought before the court to allow for a conviction—a stated minimum number of witnesses automatically led to a guilty sentence; the judge merely made the formal ruling. In more complex cases, the judge took an oath declaring that he would decide fairly based on his best judgment after hearing both parties (Sealey 1994, 41). In such a case, there was almost a return to the earlier practices when arbitrators were empowered to give ad hoc decisions for the best benefit of all parties involved.

Litigation in Athens.   The Classical Athenians did not have professional lawyers. In most suits between individuals, the litigants spoke for themselves, first to an arbitrator, and then, if necessary, within a law court. Public cases, especially ones involving crimes against the state, required authorized individuals to represent the people. This led to a number of regular public prosecutors who routinely transcribed their speeches given to the courts and the ekklesia. Such orators (*rhetors* in Greek) included Aeschines, Demosthenes, Isaios, Lysias, and Apollodoros, from whom we have several court transcripts on topics ranging from murder (such as Lysias's *Murder of Eratosthenes*) to inheritance (*Against Stephanos* by Apollodoros) to male prostitution (Aeschines's *Against Timarchus*). This last case is fascinating for the light it sheds both on the way the courts could be used as political weapons and on the Athenian ideology of the body.

In 346/345, Aeschines was embroiled in a lawsuit with a man named Timarchus. Timarchus, during a public trial, accused Aeschines of having betrayed the interests of the state when acting as ambassador—a minor form of treason. To counter this attack, Aeschines did not defend himself in court, but rather opened a counterattack on Timarchus, claiming that he was a prostitute. Self-prostitution was one of several actions that deprived an Athenian male citizen of his right to raise lawsuits and to vote in the Assembly. Others were neglecting one's parents or having abandoned one's shield in battle. If Aeschines's suit won out, Timarchus's previous suit would become null and void.

Aeschines's rhetoric (the word comes from the Greek word *rhetor*, defined above) was typical for such proceedings. He began with an address to the jurors, stating the cause that drove him before them. He then described, in lurid detail, the various crimes of Timarchus, ranging from his squandering of his family fortune on (female) prostitutes to his selling his own body in prostitution. Throughout this diatribe, Aeschines referred to the Solonic laws that Timarchus had broken. (In the text, all that is written is *nomoi* (laws), so the laws themselves must be reconstructed.) After a full account of Timarchus's crimes, Aeschines produced witnesses (*martyriai*, from which we get the word *martyr*) who verified his claims. The diatribe continues, Aeschines referencing not only the city's laws, but also "divine" precedent, referring to the actions of Achilles, Patrocles, and Hector. Finally the orator ends (196), "You have heard all that it is my duty to relate; I revealed the laws, I scrutinized the life of the accused. And now, it is you who are to judge my words; in an instant I shall be the mark of your judgments. The final decision depends on your counsel. By an equitable verdict conforming to your interests, you can, if you wish, stimulate again our passion to unmask those contemptuous of our laws."

In truth, though, there really was no proof that Timarchus ever sold himself into prostitution. He did have male lovers, who did bring him gifts, but it was only by a stretch of the evidence that Aeschines could suggest that these gifts were payment—thus prostitution. Rather than relying on his ability to prove the nature of the gifts, Aeschines focused on Timarchus's dissolute lifestyle, claiming that he lived without sophrosynê (temperance) and that he wasted his family's resources on food, drink, and his especial weakness—female prostitutes. In the end, it was not the question of whether Timarchus had at some point prostituted himself to other men that was really at issue, but whether he lived a life inappropriate for an Athenian.

By casting his disapproval of such a lifestyle into the guise of prostitution, Aeschines gave the Athenians a means of actively reprimanding Timarchus for his behavior. Typically, the Athenians were rather lenient about each other's actions, allowing citizens to act as they chose within the confines of the law. Male prostitution, however, was a legal issue, not because of the illegality of prostitution itself (Athens had state-sponsored brothels), but because it gave one man control over the body, and thus the being, of another man. This was hardly a problem if the prostitute were a slave, thus already socially dominated. But it caused a serious problem if the man were a free, adult citizen, for it suggested that this man was not an autonomous being but was under the control of another. As the Athenians worked on the "one man, one vote" system, it was not desirable to have a man under the influence of another when voting or acting in the courts—it gave excessive power to the dominant male, the "lover" (see chapter 6) (Halperin 1990, ch. 5). The theory of this law, then, was to keep power stabilized and equitable in Athens. In practice, the law allowed the Athenians to reprimand a man whose behavior they found unbecoming, whether he was actually guilty of prostitution in the purest sense or not. Law had turned from two litigants seeking arbitration to an elaborate system of rhetoric in which the law could be used as a weapon against political rivals. It was a lot like modern times.

The Athenian Court System. There were three legal bodies in Classical Athens—the ekklesia, the Areopagos council, and the popular jury courts. The ekklesia was responsible for amendments to the laws, which were infrequent. The Areopagos was the old, aristocratic legal body composed of former archons (see above). According to tradition, especially as recounted in Aeschylus's *Oresteia*, the original function of this body was to try homicide cases, the first being that of the hero Orestes, who murdered his mother Clytemnestra. Over the centuries, this council acquired increasingly greater privileges, until the mid-fifth century B.C.E., when Ephialtes and Pericles cut back their prerogatives and they were left once again with the responsibility of trying murder cases.

Beyond homicide, most legal cases went before the popular juries—the heliaia. The pool of jurors consisted of 6,000 men derived from the citizenry, who were divided up to try the various daily cases. Important disputes, like an eisangelia, could summon as many as 501 jurors at once (the idea being that no one could possibly bribe so many). By the late fifth century B.C.E., fear—or threats—of bribery caused the Athenians to establish methods of keeping any juror from knowing what case he would hear until the last minute. This was accomplished with a machine that distributed lots to the entire jury pool of 6,000, so that until a man received his lot from the machine, he had no idea what case he would hear.

Once assigned, the jurors heard the testimony of the plaintiffs and defendants. If it were a graphê paranomon—suit for unlawful behavior—wherein the "victim" was the state, a state prosecutor would speak. Women, children, and slaves were not allowed to speak for themselves in the courts and had to have their guardians speak for them. Animals and inanimate objects could also be tried if they killed someone—such as a branch falling on someone's head (Freeman 1991, 16). To the best of our knowledge today, they also were not allowed to speak in their own defense.

The testimony itself might seem rather naïve, or vicious, from a modern perspective. Only a small portion of it might actually revolve around the Athenian laws (often just written as "law" in the court transcripts, and not quoted). More important was the emotional impact made by the speakers. Defendants could bring their children before the jurors to gain sympathy. Occasionally, defendants even burst into tears, as did Pericles when defending his mistress Aspasia from an accusation of impiety. Often, defendants would remind the jurors of their (the defendants') past benefices to the city. As such, it appears that the laws themselves were almost secondary to the will of the jurors: If a defendant could mollify jurors enough, they might overlook an indiscretion or go lightly on punishment.

After hearing all the testimony, the jurors conducted an anonymous vote using pebbles. If the verdict was "guilty," the jurors might have to vote on a punishment. Most crimes had a stipulated penalty, but in some extreme cases the jurors would themselves decide a punishment. In such instances, the "people" would propose one penalty, the defendant another. Then the jurors would vote on which to accept. The most famous example of this occurred at the trial of Socrates. After his "guilty" sentence (for impiety and corrupting the youth of

Athens), the people proposed that he be executed. Socrates, contrary as ever, countered with the offer that Athens provide him with free dinner for life in the City Hall, seeing, as far as he was concerned, that he was actually doing the citizens a favor by constantly annoying them. In the end, he relented a bit and offered to pay a fine, which would be paid by his students (including Plato). The jury voted, and it is recorded that more jurors than had even voted him guilty voted for the death penalty. In the end, he was condemned to drink hemlock.

The Hellenistic Period

Hellenistic law was a composite of three separate legal systems—traditional Greek law as discussed above, the traditional legal systems of the lands ruled by Alexander's successors, and royal whim. To study Hellenistic law is to study the various Greek laws and codes discussed here; the laws of such areas as Mesopotamia, Egypt, and Persia; and the political history of the Diadokhoi (Successors). There was definitely a delicate balance between the traditional local codes, wherever they were, and royal whim. Although it is true that Hellenistic monarchs had absolute, even divine, control over their territories, the rhetoric of freedom forced them, for diplomatic reasons, to honor to some extent the traditions and autonomy of the Greek poleis.

One important innovation of the Hellenistic period, falling somewhere between the categories of law and international politics, was the growth of supranational arbitration, whereby conflicts between cities and states were submitted to third-party arbitrators. For example, in a conflict over territory boundaries between Corinth and Epidauros, delegates from Megara were called in to settle the dispute. The resolution was inscribed on stone and set up in the sanctuary of Asclepius in Epidauros, the ancient way of "publishing" a document: "The Megarians decided as follows for the Epidaurians and Corinthians concerning the land which they contested and concerning Sellanys and Spiraeus, sending a tribunal of 151 men in accordance with the decree of the Achaeans. When the judges reached the territory in question and adjudged the land to belong to the Epidaurians, the Corinthians challenged the delimitation, whereupon the Megarians again sent from among their judges 31 men to define the boundaries in accordance with the decree of the Achaeans; and these men came to the territory and delimited it thus . . ." (translation by Walbank 1992, 143).

REFERENCES

Andrewes, A. 2002. "The Government of Classical Sparta." In Whitby, M., ed. 2002. *Sparta*. New York: Routledge, 49–68.

Austin, M. M. 1981. *The Hellenistic World from Alexander to the Roman Conquest.* Cambridge, UK: Cambridge University Press.

Carlier, P. 1995. "Qa-si-re-u et qa-si-re-wi-ja." In Laffineur, R. and W.-D. Niemeier, eds. *Politeia: Society and State in the Aegean Bronze Age.* AEGAEUM 12. Liège, Belgium: Université de Liège, 355–364.

Cartledge, P. 2000. "Boiotian Swine F(or)ever? The Boiotian Superstate, 395 B.C." In Flensted-Jensen, P., T. H. Nielsen, and L. Rubinstein, eds. 2000. *Polis & Politics: Studies in Ancient Greek History.* Copenhagen: Museum Tusculanum, 397–418.

Chadwick, J. 1988. *The Mycenaean World.* Cambridge, UK: Cambridge University Press.

Davis, E. 1995. "Art and Politics in the Aegean: The Missing Ruler." In Rehak, P., ed. 1995. *The Role of the Ruler in the Prehistoric Aegean.* AEGAEUM 11. Liège, Belgium: Université de Liège, 11–22.

Davis, J. L. and J. Bennet. 1999. "Making Mycenaeans: Warfare, Territorial Expansion, and Representations of the Other in the Pylian Kingdom." In Laffineur, R., ed. 1999. *Polemos: Le Contexte guerrier en Égée à l'Âge du Bronze.* Liège, Belgium: Université de Liège, 106–120.

Ehrenberg, V. 1969. *The Greek State.* 2d ed. London: Methuen.

Freeman, K. 1991. *The Murder of Herodes and Other Trials from the Athenian Law Courts.* Indianapolis: Hackett.

Gabrielsen, V. 2000. "The Synoikized Polis of Rhodos." In Flensted-Jensen, P., T. H. Nielsen, and L. Rubinstein, eds. 2000. *Polis & Politics: Studies in Ancient Greek History.* Copenhagen: Museum Tusculanum, 177–205.

Gagarin, M. 1989. *Early Greek Law.* Berkeley: University of California Press.

Halperin, D. M. 1990. *One Hundred Years of Homosexuality.* London: Routledge.

Koehl, R. B. 1995. "The Nature of Minoan Kingship." In Rehak, P., ed. 1995. *The Role of the Ruler in the Prehistoric Aegean.* AEGAEUM 11. Liège, Belgium: Université de Liège, 23–36.

Laffineur, R. 1995. "Aspects of Rulership at Mycenae in the Shaft Grave Period." In Rehak, P., ed. 1995. *The Role of the Ruler in the Prehistoric Aegean.* AEGAEUM 11. Liège, Belgium: Université de Liège, 81–94.

McGlew, J. F. 1993. *Tyranny and Political Culture in Ancient Greece.* Ithaca, NY: Cornell University Press.

Meiggs, R. and D. Lewis. 1992. *A Selection of Greek Historical Inscriptions: To the End of the Fifth Century B.C.* Rev. ed. Oxford: Clarendon.

Ostwald, M. 2000. "Oligarchies and Oligarchs in Ancient Greece." In Flensted-Jensen, P., T. H. Nielsen, and L. Rubinstein, eds. *Polis & Politics: Studies in Ancient Greek History.* Copenhagen: Museum Tusculanum, 385–396.

Palaima, T. G. 1995. "The Nature of the Mycenaean Wanax: Non-Indo-European Origins and Priestly Functions." In Rehak, P., ed. 1995. *The Role of the Ruler in the Prehistoric Aegean.* AEGAEUM 11. Liège, Belgium: Université de Liège, 119–142.

Pelon, O. 1995. "Royauté et iconographie royale dans le Crète minoenne." In Laffineur, R. and W.-D. Niemeier, eds. *Politeia: Society and State in the Aegean Bronze Age.* AEGAEUM 12. Liège, Belgium: Université de Liège, 309–322.

Piérart, M. 2000. "Argos: Une autre démocratie." In Flensted-Jensen, P., T. H. Nielsen, and L. Rubinstein, eds. 2000. *Polis & Politics: Studies in Ancient Greek History.* Copenhagen: Museum Tusculanum, 297–314.

Rehak, P. 1995. "Enthroned Figures in Aegean Art and the Function of the Mycenaean Megaron." In Rehak, P., ed. 1995. *The Role of the Ruler in the Prehistoric Aegean.* AEGAEUM 11. Liège, Belgium: Université de Liège, 95–118.

Robinson, E. W. 1997. *The First Democracies: Early Popular Government outside Athens.* Stuttgart, Germany: F. Steiner.

Sealey, R. 1994. *The Justice of the Greeks.* Ann Arbor: University of Michigan Press.

Shipley, G. 2000. *The Greek World after Alexander, 323–30 B.C.* London: Routledge.

Stroud, R. S. 1968. *Drakon's Law on Homicide.* Berkeley: University of California Press.

Thomas, C. G. 1995. "The Components of Political Identity in Mycenaean Greece." In Laffineur, R. and W.-D. Niemeier, eds. *Politeia: Society and State in the Aegean Bronze Age.* AEGAEUM 12. Liège, Belgium: Université de Liège, 349–354.

Tod, M. N. 1985. *Greek Historical Inscriptions: From the Sixth Century B.C. to the Death of Alexander the Great in 323 B.C.* New ed. Chicago: Ares.

Walbank, F. W. 1992. *The Hellenistic World.* Rev. ed. Cambridge, MA: Harvard University Press.

Whitby, M., ed. 2002. *Sparta.* New York: Routledge.

Williams, C. K. II. 1994. "Archaic and Classical Corinth." In *Corinto e l'Occidente.* Taranto, Italy: Instituto per la Storia e l'Archeologia della Magna Grecia-Taranto.

Wright, J. C. 1995. "From Chief to King in Mycenaean Greece." In Rehak, P., ed. 1995. *The Role of the Ruler in the Prehistoric Aegean.* AEGAEUM 11. Liège, Belgium: Université de Liège, 63–80.

CHAPTER 8

Religion and Ideology

MINOAN RELIGION

Minoan religion, already a difficult topic to study because of the lack of texts, has been additionally complicated over the past century due to the ideologies of the Cambridge School. Following the lead of Sir James Frazer in his work *The Golden Bough,* many scholars have long believed that ancient religions revolved around fertility. All goddesses were "earth mothers," and most gods were "vegetation deities," usually the son/consort of the Mother Goddess, whose annual death and resurrection mirrored the agricultural cycle. For a century, then, most scholarship on Minoan (and just about every other) religion was reduced to fertility issues. Only in the past few decades have new theories and archaeological finds opened the doors to new interpretations.

The Deities—Iconography

Goddesses.   The earliest known representation of a goddess in the Minoan repertoire is the so-called Goddess of Myrtos from Room 92 of the Early Minoan II settlement of Myrtos Fournou Koriphi. The presence of this image, the presence of a bench structure, and the proximity of storerooms suggest that Room 92 was a shrine. The figurine (see Image 8.1) is a hollow, bell-shaped image with a long, solid neck; tiny head; molded breasts; and spindly arms holding a water jug. Paint decorates the body with what appears to be a skirt, a necklace, and a pubic triangle. Although this piece looks like a kindergartener's arts and crafts project, its identification as a deity is based on the thin neck and other nonrealistic attributes, in contrast to Early Minoan images of humans, which were basically realistic. The weird appearance puts the female outside human realms, thus, divine. Furthermore, the fragile yet unbroken condition of the figurine indicates that it could not have been useful for any "practical" functions.

The next goddess image is a figurine from a funerary complex at Koumasa dating between the Early Minoan III and Middle Minoan I periods. This is a stylized image with a simplistic head and a trapezoidal body, molded breasts, and painted clothing. Of special interest is the roll of clay around the figurine's shoulders, which may represent a snake. As snake goddesses were common in the later Minoan repertoire, this may be the earliest portrayal of one. The fact that an early version of a snake tube was also found at the site seems to confirm this identity, as snake goddesses and tubes usually came in pairs.

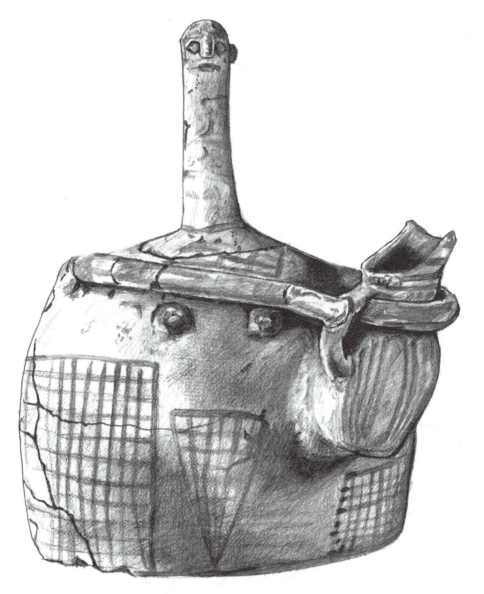

8.1 Goddess of Myrtos (Courtesy of Paul Butler)

Four more goddess images come from the Middle Minoan. Two of these come from Phaistos on an offering table and a fruit bowl. The offering table, after being heavily restored, shows three females in full skirts dancing in a row. The two flanking females are smaller in scale than the center figure, and both look to the larger female in the center. This female (perhaps a goddess) raises her hands, in which she holds flowers, possibly lilies. All three have somewhat bird-like beaks, either indicating an animal aspect to their personae (identifying them as goddesses), or indicating that they are wearing masks (suggesting participation in religious ritual). Whether they are goddesses, priestesses, or a combination of both, the main focus of the ritual "dance" seems to be the flowers, suggesting some manner of floral, vegetal, or even spring rite (Goodison and Morris 1998, 123).

The fruit bowl shows two women, skirted and beaked similarly to the ones on the offering table, gesticulating on either side of a scalloped lump in the ground, from which a female face emerges. Next to this human-headed lump is a flower. Once again, it appears that bird-beaked females are dancing on either side of some manner of supernatural female creature. Some archaeologists have suggested that the central character is a snake goddess, interpreting the scallops as snakes. However, the scallops have neither heads nor tails, so a snake identification does not seem likely. More probable is an interpretation of this center female as a flower deity. This is based on the presence of the blooming flower next to the ambiguous character, the fact that she is "growing" out of the ground, and that the same dancing figures who flanked the "flower goddess" on the offering table now flank her. Thus, we appear to have a flower goddess at Middle Minoan Phaistos.

The other two Middle Minoan images are the faience "snake goddesses" from the Temple Repositories at Knossos (see Image 8.2). One female has a snake coiled about her hat, another two wrapped about her forward-extended arms, and at least one more curling about her waist. The other, a smaller figurine with upraised arms, holds a small snake in each hand; a cat on her cap was probably added mistakenly during restoration. The sacred location, the elaborate materials and decoration, the snakes, and the gestures of these figurines all contribute to their identification as snake goddesses, suggesting that there was more than just one such goddess. Other objects found buried with the figurines were nautical—painted seashells and flying fish images—as well as faience images of mother cows and goats suckling their kids (Goodison and Morris 1998, 125). Once again, nature motifs are associated with goddess images, but now featuring animal rather than floral/vegetal life.

All of nature comes together in the goddess portrayed in the Xeste 3 Building at Akrotiri on Thera. Here, we are speaking of an island other than Crete, but the Minoans colonized at least part of Thera by 1700 B.C.E. (see chapter 4), and the iconography that emerges from Santorini is predominately Minoan in character. This goddess appears in Room 3b, in the middle of a crocus-gathering scene. Researchers can tell that she is a goddess because, first, she is seated on a tripartite shrine, a common religious motif in Minoan art. Furthermore, right behind her is a rearing griffin—a creature with the head and wings of an eagle and the body of a lion. The fact that she is attended by a magical creature emphasizes her divine status.

Looking at her personal attributes, we see she wears elaborate jewelry, one necklace composed of ducks, another of dragonflies. During a lecture several years ago, one Thera excavator, Christos Doumas, suggested that the tress curling down her back is symbolic of a snake. As such, we can at least partially interpret her as an animal goddess, a potnia therôn (mistress of animals). This idea is further supported by the presence of a monkey standing before the goddess, offering her flowers.

The ritual in which the goddess takes part casts light on another aspect of

8.2 Minoan Snake Goddess (Archivo Iconografico, S.A./Corbis)

her persona. Behind the monkey is a girl carrying a basket of crocus stamens. She is dumping these out into a shallow basket that looks almost identical to the basket before the goddess's feet. Thus, we might infer that the girl is dedicating flower parts to the goddess herself. Behind the goddess, and wrapping around the adjacent wall of the room, are more young women gathering cro-

8.3 Seal from Mycenae with Religious Scene (Ministry of Culture/Archaeological Receipts Fund/National Archaeological Museum, Athens)

cuses and carrying baskets of flowers to the goddess. It appears that what is taking place is a (perhaps annual) gathering of crocus stamens, also called saffron, which are being ritually offered to the goddess. This would suggest that in addition to being an animal deity, the Xeste 3 goddess is some manner of floral deity, a divine type well attested to in the Minoan world. However, one must remember that saffron served several important functions in the ancient Mediterranean, ranging from the medicinal to the culinary to the textile (being a common source of yellow dye). Any or all of these may have fallen under the auspices of the goddess, suggesting she was some manner of "great goddess" of nature.

Further examples of Minoan goddess iconography are present in glyptic art, scenes that appear on jewelry such as signet rings. Although only a tiny amount of detail is possible in this medium, it is evident that religious scenes featuring goddesses take place out of doors. Sometimes the goddess is standing (or hovering) in a field of flowers, as on a sealing discovered at Mycenae but clearly showing Minoan iconography (see Image 8.3). At other times, she is in a more "constructed" environment, with a paved floor and a tripartite shrine, as on an example from Archanes (Goodison and Morris 1998, 129). Even on this latter example, however, the presence of a tree growing right out of the shrine still places the religious scene in a natural setting, strengthening our notion of a goddess/goddesses of nature. It would appear that the Minoan goddesses were associated with flowers, trees, snakes, monkeys, and even birds—in short, they were nature goddesses. But, we must remember that for the Minoans, there was not really a life outside of the natural (unlike today, when people go camping or hiking to "get back to nature"). For the Minoans, to be a goddess of nature implied being a goddess of life, health, sustenance, healing, technology, and the economy.

Gods. Until recently, it has been assumed that there were no gods in Minoan religion. Or, if there was a god, it was the relatively powerless vegetation god who died every year with the crops, to be reborn the next year through the will of the Earth Mother. Once scholars began to abandon the Cambridge School way of thinking, though, it became apparent that there were gods in the Minoan pantheon. Nevertheless, there appear to have been fewer gods than goddesses; there are certainly fewer artistic representations of gods. But these representations do exist, and they tell us something about the male elements of Minoan religion.

One piece of Minoan god iconography is the master impression from Khania. Here is shown a male, nude save for a tight belt, a codpiece, sandals, a necklace, and an armband. He poses in proud fashion holding a staff on what almost resembles a tripartite shrine, except one would really have to call it a multipartite shrine, since there are so many levels and architectural elements. Many of these elements are capped with horns of consecration (see below), suggesting a religious orientation. Below the architecture is what appears to be a beach, and at the bottom of the seal, there is water. In short, the god stands upon a city that is located on a beachfront. The male's size in relation to the city identifies him as a deity, as does the fact that he stands between two horns of consecration. All this shows his dominion over the city with its adjacent beach. This notion of domination is further emphasized if we compare the man-with-staff pose with similar stances in Near Eastern iconography, in which such imagery portrayed a victorious god or king over his domain. Judging from this, it appears that we have here a city god, owner and protector of the urbs (city).

Perhaps the most important piece of Minoan god iconography is the Palaikastro Kouros, a chryselephantine (gold and ivory) statuette from Palaikastro. The statuette is one-half meter tall and stands in a standard worship pose for Minoan males, although a slight stride given to the legs probably comes from Egyptian influence (Moak 2000, 65–66). Rather than a worshipper, though, this image appears to be a god. This is evident first in the materials used in its construction. Both the gold and the ivory had to be imported, probably from Egypt. Such precious materials were probably reserved for divine images; male votives were made of clay. The elaborate workmanship that went into making the Kouros also speaks for its importance, thus its divine nature. In contrast to the rather rude votive images from Crete, there is exceptional anatomical detail in the Palaikastro Kouros, even down to the veins in its arms. The image was found by a city shrine (see below), apparently situated in a place of visual prominence, suggesting that it was intended to be the center of attention (Driessen 2000a, 95). This idea is strengthened by the fact that the statuette was originally set upon a stand: There are tangs on his feet, which fit into a blue faience mounting disc. All in all, it appears that the Palaikastro Kouros is a cult image of a Minoan god.

What type of god is a more difficult matter, and all identifications must be tentative. J. A. MacGillivray, who has done considerable work on this image, has suggested that the Palaikastro Kouros is some manner of dying and rising vegetation deity, possibly the Minoan version of Diktaian Zeus, with some Near Eastern influence in the form of Osiris, the Egyptian god of the dead. MacGillivray has even suggested that a small repository in the shrine's floor is where the image was stored during the sowing season, when the god would have been in the underworld (along with the seeds the people had sown) (MacGillivray and Sackett 2000, 169).

The Deities—Linear B

Linear B is Greek. It was developed by the Mycenaeans from Linear A (see chapter 3) to express the Greek language. Therefore, one must be very cautious when using it to determine anything about Minoan religion, as, inevitably, it involves a foreigner (Greek) looking at a local (Minoan) belief system. That much said, though, there are some data about Minoan religion that we might derive from the Linear B tablets: specifically, the deities' names and where they were worshipped.

Linear B tablets come from Mycenae, Thebes, and Pylos on the mainland, and from Knossos and Khania on Crete. A handful of divine names appear on tablets from both the mainland and the island: Zeus, Poseidon, Ares, Dionysos, Drimios, Diwiya, Hermes, and Marineus (thought to be some manner of wool god) (Hägg 1997, 165). Otherwise, the deities mentioned were specific to either the Minoans or the Mycenaeans, and it is here where we derive some information about Minoan religion from the tablets. Names specific to the Knossos archive are Atana Potnija, Potnija Dapurito, Pade, Qerasija, Pipituna, Eluthia, Erinus, Enualios, and Paiawon (Hägg 1997, 165). In spite of the odd spellings, many of these names are familiar to the student of Greek mythology. Eluthia is probably Eileithyia, goddess of childbirth. According to the Linear B tablets, this goddess had a cave sanctuary near Amnissos, where she received, among other things, dedications of honey. Erinus may refer to the Erinyes, also known as the Furies, those dread goddesses who punished crimes against blood kin. Enualios is a later epithet for Ares, just as Paiawon becomes an epithet for Apollo in his healing aspect; both may have been Minoan deities absorbed/replaced by Greek gods. Potnija Dapurito is the Mistress of the Labyrinth, probably a goddess associated especially with Knossos. Atana Potnija is almost certainly Athena, the Mistress of Athens. Finding this goddess in Knossos but not on the mainland is particularly surprising, suggesting that there was probably more overlap between the deities of the island and the mainland than the tablets reveal.

Sacred Objects

The Minoans had many objects that they understood to be divine; their presence on an object or in a picture indicated a religious context or setting. Three of the most important of these were labrydes, horns of consecration, and

8.4 Horns of Consecration, Knossos (Courtesy of Tobia Worth)

baetyls. A labrys (sing.) is a double-headed axe. How it came to be a sacred symbol is still in debate, although some suggest that it was because of its use as a sacrificial weapon. This image appears in several media and sizes in a wide variety of religious contexts on Crete. The Arkalokhori cave sanctuary produced dozens of fine labrydes in gold, silver, and copper/bronze sheet metal—all obviously too delicate for practical uses. Images of labrydes appear on art ranging from gold signets (see Image 8.3) to pottery.

Real (i.e., functional) labrydes have come to light in caves, shrines, villas, and palaces. The palace of Knossos, with its elaborate and confusing architecture (see chapter 9), was specifically known as the Palace of the Double Axe, leading to the modern word *labyrinth*. Artistic representations offer only a few clues as to the use of these objects (assuming they had a specific use). There are no portrayals of anyone killing anything with a double axe. There are, however, images of either goddesses or priestesses holding aloft labrydes in either hand, or of labrydes standing upright during rituals, with the Haghia Triadha Sarcophagus being an excellent example (see Images 8.6 and 8.7). The fact that labrydes were erected in Minoan shrines is supported by the presence of stone bases with holes for axe shafts found in a number of sacred sites, as well as by depictions of labrydes on Knossian frescoes (Davaras 1976, 72–74).

Horns of consecration are U-shaped images (see Image 8.4) that began to appear in Minoan iconography in the Middle Minoan period. The U shape is understood by scholars to be a stylized rendering of a bull's head with horns, thus the name *horns* of consecration. Another possible origin is that they represent a valley between two mountains, an image from Egypt. Although horns of consecration started out as smallish images on vases and altars, by the Late Bronze Age, they existed in three types: monumental, medium decorative, and miniature. The only monumental examples come from the palace of Knossos and its related peak sanctuary at Mt. Jouktas. Medium horns of consecration (10 cm to 1 m high) come from palaces and mansions in central and eastern Crete. In general, no more than two examples come from any given context; usually only one is found. Miniature examples appear in vase paintings and in glyptic representations. Even in the glyptic art, their presence tended to be associated with architecture, suggesting that some of the miniature versions depict the monumental ones.

Horns of consecration briefly went out of use when the Mycenaeans first took over Crete (see chapter 4). But by the Late Minoan III period, they were back in use. Medium ceramic examples with sockets for labrydes have appeared at the Villa Ariadne near Knossos and the shrine at Haghia Triadha. By the end of the Bronze Age, painted, hollow horns of consecration were common votive offerings in open-air and cave sanctuaries. What their ultimate origin and meaning were remains uncertain, but it is clear that from the Middle Minoan period onward, horns of consecration marked out sacred space (D'Agata 1992, passim).

A baetyl is a nonrepresentational depiction of a deity, usually a stone. The word comes from the Semitic languages and means "house of God" (*beth* = house, *el* = god). Several pieces of Minoan glyptic art suggest that such images played a role in Minoan worship. In some instances, worshippers, often nude, appear to be embracing baetyls, while birds or butterflies (perhaps manifestations of the deity) float nearby. A possible baetyl is located in the west court of the palace at Mallia, where the baetyl may have served in rites of epiphany (appearance of the deity to humans).

Sacred Space

Peak Sanctuaries. Peatfield defines a peak sanctuary as "a site on or near the summit of a mountain, situated to maximize human interaction (visually and physically accessible from areas of human habitation and exploitation), and identified as a shrine by the presence of specific groups of animal and human clay figurines, including anatomical models, all interpreted as votive offerings" (Peatfield 1992, 60). When peak sanctuaries first appeared is still in debate. The earliest one appears to have been on Mt. Jouktas, associated with Crete's first "city" at Knossos. The material remains here date back to the Early Minoan II period, although the extent to which the space was viewed as sacred remains debatable (Nowicki 2001, 35). Otherwise, most peak sanctuaries date from Early Minoan III to Middle Minoan I, with their high point (no pun intended) occurring in the Middle Minoan period (Nowicki 2001, 35).

From 2000 to 1650 B.C.E., there were as many as twenty-five peak sanctuaries on Crete, mostly concentrated in the east. Although high, they were accessible by foot within a few hours' walk from the nearest town, and both physical and visual links between the sanctuary and nearby residential areas seem to have been crucial in the placement of the sanctuaries (Peatfield 1992, 60). During this period, peak shrines were built up architecturally. Walls surrounded the temenos, or sacred space, and horns of consecration were common embellishments. The presence of column bases at the sites may indicate that there were roofed structures, although this would seem to contradict the point of having a sanctuary so close to the sky, and the columns may have instead been freestanding baetalic images. Several rooms are attested to at some elaborate shrines, such as the one at Mt. Jouktas, as well as built, permanent altars. Such architectural structures are not only attested to in the archaeological remains, but also in the iconography: A depiction of a peak sanctuary on a rhyton (funnel-like object) from Zakros shows a multifaceted structure with what appears to be several rooms.

Not all peak sanctuaries were so built up, though. The Atsipadhes shrine, in use through the Middle Minoan II period, was completely natural. The shrine had two terraces; the upper terrace may have functioned as some manner of adyton, or holy-of-holies. A circular area surrounded by river pebbles was, apparently, the center of the cult focus; something standing here would easily be seen from both terraces. A shallow impression may have accommodated an offering vessel, baetyl, or idol. The lower terrace was replete with clay votives, including a number of human figurines. It is probable that rituals took place here, in full view of the "deity" located on the upper terrace (Peatfield 2001, 54–55).

The votives from these sanctuaries are pretty consistent throughout Crete. Clay figurines are the most common, including both male and female humans in a variety of poses, as well as animals and individual body parts. Pebbles, and even shells, also appear in many peak sanctuaries. Less common votives, found only sporadically, are pottery, offering tables, and bronze implements, including a few labrydes.

In the Second Palace period (1650–1450 B.C.E.), the use of peak sanctuaries was deliberately limited to those few associated with the palaces. It seems that in the Middle Minoan III–Late Minoan I periods, only about six to eight sanctuaries were still in use, and by the Late Minoan II, Mt. Jouktas was the only peak sanctuary left. Early in this period, new rituals appeared at Jouktas, Kophinas, Traostalos, Vrysinas, and Petsophas. Here were found burnt and carbonized materials, occasionally even bones, showing a new use of burnt offerings.

What rites took place on the peaks of Crete, and to what deities were they dedicated? The usual assumption about the latter is that a weather god, like Zeus, was worshipped in peak sanctuaries, thus the close association with the sky. However, one of the few depictions we have of a deity on a mountaintop is the so-called Mistress of the Mountain seal from Late Minoan II Knossos. It is certainly likely that, as with the cave sanctuaries (see below), the peaks were dedicated to different deities or, following Peatfield (2001), none at all. Instead, Peatfield argues that the peaks may have been used purely for ritual action, where Minoans could gather, dance, etc., without reference to any specific deity (Peatfield 2001, passim). Other ritual performances must have included dedications of stones, shells, figurines, both human and animal, and animal sacrifice (ibid.).

Cave Sanctuaries. Caves were important to the Cretans since Neolithic times. At first, caves served as dwellings; later, they were used for laying out the dead—like a modern-day mausoleum. By the Middle Minoan period, they served religious functions. There were three categories of cave sanctuary: the grotto, which is mainly a large niche; the simple cave, which is deep but with little more than one "room"; and the complex cave, possibly bordering on the completely labyrinthine (which certainly was appropriate for the Minoans). Thirty-six such sanctuaries are attested to from Minoan Crete (Rutkowski 1986, 9). The majority contain elaborate stalagmites and stalactites, as well as water sources. These features were probably responsible for the sacred mystique of these caves, and it is likely the stalagmites and stalactites were seen as baetyls (ibid.).

Different deities were worshipped in the different cave shrines, as can be determined by the variety of votive goods dedicated. In a few very rare instances, the deity's identity has been determined by a combination of votives, Linear B evidence, and later historical references. One such example is the cave sanctuary of Eileithyia at Amnissos. Within the cave, about 10 feet from the entrance, is a smooth, rounded stone formation with a "belly-button" indentation. Farther along is a stalagmite resembling a female body (the head was chopped off in antiquity). The female imagery, especially the "pregnant belly," suggests a birth goddess. This identification is enhanced by references in the Linear B tablets to dedications to Eileithyia at Amnissos. Finally, Eileithyia's cave is mentioned in the *Odyssey.* Together, the imagery, Linear B evidence, and later literature argue that this cave was sacred to the birth goddess (Rutkowski 1986, 51).

Beyond evidence for sacrifice and drinking, we do not know what the Minoans did in the cave sanctuaries. Their dark, mystic setting, combined with later stories of shaman-like rituals taking place in them, has led Loeta Tyree, the leading expert on Minoan cave sanctuaries, to suggest that they were used in some manner of vision-quest ritual, whereby the worshipper placed herself/himself into an altered state of consciousness to encounter a deity (Tyree 2001, 43–44).

Sacred Enclosures. The term *sacred enclosure* was originally coined by the early Aegeanist M. P. Nilsson to describe what appeared to be walled, ritual structures portrayed in Minoan glyptic art. He defined a sacred enclosure as "rustic sanctuaries consisting of an enclosure with a gate-way, or free-standing portal with a sacred tree, and sometimes a baetyl, or a sacred column" (Nilsson 1950, 270–271) as per the iconography. At the time Nilsson was writing, no such sacred enclosure had ever been found on the ground.

This changed in the 1970s when A. Lebessi and P. Muhly excavated the sanctuary of Kato Symi Viannou in central Crete. This sanctuary is one of the longest-lived in ancient Greece, used continuously from the Middle Minoan period through the third century c.e. By the historical period, it was associated with Aphrodite and Hermes, although the original Minoan deities worshipped there are more difficult to determine.

By the early sixteenth century b.c.e. (Phase B of the sanctuary), the sanctuary consisted of three main structures: an area of 530 square meters surrounded by a massive enclosing/supporting wall, a paved road some 2 meters wide flanked by low curbs and separated from the wall by a drain, and a rectangular platform constructed of limestone blocks that had an initial height of more than 1.5 meters (Lebessi and Muhly 1990, 319–321). There is no evidence of a roof having been over any of these structures. The road seems to have led initially from a nearby spring, around the enclosure wall, into the enclosure on the eastern side. The platform was located within the walls, and the road must have included a ramp to allow worshippers access to the platform.

The pottery from the sanctuary is mainly gustatory in nature: chalices and goblets for drinking, libation vessels, conical cups, and dishware. The areas between the platform and walls were filled with a thick, black stratum consisting of carbonized wood mixed with animal bones. It was originally thought that the bones were the remains of sacrificial victims. However, as nothing at the site appears to have been an altar, and as the bones themselves were not burned, the hypothesis of sacrifice has been replaced with one of sacred meals celebrated at Kato Symi, with, perhaps, the head of the main course being reserved for the deity or deities. It seems that some manner of ritual picnic took place at Kato Symi (Lebessi and Muhly 1990, 327).

To date, Kato Symi is the only archaeologically recognized sacred enclosure. What is ironic is that this enclosure does not conform to the original "sacred enclosures" identified in the glyptic art. There is no clear evidence for a baetyl at Kato Symi (although there were some boulders at the site, usually avoided in construction), nor a sacred column or tree (although the latter would hardly be expected to have survived). Lebessi and Muhly have therefore revised the original definition of a sacred enclosure. Recognizing that sacred enclosures might have fulfilled a number of different ritual functions over time and across populations, they gave a more general definition: "an unroofed area serving specific cult purposes and consequently having a specific architectural plan" (Lebessi and Muhly 1990, 332). Thus, sacred enclosures accommodating tree cults would contain trees; likewise, columns would be present at sites used for column cults. Kato Symi was, rather, a feasting cult, with structures serving this purpose.

Town and House Shrines. Although the Minoans were nature-oriented in their art and sacred spaces, they did live in cities and towns (see chapter 4), and it can hardly be considered unusual that they had sacred rooms in houses and town centers as well as on mountain peaks. Such town or house shrines have been discovered at Gournia (Fournou Koriphi Myrto, possibly), Haghia Triadha, Koumasa, Malia, Pseira, Palaikastro, Haghia Iirini on Keos, Rousses Chondrou, and Khannia-Mitropolis.

What marks out a town shrine from all the buildings surrounding it in the city? There are five criteria archaeologists use to distinguish a shrine from the surrounding secular structures: (1) access from a high-traffic area, preferably a city square; (2) access through a stepped entrance (perhaps symbolic?); (3) wide entrances (for ease of entrance and egress of large bodies of worshippers); (4) axial alignment (doors on the short end of rectangular structures); and (5) architectural embellishment (think St. Peter's Cathedral) (Driessen 2000a, 90).

One town shrine is the structure near which the Palaikastro Kouros was discovered. This building (Building 5), dating to the Late Minoan I period, is located just south of Street 3-4 and the town plateia (city square). Thus, it fulfilled the first requirement above. The main, and only, entrance on the ground level led into a narrow, paved vestibule (Room 1); this led into the larger, square Room 2, which was probably the focus of whatever rituals were held in the shrine. In the floor of Room 2 was a depression containing votive items, which the archaeologists refer to as a "sacrificial pit" (Driessen 2000b, 38). Although bits and pieces of the Palaikastro Kouros were found all over the area, it was probably originally set in this room. Finally, opposite the vestibule was Room 13, a large storage room (with items still in it) and a staircase allowing access to/from the upper floors. Many of the walls were of a fine style of masonry called ashlar. The line of Rooms 1, 2, and 13 conforms to the axial alignment pattern of town shrines, and the ashlar masonry definitely counts as architectural embellishment—thus fulfilling criteria 4 and 5 above.

Minoan Ritual

How do these data come together to give us a picture of Minoan religion? We know the Minoans had a pantheon including both male and female deities, as outlined previously. The Minoans worshipped these deities on mountaintops, in caves, in houses and towns, and out in the countryside. But what form did this worship take?

The evidence from the glyptic art and the votive offerings gives some clues. Dance was certainly an aspect of Minoan worship, as evidenced in scenes of ecstatic dance in the glyptic art, dancing figures in clay found in the sanctuaries, and even "dance floors" and frescoes at Knossos portraying dancing. Eating and drinking, as well as sacrifice, were also aspects of Minoan religious ritual, as is clear from pottery assemblages and animal remains at sites such as Kato Symi and Mt. Jouktas. Offerings of flowers may have been a Minoan-Cycladic ritual, as per the frescoes at Thera, and offerings of votives, such as animal figurines, were common throughout Minoan Crete. Processional scenes in the frescoes, and the paved road preserved at Kato Symi, suggest some manner of processional ritual, possibly ancillary to other rites. Scenes of ecstasy, like those involving dance and/or baetyls, show that divine experience, be it epiphany or divine revelation, was another important aspect of Minoan religion.

In the End: The Goddess With Upraised Arms

After the fall of Knossos in the fourteenth century B.C.E. (see chapter 4), Crete went into a slow but steady decline. The palace culture that marked the Bronze Age civilizations of Crete ceased to exist, and with it the religious structures that had served the Minoans for centuries. In the place of the peak and cave

8.5 Goddess with Upraised Arms Figurine from Gazi, Crete (Courtesy of Paul Butler)

sanctuaries came a new religious structure with a new focus of veneration: The Goddess With Upraised Arms shrines. The Goddess With Upraised Arms, first appearing in Crete in the Late Minoan IIIB period, is a wheel-made ceramic figurine with a hollow "hoop" skirt. In contrast to the simple lower bodies on the figurines, the goddesses have individuated upper bodies, including a variety of hairstyles and headdresses. The consistent feature that gives these images their name is the arms, raised up on either side of the head in a posture of benediction (to judge from Near Eastern parallels) (see Image 8.5). The greatest individuality occurs in the headgear; some wear horns of consecration upon their brows, others poppies, birds, or discs. This variety in iconography, once again to judge from Near Eastern parallels, indicates that different goddesses are implied by the different figurines. That is to say, the Goddess With Upraised Arms (GWUA) icon portrays different goddesses, not one individual goddess.

These GWUA figures have come to light in shrines throughout Crete: Gazi, Gournia, Kannia, Karphi, Kavousi, Prinias, Haghia Triadha, the region of Rethymnon, and Knossos (Peatfield 1996, 29–30). Almost always found in contexts with them are snake tubes: cylindrical ceramic tubes with snake-like adfixes on either side. These tubes served as bases for offering bowls, which were also discovered in the GWUA shrines. These finds indicate that a new cult setting emerged in Late Minoan IIIB and IIIC Crete, in which the Cretan population could perform offerings (libations, perhaps) to images of their goddesses. Peatfield has argued that these new, local, and popular shrines replaced the more centralized cults originally associated with the palaces and helped the Cretans in the establishment of new political identities (Peatfield 1996, 35–36). The fact that the GWUA became a cornerstone of later Minoan ideology is evident in the image's "emigration" to Cyprus in the eleventh century B.C.E. The Minoan settlers brought this icon with them when colonizing Cyprus, where the image remained firmly entrenched well into the Classical period.

MYCENAEAN RELIGION

The Mycenaeans were fanatics for Minoan civilization, to the point of conquering Crete and taking over their civilization like some combination of hostile venture capitalists and crazed soccer fans. One result of this fanaticism was that the Mycenaeans adopted a lot of Minoan material culture, a fact especially evident in the physical manifestation of Mycenaean religion. The Mycenaeans wholeheartedly adopted Minoan iconography, to the point that early archaeologists, such as Evans and Nilsson, believed the Mycenaeans simply adopted Minoan religion upon their conquest of Crete. It was only after 1952 and the translation of Linear B that scholars realized that, although the Mycenaeans may have adopted the outer trappings of the Minoan cult, these early Greeks actually had their own distinctive religion.

The Deities—Linear B

The clearest evidence about the Mycenaean pantheon lies in the Linear B texts. As discussed above, only a handful of the deity names in these texts appear both on the mainland and on Crete. We might consider those deities mentioned only on Crete as being Minoan. For those deities mentioned on the mainland, we have at least two possibilities. On the one hand, they may be Greek, meaning that they may derive from the Indo-European civilization that gave rise to the Greek language. Some divine names do have Indo-European etymologies and cognates. On the other hand, they may be pre-Greek, belonging to the indigenous population of Greece before the Greek-speakers arrived. These deities may then have been adopted into the Greek pantheon. Some gods do have a blatantly Indo-European heritage, such as Zeus and Poseidon. Others are more difficult to determine. (The Bronze Age heritages of individual deities are discussed in a later section of this chapter.)

The deities attested to among the Mycenaeans are Zeus, Poseidon, Ares, Dionê, Marineus, Hera, Artemis, Hermes, Dionysos, Posideia, Trisheros, Manasa, Pereswa, Dopota, Dipsioi, Drimios, Iphemedeia, the Mother of Animals, the Queens, the King, the Lady of Upojo, the Lady of Asiwia, the Lady of Iqeja, the Lady of Newopeo, and the Lady of Grain, as well as simply Lady (Potnia) (Hägg 1997, 165). Much can be learned from these names not only about Mycenaean religion, but also about continuity of Greek religion into the historical periods. Many deities remained in power throughout Greek history, such as Hera and Hermes, showing that the Greek Dark Age was hardly the utter devastation and re-creation of Greece that scholars originally believed it was.

Other names in the corpus either ceased to exist after the Bronze Age or morphed into nondivine titles, such as Dipsioi, "the Thirsty," possibly referring to the dead. The most vexing of these is the name/title *Potnia*. By Homer's day, the term meant "revered female," referring either to a mortal or to a goddess. Sometimes the title was specific, as with the Potnia Therôn—Mistress of Animals—used in reference to Artemis. The question of who the Bronze Age Potnia was/were, however, is problematic.

The name/title *Potnia* appears twelve times at Pylos, five or six times at Knossos, three times at Mycenae, and once at Thebes (Boëlle 2001, 403). Thus, it is common to both Greece and Crete. In some instances, the word appears alone; in others, it is modified by a concept or place-name. At Knossos we have the a-ta-na-po-ti-ni-ja, which translates to something like Lady of Athens, and the da-pu-ri-to-jo-po-ti-ni-ja, or Lady of the Labyrinth. At Pylos we have a po-ti-ni-ja-a-si-wi-ja, Lady of Asia; po-ti-ni-ja-i-qe-ja, Lady of Horses; and at Mycenae there is the si-to-po-ti-ni-ja, or Grain Lady (Trümpy 2001, 411–413).

The question is: Is Potnia one goddess or many? Is Potnia similar to the Christian "Our Lady," in the way that Our Lady of Lourdes is also Our Lady of Fatima? Or is *Potnia* a title applicable to several separate goddesses at once? In both linguistics and occurrence, Potnia is related to the god Poseidon. The *Pot-* portion of her title may derive from the Indo-European word for possession or ownership, just as *Poseidon* means "Lord of the Land." Her strongest cult is attested to at Pylos, where Poseidon was clearly the chief god, and she even has the title of i-qe-ja, relating her to horses, just like Poseidon. One could argue that Potnia was the consort of Poseidon. Furthermore, we know from later Greek mythology that Poseidon once mated with Demeter, both of them in the form of horses. If we add this to our study, and combine it with the fact that at Mycenae there was mentioned a Grain Lady (possibly an epithet for Demeter), we might say that Potnia was one universally acknowledged Aegean goddess, understood to be a grain/horse deity, consort of Poseidon, and later manifesting as Demeter.

But then how do we understand titles like a-ta-na-po-ti-ni-ja, "Lady of Athens," which is certainly a title of an Athena-like goddess? How could an apparently Indo-European word like *Potnia* be identified with a blatantly Minoan term like *labyrinth?* Why does the name/title *Potnia* appear more than once on some Linear B tablets? Should we understand that Potnia, as one goddess, received different dedications in her different guises, or that the different Potnias referred to distinct goddesses? In the end, it seems probable that *Potnia* was a title given to various goddesses in the Aegean pantheons. In some instances, such as at Pylos, one goddess was so prominent that she could be referred to merely by the title *Lady.* At other times, adjectives were used to differentiate among goddesses.

The Deities—Iconography

As stated above, most Mycenaean iconography takes after the Minoan. Nevertheless, some elements of Mycenaean iconography are distinct. Two especially prominent Mycenaean icons are the tau, phi, and psi figurines and the Warrior Goddess. The tau, phi, and psi figurines are named after the Greek letters that they most resemble. Tau figurines (τ) have simple, straight bodies with arms extended to the sides; psi (ψ) have similar bodies to the tau but with arms curving out and up on either side of the head. Phi (φ) figurines are discoid in the torso. All frequently have small, applied breasts and are clearly female. They began to appear by the Late Helladic IIIA period and seem to have resulted from a combination of Near Eastern and Minoan influences. The Near Eastern influence is clearest in the phi figurines; these may have been simplifications of the Near Eastern Nude Goddess image, which showed a female with legs together and hands under the breasts. The psi figurines were more in tune with Minoan iconography, especially the Minoan Goddess With Upraised Arms (see above). All three varieties of figurines were quite crude. The faces were extremely simplistic, and decoration consisted of painted, vertical stripes. It is only because they showed up in shrines, as well as in graves and households, that scholars believe these common images represented goddesses.

Goddesses were not totally devoid of weaponry in Minoan iconography—some divine females were shown wielding swords in glyptic representations. But goddesses with prominent weapons and armor become more blatant in the mainland imagery. In one instance, a large-scale goddess appears on a shrine fresco at Mycenae (see below). Only her feet are preserved, but the white paint of the flesh indicates that she was female (see chapter 9). Extending down to her toes is the point of a sword with a fuller; its proximity to her body indicates that the goddess is holding the grip. Such imagery is also reflected on a plaque from Mycenae that, like the fresco, dates to the Late Helladic IIIB period. This painted plaque, partially preserved, shows a white-skinned being in the center. The fact that she is a goddess is emphasized by the small altar directly before her. She holds before her body a giant figure-eight shield and carries what appears to be a sword in her right hand. Two women stand on either side of this goddess, presumably helping her to arm herself. Both of these frescoes argue in favor of a prominent Warrior Goddess revered in Mycenae, possibly some manner of Athena forerunner (Rehak 1984, passim).

Priests and Priestesses

To judge from the Linear B tablets and the art, Mycenaean deities were served by professional priests and priestesses. Through either accident of recovery or Minoan influence, we have more information about the latter. When it is possible to determine what deities these cult functionaries served, we see that priests tended to serve gods, and priestesses, goddesses. The fact that we have the names of so many gods suggests that more priests existed than we have recovered information about so far.

At least three types of male cult officials can be identified in the Linear B corpus. These are the priest (*hiereus*), the herald (*keryx*), and the slave of the god (*doulos theou*). Two of these are mentioned on Pylos tablet Fn 187, referring to grain allocations. Except for the personal names in the text, all the titles are religious in orientation (here, just the names are given, minus the grain allocations):

1. a-pi-te-ja
2. po-si-da-i-jo-de
3. ka-ru-ke
4. pa-ki-ja-na-de
5. ka-ru-ke
6. de-do-wa-re-we
7. ku-ri-na-ze-ja
8. u-po-jo-po-ti-ni-ja
9. o-pi-tu-ra-jo
10. au-to–34*-ta-ra
11. a-ma-tu-na
12. te-qi-ri-jo-ne

13. u-do-no-o-i
14. po-te-re-we
15. a-ke-ti-ri-ja-i
16. ka-ru-ke
17. i-so-e-ko
18. po-si-da-i-je-u-si
19. 34-ke-ja
20. a-ro-ja
21. ka-ru-ke

(*34 refers to a sign without a phonetic value yet)
    (Killen 2001, 435)

A sanctuary of Poseidon is listed in line 2—Poseidaion—along with its herald/keryx in line 3. Then the sanctuary at Pakijana is mentioned in line 4, with its herald in line 5. The Potnia of Upojo appears in line 8. Line 18 mentions the priests of Poseidon—Poseidon (h)iereusi—and two more heralds appear in lines 16 and 21, probably associated with religious functionaries. The priest of Poseidon at Pylos probably functioned much as a priest in the historical periods: caring for the god's possessions and presiding at sacrifices. The idea that the heralds were religious functionaries is evident in their close associations with the sanctuaries in this tablet and by comparison with later Greek ritual. As discussed below, sacred heralds were used to call people to religious rituals.

The slave of the god/dess, of which there were male and female, is a distinct category from a common slave (see chapter 6). In contrast to the common slaves mentioned in the Linear B tablets, the slaves of the god/dess were frequently named. Furthermore, they appeared in the tablets as leasing land, showing a level of economic independence sometimes equal to that of the priests and priestesses themselves (tablet Eo 04).

The female cult officials were the priestesses (hiereiai), the key-bearers (klawiphoroi), the ki-ri-ti-wi-ja, and the slaves of the goddess (as discussed above). Mentions of priestesses appear in tablets from Pylos and Knossos. At Knossos there were references mainly about the Priestess of the Winds, who received offerings along with the deities: In tablet Fp 1+31, she receives offerings of oil, appearing at the end of a list including Diktaian Zeus, Pade, the deities of Amnissos, the Furies, and "all the gods." In the tablets from Pylos, we hear more about the priestess of a place called Pakijana, which was a popular sanctuary probably dedicated to some manifestation of Potnia. These priestesses probably presided over cult rituals such as sacrifice, as well as caring for the daily needs and affairs of their deities, such as the regulation of their property. In this they may have been aided by the key-bearers, whose keys probably belonged to the deities' sanctuaries and temples. These sanctuaries and temples themselves may have been attended on a daily basis by the slaves of the god/dess. The texts make clear that both priestesses and key-bearers managed land for their deities, as well as managing land in their own right (tablet Ep 704).

Who the ki-ri-te-wi-ja were is still uncertain. When Ventris and Chadwick first published the Linear B texts in the 1950s, they interpreted them as reapers. However, these officials show up frequently in the land-management texts, always controlling considerable amounts of land, frequently in religious contexts, and they are always listed as a communal body (as opposed to individual women). As such, Billigmeier and Turner have referred to them as "a board of women collectively possessing wealth and prestige" (1981, 7–8). These ki-ri-te-wi-ja seem to have been associated with specific deities, just as the priests and priestesses were. Pylos tablet An 607 refers to the ki-ri-te-wi-ja of the goddess Doqeta/Dopota. In each case, the women's parents were slaves of the goddess. This argues that the ki-ri-te-wi-ja were religious personnel, that they were well off financially, and that such religious functions were hereditary (Billigmeier and Turner 1981, 8).

The Haghia Triadha Sarcophagus. This ceramic coffin (see Images 8.6 and 8.7) is one of the best portrayals that we have of Minoan and Mycenaean cult ritual. The sarcophagus was created after the Mycenaean conquest of Crete, but it comes from an area where Minoan tradition remained strong. Therefore, scholars have debated whether the decorative scenes represent Minoan or Mycenaean practices. Much of the iconography is blatantly Minoan, like the labrydes with birds perched upon them. However, some of the imagery seems more in line with Mycenaean practices, like the trussed-up bull awaiting sacrifice on the altar (such scenes showed up far more often on the mainland than on the island). In general, one might simply call the sarcophagus Aegean, a fusion of Minoan and Mycenaean elements, rituals, and beliefs.

On the labrys side are two priestesses, one in an animal-hide skirt, pouring libations into a vessel between two labrydes on which birds are perched. The birds probably represent divine epiphany. Behind the priestesses is a male lyre player. Facing in the opposite direction are what researchers think are three priests, bringing offerings to an idol standing before a tomb. This would appear, then, to be a scene from a cult of the dead, possibly honoring a hero.

On the sacrifice side, we see a procession of functionaries, all behind another priestess in another animal-hide skirt (clearly a marker of religious status). This priestess stands before a small altar that is located before a temple or tomb decorated with horns of consecration. A small vessel by the priestess's hand suggests that she is pouring libations. Behind the priestess is the bull on the altar; behind him is a male flute player, the equivalent of the lyre player on the other side. Behind these in the procession are three more priestesses, although damage to their upper bodies does not permit researchers to determine what exactly they are doing. The short ends of the sarcophagus show magical females in chariots: images of the divine.

The Haghia Triadha Sarcophagus imagery suggests, as did the Linear B tablets, that priestesses play a more significant role than priests in Aegean religion, even into the Mycenaean period. Priestesses performed cult rituals in honor of the deities and the dead, including libations and animal sacrifice. Male cult functionaries also took part in these rituals, although we cannot nec-

8.6 Haghia Triadha Sarcophagos (2 views—Procession) (Kathleen Cohen/Herakleion Archaeological Museum)

essarily determine the status of the men on the sarcophagus vis-à-vis the tablets. The function of the lyre player is fairly obvious, but are the men on the labrys side priests or slaves of the god/dess? Are all the women priestesses, or only those wearing the animal-hide skirts? Perhaps those people at the end of the procession were also slaves of the god/dess; much remains unknown.

Sacred Space

There is little evidence for Mycenaean religious structures before the Late Helladic IIIA period. Only the cultic remains at the (later) sanctuary of Apollo Maleatas at Epidauros date back to the Early Mycenaean period (Wright 1996, 68). This has led some to suggest that Mycenaean cult structures were created by the palaces for the sake of propaganda. However, because at least some of the early cult places predate the palaces, as at Epidauros, it appears more likely that the palaces merely hastened a preexisting trend of building religious structures.

The Mycenaeans had three basic types of sacred space: the open-air sanctuary, the shrine building, and the megaron (Wright 1996, 37). As one might imagine, there is little archaeological evidence from the open-air sanctuaries, although textual evidence does exist for them. The most famous sanctuary known from the Linear B texts is that of Pakijana in the region of Pylos, where the priestess Erita, as well as several slaves of the god/dess, maintained land-

8.7 Haghia Triadha Sarcophagos (2 views—Sacrifice) (Kathleen Cohen/Herakleion Archaeological Museum)

holdings. Several tablets from the Pylos archive document offerings directed to Pakijana. Pakijana has not yet been "discovered," so it is entirely possible that there was some manner of cult building there. Until such is found, though, we might think of Pakijana as an open-air sanctuary.

Shrine buildings existed throughout the Mycenaean world and in the Cyclades. In some instances, they existed independently within settlements, as at Phylakopi on Melos, House G at Asine, Megaron B at Eleusis, and Amyclae. In other cases, they were located within the citadel walls of the palaces, as at Mycenae and Tiryns. All the shrine buildings had commonalities that made their identification as shrines evident. These commonalities included benches as foci of religious activity and the presence of idols serving as divine images. Nevertheless, each shrine was unique, with its own set of sacred images, arguing that the various shrines served different cults in the veneration of different deities. This certainly makes sense in the polytheistic system attested to in the Linear B tablets.

The most famous, and complex, shrine buildings are those south of Grave Circle A at Mycenae. Here, excavators found two contiguous, but not interconnected, sacred rooms abutting the citadel walls (see Image 8.8). The first of these—the Shrine of the Idols—consisted of three areas. The shrine was entered through a short vestibule to the south of the main room, dubbed the Room with the Platforms (the second part of the shrine). As you may already have guessed, one of the room's chief features was a low platform in the center of the floor. The platform was slightly concave with no signs of burning, so it may have been used for libations, but clearly not for burnt sacrifices. Beyond the platform against the far wall was a series of benches at different heights. Votives were probably placed on these benches, set before idols of the deities. One such idol still remained on the bench in the northeast corner of the room, a goddess, to judge from her prominent breasts and hair styled in a pigtail and from the upraised position of her arms. Directly before this goddess was a small table of offerings, where the devout could dedicate trinkets or first fruits.

Directly behind this idol was a staircase that led to the third component of the shrine: the Room with the Idols. Here, excavators found a quantity of similar clay figures, as well as tables of offerings, pottery, and snake models. All the idols, roughly half a meter in height, are similar in construction, yet distinctive in detail. Each was made on a potter's wheel: They have hollow, cylindrical bodies and no feet. On the torsos, the males have barrel chests, and the females have flat chests with molded breasts. Arm positions vary, and some appear to have carried now-missing items. Perhaps one male with an upraised arm carried an axe, indicative of an early manifestation of Zeus. The group of tables no doubt went with the idols, so that each deity might have had a separate place for their offerings. The meaning of the snakes has yet to be determined, although snakes were common motifs of several deities in the historical pe-

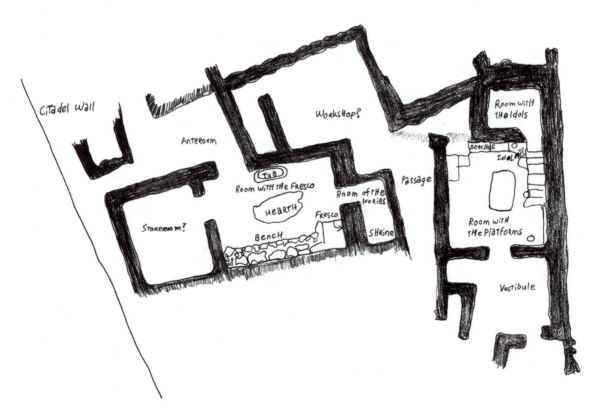

8.8 Plan of Mycenaean Shrine Complex (Courtesy of Stephanie Budin)

riod, such as Athena and Dionysos. In all events, it is clear that the Shrine of the Idols served as sacred space for several deities.

To the west of the Shrine of the Idols is the Room with the Fresco. In contrast to the axial alignment of the previous shrine, this room was relatively spread out. One entered through an anteroom to the north. Immediately left of the entrance was a bathtub containing water jugs, and it appears that one was expected to wash or purify oneself upon entering this sacred space. In the center of the room was a sunken hearth, beyond which was a bench against the south wall. No objects were found on the bench, but, as with other shrine benches, it was probably used for offerings. At the eastern edge of the bench was a white-plastered platform. This was probably an altar (Taylour 1990, 55). Immediately above this altar are the frescoes for which the shrine was named. On a lower level was a rim showing three horns of consecration, suggesting Minoan inspiration. Above these were three goddesses. The best preserved, and the smallest, shows a woman in profile carrying what appear to be sheaves of grain in both hands. Some have suggested that this is an early representation of Demeter. Above the grain goddess is a scene with two much larger females. One is the Warrior Goddess described above: She wears a fringed dress and appears to hold a sword point-down in her hand (only the bottom of the fresco remains). Facing this goddess is another female/goddess whose hem is obviously that of a Minoan flounced skirt (see chapter 9). She carries an object in her hand that appears to be a spear. To judge from the décor, this shrine was dedicated to a group of goddesses, possibly Minoan in inspiration. Behind the wall containing the frescoes was a smaller room containing several pieces of worked and raw ivory. Of particular interest to researchers is that, at a date after the room's construction, the southern wall of this room was converted into a small shrine, where was perched a little statuette of a Goddess With Upraised Arms. Apparently, one more sacred room was needed to fulfill the spiritual needs of the residents.

Finally, there is the megaron, the quintessential architectural element of the Mycenaeans. As discussed in chapter 9, the megaron—a square room with a central hearth surrounded by four columns and a throne set off to the side, approached through a porch and vestibule—was the core unit of the Mycenaean palaces. The megaron also served as the religious center of the Mycenaean palaces, and possibly of Mycenaean ideology as well. The close connection between the megaron and religion is evident both in the finds associated with the megara (pl. of megaron) and in their orientation. At Mycenae, for example, the megaron vestibule contained an altar, an offering table, and a basin possibly used for libations (Wright 1996, 54, no. 62). Thus, one was put into a ritual state of mind upon entering. At Tiryns, a special orientation heightened the religious ideology: The central hearth "looked" out through the vestibule and porch to a large piazza containing an altar. The altar was situated such that it had direct line of sight with the interior megaron hearth. Thus, the public ritual was linked to the private.

In the megaron, the hearth, columns, and throne each had symbolic meaning. The importance of the hearth as religious space probably extends well back in Indo-European tradition. It symbolized not only the concept of the house, and by extension the state, but also the notion of permanence (Wright 1996). As discussed below in the section on Hestia, the hearth was seen as the immovable center of the physical and conceptual household. To control the hearth was to control the household and, by extension, the state. The placement of the throne next to the hearth symbolized the control of the wanax (see chapter 7) over the land. The columns, possibly deriving from Minoan iconography, had at least one symbolic meaning of connecting the megaron and its hearth with the heavens. Thus, the megaron was the link between the terrestrial world of humans and the heavenly abode of the deities (ibid., 57–60). The placement of the throne right at the edge of this nexus reaffirmed the role of the wanax as mediator between the human realm and the divine.

GREEK RELIGION IN THE HISTORICAL PERIODS

Theogony (According to Hesiod)

The first four deities were Chaos, Earth (Gaia), Hell (Tartarus), and Love (Eros). Earth began the process of creation by giving birth (without a father) to Sky (Ouranos), with whom she mated through Love to produce the race of immortals. One of their sons—Kronos—castrated and overthrew father Sky at the behest of his mother, and then Kronos became king of the gods. His siblings, the children of Earth and Sky, were the Titans, the Cyclopes, and the Hundred-Handed Ones. Later, Kronos was overthrown by his son Zeus at the behest of Zeus's mother Rhea, a Titan. Zeus made sure no sons born to him could overthrow him, and thus the era of conflicts and succession (called the Succession Myth) was ended. Zeus's siblings, the children of Kronos and Rhea, were Hera, Hades, Demeter, Poseidon, and Hestia. These mated with each other and with the Titans to create the youngest generation of deities, including Apollo, Artemis, Athena, Hermes, Ares, Hephaistos, and possibly Aphrodite. Dionysos, the final Olympian god, was born of the union between Zeus and the mortal princess Semelê. Once this last generation of deities was born, the immortals turned their attention to mortals, from whom was born the race of heroes, such as Theseus, son of Poseidon, and Heracles, son of Zeus. Thus, the deities were kept to a "manageable" number.

Concerning mortals, in the earliest generations only men existed, and these lived in close contact and harmony with the gods. Unfortunately, Prometheus, a Titan, attempting to benefit mankind, caused a rift between the mortals and immortals at the Feast of Mekonê (see below). Henceforth, humans were held apart from the gods, and, if that weren't bad enough, mankind was punished with the creation of womankind. Pandora, the first woman, was presented as a "beautiful evil" gift to Prometheus's dim-witted brother Epimetheus, and from her the race of women came forth.

The Deities

Zeus. Zeus was already a prominent deity by the Mycenaean period. His name appears in Linear B texts from Knossos and Khania on Crete, as well as texts from Pylos on the mainland. In him, there appears to be a mingling of Minoan and Mycenaean influences. On the one hand, later Greek tradition recalls a "baby" Zeus, raised on Mt. Ida in Crete, who may have taken on some characteristics of an indigenous Minoan god. On the other hand, the Mycenaeans who took over Knossos in 1450 B.C.E. probably would have brought the chief of their deities with them. As such, Zeus's appearance in both Crete and Greece may derive from his initial presence in the Mycenaean pantheon, his introduction into Crete c. 1450, and his absorption of a baby god already entrenched in the Minoan pantheon.

Zeus was the king of the gods. His name is Indo-European (see chapter 1) and literally means "Sky Father." This name recalls two of Zeus's more prominent roles in Greek myth and religion. Zeus's domain was the sky, the highest, lightest place perceivable by humans. The notion of a chief deity as a sky god is quite common in world religions, especially in the Near East. However, Near Eastern sky gods tend to be older fellows, more like grandfather figures, and the more powerful deities controlled the more harrowing aspects of the sky, such as lightning. Zeus seems to have combined both types of god into his persona—although his name referred to him as a sky god, he was also the Thunderer who wielded his lightning bolts (a gift from the Cyclopes) as the ultimate weapon on heaven and Earth. As such, he was a combination of sky and storm god.

The "father" aspect recalls both the power he wielded over the other deities and his relationship to several gods and humans. Zeus was the father of many mortals and deities. On Olympos, he was father to Athena with Metis, to Ares and Hebê with Hera, to Hermes with Maia, to Apollo and Artemis with Leto, to Persephonê with Demeter, to the Muses with Mnemosynê, and to Dionysos with Semelê, not to mention his fathering of several other lesser deities. Among mortals, his most famous offspring were Heracles; the hero Perseus, who slew Medusa; the warrior Sarpedon in the *Iliad*; both Helen of Sparta and Clytemnestra (wife of Agamemnon); and Tantalos, a trickster king who was doomed to eternal torment (being tantalized) in Hades. This is only a tiny list of the thousands of children attributed to Zeus throughout the ages.

Zeus also had father-like power over the gods. In a large, family-like pantheon, his word was final, and it was he who settled disputes among the deities. In the *Homeric Hymn to Hermes*, Apollo brought his newly born brother before their mutual father to demand retribution for the cattle Hermes had stolen from him. Zeus "tried" the case, mildly rebuked Hermes, and reestablished peace and love between the two brothers. In the *Homeric Hymn to Demeter*, in a different paternal role, Zeus gave his daughter Persephonê as wife to his brother Hades. This action reflected one of the functions of mortal fathers, which was to arrange marriages for their children (see chapter 6).

Much like a typical father, Zeus had to deal with his children's discontent. Although the general understanding was that Zeus was firmly established in his role as father-king, the literature makes it clear that this stability was the result of careful planning and a lot of effort. Zeus came to power by overthrowing his own father; he had to be careful the same thing would not happen to him, that he would not have a son more powerful than he. The myths record two occasions when Zeus only narrowly escaped such a fate. In the first story, according to Hesiod, Zeus's first wife, Metis ("Intelligence"), pregnant with Athena, was destined later to give birth to a son who could overthrow Zeus. To avoid the birth of this son, Zeus swallowed Metis, who went to live in Zeus's mind. When she gave birth to Athena, Hephaistos the smith god had to crack open Zeus's skull with an axe to let her out (thus, a "splitting" headache). Metis remained within, never to conceive the dreaded son.

Likewise, in the second story, both Zeus and Poseidon once courted the sea nymph Thetis until they heard she was destined to bear a son stronger than his father. Both gods desisted in courting her, and Zeus made her marry the mortal king Peleus. Their son was Achilles, "greatest of the Achaeans," greater than his mortal father but no threat to the deities.

Zeus also had to worry about a coalition of deities ganging up on him. In Book 1 of the *Iliad* (ll. 398–406), we hear of a time when the goddess Thetis:

> defended dark-clouded Kronion [Zeus] from shameful ruin,
> when the other Olympians wished to bind him,
> Hera and Poseidon and Pallas Athena.
> But coming to him you, goddess, undid the chains,
> having quickly summoned the 100-Handed One to blessed Olympos,
> whom the gods call Briareon, but all men
> Aigaion, for he is greater in might than his father.
> He then sat by glorious Kronion, exalting,
> and the blessed gods greatly feared him, and did not bind Zeus.

Only the intervention of Thetis saved Zeus from being bound up for all eternity. (This, plus the fact that he made her marry a mortal and have a mortal son, caused Zeus to be indebted to Thetis forever, which was one of the sources of her own power.) To keep the other gods as content as possible at all times, Zeus, when overthrowing the Titans, gave each deity certain areas of power, known as their "honors." Thus, in Hesiod's *Theogony* (ll. 390–396):

> On that day, the Olympian star-lighter summoned
> all the immortal deities to blessed Olympos,
> and he said that whoever of the deities would fight the Titans by his side
> would not be without gifts, but each would have
> the honors which they had previously among the immortal deities,
> and he said that whoever was without honor and gifts under Kronos
> would enter upon such things, as was just.

Thus, Poseidon received dominion over the sea, and Demeter had the power to cause vegetal life to grow. This "balance of powers" contented the deities enough that they felt no need to struggle with Zeus for greater authority. However, it also meant that Zeus had to negotiate over certain aspects of reality. For example, after Zeus married off her daughter Persephonê to Hades, Demeter refused to allow grain to grow, thus starving humankind. Zeus could not force her to bring forth grain, but had to acquiesce to her demand to bring Persephonê up from Hades for at least part of the year. Thus, in spite of Zeus's authority, the other gods had room for their own powerful maneuverings.

Zeus was frequently worshipped as close as possible to his natural domain—the sky. Many sanctuaries and altars of Zeus are located on mountaintops, some very high, such as the one on Mt. Lykaion. Zeus, as were most deities, was worshipped with sacrifices, especially of bulls. As the king of all reality, Zeus was credited with knowing the fate of all things. His oracles, especially those at Dodona in northern Greece and Patras in Lydia, were world-renowned. In the mythology, he shared his knowledge of fate only with his son Apollo.

Hera.   Hera appears in the Linear B tablets from Pylos and Thebes. This indicates that she was revered exclusively on the mainland. Nevertheless, certain aspects of her persona indicate that she may have been a pre-Mycenaean goddess. Her name does not appear to be Indo-European, as with many of the specifically Greek Mycenaean deities. Furthermore, although later tradition records Hera as the wife of Zeus, the Linear B texts list a separate possible spouse for the king of the gods—Dionê (whose name is the feminine equivalent of Zeus's), with whom Zeus in later years was worshipped at the northern Greek site of Dodona. It is possible that Hera was a pre-Greek goddess, queenly in character, who was "married" to Zeus when the Greeks brought their own pantheon into Greece.

Hera was the queen of the gods and the goddess of marriage. Her status as sister-wife-consort of Zeus confirmed her role as queen, and the fact that she was goddess of marriage confirmed her status vis-à-vis Zeus himself. Hera plays an ambiguous role in the literature. On the one hand, Zeus's well-known extramarital escapades did not escape her notice, and many authors, Ovid, for example, have played up the image of Hera as the evil, jealous wife who wrought havoc on the lives of Zeus's mistresses and children. Far from being the powerless and bitter wife, however, she was seen at least by Homer as the second most powerful force in the universe, someone whom even Zeus had cause to fear. In Book 1 of the *Iliad* (ll. 518–519), Zeus, granting a request to Thetis, nevertheless worries because "These indeed are ruinous works, as you will set me into conflict/with Hera, who will reprimand me with reproachful words."

As she was patroness of marriage, it is interesting to note the relationship Hera had with her own husband. She clearly could not keep him faithful to her, although some ancient authors blamed this more on Aphrodite than Zeus. On the flip side, it is clear both in the literature and in the art that Zeus was extremely sexually attracted to Hera. This is evident in Hera's seduction of Zeus in Book 14 of the *Iliad*. Likewise, two votives from Hera's sanctuary on Samos show Zeus grasping Hera's breast, and metopes from Selinus and Athens show Zeus staring in rapt gaze at his wife (Burkert 1985, 132).

Although her sexual appeal was one source of her power, Hera also derived extensive power from her ability to reproduce parthenogenically (*parthenos* = maiden; *gignymi* = to create, produce), that is to say, by herself, without sexual intercourse. Thus, Hera could produce a child, a son, without Zeus's consent, a son possibly stronger than Zeus. One such attempt was made when Hera brought forth the monster Typhaon, as recounted in the *Homeric Hymn to Apollo* (ll. 306–307, 340–354):

> Awful and grievous Typhaon, scourge for mortals,
> Hera bore him in anger at Father Zeus
>
> . . . .
>
> So having spoken she smote the earth with her stout hand,
> and life-giving Gaia was moved, and she seeing this
> was happy in her heart, for she thought the matter to be perfected.
> From that time for a full year
> not once did she approach the bed of crafty Zeus,
> nor even her elaborate throne, as she had done previously
> when, sitting there, she used to speak wise counsels to him.
> But remaining in her temples of many prayers
> cow-eyed, reverend Hera rejoiced in her offerings.
> But when the months and days of the fruitful year were completed
> and the seasons came around
> she bore one resembling neither gods nor mortals.
> Immediately cow-eyed, reverend Hera, taking him,
> gave one evil to the other, and Python received him.

According to some ancient Greek tales, Hera also gave birth to Hephaistos without a father. In this way, Hera could threaten Zeus with his one and only true weakness, which, along with her sexuality, ensured her role as queen. Finally, Hera was a wise goddess. She offered "wise counsels" to Zeus, and her input was valuable to the father of gods and men.

Although the literary portrayals of Hera are rather harsh—jealous wife, mother of monsters—her true glory was evident in her cults. Hera's two most important sanctuaries were in Argos in southern Greece and on the island of Samos. Another important cult site was at Olympia, where Zeus shared her temple until a much larger one was constructed for him during the Classical period. It is logical that Hera was highly venerated at Olympia: The dominant myth at the sanctuary was the story of Pelops and Hippodameia. According to this tale, Pelops, the son of King Tantalos, had to beat the local king Oenomaüs in a chariot race in order to win the hand of Oenomaüs's daughter Hippodameia, and with her the kingship of southern Greece. Pelops bribed Oenomaüs's charioteer to sabotage the king's chariot, allowing Pelops to win. Although the duplicity of Pelops became fodder for other Greek tragedies, the "conquest" of the Peloponnese (*Pelops* + *nesos* = island) through marriage was an important theme at Olympia. Therefore, as Hera was the goddess of marriage, her role at the sanctuary was considerable. Just as Zeus had his great Panhellenic games there every four years, so, too, did Hera—the Heraia. These games were organized by sixteen local women, and the games included a girl's foot race, a procession to present new clothing to Hera, and choruses of singers (Burkert 1985, 133; Clark 1998, 20–22).

Another interesting ritual in honor of Hera, the Daidalia, took place at Plataia in Boiotia (Clark 1998, 22–25). According to Pausanias (3.5), Hera was angry with Zeus and, leaving him, went to dwell in Boiotia. To win/trick her back, Zeus made a wooden female image, dressed it as a bride, and spread the word that he was marrying the river nymph Plataia. When Hera heard about this, she stormed over and tore away the "bride's" dress, and was terribly amused to find her competitor to be a chunk of wood. She and Zeus were reconciled, and in honor of this event the Boiotians celebrated the Daidalia ("wooden images") every seven years. Based on the flight of crows, the Boiotians picked an oak from which to make a wooden image of a bride that served as the focus of the ritual. Every fifty-nine years, though, they celebrated the Greater Daidalia, at which one of fourteen "brides" was chosen by lot, along with another as "bridesmaid." These were brought by wagon to the Asopos River, where they, along with countless sacrificial animals, were burnt in a massive conflagration—a sacrifice on the altar to Zeus and Hera.

This ritual exemplifies several aspects of Hera's persona. It refers to Hera's role as Zeus's bride and to how troubled their marriage often was. It manifests the joy felt when Zeus and Hera made amends after a fight. And it demonstrates Hera's power: The "rival" bride is destroyed upon the altar as a sacrifice to the marriage goddess.

Demeter and Persephonê (with a Few Words on Hades).   Demeter has an ambiguous presence in the Greek Bronze Age. The word *da-ma-te* appears on a Linear B tablet from Pylos, but the context does not suggest a goddess's name. However, it appears to describe a unit of land, possibly grain land, calling to mind Demeter's primary function in later Greek religion (Ventris and Chadwick 1959, 242). A tablet from Mycenae refers to a Sito Potnia, "Grain Lady," and this might refer either to Demeter or to an alternately named, but related, early grain goddess. These written references are somewhat supported by a fresco from the Room of the Frescoes in Mycenae. Here we see a female, perhaps a goddess or priestess, holding sheaves of wheat in her hands. Her cap is similar to those bedecking supernatural creatures such as sphinxes in the Aegean repertoire, suggesting that this woman is more than mortal. This may be, then, our earliest portrayal of the goddess who would become Demeter.

Demeter was the goddess of grain and vegetal earthly fertility (a role she shares with Dionysos, god of wine). Her epithets (nicknames) include Chloë (Green Shoot), Sito (Grain), Haloïs (Goddess of the Ploughed Field), Hamalophoros (Bearing Sheaves of Grain), Karpophoros (Fruit-Bearing), Melophoros (Apple-Bearing), and Anesidora (Bringing Up Gifts) (Cole 2000, 136). Like all Greek deities, Demeter sometimes withheld her gift, and thus she was also a goddess of famine. This aspect of her persona comes across most clearly in the *Homeric Hymn to Demeter* (ll. 305–312), when

A most dreadful and horrible year upon the much-nourishing earth
she brought for humans, nor did earth
bring forth grain, for well-crowned Demeter hid it.

In the fields oxen drew many curved ploughs in vain;
much white barley fell onto the earth fruitlessly.
And now even the whole race of humanity she would have destroyed
with grievous famine, and she would have deprived
those who hold Olympos of their splendid right of gifts and sacrifices.

The circumstances that caused Demeter to send famine to Earth are the basis for one of her most important myths, one that explains Demeter's other important functions in Greek religion. As the *Homeric Hymn to Demeter* narrates, one day when picking flowers with girlfriends, Demeter's daughter Persephonê was seized by Hades, god of the dead, who brought her to the underworld as his wife. Neither Hades nor Zeus, Persephonê's father, had informed Demeter of their plan, which some scholars take as evidence of a tendency among the Greeks to leave mothers out of the loop regarding their children's marriage arrangements. Demeter heard her daughter's screams but was unable to find her anywhere on or above the Earth (Hades was below Earth, where Demeter did not think to look for an immortal). Eventually the deities Hecatê and Helios (the sun god who sees everything) explained to Demeter that Persephonê was taken in marriage.

First, Demeter changed herself into an old woman, went to the city of Eleusis, and became a nanny for the prince Demophoön. When she was caught setting the baby into the fire (trying to make him immortal), she revealed her true identity and demanded that the Eleusinians build her a temple on their territory. There she moped, sending famine to Earth until the gods agreed to return Persephonê to her. Zeus sent Hermes to fetch her from the underworld. Before releasing her, though, Hades had Persephonê eat a pomegranate seed, which obliged her to return to him at least once per year, usually for three to six months. Afterward, whenever Persephonê was with Hades, Demeter made the Earth infertile. At one level, then, this myth explains the origins of the agricultural dead season (winter or the hot, dry Greek summer), with Persephonê being the goddess whose annual return marked the return of the fertile season.

One must remember, though, that Persephonê (also called Korê, or "Maiden") was also the goddess of the dead, queen of the underworld, and she was more prominent in this role in the literature than Hades himself. *Hades* could serve as the name of the god as well as of the underworld, and the word seems to mean "invisible." It is possible, then, that Hades as an anthropomorphic god evolved out of a personification of death and its perceived geography. When referring to mortuary deities, the epic poets usually referred to "Dread Persephonê" either with her husband or, just as often, without. This offers a counterbalance to the view of Persephonê we get in the *Hymn to Demeter*, where she appears as a little girl, the passive victim of adult (and male) machinations. As queen of the dead, Persephonê had eventual, ultimate power over all humanity. This aspect of her persona, combined with the close relationship between Persephonê and Demeter, was the basis for the mystery cults associated with these two that offered practitioners hopes for a better afterlife, particularly the Eleusinian Mysteries (see below).

Demeter was mother to other important children in addition to Persephonê. According to Pausanias (8.25.4), Poseidon once sought out Demeter as a sexual partner. Demeter turned herself into a horse to escape her brother, but he transformed likewise, and mated with Demeter in equine fashion. From this union Demeter gave birth to Despoina ("Mistress"), a lesser-known goddess of animals worshipped mainly in the city of Lykosura along with her mother and Artemis. Elsewhere, Demeter had sex with the man Iasion on a "thrice-ploughed" field and bore Ploutos ("Wealth") from that union. This myth reveals most clearly the strong associations among Demeter, farmland, earthly fertility, and abundance.

The cults of Demeter (and Persephonê) were some of the most widespread and long-enduring. The most famous (other than the Eleusinian Mysteries) was the Thesmophoria, the Bearing of Divine Laws. This ritual was practiced exclusively by women, usually married citizens (although there may have been exceptions) throughout Greece. In Athens, it took place in October or early November; in Delos and Thasos, it occurred in late summer (Cole 2000, 138). From the scraps of literary evidence, epigraphy, and archaeology we have, we can determine a fair amount about the ritual's physical manifestation. In Athens, the women congregated near or on the Pnyx, the site of the men's Assembly (see chapter 7). Thus, women took over males' space during the ritual, fencing off the area to protect their activities from male eyes. The ritual lasted three days. The first day was the anodos, or "road up," referring to the women's arrival at the Pnyx. The second day was the nesteia, or "fasting," when the women sat on branches on the ground and did not eat all day. Not much is known about the goings-on of this day, but two possible elements—obscene language and the drinking of pennyroyal—have been related to the *Hymn to Demeter* (ll. 192–211):

But unwilling [Demeter] waited, her fair eyes cast down,
until indeed wise Iambê set down for her
a well-built seat, and upon it she cast a silvery fleece.
There sitting she held her veil before her with her hands.
A long time she sorrowed in silence, seated upon the stool,
nor did she greet anyone by word or motion.
But unlaughing, eating neither food nor drink,
she sat wasting for longing of her deep-girdled daughter,
until wise Iambê joked with her,
pleasing the reverend lady with many wily jests,
causing her to smile and laugh and her heart to be glad.
She indeed later pleased her moods.
To [Demeter] Metaneira gave a cup of honey-sweet wine,
having filled it; but she declined it, for she said it was not right
for her to drink red wine.
Then she bade them give her water
and barley mixed with soft pennyroyal to drink.
and [Metaneira], preparing a drink, brought it to the goddess, as asked.
Greatly reverend Deo [Demeter] received it for the sake of the rite.

The fasting of the second day of the Thesmophoria probably reflected Demeter's fasting in the *Hymn*. Likewise, there is some suggestion (Nixon 1995, 85–92) that the women also drank a mixture made with pennyroyal, a mint known to have contraceptive qualities. Finally on this day, there was the aiskhrologia, or "saying of obscene things." Following Iambê's lead, the women hurled obscene language and insults at each other, which not only served to amuse the goddess, but probably also helped to take the women's minds off the fact that they were really hungry and sitting on the ground all day.

The final day was the kalligenia, the "beautiful offspring," which referred either to Demeter as mother of Persephonê or to Persephonê herself. Just as Persephonê returned to mortals after Demeter's period of mourning, so too should fertility return to the land after the women had shared in the sufferings of the divine pair. At least one aspect of the Thesmophoria was fertility-oriented: Women performed the rite either just before the ploughing season (as in Attica) or right after the summer dry season (Delos). The lack of men in attendance meant that the women were chaste throughout the ritual. Sitting on the ground, literally pressing their genitalia to the Earth, hurling obscenities around, putting their own bodily fertility into abeyance through abstinence, all symbolically directed the women's fertility into the ground. In case the symbolic fertility was not enough, another aspect of the Thesmophoria was the hauling up of decomposed pig remains. Piglets were often sacrificed to Demeter, and such sacrifices were made at an earlier festival in the year, possibly the Skira four months previous. These decomposed remains were blessed and placed on Demeter's altar; later they were added to the seeds to be planted, serving as an extrapotent, religious fertilizer.

Poseidon. Poseidon appears in the Linear B tablets at both Knossos and, quite prominently, Pylos. At Pylos, the god had at least one sanctuary, the po-si-da-i-jo (Poseidaion), as well as a wife, po-si-da-e-ja (Poseidania) (Ventris and Chadwick 1959, 126). This strong connection with Pylos is reaffirmed in the Homeric epics: Nestor, king of "sandy Pylos," was the grandson of Poseidon, and when Telemachus, son of Odysseus, traveled there, he found the people on the shore making sacrifice to the "dark-haired Earthshaker."

The etymology of Poseidon's name has long been a vexing issue. The first element—*Posei*—is related to the Greek word for "lord" or "husband." The *dan* part is more troublesome. Some have suggested that the *da* of both Damater/Demeter and Poseidan/Poseidon refers to the Earth, thus "Earth Mother" and "Earth Husband." There is no proof for this, however, so at the moment all that can be said is that Poseidon and Demeter are related to some unknown element or entity.

Poseidon is god of the sea, earthquakes, and horses. Quoting Poseidon himself in the *Iliad* 15.187–192:

For we are three brothers, sons of Kronos, born of Rhea,
Zeus and I, and Hades third, ruler of the dead.
Three ways all things were divided, each received a portion:

I received the grey sea to dwell in forever when the lots were shaken,
Hades received the shadowy nether realms,
and Zeus received the broad, airy sky and clouds.

Poseidon lived in a golden palace beneath the waves at Aigai (*Iliad* 13, 17 ff.)
along with his wife Amphitrîtê, Mother of Sea Monsters.

As lord of the sea, Poseidon was responsible for sea life and, by natural extension, the fishing industry. According to the later author Athenaeus (Deipnosophistai, 297e), the first "fruits" (fish, really) of fishing expeditions, and especially those from the tunny-fishing industry, were presented to Poseidon at his sanctuaries (Burkert 1985, 137).

Poseidon was also master of the less pleasant aspects of the sea, specifically sea storms. In the *Odyssey*, the god torments Odysseus with a *very* nasty gale (5.291–296):

So speaking he drew together clouds, and he stirred up the sea
seizing his trident in his hands.
All the storm winds he roused, and with clouds he hid
earth as well as sea. Night covered the sky.
He dashed together East, South, and the stormy West winds,
and the North wind born of aither, tossing about great waves.

Of course, a sea storm isn't necessarily a bad thing if it hurts an enemy. In 480 B.C.E., when much of the Persian fleet was destroyed in a storm (see chapter 4), the Greeks offered thanks to Poseidon (Herodotus 7.192):

On the second day after the start of the storm the day-watchers, running down to the Greeks from the Euboian peaks, related everything about the shipwreck. Having heard this, the Greeks, praying to Savior Poseidon and pouring him libations, set off posthaste back to Artemision, hoping there'd be few ships to oppose them . . . From that time to even now they call Poseidon by the title "Savior."

Poseidon's important cult sites were associated with the sea, often located on peninsulas or isthmuses. His most famous, and probably oldest, sanctuary was on the Corinthian Isthmus, where evidence of bull sacrifice and ritual feasting dates back to the late eleventh century B.C.E. (Gebhard 1993, 156). In later years, this sanctuary was the site of the Isthmean Games, one of the four great Panhellenic athletic and artistic competitions of ancient Greece (along with the Olympic, Nemean, and Delphic Games).

Poseidon's association with earthquakes is clearly manifest in his epithet Earthshaker. When an earthquake hit, Greeks started singing hymns to Poseidon (*Hellenika* 4.7.4). Earthquakes were often seen as a punishment for impiety to Poseidon. Thucydides (1.128) relates that a group of Spartans once seized helot suppliants from the sanctuary of Poseidon at Tainaros and killed them. In retaliation, Poseidon sent the great earthquake of 464 B.C.E. (Burkert 1985, 137).

Counterbalancing his phenomenal destructive powers, Poseidon was also one of the chief builders among the gods. In this he definitely took second place to Hephaistos, but both Homer and Hesiod refer to his propensity for construction. In the *Iliad*, we hear that it was Poseidon who "built a wall for the Trojans about their city, wide, and very splendid, so that none could break into their city" (21.446–447). In Hesiod's *Theogony*, the poet relates that Poseidon "put in the bronze doors, and the fence that runs on both sides" of Tartarus (ll. 331–332).

Then there was the god's association with horses. He, like many deities, drove a horse-drawn chariot, in spite of his living in a watery domain. Some scholars argue that Poseidon was originally an Indo-European horse god who took on his watery aspects only when the Indo-Europeans got to Greece and needed a deity for all that ocean out there. Another possibility is that, just as the sea is a source of violent power and earthquakes are the most violent power on land, the horse is the most powerful of animals. Thus, Poseidon's relationship with horses was a manifestation of his association with powerful, elemental forces (Burkert 1985, 139), The above arguments are not mutually exclusive, and there may be an element of truth to both.

In ritual, horses were occasionally sacrificed to Poseidon, either (appropriately enough) by drowning or, in one unusual rite, attaching the horses to an empty chariot and having them run to their deaths. In myth, Poseidon was frequently the father of horses or horse-like beings, or he took on the manifestation of a horse himself. Poseidon once raped Medusa in the sanctuary of Athena (thus earning the girl, but not the god, the wrath of the goddess). Later, when Perseus beheaded Medusa, Pegasus, a winged horse whose name referred to watery springs, sprang from her neck. Wherever Pegasus kicked down, a freshwater spring emerged. In Thessaly and Athens, there was a tale that Poseidon once spilled his semen onto a rock, from which the first horse was born (Burkert 1985, 138). Finally, there is the story related above concerning his equine rape of Demeter.

Poseidon was a powerful god, but his power was not controlled. This was frequently brought up in comparisons between Poseidon and his niece Athena. Poseidon was lord of the sea; Athena invented the ship. Poseidon was the horse god; Athena invented the bit and bridle. Poseidon was the god of the elemental power; Athena figured out how to harness that power to do something with it. Poseidon was a pure nature deity whose persona was not dependent on humans or their affairs. This fact was even manifest in the location of his sanctuaries, which tended to be removed from city space (Schumacher 1993, 82–83).

Hestia. There is no evidence of the name *Hestia* in the Linear B texts discovered to date. However, the hearth was the central point of the Mycenaean megaron (see chapter 9), so some aspect of this goddess, anthropomorphic, personified or not, existed at least since the Bronze Age, if not since the discovery of fire.

Hestia was goddess of the hearth, and the word *hestia* in Greek referred to the hearth that formed the center of the home. The word also referred to the city's main hearth, located either in the prytaneion (city hall) or the agora, which formed the ideological core of the polis. When new colonies were established, fire from the mother city's main hearth was used to light the hearth of the daughter city, thus establishing a political-familial link between the two poleis (Sourvinou-Inwood 2000, 25). Hestia was omnipresent in Greek society, on both domestic and political levels.

Nevertheless, being stuck at the hearth in the center of the house, Hestia could not get about as much as other deities, and she consequently played a small role in the literature. The longest literary description we have of her appears at the beginning of the *Homeric Hymn to Aphrodite*. When discussing those goddesses immune to the works of Aphrodite, the poet tells us (ll. 19–32):

> Nor do the works of Aphrodite please the reverend maiden
> Hestia, first born of crooked-minded Kronos,
> but also the youngest, by will of Aigis-bearing Zeus,
> Queen, whom Poseidon and Apollo courted.
> But she had no such desire, and quickly declined;
> she swore a great oath, which is indeed fulfilled,
> grasping the head of Aigis-bearing, father Zeus,
> to be a maiden for all days among the deities.
> To her father Zeus has given a fine prize instead of marriage,
> and within the house she sits, drawing to herself the best (offerings).
> And in the temples of the gods she is honored.
> And among all mortals she is made first of the deities.

The idea that Hestia was "honored in the temples of the gods" derives from the fact that she was associated with fire. As sacrifice could not take place without fire, she was inevitably present at, and took an active role in, all religious festivals.

Equally important was Hestia's identity as a virgin, a trait she shared with Athena, Artemis, and Hecatê (no male god has gone on record claiming to be a virgin). Hestia's role as virgin tender of the fire is important for understanding ancient Greek conceptions of the family. The Greeks were patriarchal and patrilocal, meaning that men wielded greater control than women in politics, law, and economics, and that women left their natal families upon marriage to join their husbands' families (although this was not 100 percent consistent; see chapter 6). There was, therefore, always a certain distrust of wives—strangers in the paternal household who could still have loyalties to their own families or who could form greater bonds with their children than with a husband and his clan (as in Aeschylus's *Oresteia*, in which Clytemnestra kills her husband to avenge his murder of their daughter).

Furthermore, there was a general anxiety present in same-sex familial relationships. Sons inevitably enforced the notion of the father's mortality, and sons or grandsons in literature often caused a (grand)father's death, like Oedipus and his father Laius. Mothers and daughters could form close bonds, but those bonds were inevitably severed when the daughter left her family to join a husband's household. Thus, the closest familial bonds were between mother and son, and father and daughter. However, as with the mother-daughter bond, the father-daughter bond was constrained by the daughter's need to leave home upon marriage. In human life, then, a father's closest familial ally was only temporary (it wasn't as though he could entirely trust Mom; she was an outsider, a potential Clytemnestra).

The lives of the gods, however, were not so constrained, and in the persona of Hestia, one had the ideal paternal ally: the daughter who did not marry, who clung to the paternal hearth and was ultimately loyal to the paternal line. Just as the hearth was the solid center of the household, the virgin daughter, on the divine plane, was the solid center of the family. Hestia, being both, was more than just a hearth goddess for the Greeks: She was the personification of stability (Vernant 1983, 134).

The unmarried virgin state was not really desirable for mortal girls, though, and transfer from one family to another was common. Hestia finalized these transfers. A new bride was brought to the groom's house, and specifically to the hearth, to induct her fully into her new family. Also, in a ritual called the amphidromia, fathers walked (or ran) around the hearth holding a new baby, thus inducting the infant into the family. Babies not so inducted were viewed as strangers and could be exposed without guilt (see chapter 6). As a goddess concerned with familial transitions, Hestia was also a protectress of home and family. In Euripides's *Alkestis* (ll. 163–169), when the queen is about to die, she goes to the hearth and addresses Hestia:

> Mistress, as I proceed beneath the earth,
> for the last time I shall beseech you in supplication,
> to care for my orphaned children, to join my son in
> marriage to a dear wife, my daughter to a noble husband.
> Nor let them, as their mother was destroyed,
> die as children, before their time, but happily
> give them a joyful life in their fatherland.

Athena.   Possible references to Athena from the Bronze Age are quite intriguing. Iconographically, the most likely candidate for a goddess related to Athena is the Mycenaean Shield Goddess: A goddess who carries a shield as if she knows how to use it and a thrusting weapon speaks strongly for a later Greek goddess of war. A few earlier, small-scale depictions from Crete of females wielding weapons have led some to suggest that perhaps this Shield Goddess was not actually Mycenaean, but Minoan (Rehak 1984, 544–545). Another theory (Gesell 1984) is that the Minoan Snake Goddess was the progenitress of Athena. This is due to the frequent portrayal of snakes in Athena's iconography, and to the belief that the Minoan Snake Goddess was the protectress of house and palace. As the later Athena was protectress of the city, and often of royal families (especially Odysseus's family), scholars linked this Minoan goddess to her.

Athena's name appears once in the Linear B repertoire, on a leaf-shaped tablet from the Chariot Room at Knossos (Gulizio et al. 2001, passim). The tablet lists four deities, one of whom is a-ta-na-po-ti-ni-ja, literally "Lady of Athens"

(Gulizio et al. 2002, 454). The other three deities mentioned are Enyalios/Ares, Paiawon/Apollo, and Poseidon. All are related to warfare or horses, or both (warhorses, perhaps), suggesting that this Lady of Athens is a war/horse goddess. Once again, the evidence speaks strongly for this being Athena.

Athena was the daughter of Zeus and Metis, whose name means "cunning intelligence." As discussed above in the section on Zeus, Athena was born out of Zeus's head after he swallowed the pregnant Metis. Athena was therefore understood as having been born specifically to Zeus, explaining her intense dedication to her father and the patriarchal principle.

Athena was goddess of wisdom, war, and handicrafts, as outlined in the *Homeric Hymn to Aphrodite* (ll. 8–15):

> the maiden-daughter of Aigis-bearing Zeus, bright-eyed Athena
> . . . she does not delight in the works of golden Aphrodite,
> but rather wars please her, and the works of Ares
> and battle and combat and care for glorious deeds.
> She first taught earth-born men
> to make chariots and many-hued war-carts of bronze;
> and she taught soft-skinned
> maidens in their halls, putting glorious works in each mind.

Athena is also goddess of Athens. This aspect of her persona appears to date back to the Bronze Age, with the title of Atana Potnia, and it seems that the goddess got her name from the city, rather than vice versa. Although nowadays a goddess of both war and wisdom may seem paradoxical, Athena's character was actually quite consistent: In contrast to her brother Ares, Athena presided over the scientific aspects of war, the strategic and tactical, rather than the chaotic and bloodthirsty (see Image 5.4). Athena, as war goddess, would be just as content playing a round of chess.

Of course, except for some early conflicts with the Titans in previous generations, gods never needed to go to war, certainly not with the stability imposed by Zeus's reign. So Athena's association with warfare usually took on the aspect of "helper of heroes." In the earliest epics, she was famous as the patroness of Laërtes and his descendants, especially Odysseus and his son Telemachus. At the beginning of the *Odyssey*, it is she who convinces Zeus to free Odysseus from the goddess Calypso so that he might resume his homeward journey. It is she who led Telemachus out of Ithaca when the suitors of Penelope, his mother, were planning his murder. She, in secret, led Odysseus through the land of the Phaiakians, and she was the first to greet him on his return to Ithaca (*Odyssey* 13, 298–307):

> . . . and I among all the deities
> am revered for cunning and trickery. But you didn't recognize
> Pallas Athena, daughter of Zeus; I who always
> stand by you and guard you in all your labors,
> and who placed fondness for you among the Phaiakians.
> Now moreover I have come directly, so I might weave a plan with you,

and I shall hide as many goods as the illustrious Phaiakians
gave you to bring home by my council and mind.
And I shall relate what harsh fate you will endure
in the well-built houses.

Athena served as charioteer for Diomedes in the *Iliad*. She helped Perseus to slay Medusa, for which she received the gorgon's face as trophy. She was renowned as Heracles's helper in his various labors. Her assistance in these actions was manifest on the metopes (see chapter 9) from the temple of Zeus at Olympia. When Heracles was sent to retrieve the golden apples of the Hesperides, and was obliged to hold the sky while Atlas went to the immortal tree, Athena offered a touch of additional support.

This close association with macho heroes never progressed into romance. As the poet declared at the beginning of the *Hymn to Aphrodite*, Athena was one of the three Olympian goddesses immune to the works of Aphrodite. In some later literature, Athena was portrayed as antithetical to women, bordering on misogynistic. The epitome of this is in Aeschylus's *Eumenides* (ll. 733–740), when the goddess proclaims:

> For there is no mother who bore me,
> but I praise the male entirely, except concerning marriage,
> with all my heart; I am entirely of the father.
> So I shall not prefer a woman who brings about
> the death of her man, guardian of the house.

Nevertheless, Athena definitely had her "feminine" side, that aspect of her persona concerned with handicrafts, especially weaving. According to Homer and Hesiod, Athena made the goddesses' clothing, like the dress Hera wore to seduce Zeus in Book 14 of the *Iliad,* as well as the dress and veil that adorned Pandora when she was first presented to mankind in the *Theogony* and *Works and Days.* She also taught this art to mortal women, as with the Phaiakian women in the *Odyssey.*

Although she taught weaving to women, she taught navigation and shipbuilding to men. Athena was a patroness of carpenters, and she herself built the *Argo,* the ship used in the quest for the Golden Fleece in Apollonios's *Argonautika* (1, 111–114):

> For Athena also made the swift ship, and with her Argos
> son of Arestor built it by her counsels.
> And for this it was the best of all the ships
> which plied the sea with oars.

What these various traits—wisdom, technical skill, strategy—had in common was their close association with civilization itself (Burkert 1985, 141). Unlike Poseidon, who represented the raw forces of nature, Athena channeled these forces in ways that were productive for humans. She took the sea and made it a form of transportation, just as she did by bridling the horse. In contrast to the wild flora of the countryside, she created the cultivatable olive—a source of food, fuel, and pride to the Greeks (even today). She took raw wool and flax and turned them not merely into clothing, but into an art form: the tapestry, one of the few art forms completely available to women. Even as goddess of war, Athena tended to be the protectress of cities. Many poleis of ancient Greece had their temple of Athena on the city summit, watching over and protecting the civic space and its citizens. This was especially so in her namesake city of Athens.

Concerning Athens, Athena was, almost literally, the mother of her people. Hephaistos once tried to rape Athena. Hephaistos was not successful, but he did ejaculate on Athena's thigh. Athena wiped off the mess with a piece of wool and cast it onto the ground in Athens. From this castoff was born Erechtheus, one of the primordial kings of Athens and so-called father of his people. Thus, the Athenians not only were born of the land of Attica itself, but they might have been able to think of Athena as a stepmother.

This was because Athena adopted the baby and gave it to the daughters of Kekrops, the first king of Athens, to raise. These daughters were named Hersê, Pandrosos, and Aglauros. Athena put the baby into a box and told the girls never to look within it. Hersê and Aglauros disobeyed, looked inside, and saw the child surrounded by snakes. This frightened them so badly that they jumped off the acropolis to their deaths in fear. Pandrosos was left to raise Erechtheus, who was later worshipped with Athena and Poseidon in the acropolis temple that still bears his name: the Erechtheion. This temple, and not the Parthenon, was the original main temple of Athens, proven by the fact that the Palladion, Athena's xoanon, resided here and not in her larger temple next door.

This story of the autochthonous ("Earth-born") origins of the Athenians gave rise to one of their earliest civic rituals: the Arrhephoria, or Carrying of Secret Things. According to Pausanias (1.27.3):

> Two maidens live not far from the temple of Athena Polias; the Athenians call them Arrhephoroi. For a time they live by the goddess, but when the festival comes they do the following by night: The priestess of Athena gives them things to carry upon their heads. Neither she who gives nor they who carry know what they are. There is a sanctuary in the city not far from that of Aphrodite called in-the-Gardens, and through this is a naturally occurring underground passage, by which the maidens descend. They leave the things they carried below, and taking up something else hidden they carry it away. And then they send the maidens away, and they lead other maidens to the Acropolis in their stead.

The basket of unknown items is, of course, reminiscent of the box that the daughters of Kekrops were not supposed to open. Archaeologists have discovered what appears to be this natural underground passage, and this pathway contained an assortment of pottery dating back to Mycenaean times. This, combined with literary evidence that the Attic population had been in Attica since before the Dark Age, suggests that the Arrhephoria was an extremely ancient ritual dating back into the Bronze Age.

Aphrodite. There is no clear evidence for Aphrodite's existence in the Greek Bronze Age. There are two main theories concerning how this goddess came to join the Greek pantheon. According to one (Boedeker 1974, passim), she evolved out of an Indo-European dawn goddess and is an alternate manifestation of the dawn goddess Eos. Accordingly, Aphrodite would have been a member of the Greek pantheon since the Greeks first arrived in Greece, and her absence in the Bronze Age corpus is accidental. The other theory (Budin 2003, passim) argues that Aphrodite came to Greece by way of Crete from Cyprus during the Dark Age. The goddess evolved in Cyprus through a combination of Cypriot and Levantine (Syrian and Palestinian) influences. Thus, rather than a dawn goddess, she would be related to the Near Eastern goddesses Ishtar and Ishhara.

This ambiguity in her origins is matched by an ambiguity in her parentage. According to Homer, Aphrodite is the daughter of Zeus and the sea goddess Dionê. As such, she is a member of the youngest generation of deities, half sister to Artemis and Persephonê. According to Hesiod, however (*Theogony*, ll. 188–195), Aphrodite came into being when Kronos castrated his father Ouranos:

> When [Kronos] first cut off the genitals with adamant
> he tossed them from the land into the loudly surging sea
> where long they were borne upon the waters. White foam
> arose about the immortal flesh, and from therein a girl
> was engendered. First by the holy Kytherians
> she passed, thence she went to sea-girt Cyprus,
> and the reverend fair goddess walked forth, and about
> her slender feet grass sprang forth.

Put simply, Aphrodite was the "reincarnation" of Ouranos's penis. An Archaic Age clay figurine from Corinth shows a female with what appears to be a beard emerging from a bulbous sack. Some, such as excavator H. Payne, have suggested that this represents Ouranos's genitalia transforming into the goddess. In this instance, Aphrodite is one of the oldest deities, even older than Zeus.

Whatever her origins, Aphrodite was first and foremost a goddess of sex (see Image 9.24). According to Hesiod (*Theogony*, ll. 203–206), "this honor she has from the beginning, having received this/portion among men and immortal deities:/maidens' fond discourse and smiles and deceits/and joy and sweet love and gentleness." Likewise, at the beginning of her *Homeric Hymn*, the poet extols her thus (ll. 1–6, 34–40):

> Muses, relate to me the works of golden-throned Aphrodite,
> of Cyprus, who in deities stirs up sweet desire and

who subdues the race of mortal men
and air-borne birds and all wild creatures,
and as many creatures the mainland rears, and also the sea.
To all these are the works of well-crowned Kythera a concern.

. . . .

of all others there is none who can escape Aphrodite,
neither of the blessed gods nor of mortal men.
And she led the mind of thunder-loving Zeus astray,
who is greatest and holds the greatest share of honor.
Whenever she wishes, she easily turns his firm mind
to mingling with a mortal woman,
forgetting entirely Hera, his sister and wife.

The seventh-century poet Mimnermos further accentuated her nature, asking:

What life, what joy without golden Aphrodite?
I should die, were these things not a care to me,
Secret love and sweet gifts and the bed.

One of Aphrodite's most famous roles in Greek literature was her instigation of the Trojan War. It all began when Eris, goddess of strife, tossed a golden apple into a wedding reception and declared that it belonged to the most beautiful goddess. Immediately, Hera, Athena, and Aphrodite all claimed the apple. None of the other gods wanted to get involved in that dispute, so they picked a young Trojan prince named Paris (also called Alexandros) to play beauty pageant judge. Each goddess tried to bribe him: Hera with dominion over Asia, Athena with great wisdom, and Aphrodite with the most beautiful woman in the world. Paris chose Aphrodite, winning for himself Helen of Sparta, who was, however, already married. By carrying her off from her husband Menelaus, Paris began the Trojan War. Because it was Aphrodite who gave Helen to Paris, Aphrodite, ultimately, was held accountable for the starting of the war.

Aphrodite was also famous for her own marital infidelities. She was technically married to the smith god Hephaistos (who once stuck his mother Hera to a throne [see Image 8.12], and had to be bribed with Aphrodite to let her out again). But her affections were more inclined to the war god Ares, and on at least one awkward occasion they were caught in flagrante delicto. In Book 8 of the *Odyssey*, Hephaistos, with a magical net, trapped them having sex in bed. After inviting all the gods to have a good look and laugh at the couple, he released them. Unfortunately for Hephaistos, his plan backfired: All the gods who saw Aphrodite naked decided they wanted to have sex with her, too.

Aphrodite had two basic manifestations in ancient Greece: Pandemos ("for all the people") and Ourania ("heavenly"). For Plato, these indicated the two sides of love. Pandemos, the "common" Aphrodite, represented the baser, physical side of love. By contrast, Ourania represented the more pristine, rational, and dedicated aspect of love, devoid of crass, sexual inclinations. The title *Ourania* has two possible origins. If one follows Hesiod's account of her birth, *Ourania* associates the goddess with Ouranos, whose penis she came from. Or the name may derive from a similar epithet of Ishtar, who may be Aphrodite's progenitress. Pausanias offered a possible eastern link to this title when he claimed (1, 14, 7), "It is held that the first people to revere Ourania were the Assyrians, and after the Assyrians the Paphians of Cyprus and those of the Phoenicians who dwell in Ashkalon in Palestine; Kytherians worship her having so learned from the Phoenicians. Aigeus established [her cult] among the Athenians, believing himself to be without children—for at that time he had none—and his sisters in duress due to a curse from Ourania."

The links with Cyprus to which Pausanias refers were quite common in ancient Greece, and some of Aphrodite's more popular nicknames were Cypria, "Cyprus-born," and Paphian (see below). At the time of Homer and Hesiod, the Greeks believed that Aphrodite had first emerged on Cyprus, and by Herodotus's day, many Greeks thought her cult had actually started even farther east (see the Pausanias quote above) but had come to Greece by way of Cyprus. In either event, Aphrodite was closely associated with the island, especially at her sanctuaries at Paphos and Amathus, which were recognized as international sanctuaries in Roman times. The one at Paphos is Aphrodite's oldest known cult site, dating back into the Late Bronze Age. Unfortunately, construction of a Roman sanctuary, and then a Medieval sugar factory right on top of that, obliterated much of the early site.

In the Aegean, Aphrodite had an early sanctuary at Kato Symi Viannou on Crete, and the ancient Greeks claimed that one of her earliest cult sites was on the small island of Kythera, just south of the Peloponnese. Other literary evidence relates that Aphrodite was revered since very early times at Sparta and Corinth. At these two sites, as well as Kythera, Aphrodite's xoana (cult statues) portrayed the goddess armed. Thus, Pausanias writes (3.23.1), "Kythera is about 10 stades inland from Skandeia. The sanctuary of Ourania, the most holy and sacred, is the most ancient of all the sanctuaries of Aphrodite among the Greeks. The goddess herself is represented by an armed xoanon."

It appears, then, that in addition to her role as goddess of love and sex, Aphrodite had a martial element to her early persona.

Artemis.   Like many Greek deities, Artemis appears in the Linear B texts, specifically the ones from Pylos (Ventris and Chadwick 1959, 127). Her cult was one of the most widespread in the ancient Greek world, showing that her practical, day-to-day cult was far more important than the occasional literary references to her would imply.

The daughter of Zeus and Leto, Artemis was primarily a goddess of fertility and death, specifically of sylvan animals, although she also played a significant role in human reproduction. This may seem somewhat surprising to a modern reader, considering the other important and consistent aspect of her persona, which was that Artemis was an eternal virgin. Artemis, like her brother Apollo, never grew up; she was perpetually in her late teens. As such, she never partook in the rites of Greek womanhood: She did not marry, have sex, or bear children (Sappho fr. 44).

Artemis often appeared in literature and art as a huntress. She was depicted with a bow and arrows, wearing a short chiton (see chapter 9) with her hair pulled back but not covered. In the *Hymn to Aphrodite* (ll. 17–20), she is described as

> hallowing, golden-spindled Artemis.
> For to her is pleasing bow-hunting wild creatures in the hills,
> lyres and dancing and piercing cries
> and shady glens and cities of just men.

Nevertheless, Artemis was not merely a killer of beasts; she was the goddess of wild animals, who also loved her charges and helped them to survive. Thus, Aeschylus says of her (*Agamemnon*, 134–143):

> since for pity's sake holy Artemis holds a grudge
> against the winged hounds of her father
> who slaughter the wretched, cowering hare and her pre-born young;
> she hates the eagle's feast.
> . . . .
> How very kindly, lovely she is
> to the young and weak of devouring lions,
> and she rejoices in the breast-loving young of all wild creatures.

8.9 François Vase detail:
Potnia Therôn
(Courtesy of Paul Butler)

As the goddess who loved, protected, and also killed wild animals, Artemis acquired the title *Potnia Therôn*, Mistress of Animals (*Iliad* 21, 470). It seems possible, however, that the Potnia Therôn was originally a separate goddess whom Artemis "absorbed." This is most evident on the François Vase, created around 570 B.C.E. On side B is depicted the return of Hephaistos, in which Artemis, along with Ares and Athena, stands behind a throne on which Hephaistos has trapped Hera. However, under the vase handle is a picture of the Potnia Therôn (see Image 8.9) As was typical of her early iconography, she is winged in this representation, and she holds an animal in each hand. This iconography came from the Near East, where such winged Mistress of Animals iconography had been common for millennia. The fact that Artemis could be portrayed unwinged and named on one portion of the vase, and winged and unnamed on another, suggests that two separate goddesses are intended. Nevertheless, excavations at the sanctuary of Artemis Orthia in Sparta have revealed many small lead votives depicting a winged female. Clearly, the winged Potnia Therôn and Artemis were associated very early in the Greek Iron Age. Eventually, the winged version disappeared from Greek art, leaving Artemis as the sole Mistress of the Beasts.

Artistically, Artemis as Potnia Therôn is most blatantly expressed on the famous statue of Artemis of Ephesus (see Image 8.10). Ephesus, located in Caria (southwestern Turkey), was one of Artemis's most famous cult sites, where her temple was one of the Seven Wonders of the Ancient World. The statue is typical of Carian art: The goddess stands rigidly facing forward, wearing an "apron" called an ependitos. The ependitos—the entire statue, really—is covered with livestock, ranging from bees to bulls. It had originally been thought that the top of the apron was bedecked with several breasts, indicating Artemis's role in human fertility and lactation. However, since these "breasts" lack nipples, later art historians have argued that they are actually bull testicles, a potent fertility symbol in ancient Greece.

Artemis not only presided over sylvan animals; she was also both the protectress and the slayer of children and women. When a woman died a swift death, she was understood to have been slain by Artemis's arrows (Apollo did the same with men). This role as woman-slayer may have been responsible for her role as goddess of childbirth, especially as Artemis Lokhia, a role she shared with Eileithyia. Childbirth was a risky event for women until the end of the twentieth century C.E. Women therefore prayed to Artemis for a safe birth, protecting both mother and child. The clothing of a woman who died in childbirth was dedicated at Artemis's sanctuary at Brauron.

From their birth, Artemis took an active role in the care of children, both boys and girls. One of her titles was kourotrophos, literally "nourisher of boys." At Sparta, Artemis "supervised" the education of Spartan boys, helping to transform them into proper citizen-warriors (Vernant 1991, ch. 12–13). Perhaps more significant was her role in the maturation of girls into women. This aspect of her persona was especially evident in her epithet *Lysizonos*, "Releaser of the Belt." The zonos (belt) was an important part of female dress. Girls received their first belts at puberty, which they later dedicated to Artemis upon marriage, when the woman's belt was removed by the groom as a prelude to

8.10 Artemis of Ephesus (The Art Archive/Ephesus Museum Turkey/Dagli Orti)

sexual intercourse. The expression "to loosen the belt" referred to both defloration and childbirth. As a practical measure, the belt was loosened during childbirth, and both Theocritus and Euripides tell us that women in labor called on Artemis Lysizonos for aid (King 1983, 120–121). Furthermore, the Hippocratic corpus (see chapter 10) related that girls who were cured of amenorrhea should offer dedications to Artemis, indicating her control over menstruation (King 1983, 114).

As an adolescent huntress, Artemis was associated with wildness and youth. However, as Vernant (1991) has argued, Artemis was not exclusively a wild creature—she also loved the "cities of just men." Artemis might be understood as a semipermeable membrane who monitored the passage between the wild and the civilized/tame. This was evident in the locations of her sanctuaries, which were typically at liminal places such as swamps or at the edge of cultivated land. It was also clear from her role as kourotrophos, helping savage children become civilized adults. And it was evident in her role as huntress, the anthropomorphic entity who killed animals with weapons. In this she differed from wild animals, who kill with teeth and claw, and stood apart from the civilized person who grew grain and ate bread, a gift of Demeter.

Finally, Artemis was a plague goddess (for if she could protect and offer "medical" help, she could also do the opposite), a role she shared with her brother Apollo. At Kondylea, she sent a plague to the people until they set up a hero cult to the children who first called Artemis "Strangled" (an indication of her virginity). At Kalydon, where they forgot to offer her appropriate sacrifices, she sent the famous Kalydonian Boar, which devastated the land until brought down by the virgin huntress Atalanta and the hero Meleager. Artemis's roles as sender of plague and patroness of women's blood-rites are revealed in two of her most famous rituals in ancient Athens—both called the Arkteia.

According to legend, a bear once appeared in Attica, which eventually was tamed. One day the bear scratched the face of a girl who was teasing it. The girl's brothers killed the bear, thus angering Artemis, who sent a plague to Attica. Consulting an oracle, the Athenians learned that to appease the goddess, they must sacrifice one of their daughters to her. A man named Baros (or Embaros) offered to sacrifice his own daughter, on the condition that his family be made priests of Artemis ever after. The people agreed. Baros disguised his daughter and hid her in Artemis's sanctuary; he dressed up a goat as a girl, called it "daughter," and sacrificed it to Artemis. Henceforth, young girls "played the bear" (arktuein) at the sanctuary to appease Artemis and to save the community from plague.

One version of this Arkteia ritual featured a group of girls between ages five and ten who "played the bear" for Artemis, dressed in saffron-colored (yellow) robes. However, later commentators on ancient Greece noted that all Attic girls were required to "act as a bear" for Artemis before marriage. However, there simply wasn't enough room at the Brauron sanctuary for the full female population of Attica to pass through. C. Faraone, then, postulated that there was a second ritual associated with Artemis and bears in Attica, this one played out at the goddess's sanctuary at Mynikhion as well as at Brauron, in which girls came to offer tokens to Artemis before marriage (which would occur years after the age-ten limit of the previous ritual). Thus, there were two bear rituals in honor of Artemis, one Arkteia focusing on the goddess as sender and diverter of plague, and one Arkteia focusing on her as protectress of women at liminal points of life (Faraone 2003, passim).

Apollo (with a Few Words on the Muses and Asclepius).   Apollo is a paradox. On one hand, he was the Greek ideal: a handsome young man in the full bloom of youth, whose prerogatives included all the forces of civilization (see Image 9.26). On the other hand, he appeared to be a latecomer in the Greek pantheon who displaced gods and goddesses upon his arrival. Furthermore, in spite of his beauty and powers, he had little luck with women.

The name *Apollo* does not appear in the Linear B corpus. Instead, one of his epithets appears on the tablets from Knossos: Paiawon. In later years this epithet referred specifically to Apollo as healing deity, with the paean being a hymn inducing the god to hold off the forces of plague. At Knossos, Paiawon's name appears in lists in the Chariot Room, probably because he, like the other deities mentioned on these tablets (Athena, Poseidon, Ares), was a deity associated with war—that is, as the healer of war wounds (Gulizio et al. 2001, 459). As such, it appears that Paiawon was a Bronze Age healing god later absorbed by Apollo. A similar process occurred in the Peloponnese, where Apollo "killed" and replaced the local vegetation god Hyacinthus (see below). In other legends, Apollo replaced a series of goddesses, especially as patron of Delphi. According to Aeschylus (*Eumenides,* ll. 1–8):

> First in this prayer I give precedence to Earth,
> first prophetess of the deities. After her Themis,
> who indeed sat second as prophetess after her mother,
> as is told. Then third in this office,
> willingly, in violence to none,
> another Titan child of Earth took her place:
> Phoibê. And she gave it as a birthday gift
> to Phoibos [Apollo], who has his name from Phoibê.

Most early temples were dedicated to four deities: Hera, Artemis, Athena, and Apollo (Voyazis 1998). One of the earliest Greek temples was at the sanctuary of Apollo Daphnephoros ("laurel-bearing") at Eretria. Here, under centuries of reconstructions, archaeologists have found the foundations of a Geometric Age structure, long and narrow, with a rounded, apsidal end (see chapter 9). The idea that Apollo was the only male god associated early on with temples may derive from the fact that he displaced/absorbed some earlier Greek goddesses, which would also explain why he occasionally received jewelry (a type of item usually associated with females) as votives (Voyazis 1998, 146). This "displacement" is particularly evident at the sanctuary on Delos: The earliest sanctuary there belonged to Artemis, but by the Classical period, Apollo was revered as lord of Delos.

Apollo was the son of Zeus and the Titaness Leto, mildest of deities. His sister was Artemis. According to some legends, they were twins, but according to others, Artemis was older, present at the birth of her baby brother. This birth was not an easy one. According to his *Hymn,* no land was willing to let the new god be born upon it, either through fear of Hera or fear of Apollo himself, who would strike the ground and sink it upon his birth. Finally, Leto came to the tiny island of Delos, which agreed to accept the birth in exchange for a massive sanctuary to the new god, which greatly stimulated the Delian economy (much like a new football stadium would in modern times).

Apollo was god of youth, music, harmony, prophecy, archery, healing, and plague. He never has a beard in Greek art: The Greeks thought young men were most attractive just before the beard (and other body hair) grew in. His role as music god was clearest in his association with the Muses. The Muses were nine goddesses born of Zeus and Mnemosynê, goddess of memory. Individually these were Clio, goddess of history; Ourania, of astronomy; Thalia, of comedy; Melpomenê, of tragedy; Terpsichorê, of dance; Euterpê, of music; Polymnia, of religious poetry; Erato, of love poetry; and Calliopê, of epic poetry. They usually operated together in the literature, appearing en masse to Hesiod at the opening of his *Theogony*. They were the main singers on Olympos, with Apollo their music director and accompanist on the lyre.

The lyre was the musical instrument most commonly associated with Apollo. According to the *Homeric Hymn to Hermes*, Apollo first received the lyre as a gift from Hermes, who invented it by killing a turtle and stringing its shell with cow gut. The cows were, technically, stolen from Apollo, so Hermes presented his half brother with the new instrument in partial atonement for the theft. Apollo was delighted, and the two were best friends afterward. Apollo's association with the lyre is more significant than just pretty tunes, however: The ancient Greeks believed that musical harmony and order reflected social harmony and order (Calame 2001, 41–42). As god of the lyre, then, Apollo also took into his persona aspects of rationality and higher thinking. Nietzsche associated calm rationality with Apollo and strong emotionalism with Dionysos.

Apollo's power of prophecy was linked to his relationship with Zeus. In reality, only Zeus understood the workings of fate; the father of gods and men shared this knowledge with his favorite son. Why Apollo was Zeus's favorite son was related to his birth order. Although chronology is impossible to reckon in myth, it seems that Apollo was Zeus's first son. This is significant in light of the Succession Myth presented in Hesiod (see above), in which each of Zeus's forefathers conquered his own father to establish himself as king of the universe—Ouranos was first, then Kronos overthrew Ouranos, then Zeus overthrew Kronos. As Zeus's son, Apollo had the potential to confront his own father, plunging the universe once again into chaos. Instead:

> The deities present tremble at his passage through Zeus' house,
> and straightaway all spring from their seats
> at his drawing near, as he bends his shining bow.
> But Leto herself remains by Zeus delighting in thunder
> and straightaway she has unstrung the bow and closed the quiver
> and, taking the bow from his strong shoulders with her hands,
> she hangs it upon a golden peg on her father's pillar.
> Leading him she sits him on a throne.
> Immediately the father gave him nectar in a golden cup,
> welcoming his dear son . . .
>   (*Homeric Hymn to Apollo*, ll. 2–11)

In this story, it is clear that Apollo will be a devoted son, not a threat to his father. For love of this ally, Zeus shares his knowledge of the future, allowing Apollo himself to reveal this knowledge to human prophets and prophetesses (see below). The most famous seat of Apollo's oracular powers was at Delphi in central Greece, where the Delphic Games were held in his honor. Here, legend tells, Apollo slew the dragon Pytho and took control of her sanctuary and priestess, the Pythia. The Pythia was a prophetess whom all Greeks consulted on matters of importance. The list of those who consulted her includes not only Oedipus, the Lydian king Croesus, and Socrates himself, but also any Greek leader intending to start a colony. All Greek colonization efforts had to be approved by Apollo.

Like Artemis, Apollo carried a bow and quiver. Unlike his sister, though, Apollo was not a hunter—his bow was used against humans rather than animals. This showed Apollo in his guise as plague god, but, as he could also withhold the plague, he was a god of healing as well. Just as Artemis killed women with her arrows, Apollo killed men. This is especially evident in the beginning of the *Iliad* (ll. 43–52):

> . . . and Phoibos Apollo heard [his priest],
> and he came down from the peaks of Olympos raging at heart,
> bearing a bow and covered quiver on his shoulders.
> Straightaway the arrows screeched forth from the shoulders of the angry god,
> as he roused himself. His coming was like night.
> Then he sat himself far from the ships; he let loose an arrow;
> an awful sound came from the silver shaft.
> First on mules and swift-footed hounds he visited death,
> but then he let fly and cast the bitter shafts upon the men.
> Always the funeral pyres burnt through the night.

Here, enraged over an insult to one of his priests, Apollo attacked the Greek army with his arrows, killing all until peace was made with his devotee.

Apollo as god of healing was matched only by his son, Asclepius, a mortal born of the girl Coronis. Before the birth, Apollo was led to believe that Coronis was cheating on him, causing him to kill the girl wrongfully. Realizing too late what he had done, Apollo at least saved their son, giving him to the wise centaur Cheiron to raise. Cheiron taught Asclepius everything about the healing arts, such that Asclepius became a world-renowned doctor, even capable of curing death. This, of course, did not go over well with the underworld gods, who killed Asclepius in revenge. But in death Asclepius became a demigod. His main cult was at Epidauros, a giant healing sanctuary (see chapter 10), but his cult was also strong in Athens, where he had a sanctuary on the side of the Acropolis.

The tragic affair with Coronis was indicative of Apollo's love life in general—he did not have luck with women. This probably resulted from his eternal adolescence. Other problematic relationships of his included Cassandra, a Trojan princess who agreed to have sex with the god in exchange for the gift of prophecy but then changed her mind, and the nymph Daphnê, who preferred to become a laurel tree rather than be molested by Apollo. Daphnê was Apollo's first love, and he retained a strong attachment to laurel ever since. This was why the crowns offered at the Delphic Games, and at artistic competitions in general, are made of laurel leaves (thus, the expression *resting on one's laurels* refers to someone who relies on past achievements), and why Apollo was often revered as Daphnephoros.

As god of youth, Apollo was involved in coming-of-age rituals. A common practice throughout Greece was the dedication of a lock of hair to Apollo to mark the end of one's boyhood. As the adolescent entered a new mode of life, he literally left behind a part of himself to honor the god who had presided over his earlier life. (Girls had a similar practice devoted to Artemis.)

A more spectacular youth-oriented ritual was the Hyakinthia, celebrated by the Spartans at the sanctuary of Apollo and Hyacinthus at Amyclae (see also a later section of this chapter). According to legend, Apollo and Hyacinthus were lovers. One day while playing a game similar to Frisbee, Apollo accidentally killed the youth. For this, the first day of the Hyakinthia is set aside for ritual mourning. The true festivities began on the second day. In a theater as of yet unidentified by researchers, the Spartan youths, divided into age groups (see chapter 6), performed various songs and dances. Even more spectacular were the girls' festivities. Many took part in a procession out to Amyclae, riding on what sources, such as Pausanias, describe as early Greek floats, made of wicker instead of flowers. Then, as with the boys but all over the sanctuary, the girls, divided by age groups, sang and danced in lavish choruses. The third day was the kopis, or grand sacrifice and general cookout. Here all the Spartans gathered together to eat and worship with their households, to the point that, as later historians narrated, no one was left in the city of Sparta. The first day's focus on the death of young Hyacinthus, and the prevalence of choruses of youths and maidens on the second day, suggest that the Hyakinthia were celebrations of youth and the progression through age divisions into adulthood (Calame 2001, 174–176).

Dionysos, Mainads, Satyrs. For a long time, it was believed that Dionysos, also called Bacchus, was a newcomer to the Greek pantheon, that he had arrived around the eighth century B.C.E. along with other orgiastic cults from the east. Then his name turned up in the Linear B tablets, both on Crete and on the mainland. It immediately became clear that Dionysos was a long-standing member of the Greek pantheon and that his cult was quite extensive.

Dionysos, generally associated with wine, was the god of liminality—the crossing over of categorical boundaries and the mixing up of established states of being. The categories he crossed are god–mortal, male–female, human–animal, and sane–mad.

The crossed boundary of god–mortal began with his very conception—Dionysos was the son of Zeus and the mortal princess Semelê (who was probably once a goddess). According to myth, Hera, furious about Zeus's infidelity, played a nasty trick on Semelê. Disguised as Semelê's nurse, Hera told the princess that Zeus was an impostor, not really a god at all. To be sure, Hera recommended that Semelê ask Zeus to appear to her in all his divinity, as he appeared to his legitimate wife Hera. Semelê took the bait, made Zeus swear upon the River Styx (the most powerful oath among the gods), and demanded to see him as a true Olympian. Unfortunately, Zeus in all his divinity was a lightning bolt, which instantly incinerated Semelê. Unable to save the princess, Zeus took the unborn child out of her womb and placed it in his thigh until its birth. Once born, Dionysos proved to be immortal, although of a mortal mother. Thus, he was in between categories: a mortal-born god. Dionysos's mixing of divine and mortal categories became more blatant in the Orphic Mysteries (see below). Here, Dionysos was said to be the son of Zeus and Persephonê, queen of the dead. After his birth, he was kidnapped, killed, and eaten by the Titans at the behest of Hera. Zeus then smote the Titans in his anger, and humans were made from their flesh. As such, a small element of Dionysos, coursing through the Titans' veins, was present in all humans, providing the divine soul. Thus, Dionysos represented what is divine within mortals. The fact that Dionysos, like Athena, was born of a male introduces his role as gender-blender. Both Athena and Dionysos had mothers. Zeus swallowed Metis before Athena's birth; thus, Athena was born of a mother but emerged out of her father's head. By contrast, Dionysos's mother was dead before his birth (another aspect of his bordering between mortal and immortal), and Dionysos was born of a male. Both deities displayed significant gender reversals. Athena was militaristic, rational (these were both seen as masculine traits by the Greeks), and asexual, totally devoted to her father. Dionysos was fair-skinned (a feminine trait for the Greeks), with long, luxurious hair, and he spent most of his time (in myth at any rate) with women.

Dionysos also *caused* gender inversions. This was most evident in the god's fan club—the Mainads. Just as Artemis had a band of nymphs who accompanied her on her hunting expeditions, Dionysos had a band of (literally) wild women. The word *mainad* comes from the verb *mainazomai,* which means "to rave, to be mad." The Mainads were Dionysos's mad attendants. In art and literature, they wore fawn skins wrapped around their waists and ivy in their hair (see Image 8.11), as well as carrying a reed decorated with wool and ivy called a thyrsos, an item intimately associated with Dionysos's cult.

There were two types of Mainads. Some were the devotees of Dionysos, who followed the god much in the manner of Dead Heads following the late Jerry Garcia. The other group was those women whom Dionysos drove mad in anger, usually because their city had refused to recognize his divinity. The fact that so many stories about this god revolved around the initial rejection of his cult is one of the reasons he was believed to be a latecomer to Greece. In light of the Linear B evidence, however, it is now accepted that the Dionysos-as-outsider idea was simply a manifestation of his persona in Greek myth. At any rate, when various cities refused to accept Dionysos as a god, he drove their women mad, making them leave their homes and families to go raving out into the countryside. Such an event occurred in Euripides's *Bacchae,* when Dionysos established his cult in his home city of Thebes (ll. 32–43):

Therefore I have driven them from the houses
raving mad, they inhabit the mountain, minds frenzied;

8.11 White Figure Vase
with Mainad
(Courtesy of Paul Butler)

they wear my livery and carry out my orgies,
and all the female seed of the Cadmeians, as many
women as there are, is driven mad from the houses.
Together, with the daughters of Cadmus among them,
they sit under green pines amid roofless rocks.
For it is necessary for the city to learn this fully, even unwillingly,
being uninitiated in my Bacchic mysteries,
and for me to speak on behalf of my mother Semelê,
revealing to mortals the god she bore to Zeus.

Later we hear of the awesome power wielded by Dionysos's Mainads, when
a messenger trying to capture the women reports (ll. 733–768) that they sprang
on a herd of cattle and tore up the cows with their bare hands, cow parts flying
in all directions. Then the women attacked the towns by Kithairon, seizing
children, stealing household goods, and carrying around fire that failed to
burn them. The local citizens defended themselves, only to find that, although
their own spears had no effect on the women, the Mainads were quite adept
with their thyrsoi, wounding the men and turning them to flight. When all

was done, the women returned to the hills, washing themselves off in sacred fountains, snakes licking the blood from their cheeks.

The women were behaving like men, attacking villages like warriors. However, although the "manly" behavior of the women was remarkable, Dionysos's greatest achievement in this play was the feminization of the staunch Theban king Pentheus. There was a long-standing antipathy between the king and the god (who also happened to be first cousins), with the king at various points attempting to defeminize Dionysos. Dionysos drove Pentheus mad, dressed him as a woman, and sent him as a sacrifice to the Mainads. Just as the women became as men, Pentheus, the overmasculine man, became effeminate—another example of the god's gender-reversing effect.

The gender boundary was not the only one crossed in this instance, however. The Theban Mainads crossed the boundary between human and animal when they slaughtered the cattle bare-handed—humans use tools/weapons for such actions—ripping up flesh in a bloody spectacle called a sparagmos. Pentheus also met his end as an animal: When the Mainads discovered him spying upon them, they mistook him for a lion (Dionysos having made them crazy). His own mother Agaue began the sparagmos on her son; later she returned to Thebes waving aloft his head and bragging about her hunting prowess. The Thebans were in this way transformed into hunting and hunted animals. Even Dionysos made this transition: When Pentheus began his descent into madness, he believed he saw Dionysos in the form of a bull.

Both of these crossovers in category—male–female and human–animal—depend on one of the most important of Dionysos's "transgressions," that between sanity and madness. He drove the Theban women insane directly; Pentheus became completely mad over time. Most important for Dionysos on this continuum was drunkenness, which could be said to lie somewhere between sanity and insanity. Thus was Dionysos the god of wine. The more frightening aspects of drunkenness appear in the tale of Dionysos's introduction of wine to humanity. According to the myth, Dionysos taught the Attic farmer Ikarios how to ferment grapes into the intoxicating beverage. Delighted with the gift, Ikarios invited over his neighbors for a sampling. Never having been drunk before, the neighbors believed that Ikarios had poisoned them, and they murdered him in revenge. Later, Ikarios's daughter Erigonê came looking for her father. Finding the body, she hanged herself in grief. The gods took pity on the girl and placed her in the sky as the constellation Virgo. On Earth, she was honored with a heroine cult in which Attic girls swung on trees during the Anthesteria (see below) in her memory. Dionysos later taught the Greeks to mix their wine with water to avoid such dangerous inebriations.

The Greeks enjoyed the mild drunkenness provided by wine, and they called Dionysos the god most beneficent to mortals. Drinking wine was critical to social interaction, as Greek men enjoyed each other's company during the symposion, the men's drinking party (see chapter 6). In the *Laws*, Plato/ Socrates claimed that controlled public drinking would benefit society, as it would allow everyone (read: men) an opportunity to be perfectly honest with each other, thus clearing the political and social air. The gift of wine was especially appreciated by another group of Dionysos's followers: the satyrs. Satyrs were half-human, half-goat (or -horse) creatures who liked wine a lot. In art and literature, they appear as potbellied, joyful creatures who attended to their god in all situations. The best literary portrayal of satyrs is in Euripides's *Cyclops,* a satyr play (see chapter 10). Here, Silenos, chief satyr, laments, calling Dionysos by his epithets Bromios (Boisterous) and Bacchus (ll. 1–17):

> O Bromios, because of you I have thousands of toils,
> even now as in youth when my body was strong.
> First then, mad through Hera, you, leaving secretly,
> escaped your caretakers—the mountain nymphs.
> Then in the battle with the giants, I was your
> comrade-in-arms, your right-hand shield-man.
> I killed Enkelados, thrusting my spear half-way through
> his shield. Or wait; am I thinking of a dream?
> No, by Zeus! Since I even gave the spoils to Bacchus.
> And now I endure a greater toil than these.
> For when Hera incited a Tuscan family of pirates
> after you, so you might be sold far away,
> I, hearing this, took to sea with my kids
> seeking after you. And on the high prow
> I myself steered, holding the rudder,
> and the kids plied the oars, churning white
> the grey sea with waves, looking for you, O King!

Of course, as devotees of Dionysos, such labor was not usually the satyrs' lot, and they appear far more often in art frolicking and sexually aroused. On vases and the stage, they appeared with giant, erect phalloi, and in vase painting they were often trying to have sex with any number of unreceptive partners, including the Mainads—who generally beat them off with thyrsoi—and, on occasion, mules. Beyond the intended humor, the satyrs' sexual aggressiveness manifested the close bond the Greeks saw between wine and sexuality.

Nevertheless, wine consumption could certainly be a "decent" pursuit, even for small children. This was evident in the Attic-Ionic festival of the Anthesteria, which occurred in early spring. The festival was three days long, divided into a day of wine-tasting (pithoigia), a day of wine jugs (choes), and a day of pots (khytroi). On the first day, probably beginning near sundown, the wine made during the previous season was opened and tasted. One might liken it to Nouveau Beaujolais season in France. On this day, the Athenians carried pithoi (wine jars) down to the sanctuary of Dionysos in the Marshes, where they prayed to the god and dedicated the season's new wine to him.

The second day of the festival—the choes—was the most significant and, for modern scholars, the most confusing. One important event was the presentation of miniature wine jugs to three-year-old boys, signifying their transition from baby to child status. Archaeologists have discovered countless miniature drinking cups with pictures of babies on them, no doubt deriving from this festival. Baby boys who died before age three were often buried with such cups. For the adult men, drinking contests occurred. All the men, possibly even slaves, gathered together to drain their wineskins. When the "king" blew the trumpet, the drinking began. The winner received a small cake as a prize and, presumably, a rather amusing kind of honor among the citizens. The joyful nature of this ritual is played out at the end of Aristophanes's comedy *The Akharnians,* when the protagonist Dikaiopolis wins the competition (ll. 1227 ff.):

> Dikaiopolis: So bear me to the judges. Where's the king?
> Give me the Victory Cup!
> See how this cup here is empty;
> Hail Glorious Victory!
> Chorus: Hail, indeed, if you so bid,
> Old Fellow, Glorious Victory!
> Dikaiopolis: And first having poured it in unmixed
> I took it all in one gulp!
> Chorus: Hail now, O Gentleman!
> He goes forth taking the Victory Cup!
> Dikaiopolis: Follow now singing Ho!
> Hail, Glorious Victory!
> Chorus: But we'll follow for your sake.
> Hail! Singing Glorious Victory
> of you and your Victory Cup!

The drinking was accompanied by some odd practices: All the sanctuaries were closed and locked on this day, everyone brought their own wine and drinking vessels to the festivities, and drinking was done in silence. This stood in stark contrast to the normal drinking practices, when drinks and cups were provided by the host, and chatter, singing, and general revelry were the norm. The Athenians explained these oddities by claiming that in the heroic past, Orestes, son of Agamemnon, still ritually impure from matricide, had arrived in Athens during the choes. Telling him to go away would have been the height of discourtesy, but allowing him to participate in the festival would have risked spreading his impurity to the entire populace. The dilemma was resolved when Orestes was invited to the ritual, but the sanctuaries were closed and each participant used his own drinking materials, thus stopping Orestes's "contagion."

On the evening of the second day, further rites of Dionysos, who "himself" arrived by boat in the city, were enacted by the archon Basileus (King) and his wife, the Basilinna. References to these acts are mentioned in the fourth-century court case *Against Neaira* by Apollodoros, when a woman who was not a citizen nevertheless performed the role of Basilinna. Apollodoros complained (§73):

> And this same woman offered the unspeakable offerings on behalf of your city, and she saw things not appropriate for her to see, being a foreigner. And likewise, even being as she is, she went where no one else of those properly Athenian go, save for

the wife of the King, and she administered the oath to the venerable priestesses who preside over the rites, and she was given as wife to Dionysos, and she performed the old rituals to the deities on behalf of the city, which are most sacred and unspeakable.

The archon Basileus probably played the role of Dionysos. In myth, Dionysos was married to the Cretan girl Ariadnê, who had originally been married to, and then abandoned by, Theseus on his return from his confrontation with the Minotaur. Amusingly, Dionysos was the only Greek god known for monogamy.

The final day of the Anthesteria, the day of pots (khytroi), was dedicated to the dead, and rituals on this day were more closely associated with Hermes Psychopompos ("guide of souls") than with Dionysos. On this day an old, traditional type of porridge was made in earthen pots and either eaten or left out for the dead. In some ways, this day functioned like our earlier notions of Halloween, when the dead were said to walk among the living. At the end of the day, a herald went through the city shouting, "Out, you keres (frightful demons), the Anthesteria are over!" Many scholars have speculated as to why the final day of a springtime-, youth-, and fertility-oriented festival was a day of the dead. One might guess that the phenomenon of the hangover explains it nicely.

Beyond his association with wine, Dionysos was god of all sorts of liquid bounty, and he was one of the main fertility deities of the Greek pantheon. Although Artemis presided over animal and human fertility, and Demeter over grains and foodstuffs, Dionysos was god of juices and wines, honey, and possibly even milk. Such bounty he provided to his followers in the play *Bacchae*.

Finally, Dionysos was the god of theater. The ancient Greek theaters were his sanctuaries, and all forms of drama were sacred to him. As will be discussed in chapter 10, tragedy, comedy, and satyr plays—the three categories of ancient Greek drama—all emerged out of poetic forms dedicated to Dionysos. The orchestra section of any Greek theater had at its center a small altar for Dionysos, which was the acoustic core of the theater. All dramas were originally supposed to involve Dionysos somehow, and a shouted complaint at later Greek plays was that they had "ouden pros ton Dionyson!" ("nothing to do with Dionysos!"). In truth, just about any reference to wine or madness could be accepted as a reference to this god, and only a few surviving plays deal with Dionysos directly. These are Euripides's *Bacchae* and *Cyclops* and Aristophanes's *Frogs*. This final play, a comedy, portrays Dionysos traveling to the underworld to judge a competition between the playwrights Aeschylus and Euripides. The god, rather out of his element, is frequently scared out of his wits in the underworld, and at one point, he actually wets himself on stage. The Greeks clearly visualized Dionysos as a deity with a really good sense of humor.

Ares.   War gods were typical of Indo-European pantheons, so at least some aspect of Ares must have arrived in Greece with the Greeks. The name itself appears somewhat ambiguously in the Linear B tablets. The word *a-re* appears on a Knossos tablet, but with no context. The personal names *A-re-jo* and *A-re-i-jo* may indicate the name *Areios,* or "He of Ares" (Ventris and Chadwick 1959,

126, 288; Hägg 1997, 165). Perhaps more significant is the name *Enyalios*, appearing on tablets from Knossos and Pylos. *Enyalios* was an epithet of Ares in the historical period, and the word is related to the name of a lesser-known war goddess associated with Ares: Enyo. It is possible that, as with Paiawon and Apollo, this Enyalios was a separate Bronze Age deity who was absorbed by Ares.

Ares was one of those rare deities: an actual son of Zeus and Hera. He shares this parentage with the goddess of youth, Hebê, and, depending on which version of the story is read, Hephaistos (see below). Amusingly, being a child of the reigning deities was not an asset on Olympos. Hephaistos was the only lame god, and Ares was almost universally hated, even by his own parents. In the *Iliad*, Book 5 (ll. 889–898), Zeus yells at him:

"Do not, Two-Face, whine sitting by me!
You are most hateful to me of the deities who hold Olympos,
for ever is strife dear to you, and wars and battles.
You have the uncheckable wrath of your mother Hera,
unyielding; I with pains am undone by her words.
I believe you suffer through her promptings.
But I'll not long let you suffer pains,
for you are of my family; your mother bore you to me.
But if you were born to another of the deities, so destructive,
then indeed you'd long since have been bound lower than the Titans!"

Ares's most common epithet was *Stygeros*, "hateful." Like his half sister Athena, Ares was a war god. Unlike Athena, though, he presided over the bad aspects of war: hate, strife, pain, misery, loss, chaos. Furthermore, his harsh, chaotic domain was seen as part of his character. Athena the strategy goddess was wise; Ares the chaos god was random and ineffectual. Even in war, Ares was less than an ideal ally. He sided with the Trojans—the losing side of the Trojan War—in Homer's poems. When faced in combat by Athena and even the mortal Diomedes, he was bested and went wailing off to Olympos to be healed by Apollo.

Amusingly, Ares fared better in love than in hate. He was Aphrodite's lover, cuckolding her rightful husband Hephaistos. Ares and Aphrodite were worshipped together at Argos, Sparta, and the Cretan settlement at Sta Lenika, and they were one of the most common pairings of deities in early Greek art. From his union with the goddess of sex, Ares is the father of Harmonia, literally "Harmony." This daughter married the Phoenician immigrant Cadmus, founder of Thebes, after the hero killed another of Ares's children, a dragon. Cadmus planted the dragon's teeth, from which sprang up the original population of Thebes. In this way, Ares was father and grandfather to the Thebans. Of course, the first thing these earth- and dragon-born descendants of Ares tried to do was kill each other, but, fortunately, Cadmus was there to calm down the few remaining survivors of their first day of life.

Otherwise, Ares was usually associated with Thrace, a savage and barbaric region north of Greece. After his ill-fated tryst with Aphrodite recounted in the

Odyssey, Ares returns to Thrace, while the goddess returns to her temple in Paphos. Ares's being based in the region of Thrace may have recalled the god's original pathway into Greece, just as Aphrodite came to Greece by way of Cyprus. Or it may have been an attempt on the part of the Greeks to distance themselves culturally and geographically from a deity whose domain they were daily forced to recognize, but which they did not necessarily want to claim as their own.

Hephaistos.   Burkert, in his book on Greek religion, claims that Hephaistos was a foreign deity, worshipped originally by Tyrsenoi on the island of Lemnos, where the god's cult remained strong in antiquity (Burkert 1985, 167). Nevertheless, there may be some evidence for the god's presence in the Late Bronze Age, if the name on a Knossian Linear B tablet—a-pa-ti-jo—might be read as Hephaistios, "He of Hephaistos" (Ventris and Chadwick 1959, 127). A third possible origin for the god is Cyprus, renowned throughout history for its copper industry. Starting in the Late Bronze Age, the Cypriots made bronze statues of male deities, sometimes standing upon a copper ingot and brandishing weapons. This god ruled side by side with a nude goddess understood to have been an early manifestation of Aphrodite, goddess of Cyprus. This Cypriot combination of metallurgic and belligerent divine imagery may explain how Aphrodite came to be romantically involved with both the smith god and the war god in Greek myth.

Hephaistos was god of metallurgy, smithing, architecture, crafts, and, to a certain extent, comedy relief. We see Hephaistos working in his forge in Book 18 of the *Iliad,* when the sea goddess Thetis comes to ask him to make a new set of armor for her son Achilles (ll. 468–477):

> So speaking he left [Thetis] there, and he went to the bellows;
> he turned them to the fire and ordered them to be worked.
> And the bellows, 20 in all, blew upon the melting-vats,
> all types of strong-blowing breath they sent forth.
> And here and there he turned himself
> as Hephaistos should wish and have the work progress.
> He cast bronze into the fire, and unyielding tin
> and valuable gold and silver. And then
> he placed a great anvil on the anvil-block; in his one hand
> was a mighty hammer, in the other a pair of pincers.

The forge is filled with his creations, including sentient metal maidens who help Hephaistos get from place to place. This ability to create puts Hephaistos into a similar category as Athena, goddess, among other things, of crafts, although Athena generally tended toward more "feminine" crafts, such as weaving. Nevertheless, this close correspondence between the siblings was important, especially to the Athenians. According to their mythology, Hephaistos was the father of Erechtheus, stepson to Athena and autochthonous king of Athens (see above, in the section about Athena). Thus, Hephaistos, along with Athena, was the parent of the Athenians. This relationship was recognized both in the joint cult these deities shared in the Hephaisteion, a gem of a temple still preserved next to the Athenian Acropolis (see Image 9.7), and in Hephaistos's presence in the Athenian Apatouria festival, when family ties were celebrated (Burkert 1985, 168).

Hephaistos was also the deities' architect, to a far greater extent than Poseidon (see above). Although Poseidon may have built (and destroyed) human structures, Hephaistos created the immortals' houses, all built, according to Homer, "by means of his craftsmanship and cunning."

The most intriguing aspect of Hephaistos's persona is that he was lame, a condition otherwise unheard of among the perfect Olympians. There are two versions of how this lameness came to be, both themselves tied up with Hephaistos's confusing parentage. According to some tales, Hephaistos was alive before Athena and was the god who whacked Zeus's head with an axe to let the goddess out. In this version, Hephaistos was the son of Hera and Zeus, who tries to soften the strife between his parents. In Book 1 of the *Iliad*, Hephaistos, begging his mother Hera to stop her quarrel with Zeus, reminds her of a time that he came to her aid, infuriating Zeus, who tossed him off Olympos. Hephaistos landed a day later on the island of Lemnos, lamed by the fall. However, an alternate version of Hephaistos's birth claims that he was born after Athena. Hera was angry at Zeus for giving birth (her own prerogative, she felt), so she gave birth parthenogenically (without a man) to Hephaistos. He was born a sickly, lame god, which Hera then made worse, as Hephaistos recounts in Book 18 of the *Iliad* (ll. 395–398):

> [Thetis] saved me, when pain took me, haven fallen far
> by the desire of my bitch-faced mother. She wanted to
> hide me, being angry. Then I would have suffered pains at heart
> if Eurynome and Thetis hadn't received me to their bosom.

In this version of the tale, Hephaistos got his revenge on Hera by making her a glorious throne with magical epoxy on the seat. Once she sat down, Hera was trapped. Only Dionysos could secure her release: He got Hephaistos drunk, brought him to Olympos, and got Hera to offer him the hand of Aphrodite in marriage if he would release her. Such is the topic of one of our earliest depictions of the Olympian family on the François Vase (see Image 8.12), on which a

8.12 François Vase detail: Return of Hephaistos
(Courtesy of Paul Butler)

drunken Hephaistos on a mule led by Dionysos comes before Aphrodite and his parents.

It is this aspect of his persona that allowed (or forced) Hephaistos to play the part of comic relief. In the *Iliad*, this is a positive trait when Hephaistos can defuse tension among the gods by his antics. In Book 1, Hephaistos limps around Olympos serving nectar to the gods, a service usually performed by a far more graceful deity. The smith's bustling about stirs up immortal laughter among the gods, causing them to forget their squabbles about the Trojan War. In the *Odyssey*, however, we hear about the time Hephaistos caught his wife Aphrodite in bed with Ares. Knowing about the affair, Hephaistos set a magical net about the bed, pinning the two in a rather compromising position while he invited the other deities to come see the adulterers (8, 306–327):

"Father Zeus and other blessed, ever-living deities,
come here, so you might see laughable and harsh works,
as Aphrodite, daughter of Zeus, being spiteful
ever dishonors me; she loves destructive Ares,
since he is handsome and swift-footed, while I am
lame. But I hold nothing accountable to me for this
except my two parents; would they never had me!

. . . .

The deities stood in the forecourt, givers of good things.
Unquenchable laughter arose among the blessed deities
as they looked on the machinations of crafty Hephaistos.

This ruse did little to stop the affair, although it did tempt all the other gods into lying with Aphrodite, having gotten a good look at the goddess nude in bed. In the end, Hephaistos was a highly artistic, creative deity, but he did not always seem to have very much common sense. As stated above in the section on Athena, he attempted to rape the warrior virgin and while trying to curb his own wife's sexual proclivities, he gave all the gods on Olympos a show. The fact that their smith god could be both lame and rather clueless shows the ancient Greeks' general disdain for craftsmen and menial workers. Hephaistos was not a king like Zeus, a musician like Apollo, or a warrior like Ares. He was a worker, and as such got quite an unflattering portrayal, even for a deity.

Hermes.   Hermes appears on Linear B tablets from the mainland and, possibly, Crete (Nosch 2000, passim). The name *Hermes* derives from the word for cairn, or mound of stones. This derivation introduces many aspects of the god's persona. Cairns were used to mark boundaries, mainly of personal or political territories; Hermes was the traveling god who crossed boundaries. Cairns were used to bury the dead; Hermes is the psychopompos, or "guide of souls," who brought mortals and immortals to and from Hades. With this access to the underworld, Hermes became the patron of magic, especially of curses. Cairns were, inevitably, roughly formed; Hermes was frequently revered in the form of the herm, a stone block with the god's head on top and an erect phallus on the side (see image 8.13). These images were used to mark boundaries. Those most likely to cross boundaries were merchants and (closely related to merchants) pirates. Associations with both led to Hermes's identity as the thieving trickster, emblematic of cunning intelligence.

Hermes was the son of Zeus and the nymph Maia. He was the only Greek deity ever portrayed as an infant—all other gods emerged onto the scene fully grown, as Apollo leaping up from his own birth on Delos, or Athena springing from her father's head fully armed. By contrast, in his *Homeric Hymn*, Hermes appears as an infant in swaddling clothes, escaping from his crib. Nevertheless, he was quite precocious (ll. 17–19):

> Born at dawn, at midday he played the lyre,
> In the evening he stole the cattle of far-shooting Apollo,
> On the fourth of the month, the very day reverend Maia bore him.

His *Hymn* describes how, escaping from his mother's watchful gaze, he killed a tortoise and used its shell to make the first lyre. Then he stole a herd of cattle belonging to his older brother Apollo. Two of these he sacrificed to the Olympian gods, including himself of course, and he hid the rest in a cave. Then he sneaked back into his room through the keyhole. Later, when confronted by Apollo and Zeus about his crimes, he insisted in all honesty to Zeus (ll. 378–380):

> Believe me, for you swear to be my dear father,
> I did not take the cows home—Bless me!
> nor did I go over the threshold. What I say is completely true!

Technically, Hermes was not lying. He did not drive the cattle to his house, and he went through the keyhole, not over the threshold. Such doublespeak was one of Hermes's most famous attributes.

Hermes was the messenger of the gods, working mainly for Zeus (Hera had her own personal messenger in the rainbow goddess Iris). His speed over (and under) air, land, and sea was depicted iconographically by his winged sandals. In the *Odyssey*, he is sent to Calypso's island to demand Odysseus's release, whose time to return home has finally come. Hermes also served as an escort for humans. At the end of the *Iliad*, Hermes, in disguise, brought King Priam of Troy to Achilles's tent, as requested by Zeus (24, 334–345):

> "Hermes, since for you especially it is most dear
> to accompany men, and you listen to whom you wish,
> head over there, and lead Priam to the hollow ships
> of the Achaeans, so that no one of the Danaans sees or notices him
> before he gets to the son of Peleus."
> So [Zeus] spoke, nor did messenger Argeiphontes disobey.
> Immediately then he placed on his feet fair sandals,
> immortal, golden, which bore him equally over water as

over vast earth upon breaths of wind.
He seized his wand, with which he charms the eyes of men
when he wishes, and with which he wakes the sleeping.
Holding this in his hands strong Argeiphontes took flight.
Quickly he came to Troy and the Hellespont,
and he went forth resembling a princely youth,
one just getting his first beard, when youth is most beautiful.

The wand was the Caduceus, a rod with two snakes coiled on either side. Hermes used this to cause people or deities to fall asleep, most famously the hundred-eyed giant Argos, who once guarded Hera's sanctuary in Argos. Here the giant watched over Io, a maiden seduced by Zeus and then transformed into a cow to hide her from Hera. Hera had Argos watching her so that Zeus could not rescue the girl. Zeus, in turn, sent Hermes to distract the guard. Hermes got all 100 of Argos's eyes to close in sleep at once, at which point he killed Argos and rescued Io. For this murder, Hermes got the epithet *Argeiphontes*, "Killer of Argos."

Hermes's role as messenger and traveler extended to the realms of the dead, and it was he who led the recently dead to the underworld, as he did for Penelope's suitors, slain by Odysseus and Telemachus (*Odyssey*, 24.1–14):

Kyllenian Hermes summoned the spirits
of the suitors; he held his wand in his hands,
fair, golden, with which he charms the eyes of men
when he wishes, and with which he wakes the sleeping.
Rousing them with this he led, and the blithering dead followed.
As when bats fly out of the inner recess of a wondrous cave,
twittering, when one has fallen off
a rock clustering, and they cling to one another.
So the blithering ones went forth together. And gracious Hermes
led them down dank paths.
They went by flowing Ocean and the white rock;
by the gates of the sun and the realm of dreams
they went. Quickly they arrived in the meadow of asphodel;
there spirits dwell, images of the dead.

Hermes, at the end of the *Homeric Hymn to Demeter*, brought back Persephonê from the house of Hades, and it was he who returned Euridikê, wife of Orpheus, to that domain after the poet's attempts to resurrect her failed. For this reason, Hermes was associated with magic and curses. Many curses, often inscribed on lead tablets, were invocations to the underworld deities. As go-between for the worlds of the living and the dead, Hermes was in the best position to deliver such messages and to bring back their effects.

His proclivity for lying, stealing, and cursing notwithstanding, Hermes was beneficial to humans, much as Dionysos was, and thus his epithet *Hermes the Helper*. According to Hesiod's *Theogony*, Hermes, along with the goddess

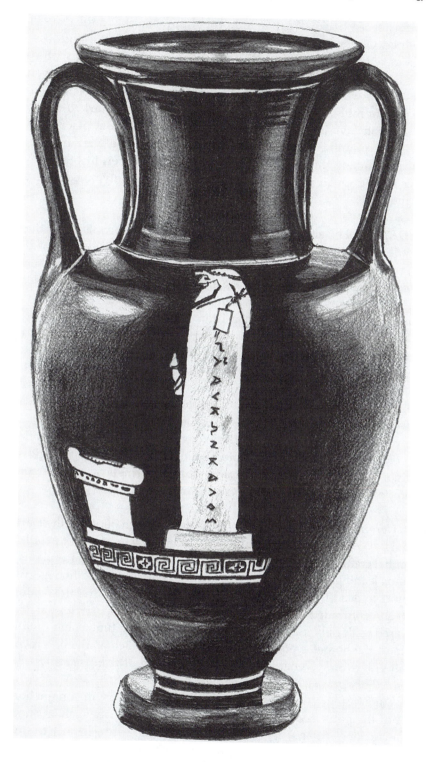

8.13 Red Figure Vase showing Herm (Courtesy of Paul Butler)

Hecatê, increased flocks of cattle and brought prosperity. In the *Odyssey*, Hermes helped Odysseus when the hero had to confront the goddess Circê: Hermes gave Odysseus the antidote to Circê's poisons. Along with Athena, Hermes aided the hero Perseus in his confrontation with Medusa, even lending Perseus his winged sandals. All in all, Hermes was an aid to humans, both heroic and humble. The herms (see Image 8.13) that marked boundaries served as protective images, keeping people safe in liminal places. The erect phallus is explained as the erection Hermes got the first time he saw Persephonê, linking this god to the underworld and to fertility. Sexually, Hermes was most popular with the nymphs, although his only noted child is Pan, god of the wilds.

Astral Deities.   The ancient Greeks, like many ancient peoples, saw the heavenly bodies as deities and worshipped them accordingly. The sun was the god Helios, who drove his chariot across the heavens every day, relaxing in his watery home past the western horizon at night. One of his sisters was Selenê, the moon; the other was Eos, "rosy-fingered" dawn. All three, according to Hesiod, were the children of Hyperion, a Titan.

The divine twins Kastor and Polydeukes (called Castor and Pollux by the Romans), who gave us the constellation Gemini, also appear to have been astral deities. Sons of sky-father Zeus, legend relates that one was mortal, the other immortal. Unwilling to be separated even after death, they chose to reside in the sky together, passing through the heavenly spheres as well as the underworld. In cult, these brothers were called the Diokouroi ("sons of Zeus"), and they were clearly revered as deities. Associated especially with horses and sea travel, they were invoked to protect sailors, and St. Elmo's fire (glow from buildup of static electricity on ship masts during storms) was understood to be a manifestation of their presence for storm-troubled ships.

Heroes, Heroines, and Tomb Cults.   Tomb cults, which began in the Dark Age, involved the veneration of a recently dead individual or group of people, often in a familial context. The worshippers may have been direct descendants of the dead, thus leading to some manner of ancestor cult, or former thanes giving final honors to dead leaders. The cults usually began right after the death of the revered and continued for a while (maybe two generations), with the names of the revered seldom being preserved (the society of the time being preliterate). Sometimes the heroes were completely unknown, such as the one revered at the shaft graves at Mycenae, whose votive read simply *emi tou herôos*, "I am of the Hero" (Snodgrass 2000, 181).

Hero cults began around the end of the eighth century in conjunction with the rise of the polis (see chapters 4 and 7). Many scholars such as Snodgrass and Coldstream see some aspect of state formation—or resistance to state formation—in their creation. Many hero-cult activities took place at Bronze Age burial sites (such as the shaft graves at Mycenae) centuries after the original burial, often after an entire change in population, so there could be no continuity between the dead entombed there and the later worshippers (a clear distinction from tomb cults).

All early hero/heroine cults appeared in central to southern mainland Greece, specifically the Peloponnese, Attica, and Boiotia, with a couple existing on the Doric- or Attic-speaking islands (Morris 1988, 757). There is actually quite a paradox in this: The Attic population saw themselves as autochthonous, meaning that they grew up out of the land itself and had always been in Attica. The Dorians saw themselves as later invaders who displaced most of the "indigenous" Greeks after the Age of Heroes (or at the fall of the Bronze Age, as we might think of it). So, hero cults sprang up among both those who thought of themselves as old and those who thought of themselves as new.

One thing both old and new groups did have in common, though, was an abundance of Bronze Age remains, especially tombs. The greatest Mycenaean sites were located in the Peloponnese, the region later dominated by Doric-speakers. Athens, as their myths suggest, showed continuity from the Bronze Age through the historical period. In both places, burial practices had changed considerably from the Bronze Age: Mass shaft graves or tholos tombs were replaced with cremations and small burials. As such, the magnificent dwellings of the dead from Mycenaean times must have struck the later Greeks as quite spectacular, even worthy of divinities. Thus, hero cults appeared in regions where Mycenaean-style burials were no longer the norm, and the local populations associated the magnificent tombs with superhuman heroes and heroines. In regions like Attica, where there was a long-standing continuity of population, the residents may have associated these cults with their own ancestors. By contrast, among the Doric-speakers, cults probably attached themselves to the names of Homeric heroes (Coldstream 1976, 17).

In its simplest definition, a hero or heroine cult is the reverence/worship of a man or woman who was (at least originally) mortal according to Greek tradition and who was still able to exert some influence over the land after he or she shed the mortal coil. According to the Greeks, there were two possible definitions of a hero/heroine. One was an individual who achieved semidivine status after death. The other was a great man recognized as a hero during his lifetime, like Heracles or Achilles (Snodgrass 2000, passim). A third possible definition, recognized by modern scholars such as Larson, is an individual who used to be a deity but who was "demoted" for whatever reason to the status of superpotent mortal, such as Helen of Sparta or Semelê, mother of Dionysos. The cult heroes and heroines had different possible fates. Often, they died and were revered at their burial spot or at some place of significance in their lives. Sometimes they achieved katasterism, meaning the gods set them in the heavens as constellations, like Orion, or the huntress Callisto, who became the bear Ursa Major. A lucky few became deities in their own right, such as Heracles and the Theban princess Ino, who became the sea goddess Leukothea. This multiplicity of origins and fates makes every hero/heroine cult unique.

An especially interesting hero cult was the joint cult of Helen and Menelaus at Therapnê, east of Sparta. Judging from the votive remains, the cult began in the early seventh century B.C.E., when "Deinis dedicated these objects to Helen wife of Menelaus" (Morris 1988, 753). In the mid-sixth century, a similar dedication was made. In the early fifth century, a limestone stele was set up at the shrine, which "Euthikrenes dedicated to Menelaus" (Antonaccio 1995, 155–158; Larson 1995, 81). This dualism in votive recipients is reflected in the early testimonials we have concerning the cult. When Herodotus tells us about the most beautiful woman in fifth-century Sparta, he relates (6.61):

> For her appearance being plain—and she being the ugly daughter of wealthy folks—her nurse, having seen that her parents thought her appearance to be a disaster, considering everything decided on the following. Every day she carried the girl to Helen's sanctuary. This is in the area called Therapnê, above Apollo's sanctuary. So the nurse carried her, setting her before the statue and invoking the goddess to deliver the child from ugliness. And indeed, once when the nurse was leaving the sanctuary, a woman, it is said, appeared and asked to see what the nurse carried in her arms. The nurse said that it was a child she bore in her arms. The woman asked her to show it to her, but the nurse said that she could not—for she was forbidden by the parents to show the child to anyone. But the woman demanded by all means to see the child, and seeing the woman making so much of seeing the girl, the nurse revealed her. The woman stroked the head of the child saying how she would be the most beautiful of all Spartan women.

According to Pausanias, however (3.19.9), "The name of Therapnê is derived from the daughter of Lelex, and in it is a temple of Menelaus; they say that Menelaus and Helen were buried here."

Based on this evidence from Pausanias, and the general belief that hero cults were mainly dedicated to males (preferably Homeric heroes), the Therapnê cult was originally thought to be dedicated to Menelaus, who was sometimes joined by his lovely wife Helen. Thus, the structure was named the Menelaion (shrine of Menelaus). However, the earlier votives and literary testimonia refer to the site as Helen's, with evidence for Menelaus's cult there only appearing in the fifth century at the earliest. The cult originally belonged to Helen; Menelaus was added in later as her consort. This early reverence of Helen may derive from the fact that she was originally a goddess, either an Indo-European astral deity or a Minoan vegetation/tree goddess. In either event, Helen was the prime recipient of honors at Therapnê. Menelaus probably joined the cult as husband, but possibly also in the capacity of well-known Homeric hero.

In some instances, a hero/ine started out as a deity (like Helen) but was demoted when the cult was taken over by a different deity, with whom the hero/ine was then worshipped. Such was the case with Hyacinthus and Apollo, worshipped together at Amyclae. The name Hyacinthus (with its -nthos ending) is pre-Greek, and Hyacinthus was an indigenous vegetation god. According to myth, Hyacinthus was Apollo's mortal friend or lover (they started off as friends in the Archaic Age, and Hyacinthus grew younger and more amorous by the Hellenistic period). One day when they were playing a Frisbee-like game, Apollo threw the disc too hard and killed Hyacinthus. In mourning, Apollo established his cult and turned his friend's remains into the flower that still bears his name: hyacinth (continuing the vegetation theme).

Concerning archaeology, Amyclae was a cult site in the Late Bronze Age, which some archaeologists recognize as a Mycenaean cult of the dead, based on the votive remains. There were about 150 years of abandonment at the site before it reemerged as Apollo's sanctuary (Antonaccio 1995, 178). However, Hyacinthus remained attached to the spot and to the cult (Ovid, *Metamorphoses*, X, 217–220):

> Nor was Sparta ashamed to have produced Hyacinthus, and his honor
> endures into this age, and as the annual festival of the
> Hyakinthia returns, it is celebrated in the manner of the forefathers.

Some heroes/heroines were simple mortals who improved their status through a heroic death, frequently sacrificing themselves for a city. One example is Aglauros, revered on the Athenian acropolis. According to legend, Aglauros was the daughter of Kekrops, a primordial king of Athens. Her sisters were Pandrosos and Hersê. In one version of their story, recounted by Pausanias (1.18.2), Athena had given them a box and told them not to open it. Aglauros disobeyed, looked into the box, and saw a baby surrounded by snakes. The sight drove her mad, and she jumped off the acropolis to kill herself. But according to another version of the myth related by Philochorus, Apollo once gave an oracle that said the Athenians would win the Eleusinian War (in which they were currently engaged) if someone killed himself for the city. Hearing this, Aglauros threw herself from the acropolis, sacrificing herself (Larson 1995, 38, 102). The first story is related to the Arrephoria (see above, in the section on Athena). The second story, however, explains not only why Aglauros has a shrine on the acropolis, but why the Athenian ephebes (young men of age for military service) swear their oath of loyalty to the city at this spot: They, like she, dedicate their lives to the welfare of Athens (see chapter 6).

There are many hero and heroine cults in the Greek repertoire, ranging from Homeric characters such as Phrontis, Odysseus's helmsman who received a cult at Sounion, to the Leuktrides, sisters who lived in Leuctra, Boiotia, and were raped by Spartans, whose cult allowed their fellow Boiotians to defeat Sparta at the Battle of Leuctra (Larson 1995, 135). Great athletic victors could also receive cults after their deaths and, by the Hellenistic period, affluent families could pay to have cults set up for themselves.

Cult Functionaries

Priests and Priestesses. The ancient Greeks had an extraordinary variety of priests and priestesses, each attached to a specific, localized deity. That is to say, there was no generic "priestess" or "priestess of Artemis," but rather a priestess of Artemis Laphria at Patras, and a priestess of Artemis Orthia at Sparta. Unlike many modern religions, in which rituals may only be performed by consecrated, career priests, the most important rites of the Greeks—sacrifice, libation—could be performed by anyone. The purpose of priest(ess)hoods, then, was to have an appropriate person look after the possessions of the deity in question and carry out specific rites.

The matter of who was an appropriate person varied according to the priest(ess)hood and cult in question. Each priest(ess)hood required an individual of a specific gender. Usually gods had priests and goddesses had priestesses, but there were exceptions. Zeus of Dodona had priestesses called doves, and higher officials in the Eleusinian Mysteries in honor of Demeter and Persephonê were male. Age was also an issue. Aphrodite's temple at Sikyon had two cult officiants, both female. One was the neokoros, an older woman who no longer had sexual relations with men; the other was the loutrophoros ("bath-carrier"), a virgin. No other people could enter the temple, and, as Burkert remarked, "the goddess of sexual life can be approached freely only by those who are excluded from her works" (Burkert 1985, 98). As age was an issue, terms of appointment also varied. Some functionaries served for one festival or for a year. Others served for life.

Many priest(ess)hoods ran in families. The Eumolpidai family provided the hierophants at Eleusis; the Eteoboutadai provided the priestess of Athena Polias in Athens; Embaros's descendants served as priests of Brauronian Artemis. In other instances, the priest or priestess merely had to come from a good (i.e., upper-class) family; the young priest of Apollo Ismenios at Thebes was such a functionary, as recorded by Pausanias (9.10.4): "The following, as I understand it, still occurs in Thebes. For Ismenian Apollo a child of excellent household (and himself good-looking and sound of body) they make annual priest. And his title is Laurel-Bearer, for the children wear crowns of laurel leaves."

In other instances, the functionary was chosen by lot. An inscription from Athens dating to 450–445 B.C.E. (Meiggs and Lewis 1992, 44 [40]) decrees the appointment, for life, of the priestess of Athena Nikê, to be chosen by lot from all free Athenian women (Meiggs and Lewis 1992, 108).

Of course, if the priestess did not come from a wealthy family, she was rather dependent on her paycheck, and this issue did arise for this priestess. According to a later inscription (Meiggs and Lewis 1992, 71 [73]) dating to c. 424 B.C.E., this priestess of Athena Nikê was paid 50 drachmai annually for her services to goddess and city (Meiggs and Lewis 1992, 204). In other instances, priests or priestesses received different types of goods in exchange for their services. A portion of all sacrifices went to them, including, usually, the animal hide (leather). Money was paid to cults and temples for certain rituals, like initiation cults, and the cult functionaries no doubt received portions of these fees.

The functions of priests and priestesses varied as much as their individual appointments. Common duties included caring for the sanctuary, temple, and divine statue. In some cases, as with the cult of Sikyonian Aphrodite mentioned above, *only* the priestesses had access to these. Although it was not necessary for a sacrifice to be enacted by a priest/ess, it was usual for them to oversee such activities in their sanctuaries. At oracular shrines, the priest(ess) may have been responsible for giving or interpreting oracles, like the Delphic Pythia and her attendant priests. Different cult functionaries were also responsible for enacting various rituals within their poleis. The Athenian Basilinna, wife of the archon Basileus, had sex with a celebrant representing Dionysos during the Anthesteria Festival (see above, in the section about Dionysos). The part of Dionysos was probably played by the archon Basileus. The priestess of Artemis Orthia oversaw the flogging of Spartan youths; the Eleusinian hierophantes revealed the sacred things that initiated initiates into the mysteries of Demeter and Korê (Persephonê). The priests of Asclepius were the earliest doctors in Greece; not only did they interpret healing dreams for their patients, but they learned quite a bit about symptom diagnosis as well (see chapter 10). Ultimately, priests and priestesses were the deities' servants, performing whatever tasks tradition required.

Oracles.   The Greeks wanted to know the mind and will of the deities, especially when disasters such as a plague struck, or when an expensive new venture such as colonization was about to take place. The commonest means of consulting the deities was through oracles, people who had special access to the divine. As in the Near East, where the Greeks may have learned the "art" of divination, there were two types of human oracles—mad/possessed and sane. The sane oracles were less common and were usually male. The most famous example in literature is the Theban Teiresias, who lived in the age of Oedipus but was still prophesying from the underworld in the age of Odysseus. According to Ovid (*Metamorphoses*), Zeus made Teiresias a prophet after he settled a debate between Zeus and Hera. Because Teiresias sided in favor of Zeus, Hera blinded him; Zeus, unable to reverse Hera's punishment, softened it by giving Teiresias the gift of prophecy—inner sight in exchange for outer sight. Thus, Teiresias was able to know fate and the hidden workings of the world, and he was able to control his knowledge and prophecies.

More common were the mad/possessed prophets, usually female. As the Greeks understood the female body to be squishy and hollow, they believed women had a greater potential for possession than men (Padel 1983, passim). With prophetesses, Zeus or Apollo took possession of the woman and, through her, spoke their will. The prophetesses therefore did not know fate, nor were they able to control their prophecies. The two most famous prophetesses in Greece were the Trojan princess Cassandra and the Delphic Pythia, both possessed by Apollo. According to Aeschylus's *Agamemnon,* Cassandra received the gift of prophecy from Apollo in exchange for agreeing to have sex with the god. However, she reneged on her promise after she received her gift. Even though she denied the god sexual access to her body, Apollo "entered" her in a violent fashion when he gave her his prophecies. Screaming "O, Apollo! Apollo!" as the god seized her body and mind, she cried (*Agamemnon,* ll. 1214–1216):

Ay! Ay! Oh! Oh! Evils!
The dread pain of true prophecy whirls again beneath me
and drives me mad with its onset, horrid beginnings!

The scenario with the Pythia was slightly less violent. Although Apollo did not "rape" this priestess, she did give her prophecies under the spell of madness. According to Greek tradition, the inquisitor underwent rites of purification, after which he/she might direct a question to Apollo through the Pythia. Upon receipt of the question, the Pythia put herself into a trance, sitting before a smoking tripod in the inner sanctum of Delphi. Then Apollo filled her mind with the answer, which the Pythia expounded as mad ravings. A handful of priests who accompanied the priestess translated her ravings into Greek hexameter for the petitioner. The Pythia was functionally mad while she prophesied, and there is no evidence that she understood, or even remembered, what she spoke. For years, there has been a debate among modern scholars about whether the Pythia was under some manner of chemical influence or drug-induced high during her ravings. It now appears that the site of the inner sanctum of Delphi is located right over two fault lines running under Greece, and that the chemical composition of the underlying geology is such that fumes escaping out through the faults in the rocks have a narcotic effect on someone located above who inhales them (Hale et al. 2003, passim). The fact that the Pythia was seated right over the literal exhaust vent for these fumes does suggest that there was a chemical element to her madness.

Zeus's prophetesses underwent less physical/mental violation in their work. Zeus's prophetess at Patara was understood to be the god's concubine; she received her oracles when shut up for the night with the god in his temple, as recounted by Herodotus. Priestesses called doves at the sanctuary of Zeus and Dionê at Dodona in northern Greece, said to be the oldest of the Greek oracles, went into a state of divine madness in Zeus's sacred oak grove, and in this state they delivered his messages. Once again, though, like the Pythia, these prophetesses were understood to be in a state of ecstasy (literally, standing outside of themselves) when they spoke, and afterward they had no knowledge of their experience. "It was when they were mad that the prophetesses of Delphi and the priestesses at Dodona achieved so much for which both states and people in Greece are grateful: when sane they did little or nothing" (Plato, *Phaidros*, 244).

For the more do-it-yourself inquisitor, there were oracles of the dead and dream oracles, cults in which the petitioner could consult with the deities semidirectly. An example of the former is the oracle of Trophonios at Lebadeia in Boiotia. Trophonios, reputedly a son of Apollo, was an architect until, as punishment for a crime, he was literally swallowed up by the Earth. Afterward, the site of his swallowing became the focus of an oracle, where, after several purification rituals a petitioner could enter (Pausanias 9.39):

> Going down there is an opening between the floor and the structure; the width is 2 spans, the height appears to be 1 span. The descender lay himself down on the floor holding barley cakes mixed with honey; and first he inserts his feet into the opening, and he himself follows, trying to get his knees into the opening. The rest of the body immediately trails after and follows the knees, just as the greatest and swiftest of rivers might subsume a man under a whirlpool. Then, for those in the sacred interior, there are different means of learning the future: one sees while another hears. The descender leaves again by the same route, feet emerging first.

Concerning dream oracles, the petitioner would go to an incubation sanctuary, perform purification rites, and sleep. The deity would send dreams, which the priests would help the petitioner to interpret. Dream oracles were prominent in the cult of Asclepius, the healing god; the sick would go to the oracles to have dreams about how to cure their illnesses.

Sacred Space

A typical place to revere the gods in ancient Greece was in a sanctuary (hieron). Hiera (pl.) were located in the countryside (including very high up on mountains), at the borders of poleis, or within cities. The nature sanctuaries were usually associated with at least one polis that provided the materials for the cult, including a family of priests and/or priestesses. The border sanctuaries often served to mark the extent of a polis's political (ideal or otherwise) control, and there were often elaborate processions from the center of a city to its border sanctuaries to establish the relationship between the two. For example, the sanctuary at Eleusis was officially attached to the city of Athens, and the yearly mysteries performed at Eleusis began with a daylong procession from Athens to this remote suburb. The urban sanctuaries were the most prime real estate for the deities, where strongly regionalistic, political rituals would be performed. In Athens, the ritual of the Panathenaia was celebrated annually at the Acropolis and served not only to extol the city goddess Athena, but also to remind the Athenians of their autochthonous origins.

A sanctuary had several constituent parts. The most important was the temenos, land that was "cut off" (*temnô* = to cut) and reserved for the deity. Once this space was consecrated, a number of pious regulations had to be observed within its limits. No one was permitted to die in a temenos, nor give birth, nor have sex. In short, nothing indicative of mortality—conception, birth, death—was allowed to happen in an area reserved for those free from the mortal condition.

Because of this prohibition on mortality-related events, a temenos often served as a sanctuary/refuge for those threatened with death, because of either a crime or, more likely, political unpopularity. A person could not be killed in a temenos, nor could he/she be forcibly removed. Such suppliants thus created an awkward situation for the surrounding community. Although they could not be killed or harmed while in the temenos, they also could not be permitted to die there, as would eventually happen through thirst and starvation. Should the suppliants die, the entire region would become polluted, bringing devastation to the local inhabitants. Thus, using temenê as sanctuaries was a tricky business, forcing a resolution to the conflict before death could occur.

In Euripides's *Heracles*, Heracles's family, condemned in his absence, wait as suppliants at a local shrine, hoping their hero will return to save them before they grow too weak to withstand their captors. Heracles shows up in the nick of time, overthrows the captors, and saves the integrity of the sanctuary (but then he goes mad and kills his wife and children anyway; tragedies are called that for a reason). In a real-life historical example, the Athenian Kylon, who attempted to make himself tyrant of Athens in the seventh century B.C.E., was overthrown and forced to seek refuge in a local temenos (Herodotus 5.71; Thucydides 1.126.10–11). Eventually, he and his men were left on the brink of starvation, forcing a crisis on the city for the above-stated reasons. The Athenians offered Kylon and/or his men safe passage out of the city and into exile if he would simply leave before profaning the sanctuary. Kylon agreed, but, not entirely trusting his adversaries, he tied a long cord between himself and the altar, thus keeping himself under divine protection (it was thought to extend along the cord) until he was outside the boundaries of Athens (and his captors' authority). On Kylon's way out of the city, the Alcmaeonidai clan cut the cord and slew him. For this, the family bore the stain of impiety for generations.

Beyond being a place of refuge, temenê served a number of other functions for the Greeks. In some instances, as at Apollo's Delphi, the sanctuary contained an oracle who predicted the future or made known the will of the gods. Some sanctuaries, especially those of Asclepius, served as hospitals, where the sick went to find cures for their ailments (see chapter 10). Technically speaking, the theaters were dedicated to Dionysos; they were where the Greeks went to see that most enjoyable of Dionysian rituals: the play. Some sanctuaries were the loci of elaborate rituals, such as Eleusis, where Greek-speakers were initiated into the rites of Demeter and Persephonê, assuring themselves of a happier afterlife.

At its simplest, the sanctuary was where the humble petitioner went to pray, to give thanks, and to offer gifts to the gods. Such gifts could consist of a smidgen of incense on the altar, a small depiction of a body part that was healed, the blood-soaked clothing of a woman who died in labor, a drawing of oneself, an elaborate bronze cauldron, or even a full-scale statue. The votive collection in the Temple of Hera at Olympia was so magnificent that Pausanias considered it a small museum.

Second in importance to the temenos was the altar, locus of the sacrifices that formed the core of ancient Greek religious expression (see below). An altar could range in style from a massive heap of ashes built up through several generations of sacrifice—such as the ash altar to Zeus Lykaios—to an elaborate and ostentatious structure of sculpted marble. Perhaps the best example of the latter is the Altar of Pergamon, a third-century altar covered with elaborate three-dimensional sculpture and which required its own staircase to reach the actual sacrificial area. Here, an animal was killed in such a way that its blood splattered the altar in a manner presumably pleasing to the receiving deity/deities. Since the altar was the focus of this critical ritual, it was an extremely important component of the temenos.

Another possible element in the temenos, by far the most famous in modern times, was the temple—*naos* in Greek. This was the deity's "house," where he or she could go to relax, enjoy religious festivities, mope, or even catch a bath!

Going to Cyprus [Aphrodite] entered the sweet-smelling temple
in Paphos, where are her temenos and fragrant altar.
And there entering she closed the shining doors,
and there the Graces bathed her and anointed her with oil
sweet and ambrosial, which was an offering to her.
  (*Homeric Hymn to Aphrodite*, ll. 58–62)

In reality, the temple was not an extremely important element of the temenos. Many temenê had no temple, and several ancient Greek temples were never even finished. The Temple of Zeus at Stratos in northern Greece was begun in the fifth century B.C.E. Sometime after starting work on the floors inside, the builders either ran out of money or lost interest, because all construction on the temple stopped. Nevertheless, the temenos with its altar continued in use well into Roman times, when a pair of second-century C.E. Roman officials dedicated statues of themselves at the site. Basically, the sanctuary was in use for over 700 years without the temple ever receiving a roof! It is clear that the Greeks did not really think of their gods as living in the temples, so the physical amenities were not always an issue. Only some very ancient naoi (pl. of naos) contained actual embodiments of the deities—xoana (see below). The Erechtheion on the Athenian Acropolis, which housed the ancient image of Athena, is one such example.

Some ancient Greek sanctuaries became humongous, coming to have Panhellenic, even international, significance. Such sanctuaries were those of Apollo at Delphi and Delos, Demeter and Persephonê at Eleusis, Zeus at Olympia, and Poseidon at Isthmia and Nemea. One reason for this popularity was the great games that took place every two or four years at Delphi, Isthmia, Nemea, and Olympia (thus the "Olympics"; see below). Another reason was the popularity of the oracle, as at Delphi. The mysteries enacted at Eleusis attracted people from all over the Greek and Roman worlds. Such popularity led to extremely large and elaborate sanctuaries, filled not just with an altar and temple, but with multiple temples to several deities, several altars, sports arenas, hotels, baths, fountains, and, presumably, snack-bars.

At the far end of the spectrum from the large, elaborate Panhellenic sanctuaries were the smaller sacred spaces. One of the most important ritual sites was the family hearth, "sanctuary" of Hestia. Some minor deities had small, natural sacred spaces. The nature god Pan and the nymphs were worshipped in groves, at especially impressive trees, in caves, or at small springs. Oracular cults as at Lebadeia and (originally) Delphi were often associated with caves or, in the case of Dodonian Zeus, an oak grove.

Images

Large-scale, 3-D images of the deities took three forms. From least to most common, these were baetyls, xoana, and statues. The name *baetyl* comes from the Semitic languages and means "House of God." In Greece, these were nonanthropomorphic or minimally anthropomorphic stone or wood renderings that manifested the deity. The most famous example was the baetyl of Aphrodite at Paphos. Still on display at the Palaipaphos Museum is this conical black stone, about one meter tall, which the ancients believed was a manifestation of Aphrodite. The baetyl was worshipped *as* Aphrodite in her temple. A more anthropomorphic example of a baetyl was the previously mentioned herm, an image of Hermes in wood or stone with a square pillar base, an erect penis halfway up, and a bearded head at the top.

A xoanon (pl. xoana) was an ancient (even for the Greeks) wooden, mostly anthropomorphic image and embodiment of a deity. The Greeks thought of these as gifts from the deities, either dropped from heaven or sent from the sea. As divine gifts, xoana manifested the gods' power and were even understood to embody the gods themselves. As such, xoana were treated as embodied deities, which had to be fed, washed, and adorned, and there were rituals involving their care and upkeep. For example, every year, the xoanon of Hera near Nauplion was bathed in the River Kanathos, thus ritually restoring her virginity, in addition to giving other benefits (Burkert 1985, 133). As manifestations of the power, and even presence, of the deities, xoana were the images most commonly used as cult statues, the portrayals of the gods that resided in their "homes" (the temples) and served as the focus of worship (as the baetyl of Aphrodite at Paphos).

Cult images (xoana) must not be confused with simple statues of the deities, whether rendered as simple kouros and korê (maiden) images (see chapter 9) or as more elaborate works, like the statue of Zeus at Olympia, which was one of the Seven Wonders of the Ancient World. Statues, as opposed to xoana, were representations made *of* the deities; they were not understood to *be* the deities as the xoana were. Such statues were gifts from humans to the gods, instead of from gods to humans as with baetyls and xoana. Statues could be enormous undertakings, like the Athena Promakhos that stood in the Parthenon and was visible from sea. This sculpture, made by Pheidias, had ivory skin and gold clothing—gold that the Athenians could borrow in times of economic duress. Although this statue was considered a wonder to behold and was located in the most lavish of Athena's temples, it was not a cult statue. Athena's cult statue on the Acropolis was the humble wooden xoanon, which "lived" in the Erechtheion, the temple next to the Parthenon. Only this xoanon was understood to embody the (power of the) goddess.

As statues were understood as merely pieces of art—and very fine art at that—a statue of any deity could be offered as a gift to any deity. Often, of course, a god/dess was honored with a statue of himself or herself, either from an individual donor or commissioned by a city. But one could also offer any random statue of a god/dess to some other deity. One example of this was the statue of Apollo in Hera's temple at Olympia. Apollo was not joined in a cult with Hera at this sanctuary, but some dedicator had decided to honor the goddess with a fine piece of art that just happened to have Apollo as its subject.

Ritual Acts

Sacrifice. The most important, and central, cult ritual among the Greeks was sacrifice, in which an animal (bull, goat, sheep, pig, even fish or dog) was killed at the altar of a deity. This action was carried out by a group of people, none of whom had to be an official priest or priestess. The animal, often consecrated to a deity from birth so that it was never subject to routine labors, was walked up to the altar along with the group performing the sacrifice. Some officiants carried sacrificial implements, such as water, grain, and a knife. Ideally, the animal would progress to the altar of its own accord.

Once the group reached the altar, the sacrificial implements were taken out.

A prayer was offered to the deity. A piece of fur was cut from the sacrificial animal's head, symbolizing that it was no longer inviolate, but formally consecrated to die. Grain was sprinkled on the altar, and one of the officiants poured water onto the head of the animal. This caused the animal to nod its head, indicating its "assent" to die for the deity. If the animal did not agree to the sacrifice, it was thought to be a very bad sign. Depending on the type of animal being sacrificed, the sacrifice could proceed in different ways. For a large animal such as a cow, the sacrificer struck the animal's spine with an axe. Once the creature was unconscious, its throat was cut, allowing the blood to spurt onto the altar, the ultimate aim of the sacrifice. The women standing around the altar gave a ritualistic scream (the "ololyge").

Depending on the type of sacrifice, the next steps could vary. Normally, the animal was dismembered. Edible portions were cooked at the sanctuary, either roasted on spits or boiled; inedible portions (bones, especially) were burned on the altar so that the receiving deity might enjoy their scent and savor. On rare occasions, the animal(s) might be burned entirely; this was called a holocaust (*holos* = entire; *kaiô* = to burn). But it was far more common for the sacrificers to eat the animal, burning only designated parts to the deity.

The fact that the receiving deity did not get the edible parts of the animal was not lost on either the ancient Greeks or modern scholars. The earliest explanation for this appears in the *Theogony* (ll. 536–556), where, at the Feast of Mekonê, the Titan Prometheus tries to trick Zeus to get humans a better food portion from slaughtered animals. His logic is that humans need food to live, whereas the ever-living gods will not eat a dead animal, merely enjoying the scent of the "bar-b-que" (*Theogony*, ll. 536–556):

At Mekonê. There [Prometheus] went forth intending at heart
to apportion out a great ox, deceiving the mind of Zeus.
For before the others he set down the flesh and innards rich with fat
on a hide, having hidden them with an ox stomach.
But before Zeus he set down the white bones of an ox
well-arranged by crafty art and hidden by shining fat.
Then indeed the father of men and gods said to him:
"Son of Iapetos, most renowned of all kings,
Egads! How unfairly you have divided the portions."
. . . .
Crafty-minded Prometheus replied to him,
smiling gently, not forgetting his devious trick:
"Most honorable Zeus, greatest of the eternal deities,
take of them whichever one your heart bids in your chest."
. . . .
In his two hands [Zeus] lifted the white fat.
Anger came to his heart, seizing his mind,
when he saw the white ox bones in the clever deception.
And from that time the race of men on earth burn
white bones to the immortals on smoking altars.

Later scholars, such as Burkert (1985, 1987) and Vernant (1991), have devised alternate theories concerning the origins of the sacrificial ritual. They argue that sacrifice was a means of reestablishing the role of humans as intermediaries between gods and animals, and, perhaps more importantly, expiating the guilt incurred with killing a living creature. All animals must kill in order to eat and thrive. Although no one gets worked up over the death of, say, a carrot, there is usually an aspect of guilt involved in killing an animal. Most religions have a sanctioned means of expiating this guilt. In the Judeo-Christian ideology, it was stated in Genesis that God gave humans dominion over the animals, suggesting that so long as humans took care of animals, they could kill them at need, guilt-free. In some Eskimo cultures, the bladders of slain animals must be preserved. Then, in a ritual, the bladders are released back into the sea, freeing the animals' souls so they can return to life. For the Greeks, killing an animal could only be fully justified by killing it for a deity. Thus, the sacrifice was done in honor of a god/dess, who was inevitably beyond reproach, and humans just happened to get a meal out of it as well.

Sacrifice as expiation of guilt comes across most clearly in an Athenian ritual known as the Bouphonia (literally "Ox Murder"). According to the myth recorded in the work *De Abstinentia* by the Neoplatonic philosopher Porphyry, a resident of Attica (but not an Athenian citizen) was once on the Acropolis when he saw an ox eating grain cakes set on Zeus's altar. Horrified at the ox's impiety, he picked up an axe and killed it. Then, horrified at his own impiety of killing an animal in sacred space, he buried the ox and banished himself to Crete. Later, a famine struck Athens. When the people sent to Delphi for help in fixing the problem, the Pythia bid them find the murderer, "resurrect" the ox, and have the entire community partake of the animal's flesh. The man was brought from Crete and made an Athenian citizen, as required by the deity. The ox-skin was sewn together and stuffed with hay. Another ox was killed like the first one, and all the Athenians partook of its flesh.

A trial was then held, but since the original murderer had now been made a citizen, his guilt was distributed onto the whole city, thinning it out. So, every year in honor of Zeus, the Bouphonia was celebrated. A work ox was brought to the Acropolis, where he ate grain at the altar. A man whacked the ox with an axe, tossed the axe behind him, and ran. The ox was flayed and the skin filled with hay. This stuffed ox was set before a wagon, like a regular work ox, thereby "resurrected." The rest of the skinned body was dismembered and eaten in typical sacrificial style. Then: "Assembling a trial for murder, they summon all who had participated in the deed to defend themselves. The water fetchers charged that the ax-sharpeners were more to blame than they. The sharpeners said the same about the ax-administrator, and this one of the throat-cutter, and this one of the knife that, being without a voice, was condemned for murder" (Vernant 1991, 302).

Not all sacrifices involved killing an animal. At the altar of Aphrodite on Paphos, only incense was burned to the goddess. At liminal points in life, often involving initiation or coming-of-age rituals, Greek boys and girls offered locks of their hair to Apollo and Artemis. "Tables" of grain or bread were offered to heroes and heroines, as per the epigraphic records.

Libations. In contrast to burning an animal up to the gods, libations involved pouring liquids down to deities, heroes, or the dead. The Greeks recognized two types of pouring rituals—the spondê and the choes. The spondê was specifically a libation to the deities, often accompanying sacrifices or drinking parties (see chapter 6). As with sacrifice, the spondê was intended to please the deity and make him/her welcome. One especially important act solemnized by the spondê was the creation of treaties and the formation of alliances. The Greeks had no specific word for the ending of hostilities (of which they had many); a spondê marked the formal end of a war. Likewise, it could be used to formalize an alliance or union, and the word *spouse* in English derives from this ancient Greek ritual. The choes, by contrast, was dedicated either to the dead or to specifically chthonic deities. Heroes and heroines also received choes in their cults (Burkert 1985, 70–73).

The liquid(s) used for both types of libation depended on the circumstances at hand and the cult being followed. Wine was the most common liquid used, especially when accompanying sacrifice or in the context of the symposion (where everyone was drinking wine anyway). Regular "civic" rituals were also generally accompanied by wine libations. When the Athenian navy was departing for its ill-fated Sicilian Expedition, Thucydides recounts that wine libations were offered into the sea (6.32.1): "Silence was signaled by the trumpeter, and prayers were offered before putting out to sea, not each ship individually, but all together, led by a herald. And the wine bowls being mixed throughout the whole army, the sailors and leaders made libation with gold and silver cups. And the rest of the crowd joined them in prayer, both those of the citizens on land and anyone else present well-minded to them. And having sung the Paian and completed the libations, they set out."

Some deities' cults, however, specifically avoided wine, such as the Eumenides ("Kindly Ones," a euphemism for the Furies, demon-like avengers of crimes against blood kin). As narrated in Sophocles's *Oedipus at Kolonos*, these dread goddesses received libations of water and honey, offered by one pure of heart, in total silence. The "thirsty" dead, likewise, received libations of water and oil rather than wine. In Aeschylus's *Libation Bearers*, Elektra brings a choes libation to her murdered father's grave. Here she pours out an offering of oil, calling out prayers to her father, the underworld gods, and Hermes, while her attendants recite hymns and deck out the grave with floral garlands.

Pompê. The pompê was a ritual procession or parade, usually enacted as a precursor to a ritual act, such as sacrifice or an initiation ritual. The pompê was actually an important aspect of a rite, as it distinguished those taking part in the ritual from those who were not. Furthermore, to partake fully in a ritual, a participant had to get to the event in a ritualized fashion. This might not seem like a problem if one was merely going down the street to perform a sacrifice, but many processions were much longer. The pompê that began the Eleusinian Mysteries, for example, was some 22 kilometers long, leading from Athens to Eleusis, which the initiates had to walk overnight. There was no option for taking a carriage and "meeting them there."

The pompê was a highly structured event, with strict regulations as to who was to take part, where they were to walk, and what they were to carry. One of our most detailed descriptions comes from a second-century B.C.E. inscription from Magnesia in Turkey:

> The Crown-Bearer in office together with the male priest and the female priest of Artemis Leukophryene shall ever after lead the procession in the month of Artemision on the twelfth day, and sacrifice the designated bull; that in the procession shall also be the council of elders the priests, the magistrates (both elected and appointed by lot), the ephebes, the youths, the boys, the victors in the Leukophyrene games, and the victors in the other crown-bearing games. The Crown-Bearer in leading the procession shall carry xoana of all twelve gods attired as beautifully as possible, and shall erect a round structure in the agora by the altar of the twelve gods, and shall lay out three couches of the finest quality, and shall also provide music, a shawm-player, a pan-pipe-player, and a lyre player. (Translation by S. Price 1999, 175, used with kind permission)

Along with the required personnel, as the inscription above indicates, ritual tools were also brought along in the pompê—the sacrificial animals, weapons used to dispatch them, barley meal and wine, and butchering equipment. Depending on the nature of the ritual, specialty items might also be brought, as in the Athenian Panathenaic Festival, in which Athena's new peplos was carried in the parade. In many rituals, statues of the deities were carried. In very rare instances, the "clergy" sought alms from the community through which they passed, a practice associated with the cult of Cybelê in Turkey (Burkert 1985, 102).

Agon.   The Greeks were an exceptionally competitive society, and athletic and artistic competitions served ritual functions for them. Both types of competition seem to have had an origin in funerary rituals. As early as the eighth century B.C.E., Hesiod won a tripod for his poetic compositions at the funeral games of Amphidamas. Likewise, our earliest description of full-scale athletic events comes from Book 23 of the *Iliad*—the funeral games in honor of Patrocles. Even the Panhellenic games, such as the Olympics, had a funerary element. Although the Olympic and Nemean Games were dedicated to Zeus, the Isthmian to Poseidon, and the Delphic to Apollo, their etiological myths recalled famous deaths. Pelops killed his father-in-law at Olympia; the infant-hero Meliqertes (probably derived from the Phoenician god Melqart) died after jumping from a cliff with his mother Ino-Leukothea and washed up at Isthmia.

Many competitions featured both athletic and artistic events, but others focused on one or the other. All over the Archaic Greek world, poets like the Homeridai recited original hymns to the deities in such competitions. In Athens starting in the sixth century B.C.E., two great civic celebrations—the Greater Dionysia and the Lenaia—were occasions when playwrights and producers competed to produce the best dramas in honor of Dionysos. By contrast, the Panathenaic Festival featured both musical and athletic competitions.

Here, rhapsodes (performing poets) competed to perform the best recitations of Homer, and runners raced for prizes of amphorae filled with precious Athenian olive oil.

The truly great competitions, though, were the four Panhellenic games: Olympic, Nemean, Isthmian, and Delphic. The Olympic Games were the earliest, dating to 776 B.C.E.; a common means of reckoning time in ancient Greece was to specify in which Olympiad an event took place. Technically, anyone was welcomed to compete, and a truce was declared throughout the Greek world a month before the festivals began so that competitors would have free access to the games. Competitions included poetry and song, foot- and chariot-racing, boxing, wrestling, and the pankration, which was a no-holds-barred fighting event at which competition got so vicious that, at one of the Olympics, the victory went to a man who had actually died in the ring. The competitions were mostly sex-segregated. The main events at the Olympics were for men; women had separate competitions at the Olympic Heraia (see above, in the section about Hera). However, in the chariot races, victory went to whoever raised the horses, and in the early fourth century B.C.E., the Spartan princess Cynisca won the four-horse chariot competition.

To win at the games brought great social status, to both the individual and his/her polis (much like the Olympics today). Honor was the main prize. Victors at the Panhellenic games got leafy circlets to wear on their heads (laurel for the Delphic Games, celery for the Nemean, for example), poetry composed in their honor by such illuminati as Pindar, and the right to dedicate pictures or statues of themselves at the sanctuary. In some poleis, such as Athens, victors got free dinner for life at the city hall.

Death

For the ancient Greeks, death occurred when breath left the body. At this point, the psychê emerged. Unlike with modern Judeo-Christian theology, in which it is believed that the soul is always present in the body, being released upon death, the Greeks believed that the psychê only existed upon an individual's death. Thus, we might consider the Greek concept of the psychê to be more like a ghost than a soul. Like a ghost, the psychê retained the individual's personality but was noncorporeal, and it could not touch or be touched.

If all went well, this psychê was brought to Hades, the underworld, the domain of dread Persephonê. In some instances, as at the end of the *Odyssey*, the Greeks thought Hermes Psychopompos led the dead to their final home. In other cases, it was the personification of death itself who did this: Thanatos. This deity gets his fullest description in Euripides's *Alkestis*, the story of a wife who willingly dies in her husband's stead. Here, Thanatos appears in dark robes, winged, carrying a sword with which he cuts off a tress of the soon-to-be-departed, consecrating him or her to the underworld gods.

The Greeks found death rather depressing. This is not to say, however, that death was avoided at all costs. From the earliest Greek times, a heroic death was the ideal for which all great soldiers strove. Even in later centuries, a glorious death was far more important than a cowardly life, and Spartan mothers especially were known for the pride they took in sons who died for the polis (and the shame they felt for sons who did not).

Nevertheless, although a heroic death might ensure a certain amount of glory among the living left behind, the afterlife that the dead endured was tedious and wearisome at best. Already from the time of Homer, the merits of a short but glorious vs. long but toilsome life were debated by none other than Achilles, the one character in Greek literature allowed to make this choice for himself. In the *Odyssey* (11.488–491), when Odysseus commends him for his legacy on Earth, Achilles confesses that the misery of the afterlife negates for him all his glory among the living:

> "Do not console me for dying, Shining Odysseus.
> I should wish to be a serf toiling for another man,
> along side one without land, one with no great livelihood,
> than be king of all the perished dead."

The dead had no knowledge of what occurred among the living, and nothing happened to the dead in Hades. But they could still worry about loved ones or fume over past injustices. A ghost with a bad reputation could be tormented or ridiculed for eternity with little redress. In contrast to the common fear of ghosts, the dead had virtually no power to harm the living: If revenge were desired, it had to be enacted by divine powers at the behest of the dead. In many instances, the deities responsible for this were the Furies, also called the Erinyes, who, on the part of the dead, punished crimes committed against blood kin. Their most famous appearance in Greek literature is their attack on Orestes for having murdered his mother Clytemnestra. Clytemnestra, now dead and therefore unable to seek revenge on her own, must goad on the dread goddesses to their work (*Eumenides,* ll. 93–115).

However, as early as Homer, an alternative to the dreary, powerless afterlife was known: the Elysian Fields. These are mentioned in the *Odyssey*, Book 11, when the Old Man of the Sea tells Menelaus of his fate (ll. 561–570):

> "For you it is not ordained, O Menelaus, fostered by Zeus,
> to die in horse-pasturing Argos and to follow death,
> but to the Elysian Field and the ends of the earth
> the immortals will lead you. There is blond Rhadamanthus,
> where the easiest life exists for humans,
> never is there snow, nor great winter storms nor shadows ever,
> but always Ocean sends forth gentle breezes of the blowing
> West Wind to refresh humans.
> This because you have Helen and are son-in-law to Zeus."

At this early date, acceptance into the Elysian Fields was dependent on having some connection with the gods. Menelaus is husband to Helen, who is daughter of Zeus and a semidivinity in her own right. As son-in-law of the king of the gods, Menelaus gets a joyous afterlife. And yet, as we have seen, such a fate is not available for Achilles, the greatest of the Homeric heroes and son of the sea goddess Thetis. It is probable that the shift in ideology from one universally dreary afterlife to various types of afterlife occurred in the final years the Homeric epics were being recorded, with both ideologies preserved in the texts.

By the sixth century B.C.E., new ideas about the nature of death and the afterlife had come into play, ideas clearly influenced by Eastern ideologies. Of these, the most important in view of later religions was metempsychosis. Metempsychosis is the belief that the soul is immortal and travels from body to body over several generations of reincarnation. As in Hindu tradition, the ancient Greeks who followed this ideology believed that one's character in this life affected the nature and quality of one's next life. If you were good and noble in this life, you could wind up a king, or even a dolphin, in the next. If you were evil in this life, you might come back as a beggar or a pig. The ultimate end was to live enough good lives in a row to gain access to "heaven," some manifestation of the Elysian Fields. According to Pindar's *Second Olympian Ode,* one had to live three good lives in a row to achieve bliss. Otherwise, punishment awaited the evildoer (ll. 56–74):

> . . . if someone having this knows the future,
> that there immediately the helpless minds of the dead
> pay the penalty—sinful acts in this realm of Zeus
> someone judges beneath the earth, giving sentences with harsh necessity.
> Always in equal nights, equal days
> they have sunlight, a life without toil
> the Good receive, not working earth with force of hand,
> nor the water of the sea for a shallow livelihood. But along side the honored ones
> of the deities, those who respected good oaths dwell tearless
> forever. But others endure pains unbeholdable.
> Those who have endured three times
> remaining in either place, keeping the soul from all unrighteousness,
> travel the path of Zeus unto the tower of Kronos.
> There Ocean breezes blow about the isle of the blessed,
> flowers of gold blaze,
> some on the shore of glorious trees, some the water nourishes.
> With chaplets and garlands of these they enwreath their hands
> according to the straight judgments of Rhadamanthus.

An interesting paradox was present in the Greek ideology of death. On the one hand, the Greeks recognized several deities whose domain was death: Hades, Persephonê, Hermes Psychopompos, and Thanatos. On the other hand, the gods were understood to despise not only the concept of death, but also anything reminiscent of the mortal condition, including death, birth, and, in some instances, even sex (which leads to conception, birth, and death). All of these acts were prohibited in sanctuaries, and a certain period of purification was required before anyone who had had contact or involvement with these events could enter sacred space.

After a family member's death, for example, worshippers had to wait twenty days *after* purification to approach a temple (Garland 1985, 44–45). Multiple purifications were applied to the island of Delos, sacred to Apollo and Artemis. Starting in 543 B.C.E., the Athenian tyrant Peisistratos had all graves removed not only from the island, but also from within sight of the island. On the nearby island of Rheneia, a tiny hospital unit was set up where those about to die or give birth could be rushed before sullying Delos's purity (Garland 1985, 44–45). At the end of Euripides's *Hippolytos*, the goddess Artemis claims she must leave the scene before her favorite human dies, for "it is not lawful for me to look upon the dead or to defile my sight with the last breath of the dying." The ever-living gods clearly loathed the mere thought of human death (although this certainly did not stop them from watching human wars).

In almost all cases, death was inevitable. The gods did bestow immortality on a few of their favorites: Heracles (the greatest mortal hero and son of Zeus), Ganymedes (Zeus's lover), and Psychê (wife of Eros), for example. Some mortals, although having to die, received divine honors after their deaths, as discussed above in the section on hero and heroine cults. But, for the most part, the Greeks had to face the prospect of death. For many, the fear of death was palliated through induction into mystery cults.

Mystery Cults

The word *mystery* comes from the Greek *mystes*, which means "initiate." A mystes (pl. mystai) was initiated into a special cult or society and, as a result, knew things that noninitiates did not. In reality, many Greek cults and rituals had their secretive aspects: In the Athenian Arrhephoria, no one knew what objects the Arrhephoroi carried from the Acropolis, and in his *Against Neaira*, Apollodoros referred to rites enacted by the priestesses of Dionysos that could not be revealed, even in court.

Mystery cults differed in that they were exclusive and voluntary. Quoting M. W. Meyer:

> The mysteries were secret religious groups composed of individuals who decided, through personal choice, to be initiated into the profound realities of one deity or another. Unlike the official religions, in which a person was expected to show outward, public allegiance to the local gods of the polis or the state, the mysteries emphasized an inwardness and privacy of worship within closed groups. The person who chose to be initiated joined an association of people united in their quest for personal salvation. (Meyer 1987, 4)

Here, a few terms should be defined. *Secret religious groups* does not mean that their existence was kept hidden from the majority of the population. Everybody knew about the mystery cults, especially the popular ones such as those of Demeter and Dionysos. Rather, they were secret in that the cult rites and symbols were known only to initiates.

The "profound realities of one deity" did not imply exclusivity. A person initiated into the rites of, say, Isis (the Greeks adopted eastern cults) could still worship, and even be devoted to, other deities. Unlike modern "religions of the Book," the ancient polytheistic religions never had a concept of exclusive worship (with the exception of a brief bout of monotheism in fourteenth-century Egypt). In fact, the last high priest of Demeter at Eleusis was also a high priest of the Aryan god Mithras.

Finally, there was more to the mystery cults than just a concern with the hereafter. Although afterlife issues were important in many mystery cults, this was not so for all of them, nor was this an exclusive concern. Initiates also expected good things from their deities in this life. Mystai dedicated to Isis, for example, could expect extra help from that goddess in healing rituals.

It is difficult to determine when mystery cults came into existence. The earliest, those of Demeter, Korê (Persephonê), and Dionysos, were in practice beginning in at least the sixth century B.C.E., probably much earlier. Excavations at Eleusis show that that site may have been used for ritual as far back as the Bronze Age, although we certainly could not argue that the rites were identical, or even related to the later cult. Most mystery cults became prominent late in Greek history, starting in the Hellenistic era, and continued in use through the Roman period. Many cults were based on eastern deities, especially the Anatolian goddess Magna Mater/Cybelê, the Aryan god Mithras (especially venerated by Roman soldiers), and the Egyptian deities Isis and Osiris. Earlier, and more local, mystery cults were dedicated to Demeter, Korê, Dionysos, Despoina (the daughter of Demeter worshipped at Lykosoura), the Kabiroi (dwarfish assistants to Hephaistos and Dionysos), Hermes, and Apollo.

As mystery cults were secret affairs, we have very little information about them. Evidence comes from obscure references in religious texts, archaeology and art history (especially for the cults of Mithras), and the testimonies of initiates who later converted to Christianity and sought to express the absurdities of their former beliefs—in other words, from people who no longer maintained their vows of silence.

Certain nonuniversal commonalities might be derived from a combination of these sources. In general, all mystery cults focused on things recited (legomena), things shown (deiknymena), and things done (dromena) (Meyer 1987, 10). The significance of the things recited was clear in the rituals at Eleusis, which admitted only Greek-speakers. The importance of things shown was manifest in the terminology used of initiates: Those who had completed initiation were called epoptes, or "beholders." Possibly related to the notion of things done was another set of words commonly used in regard to mystery cults. The word *telein* meant "to accomplish" and also "to celebrate" or "to initiate," and the related word *telestes* was the word for an initiation priest. Mystery cult rituals took place in the telesterion, or the "initiation hall," a place where "things done" could take place. The things recited, shown, and done were all intended to have a strong psychological impact on the participant, not necessarily to teach him/her something new or esoteric. According to Aristotle, those who underwent initiation should not "learn" but "experience" (Burkert 1987, 69). This is one reason why it is still so difficult to understand the mystery rites: Even when we do have some descriptions of what occurred, we do not know *how* things occurred, or the initiates' state of mind at the time. The rites had to be experienced live.

Mystery rituals took place in special locations. The Eleusinian Mysteries took place only at Eleusis. The rites of Mithras occurred in a Mithraeum, a shrine used exclusively by his initiates for his cult. Such shrines were constructed throughout the eastern Roman Empire. Temples of Isis, complete with water from the Nile, were used throughout the Hellenistic and Roman worlds. By contrast, the rites of Dionysos could take place anywhere that was adequately secluded. Different types of "clergy" attended to the cults. The positions of chief priests and priestesses of Eleusis were hereditary, running in two noble families. By contrast, the priests of Dionysos were mostly itinerant, instructed in the mysteries and then set loose into the world. The temples of Isis had a permanent staff following the Egyptian model, and the personnel of Mithras were distinguished by seven degrees of initiation, the highest being pater patrum, "father of fathers."

Mystery cults made extensive use of the written word, especially books. Aeschines, an Athenian litigator whose mother performed mystery rites, referred to the books he read to accompany his mother. Images of Mithraic priests with books have come to light at Dura Europus, and both Roman art and historiography refer to the use of books in the cults of Dionysos (Burkert 1987, 70). This is not to say that these cults had orthodoxy, or a strict code of beliefs. Except for the Eleusinian Mysteries, which were completely localized, mystery cults had regionalized beliefs and practices. Polytheistic systems tend to be remarkably open-minded and accommodating.

This open-mindedness was best expressed in the eligibility for initiation. Except for the cult of Mithras (open only to men), anyone was technically eligible for initiation—men, women, children, slaves, foreigners. There were, of course, a few catches. First, one had to be able to pay for the initiation; it was not free. Initiation at Eleusis cost 15 drachmai, more than a week's salary for a common worker (Foley 1994, 66). Second, for some cults, one had to speak Greek, so as to understand the "things said." Third, one had to be free of blood guilt—that is, not a murderer. Otherwise, the cults were quite open, cutting across class and ethnic lines perhaps better than any other aspect of ancient Greek culture. Although initiates did not form closely linked communities, the shared experience of initiation was expected to create a sense of bonding among members.

The Eleusinian rites, as stated above, may date back as far as the Bronze Age, although archaeological continuity at the sanctuary only dates to the late seventh century B.C.E. One of the longest-lasting Greek cults, these Eleusinian Mysteries endured until the end of the fourth century C.E., when Eleusis was destroyed by Alaric the Visigoth.

Our earliest document referring to these mysteries is the *Homeric Hymn to Demeter*, probably of sixth-century B.C.E. creation, which gives details concerning the mysteries' origins. The main body of the tale is related above in the section on Demeter. Relevant here is Demeter's stay in the house of Keleos (ll. 192–211, reprinted above), and her creation of the mysteries at the end of the *Hymn* (ll. 473–482):

and [Demeter] going to the law-bearing kings
showed to Triptolemos, to horse-driving Deokles,
and Eumolpos the powerful and Keleos leader of the host,
the conduct of her worship and described her rites to all,
to Triptolemos and Polyxenos and Deokles,
holy rites which in no way might be transgressed nor
revealed nor spoken of, for a great awe of the deities
restrains the voice.
Happy is he who among earth-dwelling men has seen these.
But the one uninitiated, who has taken no part in these rites,
never has an equal portion after death, down in the shadowy gloom.

The Eleusinian rites, to the best we can tell, were a reflection of the pathos of Demeter and a re-creation of Persephonê's abduction and return. The cult was dominated by two families believed to be descended from the original royal families of Eleusis. The Eumolpidai ("Good Singers") provided the hierophant ("displayer of sacred things") and the chief priestesses. The Kerykes provided the hierokeryx ("sacred herald") and the daidoukhos ("torch-bearer").

As a prelude to initiation, mystai went through the Lesser Mysteries, performed in Athens. Athens took control of Eleusis in the later sixth century B.C.E., and henceforth Athens was intimately involved in the rites. These Lesser Mysteries occurred in the spring and purified the intended initiate so that he/she was eligible for the Greater Mysteries. These took place in the middle of the month of Boedromion (September/October), and lasted about a week. Starting on the thirteenth of the month, the ephebes (boys around eighteen years old) left Athens for Eleusis to fetch the "holy objects" and escort them to Athens. These objects, tied in boxes with ribbons, were prepared by the Eleusinian priestesses. The next day, the boys returned to deposit the sacred objects in the Eleusinion in Athens.

On the fifteenth, the hierokeryx summoned the would-be mystai to the Stoa Poikilê ("Painted Stoa") in Athens. All were welcome save "those impure in hands or incomprehensible in speech," that is, murderers and non-Greek-speakers (Foley 1994, 67). Each mystes had a patron of sorts, called a mystagoge; this was an initiate who led him/her through the mysteries. The following day, the mystai walked to the beach at Phaleron harbor and purified themselves in the water. This bath was not only for themselves, though: Each initiate had to sacrifice a piglet as part of the ritual, and the piglet had to be purified in the sea, too. Pigs were, in fact, a rare offering in ancient Greek religion, but they were common in the cults of Demeter. According to myth, when Hades brought Persephonê to the Underworld, a small herd of pigs had been sucked down as well. Sending piglets to death, then, formed part of the re-creation of the abduction tale. The pig sacrifice took place later on the same day as the ritual bath (the sixteenth). On the eighteenth, the mystai remained indoors, possibly fasting in imitation of Demeter's fast in the house of Keleos.

On the nineteenth, the mystai walked the 22 kilometers from Athens to Eleusis along a path called the Sacred Way, carrying back the sacred objects brought from Eleusis several days before. Also carried along was a statue of the god Iakkhos, usually identified with Dionysos, to whom festive hymns were sung, called Iakkhoi (Herodotus 8.65). Other events breaking up the long walk were sacrifices, prayers, singing, and dancing. At a bridge over the Kephisos River, which marked the boundary between Athens and Eleusis, men and women in costumes hurled insults at the mystai. Once they crossed into Eleusis, the mystai had a small picnic. That night, the women took part in nocturnal revels, including more dancing, singing, and obscene language (Foley 1994, 67). The use of obscenities recalls the role of Iambê in the *Hymn*—it was she who, telling dirty jokes to Demeter, finally got the goddess to smile and relax.

The mystery rituals took place in the Telesterion, a giant theater-like building that could accommodate thousands of spectators. At the structure's center was the Anaktoron, or "King's Room," from which the hierophant emerged to lead the rites. Little information is available about what happened after that. We have no idea what those rites were; they were kept secret. The early Christian father Clement of Alexandria, who had undergone initiation before his conversion, related, "I fasted, I drank the kykeon, I have taken from the chest, I worked, and deposited in the basket and from the basket into the chest" (Foley 1994, 68). Kykeon was a drink of barley, water, and mint, recalling the drink Demeter took in her *Hymn* "for the sake of the rite." Clement added that another part of the ritual included a reenactment of the tale of Demeter and Korê, allowing, we presume, the spectators to share in their sufferings. At the end of the rite, according to another early Christian author, Hippolytos, in his work *Refutation of All Heresies* (8.39–8.41), "And the Athenians . . . when they make the initiations of Eleusis and display to the beholders that great and wondrous and most perfect mystery that is to be beheld there is silence, a harvested ear (of grain) . . . likewise the hierophant himself . . . , when he celebrates the great and unutterable mysteries by night at Eleusis under a brilliant light, calls out and proclaims these words: 'A holy child is born to the Lady Brimo, Brimos'— that is, to the Strong One, the Strong" (Meyer 1987, 19).

When the rituals were over, the mystai took part in sacrifices and feasts. Later, some returned to Eleusis for higher levels of initiation, provided they could afford it. The mystai's experiences with the goddesses would, as they understood it, not only bring them prosperity in life, but happiness after death. As the horde of mystai expressed it in Aristophanes's *Frogs* (ll. 440–456):

Go forth now to the goddess's sacred circle, playing in the
flowery grove, for those taking part in the holy festival.
And I go with all the maidens and women,
where they keep the all-night-revels for the goddess, bearing
the holy light.
Let us go to the rosy, flowery meadows,
our path the most beautifully danced,
playing, whom the happy Muses lead along.
For only on us shines the sun, the joyous light,
being initiates.

Orphism

The origins of Orphism are obscure, although they seem to date back at least to the sixth century B.C.E. Orphic ideology mainly concerned the mysteries of Dionysos, which many Greeks took very seriously. Thus, there was a certain reticence to speak about these mysteries, leaving modern scholars with only innuendos and side references to work with. Fortunately, archaeology has brought to light more direct data on this topic—papyri and leaves of gold buried with the dead to help them in their afterlife journeys.

Orphism, as the name implies, was attributed to the mythic poet Orpheus, son of Apollo and Calliopê, who lived one generation before the Trojan War. Orpheus reputedly composed—actually wrote—several books of metaphysical philosophy concerning the origins and natures of the gods, the creation of humanity, and the path to a just life and blissful afterlife. Orphism espoused metempsychosis and the idea that morality in this life affects the quality of one's later (after)life.

According to Orphic theology, and in contrast to Hesiod's *Theogony*, Zeus once had sex with his mother Rhea. She gave birth to Persephonê, with whom Zeus also had intercourse. Persephonê bore Dionysos, who immediately achieved "favorite son" status with Zeus. Although Zeus kept the child well guarded, Hera, always the troublemaker, convinced the Titans to kidnap and murder the child. This they did, and ate Dionysos. Only his heart was preserved—by Athena, who gave it to Zeus. When Zeus found out about all this, he smote the Titans with a lightning bolt. From their ashes, humans were formed. Orphism, then, taught that the human body was composed of dead, evil gods. However, those Titans still had Dionysos, their last meal, running through their veins when they died, and thus Orphism taught that Dionysos was also present in all humans, providing the immortal aspect of the soul. In many respects, this theology ran contrary to Greek ideology, in which the gods were understood to be definitely immortal. The idea of humanity being created from the blood and body of an evil ex-deity, however, is present in Near Eastern cosmogonies like the Enuma Elish and Atrahasis, and it appears that some of Orphism derives from eastern ideologies.

One idea deriving from this myth was that humans were, by their very creation, evil, and guilty of Dionysos's death. Orphism held that humans consisted of evil flesh (Titans) that imprisoned a divine soul (Dionysos). Dionysos's mysteries purged humanity of this guilt, overcoming the evil flesh and setting humanity into accord with divinity. The books of Orpheus established how to do this, consisting of prescriptions for daily living as well as specific rituals used to expunge impurity. These having been mysteries, of course, we know little about the rituals. Even though some philosophers such as Plato scorned these mysteries and the "priests" who enacted them, the rites received enough reverence not to be spoken of except very indirectly. The general understanding is that, as with the Eleusinian Mysteries, some re-creation of the Dionysos story was reenacted, leading to catharsis and expiation of guilt (Guthrie 1993, 206).

Concerning the daily living, we know a bit more, and in many respects the Orphic lifestyle was similar to the Pythagorean (see chapter 10). Orphism disdained the flesh, the material aspect of humanity formed from the "sinful" Titans. The Orphic lifestyle, then, was ascetic, nonsensual, attempting to purify the flesh to bring one into closer union with the divine. As with Pythagorism, vegetarianism was practiced, and there was an interesting prohibition on eating beans as well.

The ultimate goal of Orphism was communion with the divine, an event that could only occur upon death and the final shedding of the evil flesh of humanity. Even in death, though, the initiate needed help in attaining bliss, lest he/she get reincarnated back into the human condition. To help the recently deceased, the Orphics buried their dead with "instructions" to navigate the afterlife. Often, these were composed on sheets of gold, and they have come to light in Hellenistic burials from Crete, Italy, and Thessaly (Meyer 1987, 101). The text from Thessaly reads:

> I am parched with thirst, and perishing.
> But drink of me, the ever-flowing spring on the
> right, (where) there is a fair cypress.
> Who are you? Where are you from?
> I am a child of Earth and of starry Heaven, but my
> race is of Heaven (alone).
> (Translation by Meyer 1987, 101)

Orphics believed that the dead must wander through Hades, a hot and dry land. The written sheet reminded the deceased person's psychê not to drink the water of the left, which was Lethê, or Forgetfulness, but from the spring on the right, which was Memory. Then, when questioned by the afterlife judges, the initiate could claim to be a child of the divine, free from the dead and impure flesh of humanity (Meyer 1987, 101).

REFERENCES

Antonaccio, C. M. 1995. *An Archaeology of Ancestors: Tomb Cult and Hero Cult in Early Greece.* London: Rowman & Littlefield.

Billigmeier, J.-C. and J. A. Turner. 1981. "The Socioeconomic Roles of Women in Mycenaean Greece: A Brief Survey from Evidence of the Linear B Tablets." In Foley, H., ed. *Reflections of Women in Antiquity.* New York: Gordon and Breach, 1–18.

Boedeker, D. D. 1974. *Aphrodite's Entry into Greek Epic.* Leiden, Netherlands: E. J. Brill.

Boëlle, C. 2001. "Po-ti-ni-ja: Unité or Pluralité?" In Laffineur, R. and R. Hägg, eds. 2001. *Potnia: Deities and Religion in the Aegean Bronze Age.* Liège, Belgium: Université de Liège, 403–409.

Budin, S. L. 2003. *The Origin of Aphrodite.* Bethesda, MD: CDL.

Burkert, W. 1985. *Greek Religion: Archaic and Classical. Journal of Hellenic Studies.* Cambridge, MA: Basil Blackwell and Harvard University Press.

———. 1987. *Ancient Mystery Cults.* Cambridge, MA: Harvard University Press.

Calame, C. 2001. *Choruses of Young Women in Ancient Greece: Their Morphology, Religious Role, and Social Functions.* Lanham, MD: Rowman & Littlefield.

Clark, I. 1998. "The Gamos of Hera: Myth and Ritual." In Blundell, S. and M. Williamson, eds. 1998. *The Sacred and the Feminine in Ancient Greece.* London: Routledge, 13–26.

Coldstream, J. N. 1976. "Hero Cults in the Age of Homer." *Journal of Hellenic Studies 96,* 8–17.

Cole, S. G. 1998. "Domesticating Artemis." In Blundell, S. and M. Williamson, eds. 1998. *The Sacred and the Feminine in Ancient Greece.* London: Routledge, 27–43.

———. 2000. "Demeter and the Ancient Greek City and Its Countryside." In Buxton, R., ed. *Oxford Readings in Greek Religion.* Oxford, UK: Oxford University Press, 133–154.

Cosmopoulos, M. 2003. "Mycenaean Religion at Eleusis: The Architecture and Stratigraphy of Megaron B." In Cosmopoulos, M., ed. *Greek Mysteries: The Archaeology and Ritual of Ancient Greek Secret Cults.* London: Routledge, 1–24.

D'Agata, A. L. 1992. "Late Minoan Crete and Horns of Consecration: A Symbol in Action." In Laffineur, R. and J. Crowley, eds. 1992. *Aegean Bronze Age Iconography: Shaping a Methodology.* AEGAEUM 12. Liège, Belgium: Université de Liège, 247–259.

Davaras, C. 1976. *Guide to Cretan Antiquities.* Athens, Greece: Eptalofos S.A.

Driessen, J. 2000a. "A Late Minoan IB Town Shrine at Palaikastro." In MacGillivray, J. A., J. M. Driessen, and L. H. Sackett, eds. *The Palaikastro Kouros: A Minoan Chryselephantine Statuette.* Athens, Greece: British School at Athens, 3, 87–96.

———. 2000b. "The Architectural Environment." In MacGillivray, J. A., J. M. Driessen, and L. H. Sackett, eds. *The Palaikastro Kouros: A Minoan Chryselephantine Statuette.* Athens, Greece: British School at Athens, 35–48.

Faraone, C. A. 2003. "Playing the Bear and Fawn for Artemis: Female Initiation of Substitute Sacrifice?" In Dodd, D. B. and C. A. Faraone, eds. *Initiation in Ancient Greek Rituals and Narratives: New Critical Perspectives.* New York: Routledge.

Foley, H. P. 1994. *The Homeric Hymn to Demeter: Translation, Commentary, and Interpretive Essays.* Princeton, NJ: Princeton University Press.

Frazer, J. G. 1911–1915. *The Golden Bough: A Study in Magic and Religion.* London: Macmillan.

Garland, R. 1985. *The Greek Way of Death.* Ithaca, NY: Cornell University Press.

Gebhard, E. R. 1993. "The Evolution of a Pan-Hellenic Sanctuary: From Archaeology towards History at Isthmia." In Marinatos, N. and R. Hägg, eds. 1993. *Greek Sanctuaries: New Approaches.* London: Routledge, 154–177.

Gesell, G. 1984. "The Minoan Palace and Public Cult." In Hägg, R. and N. Marinatos, eds. 1984. *The Function of the Minoan Palaces.* Stockholm: Skrifter Utgivna ac Svenska Institutet, 123–126.

Goodison, L. and C. Morris, eds. 1998. *Ancient Goddesses: The Myths and the Evidence.* Madison: University of Wisconsin Press.

Gulizio, J., K. Pluta, and T. G. Palaima. 2001. "Religion in the Room of the Chariot Tablets." In Laffineur, R. and R. Hägg, eds. 2001. *Potnia: Deities and Religion in the Aegean Bronze Age.* Liège, Belgium: Université de Liège, 453–462.

Guthrie, W. K. C. 1993. *Orpheus and Greek Religion: A Study of the Orphic Movement.* Princeton, NJ: Princeton University Press.

Hägg, R. 1997. "Religious Syncretism at Knossos?" In Driessen, J. and A. Farnoux, eds. *La Crète Mycenienne: Actes de la Table Ronde Internationale organisée par l'École française d'Athènes.* BCH Supplément 30. Athens: École française d'Athènes, 163–168.

Hale, J. R., J. Z. de Boer, J. P. Chanton, and H. A. Spiller. 2003. "Questioning the Delphic Oracle." (July 15). Available at http://ScientificAmerican.com.

Kearns, E. 1998. "The Nature of Heroines." In Blundell, S. and M. Williamson, eds. 1998. *The Sacred and the Feminine in Ancient Greece.* London: Routledge, 96–110.

Killen, J. T. 2001. "Religion at Pylos: The Evidence of the Fn Tablets." In Laffineur, R. and R. Hägg, eds. 2001. *Potnia: Deities and Religion in the Aegean Bronze Age.* Liège, Belgium: Université de Liège, 435–443.

King, H. 1983. "Bound to Bleed: Artemis and Greek Woman." In Cameron, A. and A. Kuhrt, eds. 1983. *Images of Woman in Antiquity.* Detroit, MI: Wayne State University Press, 109–127.

Larson, J. 1995. *Greek Heroine Cults.* Madison: University of Wisconsin Press.

Lebessi, A. and P. Muhly. 1990. "Aspects of Minoan Cult: Sacred Enclosures: The Evidence from the Symi Sanctuary (Crete)." *Archäologischer Anzeiger* 105, 315–336.

MacGillivray, A. and H. Sackett. 2000. "The Palaikastro Kouros: The Cretan God as a Young Man." In MacGillivray, J. A., J. M. Driessen, and L. H. Sackett, eds. *The Palaikastro Kouros: A Minoan Chryselephantine Statuette.* Athens, Greece: British School at Athens, vv–oo.

Meiggs, R. and D. Lewis. 1992. *A Selection of Greek Historical Inscriptions to the End of the Fifth Century B.C.* Oxford, UK: Clarendon.

Meyer, M. W., ed. 1987. *The Ancient Mysteries: A Sourcebook.* Philadelphia: University of Pennsylvania Press.

Moak, M. 2000. "The Palaikastro Kouros." In MacGillivray, J. A., J. M. Driessen, and L. H. Sackett, eds. *The Palaikastro Kouros: A Minoan Chryselephantine Statuette.* Athens, Greece: British School at Athens, xx–yy.

Morris, I. 1988. "Tomb Cult and the 'Greek Renaissance': The Past in the Present in the Eighth Century B.C." *Antiquity* 62, 750–761.

Nilsson, M. P. 1950. *The Minoan-Mycenaean Religion and Its Survival in Greek Religion.* 2d rev. ed. Lund, Sweden: C. W. K. Gleerup.

Nixon, L. 1995. "The Cults of Demeter and Kore." In Hawley, R. and B. Levick, eds. *Women in Antiquity: New Assessments.* London: Routledge.

Nosch, M.-L. B. 2000. "Shafherden unter dem Namenspatronat von Potnia und Hermes in Knossos." In Blakolmer, F., ed. 2000. *Österreichische Forschungen zur Ägäischen Bronzezeit 1998.* Wien, Austria: Phoibos Verlag, 211–215.

Nowicki, K. 2001. "Minoan Peak Sanctuaries: Reassessing Their Origins." In Laffineur, R. and R. Hägg, eds. 2001. *Potnia: Deities and Religion in the Aegean Bronze Age.* Liège, Belgium: Université de Liège, 31–38.

Padel, R. 1983. "Women: Model for Possession by Greek Daemons." In Cameron, A. and A. Kuhrt, eds. 1983. *Images of Women in Antiquity.* Detroit, MI: Wayne State University Press, 3–19.

Peatfield, A. 1992. "Rural Ritual in Bronze Age Crete: The Peak Sanctuary at Atsipodhes." *Cambridge Archaeological Journal* 2 (1), 59–87.

———. 1996. "After the 'Big Bang'—What? or Minoan Symbols and Shrines beyond Palatial Collapse." In Alcock, S. E. and R. Osborne, eds. 1996. *Placing the Gods: Sanctuaries and Sacred Space in Ancient Greece.* Oxford, UK: Clarendon, 19–36.

———. 2001. "Divinity and Performance on Minoan Peak Sanctuaries." In Laffineur, R. and R. Hägg, eds. 2001. *Potnia: Deities and Religion in the Aegean Bronze Age.* Liège, Belgium: Université de Liège, 51–56.

Price, S. 1999. *Religions of the Ancient Greeks.* Cambridge, UK: Cambridge University Press.

Rehak, P. 1984. "New Observations on the Mycenaean 'Warrior Goddess.'" *Archäologischer Anzeiger* 99, 535–545.

Rutkowski, B. 1986. *The Cult Places of the Aegean.* New Haven, CT: Yale University Press.

Schumacher, R. W. M. 1993. "Three Related Sanctuaries of Poseidon: Geraistos, Kalaureia, and Tainaron." In Marinatos, N. and R. Hägg, eds. 1993. *Greek Sanctuaries: New Approaches.* London: Routledge, 62–87.

Snodgrass, A. 2000. "The Archaeology of the Hero." In Buxton, R., ed. *Oxford Readings in Greek Religion.* Oxford, UK: Oxford University Press, 180–190.

Sourvinou-Inwood, C. 2000. "What Is *Polis* Religion?" In Buxton, R., ed. *Oxford Readings in Greek Religion.* Oxford, UK: Oxford University Press, 13–37.

Taylour, W. 1990. *The Mycenaeans.* Rev. ed. London: Thames & Hudson.

Trümpy, C. 2001. "Potnia sans les tablettes Mycéniennes: Quelques problèmes d'interprétation." In Laffineur, R. and R. Hägg, eds. 2001. *Potnia: Deities and Religion in the Aegean Bronze Age.* Liège, Belgium: Université de Liège, 411–421.

Tyree, L. 2001. "Diachronic Changes in Minoan Cave Cult." In Laffineur, R. and R. Hägg, eds. 2001. *Potnia: Deities and Religion in the Aegean Bronze Age.* Liège, Belgium: Université de Liège, 39–50.

Ventris, M. and J. Chadwick. 1959. *Documents in Mycenaean Greek.* Cambridge, UK: Cambridge University Press.

Vernant, J.-P. 1983. *Myth and Thought Among the Greeks.* London. Routledge.

———. 1991. *Mortals and Immortals: Collected Essays.* Princeton, NJ: Princeton University Press.

Voyazis, M. 1998. "From Athena to Zeus: An A–Z Guide to the Origins of Greek Goddesses." In Goodison, L. and C. Morris, eds. 1998. *Ancient Goddesses: The Myths and the Evidence.* Madison: University of Wisconsin Press, 133–147.

Wright, J. C. 1996. "The Spatial Configuration of Belief: The Archaeology of Mycenaean Religion." In Alcock, S. E. and R. Osborne, eds. 1996. *Placing the Gods: Sanctuaries and Sacred Space in Ancient Greece.* Oxford, UK: Clarendon, 37–78.

CHAPTER 9

Material Culture

ARCHITECTURE

Cycladic

The first of the Aegean peoples to construct fortifications were the Early Cycladic residents of the Cyclades. At Khalandriani on the island of Syros, residents built a double fortification wall measuring approximately 70 meters long and strengthened it with five horseshoe-shaped towers. Similar structures were also uncovered on the island of Naxos (see chapter 6) (Vermeule 1972, 32–33).

Houses were generally made of local stones, with roofs of branches and clay supported by wooden posts. Domestic structures had no consistent layout in the Early Bronze Age—houses were rectangular, circular, or any irregular shape in between, as dictated by the lay of the land. This changed considerably in the Middle Bronze Age, possibly due to influences from Crete and Greece. A house at Aghia Irini on the island of Kea shows a typical Cycladic organization, consisting of a long series of rooms, each accessible to the rest through a series of doors running down the center of the structure. Staircases on the sides of some rooms give evidence of upper stories.

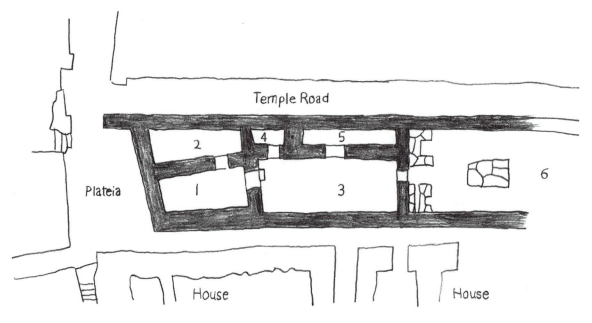

9.1 Plan of Temple at Aghia Irini, Kea (Courtesy of Stephanie Budin)

A somewhat similar organization appears at a temple in the same city, dating from the fifteenth century B.C.E. and continuing in use through the Archaic Age (see Image 9.1). This is a long, narrow, rectangular structure with an entrance hall to the southeast, giving access to two more long, rectangular rooms placed one after the other, with doors running down the center of the structure. In all respects, it resembles a house. However, this temple is slightly more elaborate than a house in organization: From the room beyond the entrance hall extend two smaller rooms, which were possibly for storage. The room at the far end of the structure also opened onto an additional room, large enough for either storage or ritual. In short, the temple followed typical domestic architecture, but with more rooms for storage and cult activity (Preziosi and Hitchcock 1999, 136).

Minoan

The Minoans mostly lived in caves during the Neolithic period and probably continued to do so in some parts of Crete into the Early Bronze Age. Nevertheless, even by the early Neolithic, a small village was already forming at the future "capital" of Knossos, and by the end of the Stone Age, another village had emerged at Phaistos (Branigan 1988, 37).

In the Early Bronze Age, "apartment-complex" structures began to appear in Crete, such as the domestic structure at Myrtos described in chapter 4. A similar creation appeared in the Early Minoan II period (2500–2200 B.C.E.) on the hilltop of Vasiliki. This unit, like that at Myrtos, rose upon a foundation of small stones bound together with clay and straw. Clay bricks were used for the upper structures, which were then covered over with a layer of fine plaster, often painted red. Timbers were set both vertically and horizontally in the walls, probably to give support and elasticity in case of earthquake (a common occurrence in the Aegean). The roofs were of reeds or possibly wood, sealed with roofing plaster against the rain. Both Vasiliki and Myrtos made use of unroofed areas called light-wells, which allowed both light and air into the complex. Inside, there were rooms with long benches, which are the closest thing to furniture that researchers have discovered. Both light-wells and benches also appeared in the palace architecture of the following era (Branigan 1988, 44–47).

Unlike the apartment complexes of the previous age, Minoan houses of the Middle and Late Bronze Age were individual and independent. Rectilinear or square in shape, they were constructed on a stone foundation with walls of stone, adobe, or mud brick, covered inside and out with plastering for protection from rain. Some windows are evident in the walls, as are permanent hearths in the floors. Flat roofs consisted of crossbeams covered with reeds or wood, and then, once again, were waterproofed with plastering. Clay chimneys in the roofs let out smoke from the hearths, a need that precluded the building of upper stories. Inside was a lot of storage space, including pithoi, wall cupboards, and plastered benches. Walls were sometimes painted, although not to such a degree as the palaces or villas (see below). Water tanks and cisterns gathered water for day-to-day living, but there is no evidence for an actual plumbing system (Waterhouse 1990, 312–313).

The palaces were the crowning glory of Minoan architecture. These were huge structures incorporating areas for residence, storage, production, archives, and ritual. As can be seen at Knossos (see Image 9.2), the palaces incorporated a continuous series of buildings around a large central court, open to the sky and usually oriented north-south. To the west of this group was usually another open court with an elaborate façade on its eastern side. This west court probably served as a place of assembly and, possibly, religious rituals. Between and around the courts at ground level were several long, narrow rooms containing storage equipment, production workshops, and columns and pillars supporting the upper stories. These upper rooms (which have seldom survived to the present day) were considerably larger than the basement rooms and were accessible through large, monumental staircases. Dotted throughout the palaces were light-wells: mini open-air courts allowing light and air into the palace interiors, and if necessary, letting smoke out. These light-wells were distinguished from "regular" rooms by their waterproof flooring, necessary as they were unroofed against rain.

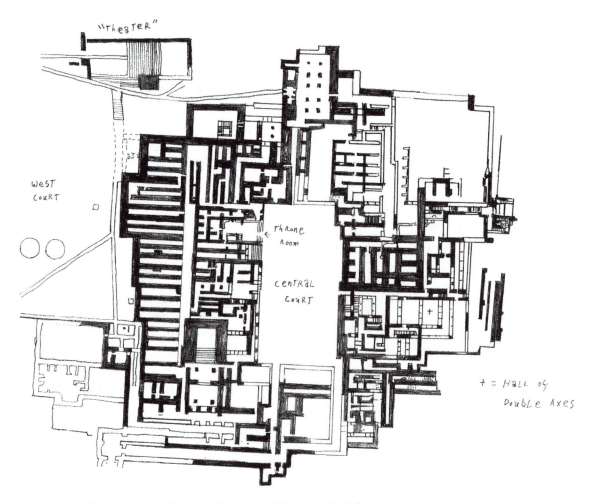

9.2 Plan of Palace at Knossos (Courtesy of Stephanie Budin)

In the upper stories, such as those that remain at Knossos, rooms could change their size and access through a Minoan architectural feature called the polythyron ("many doors") or "pier-and-door" partitions. These consisted of a series of doors that could be opened or closed to block off all of, or a portion of, a wall. With the doors closed, the room was smaller and contained. When open, they made for a larger, more accessible area. In contrast to the pier-and-door partitioned areas were smaller rooms literally sunken into the floor, with a small staircase that led from an almost loft-like level above. Evans, who first dug at Knossos (see chapter 3), dubbed these lustral basins, claiming that some manner of bathing or washing ritual took place in these sunken areas. This name is still accepted, although doubt remains as to their actual purpose.

Windows punctuated the walls of Minoan palaces, including a generally elaborate window on the west façade in each palace's west court. Wooden columns, painted red, supported the roofs. In contrast to later Greek columns, Minoan columns were thicker at the top and narrower at the bottom, which gave a sense of lightness to the construction. The roofs themselves, from what we can tell, were flat, and in later periods might have been decorated with large, monumental horns of consecration (see chapter 8). Beneath the ground, stone-lined channels and clay pipes served as plumbing (Dickinson 1994, 149). Many elements of the Minoan palaces, from light-wells to long, narrow workshops to polythyra, were incorporated into the villas, which began to appear in Crete in the Second Palace period, making them literally miniature palaces.

Inside the palaces, frescoes decorated the walls, as they would in all the more elaborate domestic architecture of the Minoan and Mycenaean periods (see Image 7.2). Unlike the style called *buon fresco*, in which paint is applied to wet plaster so as to seep into the wall itself, in the Minoan frescoes, the artist painted on dry plaster, then sealed it over with an adhesive. Painted scenes came from the daily lives of the Minoans and, later, Mycenaeans. For example, the Bull-Leaper Fresco from Knossos shows a male and two females in the process of leaping over a running bull. As is standard with Minoan (as well as Egyptian, and later Greek) iconography, females are painted with fair skin and males with darker flesh (possibly due to their spending more time outdoors). This image may provide evidence for a Minoan athletic, and possibly religious, event where trained acrobats performed over charging bulls. Likewise, the frescoes of the Minoan colony at Thera show people in various daily activities, such as fishing, boxing, and gathering flowers, giving a glimpse at their clothing, jewelry, and possibly even religious beliefs (see chapter 8).

Nature was also a favorite theme of the Minoans. Frescoes show rugged hills covered with flowers, swallows in acrobatic flight, agrimi (horned relatives of the goat) out in the countryside, and even the occasional flying fish. In the Minoan repertoire, geometric and other nonnaturalistic designs were reserved for borders. By contrast, the Mycenaeans, who adopted many Minoan styles, cultivated a more static and geometric feeling in their frescoes. When the flowers look patterned, and the background goes from flowering hills to wavy bands, researchers know they are looking at a Mycenaean creation.

Helladic

The earliest extant domestic architecture in Greece is the Neolithic A (seventh-millennium B.C.E.) village at Sesklo in Thessaly. The village contained about twenty closely grouped but independent houses (i.e., no row homes), each consisting of up to three roughly square or oblong rooms set together with irregular wall lines. These rooms could range from little more than 1 square meter to up to 8 square meters. The foundations were of smallish stones, and the walls were either of wattle-and-daub construction (reeds and mud) or possibly mud brick. The roofs were composed of reeds over a clay base. The only discernible household facilities were fixed hearths, located either in the center of a room or by the wall (which does not sound like a brilliant idea if the walls were wattle and daub). These hearths were probably for heating the house and for warming food. Outside the house structures were larger ovens, no doubt used for bread baking and possibly pottery firing (Vermeule 1972, 11).

In the Neolithic B period, a new culture emerged in Greece, best represented at Dimini, also in Thessaly (see Image 9.3). Unlike Sesklo, Dimini was a fenced settlement, surrounded by originally three, then five, low walls, arranged in concentric rings, encircling the crown of a hill measuring about 15 meters long. Within the walls was one primary domestic unit, which contained a squarish house, animal sheds, and storage facilities (Vermeule 1972, 16). Additional houses were located outside the encircling walls, suggesting either that the society had become hierarchical by this point, with a "royal family" inhabiting the main house, or that the entire structure was some manner of communal storage facility.

With the rise of the Bronze Age, a new domestic architectural style appeared in Greece—the corridor house, best represented by the House of the Tiles in Lerna, which dates to the Early Helladic II period and measures some 25 x 12 square meters (see Image 9.4). These houses, ranging from Boiotia in the north to Aigina in the east to Messenia in the southwest, are all essentially rectilinear in plan, meaning that a series of square or rectangular rooms are laid out one after the other in a row, with the row itself flanked by hallways or corridors. Some of these buildings, as at Lerna, had stairs leading to a second story. As was typical for Greek buildings henceforth, the entire house was set upon a stone socle, or base, to protect the walls from water damage. The walls were of mud brick, and the roofs consisted of timber beams covered with fired clay tiles that overhung the walls, once again providing protection from rain (Dickinson 1994, 144–145).

By the Mycenaean period, the style of Greek house that was to remain common in the Iron Age began to appear. This consisted of a group of square or rectangular rooms arranged around a central courtyard, which provided light and air to all the rooms of the house. A secondary house style, also with later appearances in Greek architecture, was a structure similar in many respects to the corridor houses of the Early Bronze Age. In this type, a series of square rooms was arranged along a corridor. The rooms had access by means of a staircase to a larger, megaron-like room (see below), possibly serving as some manner of reception hall. Around the living quarters were facilities for storage

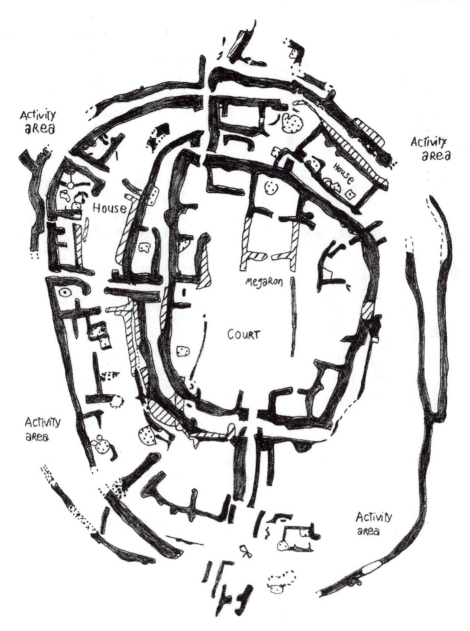

9.3 Plan of Dimini (Courtesy of Stephanie Budin)

and production, indicating a heavy economic component for these apparently upper-class houses (Kilian 1988, 32). Examples of such houses appear at Mycenae, where four residential and production-oriented homes were located just outside the city walls. These were the West House, the House of the Oil Merchant, the House of the Sphinxes, and the House of the Shields. Although generally only the basements of these structures are preserved, they show a linear arrangement for both the basement storage rooms and, based on what fell from above, the upper stories. Upper levels probably had balconies overlooking terraces, which, once again, provided light and air.

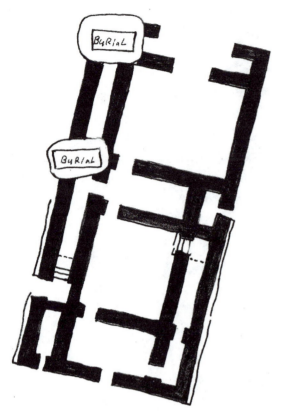

BURIAL

BURIAL

9.4 Plan of the House of the Tiles, Lerna (Courtesy of Stephanie Budin)

For a picture of true upper-class life, of course, one must turn to the Mycenaean palaces, which began to appear in the Late Helladic IIIA period with Mansions I and II at the Menelaion in Sparta; Nichoria Building IV-4, at Tiryns; and the "Megaron" on the island of Phylakopi (Dickinson 1994, 153). The most prestigious monumental architecture in Mycenaean Greece, though, was at Mycenae, Tiryns, and Pylos (see Image 9.5). The central component of the Mycenaean palace was the megaron (hall): a square room, approached through a porch and vestibule, with a hearth in the center surrounded by four pillars. Instead of an upper story, there was a gallery around the upper edge of the megaron, allowing people to look down onto the events below and also allowing smoke from the hearth to escape through an opening in the ceiling. At Pylos and Mycenae, a throne base was located in the center of the wall that stood at a right angle from the door. One approached the megaron through a long corridor of porches and anterooms, each with a full complement of smaller rooms to either side. These rooms served a variety of functions, ranging from simple offices to archives to lavatories to what may have functioned as (temporary) bedrooms. Behind the megaron were rooms for storage. Beyond the megaron-based palace proper at Pylos was a series of outer buildings, such as a wine magazine and several workshops. Altogether, the Mycenaean palaces served as royal residences and centers of redistribution and production.

It was not until the later years of the Bronze Age that the palaces, especially those at Mycenae and Tiryns, also came to function as fortresses. In the fourteenth century B.C.E., both palaces surrounded themselves with large walls, called Cyclopean, as the later Greeks believed that only the mythical giants could have moved such large stones. These walls could rise up to 13 meters high and be as thick as 8 meters (Kilian 1988, 31). They were clearly designed with defense, and specifically siege defense, in mind. The walls at Tiryns extended away from the palace proper to enclose an area probably intended to hold the general population during periods of warfare (see Image 4.3). The defensive structures at Mycenae were enlarged in the thirteenth century to enclose a spring accessible by staircase. Ultimately, such provisions did not save the Mycenaeans from the upheavals at the end of the Bronze Age, when all the palaces were burned to the ground.

Monumental architecture ceased to exist in the Dark Age, and houses built

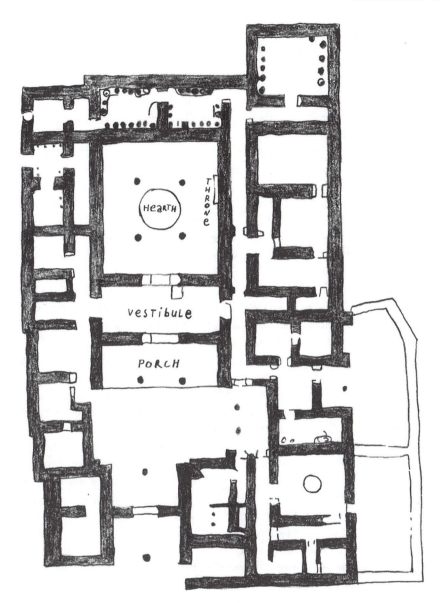

9.5 Plan of Megaron at Pylos (Courtesy of Stephanie Budin)

during that period were generally made of materials that left few remains in the archaeological record. The one major exception is the Heroön of Lefkandi (see chapter 4), which gives evidence for both domestic and funerary architecture. Otherwise, the next major phase of Greek architecture begins around 800 B.C.E. with the growth of the sanctuaries.

Greek

Sanctuaries, Temples, and Orders.   A Greek sanctuary consisted of up to three main parts. The most important part was the temenos (see chapter 8), meaning literally "cut off," which was the physical space dedicated to the deity. Often, this would be surrounded by some manner of wall, but not necessarily. Sometimes it might have been located in a cave or on a mountain peak (especially for sanctuaries of Zeus). The second part was the altar, which served as the focus of sacrifice, either of animals or possibly just burnt incense. The third part was the temple itself, which was seen as the deity's "house."

Around 800 B.C.E., temples become increasingly prominent in Greece. One of the earliest was at the sanctuary of Apollo Daphnephoros ("Laurel-Bearing") at Eretria on the island of Euboia, just southeast of Lefkandi. The original temple was a small (7.5 x 11.5 meters), apsidal (round at one end) structure, with a very low stone foundation and a number of fired clay column bases. The walls surrounding these slender columns were probably wattle and daub, which then supported a reed or other vegetal roof. The front of the structure had a small porch. To the east of the "house" was a square altar where offerings were burnt, next to which was a sacrificial pit (a bothros) into which more permanent votives could be tossed (Coldstream 1977, 322–325). All of these were surrounded by a large wall marking off the temenos.

In the eighth century B.C.E., however, the tiny "bay hut" at Eretria was replaced with a much larger structure, known as a hekatompedon. *Heka-* is Greek for "100," and this name means that the temple was 100 feet long (although bear in mind that the ancient Greeks had a different notion of what constituted one foot than we do now). The hekatompedon at Eretria was an impressive structure, measuring around 40 meters long and about 8 meters wide. It was placed a few meters east of the bay hut and made use of the same altar. A slightly older but otherwise similar hekatompedon was constructed on the island of Samos for the goddess Hera.

During the course of the eighth and seventh centuries, Greek temples slowly transformed from wooden structures into brick and/or marble buildings. This is especially evident in the columns of the Temple of Hera at Olympia. One or two earlier structures existed on the site of the final temple, which was constructed between 625 and 600 B.C.E. and lasted until the third century C.E. Originally, all forty-four columns surrounding the temple were wood; each was replaced either as necessitated by wood rot or as the townspeople could afford to replace the wooden columns with marble. So, the wooden columns were replaced with marble one at a time over several centuries, with each column representing the style that was fashionable at its time of construction (they did not match). Thus, the temple provides a complete chronology of column and capital styles from the early sixth century B.C.E. through Roman times. Pausanias, a Roman-era tourist in Greece, even claimed that upon his trip to the area, one of the columns by the back was still made of oak.

These new marble temples were rectangular rather than apsidal. The earlier temples were long and narrow for the sake of easier roofing. But, as building and roofing techniques improved, the temples became wider and more squarish in shape. The standard components of a Greek temple were the pronaos ("before the sanctuary," or the vestibule), the naos (interior sanctuary where the statues of the deity would "live"), and the opisthodomos (back room or treasury). Some later temples did not have the opisthodomos, as treasures were by then kept in a separate building called thesaurai ("treasuries"; see below). The roof overhanging the pronaos would be supported by two columns

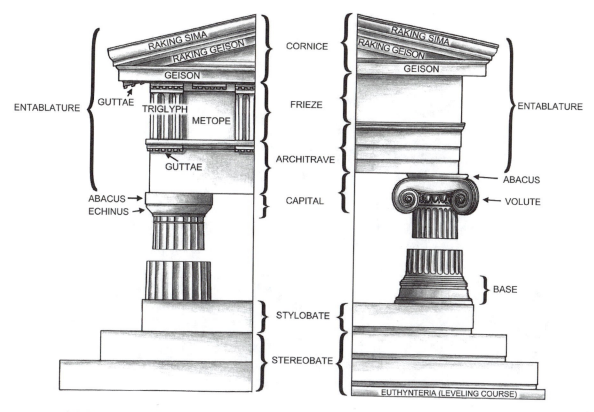

9.6 Schematics of Doric and Ionic Orders (Courtesy of Paul Butler)

at the very least, with plain walls around the rest of the structure. More often, columns would support the roof above both pronaos and opisthodomos, and, eventually, at least one row of columns would support an overhanging roof around the entire structure. Such temples are called peripteral, literally "surrounded with wings."

Most Greek temples were elevated upon a series of steps called the stereobate, which surrounded the temple (as opposed to Etrusco-Roman temples, where the steps led only up the front). These led to the floor level—the stylobate—where the columns and temple walls rested. These walls could be constructed of marble on the more expensive temples, or of sun-baked brick upon a stone base in the less elaborate versions. The stone base, a layer of paint, and the overhanging roof kept the bricks from melting in the rain. Above the walls was the roof, usually constructed of wood in the interior and covered with clay tiles on the exterior. On the front and back of the temple, the doorways to the pronaos and the opisthodomos were capped by pediments, triangular spaces often decorated with painted images or sculpture. Some elaborate temples also had akroteria on the roof—sculptures ranging from painted discs to statues of the deities, some of which functioned as gargoyles.

There were three main styles (orders) of Greek temple architecture. In order of appearance, these were Doric, Ionic, and Corinthian (eee Image 9.6).

Doric Order. The Doric style (see Image 9.7) is most readily identified by its

9.7 The Hephaisteion, Athens (Library of Congress)

columns, which have no base and rise up to be topped by simple, almost pillow-like capitals. Above the column capitals is a section called the entablature, which comprises the architrave (the area directly above the columns), the frieze, the pediment, and the roof. In the Doric order, the architrave was simple and unadorned. The frieze was decorated with a series of triglyphs and metopes. A triglyph ("thrice-cut") had three vertical grooves and probably derived from elements of an earlier wooden construction. The metopes (MET-o-pees) are flat squares between the triglyphs, which were usually painted or decorated with sculpture. The columns of a Doric structure stood directly beneath every other triglyph. This proved problematic at the corners, where the columns got rather crowded together under the final triglyphs, causing the corner columns to be a tad closer together than those along the interior. For this reason, the Doric order was thought to be essentially flawed.

Ionic Order. The Ionic order (see Image 9.8) first emerged in the sixth century B.C.E. in Ionia, at Ephesus, Didyma, and Samos. This style is more elaborate than the Doric order. Unlike the Doric columns, Ionic columns have a base between the column and the stylobate. In some cases, such as the Temple of Artemis at Ephesus, these bases could be large and elaborately sculpted. Ionic columns are capped by volute capitals with downward-tuned scrolls, somewhat resembling rams' horns. The Ionic architrave has simple horizontal pat-

9.8 Temple of Athena Nikê on Aegina (Library of Congress)

terns, and the frieze was either plain, painted, or, most elaborately, decorated with a sculptural scene. As with the Doric order, above the frieze is the pediment, which was also often decorated. One must bear in mind that the Greeks painted their sculpture, so that the more elaborate temples were covered with brightly colored statues and decorations, a far cry from the simple white buildings we see today (on which the paint has worn off).

The distinctions between Doric and Ionic were not hard and fast, and architects could combine elements from both if desired. For example, the Athenian Parthenon, built in the mid-fifth century B.C.E., was essentially Doric in style, having Doric columns, simple capitals, and a frieze decorated with triglyphs and metopes. The metopes were decorated with scenes of combat between humans and monsters. The pediments were sculpted with scenes from the life of Athena, to whom the temple was dedicated. One side shows her birth from the head of Zeus (see chapter 8), the other her victory over Poseidon for possession of the city. However, on the exterior walls of the temple (under the overhanging roof supported by the columns) is an Ionic frieze showing a procession of Athenian citizens and the presentation of an article of clothing to Athena. Thus, we have an Ionic frieze on a Doric building.

Corinthian Order.   The Corinthian order was really just a modification of the Ionic. Beginning in the fifth century B.C.E., architects created a new style of capital to place on top of the Ionic columns with their elaborate bases. These capitals were decorated with small volutes and acanthus leaves. Such capitals first appeared in the naos of the Temple of Apollo at Bassai, one of those temples with both Doric and Ionic elements. Although the exterior of the temple was Doric, the naos interior was Ionic, with a full, sculpted frieze running around the interior. A single Corinthian column stood opposite the naos entrance.

From such humble beginnings in the mid-fifth century, the Corinthian order came to dominate Greek large-scale architecture, being the preferred style of the Hellenistic regimes and the Romans. Henceforth, the Doric order was relegated to mainly secular architecture, such as stoas.

Public and Private Structures. The Greeks certainly built more than just temples, and the architectural styles that they developed in the course of temple building were used on alternate forms of public architecture. Following is a partial list of some of the more prominent public and private buildings the Greeks used in their daily affairs.

Treasuries. These buildings housed dedications given to a deity. Although smaller or more remote sanctuaries had little need for a separate treasury structure (often just the opisthodomos would do), in the larger ones, and especially the Panhellenic sanctuaries, separate treasuries were needed for several reasons. For one thing, there simply was not enough room for all the treasures dedicated to, say, Olympian Zeus in his temple at Olympia. Alternate structures were needed to guard the treasures. Furthermore, the individual poleis that made dedications preferred to keep their votives and treasures separate and distinct from those of their neighbors. Thus, the Corinthians' treasury housed dedications from Corinth; the Athenian treasury, those from Athens. Greek society was nothing if not competitive, and this spirit of competition included the vaunting of wealth, both individually and at the polis level. Treasuries were needed for appropriate flaunting, a fact manifested not only in the treasures within the buildings, but in the construction and decoration of the treasuries themselves.

Treasuries could be very elaborate. Perhaps the best example of this was the Siphnian treasury at Delphi, constructed around 530 B.C.E. This smallish structure resembled a miniature Ionic temple, except instead of Ionic columns before the pronaos, there were caryatids, columns in the shape of women. These women were dressed in elaborate, frilly clothing, and they were capped with fancy headdresses known as polos crowns. Above the caryatids was an almost fully preserved frieze depicting Trojan warriors and the battle between the gods and Titans. Above these rested a fully sculpted pediment showing Zeus arbitrating between Apollo and Heracles over the possession of the Delphic tripod. The roof was covered with tiles and decorated with sculpted-in-the-round akroteria. All the sculpture would have been painted in bright colors, creating a jewel box of a building. This was just one of dozens of elaborate treasuries at the Delphi sanctuary, flaunting the prosperity of the Greek poleis and making Delphi, even in modern times, look like the Las Vegas of ancient Greece.

Theaters. One of the most important public buildings in the ancient Greek polis was the theater, a structure that actually served as a temple to Dionysos—god of wine, madness, and liminality (see chapter 8). There were three main parts to a Greek theater: the skenê, or stage (from which we get the word *scene*); the orchestra; and the theatron, or seats. The seats, obviously, were where the spectators sat. "First-class" seats, the prohedria, were closest to the orchestra and had curved surfaces for added comfort (all other seats were flat, so people had to bring their own cushions). In contrast to modern terminology, the orchestra was where young men in costume danced and recited poetry as part of the play (see chapter 10). At the absolute center of the orchestra was a small altar to Dionysos, which was also the acoustic center of the theater—a coin dropped there could be heard at the uppermost seats. The stage was where the actors enacted the play, of course, although much of the play involved interaction with the dancers in the orchestra.

It is difficult to tell when the first theaters came into being, as they consisted of no more than a sloping hill (the seats) near a relatively flat area (orchestra and stage). The earliest indication that a specific structure was used for the skenê comes from the *Oresteia* trilogy written by Aeschylus and performed in 458 B.C.E. As one of the characters was said to be on the roof, it is clear that some sort of building was in use by that time. By the fifth and fourth centuries,

9.9 Theater at Delphi (Library of Congress)

theaters had become quite elaborate, seating up to 14,000 spectators in Athens (the Theater of Dionysos by the Acropolis) (Ley 1991, 10–14). One of the best-preserved ancient Greek theaters is the one at Delphi, which preserves a full complement of seats (see Image 9.9).

Stoas. One of the most common types of Greek public structures was the stoa, which was essentially a roofed hallway that served a variety of functions. Some stoas contained shops, making them the first shopping malls of the ancient world. Others contained art—like the Stoa Poikilê, or Painted Stoa, of Classical Athens—and so served as early museums. At their most basic, they were shelters from sun or rain, which allowed the Greeks to come together to speak in a public setting. As such, they also served as meeting halls and even law courts. In short, they were popular gathering places, some acquiring exceptional fame for the people who convened there. Zeno, the third-century philosopher, used to lecture to his followers in the Painted Stoa of Athens. For this reason, they came to be known as Stoics ("stoa dwellers").

In construction, classical stoas were combinations of Doric and Ionic elements. The standard large-scale stoa would have a tiled roof supported by two rows of columns. Those on the exterior were Doric, often appearing under a Doric-style frieze with triglyphs and metopes. On the interior, however, Ionic columns were used. By tradition, Ionic columns were taller and more slender than the massive Doric columns, and thus they allowed for more moving space inside. Unlike the temple columns, which were fully decorated with a scalloped pattern called fluting, stoa columns were often left unfluted, or they were fluted only along the top two-thirds of the column. Apparently, the Greek sculptors realized that people constantly leaning on and rubbing against the columns wore away the fluting, and they learned to save their efforts.

The Agora. The most important public gathering place in the ancient Greek city was the agora (a-go-RAH), which was the open space in or near the city center. Here, open-air markets, government buildings, altars, and small temples were located. The agora was essentially the political, economic, and social heart of the city. By the end of the fifth century B.C.E., the Athenian Agora contained three large stoas for public meetings and publications (the Royal Stoa, the Stoa of Zeus, and the South Stoa); the city mint; two law courts; the Tholos ("Round House"), where members of the city council who were on 24-hour duty lived and ate (see chapter 7); a fountain house for fresh water; the Altar of the Twelve Gods; the altar of Aphrodite Ourania; the monument of the Eponymous Heroes, where all manner of publications were posted; the city archives; the Panathenaic Way, which was used in religious processions to the Acropolis; several houses and small shops; and the open-air market and the public clock.

Homes. Private houses were less likely than temples to be constructed of durable materials such as marble, and thus fewer such structures still remain. The most common building material for houses was sun-baked bricks, which endured the elements only so long as care was taken to protect them from rain with overhanging roofs and with paint. Two large residential areas remain with enough of their foundations intact, however, to show how ancient Greek houses were constructed in the fifth and fourth centuries, one at Olynthos in

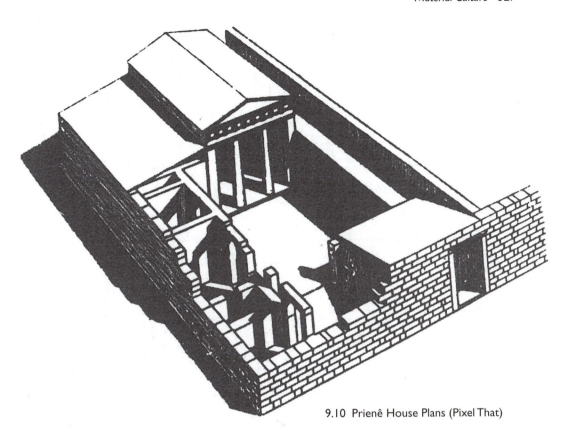

9.10 Prienê House Plans (Pixel That)

northern Greece and the other at Prienê in modern Turkey. Two texts from Classical Athens, a court case from a homicide trial and a philosophical treatise, give modern scholars an idea about the interior and daily functioning of the household.

Both Prienê and Olynthos were organized according to the Hippodamean, or planned, city structure, in which streets were aligned into a grid system and private houses were separated from public buildings. Such a layout was made famous by the fifth-century architect Hippodamos of Miletos, thus the term "Hippodamean." At Prienê, rebuilt due to the need for urban renewal in 350 B.C.E., the six east-west oriented main streets measured from 4.44 to 7.36 meters in width and crossed perpendicular north-south side streets measuring 3.5 meters wide. In the central, most public, part of the city were the public buildings, including temples, government buildings, and the gymnasion—the ancient equivalent of a sports club. Beyond the public buildings were the houses, bunched together into blocks between the main and side streets. Each block measured 47.2 x 35.4 meters and usually contained four houses (see Image 9.10). All the houses, and many of the public buildings, faced south, so as to be protected from the sun in summer but to get maximum sun and heat in winter. The entire city was surrounded by a defensive wall, and water was provided by an aqueduct that sent the water to nymphaia, or shrines to the nymphs, which also functioned as public fountains.

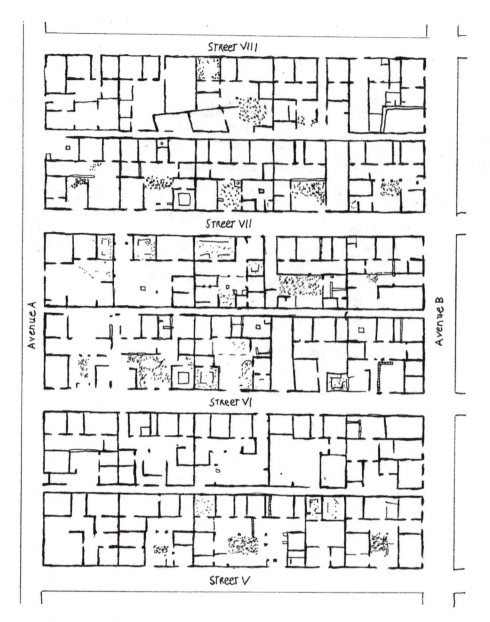

9.11 Plan of Houses at Olynthos (Courtesy of Stephanie Budin)

The houses at Olynthos were similar in date and style, with blocks measuring 110 x 40 meters, having ten houses each, arranged between main streets and side streets (see Image 9.11). The houses consisted, as did many urban Greek houses, of two-story rooms organized around a central courtyard with a well. Surrounding the central courtyard were the functional rooms, such as the kitchen, as well as the entertaining rooms, such as the dining room and the men's drinking room (called the andrôn; see chapter 6). Rooms for eating and drinking can usually be identified by their mosaic floors, which were not only impressive to look at but were easy to clean in case of spills. Upper floors contained the private chambers and may have been where the women did most of their household industries such as weaving. Contrary to some modern myths about Greek women, though, women certainly were not "confined" to the upper stories, unable to leave the house or to see people other than family.

The gendered division of the house is supported by a fifth-century legal document called "The Murder of Eratosthenes." This document records the trial of a man named Euphiletos who killed a man named Eratosthenes for having an affair with Euphiletos's wife. Concerning the organization of the house, Euphiletos tells us:

> First then, Gentlemen, (for it is necessary that all these matters be clear to you), my house is a two-story, having equal space above as below; above being for the women, below for the men. But when the child was born to us, his mother used to suckle him, and so she would not risk danger going down the stairs whenever she had to bathe him, I used to live above, and the women stayed below. And so this became customary, and often my wife went downstairs to sleep with the baby, so she could nurse him and he would not cry.

Although this text makes it clear that men and women used different areas of the home, the general understanding of space in ancient Greece actually allotted the entire house's interior to the women (minus the men's drinking room), while men were expected to work and recreate outdoors. Men were generally responsible for work in the fields, factory production, and transporting goods for sale into the cities. Women's duties are spelled out in a somewhat idealizing version of household chores presented in Xenophon's *Oikonomikos* (7, 41), where a husband tells his young wife:

> It will be necessary for you . . . to remain indoors and to send out those whose work is outside the house, and for those whose work must be done inside, you must supervise them; and you must receive what comes into the house, and you must apportion what is spent, and you must provide and take care for necessities, so that that which has to last a year does not get spent in a month. And you must attend to as much wool as is brought to you, so that there is clothing for all who need it. And indeed you must busy yourself with the flour so that it stays edible. In truth, one of your duties . . . perhaps will seem rather annoying: you must nurse anyone of the household servants who may be sick.

This list of chores gives a good idea of the daily life of a middle- to upper-class Greek woman who had a house and servants to look after. A poorer woman would take on far more physical labor herself, possibly including helping with farmwork or producing goods and selling them in the city (see chapter 5).

SCULPTURE

Cycladic

In the Early Cycladic II period, the Cycladic islands developed an elegant and unique style of sculpture that is still considered to be one of the pinnacles of

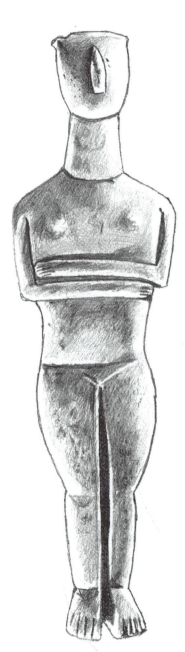

9.12 Cycladic Figurine (Courtesy of Paul Butler)

Western art. These were the Cycladic Figurines (see Image 9.12), sculpted in marble and decorated with paint (although the paint has seldom survived to the present day). Most of these figurines were female, as is evident from the molded breasts and pubic triangles. The faces, without their painted detail having survived, show little more than a nose, and the usual pose of the body has the arms folded across the chest. Many have pointed feet, meaning that the figurines could not stand erect, but some do have "flat" feet, allowing them to stand. In size, the Cycladic Figurines ranged from rather tiny, around 20 centimeters (cm) long, up to life size, around 1.5 meters high. An alternate version of these figurines is male, indicated by a phallic bulge. Unlike the females, the males are shown being active, usually playing a musical instrument, but occasionally simply walking. As with the females, the facial features on the males are usually minimal.

The Early Cycladic artists also made sculptures in clay. One of the most distinctive types of Cycladic items, and one of the most frustrating to modern scholars, is the so-called frying pan, which was a teardrop-shaped clay trivet of sorts covered with incised decoration. At the bottom (or pointed end), many of these frying pans had an incised triangle with a slit up the center, suggesting female pubic anatomy. Many also featured boats surrounded by running-spiral "seas" on the wide part of the objects. To date, no one has any ideas on what these objects were.

Minoan and Mycenaean

Neither the Minoans nor the Mycenaeans made anything as large as the life-sized figurines from the Cyclades. It is possible that either the Minoans or Mycenaeans wrought life-sized images in wood, but if so, no such statue has survived. However, both did make three-dimensional images out of a number of elegant materials, including stone, ivory, gold, and faience (a glass-like paste from Egypt).

Two fine examples of faience sculpture come from the palace of Knossos and date to the Middle Minoan period. These are the so-called Snake goddesses, two figurines composed of painted, mould-made faience, one measuring 34.5 cm high and the other measuring 29.5 cm high (see Image 8.2). They portray females in typical Minoan garb, each holding, or being enwrapped by, snakes, a long-standing slithering motif in Minoan iconography (see chapter 8).

One of the finest examples of Minoan sculpture is a chryselephantine (gold and ivory) figurine from Palaikastro, called the Palaikastro Kouros. This 50-cm-tall striding male has a torso, arms, legs, and feet of hippopotamus ivory; gold sandals and other gold accents; and a head of gray serpentine (stone) and

9.13 Lion Gate at Mycenae (Roger Wood/Corbis)

rock crystal. The posture of the arms beside the chest is typical of the Minoan male prayer stance, but the striding legs show strong influence from Egypt, an influence that would later return in the Greek Archaic Age. The pegs under the feet indicate that the statue was placed in a socle and was intended to be viewed standing upright. The artist clearly lavished extraordinary attention onto the details of this image, so that, even though the statue is only 50 cm high, the veins on the legs are clearly visible.

Some of the earliest examples of fine sculpture from the Mycenaeans are the stelai from the shaft graves at Mycenae (see Image 4.2). These limestone slabs measuring up to 1.86 meters high are decorated with relief (two-dimensional) scenes of hunting, racing, and warfare. Around these scenes are running spiral motifs, similar to the relief work on the walls of the Treasury of Atreus (see below).

The best Bronze Age example of Mycenaean sculpture is the Lion Gate from Mycenae, dating to c. 1250 B.C.E. and standing 3.3 meters high (see Image 9.13). Here, above the main entrance to the citadel, we see two heraldic (turned to

9.14 Ivory Trio from Mycenae (Courtesy of Paul Butler)

each other in mirror image) lionesses, resting their forepaws on the base of a column that rises between them. The heads are no longer preserved, but socles in the necks show that the heads were attached separately, possibly facing outward to snarl at visitors. The lionesses' bodies do not have realistic anatomies, instead being compilations of geometric forms. Nevertheless, from the height at which they were placed, they would have given a sense of monumentality that certainly would have impressed the viewer below.

On a much smaller scale is a final excellent example of Minoan-Mycenaean sculpture, this time in ivory. This Ivory Trio (see Image 9.14) comes from Mycenae and dates to the Late Helladic IIIA/B. Standing only 7 cm tall, the image portrays two women in full Minoan garb seated next to one another and sharing a shawl. On their laps is a little boy with shaven head, typical of Minoan iconography. In spite of its tiny size, it is generally supposed that this figurine depicts deities, possibly Demeter and Persephonê with the child Ploutos ("Wealth") between them.

Dark Age

Large-scale sculpture like the lions at Mycenae disappeared for a while after the Bronze Age. During the Dark Age up until the seventh century B.C.E., Greek artists produced only small-scale sculpture, usually depicting women/goddesses, men/gods, or animals. Some of these styles were inspired by styles from the Near East.

The most blatantly Near Eastern of the Dark Age and early Archaic figurines were the so-called Nude Goddesses, which first appeared in Greece in the tenth century and became extremely popular in the seventh and sixth centuries. These images, seldom larger than 20 cm high, depict fully frontal views of nude or partially nude females. The females are sometimes wearing round hats and sometimes standing on lions; their arms are shown to the sides, holding the breasts, pointing to their breasts and genitalia, or pulling away a skirt to reveal the pubic triangle. Such figurines were made of ivory, bronze, or clay, with mould-pressed clay models becoming the most popular version during the Archaic period.

The earliest Nude Goddess figurines came to light in those regions of Greece that had the closest contacts with the Near East during the Dark Age—Attica and Crete (see chapter 4). Early on, they were placed in graves, like four famous ivory examples from the Athenian Kerameikos cemetery. Later, as the Greeks began transferring more of their wealth from graves to sanctuaries, Nude Goddess figures began to show up more frequently in sanctuaries as votives. By the seventh century, they appeared all over the Greek world, from Egypt in the south to Asia Minor in the north to Italy in the west (see Image 9.15). Various interpretations have been offered for these rather erotic-looking images, ranging from their use as washabti figurines (substitute wives buried with dead men) to prayers for pregnancy to depictions of Aphrodite. It appears more likely these images were seen as oriental exotica, used by the Greeks to flaunt their far-reaching connections outside the Greek world.

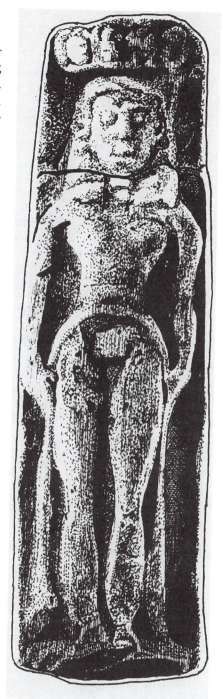

9.15 Nude Goddess from Kato Symi (Courtesy of Paul Butler)

In contrast to these exotic images, the Greeks also produced, mostly out of bronze, more "human" figurines, in which females were portrayed clothed and males were usually nude or wearing armor. Males were also sometimes accom-

9.16 Mantiklos Bronze (Courtesy of Paul Butler)

panied by horses, probably as a display of wealth and/or military service. Such figurines usually come to light in sanctuaries, possibly having served as votives. This is especially evident in one of the most famous early bronze figurines, the Mantiklos Bronze from Thebes, dated to 700–675 B.C.E. (see Image 9.16). This rather elongated nude male (20 cm high), broken off at the knees, has a dedicatory inscription running along both thighs reading: "Mantiklos dedicated me to the Far-Shooter with the Silver Bow from his tithe; grant, Apollo, something good in return" (Pedley 1998, 139).

Archaic

The real impetus for Greek large-scale sculpture came from Egypt, whence the Greeks adopted two new styles: the kouros and the korê, both of stone. The kouros ("boy") is a nude young male; the korê ("girl") is a clothed young female. The development of these styles was an excellent foil for the evolution of the Greek sculptors' skills through the Archaic Age and Classical period, in terms of both human anatomy (kouros) and the interplay of anatomy and drapery (korê).

The Kouros. This style showed a standing or striding male, arms held to the sides, fists clenched, with the left leg extended before the body. It therefore had an "active" look to it, with the "good" right side being more visible. Unlike Egyptian statues, which portrayed men in kilts, the Greeks sculpted their young men nude according to the Greek aesthetic. A good early example is the pair of kouroi known as Kleobis and Biton, who date to c. 590 B.C.E and stand 2.17 meters high. (see Image 9.17). The body is rigid, but the "striding" leg gives a sense of movement. The arms are close to the body, with the hands attached to the thighs. This design provided stability for the statue's limbs, decreasing the likelihood of breakage. Although some of the anatomical features are more or less realistic, such as the shoulders and biceps, the body on the whole has a geometric feel: the hair is a sheet of beads; the eyes are three-dimensional beads themselves; the pectorals and knees are sculpted scallops; and the abdomen, pelvis, and calves are gen-

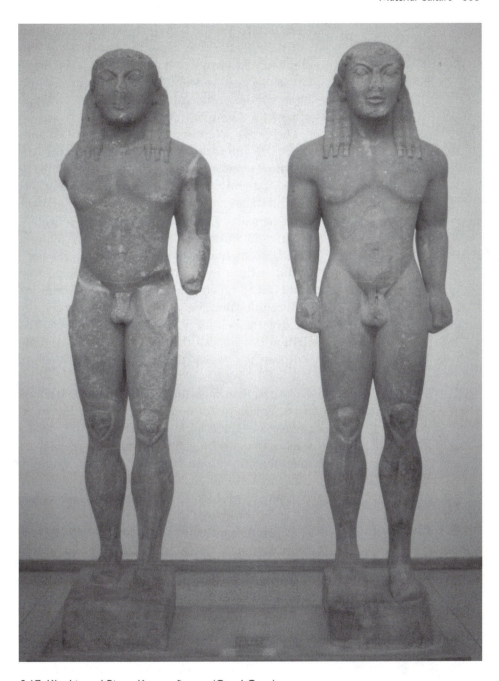

9.17 Kleobis and Biton, Kouros figures (Corel Corp)

tly curved lines. The sculptor clearly understood the general makeup of the male body but none of the underlying muscle structure.

This started to change at the end of the sixth century B.C.E. with statues like the Anavysos Kouros (sometimes called "Kroisos"), dated to c. 530 and standing 1.94 meters high (see Image 9.18). There is a rigidity to the striding body that is similar to Kleobis and Biton, and much of the hair still has that beaded

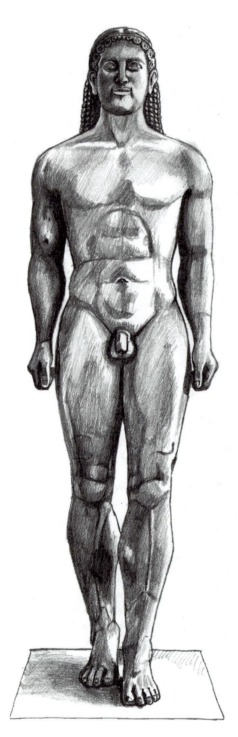

9.18 Anavysos Kouros ("Kroisos")
(Courtesy of Paul Butler)

look, but the contours of the body are more naturalistic, as is the face. Only the linear calves and elliptical abdomen retain the sense of "geometry." On the face is the so-called Archaic smile, a grin typifying all kouroi (pl. of kouros) and korai (pl. of korê) of the Archaic Age.

The Greek sculptors achieved an ideal balance of realism and idealism by 480 B.C.E. with the Kritios Boy, standing 1.17 meters high (see Image 9.19). A slightly more realistic look is given to its hair, although it is still composed of linear and circular elements. The anatomy is realistic, indicating an understanding of underlying musculature. Furthermore, the rigid, striding posture has been abandoned for the more graceful S-curve posture that typified much Greek male sculpture from the fifth century on. The hollow eyes were originally filled with shell for a more naturalistic look. The Kritios Boy marks the transition from Archaic sculpture to classical, discussed further below.

The Korê. As with the kouros, the korê derived from Egyptian influences. Like their Egyptian predecessors, the korai were clothed and, unlike the kouroi, they had static postures; the legs were together rather than striding. An early example was the Lady of Auxerre, dating to c. 640 and standing 65 cm high (see Image 9.20). Here we see the "row of boxes" hairstyle over an elliptical face. The breasts, waist, and arms have an almost naturalistic look to them, but the hands and feet appear to be composed of geometric designs, with squares and rectangles serving as toes and fingers. Furthermore, the lower body is hidden beneath a skirt covered with geometric designs that deny not only the body under the fabric, but the natural falls of the fabric itself.

One full-scale korê statue is the Nikandre statue, dating to c. 625 and standing 1.75 meters high. Its arms are similar to those of the kouros statues from this period, although the clothed body shows even less anatomical or naturalistic detail. Essentially, the statue looks like a woman's head on a tree stump. This tendency for shapelessness changed by 530 with the creation of the Peplos Korê, standing 1.21 meters tall (see Image

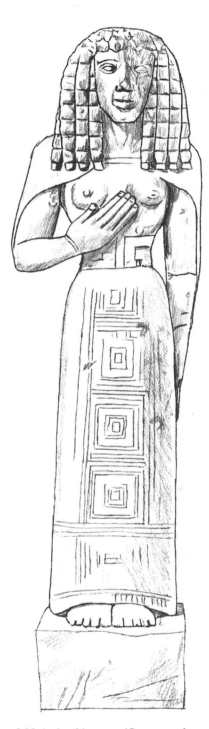

9.19 Kritios Boy (The Art Archive/Acropolis Museum Athens/Dagli Orti)

9.20 Lady of Auxerre (Courtesy of Paul Butler)

9.21 Peplos Korê (Courtesy of Paul Butler)

9.21). It has the typical Archaic face, including "goggle" eyes and the Archaic smile, but the hair, arms, and hands are more naturalistic than previous models. Furthermore, there is a sense of a body underneath the clothing, especially at the breasts, the waist, and the legs (visible as a groove in the skirt). Of particular interest are the traces of paint still visible on the face, reminding us that the Greeks originally painted all their sculpture.

The full development of the korê appears in what remains of the Euthydikos Korê, dated to c. 490 B.C.E. and standing 58 cm tall. The remains of this piece show naturalistic hair and facial features. The light draping of the dress reveals shoulders and arms that were sculpted with an understanding of the musculature. Even the overdraping mantle falling over the right shoulder does not obscure the underlying anatomy of shoulder, arm, breast, and torso. By the fifth century, then, the Greek sculptors had learned to reveal the female anatomy while still keeping the female modestly "dressed" for public display. Female nudity in public sculpture would not appear until the fourth century B.C.E.

Classical

During this period a new medium came to the fore in large-scale Greek sculpture. Although a variety of media, such as iron, ivory, and clay, were used for the smaller sculptures of early Greece, during the Archaic Age most sculpture was of marble, usually from the Penteli quarries of Athens or from the Cyclades, notably Paros. In the Classical period, bronze sculpture became prominent. For this medium, the artist carved the image in wax over a wooden frame. Then, a plaster cast was set over the wax, which was melted out of the plaster (thus the term *lost wax technique*). Melted bronze was then poured into the mould over an internal frame in a lighter material, resulting in a hollow bronze sculpture. Often, Greek bronze sculptures are preserved only in later Roman marble copies, as the bronze was eventually melted down for other uses.

Perfection of the human form was the ideal of Greek sculpture in the Classical period. The statues of men, women, gods, and goddesses created in this period showed a careful balance of naturalism and idealism, so that it looked as though the Greek world was filled with radiantly beautiful people all being seen from their "good side." Early fifth-century sculpture is dubbed the Severe style, as the statues have a lofty, unemotional, almost otherworldly look to them. The ultimate example of this is the Apollo from the Temple of Zeus at Olympia (see Image 9.26). Here is an ideal rendering of male anatomy, with every muscle present and accounted for, and the god stands with a slight S-curve in his posture. His face is calm and serene, casting an authoritative look at the event unfolding around him (which happens to be a wedding brawl involving drunken centaurs).

Later, in the fifth century B.C.E., the high degree of naturalism achieved in the kouros was combined with an interest in portraying the body in action (at least for males). Thus, the Greek sculptors created idealized statues of mortal men engaged in athletic activities. An excellent example is the Doryphoros ("Spear-Bearer") by Polykleitos, originally cast in bronze and now existing only in marble Roman copies (see Image 9.22). This sculpture, dating to c. 440 and standing 2.12 meters high, shows a full rendering of the male body with careful focus on the underlying anatomy. The torso has the typical S-curve, in which the hips are tilted in contraposition to the line of the shoulders, making the statue look as though he is casually leaning his weight on one leg. In reality, this stance is not quite possible, as the body's weight would actually fall onto the "relaxed" leg. The fact that such a stance appears both plausible and appealing in sculpture is a testimony to the talent of the Greek artists.

Greater changes occurred in the de-

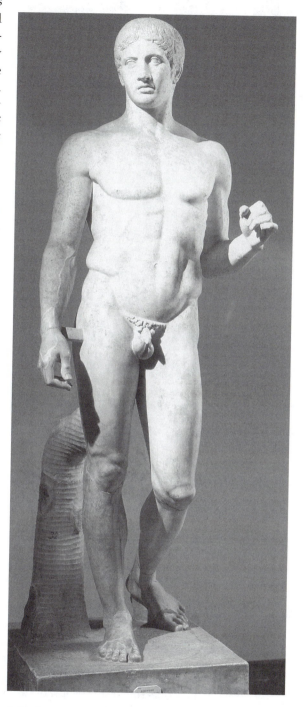

9.22 Doryphoros by Polykleitos (The Art Archive/Archaeological Museum Naples/Dagli Orti)

9.23 Nikê by Paionios (The Art Archive/Olympia Museum Greece/Dagli Orti)

velopment of female statues during the Classical period. In the fifth century B.C.E., Greek sculptors developed the "wet look" in statuary, in which the female's clothing is so transparent and snug against the body that the body is fully visible under the fabric. Perhaps the most famous example of this is the Nikê ("Victory") of Olympia, also known as the Paionian Victory after the sculptor Paionios of Mende (see Image 9.23). Here, the goddess Nikê alights from flight, her left foot just touching down upon Earth. One might imagine that the wind shear is blowing back her dress, which clings to her body, completely revealing her breasts, belly, and legs. Behind her, the diagonal alignment of her clothing gives the statue an added sense of movement and flight. So well executed is the statue that one hardly notices that the heavy cloth at the back of her dress does not match the light, clingy fabric on the front.

As visible as the female body was through the clothing, however, the Greeks still made a careful distinction between clothed and unclothed when it came to females. This was why the first nude female in Greek sculpture made such an impact. This was the Knidian Aphrodite, which the artist Praxiteles made for commission around 350 B.C.E. (see Image 9.24). According to the later Roman author Pliny (*Natural History* 36, §20):

Superior to anything not only by Praxiteles, but in truth in the whole world, is the Venus [Aphrodite], which many have sailed to Knidos to see. He had made two statues, and was selling them at the same time. The other one was of the clothed variety, and because of this the people of Cos preferred her, even though he had offered them for the same price, as they thought this was dignified and virtuous. The Knidians bought the rejected one, to far greater acclaim.

The nudity of the statue created quite a stir, such that Pliny went on to discuss men who actually tried to have sex with the statue in the sanctuary. Eventually, the Greeks got used to the idea of a nude sex goddess, and nude or partially nude images of her remained common in the Greek repertoire, such as the second-century Venus de Milo.

Hellenistic

Once the Greeks realized that they could portray the human (and divine) body to perfection, both as a static image and in motion, their next step was to create more realistic portraits, showing the human condition under less than ideal circumstances. One such example was the Dying Gaul, datable to c. 220 B.C.E. although now only known through Roman copies (see Image 9.25). Here, yet again, is an ideal portrayal of the male body, with hyperrealistic detailing of the musculature, skeletal structure, and even the flesh and a fatal wound. Realistic too are the details indicating the Celtic/Gaulish ethnicity of the subject: the torque (a solid, round neck ring favored by the Celts), the hair made spiky by application of limestone, and the full moustache. Only the subject's calm, quiet dignity in the face of death adds an idealizing element to the work, which the Greek artist clearly intended to show as the death of a noble enemy.

All the sculpture discussed above is sculpture in the round, with the exception of the Olympian Apollo. He is indicative of another style of sculpture in the Greek Archaic through Hellenistic periods—architectural sculpture. Instead of existing in the round,

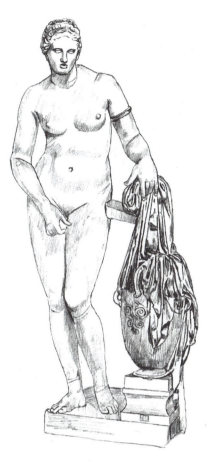

9.24 Knidian Aphrodite by Praxiteles (Courtesy of Paul Butler)

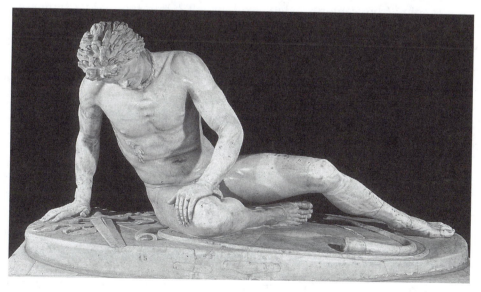

9.25 Dying Gaul (The Art Archive/Museo Capitolino Rome/Dagli Orti)

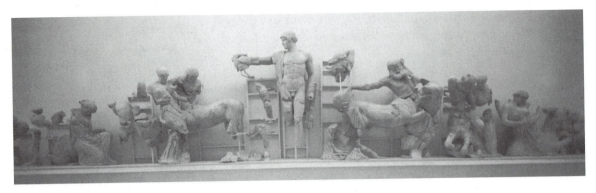

9.26 Temple of Zeus at Olympia, West Pediment (Vanni Archive/Corbis)

architectural sculpture decorated the metopes, friezes, and pediments of Greek temples and was therefore flat on the back. In general, architectural sculpture went through the same developments as sculpture in the round: Anatomy was gradually improved, human bodies went from geometric designs to naturalistic models, and clothing and drapery thinned out on females. Architectural sculpture presented an additional layer of complexity, however, and this was composition. In contrast to solitary statues, architectural sculpture usually told a story, such as the battle between the gods and Titans. This involved arranging several sculptures into a small space to produce an aesthetically pleasing yet coherent narrative.

On metopes, the artist usually showed a quick scene from a familiar story. Good examples come from the metopes of the Temple of Zeus at Olympia. These depicted the Twelve Labors of Heracles.

On pediments, the artist had to convey a narrative while simultaneously arranging all the characters coherently into a triangular space. On the west pediment of the same temple mentioned above, there is a clear hierarchy of figures ranging from center to edge (see Image 9.26). In the middle stands Apollo, calmly pointing to his right. On either side of him are men fighting inebriated centaurs who are trying to rape the women and youths in the scene. The figures closer to the edges are crouched or kneeling, giving a realistic sense to the scene while simultaneously allowing them to fit into the pediment's smaller space. In the corners are reclining figures portraying rivers or river deities, filling the smallest spaces and lending a geographic setting to the scene (i.e., showing that the action is located between rivers X and Y).

The friezes were arguably the easiest architectural sculptures to execute, as the artist had a continuous flat band on which to work. The only requirement was a scene that could fill up a long space. Both battle scenes and processional scenes fit the bill, as on the Procession Frieze on the Parthenon. Here, the Athenians are engaged in a long procession leading to the deities, who are seated at the crux of the procession. A young girl with a folded robe next to Athena identifies this scene as the Peplophoria, a ritual in which the Athenians presented Athena (or at least her cult statue) with a new dress. Not only did the frieze portray one of the most important religious festivals of the Athenian calendar, it depicted the Athenian people themselves as existing within the same space as the gods, advertising to all viewers that the Athenians were just a tad closer to divinity than everyone else.

POTTERY

Minoan

Fired pottery first appeared in Crete in the Neolithic Age, showing forms similar to those found in mainland Turkey. Distinctively Minoan styles appeared in the Early Bronze Age, notably Aghios Onoufrios Ware, Pyrgos Ware, and Vasiliki Ware, all named for the areas in Crete where they were first discovered. Aghios Onoufrios Ware had rounded shapes of light clay decorated with dark paint in linear designs. Pyrgos Ware came in clays of gray, light brown, or even red. Rather than having painted decoration, Pyrgos items were decorated with incised lines. By far the most interesting style from early Crete is the Vasiliki style (see Image 9.27). Jugs and "nose-heavy" teapots in this style are covered with a mottled pattern of oranges and browns. To date, archaeologists are not sure how the Minoan potters achieved this decoration.

In the Middle Bronze Age, a new style appeared in Crete, called Kamares Ware. Technological advances in the potter's wheel around this time allowed for much thinner pottery walls, leading to the term *Eggshell Ware* for this style. Decoration consisted of a dark paint applied to the entire surface of the item, which was then decorated with orange, red, and white paint in a variety of floral and geometric patterns. In some more elaborate instances, three-dimensional appliqués were added, giving an appearance that can only be described as tacky (see Image 9.28).

Two styles appearing in the Late Bronze Age represent, in this author's opinion, the apex of Minoan pottery. The earlier of these is called the Marine style, as the primary decorative motif is sea life, including octopi, seashells, nautili, and sea plants (see Image 9.29). These watery compositions were asymmetrical yet perfectly balanced, with compositions appropriate for whatever surface area needed to be covered, from stirrup

9.27 Vasiliki Ware (Kathleen Cohen/Herakleion Archaeological Museum)

9.28 Kamares Ware (Borromeo/Art Resource)

9.29 Palaikastro Octopus Vase (Scala/Art Resource)

jars for transporting oils to rhyta—ancient Minoan funnels. Following on the fins of the Marine style was the Floral style, in which vegetal motifs replaced marine ones (see Image 9.30). The Minoan love of naturalism was maintained in this style, including the use of asymmetry without ever sacrificing balance or grace. After 1450 B.C.E., the Mycenaeans adopted both the Marine and Floral styles, although with considerably less aesthetic success.

Helladic

The most important style of pottery to emerge from Early Bronze Age Greece was Minyan Ware, first discovered by Schliemann at the ancient city of Orchomenus and named after the city's mythical king Minyas. This style first appeared in Early Helladic III and is some of our best evidence that a new people arrived in Greece at this time, probably the Greeks themselves (see chapter 4). Minyan Ware came in two fabrics—gray and yellow—both of which had several shapes that were angular in overall appearance. It is likely that these items in clay replaced items in metal and that the angular, metallic shape was kept from the previous items. The most distinctive attribute of Minyan Ware is its soapy-to-the-touch feel.

From c. 1700 B.C.E. through the Late Bronze Age, Greek potters mostly followed Minoan potters in design and style, and thus much Helladic pottery resembles Minoan pottery of the same period. In contrast to the Minoans, however, the Bronze Age Greeks preferred repetition and symmetry in their art, as opposed to the more "flowing" Minoan compositions. For example, the Marine style, when translated into the Mycenaean style, showed small nautili arranged in a static, symmetrical pattern.

Although the Mycenaeans may have been dependent on the Minoans for pottery decoration, they did develop several new shapes of clay vessel. One of these was the Palace-style jar, which originally appeared in Greece around

1450 B.C.E. and thence at Knossos around 1400. These storage vessels measured around 80 cm high, with wide mouths for ease of access and handles for ease of transportation. The decoration of the Palace jars typified the relationship between Minoan and Mycenaean art: Both Marine and Floral styles appeared, but they tended to be symmetrical and static on the Mycenaean jars.

A second Mycenaean-style vessel was the goblet. In the fifteenth century, the Ephyrean goblet became popular, featuring a very deep cup, a short neck, two handles (a helpful feature, given how much wine they could hold), a round base, and a symmetrical motif on either side of the bowl. In later periods, the bowl became shallower, the neck lengthened, and the painted decoration became more stylized. Eventually, the bowl became almost flat, to the point that one might imagine a new generation of teetotalers. This long-necked, shallow-bowled Mycenaean goblet was the direct forerunner of the later Greek kylix.

9.30 Jug with Grass from Phaistos (Nimatallah/Art Resource)

A pictorial style featuring scenes of everyday life appeared at the end of the Aegean Bronze Age. The most famous example of this style is the Warrior Vase from Mycenae (see Image 9.31), on which a woman in a house is shown waving farewell to a line of men in armor, presumably heading off to war. This style was short-lived in Greece: Once the Bronze Age ended, representational painting on pottery mostly disappeared for centuries.

Protogeometric and Geometric

After the collapse of the Bronze Age, Greek pottery took a temporary turn for the worse, with the Subminoan and Submycenaean styles being particularly dowdy. Beginning in 1050 B.C.E., Greek pottery experienced a renaissance of sorts, with the creation of the Protogeometric style. This style, datable from 1050 to 900, is best represented by the amphora, a storage and transportation vessel with handles on either side of the neck or belly. During the Protogeometric period, these vessels were simply decorated with black paint on the bottom two-thirds of the amphora, and circles or semicircles on the shoulder. Other items decorated in this manner were the skyphos (drinking cup), the krater (a vessel for mixing wine with water), and the oinochoê (pitcher).

Around 900 B.C.E., the Greek painters began adding linear and geometric

9.31 Warrior Vase (The Art Archive/National Archaeological Museum Athens/Dagli Orti)

motifs to their pots, ushering in the Geometric period of Greek pottery. Early on, these pots were still mostly covered with the black paint typical of the Protogeometric, but the necks and/or bellies of the various vessels were decorated with a variety of motifs such as the meander, zigzags, triangles, and crosshatching. Over time, the geometric designs spread out to replace most of the black paint, so that the pottery came to be almost completely covered with decoration.

During the eighth century, a new motif was added to the decorative repertoire: humans. In some instances, little drawings of hunters or warriors would adorn the exterior of a small vessel, or dancing maidens might grace a container. The epitome of this style, and of Geometric pottery in general, is the amphorai (pl. of amphora) from the Dipylon cemetery in Athens. The most famous example is a 1.55 meter-tall belly-handled amphora dating to 750 (see Image 9.32). The majority of the body is covered with geometric patters; around the neck is a series of grazing antelopes. On the amphora shoulder is a prosthesis scene, in which a corpse is set upon a funeral pyre while men and women on either side of and below the pyre raise their arms in mourning. Such art was quite appropriate, as these large vessels were used as tomb markers.

Orientalizing and Corinthian

During the seventh century B.C.E., Greek artists were heavily influenced by eastern styles of art, especially what they saw produced by the Phoenicians (a

9.32 Dipylon Amphora (Wolfgang Kaehler/Corbis)

Semitic-speaking population originally inhabiting Lebanon, who spread out to colonize the majority of the Mediterranean). Motifs prevalent in Phoenician art included monsters and fantastic beasts such as sphinxes and griffins; rows of grazing or hunting animals such as deer and lions; nude goddess images in clay, ivory, and gold; and vegetal motifs such as flowers and trees. The Greeks adopted these images, most notably in the trading city of Corinth. Here the stark, black linear and geometric designs of the previous period were abandoned in favor of a more colorful and pictorial style. In the Protocorinthian period (up to 625 B.C.E.), jugs' exteriors were often divided into horizontal bands, each serving as the ground line for rows of natural and magical creatures. In more elaborate versions, entire scenes of battle, or mythological scenes, might appear (see Image 6.5).

Around 625, the full Corinthian style emerged. The style is easy to identify, first and foremost by its many colors. On a cream-colored background, black and red humans and beasts covered jugs, amphorai, trinket boxes, etc., the black and red figures themselves further detailed by incision (cutting) that showed up white after firing. Between the humans and animals covering the vessel were rose and flower motifs, giving the entire surface an extremely "busy" feeling.

Proto-Attic and Black Figure

The Orientalizing influence that brought about such dramatic changes in Corinth also had effects on Athenian pottery. Although less colorful than the Corinthian, and not yet making use of incision as a decorating technique, this Proto-Attic pottery was, at its best, lively and elaborate. The Athenian painters made minimal use of fanciful creatures such as sphinxes and griffins, although they came to adore another mythological beast—the gorgon. These monstrous females (of whom Medusa was the most famous) first appeared on the Eleusis amphora of 650 B.C.E. (see Image 9.33). Here were elements familiar from the Geometric and Corinthian periods, such as linear decoration on the handles and lip of the vessel, and floral decorations between figures on the body and neck of the vessel. New, however, were the depictions of mythological stories. On the body of the amphora, three gorgons chase the hero Perseus, who has just beheaded their sister. On the neck, Odysseus and his men blind the Cyclops Polyphemos, as related in the *Odyssey*. As would be standard in later styles, females were painted white and males were black, with only the faces of Odysseus, his men, and Polyphemos shown in a lighter shade.

This Proto-Attic style evolved into the Black Figure style during the late seventh and sixth centuries. Specifically an Attic innovation, Black Figure had characters such as men, women, deities, and animals painted in black upon a red background (see Image 5.2). Additional fine-tuning details were then added by incision, a process in which fine lines cut into the paint left white lines after firing. The skin of females (and often of the god Eros) was painted white, although this pigment was extremely delicate and more often than not flaked off. This Black Figure style was quite popular in the ancient Mediterranean, eclipsing the market in Corinthian Ware. Although this did lead to hostilities between Athens and Corinth (see chapter 4), it also led to the distribution of Black Figure pottery throughout Greece, Italy, and the colonies.

Red Figure and White Ground

Although Athenian painters achieved a high level of detail and realism with their Black Figure style, by 520 B.C.E., they managed to improve on this technique with a new style called Red Figure (see Image 8.13). Instead of painting black figures on a red background, they painted black backgrounds around characters who remained either the red hue of the pottery, or white in the case of females. A much greater degree of naturalism was possible with this technique, as well as a much greater degree of elaborateness. The earliest Red Figure images were on the "backs" of Black Figure vases, where the same scene was depicted on one side as Black Figure and on the other as Red Figure. Such vases are called Bilinguals. Red Figure proved to be the pinnacle of Greek vase painting and was used continually from 500 B.C.E. until well after the Roman conquest.

Even so, some variety was desirable, and a style called White Ground became popular

9.33 Eleusis Amphora (The Art Archive/Eleusis Museum Greece/ Dagli Orti)

in the fifth century. Here, the artist painted the vessel white, with the characters decorating the pot being delineated by fine lines of black paint and enhanced with soft shades of other colors (see Image 8.11). A similar style appeared during the Black Figure phase, but incorporating only black and white.

The main problem with this style was technological—the white paint was very delicate and tended to flake off easily. So the Athenian artisans limited its use to items that would not see too much action, especially pottery used in funerary ritual, such as the lekythoi (small jugs) used to pour perfumed oil onto graves. Lekythoi became the primary media of the White Ground style, and they were so common in funerary use that statues of White Ground lekythoi became common grave markers. Beyond their use in death ritual, such lekythoi are also now invaluable for the light they shed on women's lives in Classical Athens. As women were primarily responsible for funerary rites and rituals, it was usually women who brought such lekythoi (as well as floral garlands and libations) to the cemeteries. Athenian painters, knowing their market, directed the images on the lekythoi to women, decorating the vessels with scenes of women's daily lives. Thus, on these vessels we see pictures of women doing housework, raising their children, reading, talking with their husbands, and carrying out the funerary rituals for which they bought the lekythoi in the first place (see Image 9.34).

CLOTHING

We are fortunate to have several depictions of the Minoans and Mycenaeans preserved in frescoes and statuary, allowing us to see what they wore on a daily basis. The only regret is that the clothes themselves have not survived, so we are left to guess at the fabrics, although wool and linen were probably the most common materials.

Minoan

Minoan women's garb was quite elaborate (see Image 6.2). The upper body was covered with a short-sleeved, form-fitted bodice that revealed the breasts. The lower body was adorned with a flounced skirt that could be covered with an apron. A variation appearing on the Theran frescoes shows a young girl in what appears to be a short-sleeved bodice, but with the entire body covered in a thick wrap, knotted over one shoulder and descending to the floor. Necklaces, earrings, and bracelets were common.

Male costume, at least as portrayed in the art, was rather sparse. Young boys might appear nude or wearing only a belt. At a minimum, the adult males wore nothing but a penile sheath with accompanying dagger. Both Minoan and

9.34 White Ground Lekythos with Grave Scene (Courtesy of Paul Butler)

Egyptian frescoes show Minoan males wearing fuller kilts, perhaps as more formal attire. In cooler weather, a cloak covered the body. Like the women, men would sometimes wear jewelry.

Long hair seems to have been the norm for the Minoans, although children had their heads shaven so that only a few long tendrils remained (see chapter 6). Women wore their hair down or in a snood, depending on age. Older males may have had shorter hair, once again to judge from the Theran evidence.

Mycenaean

The Mycenaeans frequently copied their depictions of people, including their clothing, from the Minoans. Nevertheless, at least two facts distinguished the Mycenaean wardrobe from the Minoan. One was the cold: The Mycenaeans, especially the men, simply could not get away with the lightweight fashions of their southern neighbors. The second was what in modern times might be called a more modest view of the body, especially for women. The women of the Mycenaean frescoes, like La Parisienne at Knossos, wore straight tunics, in many ways foreshadowing the peploi and chita of the Classical period (see below). Otherwise, women might appear in Minoan garb, but with a "blouse" under the bodice to conceal the breasts.

Depictions of men are more numerous in the Mycenaean iconography. These men wore shorter tunics, once again probably of wool and/or linen, with elbow-length sleeves and flaring, knee-length skirts. A leather or woolen belt held the outfit together. Clay figurines occasionally showed men wearing pants, possibly for the very cold days in Arcadia. Also for the cold were heavy woolen cloaks, recorded in the Linear B tablets and fastened by cloak pins, which still survive (Vermeule 1972, 178–179).

Archaic and Classical Greece

For the Classical period, once again the most common fabrics were wool and linen. Cotton was originally domesticated in India and produced in Egypt as early as the sixth century B.C.E. It was not common in Greece, though, until the conquests of Alexander the Great, whose soldiers used cotton as pillow stuffing (Gullberg and Åström 1970, 17). Silk was originally cultivated in China but made its way west through Persia. Ionian women wore silk dresses, and apparently Cleopatra seduced Caesar wearing a transparent silk dress (Gullberg and Åström 1970, 17).

The textiles used for clothing could be elaborately decorated, as is evident in the vase paintings. Women did the spinning and weaving, although there was some variation as to who might dye the materials initially (see chapter 5). The preferred dye was Phoenician purple, made from the shells of the murex, a type of mollusk. Another popular color was yellow, made from saffron. Weaving was done from the earliest periods on warp-weighted looms (see Image 5.3). Loom weights have been found dating back into the Bronze Age, and often their shape and weight were indicative of the homeland of the women who used them.

There were two basic styles of women's dress. One was the Doric, in which a rectangle of cloth was wrapped as a tube around the body, going under the arms and hanging to the lower legs. Often the top was rolled down, so that there was a double layer of cloth over the upper body. Fibulai (large safety pins) fastened the fabric over the shoulders, and the whole garment was belted around the waist. This dress, called the peplos, was usually made of wool. Spartan girls wore a shorter version of this dress during athletic exercises.

The other style was an Ionic dress made of linen and called the chiton. Like the Doric style, it began as a large rectangle of fabric. Rather than being fastened with pins, however, the chiton was sewn above the arms, creating sleeves of sorts. Once again, the dress was belted at the waist, and hung down to the ankles or, more rarely, the knees.

Both dresses, but especially the chiton, could be covered by a himation (mantle). In sculptures this is often shown draped over one shoulder and hanging to the ground. The fact that women's clothing, in Athens at least, could be elegantly and elaborately layered is indicated by one of the laws passed by Solon (see chapter 7), who forbade women to wear more than three garments at a time when leaving the house.

Evidence from sculpture and vase paintings suggests that girls sometimes wore their hair long, but older girls and women usually wore theirs fastened up in a scarf. However, girls sometimes also wore flowers in their hair, if we are to trust Sappho, who says, "And you, O Dika, place about your tresses lovely garlands, binding together shoots of dill with your soft hands. For the blessed Graces look more on things adorned with flowers; they turn away from those ungarlanded."

As far as cosmetics go, the literature from Greece relates that women put lead on their faces to make their skin very white.

Men's clothing can be more difficult to study, as men were often portrayed nude in Greek art. We know that men did perform athletics in the nude, and our words *gymnasium* and *gymnastic* come from the Greek word *gymnô*, "to strip naked."

For more formal occasions, the Greek male wardrobe consisted of four main pieces: the exomis, the chiton, the himation, and the khlamys. The exomis looked very much like the modern conception of a toga. Starting as a trapezoid of fabric, the piece was pinned over one shoulder and belted at the waist. Traditionally, it fell to the knees (Losfeld 1991, 90–91).

The man's chiton was arranged like the woman's, except that it, too, usually fell only to the knees. A formal chiton, however, fell to the ankles and was worn for professional or religious purposes, such as by the priest in the Parthenon frieze mentioned above. The men's himation was also similar to the women's, being essentially a large rectangle of fabric that was draped around the body. Unlike the women, though, men could wear the himation without an undergarment. The himation could go so far as to cover the entire body, or it could be worn just around the waist almost like a sarong-skirt.

The khlamys was a cape originally developed in northern, horse-intensive Thessaly and was adopted by the rest of the Greeks only after the time of Alexander (Losfeld 1991, 176–177). This semicircle of fabric was pinned at the shoulder and could either hang down the back or, on cold days, be pulled completely around the upper half of the body (the lower body being warmed by the horse, no doubt).

To protect them from the hot sun, men also wore a light straw hat, called a petasos, featuring a round cap with a wide brim. A winged version was favored by Hermes.

ARMS AND ARMOR

Although the Minoans have acquired for themselves a certain "flower child" reputation, they were not totally without weapons. Specifically, the Minoans developed slender swords used mainly for thrusting. These bronze implements had the blade, tang, and hilt made as one continuous piece of metal, with a separate pummel and a handle of horn or wood (or, for the fancier sword, gold or silver) riveted directly to the tang (Oakeshott 1994, 27). Such armaments were more suitable for duel-style combat, possibly ritual (see chapter 6) rather than full-scale mêlé combat (Peatfield 1999, 68–70).

To judge from the remains in the shaft graves at Mycenae, the early Mycenaeans originally adopted these Minoan swords, but quickly adapted them to be more resilient in battle. They strengthened the tang/hilt region to decrease the possibility of breakage during cut-and-thrust fighting. Furthermore, they added flanges along the sides of the blade, to provide added protection for the wielder's hand (Snodgrass 1999, 16). Finally, the blade acquired a slightly leaf-like shape, with a central ridge for added strength. Such swords were far wieldier in combat than the Minoan versions (Oakeshott 1994, 32). Other than swords, the Mycenaeans of the shaft graves used heavy spears (of which only the heads remain); slender javelins; and arrows featuring tips of flint, obsidian, and even bronze.

For defense, the early Mycenaeans used two types of shield. One was the so-called figure-eight shield that they adopted from the Minoans. This shield, when seen from the front, had a figure-eight shape, although in 3-D it had an oval shape with the center sides "curled in" for carrying. Frescoes from this period show animal-hide patterns on these shields, suggesting that they were wooden frames on which animal hides were stretched. A second style was the tower shield, a large, rectangular construction consisting of either wood and hide as with the figure-eight shields or possibly an even lighter material, such as wicker. For the head, there were helmets made of rows of boars' tusks sewn onto a leather cap. Such helmets are mentioned by Homer, with one famous example belonging to Odysseus himself.

More for show than for fighting were the decorated daggers of the shaft graves and later times. These large knives had pictorial scenes on the blades, wrought in gold, silver, and niello (a thick, black, paste-like substance). Hunting scenes were especially common, in which hunters armed with spears stalked down large cats in scenery strongly resembling the banks of the Nile. For this reason, such scenes are called Nilotic. These blades were not at all practical, clearly intended to display the wealth (and possible pastimes) of the dead with whom they were buried.

Starting around 1450 B.C.E., a new fashion in defensive armor emerged:

9.35 Dendra Panoply from Midea
(Courtesy of Paul Butler)

bronze plate. The best example of this is a full panoply of armor discovered in a warrior's grave at Dendra (see Image 9.35). This had a full gorget for neck protection, pauldrons to cover the shoulders, and complete coverage down the torso to the hips, where the armor flared out for ease of motion. On the whole, it was heavy and probably did not allow for long, sustained combat, but it did offer almost full body protection (Snodgrass 1999, 21). Within the next century, new elements were added to the warrior's panoply, including a bronze helmet and, unique to the Greeks, bronze greaves, which protected the shins and ankles (Snodgrass 1999, 25).

By the end of the Bronze Age, the Greek arsenal once again reinvented itself. Two new styles of sword appeared at this time in the archaeological record. One was a short sword with a strong hilt and straight blade, which does not appear to have been longer than about 2 feet (Snodgrass 1999, 28). Far more important for the Mycenaeans was the arrival of a central European style of sword in Greece, the Naue II or Griffzungenschert sword (see Image 9.36). This solid-cast sword had a thick hilt onto which was riveted a wooden or bone handle. The nearly leaf-shaped blade had two thin relief ridges, which lightened the blade without sacrificing strength. The tip for thrusting, plus the double-edged blade for cutting, made this an excellent cut-and-thrust weapon, and it remained in the Greek repertoire for centuries (Hänsel 1988, 265).

A final piece of evidence concerning arms and armor at the twilight of the Bronze Age is the previously mentioned Warrior Vase (see Image 9.31), which depicts a row of warriors presumably heading out to battle. In contrast to heavy panoply like that from Dendra, these warriors are in light armor, consisting mainly of heavy cloth, metal greaves, and helmets with only one boar's tusk per man. They carry spears and rounded shields with an unusual scallop at the bottom. Assuming that the artist was painting from reality, then, we see a society where either lightness and ease of mobility were valued over full armor protection or bronze was more difficult to acquire, forcing the use of different materials for defense. Both are certainly possible. It is also possible that the Warrior Vase depicts a new style of fighting, which was to become far more prevalent and important in the Early Archaic Age: phalanx-style warfare, evolving eventually into the hoplite squadron (see chapter 6).

The Griffzungenschert sword that was so popular at the end of the Bronze Age remained a staple in the Dark Age, although now made in iron instead of bronze. During the Dark Age, however, spears became more important as of-

9.36 Naue II Sword (Courtesy of Paul Butler)

fensive weapons. At first, the spearheads, which were fastened onto a wooden shaft, were made of bronze, probably as the intricate shape was too difficult to hammer (iron could not be melted, but bronze could). In the Archaic Age, these would also be made of iron. The vase painting and archaeology from the time also attest to the importance of archery in the Dark Age. Eighth-century battlefields have turned up several bronze arrowheads, the only enduring part of an archery set consisting of a wood and horn bow with gut bowstring and arrows with wooden shafts and, presumably, feather fletching.

Perhaps the most important defensive item of the day was bronze armor, now of a kind far more sophisticated than the Dendra style. One nearly complete example comes from Argos. This shows a corselet (torso armor) fully fitted to the upper body, with the lines of the pectorals molded onto the front. The armor goes down to the lower waist, where it flares out, leaving the lower body free for maneuverability. The pelvis region was probably covered with leather, creating a sort of defensive kilt. A bronze helmet, possibly with horsehair decoration, covered the head. The remaining defensive armor was a bronze shield. An example of a shield from a soldier's tomb in Kaloriziki, Cyprus (Hellenized by this point in history), had a composite construction: The central boss and outer rim were of bronze, but the actual body of the shield no longer remains. This section clearly consisted of perishable materials such as wood or leather. A similar, if slightly smaller, shield was used by the Vikings.

The seventh century B.C.E. was the real renaissance of Greek arms and armor, constituting the so-called Hoplite Revolution. *Hoplite* comes from the word *hoplos,* which refers to the full panoply of armor used by a soldier in the field. This panoply consisted of a helmet, a chest plate, greaves, a shield, one to three spears, and probably a short sword.

The most famous early hoplite helmet was the Corinthian helmet, probably created in Corinth. This was a single piece of bronze hammered into a full head covering, including both nose guard and cheek guards, so that all that was exposed of the face was a T-shaped section for eyes and mouth. Hearing was definitely a problem in the Corinthian helmet, but otherwise it afforded complete protection. Later, other helmet styles evolved, including the Athenian, which was a head plate that covered the back of the neck but left the face mostly exposed, and the extremely practical Chalkidian helmet, which offered the full protection of the Corinthian helmet, but with less covering over the mouth and with cutouts over the ears, allowing for easier communication on the battlefield.

Vase paintings began to depict greaves around 675, although such armor had been in the Greek repertoire since Mycenaean times. The greaves of the Archaic Age were longer than those used previously, covering the leg from the upper knees all the way down to the ankles (Snodgrass 1999, 52–53). Such greaves, plus the helmet and thorax, or chest plate, comprised the basic hoplite armor. Remarkably, the Greeks appear to have had little sturdy protection for the groin (no iron cups have yet been found). This was certainly due to a need for mobility on the field, even though we know from the literature that the genitalia were a target in battle. The Spartan poet Tyrtaios relates, "For it is a shameful thing, really, for an older man having fallen in the midst of the van guard to lie before the youths, already having a white head of hair and a grey beard, breathing out his stout heart in the dust, holding his bloody genitals in his dear hands, and his naked flesh. These are shameful to the eyes and awful to see."

The shield was the most important item of the hoplite's accoutrements, and theirs was a shield that was truly revolutionary in construction. In contrast to the large, somewhat unwieldy Bronze Age shields and the lighter, more perishable Dark Age shields, the hoplite shield was both maneuverable and extremely durable. Probably first created in Argos, this shield consisted of strips of bronze over a wooden core, surrounded by a bronze rim. On the interior of the shield were two attachments. One was the porpax, or armband, which the Greek soldier hung on his arm. At the shield's edge was the antilabê, or handle. The porpax took the brunt of the shield's weight; the antilabê allowed for maneuverability. In later days, especially with the rise of strong civic identities, this shield often carried a device identifying the soldier, much as did the Medieval European devices.

The weapon of choice was the spear, and many spearheads have turned up in excavated battlefields and as dedications in sanctuaries. Some vase paintings show soldiers with two spears, one probably for throwing and the other for use at close range. A short sword would only be used as a weapon of last defense: If the phalanx broke up and the soldier was forced to fight at close range, the sword was an effective weapon, especially against a lightly armored opponent (see chapter 6). A new style of sword that became popular during this period was the falcata or kopis, a rather heavy, curved sword with an edge on the curve's interior. It was overbalanced to the tip of the blade, making it an effective slashing and hacking weapon (Snodgrass 1999, 97).

One interesting development in the fifth century B.C.E. was a renewed interest in archery, especially for long-range attacks. This interest probably derived from contacts with the East, especially with such archery masters as the Scythians of the Ukraine. Athenian plays make reference to such Scythians serving as a municipal police force, and Red Figure pottery shows "barbarians" on the field well equipped with an archer's paraphernalia. The Scythian archery set consisted of a gorytos (a quiver that could hold both arrows and the bow); hundreds of thin, light arrows tipped with bronze points; and a double recurve bow. Archers using such equipment could shoot both as infantry and from horseback.

The importance of the hoplite declined and ended under Alexander and his successors. Part of this was due to a renewed interest in cavalry, along with a greater interest in flexibility for impromptu movements, which the hoplite phalanx formations did not allow (see chapter 6). Under Alexander, the hoplites were replaced by the sarissaphoroi, or sarissa bearers, who fought with long pikes (sarissa) in battle alongside the cavalry (Snodgrass 1999, 119). Also novel was the armor, which, since the Dark Age, had grown consistently lighter. The full corselet of the Dark Age had been replaced by the thorax of the Archaic Age, which was now replaced by thick linen, leather, or scale armor. Scale armor consisted of a leather backing with sewn-on scales of bronze or iron. This armor was much lighter than the metal plate, allowing for greater speed and maneuverability on the field. Although it did not provide as much defense against direct blows, it was extremely effective against arrows, keeping the foot soldier safe from long-range attacks while the cavalry held off the heavier-armed fighters. Such scale armor first appeared in the Near East in the Bronze Age, once again probably for defense against arrows, and it was used minimally in Greece until the Late Classical period.

THE ART OF DEATH

Minoan Crete

Two styles of tomb were prevalent in Crete in the Early and Middle Bronze Age; they might be characterized as square and round. The square variety was more prevalent, appearing in different manifestations from Palaikastro to Gournes to Arkhanes to Mochlos. These were either square or oblong rooms, or a series of narrow rectangular chambers, arranged parallel to each other. Some scholars suggest that these square tombs should be regarded as house tombs, and that they served as houses for the dead.

Located only in southern Crete, in an area called the Mesará, were the round tholos tombs. These were slightly more elaborate in construction, combining a rubble core with a rock facing. The entrance was always to the east, probably in association with the rising sun. Whether or not these structures were roofed is still under debate. Inside, the structures had a slight corbel vault, meaning that the rocks came closer together as they rose above the ground. For large structures, the only way to secure such vaulting was with a capstone at the very top, meaning that the corbelling had to go all the way up. Such a roof has never been preserved among the tholoi of the Mesará, so it is impossible to tell if all their roofs have simply fallen in, if the corbelling went up only a short distance before being covered over by a reed roof, or if the tombs were simply left open to the sky. These structures were large enough for several burials, and they were used repeatedly over several generations, occasionally having the insides burned as a form of "housecleaning." The ultimate form of the tholos appeared much later and much farther to the north, when the Mycenaeans adapted the Minoan practice for their own nobility.

Bronze Age Greece

Before that occurred, however, the Bronze Age Greeks had their own styles of burial. Simple inhumations in cist graves generally served in the Early and Middle Bronze Age. A cist grave was a rectangular chamber dug into the ground and lined with slabs of rock to support the shape. A bedding of pebbles could line the floor, and the interred might be laid out in a crouched position, so that a smaller cist would suffice for burial. With the coming of the Mycenaeans (or at least their newfound wealth), a more elaborate style was used, specifically the shaft graves of Mycenae discussed in chapter 4. One might say that these were improved cist graves, in which the cist was deepened and enlarged to accommodate up to three people, and the walls were given additional supports to keep them from falling in upon the dead. Finally, the grave was roofed over with stone. Several such shafts are arranged together in Grave Circles A and B at Mycenae, with the circles themselves covered over with earth and the individual graves marked by sculpted stelai.

But for true ostentation, nothing beat the Mycenaean tholos tombs of the Late Helladic III period. These structures were the result of a natural evolution of the Minoan tholoi. Several smaller tholoi appeared in Greece during the Mycenaean period, all round, all with their roofs (these did have roofs) fallen in. But in the Late Helladic II, these structures took on monumental proportions. One of the later examples, the so-called Treasury of Atreus, for example, measured 15 meters in diameter and in height. The interior was entirely lined with sculpted stone and was originally decorated with gold wall ornaments. A separate, rectangular room jutted off from the circular tholos, where, past a door, the body was laid to rest. Grave robbers were prolific in the Bronze Age (and also in the Victorian era), and every attempt was made by the Greeks to protect the grave and its goods. Despite their attempts, however, nothing now remains of the treasure, but both the side chamber and the tholos were probably filled with elaborate grave goods.

Located 90° from the burial chamber was the tholos entrance, comprising a door almost 10 meters high capped off with a lintel stone weighing several tons. The entire portion of the tholos below the level of the lintel was dug into a hillside, along with a 36-meter-long dromos, or corridor, leading to the entrance. The face of the doorway, as well as the dromos walls, was lined with large, regularly cut, rectangular stones. Above the level of the lintel was the corbel vault, giving the tholos the nickname *beehive tomb,* as on the interior such corbel vaulting looked like a beehive. This kind of vaulting stayed in place through conflicting pressures—pressure that the cut stones placed on each other, and what the surrounding earth placed on them from above and around. For this reason, it was imperative that the vaulting be buried. If the ground above the capstone eroded away, the capstone eventually fell in, and the entire vault came undone.

On all the walls except the doorway, the corbelling was pretty much continuous from floor to capstone, so no one stone had to bear very much weight. This was not the case with the lintel, however, which had nothing below it for support. To relieve this stone (which is already quite heavy) of some weight, the Mycenaean architects developed the relieving triangle, a hollow triangle directly above the lintel. This triangle was covered with decoration, so as not to be visible from the outside. Of course, grave robbers inevitably knew it was there, and that was the main form of illicit access into the tholoi.

The treasury's façade was elaborately decorated with sculpted stone imported from Egypt and now on display in the National Museum in Athens. Then, once the entire complex was filled and finished, it was buried, so that only a hill was visible. One might call it a rather inconspicuous form of conspicuous consumption.

Dark Age

These grandiose shaft graves and tholos tombs of the Bronze Age were not used in later periods. For the next several centuries, the inhumations and cremations that sent the dead to their destinies did not involve architecture, but various styles of burial and sculptural memorials. The only exception is the Heroön of Lefkandi on Euboia, discussed in chapter 4.

One reason for the apparent decline in tomb expenditure was a changeover from inhumation to cremation during the Dark Age. This is especially evident in the Heroön at Lefkandi, where the "hero" was cremated and his ashes placed within a bronze jar, but the "heroine" was inhumed covered with gold. This change in funerary custom may originally have been dictated by the unstable conditions at the end of the Bronze Age, when large-scale architecture of any kind was uncommon. But it quickly became an important aspect of the heroic ethos recorded in the Homeric epics, and thus cremation came to be seen as a hero's funeral. The most famous example of this is the funeral of Patrocles in Book 23 of the *Iliad* (ll. 163–177):

> But those closest to Patrocles stayed and piled up the wood;
> they made a pyre 100 feet in both directions.
> And at the pyre's peak they cast the corpse with heavy hearts.
> And many fat sheep and rolling-gaited cows
> they flayed and dressed before the pyre, and collecting the fat from them all
> great-hearted Achilles covered the corpse with it
> from head to foot; he heaped the flayed bodies about him.
> And there he set two-handled jars of honey and olive-oil,
> leaning them upon the bier; and four horses with arching necks
> he eagerly cast onto the fire, groaning mightily.
> Nine table-fed dogs belonged to kingly Patrocles;
> he cut the throats of two of these and cast them onto the fire.
> And twelve fine sons of the great-hearted Trojans
> he cut down with bronze—evil works plotted in his mind.
> And the iron force of the fire he released to devour them.

The next day (ll. 161–177):

> First they quenched the pyre with shining wine,
> as much as the flame had covered it; the ash feel deep.
> Mourning, they gathered up the white bones of their gentle comrade
> in a gold urn with a double layer of fat,
> and placing this in his tent they covered it over with a smooth cloth.
> They rounded out the barrow and established its base
> around the pyre. Forthwith they heaped up a mound of earth
> and so doing they went home.

Archaic and Classical

The elaborate sacrifices that accompanied the funeral, especially the twelve Trojans, were not replicated in Iron Age burials. Nevertheless, until the eighth century B.C.E., burials could be very lavish. Traditionally, the body was burned on a pyre, which was quite expensive in a non-tree-intensive region such as Greece. Afterward, the remains of the body were placed in an amphora, neck-handled for the men and belly-handled for the women. This amphora was then filled with personal artifacts and covered with a bowl. The covered amphora was placed into the ground, possibly with yet more artifacts and goods, before the whole collection was buried. Early grave markers were often pottery jars, sometimes another amphora, or, for the men, large kraters (bowls used for mixing wine with water). Such receptive vessels were particularly important for the grave, as they could receive the libations to the dead brought by the family after the funeral.

As discussed in chapter 4, such conspicuous consumption moved from the grave to the sanctuary during the eighth century B.C.E., although even as late as the sixth century, Solon of Athens had to establish laws limiting the amount of money families could spend on funerals. The interred could have no more than a rounded stone bearing his or her name, father's name, and deme (the "neighborhood" to which one belonged as a citizen). According to Plutarch, the Spartans buried their dead with no markers at all, except for soldiers who died in battle and women who died in childbirth.

By the mid-fifth century B.C.E., a new desire sprang up in Athens to commemorate the dead with sculpted monuments. These often portrayed an idealized version of the departed, along with an inscription mentioning the individual's name, patronymic, and deme, as well as a few words of remembrance composed by the dedicator. One such stele dating from c. 400 B.C.E. and executed in pristine Classical style was the grave stele of Hegeso from the Kerameikos cemetery (see Image 9.37). Here, the departed sits upon a chair examining the contents of her jewel box; a painted necklace that no longer survives would have been hanging from her upturned fingers. Before Hegeso stands a young maid, probably Hegeso's serving girl. The fine quality of the chair, the jewelry box, and the servant all attest to Hegeso's wealth in life, thus, along with the elaborate monument, doubly flaunting the wealth of her family. Such lavish funerary displays were outlawed once again at the end of the fourth century in Athens.

It was in the fourth century B.C.E. when funerary expenditure once again gained (literal) ground in the Greek world. Specifically, this was when large-scale architecture was applied to tombs. The most famous example was the fourth-century funerary monument of King Mausoleus of Halicarnassus (modern Bodrum) in southwestern Turkey, whose tomb—the Mausoleum—was one of the Seven Wonders of the Ancient World. Unfortunately, nothing now remains of this monument except a very large hole in the ground, and opinions range widely concerning the building's appearance when it existed.

The most impressive burial complex to arise since the Mycenaean tholoi was the Great Tumulus of Vergina in Macedonia, located at the western edge of the so-called Tumulus cemetery and measuring 110 meters in diameter (Touratsoglou 1996, 221). Within this mound were no fewer than three royal tombs. The largest of these was the so-called Tomb of Philip II, which measures 8.12 meters long by 4.46 meters wide by 5.3 meters high. The tomb's façade resem-

9.37 Hegeso Stele (Instructional Resource Corp.)

bles a Doric temple, only instead of a pediment there was a painted frieze above the entablature. The façade's painted decoration has been preserved marvelously (because it was buried), allowing not only a glimpse of what the structure looked like back in the fourth century, but also an idea of how colorful many of the Greek temples must have appeared.

The tomb's interior is vaulted and consists of two chambers, an antechamber of sorts, and a "main room." Within the antechamber was a marble ossuary (box for bones) containing a gold box, which held burned bones wrapped in gold and purple cloth and topped by a lovely wreath of gold leaves. On the floor were several gold items, including an arrow quiver and a pair of greaves. The "main room" contained another ossuary with another set of bones, also wrapped in gold and purple cloth within another gold chest. Around the room were the burial goods, including an iron cuirass and helmet, bronze and ceramic vases, a sword with ivory handle, a shield, and ivory decorations from a piece of furniture that no longer remains. It is evident that whoever was buried in this tomb engaged in a martial lifestyle and was proud of it.

REFERENCES

Branigan, K. 1988. *Pre-Palatial: The Foundations of Palatial Crete: A Survey of Crete in the Early Bronze Age.* Amsterdam: Adolf M. Hakkert.

Coldstream, J. N. 1977. *Geometric Greece.* Cambridge, UK: Cambridge University Press.

Dickinson, O. 1994. *The Aegean Bronze Age.* Cambridge World Archaeology. Cambridge, UK: Cambridge University Press.

Gullberg, E. and P. Åström. 1970. *The Thread of Ariadne: A Study of Ancient Greek Dress.* Studies in Mediterranean Archaeology XXI. Göteborg: Paul Åströms Förlag.

Hänsel, B. 1988. "Catalogue." In *The Mycenaean World: Five Centuries of Early Greek Culture 1600–1100 B.C.* Athens: National Archaeological Museum.

Kilian, K. 1988. "Mycenaean Architecture." In *The Mycenaean World: Five Centuries of Early Greek Culture 1600–1100 B.C.* Athens: National Archaeological Museum.

Ley, G. 1991. *A Short Introduction to the Ancient Greek Theater.* Chicago: University of Chicago Press.

Losfeld, G. 1991. *Essai sur le costume Grec.* Paris: Éditions de Boccard.

Oakeshott, E. 1994. *The Archaeology of Weapons: Arms and Armor from Prehistory to the Age of Chivalry.* New York: Barnes & Noble.

Peatfield, A. 1999. "The Paradox of Violence: Weaponry and Martial Art in Minoan Crete." In Laffineur, R., ed. *Polemos: Le Contexte guerrier en Égée à l'Âge du Bronze.* Liège, Belgium: Université de Liège, 67–75.

Pedley, J. G. 1998. *Greek Art and Archaeology.* 2d ed. Upper Saddle River, NJ: Prentice-Hall.

Preziosi, D. and L. Hitchcock. 1999. *Aegean Art and Architecture.* Oxford: Oxford University Press.

Snodgrass, A. M. 1999. *Arms & Armor of the Greeks.* Baltimore: Johns Hopkins University Press.

Touratsoglou, I. 1996. *Macedonia: History, Monuments, Museums.* Athens: Ekdotike Athenon.

Vermeule, E. 1972. *Greece in the Bronze Age.* Chicago: University of Chicago Press.

Waterhouse, H. 1990. "Middle Minoan Houses." In Krzyszkowska, O. and L. Nixon, eds. *Minoan Society.* Bristol, UK: Bristol Classical Press, 323–346.

CHAPTER 10
Intellectual Accomplishments

This is the only chapter in this book that will not touch upon the Bronze Age. This is not because the Bronze Age Greeks had no literature, science, or philosophy. Quite to the contrary; the divine names in the Linear B texts suggest a full pantheon ripe with mythic content, just as the fabulous items of gold, silver, and bronze from that era show great familiarity with aspects of metallurgy. Likewise, the lavish funerary architecture and the vast supplies furnishing the tombs of the rich and famous hint strongly at an elaborate conception of the afterlife, thus of humanity's place in the cosmos.

The problem is that none of this has been recorded for us. The Linear B tablets that tell us the names of the deities do not record the actual myths associated with these deities. Although we know that bronzesmiths understood the working of copper and tin, we have no way of knowing *why* they thought these metals combined as they did to produce arms and armor. And although we may look at possible parallels in Egypt or the Levant to try to understand what the Bronze Age Minoans and Greeks believed the afterlife to be like, we have none of their own words to describe their view of these concepts. In short, we have no extensive writings, the only real means for understanding the mental workings of a society—the workings expressed through literature, science, and philosophy. The fact that this chapter begins with Homer instead of Minos does not imply that the Minoans and Mycenaeans had no intellectual accomplishments, only that they failed to record them in a way available to a twenty-first-century public.

LITERATURE

Early Epics: Homer

Greek literature begins with Homer, a semimythic, supposedly blind poet who composed the *Iliad* and the *Odyssey,* both several thousand lines long and composed in dactylic hexameter (see sidebar on meter). The *Iliad* records a brief episode in the last year of the Trojan War, when "The Best of the Achaeans," Achilles, got into a spat with the "King of Men," Agamemnon, over the woman Briseis. Infuriated that Agamemnon took Briseis from him, Achilles refused to join his comrades, the Greek army, in battle, while simultaneously asking the gods to give extra strength to the Trojans. The Greeks—called Achaeans, Argives, and Danaans—suffered so terribly at Trojan hands as a result that Achilles's close friend Patrocles finally disguised himself as Achilles to frighten off the enemy. Unfortunately, in so doing, he was mistaken for Achilles and was killed by the best of the Trojans—Hector. This angered Achilles even more than the loss of Briseis; he reentered the war and killed Hector, thus eventuating his own death beneath the walls of Ilion, another name for Troy.

The *Odyssey* tells the story of the king and hero Odysseus and the trials he suffered on his way home from Troy, a ten-year journey. On his way home, Odysseus met with giants; Cyclopes (see Image 9.33); Sirens; the goddess Circê, who turned his crew into pigs; the goddess Calypso, who wanted to marry Odysseus; and the Phaiakians, a blessed population who lived at the edge of the civilized world. He even traveled to Hades to meet with the great prophet of Thebes, Teiresias. Arriving on Ithaca, his home island, Odysseus had to rid his palace of several dozen suitors who had been courting his wife Penelope and eating him literally out of house and home. Through all this, Odysseus had to rely on his wit and perseverance, and occasional help from his patron goddess, Athena.

For years, the study of these epics focused on two problems: When were they composed, and how? The question of when became especially acute once Schliemann discovered that places such as Troy and Mycenae actually existed (see chapter 3), showing that the epics had some basis in historical fact. The problem was that, although the epics seemed to be primarily Bronze Age in feel, some of the details were clearly from a later date. References to iron, for example, simply could not have originated in a strictly Bronze Age composition. However, many of the details, such as the importance of the "capital" city of Mycenae, not only were inaccurate after the Bronze Age, but they would have been unknown after the Dark Age, by which time Mycenae was little more than a shantytown with some old walls. When, then, could the stories have been composed so as to take into account cultural facts from so many periods?

Even before the issue of historicity arose, though, there was an interest in how the poems came into being. As discussed in chapter 3, the Iron Age Greeks did not adopt a writing system until the eighth century (in fact, some people have suggested that writing was specifically adopted to record the Homeric epics). As at least some of the Homeric poetry derives from the Bronze and Dark Ages, it is generally agreed that the poems were not originally written down, but were composed and performed orally. How, then, could one individual remember so much poetry off the top of his (or her) head? And was Homer one individual, or a composite of several composers, or maybe the last in a long line of composers?

For a long time, the debate was dominated by two schools: the Unitarians and the Analysts. The Unitarians believed that the *Iliad* and the *Odyssey* were the work of one extremely gifted poet. The Analysts suggested that both were composed by several poets, only one of whom might be dubbed the mythic Homer (Schein 1984, 10).

But in the early twentieth century, Milman Parry and Albert Lord conducted field research in one of the few closely related places where an oral epic tradition still thrived—Yugoslavia (Lord 2000, passim). Parry and Lord discovered

A Note on Meter

Meter refers to the rhythm of a poem, how it might sound if it were sung. For English poetry, meter refers to where the stresses fall in a line. Thus, in a limerick, we say: There ONce was a WOMan from BOSton.

By contrast, ancient Greek meter was based not on stress but vowel length, so you might say: There ooooonce was a wooooman from Booooston.

The ancient Greeks had several different meters that they used when composing poetry. Each meter was identified based on the pattern of long and short syllables in a line and how many "feet" there were to a line. For example, a common early meter was dactylic hexameter, in which Homer and Hesiod composed their epics. *Dactylic* means that vowel length consisted of a long-short-short or long-long (with two shorts equaling one long, or spondee) pattern. *Hexameter* means that each line of poetry contains six (*hex-*) "feet," each foot being one of those long-short-short or long-long combinations. Thus, in rhythm, a line of Homeric poetry went something like:

— ∪ ∪, — ∪ ∪, — —, — —, — ∪ ∪, — x

Long-short-short, long-short-short, long-long, long-long, long-short-short, long-either

The last foot was generally shorter than the rest. This modern, stress-based, English example of dactylic comes from "In Spring" by e. e. cummings:

— ∪ ∪ — ∪ ∪ — ∪ ∪ — ∪ ∪ — ∪ ∪ — ∪ ∪ —∪∪ —

sweet spring is your time is my time is our time for sweet spring is love time and viva sweet love!

(Read it out loud and you'll get the sense of it.)

All the Greek meters were made up of series of specific long-short combinations, arranged into a certain number of feet. Some different combinations were:

Iamb: x — ∪ — (remember, "x" means either long or short)
Trochee: — ∪ — x
Cretic: — ∪ —
Bacchiac: ∪ — —
Lekythion: — ∪ — x — ∪ —
Ithyphallic: — ∪ — ∪ — —
Dactyl: see above
Anapest: — ∪ ∪ — ∪ ∪ or ∪ ∪ — ∪ ∪ —
Ionic: ∪ ∪ — —
Choriamb: — ∪ ∪ —
Anaklast: ∪ ∪ — ∪ — ∪ — —
Diochmiac: x — — ∪ —

(continues)

A Note on Meter (continued)

Glykonic: x x — ∪ ∪ — —
Pherekratean: x x — ∪ ∪ — —
Hipponaktean: x x — ∪ ∪ — ∪ — —

Each of these rhythms could be combined in a number of feet to produce different meters, each seen as appropriate to certain types of poetry (for example, you probably wouldn't compose a love poem in limerick meter, unless your sweetheart had a really good sense of humor). Epic poetry, for example, was composed in dactylic hexameter, as discussed above. By contrast, much tragedy and comedy were composed in iambic trimeter (three feet), which went thus:

x — ∪ — | x — ∪ — | x — ∪ —.

Noting the type of long-short combination and the number of such combinations (feet) in a line is how all ancient Greek poetry is categorized.

The modern convention of showing translated (and even the original Greek) poetry as broken up into stanzas and lines is accomplished through the proper understanding of meter. As with all original Greek texts, such as the papyri from Egypt, Greek poetry was written in lines as long as the papyrus would allow, all in capital letters. There were no "lines" of poetry as such. It is only by understanding and expressing the meter that ancient Greek poetry is broken up into the lines and stanzas typical of traditional European poetry. All poems quoted in this text have been subjected to this modern interpretation.

REFERENCES

Barnstone, W. 1988. *Sappho and the Greek Lyric Poets*. New York: Schocken.
Halporn, J. W., M. Ostwald, and T. G. Rosenmeyer. 1994. *The Meters of Greek and Latin Poetry*. Indianapolis, IN: Hackett.
Lesky, A. 1996. *A History of Greek Literature*. Indianapolis, IN: Hackett.

that oral epic creation was a combined process of learning stories and memorizing formulae in the appropriate meter. So, the young, would-be poet (usually someone who was illiterate and seldom a poet by trade) would spend several years of his/her youth listening to elders recite the great epics. From this, the poet would at least learn the tales, just as modern children learn about Cinderella and Peter Pan. But more importantly, the poet would learn what Parry and Lord called the formulae: groups of words, possibly even as long as entire lines, that were in the appropriate meter and that could be combined in various ways to narrate a story (much like the way limericks always seem to begin with "There once was a . . ."). What this means is that the poet did not have to memorize a poem verbatim (hardly possible, anyway, with the length of the poems in question). He/she merely learned the plot, and then combined the formulae to tell the story in the appropriate poetic form. As such, there was no one standard form of any epic; in each recitation, the epic poem was created anew—an eternal re-creation.

This discovery answered many questions about the Homeric epics. The time range perceptible in the verses was attributed to changes that occurred in Greek society over the centuries when the epics were being re-created. The hypothesis of there being one single artist—Homer—was abandoned in favor of the Parry-Lord model, with possibly one fellow named Homer who popularized the tales just before they were written down.

This act of writing down crystallized the epics—turned them from mutable, oral poems into "authoritative texts." Perhaps Homer dictated this finalized version, giving his name to epics that had been in existence for centuries before he was born. This writing down probably occurred in the eighth century B.C.E. Although there are several elements in the epics that clearly belong to the Bronze and Dark Ages, many references seem appropriate for the dawn of the Archaic Age, and there is little in either poem that suggests a later date. Thus, although some have argued that the poems may have to be down-dated to as late as the sixth century, it is generally accepted that the *Iliad* and *Odyssey* began being written down somewhere between 750 and 700 B.C.E.

The Epic Cycle

The *Iliad* and *Odyssey* were only two, although apparently the best, of a series of epics recounting the lives of the gods and the events surrounding the Trojan War. Unfortunately, these other poems no longer exist and can only be vaguely reconstructed through references in other poems, such as the *Iliad* and *Odyssey*, and through commentaries written about them during the Hellenistic period and after. According to a quote preserved in the writings of Photius (see chapter 3), the Epic Cycle dealt with everything from the marriage between Heaven and Earth through the death of Odysseus (Lesky 1996, 79). Arranged chronologically according to subject, the first are the three Theban epics—the *Oedipodea*, the *Thebaid*, and the *Epigoni*. The *Oedipodea* was some 6,600 lines long and was attributed to a man named Kinaithon. It recounted the story of Oedipus (Oidipous), his murder of his father, and his ill-fated marriage to his mother. The *Thebaid*, possibly written by one Kallinos, told the tale of Oedipus's family, from Oedipus's curse on his sons Eteocles and Polyneices to the death of both in the battle of the Seven Against Thebes (referred to often in the Homeric epics). The city of Thebes is finally seized in the next generation according to the *Epigoni*, which Herodotus somewhat dubiously ascribed to Homer (Lesky 1996, 80–81).

The *Kypria*, composed by Stasinos, Hegesias, or possibly Hegesinos, tells in eleven books the story of the Trojan War before the events of the *Iliad*: the meeting of Helen and Paris, their escape to Troy, and Menelaus's attempt to negotiate a return and settlement. In mythic time, the *Kypria* is followed by the *Iliad*, which itself is followed by the five books of the *Aithiopis*, ascribed to one Arctinus of Miletos. This poem deals with the final exploits of Achilles, his fight with the Amazon Penthesilea, his fight with Memnos—son of the dawn goddess—and his final death at the hands of Paris and Apollo. All of this is followed by Arctinus's second poem, the *Iliu Persis*, or *Sack of Troy*, in which the final days, and eventual destruction, of Ilion are recorded. An alternate version, attributed to Lesches or Kinaithon, is recorded in the so-called *Little Iliad*.

The *Odyssey* is but one narrative in the general collection of homecoming stories that took place after the fall of Troy. These tales are called Nostoi ("Homecomings") and were composed either by Homer or by Hagias from Troizen. The final poem in the Epic Cycle is the *Telegonia*, which is a continuation of the *Odyssey*. Part of this tale is foreshadowed in the *Odyssey*, when Odysseus must go on a final journey to placate the wrath of Poseidon. Odysseus is killed by Telegonos, his son with Circê (not mentioned in the *Odyssey*). In the end, Penelope, Odysseus's widow, marries Telegonos, and Circê marries Telemachus—Odysseus's son with Penelope (Lesky 1996, 82–83).

Early Epics: Hesiod

Unlike the amorphous character of Homer, Hesiod was a historically verifiable person who did, single-handedly, compose and probably write his own poems (although to what extent he was influenced by a tradition like the Yugoslav one is hard to tell). He has two main epics, the *Theogony* and the *Works and Days*, and two lesser works, the *Shield of Heracles* and the *Catalogue of Women*. Like Homer's works, these are composed in the "Epic Meter"—dactylic hexameter.

From what we can tell from his poetry, Hesiod's father originally came from a town called Cymê on the west coast of Turkey. Trying his luck as a traveling merchant, he was a spectacular failure and ultimately settled down in the village of Askra in Boiotia (*Works and Days* 633–640):

> As indeed my father and yours, greatly foolish Perses,
> used to sail off in ships, lacking a good life.
> He then came to this place, having crossed a large stretch of sea,
> leaving Aiolian Cymê, in a black ship,
> not fleeing riches nor wealth nor joy,
> but evil poverty, which Zeus gives to men.
> He settled by Helikon in a wretched village,
> Askra, evil in winter, painful in summer, never pleasant.

It is difficult to tell whether Hesiod had always wanted to be a poet. According to his poems, he started out as a farmer (*Works and Days*) and a shepherd (*Theogony*). While he was engaged in this latter activity, the nine Muses (see chapter 8) came to him from Mt. Helikon. First they verbally abused him ("Oaf! Nothing but a belly!"); then they inspired him to sing of gods and men.

He sang of gods in the *Theogony*. The poem's main theme is the rise of all creation, from the first four primordial gods, Chaos, Earth (Gaia), Love (Eros), and Hell (Tartarus), to the generation of the entire divine family with Zeus as its king, and the eventual creation of women. This is discussed in detail in chapter 8.

The *Works and Days,* less grandiose in scope, is a didactic poem discussing the appropriate way to run a farm. Poetry was used for composition long before prose, and such "how to" manuals were originally written in verse. The pretext for this manual was the legal debate between Hesiod and his brother Perses over their father's land after his death. After encouraging Perses to be fair and honest about the proceedings, Hesiod discusses how and when to raise crops and livestock, and how generally to be economically prosperous. Dotted throughout this text are bits of insight and philosophy. For example, Hesiod mentions that there are two goddesses of strife—both named Eris. The one is nasty, and she provokes hatred and wars among men. But the beneficial Eris promotes healthy competition, causing men to be their best through direct competition with one another (one might think of her as the patron goddess of capitalism).

The Homeric Hymns

The last set of poems in the epic style, although much shorter, is the Homeric Hymns. Because of their meter and vocabulary, they were originally attributed to Homer, thus the name. Since then, however, it has been determined that they are actually later in date than the *Iliad* and *Odyssey.* The Hymns are tales and praises of different deities. Some are long and tell full stories; others are short and refer to the awesome powers and beneficence of the gods. The poems appear to have been composed by traveling rhapsodes, or poets, who, to judge from the evidence of the poems themselves, recited their poetry in competition with each other. Even Hesiod claimed once to have traveled to Chalkis to compete in a poetic competition at a funeral. The peripatetic (itinerant) nature of such performers is shown in the *Homeric Hymn to Apollo,* in which the rhapsode sings (ll. 166–175):

> Greetings to you all; and afterwards remember me,
> whenever someone of earthy humanity,
> a wandering stranger, coming here asks:
> "O Maidens, what man was most sweet in singing to you,
> who wandered along here and in whom you took greatest joy?"
> "A blind man, dwelling in craggy Chios.
> All his songs ever after are the best!"
> And we shall carry forth your glory, wherever
> upon the earth of mortals we should roam,
> to well-inhabited cities.

Lyric Poems

The term *lyric* (from Greek *lyrikos*) was first coined in the Hellenistic period to describe poetry that was sung, usually accompanied by a stringed instrument such as the lyre (Lesky 1996, 108). It appears that such poetry consisted not merely of song and music, but dance as well (much like traditional flamenco), and that this combination of voice, music, and movement was used in religious rituals. Such was the case with another form of Greek poetry—drama (see below).

By the time this poetry was written down starting in the seventh century B.C.E., two distinct forms of lyric existed: choral and monody. Choral, like modern choruses, was sung in groups. Monody (*mono* = one, *oidos* = song) was what we might think of as a more traditional song, sung by one individual in one voice. There were subdivisions within these two categories, based on what each poem was meant to express. For the choral category, there was the threnos, a dirge for the dead; the hymnaion, a wedding song; the prosodion, a processional song; the paian, originally a hymn to Apollo but later a hymn to other gods as well; and, one of our earliest recorded forms, the parthenaion, or maiden song, sung by choruses of young girls in competition. In the sixth century B.C.E., the epinikion and enkomion were added, poems that praised athletic victors and their families (Barnstone 1988, 3). Back in ancient Greece, having such a poem written about one by a great poet such as Pindar was great public recognition.

All choral pieces had certain common characteristics. The first was use of elaborate language, with elements of the Doric dialect (see chapter 6). The poems were arranged in series of paired and metrically identical stanzas, one spoken by one half of the chorus—the strophe, and the other by the other half—the antistrophe. Finally, all choral odes had certain consistent features of content. First, there was a myth retold or referred to. Then, there was an opinion or maxim, the gnomê. Finally, there was the personal element, in which the dead was remembered or the victor hailed (Barnstone 1988, 4; Lesky 1996, 148–149).

According to Hellenistic scholars, the great choral poets were Alcman, Stesichorus, Ibycus, Simonides, Bacchylides, and Pindar (Lesky 1996, 108). Alcman, who lived in the mid-seventh century B.C.E., is the earliest for whom we have recovered any written poetry. He is most famous for his *Maidens' Songs*, performed by troupes of young girls, possibly subdivided into two "rival" groups. In one of his remaining poems, the entire choir begins with a truism:

> There is a vengeance of the gods,
> but he is blissful, whoever is wise,
> weaves out his days tearless.

From here, the two groups divide, headed by the group leaders Agido and Hagesikhora. The song ends with the whole chorus singing again in unison, praising their own talents.

Pindar, who lived in the fifth century B.C.E., left us more writings than almost all of the other poets. His Nemean, Olympian, Isthmean, and Pythian odes are enkomia and epinikia to the victors of the Panhellenic games. Following is an excerpt from his eleventh Olympian ode to a Lokrian named Hagesidamos who won at boxing:

> Free of envy is the praise dedicated
> to Olympic victors. Our tongue

wishes to cherish such themes,
but from a god a man blossoms in mental skills as well.
Know now, child of Arkhestratos,
Hagesidamos, on account of your boxing
I shall celebrate loudly in sweet song the adornment
of your crown with golden olive,
giving heed to the race of Zephyrian Lokris.
Then let us revel! I shall pledge,
O Muses, neither people inhospitable nor
ignorant of beautiful things will you meet,
but those of high wisdom and wieldy with spears.
For neither shining fox nor
roaring lions might change their innate natures.

Monody was a personal kind of poetry, often expressing the poet's own thoughts and feelings and presented in the company of close associates. In form, these poems were composed of short, repeated stanza patterns (Barnstone 1988, 5). In type, they included skolia—drinking songs sung at symposia (see chapter 6), personal reflections and prayers, and iambic and elegy. These final two were categorized differently than traditional lyric, probably because they either were not sung or were accompanied by flute rather than stringed instruments. Iambic poetry (see the "Meter" sidebar) was often used to express mockery, satire, abuse, or polemic. The meter itself was thought of as innately obscene or harsh. According to the *Homeric Hymn to Demeter*, it was named for a scullery maid who made Demeter laugh by telling her dirty jokes or, in other versions, flashing her.

The elegy consists of repeated combinations of a dactylic hexameter and pentameter (see the "Meter" sidebar). This form had a wide range of uses. At the most frivolous, it could be used for skolia (drinking songs) at the symposia. On a more serious note, it was used for military harangues and epitaphs, and, following logically from there, laments.

The Hellenistic Greeks recorded that the greatest monodic lyric poets were Alcaeus, Sappho, and Anacreon (Lesky 1996, 108). To these we must add the earliest iambic poet, Archilochus. Archilochus, who lived around the early seventh century B.C.E., is sometimes seen as the inventor of the monodic spirit, placing himself personally into his verses. He was definitely a unique character. The illegitimate son of a nobleman and a slave, he led his life as a colonist and mercenary. He is famous for his rejection of the warrior ideal presented in the works of Homer, especially that Spartan ideal of coming home either with one's shield (victorious) or on it (dead). Quite to the contrary, one of his most famous poems, elegiac in form, claims:

Someone of the Thracians delights in my shield, which
I abandoned by a bush, blameless, unwillingly;
I saved myself then. What do I care for this shield?
To heck with it! I'll get another one just as good.

In contrast to the "masculine" obsessions with militarism and politics, Sappho of Lesbos wrote her lyrics about love, although often employing military allusions. Her one complete poem, "To Aphrodite," was preserved in a work of Dionysios of Halicarnassus as an example of "perfect" poetry:

Ornate-throned, immortal Aphrodite
Child of Zeus, while-weaving, I beseech you,
do not, with ache and anguish overwhelm,
Mistress, my heart.
But, come here, if ever before
hearing my prayers from afar
listening, leaving your father's house
of gold, you came.
On a yoked chariot, beautiful swift sparrows brought you
on fluttering wings to the dark earth from heaven
through the middle air.
Quickly you came. And you, O blessed one,
smiling on your immortal face,
asked on what account I am suffering again, and
on what account was I summoning again,
and what did I want most in my raving heart to happen.
"Whom do I persuade on this account
to lead you back to her dearest love?
Who, O Sappho, wrongs you?
For if she flees, soon will she follow;
and if she does not receive gifts, then she will give.
And if she does not love, soon she will love even if she does not wish it."
Come to me now, release me from this grievous care!
What my heart desires to come to pass, make happen.
and you yourself be my ally.

It was such references to what appeared to be Sappho's erotic love for other females that led to the modern term *lesbian* for female homosexuality (Sappho lived on the isle of Lesbos). However, the exact context of any of Sappho's poetry, or that of any other female poet, is still in debate. Some have argued that Sappho was a priestess of Aphrodite and that her poems were sung in religious rituals. Others have suggested that she was a teacher in some manner of "finishing school" and the girls she refers to were her students. Another possibility is that woman got together in their own symposia just like men and shared each other's company and voices. Such might be the case for the Boiotian poet Corinna, who tells us:

Terpsichora bids me
to sing lovely things to
the white-robed women of Tanagra;
and the city greatly rejoices in my
clear-twittering voice.

It was possibly the female lyricists who gave rise to a style popular in Hellenistic times—the epigram. These were originally brief verses put on grave markers to commemorate the dead. This practice, combined with the sentiments of elegy, produced an art form in its own right. An elegant example of the high art, and even philosophy, of this style comes from the Hellenistic Arcadian poet Anytê, who wrote of a slave:

> Alive, this man was Manes, a common slave.
> Dead, even great Darius is not his peer.
>> (Translation by Barnstone 1988, 186)

Slightly less sublime, but certainly honest, is an epigram by Callimachus, a Hellenistic poet from Cyrenê in northern Africa. In his "Epitaph of an Enemy," he writes:

> Passerby, do not wish me well with your sour heart.
> Go away. And I shall be well by your being gone.
>> (Translation by Barnstone 1988, 188)

Theater

When discussing drama, we are discussing an Athenian art. This is not because theater did not exist in other parts of Greece. Quite to the contrary, there were theaters all over the Greek world, with some of the best-preserved examples existing outside of Attica (see chapter 9). However, all of the dramatic texts that survive to this day and have been found by researchers are Athenian. As such, when discussing theater as a literary form, we must keep in mind that we are speaking exclusively of Athens.

There were three types of Attic drama: tragedy, satyr play, and comedy. The tragedy (*tragos* = goat + *oidos* = song = "goat song") dealt with mythic themes taken from Homer or the Epic Cycle. They were of a serious bent and generally ended sadly, such as when a hero discovers that he has murdered, had sex with, and/or eaten a member of his immediate family and/or alternate species. In Euripides's *Bacchae*, for example, the princess Agaue mistakes her son Pentheus for a lion, and she rips off his head with her bare hands before returning to sanity. In Sophocles's *Oedipus Tyrannos*, the hero murders his father and marries his mother, bringing a plague onto his people.

A satyr play was a slapstick show, featuring, among the other characters, satyrs—part human, part goat (or horse), completely lecherous males who served Dionysos. Sexually lewd and scatological humor typified such shows, of which only one—Euripides's *Cyclops*—survives.

There were two distinct types of comedy—Old Comedy, which appeared at the end of the fifth century B.C.E., and New Comedy, which appeared at the end of the fourth. Old Comedy showed both the world of the gods and the political world of men in irreverent light. In *The Frogs*, for example, the god Dionysos wets himself on stage when frightened while visiting the underworld. In the *Lysistrata*, the male citizens of Athens and Sparta suffer incurable erections when their wives go on a sex strike to end the Peloponnesian War.

New Comedy, on the other hand, produced in the less-than-open atmosphere of the Macedonian monarchies, was more a comedy of manners, featuring set plots of long-lost children, mischievous slaves, and love.

All drama was associated with Dionysos, god of wine, fertility, and liminality. Although the origins of the art forms are in debate among modern researchers, it appears that tragedy evolved out of the lyric form of the dithyramb, which Archilochus tells us was specifically the song of Dionysos (fr. 77). This dithyramb was recited by the strophe and antistrophe, alternating with each other. Two men are credited with transforming the dithyramb into what would become tragedy—Arion of Corinth and Thespis of Ikaria. Arion, who lived around 600 B.C.E., wrote dithyrambs for a choir (as opposed to for a group of men drinking, as with Archilochus), and had them treat a specific subject. According to Aristotle (*Poetics* 3–5), Thespis, who performed in Athens in the mid-sixth century, brought an individual speaker out of the chorus, thus beginning the tradition of an actor who could address the chorus and audience independently of the other actors. It is generally accepted, then, that the earliest tragedy consisted of a two-part chorus that recited lyric odes, interspersed with speeches from an actor who recited the episodes (*epi* = around; "around the odes").

The poetic meters used in tragedies moved beyond the standard dithyramb. Thespis was said to have introduced the trochaic tetrameter, and iambic trimeter came to the fore in the fifth century for the actors' dialogues (see the "Meter" sidebar). Although the dialect of the plays was mostly Attic (being written by Athenians), there remained Doric elements, strengthening the argument that the art form first appeared in Arion's land of Corinth.

Comedy evolved out of two traditions. One was the lyric, specifically the work of the monodic iambic poets. As with tragedy, this meter was standard for the actors performing the drama. The second tradition was that of the komos, or revelers' band, with the word *comedy* coming from the words *komos oidos*—reveler's song. The ritual of the komos was part of the general practice of carnival, a festive rite occurring throughout the world where inversion was the rule of the day. In Medieval times, a King of Fools was revered for a day, instead of the actual monarch. In the modern tradition of carnival, excess and public frivolity take the place of the workaday world. During such festivals, authority is flouted and derided, serving as a vent for public indignation without leading to full-scale revolt or revolution. An aspect of such carnivals for ancient Greece was the komoi-bands, who disguised themselves and went about the city, ridiculing the important and powerful. A further element of this practice was the phallophoros, or carrying around of a giant phallus. Display of sexual items, use of obscene language and (presumably) gestures, and insults typified the early komoi. Over time, they were organized into poetic bands, hurling poetic insults at one another as well as at society at large. In the end, they were brought into the dramatic tradition, serving as a chorus for an iamb-chanting hero/actor ridiculing society in general from the stage (Henderson 1996, 8–11).

The two main dramatic festivals in Athens were the City Dionysia, probably founded by Peisistratos (see chapter 4), and the Lenaia, established in the mid-fifth century B.C.E. As with most things in ancient Greece, the plays were presented in competition with each other. The competitions were divided between the tragedians and the comedians. The tragedians presented three tragedies in a row, followed by a satyr play as comic relief. The comedians would present one comedy each. Funding for the plays was provided as a required city benefit by a wealthy citizen, who, of course, was extolled along with the dramatist if the plays he funded won the competition (see chapter 5). Beyond the main theatrical events, there were also smaller venues for theater, where either older plays could be redone or new plays could be tested before the festivals.

Of all the plays that existed, only a small number have survived. These are plays written by the tragedians Aeschylus, Sophocles, and Euripides, and the comedians Aristophanes and Menander (all in chronological order). Aeschylus, who wrote in the early fifth century B.C.E., was credited with introducing a second actor to the play, in addition to Thespis's one. Eventually, there were three speaking actors total, along with the chorus and the nonspeaking actors.

There were, of course, more than three speaking characters in a play, meaning that the three actors had to change roles throughout the performance. This was facilitated by the traditional use of masks as costume (an aspect of Dionysos's cult). Merely by changing masks and a bit of costume, the actor could quickly go from being Aigisthus to Clytemnestra. Men played all roles, both male and female, and there is debate as to whether women even attended the theater. What was probably the first play to feature all three speaking characters was Aeschylus's trilogy, the *Oresteia.* This tells the story of the return of Agamemnon from the Trojan War, his murder by his wife Clytemnestra, her murder at the hands of their son Orestes, and Orestes's trial at Athens. In the first play, *Agamemnon,* the king returns home and confronts his wife before a chorus of old men. She persuades her husband to enter the house on a wine-colored carpet (one of the earliest examples of the "red carpet treatment"), after which she stabs him as he bathes in the tub (a motif adopted by Hitchcock in modern times). At this point, the two expected speaking actors have left the scene, when a surprise third actor—Cassandra—begins to speak. This number of actors remains constant throughout Greek drama from this point in history forward.

Sophocles and Euripides were roughly contemporary, writing in the mid- to late fifth century B.C.E. Sophocles is now most famous for his plays about Oedipus (spelled *Oidipous* in Greek), although, contrary to modern understanding, they were not a trilogy. The first play performed was the "last"—*Antigone*—performed in 458 B.C.E. *Oedipus the King* came out in 431, and *Oedipus at Colonus* in 401 (Ley 1991, 75–76). Euripides produced a number of plays, including our only surviving satyr play, *The Cyclops.* This tells the story of Odysseus's confrontation with the Cyclops Polyphemos, recounted in Book 9 of the *Odyssey.* Living with Polyphemos are a group of satyrs who were shipwrecked on the island when chasing a band of pirates who had kidnapped Dionysos. After getting a bit tipsy on Odysseus's wine (itself a manifestation of

Dionysos), the head satyr asks about the Trojan War, focusing on the baser aspects of Helen specifically:

> So then, when you caught the girl,
> did you all bang her one at a time,
> since she really enjoyed mating with lots of men,
> the traitor? She seeing a guy wearing colorful trousers on
> his legs and a gold collar on his neck
> went all aflutter, leaving Menelaus,
> the better fellow. I wish there were never
> any race of women, except one for me alone!

Euripides's tragedies, like the others, focused on the traditional myths. There were clear differences among the works of Aeschylus, Sophocles, and Euripides, though. Aeschylus wrote during the heyday of Athens, after the defeat of the Persian armies at Marathon (see chapter 4). His plays were very pro-military and, especially with Clytemnestra, rather misogynistic. By contrast, Sophocles experienced the decline of Athens in the later fifth century B.C.E. His plays, especially *Oedipus at Colonus,* showed the horrors of war in contrast to the peace and devotion that are (or at least should be) present in the female domain of the family. Sophocles was an idealist. He is credited with showing people as they should be and with showing the gods as supreme and inscrutable. By contrast, Euripides showed people as they were and held the gods responsible for the atrocities they committed. It is a testament to the freedom of speech in fifth-century Athens that Euripides's plays were produced, rather than being destroyed as "heresy."

The same might be said for Aristophanes's works, produced in the late fifth to early fourth centuries B.C.E. From the gods to city officials to other playwrights, no one was free from his cutting remarks. Dionysos is set out for ridicule in *The Frogs,* and the philosopher Socrates is maligned in *The Clouds.* With Aristophanes's acrimony, however, came idealism and advice for the city. During the tribulations of the Peloponnesian War, Aristophanes produced *Lysistrata,* a play about the women of Greece attempting to force an end to the war. Not only do they hold a sex strike, but the women of Athens also seize control of the Acropolis and, with it, the city finances. In this exchange, Aristophanes comments not only on corruption in the city government, but on the responsible, and undervalued, role played by the city's women (ll. 486–496):

> Magistrate: And really, this first I'd like to learn from them, by Zeus:
>   What are you hoping, barring us from the Acropolis?
> Lysistrata: That we might keep the money safe and you might not use it for war.
> Magistrate: So we make war for money?
> Lysistrata: *And* why all the other things are in a mess: for in this way Peisandros and
>   the officers attached to him are able to steal it—they constantly stir up trouble.
>   And so by this they do whatever they want. But no longer will they steal the
>   money.

Magistrate: But what will *you* do?

Lysistrata: You ask me this? We shall be the treasurers!

Magistrate: *You'll* manage the money?!?

Lysistrata: Why do you find that so awful? Don't we manage the household finances for you?

Magistrate: That's not the same thing!

Lysistrata: How not?

Magistrate: These funds are for war!

Lysistrata: But there shouldn't be a war in the first place.

The chorus of women go on to note that they have the greatest stake in the war, for it is their sons who are killed daily. It is an interesting irony that the voice of women was heard only in drama through the pen, and mouth, of a man.

This freedom of public political condemnation came to an end with the conquests of Philip and Alexander, and the New Comedy of this era was typified by its focus on the common people, rather than on the higher-ups. The only complete play of this genre is Menander's *Dyskolos*, performed around 316 B.C.E. (Lesky 1996, 650). Here we meet the archetype of the old miserly man with the young, beautiful daughter who falls in love with the charming, handsome suitor. The play revolves around the suitor trying to win permission to marry the daughter, with side scenes referring to gossiping, meddlesome, and often clumsy servants. In the end, there is not one but two marriages, prefiguring the happy endings of Jane Austen. Such comedies of errors became standard in both Greek and Roman theaters until Late Antiquity, and have a revival in *Something Funny Happened on the Way to the Forum*.

In the End—the Alexandrians

The last great phase of Greek literature before the Roman conquests took place in Alexandria. Ptolemy II sought to legitimize his rule by turning Alexander's city on the coast into a great intellectual power, a rival to Athens in the north. He brought over Demetrios of Phaleron, a compatriot of Aristotle, to establish a library and museion (sanctuary of the Muses, from which we get our modern word *museum*). The great library of Alexandria ended up with some 700,000 scrolls, the largest library of its day and many later days (see chapter 3). The literature of this period was dominated by three great poets: Theocritus, Callimachus, and Apollonios of Rhodes.

Theocritus of Syracuse was most famous for his series of poems called the *Idylls*, which dealt with the simple lives of peasants. These were, of course, utter idealizations of country life, presenting scenes of frolicking shepherdesses in rosy scenery rather than malnourished farmers struggling with locust invasions and tax collectors. One might liken them to Marie Antoinette's Bergerie at Versailles, where the last queen of France used to play shepherdess with perfumed sheep, color-coordinated to match her shepherdess costumes. These poems were written, ultimately, for the entertainment of Ptolemy himself, in exchange for his patronage (i.e., financial support). As the poet himself expresses it: "The spokesman of the Muses celebrates Ptolemy in return for his benefactions" (*Idylls* 17.115–116).

Callimachus of Cyrenê in northern Africa was the poetic trendsetter of his day. He scorned the repetitive nature of the Homeric epics and believed that poems should be refined art in themselves, rather than a means of telling a long and possibly tedious story. He was famous for his epigrams (see above). When he did delve into the dactylic hexameter form, it was more to parody epic than to follow it. In his "great epic" *Hekalê*, he narrates an event in the life of Theseus, focusing not on heroic deeds, but on Theseus's relationship with an old woman who served him dinner. Callimachus's greatest, and longest (some 7,000 lines), work was the *Aitia—Causes of Things*. This semiscientific poetry style was later taken up by the Roman poet Lucretius in his work *De Rerum Natura—On the Nature of Things*.

Quite dissimilar to both Theocritus and Callimachus was Apollonios of Rhodes, who was actually from Alexandria in spite of his epithet, and who became the head librarian there. His major work returns us to the beginnings of Greek literature: His epic *Argonautika*, or *Voyage of the Argo*, tells the tale of Jason and his band of heroes, who sought the Golden Fleece and returned victorious with the "witch" Medea. In this work, Apollonios was clearly imitating the works of Homer, defying the dictates of his supposed teacher Callimachus. It is reported that the story received such bad press when first published that Apollonios moved to Rhodes for a time to escape the censure of Alexandria and to edit the poem. When republished, it was heralded with great acclaim, and the Rhodians honored Apollonios with full citizenship, thus his title "of Rhodes."

The story of Jason and Medea is actually quite old. There are references to the *Argo* in the *Odyssey*, and the story of Medea was intimately bound up with the cult of Hera at Perachora (near Corinth), one of the oldest large-scale sanctuaries in Greece. Euripides presented a rather unusual version of the tale in his play *Medea*, in which the "witch from Colchis" murdered her and Jason's sons in revenge for Jason's infidelity. According to all other versions of the myth, Medea was persecuted by the people of Corinth, who formed a mob and murdered her children themselves.

Apollonios's *Argonautika* is a fascinating mixture of Homeric style and Hellenistic scientific reasoning. When the characters are traveling in the Mediterranean—Homer's territory—Apollonios is vague about geography, leaving the terrain much as Homer described it. When branching out into other regions, however, such as Germany and Russia, the poet describes rivers and mountains such that later scholars have attempted to trace his path. Prayers and divination in the poem reflect those practices described in Homer, but Medea's use of magic, especially magical potions, shows influence from the recently conquered Near East, where the "science of magic" had long been studied. Even Jason is distinct from the Homeric heroes. Rather than being the best and brightest all rolled up into one immanent figure, Jason is a "managerial" hero. He delegates authority, lets others use their talents to his best advantage, and generally wins the day himself through charm. He is perhaps the earliest prefiguring of the modern notion of the hero.

SCIENCE

The Early Natural Philosophers

It is impossible to differentiate between the early origins of Greek science and of Greek philosophy, as they are the same thing. The word *philosophy* comes from the Greek words *philos* (love) and *sophia* (wisdom). The Greek philosophers were interested in everything: the natural world, the nature of the gods, the meaning of life. As such, many of the early philosophers delved into questions that today we would regard as science. In many ways, of course, this is no different from modern times, when theories of quantum physics and the neurosciences are once again challenging our notions of reality and perception. Thus, the reader should understand that early Greek science and philosophy overlap. This section will cover "science-philosophy" through the Archaic Age, then continue into what might be deemed the hard sciences. The last section of this chapter deals with the more nonscientific aspects of Greek philosophy.

The Presocratics

The first wave of natural philosophers lived and thought between c. 600 and 400 B.C.E. They are called the Presocratics, although some of them were actually contemporaries of Socrates. All of them believed that the universe, or cosmos, could be explained through a consistent set of rules that could be grasped with either the senses or the mind. Although not atheists, they did attribute to nature, or physis, more mechanical explanations than did Homer or Hesiod. Each in his own way sought an arkhê—the original principle of existence and change (or lack of change, depending on the philosopher). For some, this might be air; for others, fire; or for others, even atoms. No original texts from these philosophers survive, and their words are preserved only in the writings of later philosophers and historians.

The person usually designated the first Greek philosopher was Thales of Miletos (625–585 B.C.E.). Concerning his astronomical work, he is famous for predicting a solar eclipse based on his own study of their periodic recurrences and, probably, having access to data kept in the Near East for the previous millennia. Likewise, he is credited with the theories that Earth was a "bubble" of air in the midst of an aqueous mass, that the light of the moon was actually reflected sunlight, and that all of creation was a form of water, which he believed was the cosmic arkhê. On a more metaphysical level, he argued that all creatures, even stones, had souls, and that this accounted for their ability to provoke movement. He was specifically referring to magnets when composing this theory.

Following in the wake of Thales was Anaximander, also of Miletos, who lived around 570 B.C.E. Contrary to Thales's views, Anaximander believed that the primordial arkhê was infinite, from which all the "stuffs" of the universe came into being. These interacted with one another through contrasts of hot and cold. Like Thales, Anaximander believed that the Earth, as the center of the universe, was suspended in an immovable state, equidistant from every other point in the outer heavens (Barnes 1987, 37). The third great Milesian philosopher was Anaximenes, who followed many of Anaximander's precepts, but who believed that the arkhê of the universe was air (Barnes 1987, 37).

Coming after the Milesians were the Pythagoreans, so named for their founder, Pythagoras. In terms of astronomy specifically, Pythagoras was credited with figuring out the order of the then-known heavenly bodies: Earth, moon, Mercury, Venus, sun, Mars, Jupiter, Saturn (Nicolaidis 2001, 185). In terms of mathematics, he was said to have discovered the Pythagorean Theorem ($a^2 + b^2 = c^2$), although this attribution was probably a later invention. In the realms of "abstract" philosophy, the Pythagoreans introduced the idea that the cosmos incarnated a rational order and divine harmony. They believed that below the moon was where generation, corruption, disorder, and general chaos held sway, and above the moon was an area of eternal order and purity. They believed that humans lived below the moon; the gods lived above.

Finally, Pythagoras and his followers propagated the ideology of metempsychosis, or what we might call reincarnation. Pythagoras suggested that unlike the body, the soul was immortal, and it passed into different bodies over the course of several lifetimes. In his *Life of Pythagoras*, the later philosopher Porphyry stated, "But it became very well known to everyone that he said, first, that the soul is immortal; then, that it changes into other kinds of animals; and further, that at certain periods whatever has happened happens again, there being absolutely nothing new; and that all living things should be considered as belonging to the same kind" (Barnes 1987, 86).

One of the most influential Presocratic philosophers was Heracleitus (late sixth century B.C.E.), occasionally called the Riddler because of the confusing nature of his theories. On a simple level, he believed that fire was the primordial arkhê. Somewhat more complex were his three most popular theories of reality: First, the world was eternal, rather than created or evolved as in Hesiod's *Theogony*. Second, everything in the world was always in a state of flux or change. Finally, and most obscurely, was the Unity of Opposites, whereby all things were manifestations of contradictory opposites whose tug-of-war was essential to their continued existence. Thus, "the world is an eternal and ever-changing modification of fire, its various contents each unified and held together by a dynamic tension of contrarieties" (Barnes 1987, 39).

The next wave of Presocratic philosophers—the Eleans—was led by Parmenides (c. 510–450 B.C.E.). As far as clarity goes, his work was not much better than that of Heracleitus. All his references to the natural sciences occur in a section of his poem *On Nature*, which he himself called the Way of Opinion, and which he claimed was false and deceitful. This caveat aside, he rejected the beliefs of the Milesians by claiming that there were actually two arkhai (pl. of arkhê), light and darkness, and that all things partook of both.

Concerning the structure of the universe, Parmenides argued that the cosmos was organized into rings or spheres. The innermost was the primary cause of creation and movement, which Parmenides identified as a goddess. Then came the ring of air, and then the sun and the Milky Way, which were exhalations of fire. Then there was the moon, composed of air and fire; the aither, or the sky; and finally the Earth itself, densest of them all (Allen 1985, 46). In his section called "True Things," Parmenides was more philosophical than scientific, focusing on epistemology, or the ability to know anything. He argued that reality did exist, and that all things were unchanging and graspable by the human mind.

Parmenides's two main followers were Melissos and Zeno, both of whom involved themselves in questions of the infinite. Melissos argued that existence was infinite and filled with only one, unmoving "thing." In a similar vein, Zeno, in his forty-odd series of arguments, suggested that existence was a unified entity. If more than one "thing" existed, paradoxes, which were impossible, would follow. Both philosophers believed that human perceptive senses (sight, smell, etc.) were deceptive and could not be used to comprehend reality.

The last Presocratics were Empedocles of Acragas (493–433 B.C.E.), Anaxagoras of Athens (500–428 B.C.E.), and Democritus of Abdera (born c. 460 B.C.E.), often called the Pluralists. Empedocles was the first to suggest that all creation was composed of the four elements—air, fire, water, and earth. The impetus for their mixing or dissolution was love (philia) and strife (neikos). The cosmos, he taught, began with the separation of these elements and the formation of light and darkness.

Anaxagoras argued that all creation emerged from one universal mass, which underwent a period of differentiation leading to the apparently different "stuff" now composing the cosmos. However, Anaxagoras held that none of this "stuff" was totally separated from all the other "stuff," so that all creation contains bits of all the rest of creation. As such, there was, say, a bit of iron in blood, and a bit of gold in iron. The mover and shaker of all these "stuffs" was Mind (Nous), the one thing in the universe that was eternal and unchanging. This Mind set all things into motion, with the dense, moist, cold, and dark heading together into a "center" (basically, Earth), while their opposites went to the periphery (heavens). The one exception was "heavy" stars, which, according to Anaxagoras, were stones torn from Earth, rendered red-hot by their swift motion.

Democritus argued that all reality was made up of very tiny, indivisible parts, which come together in different ways to make up the stuff of the universe. In many respects, then, he was the father of modern atomic (a = not, *tomos* = cut apart) theory. Beyond the "hard" sciences, Democritus was also a fan of anthropology, and he wrote on such topics as the origins of religion and the nature of language (Barnes 1987, 47).

All the Presocratics worked in a bit of a vacuum. Although they had access to each other and to data from the Near East, such issues as eschatology and the reliability of the senses were new to the world of philosophic inquiry: A person, or a civilization, has to have a lot of leisure time to start considering whether reality exists or not. To their credit, the Presocratics established the idea that the universe was governed by laws, laws that were applicable to all aspects of reality. They tested their hypotheses of these laws, rather than just accepting them. And they did teach people to question their assumptions about reality, leading ultimately to the understanding that the Earth is not the center of the universe, and that, as quantum theory now tells us, the observer is an integral component of any observation.

Astronomy after the Presocratics

After the Presocratics, one of the earliest astronomers about whom we have any information is Meton, a contemporary of Socrates, who, through observations made at Athens, reconciled the solar and lunar calendars, noting that they realigned themselves every nineteen years. Such information was especially important in the regulation of the calendar. The Greeks mainly kept time according to the moon, but the agricultural year progressed according to the solar cycles (summer is summer, no matter what phase of the moon). Coordinating the solar and lunar cycles was a concern in many ancient societies.

Eudoxos of Knidos (390–340 B.C.E.) was the first Greek astronomer to construct a mathematical system to explain the apparent movements of the heavenly bodies: that of the Homocentric Spheres, discussed in a work entitled *Peri Takhon*. It was a great feat of mathematical evidence and, apparently, involved no observation whatsoever. Eudoxos believed that all heavenly movements were caused by the interactions of twenty-seven intertwined concentric spheres, with the Earth at the center. All the stars existed on the single, outermost sphere, and each of the planets made use of no fewer than four concentric spheres, which spun along different axes to produce the planets' apparently irregular courses. Likewise, the sun and moon were governed by three spheres each. All this complexity existed to explain the retrograde motion of the planets within a presumed geocentric system. Perhaps more influential were his descriptions of the constellations, including calendrical notices of their risings and settings.

Later, Eudoxos's theories were "corrected" by Callipus of Cyzicus (c. 330 B.C.E.), who added two more spheres for the sun and moon and one more for each of the planets. This did not simplify matters.

Following closely on the heels of Callipus was Aristarchus of Samos (c. 320 B.C.E.). Rather than further complicating the Homocentric Spheres theory, he derived a (semi-) heliocentric theory of astral movements, suggesting that the stars and sun were fixed in space and that the Earth revolved around the sun in a circle. A different means of explaining the "irrational" movements of the heavenly bodies was presented by the third-century mathematician Apollonios of Perge, who calculated the eccentric and epicyclical models of planetary motion. His work was to be of critical importance to the master of Greek astronomy, Ptolemy (see below).

Eratosthenes of Cyrenê (276–197 B.C.E.), although best remembered for his work in mathematics (especially on the subject of prime numbers), is famous in astronomy/geometry for his extremely accurate measurement of the Earth's surface. To attain this, he compared the noon shadows in midsummer between Aswan and Alexandria in Egypt. He gave the Earth's circumference as 250,00 stadia, the distance to the sun as 804,000,000 stadia, and the distance to the moon as 780,000 stadia. Furthermore, he measured the tilt of the Earth's axis and attained a measurement of 23° 51'15. Finally, he compiled a catalogue of 675 stars. This is especially important because here, for the first time in centuries, the Greeks were learning the art of accurate observation from their eastern neighbors (fortunately, the Greek astronomers were willing to accept the perceptions of their senses).

The pinnacle of astronomy in ancient Greece was reached under Hipparchus of Nicaea (190–126 B.C.E.) and Claudius Ptolemy, who lived in Egypt in the mid-second century C.E. (although this late date rather puts him out of the scope of this book, he is included for the sake of completeness). Hipparchus was the first Greek to construct a full theory of the motion of the sun and moon that was properly based on observational data. He combined the mathematical system of Apollonios of Perge and his own observations with the Babylonian eclipse record (dating back to the eighth century B.C.E.), and thus extracted accurate estimates of the mean motions of the sun and moon, as well as the length of the tropical year (which he put at 365.26 minus 1/300th days). He is famous for his discovery of the procession of the equinoxes, which he did by comparing his own observation of the distance of the star Spica at the autumnal equinox with that recorded 160 years earlier. Hipparchus noted that, in its annual movement, it took the sun a little more time to reach the same zodiacal point than to reach the equator: The sidereal year would thus be different from the solar year. Hipparchus interpreted this phenomenon as a very slow movement of the sphere of the stars, from west to east (about 1 degree per century, although the actual value is 1 degree, 23 minutes, 30 seconds). Furthermore, he studied the problem of parallax, and thus came to devise the first practical method for determining the sizes of and distances to the sun and moon (the latter he actually calculated correctly).

The work of Claudius Ptolemy has survived in a tome entitled the *Almagest,* an Arabic translation of *O Magiste,* the "Greatest" (see chapter 3 on Arabic preservations of Greek scientific texts). Based on his own observations, Ptolemy compiled a list of stars, giving their ecliptic coordinates and magnitudes. He constructed a theory of motion for the five known planets, for which he used the established theories of eccentric and epistyle motion. He showed that the heavenly bodies did not move in perfect circles, as suggested by Aristotle (see below), but in ellipses. This made it possible to predict the position of all known heavenly bodies at any given moment, all the details of the eclipses, the retrograde motions of the planets, and the appearance and disappearance of the planets and stars.

The Greek study of astronomy was based primarily on geometry, with little or no attention paid to physics or chemistry since the days of Anaxagoras. The Greek astronomers could say what was there and where things would be later, but they could not explain the composition of the stars or why the planets moved as they did. This was to be the concern of Renaissance and modern research.

Medicine

The earliest references to what we would term medicine in ancient Greece come from Homer. In the *Iliad,* the poet refers to Podalirios and Machaon (sons of Asclepius), who treated wounded Greek soldiers. When Menelaus was struck with a barbed arrow, Machaon was summoned (*Iliad,* Book 4, ll. 217–219):

But when he saw the wound where the sharp arrow burst in,
squeezing out the blood, he spread soothing medicines upon it
expertly, which once wise Cheiron gave his father in friendship.

From this period until the fifth century B.C.E., ancient Greek medicine was an aspect of religion, especially the cult of Asclepius. According to legend, Asclepius was the mortal son of Apollo and Coronis, who, after his mother's death, was given over to the centaur Cheiron to learn the healing arts. Asclepius became a world-renowned healer. According to some versions of the myth, though, he eventually became too full of conceit, either going so far as to raise the dead or, even worse, actually charging for his services. The gods brought about his death. In some regions, however, he became a demigod, the patron of healing, especially in the city of Epidauros. His sanctuary there was one of the earliest hospitals. Those ill or out of sorts would come to the sanctuary, engage in purification rituals (often involving food restrictions and bathing), bring offerings to the deity, and then sleep in the sanctuary's dormitory, the abaton. During this sleep—or incubation, as it was called—the patient would receive a dream from Asclepius explaining what was necessary to cure the problem. The priests of Asclepius interpreted the dream, and the patient was hopefully cured (Kasas and Struckmann 1990, 37).

Countless tokens of cures have been discovered at the various sanctuaries of Asclepius, especially in Epidauros and Corinth, consisting of terra-cotta body parts indicating what the god cured for the patients. Eyes and ears bespeak corrected vision and hearing; legs and arms, cured limbs; and breasts, cured problems with lactation. Also present among the items found at the sanctuaries were medical tools, indicating that efforts beyond merely the dreams were used in treating pilgrims.

In the early fifth century B.C.E., the ordering of the natural world studied by the Presocratic philosophers came to be applied to the human body. This, combined with the observations of the Asclepian priests, engendered the rise of medical science. Two fifth-century philosophers who contributed early theories of human physical well-being were Empedocles of Acragas and Alcmaeon of Croton. The former devised the notion of the four humors, stating that the human body was mainly an ambulatory sack of different fluids and that the combination of those fluids resulted in different states of physical and emotional well-being (DeWaal 2001, 1023). The latter argued that good health depended on the proper balance of all conflicting qualities in the body: hot and cold, wet and dry. The word *isonomia* (balance) referred to a healthy state of body, just as the word was used in political writings to refer to a balanced, open, thriving government. Disease occurred when one quality "tyrannized" the rest (King 2001, 8).

Emerging from these traditions was Hippocrates of Cos, called the Father of Medicine (c. 460–377 B.C.E.). The so-called Hippocratic Corpus, attributed to him, consisted of some sixty or seventy treatises on various aspects of the nature and treatment of the human body. On an ideological level, Hippocrates was heavily influenced by the theories of Empedocles, believing that the health of the human body was dependent on the proper balance of the humors. As a result, remedial techniques such as bloodletting, purgations, and diet were common in Hippocrates's repertoire. But, true to science, the Hippocratic technique included a keen awareness of the importance of direct observation. This was most clearly expressed in the books of the *Epidemics*. Contrary to the modern meaning of this word (*epi* = around; *demos* = people/neighborhood), the *Epidemics* do not refer to an illness that spreads about an area, but to a doctor who travels about, making house calls. The *Epidemics* are like a journal in which the doctor recorded progressions of symptoms, and also his own observations and thoughts (King 2001, 12):

> At Larissa, a bald man suddenly has a pain in the right leg. Of the treatments, none helped.
>
> Day 1: Sharp, burning fever, he did not tremble, but the pain persisted.
>
> Day 2: The pains in the thigh abated, but the fever was worse. He became rather restless and did not sleep; cold extremities. He passed a lot of urine but this was not of a favorable kind.
>
> Day 3: The pain in the thigh stopped. His mind was deranged, with disturbance and much tossing about.
>
> Day 4: Near midday: he died.

Through the end of the Classical period, Cos, along with nearby Knidos, was the center of medical studies in ancient Greece. The Hippocratic Corpus was written here, and this was also where the largest medical library was preserved. Contributing to the growth of medical knowledge was Aristotle (see below), who was himself the son of a physician. Aristotle did not study medicine per se, but his strict categorization of the natural world, and especially his work on comparative anatomies and embryology, greatly influenced the study of Hellenistic medicine.

The intellectual capital of the Hellenistic world emerged in Alexandria in northern Egypt. The Ptolemaic rulers of the kingdom invested heavily in bringing all aspects of culture to their realm, and this included building the finest library in the world. Included in their acquisitions was the complete Hippocratic Corpus. A unique development in the Alexandrian pursuit of medical knowledge was a brief lifting of the general ban on human dissection. For the first time, medical students were allowed controlled opportunities actually to see what went on inside the human body, rather than relying on accidental wounds or on analogies with animal bodies (King 2001, 29–31).

Two people to benefit from this new opportunity were Herophilos of Chalcedon (c. 335–280 B.C.E.) and Erasistratos of Chios (c. 304–250 B.C.E.). The former might be considered the father of modern neurology. He studied the nervous system and the brain, and he was the first to determine that these two were actually related. Until this point, Greeks from Hesiod to Aristotle had been convinced that the center of human thought was in the heart and lungs. It was Herophilos who suggested that it was, in fact, the brain. He also made extensive examinations of the human reproductive systems, he studied the liver, and he is the first recorded doctor in the Western world to study the relation-ship between the pulse and health (King 2001, 27–28). Erasistratos is consid-ered to be the founder of physiology. His main works were on the digestive tract and the circulatory system, wherein he determined that the heart func-tioned as some manner of pump.

Both of these physicians still believed in the four-balanced-humors theory of human health. Thus, typical remedies used were still diet, bloodletting, and so forth. In contrast, Asclepiades of Bithynia (flourished c. 150 B.C.E.), the first Greek physician to practice widely in Rome, was influenced by the theories of Democritus of Abdera (see above). Rather than from fluids, Asclepiades be-lieved that disease resulted from overly relaxed or overly excited states of the tiny particles making up the body. To get these back to normal, Asclepiades and his followers prescribed therapeutic massages, fresh air, and adjusted di-ets (DeWaal 2001, 1024). When faced with a choice between massage and leeches, it is easy to see how his school became popular with patients.

Mathematics

The Greeks certainly did not invent mathematics, or even higher math. The Greeks themselves attributed the invention of geometry to the Egyptians (Herodotus, 2, 109), and the Mesopotamians had previously developed an al-gebraic system. What the Greeks are credited with is the invention of the math-ematical process, wherein the "laws" of numbers are reduced to the simplest axioms possible and are then used in proofs to solve complex problems. The earliest mathematical treatises we have from ancient Greece are those of Eu-clides, who lived in the late fourth century B.C.E. Before this, the development of mathematics is recorded as having been a combination of philosophical en-deavors, such as those of the Pythagoreans (see above), and the attempt to solve certain specifically geometric problems. Three of these became quite fa-mous, much as in modern times the attempt to reconcile relativity theory with quantum theory is a well-known debate in physics. The first of these was the so-called Delian problem, which sought how to double the size of a cube. Ac-cording to legend, the population of Delos was told it could cure a plague by doubling the size of Apollo's cubical altar on the island. The problem was sent forth to all the Greeks, and various solutions are attributed to schools from the Platonic in Athens (see below) to one Archytas of the Pythagoreans (Wallace 2001, 1012).

The second great question was how to determine the area of a circle, as the value of $\pi = 3.14$ had not yet been discovered. Various early mathematicians attempted to solve this problem, often making use of measurable polygons that "fit into" the body of a circle so as to approximate its area. Although the early astronomer Eudoxos reached a reasonable approximation, it was ulti-mately the mathematician-physicist Archimedes who (almost) calculated π (see below).

One of the first steps in this eventual direction emerged out of the third great mathematical question, which involved calculating the trisection of an angle. Hippias of Elis approached this problem using the quadratrix, which observed the contact points between the radius of a circle moving 90° within a circle, and a straight line starting out perpendicular to the radius and moving from the edge to the center of the circle (Wallace 2001, 1012).

In the Hellenistic period, the three great Greek mathematicians were Euclides, Apollonios of Perge, and Archimedes. Tradition related that Euclides was educated in Athens by the students of Plato before founding a school in Alexandria during the reign of Ptolemy I (306–283 B.C.E.). His most important writing was *The Elements,* which came to be used as the standard textbook of mathematics in the West soon after completion. In this work, he assembled all the mathematical works of his predecessors, such as Eudoxos, while "correcting" them and adding his own systems. The work consists of a series of definitions ("A point is that which has no part"; "A line is a length with no width") and propositions, which are solved with proofs derived from the definitions and previously ascertained propositions. For example, Proposition 15 of Book 1 of *The Elements* states:

If two straight lines cut each other, they make vertical angles equal to each other.

For the two straight lines AB and GD cut each other at point E; I say that angle AEG is equal to angle DEB, and that GEB is equal to AED. For since line AE stands upon line GD, forming angles GEA and AED, then the angles GEA and AED are equal to right angles. Again, since line DE stands upon line AB, making angles AED and DEB, then angles AED and DEB are equal to right angles. And it is evident that angles GEA and AED are equal to right angles; then angles GEA and AED are equal to AED and DEB. Let angle AED be subtracted from both; the remainder then from angle GEA is equal to that from BED. Likewise it will be evident that angles GEB and DEA are also equal.

Apollonios of Perge, whose work was so influential in astronomy (see above), was renowned in ancient mathematics for his work on conics. Of the eight books of his work of that title, four remain in Greek, three remain in Arabic translations, and the last has been lost. Working out the values of sections "cut" from circular cones by linear planes, he calculated the parabola, the ellipse, and the hyperbola.

Living and working slightly earlier than Apollonios was Archimedes of Syracuse, perhaps the most famous name in ancient Greek math and science. Born in Syracuse around 287 B.C.E., Archimedes traveled in the highest levels of Syracusan society, befriending the kings Gelo and Hieron. His work might be divided into the theoretical and the practical, with Archimedes himself rather despising his work in that latter category. In terms of theoretical mathematics, his greatest contribution was almost discovering π (the values he derived were 3.14282, some 0.0012 too large, or 3.1409, some 0.0007 too small) (Stein 1999, 116). His calculations are preserved in a work entitled "Measurement of a Circle," in which Archimedes "fills" the circle with a ninety-six-sided polygon, the area of which he calculates in order to estimate the area of the circle (Stein 1999, 116). His other contributions to theoretical mathematics include his computation of the volumes of the sphere and cylinder (of which he was so proud he had those two forms set on his grave marker), his computations of the spiral, and his work on conic sections.

Archimedes's practical work might be dubbed physics. Archimedes is perhaps most famous for his discovery of specific gravity. As the story goes, King Hieron had a golden wreath that he wanted to verify was pure gold. He gave it to Archimedes and asked him to prove the content of the object. The mathematician was at a bit of a loss when, reclining in a tub at the bath house, he noticed how much water was displaced by his body and realized that a similar "calculation" would apply to any object, wreath included. According to the Roman architect Vitruvius, Archimedes got so excited that he ran home, completely naked, shouting "Eureka!" ("I have found it!").

Archimedes's other famous discoveries were centers of gravity and levers. Later tradition credits him with saying, "Give me someplace to stand and I shall move the Earth!" Closer to the truth was the proof of his theories to the people of Syracuse: He contrived a device that allowed him, with one arm, to lift up a full ship, cargo, and crew, which could not be moved by the rest of the city's population. On that day, King Hieron decreed that "Archimedes was to be believed in everything he said" (Heath 1996b, 399). In an action of a more militaristic nature, Archimedes invented variable-sized catapults for holding off the Roman fleets that were attacking Syracuse at the end of the third century B.C.E. These allowed the Syracusans to hit Roman ships from different distances. In preparation for the point in battle when the ships came too close for the long-range weapons, Archimedes devised grappling hooks with which the population pulled the ships, crews and all, right out of the water. Some have even claimed, although it is not supported by any evidence, that Archimedes used giant mirrors to set Roman ships on fire.

Archimedes died in 212 B.C.E., when the Roman general Marcellus took Syracuse by treachery and guile (he had not been able to take it by force, not with Archimedes ruining all his ships). There are various stories about the mathematician's final end. The general consensus is that he was working on a mathematical proof when a Roman soldier stormed in and demanded that Archimedes come to Marcellus. Archimedes was slow to comply, claiming that he wanted to finish the problem he was working on first. The soldier, in a pique, killed the scholar.

PHILOSOPHY

After the Presocratics came the era of the Schools of Philosophy, when individual philosophers drew followers to themselves—leading, in some instances, as with Plato, to the rise of long-enduring learning institutions, and in other instances to the formation of actual communes. Generally, the scholars of this phase divided their inquiries into the categories of physics (the natural sciences), logic, and ethics. The earlier philosophers Socrates, Plato, and Aristotle are most famous for their works in the first two categories, and the founders of the later popular schools of Cynicism, Epicureanism, and Stoicism are more famous for their strides in the latter.

Socrates and Plato

There is a joke in academia that Socrates could never get tenure at a modern university because he never published. All we know of his philosophy is what was preserved by his students, notably Plato and Xenophon.

Socrates (469–399 B.C.E.) was an Athenian citizen of modest means who, during the Peloponnesian War (see chapter 4), served as a hoplite in the Athenian army. When not fighting, he involved himself deeply in the contemplation of philosophy (and somewhat less deeply in the care of his wife and children). According to his/Plato's *Apology* (§21), or court defense, Socrates's friend Chaerephon once asked the Delphic oracle (see chapter 8) if there were any man wiser than Socrates, to which the oracle answered "No." When Socrates heard this, he took it as a moral obligation to test the meaning of the oracle, and so he began to probe the wisdom of the great thinkers of his day. His quest led him to the discovery that much of the so-called wisdom of his contemporaries was faulty, based on opinion rather than fact. Socrates came to the conclusion that all he (or anyone else, really) knew was that he knew nothing, but that this bit of self-realization gave him an edge over his contemporaries, who were calculating doctrines based on inaccurate data.

Socrates's method of inquiry was through dialogue: He asked questions of philosophers, teachers, and students alike, and then subjected their replies to vigorous scrutiny to see if their thoughts or ideas were logical, consistent, and possibly even accurate. Each idea was broken down into its constituent parts and tested individually, then put back together again to see if the ideas, functioning independently, would also function as a whole. Such philosophical probing is now called the Socratic Method.

What we know of Socrates through Plato and Xenophon is that he was especially concerned with ethics and how to lead a "good" life. He believed that all people were innately good and they only acted badly through lack of knowledge. If people truly understood what was good, right, and beneficial, they would always act with virtue. However, because people were confused about what was truly good, overvaluing money, power, and prestige, they acted with vice (Luce 1992, 91). Socrates also believed that the gods were ideally good, being all-knowing, and he disapproved of their portrayals in Homer and Hesiod as being subject to the weaknesses and failings of mortals.

This reproach led some to suggest that Socrates was an atheist. Furthermore, his tendency to teach nonmaterialistic ideals to the youth of Athens, and to uncover the inadequacies of their teachers, bought Socrates several enemies. He was accused of impiety and corrupting the youth, brought to trial in 399 B.C.E., found guilty, and condemned to death. Proving his lifelong loyalty to his city, he willingly accepted the verdict and drank hemlock in the company of his friends, including Plato.

Plato (427–347 B.C.E.) was an aristocratic Athenian who was very hard hit by Socrates's death. After traveling to Magna Graecia, and after a brief love affair with Dion of Syracuse, he returned to Athens to dedicate himself to philosophy and teaching. Unlike Socrates, Plato was an avid writer, and all of his treatises and one of his letters are preserved to the present day. Many scholars have attempted to arrange his dialogues, as they are called, into some chronological order, to see how Plato's theories evolved over time. His early works revolved mainly around Socrates. These include the *Apology, Crito, Protagoras,* and *Gorgias.* In his "middle" period, he composed the *Republic,* his most influential work, as well as the *Phaidon, Symposion, Parmenides,* and *Theaeteus.* In his later years came such works as the *Sophists, Statesman, Timaeus,* and the *Laws.* He was working on revisions to this last dialogue when he died (Luce 1992, 97–98).

Plato's inquiries touched on all aspects of knowledge, including mathematics (*Meno*), the nature of the universe (*Timaeus*), the nature of love (*Symposion*), and linguistics (*Kratylos*). However, some of his more influential, overarching ideas were metaphysical in nature, focused on the nature of reality and the soul.

One of Plato's most important themes was that of the Ideal Forms. Plato, influenced by the works of the Presocratic philosophers, was caught in the debate between the changeability and unchangeability of reality. Was the universe always in a state of flux? Or was the Real permanent and unchanging? Plato opted for both. He believed that the physical world around us was always changing, always, technically, in some state of decay. However, he also thought that the universe perceived by human senses was only a reflection of the "true," everlasting, unchanging reality, the reality of the Ideal Forms. The chair we see and sit on is only an imperfect, temporary manifestation of the Ideal Form of Chair. When we perceive something as being pretty, it is because we vaguely perceive the Ideal Form of Beauty emanating through it.

For Plato, the Forms were more real than physical reality, and he thought that it was a sorrowful aspect of the human condition that we could perceive only the changeable, physical forms instead of the true Ideal Forms. As such, humans did not perceive reality, but shadows of reality. This ideology was best presented in his *Republic* in the allegory of the prisoners in the cave. At the beginning of Book 7, Plato paints a picture of "prisoners" who have spent their entire life in a cave, chained at the neck, with the light of the outside world behind them. All they can see are the shadows of things against the wall they face, and, being used to this portrayal of reality all their lives, they assume that this is an accurate portrayal of the world. Then one of them is brought up to the outer world. At first, the brightness of the sun dazes and confuses him, but over time, he becomes accustomed to the light. He first sees reflections of this upper reality in water and in shadows, but after a while, his eyes grow accustomed to the light, and he can see reality as opposed to the mere shadows on the wall. Such, Plato argued, was the quest of the philosopher, to seek out the higher, "realer" truth, recognizing the shadows of common "reality" for what they are. Such higher truth was accessible only through the mind, Plato taught, for the physical senses were inevitably tied to the "shadowy" world of temporary existence.

How, then, could a physical person perceive and learn of the Forms? In this question, Plato was influenced by the Pythagoreans, especially their ideology of metempsychosis. As Plato understood it, in between lifetimes, the soul traveled to the realm of Ideal Forms. Once shoved back into a body, the soul forgot most of these Forms, but it was still capable of vague recollections of that ideal plane. Through the study of philosophy, the mind was capable of recollecting some of what it knew between lives, and thus the process of learning was really just the process of remembering. This was most clearly discussed in the dialogue *Phaidros,* which presented the soul as a charioteer with flying horses. The soul attempts to soar to the divine plane of Ideal Forms, where the deities live (§248A-B, 249C–D):

> . . . but of the other souls: The best of them, following after and resembling a deity, raises the head of the charioteer to the upper path, and is carried about the higher plain. But being tossed about by the horses she can barely perceive reality. At one point she rises, then falls, through the unruliness of the horses, so now she sees, then not. And indeed all the other souls being eager for the upper realms follow, but are unable, being carried about as under water; they fly about crashing into each other, each striving to get ahead of the others. And so the uproar and striving and sweat become extreme; many indeed are lamed by the evil of the charioteers, many have their wings completely broken. But all having great toil depart unfulfilled from god's reality, and departing they are subject to the food of semblance . . . Therefore, only the mind of the philosopher justly is bewinged, for it is always to the best of their power to be in memory before such things by which god is godly. And indeed by such things a man using memory well, always completing the mysteries in perfection, alone becomes perfect. And standing apart from the mundane hurley-burley and being near the divine, he is reprimanded by the masses for being a trouble-maker, and they do not see that he is divinely inspired.

Plato also wrote copiously about the ideal organization of a political body. This is the subject of his two longest works, the *Republic* and the *Laws*. The *Laws* is perhaps the more pragmatic of the two, considering issues of population density, education, and the like. Of general amusement, in Book 2 Plato suggests that all the men of all cities should get together once each month and drink to excess (making certain that sober guards are about, to prevent any real damage). As men are more open and honest when intoxicated, such gatherings would allow all male citizens to speak honestly to each other, thus serving as some manner of civic catharsis and allowing for greater friendship among the people.

The *Republic,* although couched in terms of politics, is actually an inquiry into the nature of justice and the human psyche. In it, Plato posits that a man's self-control is similar to the administration of a state. A person who exhibits self-control and temperance is like a state ruled by a philosopher-king, a wise monarch looking out for the welfare of all citizens. By contrast, a person eternally subject to irrational passions is like a city ruled by a mob, where instability and chaos are the norm.

This ideology got Plato a reputation for being opposed to democracy, which was not altogether untrue, as he was not at all fond of the democratic "rabble" that had condemned Socrates. On a psychological level, though, one sees in the *Republic* an early version of Freud's theories about the ego, the superego, and the id. Plato claimed that each psyche is composed of three levels: the appetitive element, much like the base, physical id; the spirited element, where emotions and sense of self reside—the ego; and the rational element, the mind or superego (Luce 1992, 103). Plato suggested that all were necessary for survival—the population would crash without a sex drive—but the lower faculties were ideally under the control of the higher, just as a good society thrived under the direction of a philosopher-king.

To instruct as many people as possible in the way of philosophy, Plato, in 388/387 B.C.E., established the Academy, named for a nearby sanctuary of the hero Academus. Created as a corporation, the institution endured long after Plato's death. "Deanship" of the Academy passed from elected scholar to elected scholar until the school was finally closed by Emperor Justinian in 529 C.E. At this site, Plato had a building constructed that housed classrooms, a gymnasium, and a common dining hall. Here, men and women congregated to study philosophy and share their thoughts. The reputation of the Academy was such that students came from all over the Greek world to study there, making it one of the first truly cosmopolitan centers of the West. Its most famous student, the hallmark of late Classical philosophical inquiry, was Aristotle.

Aristotle

It is not really possible to summarize Aristotle's work; it would be like trying to summarize the *Encyclopedia Britannica*. Although some people of a more malicious bent might suggest that one could shorten such a presentation by discussing only the things Aristotle actually got right—which, in the end, were few—this would downplay the vast subject range that Aristotle and his students studied and systematized. In his own way, Aristotle *was* the ancient Greek *Encyclopedia Britannica*.

Aristotle was born in 384 B.C.E. in the town of Stagira in Macedon. His father was court physician to King Amyntas, the father of Philip II and grandfather of Alexander the Great. At age seventeen, Aristotle went to Athens to study with Plato at the Academy, where he remained for the next twenty years. He finally left when Plato died of old age in 347 B.C.E., and in 343 he went north to the city of Pella at the invitation of Philip II to tutor the young prince, Alexander. Aristotle served as personal instructor until Alexander began his regency in 340 B.C.E. Even after this, there remained a strong bond between the two, and Alexander greatly facilitated Aristotle's continued studies and his establishment of a school (see below).

The "complete works of Aristotle" (or most of them, anyway) have been preserved from ancient times in a distinct set of groupings. First are his works on logic, a body of treatises called the *Organon* ("Instrument" of thought). These include the *Categories, On Interpretation, Sophistic Refutations,* and *Prior Analytics*. One important idea from these works is the syllogism: According to this logical construct, if A = B and B = C, then A = C.

Following his logic treatises are Aristotle's works on the natural sciences, beginning with eight books on physics, including astronomy, meteorology, and what we might consider an early form of chemistry. Next come his works entitled *On the Soul*. Next, and perhaps most importantly, are Aristotle's works on biology and related sciences. His *Short Physical Treatises* include what today we consider psychology, with essays on memory, sleep, and sensory observation. In his *Biological Treatises*, Aristotle categorized just about every form of life he could observe, which was an appreciable number, considering that Alexander the Great himself had all new species that were discovered sent to his old teacher. Aristotle noted how animals lived, moved, and propagated.

After the *Physics* were the *Metaphysics* (literally, "after physics"). This was where Aristotle was at his most abstract. The Medieval philosopher Avicenna claimed that he finally started to understand the *Metaphysics* after reading the several essays some forty times. Here Aristotle discusses the concepts of matter and change, literally the building blocks of reality. In this corpus, Aristotle discusses the four causes of being. He claimed that every being must be explained according to four criteria. First was the material cause, which noted what a being was made of (bronze, flesh, water, etc.). Then there was the formal cause, which explained why a being was formed or shaped the way it was. Third was the efficient cause, which explained how the being came into being (e.g., born, carved), and finally came the final cause, which explained why the being came into being in the first place (Luce 1992, 116). As Aristotle puts it (*Metaphysics*, 5.2):

"Cause" is said on the one hand to be that by which means something comes into being, as bronze for the statue and silver for the cup, and such classes of things. Second, the form and the shape. That is: the logic of that which is and the classes of it . . . Third, from what initial beginning either a change or lack of change occurs, as the planner of the action, the father of the child, and in all other respects the doing of the thing done and the changer of the changed. Then the end result—that on which account the thing is done, as walking for health.

Put more simply, the material cause of a house is wood and brick. The formal cause is the practicality of four walls and a roof. The efficient cause is the architect and builder. The final cause is residence.

Following the *Metaphysics* are the *Eudemian Ethics* and *Nicomachean Ethics*, both ethical treatises. Finally, there are Aristotle's works on politics and literary criticism, including the books *Rhetoric* and *Poetics*. In this last study, Aristotle claimed that the purpose of drama was mass, emotional catharsis. This book was also where he established the three unities of theater: A drama should have one plot, be set in one place, and occur in one day. These unities were revered for 2,000 years. The seventeenth-century French dramatists Corneille and Racine followed them to the letter, even though this occasionally meant that the hero had to travel from France to Spain, vanquish an enemy army, and return in one day.

In 335 B.C.E., with financial backing from Alexander the Great, Aristotle established the Lyceum, a school like Plato's Academy, located near a sacred grove of Apollo Lykeios. The most notable physical structure of the complex was a colonnaded courtyard called the Peripatos, around which Aristotle

10.1 The School of Athens. Detail: Plato and Aristotle (Ted Spiegel/Corbis)

walked while discussing philosophy (and everything else). From this his students got the name Peripatetics. The main difference between Aristotle's school and Plato's was the perception of physical reality taught in each school. Plato believed very strongly in the Forms; the physical reality perceived with the bodily senses was merely temporary and not to be trusted. True reality existed on a higher plane. Aristotle, on the other hand, believed that physical reality, perceived through the senses, was the path to all knowledge. The Lyceum involved itself in all branches of philosophical and scientific inquiry, pursuing knowledge through the study, categorization, and explanation of all aspects of the world around it. Aristotle was of this world, Plato of a world beyond (see Image 10.1).

Cynicism

The word *Cynic* comes from the Greek kunos (dog) and refers to the supposedly dog-like lifestyles of the followers of this branch of moral philosophy. The school's founder was Diogenes of Sinopê (400–325 B.C.E.). His belief, passed on to his followers, was that humans should have a minimalist lifestyle, be self-sufficient, and conform to nature in all things. Living according to his word, Diogenes, as legend has it, lived in Athens with a barrel for a home, and he seldom bothered with clothes. As he felt that nature was always right, he took care of all his bodily needs, including urination, masturbation, and sex, out in public whenever the mood (and a possible partner) grabbed him. It is also recorded that Alexander the Great, admiring the philosopher's austere style of living, once stood over the reclining philosopher and offered him anything he wanted in the world. Diogenes supposedly replied, "Please move; you're blocking my sun."

Diogenes's greatest followers, responsible for spreading the Cynic philosophy, were Crates of Thebes (c. 368–288 B.C.E.) and his wife Hipparchia. The fact that these two were married shows a slight variation on the Cynic ideal, which would originally not have recognized that human institution or any need for it. Nevertheless, it does demonstrate a common aspect of the Cynic school—there was no clear "doctrine" of Cynicism, no code of beliefs or orthodoxy. The followers of Diogenes and Crates could pretty much adopt whatever aspects of the philosophy appealed to them, ultimately making it rather difficult to determine later who was a "real" Cynic. Crates was drawn to the ascetic aspect of Cynicism, preaching the happiness that comes from leading a simple, austere life, avoiding the complexities and dangers of political and social entanglements. He wandered all over Greece—carrying all his worldly possessions in a knapsack, as legend has it—preaching his philosophy and comforting people during the civil wars that marked the early Hellenistic era (see chapter 4). He was so beloved by the Greeks that the Roman author Julian recorded that people wrote on their doors "Welcome to Crates, the good spirit." Concerning Hipparchia, we know a bit less. Nevertheless, her epigram, recorded by Antipater of Thessalonica in the first century B.C.E., well embodies the Cynic free spirit:

> I, Hipparchia, have no use for the works of deep-robed women; I have chosen the Cynics virile life. I don't need capes with brooches or deep-soled slippers; I don't need glossy nets for my hair. My wallet is my staff's traveling companion, and the double cloak that goes with them, the cover for my bed on the ground. I'm much stronger than Atalanta from Mainalos, because my wisdom is better than racing over the mountain. (Lefkowitz and Fant 1992, 168)

Cynicism made its greatest impact in Greek (and, some would argue, even Roman) literature in the works of Bion of Borysthenes (325–255 B.C.E.) and Menippos of Gadara, a Syrian slave who eventually became a Theban citizen. The former invented the literary form known as the diatribe, a dialogue like those used by Plato but marked by caustic wit and satire with a strongly polemic voice. Very little of Bion's work remains, but it is evident that he attacked and condemned various types of excessive passions and cultural prejudices (Lesky 1996, 670). Better preserved are the works of Menippos, who is credited with inventing the spoudogeloion, or seriocomic style of philosophical commentary. His thirteen books are a combination of prose and poetry, filled with attacks on humanity's foolishness and the absurdities of the (other) schools of philosophy. His *Arcesilaus* poked fun at the Athenian Academy, and his *Nekyia* satirized traditional views of life after death (Lesky 1996, 671). It was this kind of harsh, critical, and yet humorous critique of the social mores of the day that led to the modern conception of a cynic as a curmudgeon who sees all that is wrong in the world.

Epicureanism

This school was named after its founder, Epicurus, an Athenian citizen born on Samos in 341 B.C.E. Epicurus was a prolific writer and composed some 300 scrolls of his theories on the nature of reality and humanity's place therein. Only a few scraps of his works have survived, including three of his letters preserved in the works of the later author Diogenes Laertius; a set of forty-three maxims called *The Principle Doctrines*; and part of his treatise *On Nature* discovered in the remains of Hurculaneum, a city destroyed by the same volcanic eruption that buried Pompeii (Luce 1992, 139–140).

Epicureanism is perhaps best known for its doctrine that pleasure was the ultimate purpose of life. One would think that unfettered hedonism would have been the lifestyle espoused by this school, but in truth, Epicurus believed that the only real pleasure was the absence of pain and want, and thus the true path to pleasure was the avoidance of pains and desires. Epicurus distinguished between kinetic and static pleasures. Kinetic pleasures, he said, were short-lived and generally caused more problems than they were worth. One might think of heroin addiction as an example. By contrast, static pleasures were mainly associated with the mind and produced a joy that was mostly divorced from the body. Contemplation of the perfection of the gods and the study of philosophy were static pleasures that led to happiness and had no drawbacks (Luce 1992, 145). Some pleasures more physical in nature that were allowed by Epicurean doctrine were drinking when one was thirsty and eating when hungry, but Epicurus taught that neither of these should be done to excess. Desire for fame, money, or power was seen as bad, as there was no natural fulfillment to these desires: No matter how much any individual had of them, there was no cessation of the desire for more.

Epicurus was no atheist. He believed in the gods, but he believed that they were beyond the human realm of existence. Like humans, gods would seek their own pleasure, and, as far as Epicurus was concerned, this did not include involving themselves in the affairs of men. That being the case, Epicurus taught, there were gods, perfect in all ways, who had little or nothing to do with people. Epicurus also had certain novel ideas concerning the nature of the soul. Unlike many of his predecessors, Plato especially, Epicurus believed that the soul was a physical entity that grew up with and in the body. Following the atomic theory (see above) line of reasoning, Epicurus taught that the body and soul were composed of atoms, those of the soul being smaller than those of the body, but just as physical. As such, there was no incorporeal, immortal aspect of the human persona (Diogenes Laertius 10, 67):

> But it is impossible to think of the incorporeal except for nothingness. And nothingness is able neither to act nor to be acted upon; it merely provides energy for bodies

to move through it. And so those who say that the soul is incorporeal are deceived. For it would not act or suffer, if that were so. But now, clearly, both of these are properties of the soul.

As there was no existence after death, the Epicureans believed that people should not waste time worrying about the afterlife. Instead, Epicurus developed the Tetrapharmakon, or Four-Part Remedy, for human sorrow: First, one should meditate, especially on the perfect nature of divinity. Second, one should accept death as the end and not worry about it. Third, one must accept a simple lifestyle. Finally, one should relax with friends and study philosophy as much as possible (Luce 1992, 148).

In an effort to facilitate that last remedy, Epicurus established schools where his followers could gather, study, and live Epicurean lifestyles together. He himself bought a house with a garden in Athens, and his school came to be known as the Garden (like Plato's Academy and Aristotle's Lyceum). The Garden endured into the second century C.E. Other schools were established in Egypt and Asia, and Epicurus wrote some of his letters to these schools. Membership was open to all levels of society—men, women, slaves, free, rich, poor—with the only requirement being that the members swear an oath of loyalty to Epicurus. The Epicurean theories of "absentee" deities and the mortality of the soul made them anathema to the Christians, who criticized them heavily, leading to the modern conception of an Epicurean as one who leads a hedonistic lifestyle.

Stoicism

This philosophy was devised in Athens by Zeno of Kition in the later fourth century B.C.E. Originally educated in Cynical theory, he devised his own ideas and discussed them with other students at the Stoa Poikilê (Painted Portico), giving rise to the name *Stoicism*. Almost all information we have about Stoic philosophy derives from later, Roman authors. Most notable are Diogenes Laertius, especially his *Life of the Stoics;* Cicero in his work *Academia;* and the Roman Stoic philosophers Epictetus and Emperor Marcus Aurelius, whose *Meditations* is considered one of the finest treatises on Stoic philosophy.

The Stoics believed that all reality was physical and that this physicality could be grasped by the human mind. Thus, it was possible for people to understand reality. They saw the world as a vast mechanism run by Deity or Mind, where all aspects of reality were linked to all other aspects in a grand, unified cosmos. This unity meant that any and all actions in the world affected all others. Rather than producing chaos, though, this grand unity, guided by Deity, was already set upon its appropriate course, where everything was predestined and occurred according to fate. As all things were predetermined by the Deity running the cosmos, and as the Stoics understood Deity as essentially beneficent, then all things always occurred as they were supposed to for the ultimate good of the universe (to quote Voltaire's Dr. Pangloss, "It's the best of all possible worlds"). Thus, there was no reason to get upset about (inevitable) problems in life, and the Stoics preached the ideal of reason and self-control over irrational, emotional reactions to day-to-day life. Such apatheia (lack of passion) is one of the most popular understandings of Stoic philosophy, best expressed in the Vulcans of *Star Trek* fame.

Influenced by Cynic beliefs, Zeno believed that an appropriate life was one led according to nature. But although the Cynics maintained that "according to nature" meant stripped of artificial civilization, Zeno believed that this meant according to humanity's rational nature. As reality was already predetermined, the "right" path was to follow one's predetermined calling. Living according to these dictates of Deity was virtue; to attempt resistance was vice. Because the Stoic universe was completely integrated, following the "natural" path inevitably meant that one was involved with all the affairs of the world. The Stoic was inevitably (at least ideally) political, and his/her outlook was cosmopolitan rather than limited to the polis or Greece. The Stoics saw themselves as citizens of the world.

In its earliest, purest form, Stoicism was rather extremist in its philosophical doctrines. Emotions were bad; reason was good. Vice was bad; virtue was good. Pretty much everything else fell into the category of "indifferent," meaning not worthy of thought or even necessarily of existence. Later, however, the Stoics lightened up a bit. Certain emotions were deemed acceptable, such as general cheerfulness (perhaps they realized that feeling happy about being a good Stoic suddenly put you back at square one). And though virtue remained the only true Good, certain other aspects of reality were considered at least to have value, such as health (Luce 1992, 137).

Stoic philosophy was the longest enduring of the Hellenistic philosophies, being adopted by many of the Roman intelligentsia. One of the greatest Stoic philosophers was the Roman emperor Marcus Aurelius, and Stoic philosophy pervades Vergil's *Aeneid.* The recognition of Deity as running the mechanisms of reality, and the focus on self-control, made the Christians less antagonistic to Stoicism than they were to some of the other Greek philosophies, allowing many of its ideologies to pervade Medieval and Renaissance ideologies.

REFERENCES

Allen, R. E. 1985. *Greek Philosophy: Thales to Aristotle.* 2d ed. New York: Free Press.

Athanassakis, A. 1976. *The Homeric Hymns: Translation, Introduction, and Notes.* Baltimore: Johns Hopkins University Press.

Barnes, J. 1987. *Early Greek Philosophy.* London: Penguin.

Barnstone, W. 1988. *Sappho and the Greek Lyric Poets.* New York: Schocken.

Beye, C. R. 1993. *Ancient Epic Poetry: Homer, Apollonius, Virgil.* Ithaca, NY: Cornell University Press.

DeWaal, C. 2001. "Medicine." In Speake, G., ed. *Encyclopedia of Greece and the Hellenic Tradition.* London: Fitzroy Dearborn.

Foley, H. P., ed. 1994. *The Homeric Hymn to Demeter: Translation, Commentary, and Interpretive Essays.* Princeton, NJ: Princeton University Press.

Hackforth, R. 1993. *Plato's Phaidros.* Cambridge, UK: Cambridge University Press.

Halporn, J. W., M. Ostwald, and T. G. Rosenmeyer. 1994. *The Meters of Greek and Latin Poetry.* Indianapolis, IN: Hackett.

Heath, T. L. 1996a. "Euklides's Elements." In Adler, M., ed. *Euklides, Arkhimedes, Nicomachus.* Chicago: Encyclopedia Britannica.

————. 1996b. "The Works of Arkhimedes." In Adler, M., ed. *Euklides, Arkhimedes, Nicomachus.* Chicago: Encyclopedia Britannica.

Henderson, J. 1996. *Three Plays by Aristophanes: Staging Women.* New York: Routledge.

Hutchins, R. M., ed. 1952. *Aristotle.* Chicago: Encyclopedia Britannica.

Inwood, B. and L. P. Gerson. 1988. *Hellenistic Philosophy: Introductory Readings.* Indianapolis, IN: Hackett.

Kasas, S. and R. Struckmann. 1990. *Importants centres médicaux de l'antiquité: Épidaure et Corinthe.* Athens, Greece: Editions Kasas.

King, H. 2001. *Greek and Roman Medicine.* London: Bristol Classics.

Lefkowitz, M. R. and M. B. Fant. 1992. *Women's Life in Greece & Rome: A Source Book in Translation.* Baltimore: Johns Hopkins University Press.

Lesky, A. 1996. *A History of Greek Literature.* Indianapolis, IN: Hackett.

Ley, G. 1991. *A Short Introduction to the Ancient Greek Theater.* Chicago: University of Chicago Press.

Lord. A. 2000. *The Singer of Tales.* 2d ed. Cambridge, MA: Harvard University Press.

Luce, J. V. 1992. *An Introduction to Greek Philosophy.* London: Thames & Hudson.

Nicolaidis, E. 2001. "Astronomy." In Speake, G., ed. *Encyclopedia of Greece and the Hellenic Tradition.* London: Fitzroy Dearborn, 185–187.

Schein, S. L. 1984. *The Mortal Hero: An Introduction to Homer's* Iliad. Berkeley: University of California Press.

Stein, S. 1999. *Arkhimedes: What Did He Do besides Cry Eureka?* Davis: University of California Press.

Wallace, R. 2001. "Mathematics." In Speake, G., ed. 2000. *Encyclopedia of Greece and the Hellenic Tradition.* London: Fitzroy Dearborn, 1011–1013.

Wender, D. 1973. *Hesiod and Theognis.* New York: Penguin.

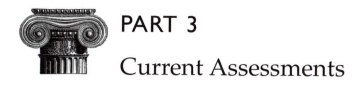

PART 3

Current Assessments

CHAPTER 11

Major Controversies and Future Directions in the Study of Greek Civilization

I t would be impossible here to recount and explain all of the controversies and needed foci of research in the study of Greek history. This is mainly because every Hellenist, archaeologist, papyrologist, numismatist, and Classicist is going to have a different idea of what those controversies are and what is needed to resolve them. Therefore, this chapter is quite subjective. I have listed and discussed here a few of the issues currently being debated in the fields of ancient history and Classics.

EXCAVATION

One universal desire among researchers is for more archaeological excavations and, just as importantly, for those excavations to be published in a timely manner. Every few years, the Greek Department of Antiquities suggests that Greek archaeologists should not be allowed to start new excavations until their old ones are published. Unfortunately, such policy never seems to materialize, and excavated sites remain unknown and inaccessible to all but the excavator himself/herself and those students working on the site. To give one example, the sanctuary of Apollo at Thermon was excavated decades ago but has yet to be appropriately published. The many excellent finds from the site are on display at the on-site museum, carefully watched over by guards who allow no photographs to be taken and no drawings to be made of the items.

More scientific analysis is also needed in the field of archaeology, especially for neutron and chemical analyses (see chapter 3). The work now taking place at such institutions as MASCA (Museum Applied Science Center for Archaeology) at the University Museum of the University of Pennsylvania can provide information, such as where pottery was made (through chemical analysis of the clays used in production) and what organic materials were contained in such vessels. To give an example, Patrick McGovern of MASCA, working with archaeologists excavating the Phrygian site of Gordion, famed capital of King Midas of the Golden Touch, analyzed the funerary banquet that sent the king off to his afterlife. It turned out that the liquid used in the libations consisted of honey, barley, and grapes—mead, beer, and wine, not far off from the potion described in the Homeric epics (McGovern et al. 1999, passim). Thus, archaeology shows the reality behind the Homeric "myths." (As an interesting aside, ancient beer contained no hops; these were a Medieval German addition. Therefore, ancient beer was sweet, not contrasting in flavor with the wine and mead.)

LINEAR A

One of the most important areas of research in Aegean prehistory is the translation of Linear A, the writing system used by the Minoans before the Mycenaean conquest (see chapters 3 and 4). It would appear that certain elements of a pre-Greek language have made their way into Greek, usually names ending in -nthos, -ssos, or -eus such as Knossos, Corinth(os), basileus, and Odysseus. The language that provided such words, then, should be the language (or at least a related group of languages) that was recorded in Linear A.

To this date, not only can we not read the language, we do not even know to what language family, if any, it belongs. For a while, some believed that Linear A was a Semitic language, thus related to Arabic and Hebrew. Although there may have been some loan words, especially for imported items (think of the word karate being used in English now), no aspect of what is known of the language seems to conform to the linguistics of Semitic languages. For example, the consonant cluster beginning place-names such as Knossos would not be likely to exist in a Semitic language. Others have suggested, and some now do still maintain, that the language is Indo-European, possibly related to the Luwian dialects spoken in nearby Turkey. Yet others think the language may be the elusive Pelasgian, the pre-Greek dialect occasionally referred to in the writings of the ancient Greeks themselves. As the language certainly appears to be pre-Greek, such a hypothesis is not unfounded. But it provides no actual help either, as the "Pelasgians" are even less well understood in Greek history than the Minoans themselves. Finally, there are those who see the Linear A language as simply Minoan, not related to any other languages, much as modern Basque.

Ultimately, the problem is that there is so little Linear A to work with. Ventris, Chadwick, and their colleagues had copious supplies of Linear B tablets with which to decode the language, many several lines long. What remains of Linear A is quite paltry, usually just a few signs on a pot or column. Add to this the fact that we really have no certain way of knowing if the phonetics discerned for Linear B are the same as those for Linear A. Thus, we cannot tell if we are even sounding the short words correctly (although see Godart 1984, 121–128, for more on this issue).

Nevertheless, once this language is decoded and translated, it is expected to provide many new data concerning the life of the ancient Minoans. Some important scholars currently working on this problem are John Younger, Jean-Pierre Olivier, and Louis Godart. The latter two have published much of the Linear A corpus in their *Recueil des inscriptions en Linéaire A* (Godart and Olivier 1976–1985).

MINOAN DEITIES

Another problem now being reconsidered is the nature of Minoan religion (which would probably be helped a lot by the translation of Linear A). Sir Arthur Evans, who first brought Knossos, and thus the Minoans, to light, was heavily influenced by a school of thought known as the Cambridge School, best expressed in the work *The Golden Bough* by Sir James Frazer. Much of this school claimed that ancient, "primitive" religions functioned around the need for fertility. Thus, ancient myths, ancient rites, and even ancient gods were all understood as aspects of some massive fertility cult. The center point of such religions, as the ancients understood it, was an Earth Mother/fertility goddess, who usually had a son-consort vegetation god who died and was reborn annually. Even to this day, Stone Age figurines such as the Venus of Willendorf are understood as "fertility idols." So influenced, Evans, and other scholars after him, seeing the prominence of females in Minoan iconography (see chapter 8), have suggested that the Minoans had a fertility cult surrounding the Great Minoan Mother Goddess. This symbolism was believed to explain such "awkward" images as the prominently displayed breasts of the Middle Minoan Snake Goddesses—lactation imagery, according to the Cambridge School.

In recent years, though, scholars such as Christine Morris and Lucy Goodison have challenged such notions, most accessibly in their 1998 publication *Ancient Goddesses* (Goodison and Morris 1998). Here, they consider such facts as the utter lack of any pregnant goddess imagery in the Minoan repertoire, the fact that none of these "mother goddesses" are ever shown with children, and the fact that the various items decorating the different goddess images—snakes, birds, labrydes—suggest that we are dealing with several goddesses, not just one major one. In point of fact, monotheism was almost unheard of in the ancient world until the rise of Akhnaten of Egypt in the fourteenth century.

Furthermore, the evidence from the Linear B tablets shows that there were several goddesses and gods in the Minoan repertoire (names appear in the tablets that are non-Greek and that are associated predominantly with Crete, having few to no cults on the mainland). Thus, deities such as Pade, Pipituna, and Qerasija appear from the records in Knossos, indicating Cretan but not Greek deities (Hiller 1997, 211). Some of the male deities, such as Enyalios and Paiawon, were apparently later absorbed by Greek gods—they became Ares Enyalios and Apollo Paean. Even the Minoan iconography shows male deities worshipped in sanctuaries, most notably the Palaikastro Kouros discussed in chapter 8. The notion of a single Mother Goddess and her Dying God consort must now be seriously reconsidered and replaced in the literature.

THE DARK AGE

Remarkably little is known about these centuries of Greek history except for the pottery sequences and the extraordinary finds from Lefkandi on the island of Euboia. The actual causes of the fall at the end of the Bronze Age are still in debate, although a current consensus more or less now states that a breakdown in the international relations and trade of the eastern Mediterranean provoked an upsurge of piracy, which destabilized the population such that they either went wandering in search of new homes or relocated as far from the wealthy, pirate-targeted urban centers as possible.

Those Greeks looking for new homes were one part of that movement, including the Sea Peoples recorded in the Egyptian records. The work of Trude Dothan has established that at least some aspects of Philistine culture were originally Mycenaean, later heavily influenced by Cyprus and Egypt (Dothan 1982, passim). More work is necessary, however, to determine how the Greeks related to the other groups of Sea Peoples, and where these wound up in their peregrinations around the Mediterranean. Several of the chapters in Eliezer Oren's (2000) *The Sea Peoples and Their World: A Reassessment* consider various aspects of this issue.

Likewise, the nature of the early Greek settlements in Cyprus is still in debate. It is generally now accepted that the Greeks arrived in Cyprus in two distinct "waves," one in about 1190 B.C.E. settling the western edge of the island at Maa-Palaikastro, the other settling farther north around 1075. Although originally these settlers were seen as Homeric warrior-pirates, seizing the island and Hellenizing it by force, scholars now believe that the Greeks arrived as humble refugees, wives and children in tow, bringing their language with them but in other ways adopting the local culture, including the local goddess Aphrodite.

However, the "two-wave" hypothesis has now come into debate. Most notably, Maria Iacovou, in her article "Cyprus at the Dawn of the First Millennium B.C.: Cultural Homogenisation versus the Tyranny of Ethnic Identifications" (in press), argues that there was only one twelfth-century wave and that there is, in fact, no clear evidence for an eleventh-century wave of Greek immigration onto the island. Rather, the minor cultural innovations of the eleventh century were due to the merging of the indigenous and Greek cultures into a new, Iron Age Cypriot society. If her hypotheses are correct, the history of the Hellenization of Cyprus must be reconsidered.

NON-ATHENIAN CULTURE

The Athenians, especially those of the fifth and fourth centuries B.C.E., left us an amazing wealth of materials from which to reconstruct their religion, culture, laws, and politics. This embarrassment of riches has led to an extraordinary focus on Athens in the study of ancient Greece. Almost any general book on Greek history is roughly 25–33 percent pure Athenian material, and Classical Athenian at that, and in any library, well over half of the books on ancient Greek politics, law, philosophy, or literature focus on Athens exclusively. This has led to a somewhat skewed view of ancient Greece in which it appears that only the Athenians had a democratic government or a literary heritage. It also tends to obscure the fact that Athens was not necessarily "typical" and that one cannot extrapolate from Athens to the rest of Greece. It is really only in recent times that any concerted efforts have been made to learn more about the cultures and societies of the various Greek poleis outside of Athens.

For example, it is a common misconception that democracy in ancient Greece was "invented" in Athens. All standard textbooks give the progression from Solon to Kleisthenes to Pericles as the evolution of Greek democracy (see chapter 7). By contrast, Eric Robinson, in his book *The First Democracies: Early Popular Government Outside Athens* (1997), has argued that democratic ideologies might be attributed to the relative egalitarianism associated with colonization. Every (adult male) colonist received equal portions of land and, by extension, an equal say in city politics. This system led to democratic elements in some colonial poleis as early as the mid-sixth century B.C.E., well before the first real manifestations of democracy in Athens under Kleisthenes. As such, rather than being in the vanguard of democratic reforms, Athens may have been acting under the general stimulus of egalitarianism spreading out from the colonies in the seventh and sixth centuries, which affected several of the Greek city-states in the Archaic Age.

FOREIGN RELATIONS

This is an area very much in need of further research, especially concerning Greek relations with the Near East and with the Black Sea region. Greek relations with the Near East have been a topic of interest for several years now, beginning in modern times as early as Astour's *Hellenosemitica* (1965) and being brought into sharp relief by such works as Boardman's *The Greeks Overseas* (1999), Burkert's *The Orientalizing Revolution* (1992), Bernal's *Black Athena* (1987), and the various articles in *Greeks and Barbarians* (Coleman and Walz 1997). For a long time, the main focus was on the Hellenization of the East under the successors of Alexander the Great. Then, as with Burkert, the focus shifted more to the "Oriental" influences that stimulated the Greeks during the Archaic Age, leading, among other things, to the invention of Greek writing (see chapter 3). Now, focus is once again shifting to relations between Greece and the Near East in the Bronze Age, especially in such publications as Lambrou-Phillipson's *Hellenorientalia* (1990) and George Bass's publications of the Ulu Burun and Gelidonya shipwrecks (Bass 1967; 1986).

A major problem is that there is as yet insufficient crossover between the fields of Classics and Classical history on the one side and Near Eastern studies on the other. Too many Hellenists discuss transference of culture between East and West without sufficient understanding of the Near Eastern cultures. To offer but one example, it has long been accepted that the goddess Aphrodite evolved from the Phoenician goddess Astarte, understood to be the Near Eastern goddess of love and fertility (see above, in the discussion about the Cambridge School). However, the Phoenician texts that refer to the goddess Astarte, and the Bronze Age Ugaritic texts as well, show her to be a goddess associated with warfare, hunting, and justice. In many respects, one might say she was more like a combination of Athena and Artemis than Aphrodite. Failing to consult the Phoenician sources, however, the majority of Classicists continue to see Aphrodite and Astarte as the same creature, not only confusing the origins of the Greek goddess, but perpetuating a false stereotype about the

Phoenician goddess as well (Budin 2003, ch. 9). Until such time as scholars look at both sides of an exchange, there will be only halting progress in this aspect of Greek studies.

WOMEN IN ANCIENT GREECE

Since the publication of Sarah B. Pomeroy's book *Goddesses, Whores, Wives, and Slaves: Women in Classical Antiquity* in 1975, there has been no lack of research on women in ancient Greece (and Rome, and now the Near East as well). As Greece was a very andocentric society, the study of women is hampered (to say the least) by the utter lack of female voices in the literary record. The few verses we have from Sappho or Corinna hardly make up for the otherwise exclusively male voice of the sources. Almost invariably, women must be studied and understood through what men have said about them. It is worth noting that, in all the hundreds of pages on women in ancient Greece in Lefkowitz and Fant's *Women's Life in Greece & Rome* (1992), only ten pages bear women's words, ranging from poetry to funerary inscriptions.

Part of this quandary has been solved in recent years through the application of women's studies and gender theory to the classical texts. Works such as Page DuBois's *Sowing the Body* (1998) and Helen King's *Hippocrates' Woman* (1998), for example, reveal how the ancient Greeks (by which I mostly mean men) understood the female body, both physically and ideologically. The literary texts, combined with epigraphy and archaeology, have yielded considerable data on the day-to-day lives of women, with Nancy Demand's *Birth, Death, and Motherhood in Classical Greece* (1994) being an excellent example of such a synthesis.

But more work needs to be done. As is applicable for far too many Greek studies, we have a preponderance of information for Athens, with much work still needed for the rest of Greece, although Sarah B. Pomeroy's *Spartan Women* (2002) is an excellent start. The effects of colonization for women must still be considered, as are the effects of class and domestic setting (urban vs. rural). Perhaps most importantly, more research is needed in the study of women during the Aegean Bronze Age. For decades, the idea of a Minoan matriarchy thrived, fueled by notions of the Minoan Great Mother Goddess (see above). Only now are scholars such as Barbara Olsen (1999) studying the available records to determine the status of women in Bronze Age Crete and Greece. According to Olsen's findings, the Linear B tablets show that it was far more common for women to own land independently in Crete than in mainland Greece during Late Helladic III. Furthermore, although secular women might have owned their own farms or orchards in Crete, only women serving as religious functionaries had land in Greece, suggesting that ownership for women was dependent on their duties to a deity. If such a system of landholding was a remnant from earlier practices, it may serve as conclusive evidence that the Minoans were at least more egalitarian than the Mycenaeans, if not strictly matriarchal (which is actually quite unlikely) (Olsen 1999, 296).

As mentioned in the beginning of this chapter, the subjects outlined here are only a tiny fraction of the topics in need of further research in the study of ancient Greece. Other scholars who see this chapter may be disappointed that it leaves out their pet projects, such as the evolution of the cross-bar alpha in Attic epigraphy, or the use of Queer Theory in the analysis of New Comedy. What the student of ancient Greece should take away from this ever-so-brief chapter is a sense of how much work is still needed in the exploration of the ancient Greek world. People have been studying Greece since the days of Homer himself (and, for the record, we still have no idea who Homer even was), and thousands of questions and topics still remain to be examined. It is a very rich field offering eternal intellectual fodder to the enthusiastic Hellenist.

REFERENCES

Astour, M. C. 1965. *Hellenosemitica: An Ethnic and Cultural Study in West Semitic Impact on Mycenaean Greece.* Leiden, Netherlands: E. J. Brill.

Bass, G. F. 1967. *Cape Gelidonya: A Bronze Age Shipwreck.* Transactions of the American Philological Association. New Series 57 (8). Philadelphia: American Philological Association.

————. 1986. "A Bronze Age Shipwreck at Ulu Burun (Kas): 1984 Campaign." *American Journal of Archaeology* 90, 269–296.

Bernal, M. 1987. *Black Athena: The Afroasiatic Roots of Classical Civilization.* New Brunswick, NJ: Rutgers University Press.

Boardman, J. 1999. *The Greeks Overseas: Their Early Colonies and Trade.* London: Thames & Hudson.

Budin, S. L. 2003. *The Origin of Aphrodite.* Bethesda, MD: CDL.

Burkert, W. 1992. *The Orientalizing Revolution: Near Eastern Influence on Greek Culture in the Early Archaic Age.* Cambridge, MA: Harvard University Press.

Coleman, J. E. and C. A. Walz, eds. 1997. *Greeks and Barbarians: Essays on the Interactions between Greeks and Non-Greeks in Antiquity and the Consequences for Eurocentrism.* Bethesda, MD: CDL.

Demand, N. 1994. *Birth, Death, and Motherhood in Classical Greece.* Baltimore, MD: Johns Hopkins University Press.

Dothan, T. 1982. *The Philistines and Their Material Culture.* New Haven, CT: Yale University Press.

DuBois, P. 1988. *Sowing the Body: Psychoanalysis and Ancient Representations of Women.* Chicago: University of Chicago Press.

Godart, L. 1984. "Du Linéaire A au Linéaire B." In *Aux origines de l'Hellénisme: La Crète et la Grèce. Hommage à Henri van Effenterre.* Paris: Publications de la Sorbonne, Histoire Ancienne et Médiévale 15.

Godart, L. and J.-P. Olivier. 1976–1985. *Recueil des inscriptions en Linéaire A. Études Crétoises 21,* vols. 1–5. Paris: Librairie orientaliste Paul Geuthner.

Goodison, L. and C. Morris, eds. 1998. *Ancient Goddesses: The Myths and the Evidence.* London: British Museum Press.

Hiller, S. 1997. "Cretan Sanctuaries and Mycenaean Palatial Administration at Knossos." In Driessen, J. and A. Farnoux, eds. *La Crète Mycenienne: Actes de la Table Ronde Internationale organisée par l'École française d'Athènes.* BCH Supplément 30. Athens: École française d'Athènes, 205–212.

Iacovou, M. (in press). "Cyprus at the Dawn of the First Millennium B.C.: Cultural Homogenisation versus the Tyranny of Ethnic Identifications." In Clarke, J., ed. (in press). *Archaeological Perspectives on the Transmission and Transformation of Culture in the Eastern Mediterranean.* London: Council for British Research in the Levant. Oxbow.

King, H. 1998. *Hippocrates' Woman: Reading the Female Body in Ancient Greece.* London: Routledge.

Lambrou-Phillipson, C. 1990. *Hellenorientalia: The Near Eastern Presence in the Bronze Age Aegean, c. 3000–1100 B.C.: Interconnections Based on the Material Record and the Written Evidence: Plus Orientalia: A Catalogue of Egyptian, Mesopotamia, Mitannian, Syro-Palestinian, Cypriot, and Asian Minor Objects from the Bronze Age Aegean.* Göteborg: Paul Åströms Förlag.

Lefkowitz, M. R. and M. B. Fant. 1992. *Women's Life in Greece & Rome: A Source Book in Translation.* 2d ed. Baltimore: Johns Hopkins University Press.

McGovern, P. E., et al. 1999. "A Funerary Feast Fit for King Midas." *Nature* 402 (December 23), 863–864.

Olsen, B. 1999. "Gender Ideologies and Economic Roles: The Land Tenure Tablets at Pylos and Knossos." *American Journal of Archaeology* 103, 296.

Oren, E. D. 2000. *The Sea Peoples and Their World: A Reassessment.* Philadelphia: University Museum Press.

Pomeroy, S. B. 1975. *Goddesses, Whores, Wives, and Slaves: Woman in Classical Antiquity.* New York: Schocken.

———. 2002. *Spartan Women.* Oxford: Oxford University Press.

Robinson, E. W. 1997. *The First Democracies: Early Popular Government Outside Athens.* Stuttgart: F. Steiner.

Glossary

(All dates B.C.E. unless otherwise noted.)

ABATON: "Not to be tread upon," an extra-sacred space in a sanctuary.

ABSOLUTE CHRONOLOGY: The establishment of when an event occurred by year, month, or exact day. Also see CHRONOLOGY.

ACADEMY: A school for the study of philosophy and all other types of knowledge, established by Plato around 385 in the vicinity of the sanctuary of Academas (hence the name). It lasted well into the fifth century C.E. and became the center for Neoplatonic philosophy.

ACHAEANS (AKHAIANS): One of the names used to identify the Greeks in Homer's writings.

ACHILLES (AKHILLEUS): "Best of the Achaeans." Primary hero of the *Iliad*.

ACROCORINTH: Acropolis of Corinth.

ACROPOLIS: Topographic high point of a city, often where the city deity had his/her main temple.

ADONIS: "Lord." Mortal lover of Aphrodite; his death was mourned by Greek women. Adonis derives from a Near Eastern dying-and-rising god, probably the Phoenician god Melqart.

ADYTON: The "holy-of-holies," the innermost sanctum of a temple.

AEOLIC: Of or relating to the speakers of the Aeolic dialect and/or the people living on the islands and mainland of the northwest coast of Asia Minor.

AESCHINES (AISKHINES): (397–322) Athenian orator and ambassador to Macedon.

AESCHYLUS (AISKHYLOS): (525/4–456) Athenian tragic playwright, earliest of the recorded tragedians.

AGAMEMNON: Mythic king of Mycenae, called King of Men. War leader in the *Iliad*.

AGHIOS ONOUFRIOS WARE: Early Minoan style of pottery typified by light clay with dark, painted linear designs.

AGLAUROS (AGRAULOS): Athenian heroine, daughter of the mythical King Kekrops, who leapt from the acropolis either in madness or to save the city. Her shrine on the acropolis was where the ephebes made their vow to preserve the city.

AGOGÊ: State-sponsored educational system for boys at Sparta.

AGORA: Civil, commercial, and religious center of a Greek city.

AISKHROLOGIA: The saying of obscene things.

AITHIOPIS: Epic of the Epic Cycle attributed to Arctinus of Miletos relating the final exploits of Achilles.

AKMAZONTES: Men at the "peak" of youth.

ALCAEUS (ALKAIOS): (b. c. 620) Lyric poet from Mytilene, Lesbos.

ALKIBIADES: (450–404) The "bad boy" of Athens. Nephew of Pericles, lover of Socrates, he was accused of profaning the Eleusinian Mysteries and defacing the Herms of Athens. Escaping trial, he fled to Sparta where he helped his new city defeat Athens. Accused of sleeping with one of the queens, he was banished from Sparta, too.

ALCMAEON (ALKMAION) OF CROTON: (fifth century) Medical writer who argued that good health depended on isonomia, or balance among all opposing forces in the body.

ALCMAEONIDAI (ALKMAIONIDAE): Noble clan of Athens, under atimia for the murder of Kylon in 632. Famous members were Pericles and Alcibiades.

ALCMAN (ALKMAN): (fl. 654–611) Lyric poet from Laconia. Author of the Partheneia, or "Maidens' Songs."

ALEXANDER IV: (323–310) Posthumous son of Alexander the Great with Roxana. One of Alexander the Great's heirs.

ALEXANDER THE GREAT: (356–323) Son of Philip II and Olympias of Macedon. Became king of Macedon and Greece upon the death of his father in 336 and proceeded to conquer all territories from Greece to India to Egypt.

ALKINÒÒS: In the *Odyssey,* the King of the Phaiakians.

ALMAGEST: "O Magistê," the greatest work of Claudius Ptolemy, a first-century C.E. astronomer.

AMPHICTIONY: An alliance, originally religious in orientation, among several poleis.

AMPHIPOLIS: Athenian colony in the Black Sea, and Athens's main supplier of grain. Hometown of Xena.

AMPHORA: Two-handled vessel used to store and transport liquids. In the Dark Age, cremated remains were often buried in these vessels—neck-handled ones for men, belly-handled ones for women.

AMYKLAI: Site just outside of Sparta famous for its sanctuary to Hyacinthus and Apollo.

ANACREON (ANAKREON): (b. c. 570) Lyric poet from Teos, considered to be the premier sympotic poet.

ANAKALYPTERIA: Part of the wedding ceremony in which the bride lifts her veil, symbolically giving herself to her new husband.

ANAXAGORAS: (500–428) Athenian natural philosopher who argued that all existence diverged from one primordial mass, and that all things still contain a bit of everything else. He taught that all things were moved by Mind, the one thing that was both universal and unchanging.

ANAXIMANDER OF MILETOS: (610–540) Natural philosopher and astronomer.

ANAXIMENES OF MILETOS: (fl. 546) Natural philosopher and astronomer, probably a student of Anaximander.

ANCHISTEIA: One's close family, extending out as far as second cousins.

ANDROMAKHÊ: Wife of Hector in the *Iliad.*

ANDRÔN: The "men's room" in a Greek house; the room where symposia were held.

ANTIGONID: Of or relating to the dynasty that controlled Greece after the death of Alexander the Great.

ANTIGONOS I: (382–301) Called Antigonos One-Eyed. General under Alexander the Great and satrap of Phrygia in Asia Minor. After Alexander's death, he attempted to reunite the empire under his own command, eventually being defeated at the Battle of Ipsos.

ANTIGONOS II: (320–239) Also known by the epithet "Gonatas." Son of Demetrios I, the first acknowledged Antigonid king of Macedon. Well-known as a statesman and philosopher.

ANTIPATER: (397–319) General under Philip II, governor of Macedon and general of Europe during Alexander the Great's eastern travels. Regent for Alexander's heirs.

ANYTÊ: (third century) Poet from Tegea, Arcadia, famous for her epigrams.

APATOURIA: Attic-Ionic religious festival celebrating the family and clan.

APETAIROS: A resident alien in a Cretan city.

APHRODITE: Goddess of sex and love.

APOLLO: God of music, light, prophecy, healing, plague, youth, and archery.

APOLLONIOS OF PERGÊ: (third century) Astronomer and mathematician who calculated the eccentric and epicyclical models of planetary motion. He also published works on conics.

APOLLONIOS OF RHODES: (third century) Librarian at Alexandria and last great epic poet. Defying the styles dictated by Callimachus, he composed the *Argonautika* in traditional Homeric style. Received honorary citizenship at Rhodes for his work.

APSIDAL: Architectural term referring to a building with a rounded end.

ARCADIA (ARKADIA): Territory in central Peloponnese. Primary cities were Mantinea and Tegea.

ARCHIDAMAS II: (r. 469–426) King of Sparta who led the Spartan attacks on Athens in the early years of the Peloponnesian War.

ARCHIDAMAS III: (r. 361–338) King of Sparta who fought at the Battles of Leuctra and Mantinea.

ARCHILOCHUS (ARKHILOKHOS): (seventh century) From Paros, iambic and elegiac poet, seen as the inventor of the monodic spirit.

ARCHIMEDES (ARKHIMEDES): (287–212) Mathematician and inventor from Syracuse. He is most famous for his discovery of specific gravity ("Eureka!") and for his war machines used against the Roman navy c. 213. Killed by a Roman soldier in the 212 invasion of Syracuse.

ARCHON (ARKHON): State officeholder, usually the highest executive officer.

AREOPAGOS: "Hill of Ares." An Athenian council composed of former archons. Its primary function was to serve as court and jury for homicide cases.

ARES: God of war.

ARETÊ: (1) Virtue, excellence, the Greek ideal. (2) In the *Odyssey,* the Queen of the Phaiakians.

ARGIVES: A name used to identify the Greeks in Homer's epics.

ARGOLID: Territory in the southeastern Peloponnese along the Gulf of Argos. Dominated by Mycenae in the Bronze Age and Argos in the Iron Age.

ARGOS: City of the Argolid. Ruled by Diomedes in the Homeric epics, and by Pheidon in the seventh century (?). Famous for its Archaic sanctuary of Hera.

ARION OF CORINTH: (fl. c. 600) Lyric poet who composed dithyrambs on specific themes, leading eventually to the rise of tragedy.

ARISTARKHOS OF SAMOS: (fl. 330) First Greek astronomer to suggest that the Earth revolved around the sun and that the Earth rotated on its axis.

ARISTIDES: (late sixth–early fifth century) Called The Just. Athenian statesman and general, ostracized before the Persian Invasions and recalled to face the Persian forces at Plataia.

ARISTOPHANES: (d. 385) Athenian comic playwright whose comedies are the only ones remaining in the Old Comedy style.

ARISTOTLE: (384–322) Philosopher, student of Plato, and tutor of Alexander the Great. His work touched on almost everything, and his theories were revered well into the Renaissance. Founder of the Lyceum in Athens.

ARKTEIA: Name of one or two rituals in Attica in which girls of different ages "played the bear" for Artemis.

ARTEMIS: Goddess of the hunt, goddess of animal fertility, and protectress of children and women.

ASCLEPIADES OF BITHYNIA: (second century) Greek physician practicing in Rome who argued that illness comes from the over- or underexcited nature of the atoms composing the body.

ASCLEPIUS (ASKLEPIOS): Semidivine son of Apollo and Coronis; he was revered as the demigod of physicians and healing.

ASIA MINOR: The peninsula of Turkey.

ASPASIA: (fifth century) Milesian woman who moved to Athens and became the consort of Pericles of Athens. Regarded as a philosopher by Socrates in the works of Plato.

ASTARTE: Canaanite and Phoenician queen deity and goddess of warfare, hunting, and the royal family.

ATHENA: Goddess of wisdom, war, handicrafts, and the city of Athens.

ATHENS: Capital city of Attica. Politically dominant during the fifth century.

ATIMIA: Dishonor, a severe punishment in Greece including loss of civic rights.

ATTICA (ATTIKA): Territory of central Greece, politically united under the leadership of Athens.

AULOS: Woodwind instrument, either single- or double-bodied.

AUTARKEIA: Self-sufficiency, the economic ideal of the ancient Greeks.

BACCHIADAE (BAKKHIADAI): Dominant clan in Early Archaic Corinth.

BACCHILIDES (BAKKHILIDES): (fl. fifth century) Lyric poet from Iulis on Keos.

BAETYL: "House of God." A (mostly) unworked stone understood to house the presence of a deity. Often associated with Aphrodite and Hermes.

BASILEUS: In the Bronze Age, some manner of industrial foreman and civic leader. In the Dark and Archaic Ages, this was the term for *king*, of which there could be many in each city. By the Classical period, this title was reserved for the emperor of Persia.

BASS, GEORGE: Present-day father of modern underwater archaeology.

BION OF BORYSTHENES: (325–255) Cynic philosopher credited with inventing the literary style of the diatribe.

BLACK FIGURE: Style of vase painting prevalent until 500. Figures were painted black on a natural background, with additional details added by incision. Women's skin was then painted white.

BLEGEN, CARL: (1887–1971 C.E.) Pioneer in Bronze Age Aegean archaeology; excavated Nestor's palace at Pylos.

BOIOTIA: "Cow-Land." Territory of central Greece. Capital is Thebes.

BOULÊ: Political council, usually the administrative aspect of the ekklesia.

BOYD-HAWES, HARRIET: (1871–1945 C.E.) Pioneer in Bronze Age Aegean archaeology; excavated the town of Gournia.

BRAURON: Site in Attica near Athens, famous for a sanctuary of Artemis. Here, Attic girls came to "play the bear" as children and before marriage.

BRIDE PRICE: Money or goods paid by a groom's family to a bride's family upon the arrangement of a wedding.

BYZANTIUM: Greek colony on the Sea of Marmara.

CADMUS (KADMOS): In myth, the Phoenician founder of Thebes, grandfather of Dionysos.

CALLIMACHUS (KALLIMAKHOS): (305–240) Extremely influential poet at Alexandria. He scorned the epic style, preferring short, elegant verses. His greatest work is the *Aitia*, or "Causes of Things."

CALLIPUS (KALLIPOS) OF CYZICUS: (fl. 330) Astronomer who added to Eudoxos's homocentric spheres theory and who calculated the solar year to be 365 and one-fourth days.

CAPE GELIDONIYA: Site of a late thirteenth-century shipwreck excavated by George Bass.

CARBON DATING: Measuring the breakdown of Carbon 14 into Carbon 12 in organic items from archaeological sites. As Carbon 14 decays at a predictable rate, the ratio of Carbon 14 to Carbon 12 in the item allows scientists to determine the item's age.

CARIA: Region of southwestern Asia Minor.

CASSANDER (KASSANDER): (358–297) Soldier in Alexander the Great's army and son of Antipater, he seized control of Greece from Polyperchon and attempted to reunite Alexander's empire for himself. He reigned in Greece until his death, establishing the city of Thessalonica and rebuilding Thebes.

CASSANDRA (KASSANDRA): In myth, the prophetic princess of Troy, raped by Ajax, enslaved by Agamemnon, and murdered by Clytemnestra.

CHADWICK, JOHN: Present-day British classicist active in the translation of Linear B.

CHAERONEA (KHAIRONEIA), BATTLE OF: (338) Battle in which the combined forces of Greece, led by Athens and Thebes, faced the Macedonians under Philip II. Philip won, signaling the end of Greek independence and initiating the period of Macedonian hegemony that would culminate under Alexander and the Antigonid monarchies.

CHALKIS (KHALKIS): City on Euboia that thrived during the Dark and Early

Archaic Ages. As indicated by its name (*khalkos* = bronze), the early city appears to have had an active bronzesmithing industry. Cofounder of Pithekoussai with Eretria.

CHAOS: One of the four primordial deities in Hesiod's *Theogony.*

CHITON (KHITON): Woman's dress made of a sheet of linen and usually sewn above the shoulders.

CHRONOLOGY: The study of time, specifically a list of when particular events occurred.

CHRYSELEPHANTINE: Made of gold and ivory.

CIST GRAVE: Sunken, roughly rectangular grave, usually lined with pebbles.

CLEOPATRA VII (KLEOPATRA): (69–31) Final Hellenistic monarch, pharaoh of Egypt. Her forces, combined with those of Marc Antony, were defeated at the Battle of Actium in 31, after which she committed suicide, leaving Egypt in the hands of Rome.

COMEDY: From the Greek term for "village revel," a humorous drama usually based on contemporary events, used in the worship of Dionysos. All extant Old Comedies were written by the Athenian Aristophanes. All extant New Comedies were written by the Athenian Menander.

CORINTH: City located at the isthmus founded in the Geometric period. Famous for its contacts with the Near Eastern civilizations, its port, its pottery, and its sanctuary of Aphrodite.

CORINTHIAN ORDER: Architectural style typified by a combination of Doric and Ionic styles and by the use of acanthus leaf decorations on column capitals.

CORINTHIAN STYLE: Pottery style from Corinth starting in 625. Typified by many colors (buff, black, red), fantastic creatures, and a "busy" feel.

CRATES (KRATES) OF THEBES: (368–288) Cynic philosopher and husband of Hipparchia, who propagated his beliefs throughout the Greek world. Was so well loved that he was deemed a "good spirit" by the Greek people.

CRETE: Island south of mainland Greece, home of the Minoan civilization in the Bronze Age. Doric territory in the Iron Age.

CROESUS (KROISOS): (r. 560–546) Wealthy king of Lydia, host to Solon, defeated by the Persians.

CULT: The physical manifestation of a religion, including items and acts such as rituals, clothing, and dedications.

CYCLADES: The "circle" of islands surrounding Delos in the Aegean.

CYCLOPEAN CONSTRUCTION: Style of building construction characterized by the use of huge stones and boulders, typical of the Mycenaean period. Later Greeks believed that only the Cyclopes could have moved such large stones.

CYNICISM: Hellenistic philosophy founded by Diogenes of Sinope, espousing natural living.

CYNISCA (KYNISKA): (early fourth century) Spartan princess, first female victor at the Olympics.

CYPRO-ARCADIAN: Of or relating to the speakers of the Greek dialect spoken in Arcadia in the central Peloponnese and Cyprus.

CYPRUS (KYPROS): Island south of Turkey off the Levantine coast. Named for its principal commodity, copper, it was settled by Greeks starting in the twelfth century, and by Phoenicians in the ninth.

CYPSELUS (KYPSELOS): (r. 657–625) Member of the Bacchiadae clan who over-threw his family to establish a tyranny in Corinth.

CYRENÊ (KYRENÊ): Prosperous Greek colony/city in Libya.

DANAANS: A name used to identify the Greeks in Homer's epics.

DELIAN LEAGUE: Also called the First Athenian Empire. A defensive league established after the Persian Invasions of 479. Headed by Athens. All member poleis contributed ships for the naval defense of Greece, or money to fund said navy. By 450, membership ceased being voluntary and tribute to Athens became mandatory.

DELOS: Small island in the center of the Cyclades. Mythic birthplace of Apollo, it was famous for its sanctuaries of Artemis and Apollo. Its religious character made it a Panhellenic sanctuary and the original treasury of the fifth-century Delian League.

DELPHI: City in central Greece famous for its sanctuary of Apollo and its Panhellenic games. Home of the Pythia, Apollo's primary oracle priestess.

DEME: Literally, "neighborhood." The smallest political unit in Athens, as es-tablished by Kleisthenes in 508. Membership in the citizen body was depend-ent on deme membership.

DEMETER: Goddess of vegetal fertility, especially of grain.

DEMETRIOS I: (336–283) Also known by the epithet "Poliorcetes." Son of Antigonos I who helped his father try to reunite Alexander the Great's empire. After a setback at the Battle of Ipsos, Demetrios led a sea-based regime until the death of Olympias, when the army recognized him as the legitimate king of Macedon.

DEMETRIOS OF PHALERON: (b. c. 350) Athenian Peripatetic philosopher, made governor of Athens under Cassander; eventually became chief librarian at Alexandria in 297.

DEMOCRITUS OF ABDERA: (b. c. 460–457) The first atomist, arguing that all things are composed of very tiny, indivisible units. Also wrote on anthropolog-ical topics.

DEMOSTHENES: (384–322) Greatest Athenian orator, especially famous for his declamations against the rise of Macedon under Philip II.

DENDROCHRONOLOGY: The study of tree rings in ancient wood to determine chronology.

DESPOINA: "Mistress" goddess of wildlife, worshipped mainly at Lykosura.

DIAGORAS OF RHODES: (fifth century) A boxer renowned throughout Greece.

DIKÊ: Justice, especially as enforced by Zeus.

DIODORUS SICULUS: (first century) Wrote a world history providing much information on ancient Greece.

DIOGENES LAERTIUS: (third century C.E.) Author of a compendium on the lives and doctrines of philosophers from Thales to Epicurus.

DIOGENES OF SINOPÊ: (400–325) Founder of the Cynic school of philosophy, which preached that happiness was attainable by attending to the body's natu-ral needs and scorning artificiality. Lived in Athens in a barrel.

DIONYSOS BAKKHOS: God of wine, liquid fertility, and liminality.

DITHYRAMB: Choral lyric poem sacred to Dionysos.

DODECANESE (DODEKANESE): The twelve islands off the southwest coast of Asia Minor, led by the administration of the island of Rhodes.

DORIC: Of or relating to speakers of the Doric dialect, usually comprising the people of the southern Peloponnese, Crete, and the Cyclades.

DORIC ORDER: Architectural style featuring simple column capitals and a frieze of triglyphs and metopes.

DOWRY: Daughter's share of her inheritance, received upon her marriage and passed on to her own children.

DRACHMA (DRAKHMA): "Handful." A coin worth six obols.

DROMOS: (1) Entrance corridor to a tomb in the Mycenaean period. (2) A racetrack.

EARTH (GE OR GAIA): One of the four primordial deities in Hesiod's *Theogony*.

EKDOSIS: The "giving away of the bride" part of the wedding ceremony.

EKKLESIA: Political assembly, composed of all citizens of a polis who were eligible to vote as based on sex and class.

EKPHORA: Carrying out of a corpse, a common motif on Late Geometric pottery.

ELEUSINIAN MYSTERIES: One of the oldest mystery cults, held annually at Eleusis in Attica. Sacred to Demeter and Persephonê/Korê, they offered the initiate hopes of a better life and afterlife.

EMPEDOKLES OF ACRAGAS: (493–433) Natural philosopher who first argued that physical reality was composed of the four elements of air, fire, water, and earth. Extending this notion, he suggested that the human body was composed of four humors, a balance among which was necessary for good health.

ENGYÊ: Betrothal, the first step in a marriage ritual.

ENKOMION: Choral poem praising a victor and his family.

ENYALIOS: Bronze Age war deity who later merged with Ares.

EPAMEINONDAS: (d. 362) Leader of Thebes during its period as hegemon of Greece. Brought Philip II to Thebes as hostage and taught Philip everything he knew about warfare. Was killed at the Battle of Mantinea.

EPHEBE: A boy just under the age of adulthood, somewhere between ages fifteen and twenty (usually eighteen or nineteen).

EPHOR: Spartan politician responsible for maintaining law and keeping the kings in line. Five ephors served at a time.

EPICURUS (EPIKYROS): (341–270) Greek natural and moral philosopher who taught that happiness and pleasure of the soul were the principal aims of life and that one should limit one's desires so as to achieve both.

EPIDAUROS: City in north-central Greece famous for its sanctuary of Asclepius and its well-preserved theater.

EPIGONI: Epic in the Epic Cycle, tentatively attributed to Homer, relating the end of the Seven Against Thebes.

EPIGRAM: Two-line inscribed poem appearing in Greek literature since the eighth century. Often used for funerary epitaphs starting in the Classical period.

EPIGRAPHY: The study of inscriptions.

EPIKLEROS: An heiress, as named in Athens. A girl with no brothers whose father has died; she must therefore marry a close male relative on her father's side to pass on the patrimony.

EPINIKION: Choral victory poem.

ERASISTRATOS OF CHIOS: (304–250) Greek father of physiology who determined that the heart was a pump for the circulatory system.

ERASTES: The "dominant" partner in a sexual union; the penetrator.

ERATOSTHENES OF CYRENÊ: (276–197) Astronomer/mathematician famous for his work on prime numbers and his accurate measurement of the Earth's surface.

ERECHTHONIUS: "The Earth-Born"; mythical foster son of Athena and early king of Athens.

ERETRIA: City on the island of Euboia, one of the first poleis to send off colonies in the eighth century. Cofounder of Pithekoussai with Chalkis.

ERINYES (THE FURIES): Dread goddesses who punished crimes against blood kin.

ERIS: Goddess of strife.

EROMENOS: The "submissive" partner in a sexual union; the penetratee.

EROS: God of love. Either one of the four primordial deities or, later, the son of Aphrodite.

ETHNIC LEAGUE: An equal alliance between poleis originally based on a common ethnic identity.

ETHNOS: A recognized ethnic group, distinguished primarily by language.

EUBOIA: Island off the coast of Attica. Unusually prosperous during the Dark Age, featuring towns such as Eretria, Chalkis, and Xeropolis (= Lefkandi). Pottery from Euboia was widely dispersed in the Dark and Early Archaic Ages.

EUCLIDES (EUCLID): (fl. c. 300) Prolific author on mathematics and music theory, especially well-known for his works on geometry, summarized in his book *Elements.*

EUDOXOS OF KNIDOS: (390–340) Astronomer who developed the theory of the homocentric spheres, by which he attempted to explain the retrograde motion of the planets. He also compiled a list of the constellations, including their calendrical risings and settings.

EURIPIDES: (485–406) Athenian tragic playwright. Although he was primarily a tragedian, his *Cyclops* is the only complete surviving satyr play.

EVANS, SIR ARTHUR: (1851–1941 C.E.) Pioneer in Bronze Age Aegean archaeology. Excavator of Knossos, "founder" city of Minoan civilization. Knighted in 1911.

EXOMIS: Man's garment made of a trapezoid of cloth wrapped around the body and falling to the knees.

FAIENCE: Glass-like substance developed in Egypt, used in both glaze and solid form.

FIBULA: Dress pin with a clasp.

FLORAL STYLE: Name for the style of decoration typifying Late Minoan IB pottery.

FLUTING: Vertical scalloped patterning on a column.

FOLLOWERS (HEQUETAI): Companions to the wanax in the Linear B tablets, high functionaries in the Bronze Age palatial bureaucracy.

FORMULA: Set phrase in appropriate meter; the building block of oral epic poetry.

FRESCO: Wall-painting technique in which pigments are applied directly onto the wall plaster.

FRIEZE: Continuous zone below a temple pediment, decorated with metopes and triglyphs in the Doric order and with sculpture in the Ionic and Corinthian orders.

GAMOS: Literally, "marriage." Also referring to that part of the wedding ritual in which the couple consummated the marriage.

GELON: (540–478) Military leader who became master of Gela, then tyrant of Syracuse, through his military victories against the Carthaginians. Founder of the Deinomenid dynasty.

GENOS: A clan or family, specifically a noble family, which maintained control over political and religious functions in a polis.

GEOMETRIC: Of or relating to the arts or culture of Greece from 900 to 700.

GEROUSIA: In Sparta, the council of twenty-eight elders who served as the advisory board to the kings. Such a group also existed in Cyrenê, Libya.

GODDESS WITH UPRAISED ARMS: Idol type prolific in the Late Minoan IIIC period on Crete and, starting in the eleventh century, on Cyprus.

GORTYN: City in Crete famous for its Archaic/Classical law code, preserved in inscriptions.

GOURNIA: Site of a Minoan city in eastern Crete.

GRIFFIN: Mythical animal with the body of a lion and the head and wings of an eagle.

HADES: (1) God of death and the underworld. (2) The underworld itself.

HAGHIA IRINI: Site on the island of Keos famous for its Bronze Age fortifications and its sanctuary, which remained in use from the Bronze Age through Archaic times.

HAGHIA TRIADHA: "Holy Trinity." Site in central Crete featuring a village dating from Early Minoan times and also featuring a Late Bronze Age villa.

HAGHIA TRIADHA SARCOPHAGUS: Small, painted, terra-cotta coffin decorated with frescoes of religious rituals typical of Minoan and possibly Mycenaean cults.

HALBHERR, FREDERICO: (late nineteenth–early twentieth century C.E.) Pioneer in Bronze Age Aegean archaeology. Excavator of the palace of Phaistos.

HEBÊ: Goddess of youth.

HECATÊ (HEKATÊ): Goddess associated with good luck and magic, especially prominent in Hesiod's *Theogony*.

HECTOR (HEKTOR): Chief soldier and prince of the Trojans in the *Iliad*.

HECUBA (HEKABÊ): Queen of Troy in the *Iliad*.

HEGEMON: Leader.

HEGEMONIC LEAGUE: An alliance among poleis in which one polis is recognized as group leader.

HELEN OF TROY (HELEN OF SPARTA): Mythical queen of Sparta who left her husband Menelaos for Paris/Alexandros, prince of Troy. Originally a goddess, either of vegetation or dawn, later demoted to heroine status.

HELLADIC: Of or referring to mainland Greece in the Bronze Age.

HELLAS: Greek word for Greece, root of such words as *Helladic, Hellenistic,* and *Panhellenic.*

HELLENISTIC: (323–31) Of or relating to the Greek-speaking world from the death of Alexander the Great until the death of Cleopatra VII.

HELOTS: The conquered Messenian population, enslaved by the Spartans in the seventh century B.C.E. and freed in the fourth century B.C.E.

HEPHAISTOS (HEPHAESTUS): God of metalworking and smiths.

HERA: Goddess of marriage, queen of the deities.

HERACLES (HERCULES): "Glory of Hera." Greatest hero in Greek mythology. Son of Zeus and Alkmenê ("Strength"), he was extremely strong. Often driven mad by Hera and Lyssa, he committed crimes for which he absolved himself by performing labors. He is most famous for his Twelve Labors, including slaying the Nemean lion, Lernaian hydra, and Stymphalian harpies, and for capturing Kerberos. In early tradition, he was mortal, but by the Archaic Age, legend tells that he was divinized after his death and married the goddess Hebê.

HERACLITUS (HERAKLEITOS): (fl. 500) Natural philosopher and astronomer from Ephesus. Called The Riddler for the obtuse nature of much of his writing.

HERM: Rectangular block of stone or wood topped with the head of Hermes and with his erect phallus on the side. Used as a boundary marker.

HERMES: Messenger of the deities. God of athletics, herding, trade, and trickery. As Psychopompos, he brought souls to and from Hades.

HERO/HEROINE: An individual formerly mortal but revered after death as semidivine.

HERODOTUS: (c. 500–c. 430) Called the Father of History. Born in Halicarnassus, Turkey. He wrote the *Histories,* a study of the peoples of Greece and the Near East, culminating in the Persian Invasions of Greece.

HEROÖN: Temple in which a hero or heroine was revered.

HEROPHILOS OF CHALCIDON: (335–280) Greek father of neurology. He studied the nervous system, liver, reproductive system, and circulatory system. Famous for determining that the brain was the center of thought and that the pulse was related to health.

HESIOD: (eighth century) Epic poet who lived in Askra, Boiotia, and who composed the *Theogony, Works and Days, Shield of Heracles,* and *Catalogue of Women.*

HESTIA: (1) Goddess of the hearth. (2) The hearth itself.

HETAIRA: Literally, "female companion." An upper-class, self-employed prostitute.

HIEROKERYX: "Sacred Herald." A cult functionary at Eleusis.

HIERON: Sacred space dedicated to a deity, usually translated as "sanctuary."

HIERON I: (d. 467/466) Brother of Gelon, tyrant of Syracuse. Became tyrant of Gela when Gelon moved to Syracuse, and eventually Hieron succeeded to the rule of Syracuse himself. Chief power in Sicily in the early fifth century; his court hosted many philosophers and poets.

HIERON II: (306–215) Military leader who became tyrant of Syracuse c. 275. Originally a supporter of Carthage, he allied himself with Rome in 263 and remained a steadfast Roman ally until his death.

HIEROPHANT: Literally, "One Who Shows Sacred Things." High priest at Eleusis.

HIMATION: Cloak or mantle worn by men and women.

HIPPARKHIA: (fourth century) Cynic philosopher and wife of Crates of Thebes. She traveled throughout the Greek world spreading the Cynic philosophy.

HIPPARCHUS (HIPPARKHOS) OF NICAEA: (190–126) First Greek to construct a full theory of the motion of the sun and moon. He also discovered the procession of the equinoxes and used parallax to determine the size and distances of the sun and moon.

HIPPEIS: "Knights." Second highest class in Solon's class system for Athens. A knight's property could furnish 300 units of grain, wine, or oil, enough to purchase a complete set of armor and maintain a horse.

HIPPIAS OF ELIS: (485–415) Sophist and mathematician who calculated the quadratrix.

HIPPOCRATES (HIPPOKRATES) OF COS: (460–377) Physician and medical writer who established a medical school and hospital on his home island. Studied medicine through direct observation and recorded his findings and conclusions.

HOMER: (c. eighth century) Semimythical epic poet credited with composing several epics relating to the Trojan War. Of these, only the *Iliad* and *Odyssey* remain.

HOMERIDAI: Poets who composed hymns to the deities in the style, meter, and language of the Homeric epics.

HOPLITE: Heavily armored foot soldier, usually equipped with helmet, shield, spears, sword, and greaves.

HORNS OF CONSECRATION: Sacred symbol in Minoan Crete, derived either from a schematic rendering of a bull's head or from the Egyptian hieroglyph of a valley.

HYACINTHUS (HYAKINTHOS): Pre-Greek nature deity worshipped in the Peloponnese. Later replaced by Apollo and demoted to position of that god's friend and victim.

HYDRIA: Three-handled water jug.

HYMNAION: Choral poem used as a wedding song.

HYPOMAIONES: Former Spartan citizens who had lost citizenship by not being able to pay their sysition dues.

IBYCUS (IBYKOS): (sixth century) Choral lyric poet from Rhegion.

IDEOGRAM: In a writing system, an image that represents an idea, such as the modern happy face ☺.

ILIAD: Epic attributed to Homer, relating the story of the wrath of Achilles and the death of Hector.

ILIU PERSIS: Epic of the Epic Cycle attributed to Arctinus of Miletos, describing the end of the Trojan War.

INDO-EUROPEAN: (1) Language family including Greek, Irish, German, Latin, Persian, and Vedic. (2) Of or referring to speakers of these languages.

IONIC: Of or relating to the speakers of the Attic-Ionic dialect and/or the people living along the western coast of Asia Minor.

IONIC ORDER: Architectural style originating in western Asia Minor featuring volute capitals and a continuous frieze.

IPHIGENEIA (IPHIANASSA): Daughter of Agamemnon and Clytemnestra, sacrificed by her father to bring good winds to the fleet heading for Troy. She didn't actually die, and she later became high priestess to Artemis at Brauron.

IPSOS, BATTLE OF: (301) Battle between Antigonos "One-Eyed" against Seleucus, Ptolemy, and Cassander. Antigonos lost and was killed.

IRIS: Goddess of the rainbow, messenger for Hera.

KADMEIA: The acropolis of Thebes.

KAMARES WARE: Minoan black-, white-, and orange-painted pottery typically decorated with floral motifs, appearing in the Middle Minoan period.

KANTHAROS: Drinking cup with high, arched handles.

KATO ZAKRO: Site in eastern Crete of a Bronze Age palace and port. Especially famous for Near Eastern goods dating back into Middle Minoan times.

KEKROPS: Mythical early king of Athens.

KERBEROS (CERBERUS): Three-headed dog, guardian of Hades.

KHLAMYS: Man's half-cape, originally developed in Thessaly.

KITION: City in eastern Cyprus, well inhabited in the Bronze Age and colonized in the ninth century by the Phoenicians.

KLEISTHENES: (fl. 508) Athenian statesman elected Archon in 508. In this capacity, he reorganized the political structure of Athens, further democratizing the city.

KLEOS: Honor and glory for which all Homeric heroes strove.

KLERUKHY: Allotment of land loaned to a soldier in exchange for military service. Over time, these became hereditary in the Hellenistic period.

KLYTAIMNESTRA: Mythical queen of Mycenae who murdered her husband, Agamemnon.

KNOSSOS: Capital of ancient (and modern) Crete. Inhabited since the Neolithic era. The earliest monumental architecture in Crete also began here.

KOMMOS: Site in south-central Crete famous for its Bronze Age settlement, Dark Age Phoenician shrine, and later Classical settlement.

KORÊ: Literally, "maiden." The name given to the standing female statues developed in the Archaic Age. See also PERSEPHONÊ.

KORINNA: (c. fifth century) Lyric poet from Tanagra, Boiotia, thought to be a contemporary of Pindar and to have beaten him in competitions.

KOUREOTIS: Event at the Apatouria where new phratry members (babies and youths) were introduced to their phratriai.

KOUROS: Literally, "guy." The name given to the striding, nude male statues developed in the Archaic Age.

KRATER: Wine-mixing bowl, in which wine was mixed with water.

KRYPTEIA: Final phase of Spartan military education, engaged in by men aged nineteen to twenty, in which they lived in helot territory, terrorizing and killing the helots.

KYKLOPS: "Round Face." Giant with one eye in the center of the forehead.

KYLIX: Shallow-dished, long-stemmed wine cup.

KYLON: (d. 632) Athenian who tried to establish a tyranny in Athens. Sought sanctuary at a local shrine and was slaughtered while still under its protection by the Alcmaeonidai clan.

KYPRIA: Epic in the Epic Cycle attributed to Stasinos, Hegesias, or Hegesinos and relating the events leading up to the Trojan War.

LABRYS: Double-headed axe, prominent in Minoan religious iconography. The Palace of the Labrys at Knossos came to be known as the Labyrinth.

LACONIA (LAKONIA): Territory in the Peloponnese. Its capital was Sparta.

LAWAGETAS: Mycenaean military leader, second in rank to the wanax.

LEBES GAMIKOS: Tall vessel used to carry the water used in the ritual bridal bath.

LEFKANDI: Dark Age settlement at the site of Xeropolis on Euboia. Famous for its five wealthy Dark Age cemeteries and the Heroön of Lefkandi, wherein were discovered the remains of sacrificed horses, an inhumed "heroine," and (possibly) a cremated "hero."

LEKYTHOS: Slender vessel used to carry oil. So commonly used for funerary libations that the vessel came to be associated with graves. Eventually, large, marble versions were used as grave markers.

LERNA: City in the Argolid, well inhabited in the Early Helladic II period before being destroyed by invaders at the dawn of Early Helladic III. Location of the House of the Tiles. In later myth, the multiheaded hydra slain by Heracles resided here.

LESBOS: Island off the western coast of Turkey; capital was Mytilene. Famed for the beauty of its women and as being home to Sappho and Alcaeus.

LEUCTRA, BATTLE OF: (371) A battle in which the Thebans defeated the Spartans, ending the period of Spartan hegemony and ushering in the period of Theban hegemony under Epameinondas.

LEVANT: The eastern coast of the Mediterranean Sea.

LILY PRINCE FRESCO: A Minoan image restored by Evans, showing a youth with an elaborate headdress, identified as a priest-king. Later shown to be a composite of three different frescoes, including a female and a sphinx.

LINEAR A: As-yet-untranslated writing from Minoan Crete.

LINEAR B: Earliest attested written form of Greek, adapted from Linear A, in use as early as 1400 B.C.E.

LITTLE ILIAD: Epic of the Epic Cycle attributed to Leskhes or Kinaithon, relating the final days of the Trojan War.

LYCURGUS (LYCOURGOS): Semimythical reformer of Spartan law and society.

LYRE: Stringed instrument on which the strings are attached outside of the soundbox. Sacred to Apollo, usually used as accompaniment to lyric poetry.

LYSANDER: (d. 395) Spartan general and statesman leading the Spartan military forces at the conclusion of the Peloponnesian War. His obnoxious personality lost him favor in Sparta, and he was removed from the city.

LYSIAS: (459–380) Speechwriter and owner of a prosperous shield factory who dwelled as a metic in Athens.

LYSIMACHUS (LYSIMAKHOS): (360–281) Companion and successor to Alexander the Great, he took charge of Thrace upon Alexander's death.

LYSSA: Goddess of madness.

MAA-PALAIKASTRO: Site in western Cyprus where the earliest Greek settlement on the island was established in 1190.

MACEDON: Territory north of Mt. Olympos, united by Philip II.

MACHAON: In the *Iliad*, a son of Asclepius and a physician.

MAGNA GRAECIA: "Great Greece," an area of Sicily and southern Italy settled by Greeks.

MAINAD (MAENAD): Maddened follower of Dionysos, either a permanent devotee or a woman driven temporarily insane.

MALLIA: Bronze Age palatial site in north-central Crete.

MANTINEA, BATTLE OF: (362) Confrontation between Thebes and Sparta. Thebes won, although their leader—Epameinondas—later died from wounds sustained here.

MARINE STYLE: Style of decoration typifying Late Minoan IA pottery.

MEGARON: Core of Mycenaean domestic architecture. A rectangular room with a hearth at the center, surrounded by four pillars supporting the roof. Entered by a vestibule.

MELISSOS: (fifth century) Samian naval commander and philosopher who expounded on the infinitude and changelessness of existence.

MENANDER: (342–293/289) The only writer of New Comedy plays whose works have survived. His one completely preserved comedy, *Dyskolos,* won a competition in 317.

MENELAUS: Mythical king of Sparta, husband of Helen of Troy.

MENIPPOS OF GADARA: (early third century) Cynic philosopher who began as a Syrian slave and ended up a Theban citizen. Invented the spoudogeloion.

MESARÁ: Area of south-central Crete.

MESSENIA: Territory in the central Peloponnese, conquered by Sparta in the eighth century, when the inhabitants were reduced to helotry. Liberated in the fourth century. Messenê was established in 369 as a capital city.

METEMPSYCHOSIS: The belief that all souls travel from body to body over the course of several lifetimes. Comparable to reincarnation.

METER: The rhythm of poetry. In ancient Greek poetry, this was length-based rather than stress-based.

METIC (METOIKOS): A resident alien in Athens.

METIS: "Intelligence." Goddess of cunning wisdom and mother of Athena.

METON: (fifth century) Athenian astronomer who reconciled the solar and lunar years.

METOPE: The flat square, often decorated with paint or sculpture, between the triglyphs of a Doric frieze.

METROPOLIS: "Mother City." A city that sent out a colony.

MILETOS: Site on the west coast of Asia Minor, originally colonized by the Minoans and taken over by the Mycenaeans, for whom it served as an eastern capital city. It was a thriving town in the historical period, producing the first Greek natural philosophers and several colonies.

MINOAN: Of or referring to Crete during the Bronze Age.

MINOS: Mythical king of Knossos, one of the underworld judges of the dead.

MINOTAUR: Mythical beast with the body of a man but the head of a bull. Born of Queen Pasiphaë of Knossos.

MINYAN WARE: Two styles of pottery—yellow and gray—that first appeared in Greece in the Early Helladic III and Middle Helladic I periods, signaling the arrival of a new population. Typified by a linear silhouette and a soapy surface feel.

MNEMOSYNÊ: Goddess of memory, mother of the Muses.

MOCHLOS: Site in northeastern Crete inhabited from Early Minoan through Byzantine times. Especially famous for its tombs and pottery sequence.

MONODY: Lyric poetry composed for, and sung by, a single voice.

MOTHAKES: Lower-class mixed-blood residents of Sparta, raised and educated with Spartan children, thus raised in class/status.

MUSES: Nine sisters, goddesses of the arts. Their names were Clio (history), Ourania (astronomy), Melpomenê (tragedy), Thalia (comedy), Erato (love poetry), Eutrepê (music), Terpsichorê (dance), Polymnia (religious poetry), and Calliopê (epic poetry).

MYCENAE (MYKENAI): Bronze Age palatial center in the Argolid, well fortified in the thirteenth century and home of the wanax, or high king.

MYIA: (late sixth–early fifth century) Pythagorean philosopher, daughter of Pythagoras.

MYRTOS: Site of an extensive Early Minoan familial domestic structure in Crete.

MYSTERY CULT: Religious ritual marked by an exclusive and initiatory nature. Many such cults dealt with issues of divine empathy and happier afterlife experiences. The most famous are those dedicated to Demeter and Persephonê, Dionysos, Isis, Cybelê, and Mithras.

MYTILENE: Capital of Lesbos.

NAOS: Central room of a temple, where the deity "lived."

NIELLO: Black, sticky substance of copper, lead, sulfur, and borax used to inlay metal.

NIKÊ: "Victory." Conceptualized either as a separate winged goddess or as a manifestation of Athena.

NOSTOS: "Homecoming." The Nostoi (pl.) are the tales relating the homecomings of the heroes of the Trojan War, with that of Odysseus being the best known.

NOTHOS: "Bastard." Mixed-blood Spartan-helot children used to fill the Spartan army ranks.

NUMISMATICS: The study of coins.

NYMPH: Immortal or semi-immortal nature spirit.

OBAI: The five villages that synoecized to form the polis of Sparta.

OBOL: (1) An iron spit. (2) The smallest unit of Greek currency. Six obols = one drachma.

OBVERSE: The front side of a coin.

ODYSSEUS: Trickster hero, mythical king of Ithaca, and protagonist of Homer's *Odyssey*.

ODYSSEY: Epic attributed to Homer, relating the travels and homecoming of Odysseus.

OEDIPODEA: Epic in the Epic Cycle attributed to Kinaithon, recounting the story of Oedipus.

OEDIPUS (OIDIPOUS): Mythical king of Thebes who killed his father Laius and married his mother Jocausta. Received hero status upon his death in Athens.

OIKOS: The household, including all family members living together as well as the household slaves and workers.

OLIGARCHY: "Rule of the few." Governmental system in which a limited number of people, usually fulfilling specific property ownership requirements, may participate.

OLYMPIA: City in the central Peloponnese, famous for its great sanctuary of Zeus and Hera and for the Panhellenic games, which occurred there every four years starting in 776.

OLYMPIAS: (fl. 330) Macedonian queen, mother of Alexander the Great.

OLYMPOS (OLYMPUS): Highest mountain on mainland Greece, forming the boundary between Hellas and Macedon. Believed to be the home of the deities.

OPISTHODOMOS: Back room of a temple, sometimes serving as a treasury.

ORCHESTRA: Round, flat area in front of the skenê/stage of a Greek theater, where the chorus performed and the altar of Dionysos was located.

ORCHOMENUS: Site in north-central Greece. A palatial center in the Bronze Age, mythically ruled by the Minyan dynasty. A city in Classical times as well.

ORPHEUS: In myth, the greatest poet and musician. Son of Apollo and Calliopê, he founded the Dionysian Mysteries and nearly brought his wife Euridikê back from the dead.

OURANOS: "Sky." A male deity; first son and consort of Earth.

PAEAN: Choral hymn intended to invoke Apollo as healing god.

PAIAWON: Bronze Age healing deity, who later merged with Apollo.

PAIONIOS: Fifth-century sculptor from Mende in Thrace. Especially famous for his sculpture of Olympian Nikê.

PALAEOGRAPHY: The study of ancient writing, especially as it is preserved on papyrus, wax, and parchment.

PALAIKASTRO: "Old Castle." Site of a Minoan city with an urban sanctuary in eastern Crete.

PALAISTRA: Ancient Greek sports club building.

PAN: God of nature.

PANHELLENIC: Referring to all of Greece or the Greek-speaking peoples.

PAPHOS: City on Cyprus famous for its sanctuary of Aphrodite.

PAPYRUS: Fibrous plant from Egypt. Its unrolled stem furnished a paper-like material on which the ancients wrote.

PARIS (ALEXANDROS): Trojan prince who ran away with Helen of Troy, instigating the Trojan War.

PARMENIDES: (c. 510–450) Natural philosopher from Elis. First philosopher to consider the meaning of being.

PARTHENAION: Choral song sung by girls, usually with an educational component.

PARTHENON: Temple dedicated to Athena on the Athenian Acropolis. Originally constructed in the sixth century, it was destroyed by the Persians and then was rebuilt under the auspices of Pericles in the fifth century. It remained intact until the seventeenth century C.E., when it was used to store gunpowder and was hit with a missile.

PARTHENOS: A girl or woman who has not yet been socially recognized as a mother. Often translated as "maiden" or "virgin."

PASIO (PASION): (d. 370) Former slave who became the wealthiest banker in Athens.

PATROIOKOS: "Of the father's house." An heiress, so named in Gortyn. A girl with no brothers, whose father has died. She was strongly encouraged to marry a close male relative on her father's side, in order to pass on the patrimony.

PATROUKHOS: An heiress, so named in Sparta. A girl with no brothers, whose father has died. Her marriage was designated by one of the kings for appropriate passing on of the patrimony.

PAUSANIAS: (fl. c. 150 C.E.) Greek traveler and historian, most famous for his *Description of Greece.*

PAUSANIAS I OF SPARTA: (d. c. 470) Son of the Spartan king Kleombrotos. Led the Spartan forces against the Persians at Plataia. Having outraged Greece with his arrogant behavior, and threatening to ally himself with Persia, he was put to death in Sparta.

PAUSANIAS II OF SPARTA: (d. 394) King of Sparta in 445–426 and 408–394. He ruled Sparta at the end of the Peloponnesian War and was active in ameliorating political and social affairs in Athens after its defeat.

PEDIMENT: Triangular space above the entrance and beneath the roofline of a temple, usually decorated with paint or sculpture.

PELESET (PHILISTINES): Group of Sea Peoples, originally Greeks, recorded in the Medinet Habu inscription, who ultimately settled in the southern Levant.

PELOPONNESE: The southern half of mainland Greece, south of the isthmus. Literally, the "Island of Pelops."

PELOPS: In myth, the son of Tantalos, who killed him and served him in a stew to the deities. Resurrected, Pelops killed Oenomaüs and married his daughter Hippodameia, who brought with her the entire southern portion of Greece as her dowry, a region henceforth named for Pelops.

PELTAST: Lightly armed soldier, usually equipped with short sword and shield.

PENELOPÊ: Wife of Odysseus in the *Odyssey.*

PENNYROYAL: Mint used in the rites of Demeter, possibly having contraceptive qualities.

PENTAKOSIOMEDIMNOI: Highest class in Solon's class system for Athens. Their property could furnish 500 units of grain, wine, or oil.

PENTECONTAETIA: The fifty years between the Persian Invasions and the Peloponnesian War, marked by the rise of the First Athenian Empire.

PEPLOS: Woman's dress made of a sheet of wool and fastened at the shoulders with pins.

PERDICCAS (PERDIKKAS): (d. 321) Alexander the Great's military second-in-command and regent for Macedon upon Alexander's death.

PERIANDROS (PERIANDER): (r. 625–585) Tyrant of Corinth, son of Cypselus.

PERICLES (PERIKLES): (495–429) Athenian statesman who governed Athens in the years preceding the Peloponnesian War.

PERIOIKOS: A resident alien in Sparta. This group conducted most production and trade in the state.

PERISTYLE: Covered colonnade surrounding a building or court.

PERSEPHONÊ (KORÊ): Queen of the underworld and goddess of spring or autumn.

PHAISTOS: Bronze Age palatial site in south-central Crete.

PHALANX: Unit of foot soldiers arranged into lines, usually around eight lines deep, who fought together as an integral whole.

PHEIDON OF ARGOS: (c. seventh century) King of Argos, reputed to have seized control of the Olympics one year and to have given the Greeks their system of weights and measures.

PHIDIAS: (b. c. 490) Athenian sculptor, most famous for his statue of Athena Promakhos and his work on the Parthenon.

PHILIP II: (359–336) Macedonian king, conqueror of Greece and father of Alexander the Great.

PHILIP III (ARRHIDAIOS): (358–317) Son of Philip II and one of Alexander the Great's heirs.

PHILIP V: (238–179) Final Antigonid king of Macedon before the Roman conquest.

PHORMIO: (early fourth century) A slave adopted by Pasio, eventually manumitted, who became one of the wealthiest bankers in Athens.

PHRATRY: "Brotherhood." A recognized social/political/religious body, often with its own traditions and even constitutions, composed of people believed to come from a common ancestor. A smaller subdivision than a phylê.

PHYLAKOPI: Site on the island of Melos famous for its Bronze Age sanctuary and fortifications.

PHYLÊ: "Tribe." A pseudo-familial subdivision of an ethnos. The Ionians had four; the Dorians three. In the Early Archaic Age, political and military groupings were often done by phylê.

PINDAR: (518–438) Boiotian lyric poet who composed victory songs for athletic victors at the Panhellenic competitions, such as the Olympics.

PITHEKOUSSAI (PITHECUSSAE): First Greek colony, established c. 750 on the island of Ischia, just west of the Italian peninsula. Founded by the Euboian poleis of Eretria and Chalkis.

PLATO: (429–347) Athenian philosopher and disciple of Socrates. He recorded the majority of Socrates's dialogues and was the founder of the Academy.

PNYX: Hill in Athens where the ekklesia met.

PODALIRIOS: In the *Iliad*, a son of Asclepius and a physician.

POLIS: Greek city-state, with autonomous laws and cults, consisting of a city region and the farmlands outside of the city.

POLOS: Round hat resembling a tambourine.

POLYPERCHON: (b. c. 380) Cavalry officer under Alexander the Great. Succeeded Antipater as regent for Alexander's heirs.

POMMEL: Attachment at the end of a sword or dagger handle, which holds the handle on and keeps the hand from slipping.

PORNÊ: A lower-class sex worker, usually a slave.

POSEIDON: God of the sea.

POTNIA: Name/title referring to a goddess or goddesses in the Bronze Age, a revered lady or goddess in the historical period.

PRAXITELES: (mid-fourth century) Athenian sculptor most famous for his Knidian Aphrodite.

PRIAM: In myth, the king of Troy during the Trojan War.

PROEDRIA: The best seats in a theater.

PRONAOS: Front room or vestibule of a temple.

PROSODION: Choral poem, used as a processional song.

PROTO-ATTIC: Pottery style of Athens from 700 to about 620. Replaced by Black Figure.

PROTOCORINTHIAN: Pottery style of Corinth from 700 to 625. Replaced by the Corinthian style.

PROTOGEOMETRIC: Of or relating to the arts or culture of Greece from 1050 to 900.

PRYTANEION: City hall.

PRYTANEIS: The Athenian "presidents": those members of the boulê who remained on twenty-four-hour call for one-tenth of the year.

PSYCHÊ (PSYKHÊ): (1) A ghost, one's incorporeal manifestation after death. (2) Wife of Eros.

PTOLEMAIC: Of or relating to the dynasty that took control of Egypt after the death of Alexander the Great.

PTOLEMY: Name used by all Hellenistic kings of Egypt.

PTOLEMY I: (367–282) Called Savior. He became satrap of Egypt upon Alexander's death and made himself king of that region in 304, later conquering Palestine and Cyprus. Founder of the Ptolemaic dynasty.

PTOLEMY XIII: (63–47) Brother and husband of Cleopatra VII. Defied Julius Caesar, lost, and later drowned in the Nile.

PTOLEMY XIV: (59–44) Another brother and husband of Cleopatra VII. Killed on her orders.

PYLOS: Site in the western Peloponnese famous for its Mycenaean palace and archives, from which many Linear B tablets derive. In myth, it was ruled by Nestor, descendant of Poseidon.

PYRGOS WARE: Early Minoan style of pottery typified by dark clay and incised linear decoration.

PYTHAGORAS: (late sixth century) Philosopher originally from Samos but generally associated with Croton. His philosophies touched on many topics, but he is most famous for his mathematical work (such as the Pythagorean Theorem) and his theories on metempsychosis.

PYTHIA: Priestess and oracle of Apollo at Delphi.

PYTHON: In myth, a dragon-like monster that possessed Delphi before being slain by Apollo.

RED FIGURE: Vase-painting technique prevalent after 520. Figures are left the color of the pottery (red in Attica, thus the name), and the background was painted black.

RELATIVE CHRONOLOGY: The sequence in which events occurred or in which objects were made relative to one another, regardless of specific date. See also **CHRONOLOGY**.

RELIEF SCULPTURE: Sculpture in which the images project from a sunken background. In low relief, this is a mostly two-dimensional rendering. In high relief, the sculpture is almost in the round, projecting extensively from the background.

RELIEVING TRIANGLE: In Mycenaean tholoi, the space above a building's lintel at ground level left free of stones so as to decrease the weight upon the lintel stone.

REVERSE: The back side of a coin.

RHADAMANTHYS: Mythical king of Phaistos, underworld judge of the dead.

RHETRA: The divine mandates of the Spartan constitution, established by Lycurgus.

RHYTON: A funnel, often with ritual purposes in Minoan cult.

ROXANA: (fl. 327) Sogdian princess, wife of Alexander the Great.

SANTORINI: Island famous for its well-preserved Minoan architecture and frescoes. See THERA

SAPPHO (PSAPPHO): (b. c. 612) Lyric poet from the island of Lesbos. Composed choral wedding songs as well as more personal works.

SARISSA: Extremely long pike, a favorite in the armies of Alexander the Great.

SATRAP: Persian term meaning "governor." A title later adopted by, and used in the administration of, Alexander the Great and his successors.

SATYR: In mythology, creatures that were half-man, half-goat or -horse, who were especially dedicated to the god Dionysos.

SATYR PLAY: Type of Greek drama that was especially slapstick and obscene, featuring choruses of satyrs. It was shown in the competitions after the tragedies. Used in the worship of Dionysos. The only fully extant satyr play is Euripides's *Cyclops*.

SCHLIEMANN, HEINRICH: (1822–1890 C.E.) Father of Bronze Age Aegean archaeology. Wealthy German businessman who financed his own excavations of Troy and Mycenae.

SCYTHIA: Ancient area of the Ukraine. The Scythians were nomads famous for their archery and art.

SEISAKHTHEIA: "Shaking off of burdens" or releasing of debts, enacted by Solon in 594 to help relieve the high level of poverty plaguing Athens.

SELEUCID (SELEUKID): Of or relating to the dynasty that took control of Asia after the death of Alexander the Great.

SELEUCUS (SELEUKOS) I: (358–281) Called Nikator. General under Alexander the Great, named satrap of Babylon upon Alexander's death. Crowned king of Asia in 304 and was founder of the Seleucid dynasty.

SEMELÊ: Mythic Theban princess and mother of Dionysos.

SEMITIC: (1) Language family including Arabic, Hebrew, and Phoenician. (2) Of or referring to the speakers of these languages.

SEMONIDES: (late seventh century) Iambic and elegiac poet from Samos. His work had misogynist overtones.

SHAFT GRAVE: Deep, rectangular grave lined with stone, floored with pebbles, and roofed, used as a prestige burial plot in Mycenaean times. Generally communal.

SILPHIUM: Herbal and pharmaceutical plant, mainly grown in Cyrenê, popular in ancient Greece as a garnish and contraceptive.

SIMONIDES: (556–468) Lyric and elegiac poet from Iulis on Keos.

SISTRA: Rattling percussion instrument, used in the cult of Dionysos.

SKENÊ: Name of the stage on which dramatic actors performed.

SKOLION: Drinking song.

SKYPHOS: Deep, two-handled drinking cup.

SOCRATES (SOKRATES): (469–399) Athenian philosopher executed by the state for impiety and corrupting the youth. His philosophical arguments, composed in dialogue format, were recorded by his students Plato and Xenophon.

SOLON: (fl. 600) Athenian poet and statesman, elected chief archon in 594/593. He called off all debts in Athens and restructured the class system so that it was based on wealth rather than birth.

SOPHOCLES (SOPHOKLES): (496–406) Athenian tragic playwright. Most famous for his works on the Oedipus myths: *Oedipus the King, Oedipus at Kolonos,* and *Antigone.*

SOPHROSYNÊ: Temperance, self-control. A Greek ideal and special quality of Odysseus.

SPARTA: City in Laconia, Peloponnese. Politically dominant during the Late Archaic Age and Classical period.

SPHINX: Mythical animal with the body of a lion and the head of a woman.

SPOUDOGELOION: Seriocomic style of philosophic/political commentary. Invented by Menippos of Gadara.

STELAI: Commemorative stone pillars.

STEREOBATE: Stone, stepped foundation of a temple.

STESIKHOROS: (632–553) Lyric and epic poet from Mataurus who composed the *Iliu Persis.*

STIRRUP JAR: Rounded vessel with a double handle on the top and a narrow spout, used to transport and pour oils and perfumes during the Bronze Age.

STOA: Long, roofed structure enclosed on three sides and with a row of columns on the fourth. Used for a variety of purposes in the Classical period and after, such as museum, meeting house, and mall.

STRABO: (64 B.C.E.–21 C.E.) Greek historian and geographer of the Roman Empire, most famous for his *Geography.*

STRATIGRAPHY: The layering, usually horizontal but also possibly vertical, of archaeological sites. Generally, deeper layers represent older periods of time, and layers closer to the surface represent more recent times. Used by archaeologists to determine chronology.

STYLOBATE: Floor level of a temple, on which columns are set.

SUDA: Name of the lexicon compiled in tenth-century C.E. Byzantium, recording all then-known knowledge of the classics.

SYGGENEIA: One's family, extending out to include all blood relatives as far as anyone can remember.

SYLLABIC SCRIPT: Writing system in which each sign represents a syllable, usually either a vowel, a consonant-vowel combination, or even a consonant-vowel-consonant combination.

SYMPOSION (SYMPOSIUM): A drinking party. Emerged as a significant aspect of Greek (male) social life in the Late Archaic Age.

SYNOECISM (SYNOIKISM): The political unification of households and villages into a single autonomous city/polis.

SYRACUSE: Capital city of Sicily, founded as a colony from Corinth. In the fifth to third centuries, the tyrants of Syracuse were the functional rulers of Greek Sicily.

SYSITIA: Communal mess halls in which all Spartan males had to maintain membership through obligatory food donations. Loss of sysition membership equaled loss of citizen status.

TANG: Portion of a blade extending into the handle and attached to the pommel.

TARTARUS: Hell. One of the four primordial deities in Hesiod's *Theogony.*

TELEGONIA: Epic of the Epic Cycle relating the death of Odysseus and the affairs of his family after his death.

TELEMACHUS (TELEMAKHOS): Son of Odysseus in the *Odyssey.*

TEMENOS: Land "cut off" and dedicated to a deity, usually translated as "sanctuary."

TERRA-COTTA: Fired clay.

THALASSOCRACY: Rule of the sea, a naval empire.

THALES OF MILETOS: (625–585) Considered to be the first Greek natural philosopher. Most famous for his prediction of a solar eclipse.

THANATOS: (1) The concept of death. (2) Death anthropomorphized as a winged god.

THEANO: (late sixth century) Pythagorean philosopher, wife of Pythagoras.

THEBAID: Epic in the Epic Cycle attributed to Kallinos, relating Oedipus's curse of his sons and the Seven Against Thebes.

THEBES: Capital of Boiotia, hometown of Dionysos and Oedipus.

THEMISTOCLES: (528–462) Athenian statesman who convinced the Athenians to build up their navy in the 480s. As general, he led the naval defense of Athens in the second Persian Invasion in 480–479, even tricking King Xerxes to attack in an inauspicious (for the Persians) location at Salamis. Connived to have the Athenians rebuild their walls against Spartan opposition. Eventually banished from Athens, he ironically wound up an honored guest at the Persian court.

THEOCRITUS (THEOKRITOS): (300–260) Poet from Syracuse who wound up serving the Ptolemies in Alexandria. Most famous for his *Idylls,* poems of a bucolic nature.

THERA: Cycladic island colonized by the Minoans during the Middle Minoan period.

THERAMENES: (d. 403) Athenian statesman active at the end of the Peloponnesian War. He was the chief Athenian negotiator with the Spartan Lysander and was one of the Thirty Tyrants established in Athens at the end of the war.

THESEUS: Athenian mythic hero, famous for slaying the Minotaur.

THESMOPHORIA: Women-only ritual in honor of Demeter and Persephonê, held throughout the Greek world.

THESPIS OF IKARIA: (mid-sixth century) Lyric poet who first separated one actor from a chorus, leading to dramatic distinction between chorus and actor.

THESSALY: Region of northern Greece, famed for its horses.

THETE: "Laborer." The lowest member of the Athenian class system.

THETIS: Sea goddess, mother of Achilles, preserver of the cosmic order.

THIASOS: Band accompanying certain deities. Artemis had her hunting nymphs, Dionysos his satyrs and Mainads.

THOLOS: (1) Round tomb first appearing as a mass grave in the Mesará of Bronze Age Crete. Later adapted and greatly enlarged by the Mycenaeans and used as a royal tomb. (2) Round temple-like structure dedicated to deities during the Classical period.

THRACE: "Barbaric" region northeast of mainland Greece, seen by the Greeks primarily as a source of slaves.

THRENOS: Choral poem, used as a dirge for the dead.

THUCYDIDES (THOUKYDIDES): (c. 460–c. 400) Athenian general and historian who wrote *The History of the Peloponnesian War.*

THYRSOS: Staff made of fennel wrapped with ivy, a symbol of the cult of Dionysos.

TIMARCHUS (TIMARKHOS): (fourth century) Athenian noble prosecuted by Aeschines for prostitution and debauchery.

TITAN: One of twelve anthropomorphic deities born to Earth and Ouranos.

TOMB CULT: Cult of reverence for an unknown hero or heroine at his/her tomb.

TRAGEDY: From the Greek words for "goat song," a drama based on mythological themes that portrayed a depressing story. Used in the worship of Dionysos. All extant tragedies come from Athens and were written by Aeschylus, Sophocles, and Euripides.

TRIGLYPH: The triple-grooved slab between metopes on a Doric frieze.

TRITTYES: The thirds into which Kleisthenes divided up the political composition of Athens in 508. Each consisted of demes either along the coast, in the countryside, or in the city of Athens.

TYRTAIOS (TYRTAEUS): (seventh century) Elegiac poet and general from Sparta.

ULU BURUN: Site of a late-fourteenth-century shipwreck excavated by George Bass.

VASILIKI WARE: Early Minoan style of pottery decorated with a blotchy red, orange, and black pattern.

VENTRIS, MICHAEL: (d. 1953 C.E.) British architect who translated Linear B.

WANAX: Mycenaean king, as attested to in the Linear B tablets.

WHITE GROUND: Vase-painting technique in which the vase surface was painted white, with pictures added with black outlines and soft colors upon the white surface. As the white pigment was fragile, this technique was reserved for objects that would not see much use, such as funerary vases.

XENIA: Guest-friendship. A tight alliance formed between two strangers, in which one was offered hospitality by the other. Such relationships of goodwill and mutual obligation endured throughout several generations, and they took precedence over almost all other types of alliance, even during periods of war.

XENOPHON: (428/427–354) Athenian historian and philosopher. He recorded a number of the Socratic dialogues, and he wrote several historical treatises, such as the *Anabasis,* the *Spartan Constitution,* and the *Oikonomikos.*

XOANON: Cult statue of a deity, understood to be a gift from the deity and to encompass that deity's presence.

ZENO OF ELEA: (b. c. 490) Natural philosopher who argued that existence was a unified entity. Student of Parmenides.

ZENO OF KITION: (335–263) Founder of the Stoic school of philosophy in Athens.

ZEUGETAI: Third highest class in Solon's class system for Athens. Their property could furnish 200 units of grain, wine, or oil.

ZEUS: King of the deities, god of the sky and lightning.

Chronology

(All dates approximate. For Bronze Age, see also the chronology chart in chapter 3.)

BEFORE THE COMMON ERA

Seventh millennium B.C.E.	Settlement of Crete.
3300–1050	Bronze Age.
3000–2100	Rise of indigenous culture in Early Helladic Greece.
2100	Destruction of the House of the Tiles at Lerna; possible date for the Greeks' arrival in Greece.
2000	Rise of the first palaces in Crete.
1650	Earliest shaft graves in Circle B at Mycenae. Dawn of the Mycenaean period.
1650–1550	Burials in Grave Circle B.
1638	Eruption of Thera volcano. Beginning of the Second Palace period on Crete.
1600–1500/1450	Burials in Grave Circle A.
1500–1450	Rise of the tholos tombs in Greece.
1450	Mycenaean conquest of Knossos.
1450–1200	Third Palace period in Crete. Apex of Mycenaean civilization.
1400	Rise of Mycenaean palaces.
1375	Destruction of Knossos. First destruction of Thebes.
Thirteenth century	Fortification of the Mycenaean palaces.
1240	Second destruction of Thebes.
1200	Destruction of the Mycenaean palaces. End of the Mycenaean and Third Palace periods.
Twelfth century	Ionian migrations.
1190	Initial Greek settlement on Cyprus at Maa-Palaikastro.
1186	Egyptian Medinet Habu inscription, recording invasions of the Sea Peoples.
1185	Traditional date of the fall of Troy.
1075	Minoan colonists settle on Cyprus.
1050	End of the Bronze Age.
1050–750	Dark Age.

1000	Heroön of Lefkandi.
850	Establishment of emporion at Al-Mina.
Eighth–sixth centuries	Orientalizing revolution.
776	Traditional date of the first Olympics (Olympiad 1).
770–550	Era of colonization, begun with the foundation of Pithekoussai.
750	Traditional date for heyday of Homer and Hesiod.
750–490	Archaic Age.
733	Foundation of Syracuse.
730–710	Sparta's invasion of Messenia in the First Messenian War.
725	Nestor's Cup inscription, earliest attested written Greek after the Bronze Age.
700	Lelantine War.
700–650	Rise of hoplite warfare.
Seventh century	Rise of lyric poetry.
660	Approximate date of Lycurgan reforms in Sparta. Helotry established.
657–627	Tyranny of Cypselus in Corinth.
640–630	Second Messenian War.
632	Kylon's attempt at tyranny in Athens.
625–585	Tyranny of Periandros in Corinth.
621	Reforms of Drako in Athens.
585–400	Age of the Presocratic philosophers.
546–510	Tyranny of Peisistratos and Hippias in Athens.
508	Reforms of Kleisthenes in Athens.
490–323	Classical period.
Fifth century	Rise of drama.
499–494	Ionian revolt against Persia.
490	First Persian Invasion. Battle of Marathon.
483	Discovery of the silver mines at Laurion. Rise of the Athenian navy.
480–479	Second Persian Invasion. Battles of Thermopylai, Salamis, and Plateia.
479	Gelon becomes tyrant of Syracuse and founds Deinomenid dynasty.
478	Formation of the Delian League.
465	Earthquake and helot revolt in Sparta.
462	Ephialtes's reforms of the Areopagos in Athens.
460–429	Age of Pericles in Athens.
454	Delian League treasury transferred to Athens.
449	Peace of Kallias signed between Persia and Greece.
446	Signing of the (tragically misnamed) Thirty Years' Peace between Athens and Sparta.
431–421	Archidamian War.
431–404	Peloponnesian War.

421	Peace of Nikias.
415–413	Sicilian Expedition.
413–404	Dekeleian War.
404	Athenian defeat at Aigospotamoi. End of the Peloponnesian War.
404–371	Period of Spartan hegemony.
395–386	Corinthian War.
388	Foundation of Plato's Academy.
386	King's Peace between Sparta and Persia.
377	Establishment of the Second Athenian Empire.
371	Battle of Leuctra.
371–362	Period of Theban hegemony.
362	Battle of Mantinea; death of Epameinondas.
359–336	Reign of Philip II of Macedon.
357–355	End of the Second Athenian Empire.
346	Peace of Philokrates.
338	Battle of Chaeronea. Foundation of the League of Corinth.
336–323	Reign of Alexander the Great.
335	Aristotle's founding of the Lyceum.
334	Alexander leaves Greece for Asia. Battle at Granikos River.
332	Alexander conquers Tyre in Lebanon.
331	Founding of Alexandria in Egypt. Victory over Darius of Persia at Gaugamela.
327	Alexander conquers Bactria and Sogdiana; marries Roxana.
326	Alexander's army mutinies at Hyphasis River in India.
323	Death of Alexander the Great.
323–31	Hellenistic period.
322–321	Civil war against Perdiccas. Death of Perdiccas.
317	Death of Philip III.
310	Death of Alexander IV. Zeno establishes Stoicism in Athens.
307	Epicurus establishes Epicureanism in Athens.
306	Rise of the Antigonid dynasty.
305	Rise of the Ptolemaic dynasty.
304	Rise of the Seleucid dynasty.
303	Seleucus cedes his eastern territories to King Chandragupta of India.
284	Foundation of Achaean League.
280–275	Pyrrhic War; Rome wins Greek Italy.
279	Gauls invade Greece.
269–215	Tyranny of Hieron II in Syracuse.
264	Roman conquest of Sicily.
263	Foundation of Pergamon.
215–146	Roman-Macedonian Wars.
211–205	First Macedonian War.
200–196	Second Macedonian War.
171–167	Third Macedonian War.
149–146	Fourth Macedonian War.

148	Macedonia becomes Roman province.
146	Roman destruction of Corinth.
133	Attalos III bequeaths Hellenistic kingdom of Pergamon to Rome.
129	Roman conquest of the Seleucid Empire.
31	Defeat of Cleopatra VII and Marc Antony at Actium.
1st century B.C.E.–C.E.	Writings of Strabo.

THE COMMON ERA

Second century	Rise of Atticism. Writings of Pausanias.
117–138	Reign of Roman emperor Hadrian, the Philhellên. Beginnings of the Second Sophistic.
324	Foundation of Constantinople.
396	Alaric the Visigoth sacks Athens. End of the Eleusinian Mysteries.
529	Emperor Justinian closes the Academy.
970	Writing of the *Suda.*
1204	Fourth Crusade. Venice attacks Byzantium.
1453	Turkish conquest of Constantinople. Greek refugees flee west.
1777	*Homeric Hymn to Demeter* discovered in Moscow.
1788	Discovery of the Oxyrhincus Papyri.
1870	H. Schliemann begins excavations at Hissarlik, Turkey.
1871–1873	Schliemann discovers several layers of Troy.
1876	Schliemann begins excavations at Mycenae.
1900	Sir Arthur Evans begins excavations at Knossos. Federigo Halbherr and Luigi Pernier excavate Phaistos and Haghia Triadha.
1908	Harriet Boyd-Hawes publishes the excavations of Gournia.
1920	Evans's publication of *The Palace of Knossos.*
1952	Michael Ventris translates Linear B.

Resources for Further Study

Note: Many of the resources in this list are tagged as follows:
* Highly recommended for neophytes
‡ Excellent for more advanced research

ARCHAEOLOGY AND HISTORIOGRAPHY

Biers, W. R. 1987. *The Archaeology of Greece: An Introduction.* Ithaca, NY: Cornell University Press.

Ceram, C. W. 1986. *Gods, Graves, & Scholars: The Story of Archaeology.* 2d ed. New York: Vintage.

Fagan, B. M. 1991. *In the Beginning: An Introduction to Archaeology.* 7th ed. New York: HarperCollins.

Reynolds, L. D. and N. G. Wilson. 1991. *Scribes and Scholars: A Guide to the Transmission of Greek and Latin Literature.* 3d ed. Oxford: Clarendon.

Wilson, N. G. 1983. *Scholars of Byzantium.* Baltimore: Johns Hopkins University Press.

Bronze Age

General

‡Broodbank, C. 2000. *An Island Archaeology of the Early Cyclades.* Cambridge, UK: Cambridge University Press.

‡Cullen, T., ed. 2001. *Aegean Prehistory: A Review.* Boston: American Journal of Archaeology. Supplement 1.

*Dickinson, O. 1994. *The Aegean Bronze Age.* Cambridge World Archaeology. Cambridge, UK: Cambridge University Press.

Drews, R. 1988. *The Coming of the Greeks: Indo-European Conquests in the Aegean and the Near East.* Princeton, NJ: Princeton University Press.

Renfrew, C. 1972. *The Emergence of Civilization: The Cyclades and the Aegean in the Third Millennium B.C.* London: Methuen.

*Taylour, W. 1990. *The Mycenaeans.* Rev. ed. New York: Thames & Hudson.

Thimme, J., ed. 1977. *Art and Culture of the Cyclades in the Third Millennium B.C.* Chicago: University of Chicago Press.

Vermeule, E. 1972. *Greece in the Bronze Age.* Chicago: University of Chicago Press.

Warren, P. 1990. *The Aegean Civilizations.* New York: Peter Bedrick.

Art

Davaras, C. 1976. *Guide to Cretan Antiquities.* Athens: Eptalofos S.A.

Davis, E. 1986. "Youth and Age in the Thera Frescoes." *American Journal of Archaeology* 90, 399–406.

Doumas, C. and A. Doumas. 1992. *The Wall-Paintings of Thera.* Athens: Thera Foundation.

Getz-Preziosi, P. 1994. *Early Cycladic Sculpture: An Introduction.* Rev. ed. Malibu, CA: J. Paul Getty Museum.

Hampe, R. and E. Simon. 1981. *The Birth of Greek Art, from the Mycenaean to the Archaic Period.* New York: Oxford University Press.

Hänsel, B. 1988. In *The Mycenaean World: Five Centuries of Early Greek Culture: 1600–1100 B.C.* Athens: National Archaeological Museum.

Higgins, R. 1989. *Minoan and Mycenaean Art.* New York: Thames & Hudson.

‡Laffineur, L. and P. P. Betancourt, eds. 1997. *TEXNH: Craftsmen, Craftswomen, and Craftsmanship in the Aegean Bronze Age.* Liège, Belgium: Université de Liège.

MacGillivray, J. A., J. M. Driessen, and L. H. Sackett. 2000. *The Palaikastro Kouros: A Minoan Chryselephantine Statuette.* Athens: British School at Athens.

Preziosi, D. and L. A. Hitchcock. 1999. *Aegean Art and Architecture.* Oxford: Oxford University Press.

Foreign Relations

Bass, G. 1967. *Cape Gelidonya: A Bronze Age Shipwreck. Transactions of the American Philological Association,* New Series 57 (8). Philadelphia: American Philological Association.

———. 1986. "A Bronze Age Shipwreck at Ulu Burun (Kas): 1984 Campaign." *American Journal of Archaeology* 90, 269–296.

Crowley, J. L. 1989. *The Aegean and the East: An Investigation into the Transference of Artistic Motifs between the Aegean, Egypt, and the Near East in the Bronze Age.* Jonsered, Sweden: Paul Åströms Förlag.

Dothan, T. 1982. *The Philistines and Their Material Culture.* New Haven, CT: Yale University Press.

‡Lambrou-Phillipson, C. 1990. *Hellenorientalia: The Near Eastern Presence in the Bronze Age Aegean, c. 3000–1100 B.C.: Interconnections Based on the Material Record and the Written Evidence: Plus Orientalia: A Catalogue of Egyptian, Mesopotamia, Mitannian, Syro-Palestinian, Cypriot, and Asian Minor Objects from the Bronze Age Aegean.* Göteborg: Paul Åströms Förlag.

Lolos, Y. G. 1995. "Late Cypro-Mycenaean Seafaring: New Evidence from Sites in the Saronic and the Argolic Gulfs." In Karageorghis, V. and D. Michaelides, eds. 1995. *Cyprus and the Sea.* Nicosia, Cyprus: University of Cyprus, 65–88.

Negbi, O. 1988. "Levantine Elements in the Sacred Architecture of the Aegean at the Close of the Bronze Age." *British School Annual* 83, 339–357.

‡Oren, E. D., ed. 2000. *The Sea Peoples and Their World: A Reassessment.* Philadelphia: University Museum Press.

Vichos, Y. and Y. Lolos. 1995. " The Cypro-Mycenaean Wreck at Point Iria in the Argolic Gulf: First Thoughts on the Origin and the Nature of the Vessel." In *In Poseidon's Reich: Archäologie unter Wasser.* Zaberns Bildbände zur Archäologie, 23. Germany: Mainz von Zabern, 321–335.

Language

*Chadwick, J. 1980. *The Mycenaean World.* Cambridge, UK: Cambridge University Press.

Finkelberg, M. 1990. "Minoan Inscriptions on Libation Vessels." *Minos* 25/26, 43–85.

Godart, L. 1984. "Du Lineaire A au Lineaire B." In *Aux origines de l'hellénisme: La Crète et la Grèce. Hommage à Henri van Effenterre.* Paris: Publications de la Sorbonne, Histoire Ancienne et Médiévale 15, 121–128.

Godart, L. and J.-P. Olivier. 1976–1985. *Recueil des inscriptions en Linéaire A. Études crétoises 21,* vols. 1–5. Paris: Librairie Orientaliste Paul Geuthner.

*Hooker, J. T. 1980. *Linear B: An Introduction.* Bristol, UK: Bristol Classics.

Melena, J. L. and J.-P. Olivier. 1991. *Tithemy: The Tablets and Nodules in Linear B from Tiryns, Thebes, and Mycenae.* Minos Supplement #12. Solamanca, Spain: Editiones Universidad de Solamanca.

Olivier, J.-P., L. Godart, C. Seydel, and C. Sourvinou. 1973. *Index généraux du Linéaire B.* Incunabula Graeca, vol. 52. Rome: École française d'Athènes.

Palaima, T. G. 1988. *The Scribes of Pylos.* Incunabula Graeca, vol. 87. Rome: École française d'Athènes.

Ventris, M. and J. Chadwick. 1959. *Documents in Mycenaean Greek: 300 Selected Tablets from Knossos, Pylos, & Mycenae.* Cambridge, UK: Cambridge University Press.

Religion

Burdajewicz, M. 1990. *The Aegean Sea Peoples and Religious Architecture in the Eastern Mediterranean at the Close of the Late Bronze Age.* BAR International Series 558. Oxford: Oxford University Press.

Chadwick, J. 1957. "Potnia." *Minos* 6, 117–129.

French, E. 1971. "Development of Mycenaean Terracotta Figurines." *British School Annual* 66, 102–187.

Gesell, G. C. 1985. *Town, Palace, and House Cult in Minoan Crete.* Göteborg: Paul Åströms Förlag.

*‡Goodison, L. and C. Morris, eds. 1998. *Ancient Goddesses: The Myths and the Evidence.* Madison: University of Wisconsin Press.

‡Hägg, R. and N. Marinatos, eds. 1981. *Sanctuaries and Cults in the Aegean Bronze Age.* Stockholm: Swedish Institute at Athens.

Laffineur, R. and J. Crowley, eds. 1992. *Eikon Aegean Bronze Age Iconography: Shaping a Methodology.* AEGAEUM 8. Liège, Belgium: Université de Liège.

‡Laffineur, R. and R. Hägg, eds. 2001. *Potnia: Deities and Religion in the Aegean Bronze Age.* Liège, Belgium: Université de Liège.

Lebessi, A. and P. Muhly. 1990. "Aspects of Minoan Cult: Sacred Enclosures: The Evidence from the Symi Sanctuary (Crete)." *Archäologischer Anzeiger* 3: 15–336.

Palmer, L. R. 1979. "Some New Mycenaean Functional Gods?" *Nestor* 6 (2), 1338–1339.

Peatfield, A. 1992. "Rural Ritual in Bronze Age Crete: The Peak Sanctuary at Atsipadhes." *Cambridge Archaeological Journal* 2 (1), 59–87.

Rehak, P. 1984. "New Observations on the Mycenaean 'Warrior Goddess.'" *Archäologischer Anzeiger* 99, 535–545.

*Rutkowski, B. 1986. *The Cult Places of the Aegean.* New Haven, CT: Yale University Press.

Ruud, I. M. 1996. *Minoan Religion: A Bibliography.* Jonsered, Sweden: Paul Åströms Förlag.

Warren, P. 1988. *Minoan Religion as Ritual Action.* Gothenburg, Sweden: Paul Åströms Förlag.

Watrous, L. V. 1996. *The Cave Sanctuary of Zeus at Psychro: A Study of Extra-Urban Sanctuaries in Minoan and Early Iron Age Crete.* AEGAEUM 15. Liège, Belgium: Université de Liège.

Society

Branigan, K. 1988. *Pre-Palatial: The Foundations of Palatial Crete, a Survey of Crete in the Early Bronze Age.* Amsterdam: Adolf M. Hakkert.

*Chadwick, J. 1988. *The Mycenaean World.* Cambridge, UK: Cambridge University Press.

‡Driessen, J. and A. Farnoux, eds. 1997. *La Crète mycenienne: Actes de la Table Ronde Internationale organisée par l'École française d'Athènes.* Supplément 30. Athens: BCH.

Galaty, M. L. and W. A. Parkinson, eds. 1999. *Rethinking Mycenaean Palaces: New Inter-*

pretations of an Old Idea. Monograph 41. Los Angeles: Cotsen Institute of Archaeology, UCLA.

Hägg, R., ed. 1997. *The Function of the "Minoan Villa."* Stockholm: Paul Ånstöms Förlag.

Hägg, R. and N. Marinatos, eds. 1984. *The Minoan Thalassocracy: Myth and Reality.* Stockholm: Paul Åströms Förlag.

———. 1987. *The Function of the Minoan Palaces.* Stockholm: Skrifter Utgivna ac Svenska Institutet.

Krzyszkowska, O. and L. Nixon, eds. 1990. *Minoan Society.* Bristol, UK: Bristol Classics.

‡Laffineur, R., ed. 1999. *Polemos: Le Contexte guerrier en Égée à l'Âge du Bronze.* Liège, Belgium: Université de Liège.

‡Laffineur, R. and W.-D. Niemeier, eds. 1995. *Politeia: Society and State in the Aegean Bronze Age.* AEGAEUM 12. Liège, Belgium: Université de Liège.

Olsen, B. 1998. "Women, Children, and the Family in the Late Aegean Bronze Age: Differences in Minoan and Mycenaean Constructions of Gender." *World Archaeology* 29 (3), 380–392.

Rehak, P., ed. 1995. *The Role of the Ruler in the Prehistoric Aegean.* AEGAEUM 11. Liège, Belgium: Université de Liège.

Voutsaki, S. and J. Killen, eds. 2001. *Economy and Politics in the Mycenaean Palace States.* Cambridge, UK: Cambridge Philological Society.

Historical Periods

General

*Speake, G., ed. 2000. *Encyclopedia of Greece and the Hellenic Tradition.* London: Fitzroy Dearborn.

Art and Archaeology

Coldstream, J. N. 1977. *Geometric Greece.* London: Methuen.

Gullberg, E. and P. Åström. 1970. *The Thread of Ariadne: A Study of Ancient Greek Dress.* Studies in Mediterranean Archaeology 21. Göteborg: Paul Åströms Förlag.

Hurwit, J. M. 1985. *The Art and Culture of Early Greece: 1100–480 B.C.* Ithaca, NY: Cornell University Press.

Losfeld, G. 1991. *Essai sur le costume grec.* Paris: Éditions de Boccard.

*Pedley, J. G. 1993. *Greek Art and Archaeology.* 2d ed. Upper Saddle River, NJ: Prentice-Hall.

Rasmussen, T. and N. Spivey, eds. *Looking at Greek Vases.* Cambridge, UK: Cambridge University Press.

Touratsoglou, I. 1996. *Macedonia: History, Monuments, Museums.* Athens: Ekdotike Athenon.

Daily Life

*‡Garland, R. 1985. *The Greek Way of Death.* Ithaca, NY: Cornell University Press.

*‡———. 1990. *The Greek Way of Life: From Conception to Old Age.* Ithaca, NY: Cornell University Press.

Golden, M. 1981. "The Exposure of Girls at Athens." *Phoenix* 35, 316–331.

———. 1990. *Children and Childhood in Classical Athens.* Baltimore: Johns Hopkins University Press.

Murray, O. 1994. "Nestor's Cup and the Origins of the Symposion." *Annali di Archeologia e Storia Antica,* 1, 47–54.

———. 1999. *Sympotica: A Symposium on the Symposion.* Oxford: Clarendon.

*Pomeroy, S. B. 1997. *Families in Classical and Hellenistic Greece: Representations and Realities.* Oxford: Clarendon.

Economics

‡Cohen, E. E. 1992. *Athenian Economy and Society: A Banking Perspective.* Princeton, NJ: Princeton University Press.

Finley, M. I. 1973. *The Ancient Economy.* Berkeley: University of California Press.

Kraay, C. 1976. *Archaic and Classical Greek Coins.* Berkeley: University of California Press.

Epigraphy

Meiggs, R. and D. Lewis. 1992. *A Selection of Greek Historical Inscription to the End of the Fifth Century B.C.* Oxford: Clarendon.

Tod, M. N. 1985. *Greek Historical Inscriptions.* Chicago: Ares.

*Woodhead, A. G. 1992. *The Study of Greek Inscriptions.* Norman: University of Oklahoma Press.

Foreign Relations

Bernal, M. 1987. *Black Athena: The Afroasiatic Roots of Classical Civilization.* New Brunswick, NJ: Rutgers University Press.

*Boardman, J. 1980. *The Greeks Overseas: Their Early Colonies and Trade.* New York: Thames & Hudson.

Burkert, W. 1992. *The Orientalizing Revolution: Near Eastern Influence on Greek Culture in the Early Archaic Age.* Cambridge, MA: Harvard University Press.

Coldstream, J. N. and P. M. Bikai. 1988. "Early Greek Pottery in Tyre and Cyprus: Some Preliminary Comparisons." *Report of the Department of Antiquities, Cyprus,* 35–44.

Coleman, J. E. and C. A. Walz. 1997. *Greeks and Barbarians.* Bethesda, MD: CDL.

Demetriou, A. 1989. *Cypro-Aegean Relations in the Early Iron Age.* Studies in Mediterranean Archaeology 83. Göteborg: Paul Åströms Förlag.

*Harrison, T., ed. 2002. *Greeks and Barbarians.* New York: Routledge.

‡West, M. L. 1997. *The East Face of Helicon: West Asiatic Elements in Greek Poetry and Myth.* Oxford: Clarendon.

History, Politics, and Warfare

Austin, M. M. 1981. *The Hellenistic World from Alexander to the Roman Conquest.* Cambridge, UK: Cambridge University Press.

Ducrey, P. 1986. *Warfare in Ancient Greece.* New York: Schocken.

*Ehrenberg, V. 1969. *The Greek State.* 2d ed. London: Methuen.

‡Flensted-Jensen, P., T. H. Nielsen, and L. Rubinstein. 2000. *Polis & Politics: Studies in Ancient Greek History.* Copenhagen: Museum Tusculanum.

Graham, A. J. 1970. "The Colonial Expansion of Greece." In *Cambridge Ancient History.* London: Cambridge University Press, 83–195.

*———. 1983. *Colony and Mother City in Ancient Greece.* 2d ed. Chicago: Ares.

McGlew, J. F. 1993. *Tyranny and Political Culture in Ancient Greece.* Ithaca, NY: Cornell University Press.

*Oakeshott, E. 1994. *The Archaeology of Weapons: Arms and Armor from Prehistory to the Age of Chivalry.* New York: Barnes & Noble.

*Osborne, R. 1996. *Greece in the Making: 1200–479 B.C.* London: Routledge.

Ridgeway, D. 1992. *The First Western Greeks.* Cambridge, UK: Cambridge University Press.

‡Robinson, E. W. 1997. *The First Democracies: Early Popular Government Outside Athens.* Stuttgart: F. Steiner.

Robinson, E. W., ed. 2004. *Ancient Greek Democracy: Readings and Sources.* Oxford, UK: Blackwell.

*‡Sage, M. M. 1996. *Warfare in Ancient Greece: A Sourcebook.* New York: Routledge.

*Shipley, G. 2000. *The Greek World after Alexander, 323–30 B.C.* London: Routledge.

Snodgrass, A. 1980. *Archaic Greece: The Age of Experiment.* Berkeley: University of California Press.

*———. 1999. *Arms & Armor of the Greeks.* Baltimore: Johns Hopkins University Press.

‡Tritle, L. A., ed. 1997. *The Greek World in the Fourth Century: From the Fall of the Athenian Empire to the Successors of Alexander.* New York: Routledge.

*Walbank, F. W. 1992. *The Hellenistic World.* Rev. ed. Cambridge, MA: Harvard University Press.

Language and Script

Allen, W. S. 1991. *Vox Graeca: The Pronunciation of Classical Greek.* 3d ed. Cambridge, UK: Cambridge University Press.

Horrocks, G. G. 1997. *Greek: A History of the Language and Its Speakers.* London: Longman.

Jeffery, L. 1961. *The Local Scripts of Archaic Greece: A Study of the Origins of the Greek Alphabet and Its Development from the Eighth to the Fifth Centuries B.C.* Oxford: Clarendon.

Law

Freeman, K. 1991. *The Murder of Herodes and Other Trials from the Athenian Law Courts.* Indianapolis: Hackett.

*Gagarin, M. 1989. *Early Greek Law.* Berkeley: University of California Press.

Sealey, R. 1994. *The Justice of the Greeks.* Ann Arbor: University of Michigan Press.

Stroud, R. S. 1968. *Drakon's Law on Homicide.* Berkeley: University of California Press.

Literature

*‡Athanassakis, A. 1976. *The Homeric Hymns: Translation, Introduction, and Notes.* Baltimore: Johns Hopkins University Press.

*Barnstone, W. 1988. *Sappho and the Greek Lyric Poets.* New York: Schocken.

Beye, C. R. 1993. *Ancient Epic Poetry: Homer, Apollonius, Virgil.* Ithaca, NY: Cornell University Press.

Halporn, J. W., M. Ostwald, and T. G. Rosenmeyer. 1994. *The Meters of Greek and Latin Poetry.* Indianapolis: Hackett.

Henderson, J. 1996. *Three Plays by Aristophanes: Staging Women.* New York: Routledge.

Lesky, A. 1996. *A History of Greek Literature.* Indianapolis: Hackett.

*Ley, G. 1991. *A Short Introduction to the Ancient Greek Theater.* Chicago: University of Chicago Press.

Lord, A. 2001. *The Singer of Tales.* Cambridge, MA: Harvard University Press.

Rehm, R. 1994. *Marriage to Death: The Conflation of Wedding and Funeral Rituals in Greek Tragedy.* Princeton, NJ: Princeton University Press.

*Schein, S. L. 1984. *The Mortal Hero: An Introduction to Homer's Iliad.* Berkeley: University of California Press.

Philosophy

Allen, R. E. 1985. *Greek Philosophy: Thales to Aristotle.* 2d ed. New York: Free Press.

Barnes, J. 1987. *Early Greek Philosophy.* London: Penguin.

Inwood, B. and L. P. Gerson. 1988. *Hellenistic Philosophy: Introductory Readings.* Indianapolis: Hackett.

*Luce, J. V. 1992. *An Introduction to Greek Philosophy.* London: Thames & Hudson.

Religion

‡Alcock, S. E. and R. Osborne. 1996. *Placing the Gods: Sanctuaries and Sacred Space in Ancient Greece.* Oxford: Clarendon.

Antonaccio, C. M. 1995. *An Archaeology of Ancestors: Tomb Cult and Hero Cult in Early Greece.* London: Rowman & Littlefield.

Budin, S. L. 2003. *The Origin of Aphrodite.* Bethesda, MD: CDL.

Burkert, W. 1985. *Greek Religion: Archaic and Classical.* Cambridge, MA: Basil Blackwell and Harvard University Press.

*‡————. 1987. *Ancient Mystery Cults.* Cambridge, MA: Harvard University Press.

‡Buxton, R., ed. 2000. *Oxford Readings in Greek Religion.* Oxford: Oxford University Press.

Calame, C. 2001. *Choruses of Young Women in Ancient Greece: Their Morphology, Religious Role, and Social Functions.* Lanham, MD: Rowman & Littlefield.

Coldstream, J. N. 1976. "Hero Cults in the Age of Homer." *Journal of Hellenic Studies* 96, 8–17.

Cosmopoulos, M., ed. 2003. *Greek Mysteries: The Archaeology and Ritual of Ancient Greek Secret Cults.* London: Routledge.

Dodd, D. B., and C. A. Faraone, eds. 2003. *Initiation in Ancient Greek Rituals and Narratives: New Critical Perspectives.* New York: Routledge.

Foley, H. P. 1994. *The Homeric Hymn to Demeter: Translation, Commentary, and Interpretive Essays.* Princeton, NJ: Princeton University Press.

*‡Goodison, L. and C. Morris, eds. 1998. *Ancient Goddesses: The Myths and the Evidence.* Madison: University of Wisconsin Press.

Guthrie, W. K. C. 1993. *Orpheus and Greek Religion: A Study of the Orphic Movement.* Princeton, NJ: Princeton University Press.

Larson, J. 1995. *Greek Heroine Cults.* Madison: University of Wisconsin Press.

Marinatos, N. and R. Hägg, eds. 1993. *Greek Sanctuaries: New Approaches.* London: Routledge.

*Meyer, M. W., ed. 1987. *The Ancient Mysteries: A Sourcebook.* Philadelphia: University of Pennsylvania Press.

Morris, I. 1988. "Tomb Cult and the 'Greek Renaissance': The Past in the Present in the Eighth Century B.C." *Antiquity* 62, 750–761.

Pozzi, D. C. and J. M. Wickersham, eds. 1991. *Myth and the Polis.* Ithaca, NY: Cornell University Press.

*‡Price, S. 1999. *Religions of the Ancient Greeks.* Cambridge, UK: Cambridge University Press.

Vernant, J.-P. 1991. *Mortals and Immortals: Collected Essays.* Princeton, NJ: Princeton University Press.

Science

Kasas, S. and R. Struckmann. 1990. *Importants centres médicaux de l'antiquité: Épidaure et Corinthe.* Athens: Editions Kasas.

*King, H. 2001. *Greek and Roman Medicine.* London: Bristol Classics.

Stein, S. 1999. *Archimedes: What Did He Do Besides Cry Eureka?* Davis: University of California.

Sex

Dover, K. J. 1989. *Greek Homosexuality.* Cambridge, MA: Harvard University Press.

Halperin, D. M. 1990. *One Hundred Years of Homosexuality*. London: Routledge.

Halperin, D. M., J. J. Winkler, and F. I. Zeitlin, eds. 1990. *Before Sexuality: The Construction of Erotic Experience in the Ancient Greek World*. Princeton, NJ: Princeton University Press.

Sparta

*Cartledge, P. 2001. *Spartan Reflections*. London: Duckworth.

‡———. 2002. *Sparta and Lakonia: A Regional History 1300 to 362 B.C.* 2d ed. London: Routledge.

———. 2003. *The Spartans: The World of the Warrior-Heroes in Ancient Greece, from Utopia to Crisis and Collapse*. Woodstock, NY: Overlook.

Whitby, M., ed. 2002. *Sparta*. New York: Routledge.

Women and Gender

Billigmeier, J.-C. 1985. "Studies on the Family in the Aegean Bronze Age and in Homer." *Journal of Family History* 3 (3/4), 9–18.

Blundell, S. and M. Williamson, eds. 1998. *The Sacred and the Feminine in Ancient Greece*. London: Routledge.

Bolger, D. and N. Serwint, eds. 2002. *Engendering Aphrodite: Women and Society in Ancient Cyprus*. Atlanta: American Schools of Oriental Research.

‡Cameron, A. and A. Kuhrt, eds. 1983. *Images of Woman in Antiquity*. Detroit: Wayne State University Press.

Cohen, B., ed. 1995. *The Distaff Side: Representing the Female in Homer's Odyssey*. Oxford: Oxford University Press.

DuBois, P. 1988. *Sowing the Body: Psychoanalysis and Ancient Representations of Women*. Chicago: University of Chicago Press.

‡Foley, H., ed. 1981. *Reflections of Women in Antiquity*. New York: Gordon and Breach Science.

King, H. 1998. *Hippocrates' Woman: Reading the Female Body in Ancient Greece*. London: Routledge.

*‡Lefkowitz, M. R. and M. B. Fant.1992. *Women's Life in Greece & Rome: A Source Book in Translation*. 2d ed. Baltimore: Johns Hopkins University Press.

Pomeroy, S. B. 1975. *Goddesses, Whores, Wives, and Slaves: Woman in Classical Antiquity*. New York: Schocken.

*———. 2002. *Spartan Women*. Oxford: Oxford University Press.

Rabinowitz, N. S. and L. Auanger. 2002. *Among Women: From the Homosocial to the Homoerotic in the Ancient World*. Austin: University of Texas Press.

WEB PAGES

American Philological Association: http://www.apaclassics.org

Archaeological Institute of America: http://www.archaeological.org

Diotima (one of the best sources for new research on women and gender in the ancient world): http://www.stoa.org/diotima/

Hellenic Culture (a full database—with images—of Greek museums and archaeological sites): http://www.culture.gr

Nestor (an extensive database for the study of Aegean prehistory, with copious additional links): http://asweb.artsci.uc.edu/classics/nestor/

The Perseus Project (an excellent source for classical texts in Latin, Greek, and English): http://www.perseus.tufts.edu

TOCS-IN (an archive of the contents of 150 classics journals): http://www.chass. utoronto.ca/amphoras/tocs.html

Index

About the Author

STEPHANIE LYNN BUDIN received her Ph.D. in Ancient History from the University of Pennsylvania, where her areas of concentration were ancient Greece and the Near East. Her main areas of interest are ancient mythology and religion, sex and gender, and cross-cultural contacts among the societies of the ancient Mediterranean. Much of her research concentrates on the combination of all these interests. Her first book, *The Origin of Aphrodite* (2003), concerns the transmission and evolution of what would become for the Greeks the goddess Aphrodite from her origins in Syria through Cyprus to Crete in the Late Bronze and Dark Ages. Her two current research projects are a study of Nude Goddess iconography throughout the Near East and Mediterranean, and the myth of sacred prostitution. Dr. Budin lives in New Jersey with her husband Paul Butler and several pets.